ORACLE®　　*Oracle Press*™

Real-World SQL and PL/SQL

About the Authors

Arup Nanda, Oracle ACE Director, Oak Table Network member, and winner of Oracle's DBA of the Year award in 2003 and Enterprise Architect of the Year in 2012, has been an Oracle DBA and developer for 22 years and counting. He is the principal global database architect of a New York–area multinational company. He has coauthored six books, written more than 500 published articles, presented more than 300 sessions, and taught multi-day-long seminars in over 20 countries. He is an editor of *SELECT Journal,* the International Oracle User Group publication, and is a member of the board of directors of Exadata SIG.

Twitter: @ArupNanda
Blog: arup.blogspot.com
Email: arup@proligence.com

Brendan Tierney, Oracle ACE Director, is an independent consultant (Oralytics) and lectures on data science, databases, and Big Data in the Dublin Institute of Technology/Dublin Technological University. He has 24+ years of experience working in the areas of data mining, data science, Big Data, and data warehousing. Brendan is a recognized data science and Big Data expert and has worked on projects in Ireland, the UK, Belgium, Holland, Norway, Spain, Canada, and the U.S. Brendan is active in the Oracle User Group community, where he is one of the leaders for the OUG in Ireland. Brendan is the editor of the *UKOUG Oracle Scene* magazine, a regular speaker at conferences around the world, and an active blogger, and he also writes articles for OTN, *Oracle Scene, IOUG SELECT Journal, ODTUG Technical Journal,* and ToadWorld. He is also on the board of directors for DAMA in Ireland. Brendan has published two other books with Oracle Press (*Predictive Analytics Using Oracle Data Miner* and *Oracle R Enterprise: Harnessing the Power of R in Oracle Database*). These books are available online.

Twitter: @brendantierney
Web and Blog: www.oralytics.com
Email: brendan.tierney@oralytics.com

Heli Helskyaho, Oracle ACE Director, is the CEO of Miracle Finland Oy and an ambassador for EOUC (EMEA Oracle Users Group Community). Heli holds a master's degree in computer science from Helsinki University and she specializes in databases. At the moment she is working on her doctoral studies on Big Data, schema discovery, and semi-structured data. She has been working in IT since 1990 and with Oracle products since 1993. She has been in several positions, but every role has always included database design. Heli believes that good database design and good documentation reduce performance problems and make solving them easier. Heli is also an Oracle ACE Director and a frequent speaker at many conferences. She is the author of *Oracle SQL Developer Data Modeler for Database Design Mastery* (Oracle Press, 2015) and one of the first winners of Oracle Database Developer Choice Award (Devvy) in the Database Design category in 2015.

Twitter: @helifromfinland
Blog: helifromfinland.wordpress.com
Email: heli@miracleoy.fi

Martin Widlake, Oracle ACE Director and OakTable Network member, has been working with Oracle technology since 1992 when he started as a Forms 3 and CASE developer, so he has been using PL/SQL for 24+ years. Martin has been a development DBA for the last two decades, mostly working on VLDBs and the latest versions of Oracle. He was named Oracle Beta Tester of the year in 2003. For the last eight years he has been an independent consultant (ORA600, Ltd.) specializing in database design, performance, and PL/SQL development. Martin has been a regular presenter at conferences and user groups since 2002, both at home (the UK) and internationally, and also writes articles for magazines. He is a strong advocate of user groups and is an active member of the UKOUG, chairing Special Interest Groups and helping organize the annual technical conference for the last few years. He is also deputy editor of *Oracle Scene* magazine. Martin maintains a blog that is both technical and also includes his popular "Friday Philosophies"—light-hearted articles about IT management and the odder aspects of our working lives.

Twitter: @MDWidlake
Blog: mwidlake.wordpress.com
Email: mwidlake@ora600.org.uk

Alex Nuijten, Oracle ACE Director, is an independent consultant (allAPEX), specializing in Oracle database development with PL/SQL and Oracle Application Express (APEX). Besides his consultancy work, he conducts training classes, mainly in APEX, SQL, and PL/SQL. Alex has been a speaker at numerous international conferences, such as ODTUG, Oracle Open World, UKOUG, IOUG, OUGF, BGOUG, OGH APEX World, and OBUG. For his presentations, Alex received several Best Speaker awards. He has written many articles in Oracle-related magazines, and at regular intervals he writes about Oracle Application Express and Oracle database development on his blog "Notes on Oracle" (nuijten.blogspot .com). Alex is co-author of the book *Oracle APEX Best Practices* (published by Packt Publishers).

Twitter: @alexnuijten
Blog: nuijten.blogspot.nl
Email: alex@allapex.nl

About the Technical Editor

Chet Justice, Oracle ACE Director, has been an Oracle professional since 2002. He began by being given SQL*Plus and a tnsnames file, and he quickly connected Microsoft Access to it so he could see the tables. He began working extensively with PL/SQL and testing that PL/SQL with SQLUnit. He learned some database administration skills along the way while setting up testing environments. Then he found and fell in love with APEX. Since he lacks any serious focus, he took a job in a data warehousing environment writing ETL in PL/SQL—then back to OLTP systems, more PL/SQL, and modeling data, before finally finding fulfillment in the chaos of consultancy. He is currently working in the OBIEE realm.

ORACLE® *Oracle Press*™

Real-World SQL and PL/SQL: Advice from the Experts

Arup Nanda
Brendan Tierney
Heli Helskyaho
Martin Widlake
Alex Nuijten

New York   Chicago   San Francisco
Athens   London   Madrid   Mexico City
Milan   New Delhi   Singapore   Sydney   Toronto

Cataloging-in-Publication Data is on file with the Library of Congress

McGraw-Hill Education books are available at special quantity discounts to use as premiums and sales promotions, or for use in corporate training programs. To contact a representative, please visit the Contact Us pages at www.mhprofessional.com.

Real-World SQL and PL/SQL: Advice from the Experts

1 2 3 4 5 6 7 8 9   DOC   21 20 19 18 17 16

ISBN   978-1-25-964097-1
MHID   1-25-964097-3

Sponsoring Editor Wendy Rinaldi	**Copy Editor** Bart Reed	**Composition** Cenveo® Publisher Services
Editorial Supervisor Janet Walden	**Proofreader** Lisa McCoy	**Illustration** Cenveo Publisher Services
Project Editor LeeAnn Pickrell	**Indexer** Rebecca Plunkett	**Art Director, Cover** Jeff Weeks
Technical Editor Chet Justice	**Production Supervisor** Pamela Pelton	

Contents at a Glance

PART V
Database Security

Contents

PART I
The Importance of SQL, PL/SQL, and a Good Data Model

PART II
Underutilized Advanced SQL Functionality

PART III
Essential Everyday Advanced PL/SQL

PART IV
Advanced Analytics

PART V
Database Security

Foreword

You are working with an Oracle database and you need to make a decision about which programming languages your application development will focus on. The following three options are put on the table for you to consider:

- SQL
- PL/SQL
- Something outside the database (Java, C#, JavaScript, and so on)

Which should you pick? Let's discuss it.

The Case for SQL

SQL is at the heart of a relational database. It's how the database manages itself internally. You send a SQL statement to the database server, and recursive SQL is used during every step of the processing—to make sure your statement is valid, check if you have the privileges to access the objects, and decide on the execution plan, which determines how to retrieve the data. There is very little happening inside a relational database that doesn't involve SQL somewhere.

Let's think about that for a minute. As a developer of a relational database engine (Oracle, MySQL, SQL Server), if you improve the performance of SQL, you not only improve the performance of other people's applications, you actually improve the performance of the internals of the database engine itself. So it makes a lot of sense for the developers of relational database engines to obsess about the performance of SQL—which they do.

SQL is not just about basic inserts, updates, deletes, and queries with a few table joins in them. Modern relational database engines include crazy amounts of SQL functionality that allows you to massively reduce the number of lines of code in your applications. Functionality such as analytic functions, pattern matching, and the model clause allow you to perform analytics on your data without ever having to leave SQL. Generation and consumption of XML and JSON data are trivial in SQL, making web services possible with almost no additional code.

From a performance perspective, SQL is the king. There are very few occasions where a non-SQL solution will outperform a SQL solution for processing data held in a relational database. Most languages encourage you to process data in a row-by-row manner, which is completely the opposite of what a relational database wants to do. By using SQL and focusing on set processing, you will often see the performance of batch processing and analytics increase by orders of magnitude.

With that in mind, it should be obvious the best language for interacting with data in a relational database is SQL. Whenever you use any language that is not SQL, you are taking the database further away from what it does best, which will ultimately reduce the performance and scalability of your application.

The Case for PL/SQL

PL/SQL is a procedural extension of SQL, allowing you to add procedural logic into your data processing, without having to leave the database engine itself. The location of the PL/SQL engine is a really important factor in what makes PL/SQL great.

Imagine a scenario where we have two equally competent programming languages, but one is running inside the database and one is running on an application server on a separate machine. When the language running inside the database needs some data, it's there for the taking. When the language running on the application server needs some data, it has to make a request over the network to the database server, and all the data that is returned has to travel back over the network. Now imagine a "chatty" application that makes repeated calls to the database to complete one task, and I think you can see how the code on the application server will fail to scale.

One solution to the scaling problem is to add more hardware and caching layers outside the database. The other solution is to simply move the functionality into the database itself by rewriting it as PL/SQL.

Over the years I've worked on a number of projects that have tried to focus entirely on the middle tier and use the database as a basic data bucket. Invariably they come across performance problems, especially when it comes to batch processing, and the solution is almost always to rewrite those data-intensive processes into PL/SQL so they are close to the data. Keep your data-centric processing in the database, and you will reap rewards from a scalability and performance perspective, as well as make it much easier to share functionality between different client tools, presentation layers, and interfaces.

The PL/SQL language is tightly integrated with SQL, making the transition between SQL and the procedural logic almost seamless. In contrast, every other language I've used over the last 20+ years feels incredibly clumsy when dealing with the database.

So PL/SQL is just for batch processing then? Not at all! It really shines where data-centric code is concerned, but PL/SQL has become an incredibly rich development platform over the years. Take a look at the functionality available through a development tool like Oracle Application Express (APEX), which is written in PL/SQL, and you will realize just how capable a language PL/SQL is.

The Case for Other Languages

There will always be requirements for specialist languages that target a specific niche, like Oracle R Enterprise, which allows you to run R inside the Oracle database and integrates into SQL and PL/SQL, but what about languages outside the database?

As part of my job I am constantly using a variety of programming languages, including Perl, Python, PHP, JavaScript, and numerous OS scripting languages. In the past I've developed using Java, C#, and C, among others. Each language has its sweet spot, but where database interaction is concerned, nothing beats PL/SQL.

You will invariably use other programming languages and frameworks for your presentation layers, and maybe even for some of your business logic, but the further you get away from the database, the harder your life will become.

Conclusion

Most database developers and DBAs have come to a similar conclusion. If you can, do it in SQL. If you can't do it in SQL, do it in PL/SQL. If you can't do it in PL/SQL, do it in another language.

Tim Hall
DBA/Developer
oracle-base.com
Oracle ACE Director

Preface

Brendan Tierney and Heli Helskyaho approached me in March 2015 about being an author on this book, along with Arup Nanda and Alex Nuijten. Soon after, we picked up Martin Widlake. To say that I was honored to be asked would be a gross understatement. Rather quickly, though, I realized that I did not have the mental energy to devote to the project and didn't want to put the other authors at risk. Still wanting to be part of the book, I suggested that I be the technical editor, and they graciously accepted my new role.

This is my first official role as technical editor, but I've been doing it for years through work: checking my work, checking others' work, and so on. Having a touch of obsessive-compulsive disorder (OCD) helps greatly.

All testing was done with the prebuilt Database App Development VM provided by OTN/Oracle, which made things easy. Configuration for testing was simple with the instructions provided in those chapters that required it.

One of my biggest challenges was the multitenant architecture of Oracle 12c. I haven't done DBA-type work in a few years, so trying to figure out if I should be doing something in the root container (CDB) or the pluggable database (PDB) was fun. Other than that, though, the instructions provided by the authors were pretty easy to follow.

Design (data modeling, Edition-Based Redefinition, VPD), security (redaction/masking, encryption/hashing), coding (Regex, PL/SQL, SQL), instrumentation, and "reporting" or turning that raw data into actionable information (data mining, Oracle R, predictive queries)—all these topics are covered in detail throughout this book. This is everything a developer would need to build an application from scratch.

Probably my favorite part of this endeavor is that I was forced to do more than simply see if it works. Typically when reading a book or blog entry, I'll grab the technical solution and move on, often skipping the why, when, and where. How, to me, is relatively easy. I read AskTom daily for many years; it was my way of taking a break without getting in trouble. At first, it was to see how particular solutions were solved, occasionally using them for my own problems. After a year or two, I wanted to understand the why of doing something a certain way and would look for those responses where Tom provided insight into his approach.

That's what I got reviewing this book. I was allowed into the authors' minds, to not only see *how* they solved technical problems, but why. This is invaluable for developers and DBAs. Most of us can figure out how to solve specific technical issues, but to reach that next level we need to understand the why, when, and where. This book provides that.

Chet Justice
Oracle ACE Director
Technical Editor

Acknowledgments

My special thanks to my wife, Ani, and son, Anish, for letting me steal precious time from you to work on this project.

Arup Nanda

Special thanks to Charlie Berger (Product Manager for Oracle Data Mining and Oracle Advanced Analytics), Mark Kelly, Mark Hornick, Marat Spivak, Denny Wong, and all the members of the Oracle Advanced Analytics team who have supported my work over the years. I would also like to thank my fellow coauthors Martin, Arup, Alex, and Heli. Also, thanks to Chet Justice (aka oraclenerd) for tech editing the book.

The biggest personal thanks I owe is to Grace, Daniel, and Eleanor, who through their constant encouragement and support made this book and my other books possible, by giving me the time and space to work on them. These books would not have happened without you.

Brendan Tierney

Thank you to my loving family: Marko, Patrik, and Matias. Thank you for your continuous support and encouragement for whatever I decide to do.

Thank you Bryn Llewellyn, Chet Justice, Alex Nuijten, Martin Widlake, Arup Nanda, Brendan Tierney, Tim Hall, Steven Feuerstein, and everybody who gave me advice and support during our project. This project was fun!

Heli Helskyaho

A lot of people have helped me with SQL and PL/SQL (and Oracle in general) over the years, and particularly while I was writing my chapters of this book. I'd like to specifically thank Tim Hall, Mike Cox, Adrian Billington, Neil Chandler, Steven Feuerstein, Frits Hoogland, Oren Nakdimon, Dawn Rigby, and Jonathan Lewis, with a special thanks to Babak Tourani, who helped me with some examples and text for one section.

I'd like to especially thank my coauthors who have graciously helped and guided me on this, my first book. Brendan, Alex, Heli, Chet, and Arup, thank you for your patience.

Finally, I want to thank my wife for her patience and support while I have been chained to my desk and computer working on this book. Normal domestic duties will now resume.

Martin Widlake

There are so many people who have helped me in my Oracle career that it is impossible to name them all. To name a few would do injustice to the ones who aren't named.

I would like to thank Heli, Arup, Brendan, and Martin for allowing me to join in this project. While working on this book I learned a great deal from all of you. Thanks, Chet Justice, for your technical reviews; the feedback was very insightful.

Without the continuing support of my wife Rian, son Tim, and daughter Lara, I could never have worked on this project. Preparing presentations and writing articles and chapters takes an enormous amount of time, and you understand this and are alright with it. I could never do all that without your support. I love you so much.

Alex Nuijten

Introduction

While attempting to give you an idea into our original thinking behind the need for this book and why we wanted to write it, the words of Rod Stewart's song "Sailing" kept popping into my mind: "We are sailing, we are sailing, home again 'cross the sea." This is because the idea for this book was born on a boat. Some call it a ship. Some call it a cruise ship. Whatever you want to call it, this book was born at the OUG Norway conference in March 2015. What makes the OUG Norway conference special is that it is held on a cruise ship that goes between Oslo in Norway and Kiel in Germany and back again. This means as a speaker and conference attendee, you are "trapped" on the cruise ship for two days filled with presentations, workshops, discussions, and idea sharing for the Oracle community.

It was during this conference that Heli and Brendan got to talking about their books. Heli had just published her Oracle SQL Developer Data Modeler book and Brendan had published his book on Oracle Data Miner the previous year. While they were discussing their experiences of writing and sharing their knowledge and how much they enjoyed it, they both recognized that there are a lot of books for the people starting out in their Oracle career and then there are lots of books on specialized topics. What was missing were books that covered the middle group. A question they kept asking but struggled to answer was, after reading the introductory books, what book would they read next before getting on to the specialized books? This was particularly true of SQL and PL/SQL.

They also felt that something missing from many books, especially introductory ones, was the "why and how" of doing things in certain ways that comes from experience. It is all well and good knowing the syntax of commands and the options, but what takes people from understanding a language to being productive in using it is that real-world derived knowledge that comes from using the language for real tasks. It would be great to share some of that experience.

Then over breakfast on the final day of the OUG Norway conference, as the cruise ship was sailing through the fjord and around the islands that lead back to Oslo, Heli and Brendan finally agreed that this book should happen. They then listed the type of content they thought would be in such a book and who the recognized experts (or superheroes) are for these topics. This list of experts was very easy to come up with, and the writing team of

Oracle ACE Directors was formed, consisting of Arup Nanda, Martin Widlake, and Alex Nuijten, along with Heli Helskyaho and Brendan Tierney. The author team then got to work defining the chapters and their contents. Using their combined 120+ years of SQL and PL/SQL experience, they finally came up with the scope and content for the book at Oracle Open World.

The book is divided into four sections, and each of these sections is aimed at helping an Oracle Developer to better understand the core technology they use on a daily basis—that is, SQL and PL/SQL.

The first section of the book looks at one of the absolute core parts of any database project—the design of your data model—and addresses the fundamental question of when to use SQL and when to use PL/SQL. This first section of the book also introduces Oracle SQL Developer Data Modeler, a tool for database designing.

The second section looks at some underused but extremely useful tools in SQL and PL/SQL, such as handling complex data sets, regular expressions, and edition-based redefinition, to significantly boost the availability of the applications during structural changes. It also looks at using PL/SQL in areas where it's not used much but, given its power and flexibility, should be used to the fullest extent. You will see how you can extend SQL with PL/SQL while avoiding some common but rarely handled issues that this can introduce. You will learn how to instrument your code for profiling and diagnosing performance issues, how to effectively use dynamic SQL (and, by extension, PL/SQL), and how to leverage the power of PL/SQL for automating tasks and aiding database management.

The third section looks at how you can use the Oracle Database features that support the area of data science. These include how you can use the Oracle Data Mining algorithms using the PL/SQL and SQL functions, as well as how to use Predictive Queries, a new feature in Oracle 12*c* that allows you to perform automated data mining without having to know anything about the algorithms. This section also shows you how to use the R language as part of the Oracle Database engine. Now, not only can you analyze your data, but you can use Oracle R Enterprise with SQL and PL/SQL. These advanced analytics capabilities of the Oracle Database allow you to quickly and efficiently (without any data movement) analyze your data using the various data mining and machine learning techniques.

The fourth section looks at incorporating security in PL/SQL coding to ensure that the overall system, including database and applications, remains secure. This section talks in detail about fortifying the code to secure against SQL injection attacks and insider hacking, as well as redacting and encrypting sensitive production data to protect from unauthorized access. This section is not about database infrastructure security but rather about coding while keeping security in mind and using the tools Oracle provides to build secure applications.

In keeping with the mission statement, the book aims to bridge the gap between the beginner and advanced SQL and PL/SQL user. Our objective is to cover the powerful but not-so-often used features that the PL/SQL and SQL infrastructure offers to make you a better informed, more efficient, and security-minded technology professional regardless of your role—be it a developer, an architect, or even a DBA. Everyone working with the Oracle Database will benefit from this book.

Code Available for Download

Most of the chapters in this book come with extensive examples. To save you the time of having to retype these, along with fixing all the typing errors, we have created a set of code files. For the chapters where there is code, all the code is available in a separate file. This will allow you to quickly try out the examples shown in each of the chapters.

You can download the ZIP file from the McGraw-Hill Professional website at

www.mhprofessional.com

Simply enter this book's title or ISBN in the search box and then click the Downloads & Resources tab on the book's home page.

PART
I

The Importance of SQL, PL/SQL, and a Good Data Model

CHAPTER
1

SQL and PL/SQL

B usiness is often based on knowledge and information, and all the important information is usually in a database. A relational database can only be accessed using the Structured Query Language (SQL), which is a standardized language for managing data held in a relational database management system (RDBMS). The Procedural Language/Structured Query Language (PL/SQL) is Oracle Corporation's extension of the SQL language that gives you the ability to develop procedural code (for example, IF...THEN...ELSE, loops, and so on) for an Oracle RDBMS.

Introduction to SQL and PL/SQL

The database is the place where all important information is located, and, of course, the user needs a way to get that information from the database as well as a way to keep the information up to date. It is very important that the database is well designed for its intended purpose. A good design guarantees the performance needed and the quality of the data, among other things. You can read more about designing databases in Chapter 2. Because it is important that the data is up to date, there must be a way to maintain it.

SQL is a standardized language for managing the information in an RDBMS. SQL allows you to query the information and to manipulate it. It supports inserting, updating, deleting, and, of course, selecting data from a database. Using SQL is the most efficient way of handling data, meaning that it performs every action in the database and retrieves only the rows needed outside the database, which makes handling and moving data safer and performance better. Some people like to drag all the data to the application server, the middle tier, and do the filtering and joining there, but that is certainly not the safest and most efficient way of performing the task. Using the combination of the database and SQL is the best method for handling data because they were invented for that purpose. What's more, SQL is the only language the database understands.

On the other hand, SQL only supports single SQL clauses at a time, and in many cases that is not enough: you need procedural structures to get the business logic and results required. To fill this gap, Oracle offers PL/SQL, which is a procedural extension to SQL for the Oracle RDBMS. PL/SQL allows you to use procedural programming structures, such as IF...THEN...ELSE and loops, and makes it possible to save the program code into the database to be called both from inside and outside the database. Since Oracle 12c there have been a lot of improvements to the performance of PL/SQL. Although using SQL is considered the fastest method, since version 12.1 you can define schema-level functions/procedures with pragma UDF, which is almost as fast as using pure SQL. Using a function/procedure in a WITH clause is almost as fast as pragma UDF. The ordinary schema-level function/procedure used before Oracle 12.1 is much slower.

SQL

SQL was created for interacting with RDBMSs and provides the only way to communicate with them. Like any invention, though, it's not perfect. The problem is that the relational model is based on relational theory, but SQL is unfortunately not relational in every sense of the word—and that will cause problems. To avoid those loopholes, you must understand relational theory, how SQL departs from it, and how to write SQL relationally. To understand the relational model, read C. J. Date's book *Database in Depth: Relational Theory for Practitioners* (O'Reilly, 2005). In this chapter, we examine some examples of nonrelational features of SQL, but if you want to learn more about the relational model and how to write truly relational SQL, read C. J. Date's book *SQL and Relational Theory: How to Write Accurate SQL Code* (O'Reilly, 2009).

The best examples of nonrelational implementations in SQL are duplicate rows and nulls. Let's look at duplicates first. A table can never contain duplicates because a table structure is a result set (that is, a set of tuples), and sets in mathematics never contain duplicate elements. Thus, the optimizer might rely on this known fact when rewriting a query for better performance, but in some cases will end up with an incorrect result because the assumption of not having duplicate rows was wrong. Another example is error handling. It might be difficult if duplicates are allowed because you wouldn't know whether the duplicate row was correct or an error.

So how do you end up getting duplicates? One way is when the database designer does not define a primary key (PK), or at least a unique key for a table, and thus allows duplicate rows in the table. Alternatively, the designer might define a surrogate key without a unique constraint, and so there is no constraint really watching for the data integrity and data quality. If we assume the database designer knows enough to define a PK (and a unique constraint if using a surrogate PK) for each and every table, we might think there is no risk of duplicates—but we would be wrong. Due to the way SQL behaves, the risk exists—not for the base table in the database but for the result set after the SQL query.

Let's consider a database with two tables: Customers and Orders. In this case, we have a table for customers that has columns named customer_no and customer_name, as well as a denormalized, summarized column for the total number of orders for each customer named tot_order_count. In the ORDERS table, we have all orders for the customer as well as columns named order_no, customer_customer_no, and order_amount (the monetary value of this order). We have a column named customer_customer_no because in our naming standards we have defined the foreign key columns to follow the convention *parent tablename_column name*. Defining the naming standards for your design work is very important for better consistency and quality. Good database design tools support naming standards.

DISTINCT is only defined as the default for UNION, INTERSECT, and EXCEPT, but ALL is the default for all the other commands like SELECT ALL or UNION ALL, for instance. Suppose we have a history table for customers (CUSTOMERS_HISTORY). For some reason, the business rule dictates that this history table include both current and previous customers.

```
SELECT CUSTOMER_NO, CUSTOMER_NAME, TOT_ORDER_COUNT FROM CUSTOMERS_HISTORY

CUSTOMER_NO     CUSTOMER_NAME     TOT_ORDER_COUNT
1               Customer_A        -
2               Customer_B        1
42              Customer_42       10000
```

If we are not aware of this implementation, we might expect current customers to be in CUSTOMERS and only the past customers to be in CUSTOMERS_HISTORY and therefore use UNION ALL to find all the customers, like so:

```
SELECT CUSTOMER_NAME FROM CUSTOMERS
UNION ALL
SELECT CUSTOMER_NAME FROM CUSTOMERS_HISTORY

CUSTOMER_NAME
Customer_A
Customer_B
```

```
Customer_A
Customer_B
Customer_42
```

As you can see, the result is not what we expect: we have all the existing customers twice in the result set. In this case, the right way to query would have been like this:

```
SELECT CUSTOMER_NAME FROM CUSTOMERS
UNION
SELECT CUSTOMER_NAME FROM CUSTOMERS_HISTORY

CUSTOMER_NAME
Customer_42
Customer_A
Customer_B
```

This example provides two lessons:

■ If you define data structures (for performance or any other reason) that are not self-documenting (for example, following relational theory, like the CUSTOMERS_HISTORY table in our example), you need to make sure everybody is aware of the logic for how the data is saved and the way it should be retrieved.

■ If you use ALL operations, remember that all the rows for all the tables in the query will be in the result set, even possible duplicates.

Of course, the classical example of nonrelational behavior in a result set is the Cartesian join. A Cartesian join is a typical result when the tables in a SQL query are not joined correctly. For instance, here we query the tables CUSTOMERS and ORDERS without a join on customer number:

```
SELECT CUSTOMER_NO, CUSTOMER_NAME, ORDER_NO FROM CUSTOMERS, ORDERS

CUSTOMER_NO     CUSTOMER_NAME     ORDER_NO
1               Customer_A        99
2               Customer_B        99
```

This shows that **order_no=99** is an order made by both of our customers, which is, of course, not true. Understanding when to join tables, and how, is very important. Also, defining the foreign keys correctly really helps in building the joins (and maintaining the data quality).

Another troublemaker is NULL. In theory, table structures never contain nulls because they are sets of tuples, and tuples never contain nulls. Having nulls means having three-valued logic: true, false, and unknown. So if a value is NULL, what does it mean? It can mean that there is no information, we do not know the information (unknown), or we simply do not have privileges to that information even though it does exist. SQL only partly supports three-valued logic. For instance, the BOOLEAN data type only contains two values: true and false. This mismatch causes problems. As you can see, NULL is not an easy concept and therefore makes a lot of trouble in databases.

The NULL problem can occur if NULLs are allowed in a database. Usually that is done because the information is not always available or the business cannot define the data to be mandatory for some reason. The database designer should be the one saying that NULLs are not allowed and demand that the business define at least a default value in case the data is not otherwise available. In a database, a "not NULL" constraint is used to define that this data is mandatory. Since Oracle 12.1, users have been able to define a default value on explicit NULLs. That default is defined in the CREATE TABLE clause for a column that might have NULL values.

For example, let's consider a customer who has not yet ordered anything. For some reason, the tot_order_amount has been defined as nullable, meaning that NULLs are allowed, and it is only updated when the customer makes an order. Therefore, when a customer has not ordered anything, the value is NULL.

```
SELECT CUSTOMER_NO, CUSTOMER_NAME, TOT_ORDER_COUNT FROM CUSTOMERS

CUSTOMER_NO      CUSTOMER_NAME      TOT_ORDER_COUNT
1                Customer_A         -
2                Customer_B         1

SELECT ORDER_NO, ORDER_AMOUNT, CUSTOMER_CUSTOMER_NO FROM ORDERS

ORDER_NO      ORDER_AMOUNT      CUSTOMER_CUSTOMER_NO
99            12.5              2
```

Here, you can see that the customer with customer number 1 has not ordered anything, and the customer with customer number 2 has placed one order (**order_no 99**). If we do not know the implementation of the requirement, we might not be aware that the result set could include NULL values and therefore we might not be prepared for them when handling the data in the result set. For instance, we might query CUSTOMERS with **tot_order_count=0**, or we might summarize the total number of orders in the Helsinki area, not realizing that the NULLs will destroy our result set. If your database contains NULL values, be aware of that fact and make sure they are handled correctly.

Another possibility is that for some reason the result set returns NULLs even though there are no NULLs in the database. For instance, most of the aggregate functions return NULL for an empty result set. For instance, the query

```
SELECT SUM(ORDER_AMOUNT) FROM ORDERS WHERE CUSTOMER_CUSTOMER_NO=1
```

would return a NULL value if there are no rows for the customer with customer_no 1:

```
SUM(ORDER_AMOUNT)
-
```

Also, if you are not aware of this behavior, you might use this result set for another counting operation and get a completely incorrect result. For instance, suppose you use it for counting a 10 percent commission:

```
SELECT (SUM(ORDER_AMOUNT))*0.1 AS COMMISSION FROM ORDERS WHERE CUSTOMER_CUSTOMER_NO=1

COMMISSION
-
```

A commission of zero would be understandable, but what does a commission NULL mean?

One exception on aggregate functions that returns zero on NULL values is COUNT. But unfortunately COUNT has its own risks if you are not aware of its behavior. Think about a query where we want to find customers who have a denormalized tot_order_count equal to the count of orders:

```
SELECT CUSTOMER_NO, CUSTOMER_NAME FROM CUSTOMERS C
WHERE TOT_ORDER_COUNT = (
SELECT COUNT(ORDER_AMOUNT) FROM ORDERS O
WHERE O.CUSTOMER_CUSTOMER_NO=C.CUSTOMER_NO)
```

```
CUSTOMER_NO       CUSTOMER_NAME
2                 Customer_B
```

In this case, you would probably expect to see all the customers. You might think that Customer_A should also be in the result set because that customer has zero orders. However, because we defined that the tot_order_count column would be updated only when the first order was made, a customer without any orders is not in the result set. To be able to have this customer in the result set, the total amount for the customer should be zero and the row should be returned. Another surprise with COUNT can arise with nested SQL queries if the value to compare to in the outer query is zero and the value in the inner query is COUNT(NULL), meaning there are no rows in the inner query that satisfy the criteria. In that case, the query would be true (0=0), even though in real life it is not. Sometimes when you're optimizing a query and changing it from a flat query to a nested query, or the opposite, the result set might change.

An outer join is another example of a SQL feature that might cause NULL values in the result set, even though the data itself does not have NULLs. Let's look at this query:

```
SELECT CUSTOMER_NAME, ORDER_NO FROM CUSTOMERS C, ORDERS O WHERE O.CUSTOMER_
CUSTOMER_NO (+)= C.CUSTOMER_NO
```

```
CUSTOMER_NAME     ORDER_NO
Customer_A        -
Customer_B        99
```

If a customer has no orders, the query would return (in our example) Customer_A, NULL. To avoid outer joins, it is very important that you define a mandatory relationship whenever possible and that you understand what you really need to query for. For instance, our sample query actually makes no sense. If we needed to know all the customers, we would query just the Customers table, and if we needed to know all the orders and add the customer information to that, we should use an inner join (natural join).

But nevertheless, SQL is the only language for querying and manipulating data in an RDBMS database, and if you know how it works you can avoid the problems related to nonrelational behavior. Actually, none of the problems described earlier is relevant if you know what you are doing: just be sure to design your database well, know how business rules are implemented in your database, and understand how SQL works. Keep in mind that the power of SQL does not reach the more complex business logic because SQL only allows you to write single SQL clauses. After all, it is a query language, not a programming language. SQL clauses can be very long and complicated and perform unbelievable tasks, especially when all possible functions and procedures are being used, but writing SQL clauses that are too complicated is not wise. Why? What if you have a wonderful and super-smart SQL clause that is ten pages long, but you realize it is not performing as well as it should or is not returning the right result set. How do you change that query into a better one? How about if the requirements change and you need to change the SQL clause accordingly. Could you do it and would the query still work? If the query is too complicated, tuning and maintaining it will be an impossible mission. Writing simple and understandable SQL is always the best—not just for other people, but also yourself. (Six months later you probably won't remember what the great idea in that particular SQL clause was.) Anything can be done using SQL, but if the query becomes too complicated or if elements such as loops and IF...THEN...ELSE structures are needed, then it's time to think about using PL/SQL.

PL/SQL

PL/SQL (Procedural Language/Structured Query Language) is Oracle Corporation's procedural extension for SQL for the Oracle RDBMS. PL/SQL extends SQL by adding constructs used in procedural languages to enable more complex programming than SQL provides. Examples of these structures are IF...THEN...ELSE, basic loops, FOR loops, and WHILE loops. PL/SQL also offers the possibility of using a SQL cursor, which is a private Oracle SQL working area. There are two types of SQL cursors: implicit cursors and explicit cursors. The implicit cursors are used by Oracle Server to test and parse SQL statements, and the explicit cursors are declared by programmers and used in the code. A PL/SQL code can also be saved in the database and reused from there. A batch routine (that is, code that processes a large number of records at the same time) is a good example of a routine that should be written in PL/SQL.

Only two procedural languages can run inside Oracle Database: PL/SQL and Java. A major difference between those two is that Java only has subroutine support for SQL, whereas PL/SQL has subroutine support for both SQL and embedded SQL. PL/SQL was invented for this purpose; Java was not. PL/SQL also has support for dynamic SQL, which is explained in Chapter 8, and it supports all SQL data types and bulk load operations. What's more, privileges can be defined very well for PL/SQL objects without giving any privileges to the actual database tables, and since Oracle 12.1, whitelists can be used for defining programs that are privileged to call a program. PL/SQL understands the Oracle errors, and exceptions are easier to build. Since Oracle Database 12.1, pragma UDF can be used to get almost as good a performance as with SQL, and with the clarity and reusability of PL/SQL. Edition-based redefinition (EBR) can be used to upgrade PL/SQL code or object structures in the database without interrupting application availability. You can read more about EBR in Chapter 5. There are many other features that make PL/SQL the best choice for programming in the Oracle Database. For instance, PL/SQL is a strongly typed language; all the variables must be declared, and they must have types. PL/SQL supports overloading, meaning that there can be procedures/functions with the same name but different parameters. This is very useful when two versions of the same program unit are needed.

The basic unit in PL/SQL is the block, and all PL/SQL programs are built of blocks. These blocks can be nested within each other. Usually each block performs a logical action in the program, and each block can be given a name. The logic is always performed in the database and compiled in it. When you're writing PL/SQL code, you might find it useful from a productivity standpoint to first execute it without saving to the database; then, when you are ready, you save it. The code can be saved in the database as a function, procedure, package, type, or trigger.

Both functions and procedures are known as *subprograms*. A subprogram can be created as a database object, being a stand-alone subprogram on the schema level, or as a packaged subprogram inside a package or inside a PL/SQL block. A function is generally used for calculations (for instance, calculating the discounted price for a product), and a procedure is generally used for performing an action (for instance, creating a new customer in the database). PL/SQL functions support recursion, meaning you can call the function itself. As in any programming language, PL/SQL functions return a value, but a procedure does not return anything. Both functions and procedures can have parameters for input (IN) and output (OUT), but a parameter can also be both ways (IN OUT). An IN OUT parameter passes a value to a subprogram and returns an updated value to the caller. Each subprogram has three parts: declaration, executable, and exception handling. Only the executable part is mandatory, but all parts are recommended. To show your level of professionalism, you should always include exception handling. It is quite confusing for end users to get unhandled exceptions.

A *package* is a database object that groups logically related PL/SQL types, variables, objects, and subprograms. Packages usually have two parts: a specification and a body. The specification is the interface to the package. It declares (DECLARE) the types, variables, constants, exceptions, cursors, and subprograms available to be called outside the package. The body contains the code, divided into procedures and functions, and there can also be an initialization section that is executed only once during a session. All objects in the specification are public objects, whereas the objects in the body are private objects. You can debug, improve, change, or replace a package body without changing the package specification (the interface).

A *type* is a definition of an object. CREATE TYPE can be used to create the specification of an object type, a SQLJ object type, a named varying array (varray), a nested table type, or an incomplete object type. Just like packages, types have a definition and a body. The definition of a type is a defined list of attributes and possibly member functions and packages. If the type contains member functions or procedures, the code is defined in the TYPE BODY. Those objects defined using types can be used, for instance, as a data type for a column in a table.

A *trigger* is a database object in a DBMS that can be used to execute code automatically in a database. There are four types of database triggers: table-, view-, database-, and session-level triggers. You can use triggers, for instance, to populate a history table automatically.

Oracle also allows you to embed code in database views. This is extremely useful if you are using views on the application API. You may use a function in the SELECT part of the SQL statement for the view. For instance, if you want to return the age of a customer instead of his or her birthday, you can do so easily in the SQL statement for the view by calling the appropriate function. Alternatively, you can embed the PL/SQL code in INSTEAD OF triggers on a view. Using these triggers, you can perform INSERT, UPDATE, and DELETE operations on complex views.

Summary

SQL is the only interface to a relational database, and PL/SQL is a procedural extension to SQL. It is important to understand how SQL works and to design databases and business logic correctly to get the right result set. PL/SQL can be used inside the database, and it has many powerful features. There are a lot of improvements to PL/SQL in Oracle Database 12.1. Use SQL whenever possible, but if your query gets too complicated or procedural features are needed, it is best to use PL/SQL instead.

CHAPTER
2

Expert Data Modeling and Implementing Business Logic

B usiness logic is what makes software right for a given purpose. If that is understood but the software is implemented incorrectly and doesn't serve its purpose, it is no help to its users. Some business logic can be implemented in database objects through the database design, but more complex logic cannot. It is important to make decisions about implementing business logic in a way that recognizes maintainability, security, performance, and the existing skillsets people have.

Database design is central to guaranteeing the quality of the data and the performance needed. All the business logic that possibly can be implemented in a database structure's design should be implemented there.

Designing a database is much easier if you have a tool for that purpose, and it is important that the tool fully support the database design work. Oracle SQL Developer Data Modeler is one possibility, and it is free to use.

Implementing Business Logic

Business logic is what makes software behave in the way the users want and makes it different from other software. During requirements analysis and conceptual design, end users state their requirements for the application. Also, the business logic is documented and is implemented later on in the process.

Business Logic in Database Objects

Some business logic is clear and easy to implement while designing the database. For instance, the price of a product is numeric information with a length of 15 numbers and two decimal places. This business logic will be implemented in the database as a data type and a length. If you want to be even more thorough in the database design work, you can even define it as a domain and use it in every attribute that would be a type of money. Another example might be that every customer must have a customer number and a name. This business logic can be implemented in the database as mandatory columns. One more example of business logic that can and should be implemented in the database is that an order must belong to a customer; in other words, there cannot be orders that do not belong to a customer. This is implemented as a mandatory relationship. These are typical examples of business logic that can and must be implemented in the database during the database design phase. While the database is being designed, the rules for data are implemented in the database (mandatory columns, relationships, and so on) as well as they can be. However, not all the rules can be implemented in tables, columns, or constraints.

More complex examples might be that the order date cannot be prior to the birth date of a customer or that a customer cannot have more than two addresses. These can be implemented in the database, too: the first one as a constraint and the second one by creating two columns for addresses, for instance, and no more than that. This kind of business logic can be added to the program code of the application, too. However, there is also more complex business logic that cannot be implemented in the database design—it can only be implemented programmatically. This program code can be located either in the database or outside the database in any programming language. It is important to decide where the business logic is implemented and how. Some important aspects to think about when making this decision are maintainability, security, performance, and the existing skillsets of the users.

Business Logic in the Code

It is a known fact that it is more efficient and less error prone to build the business logic on components or modules that can be combined, where one module includes a single piece of business logic. Those modules can be called from other modules, and they can be joined to other modules to get more complex business logic. If a single piece of business logic is programmed only once, in one module, it guarantees that this business logic always works the same way no matter where this module is called from. Also, if the requirement for the business logic changes, it will be easier to change just one module. For instance, calculating the interest for a loan and calculating the discounted price for a product are examples of a single piece of business logic and thus candidates for a module.

Security is an important factor in deciding the implementation of the business logic. Different aspects of security must be considered because data can leak in several places. The simple example of security is privileges. Privileges must be defined and implemented in all locations where the data is saved and to which it is moved. Of course, the data should be saved and moved safely, possibly encrypted, and there is no point in moving data that is not needed—the more data is moved, the bigger the risk of leaking the data.

Also, in terms of performance, it is not wise to move unnecessary data; only the data needed should be moved. The bandwidth required to move unnecessary data can be huge, and although the technology is getting better every day, common sense is still king. Therefore, do not move data that does not need to be moved.

This leads to another point: joining data. The best place for joining data from different tables is the database; it's designed for joins and handling data. There is no point in moving all the possibly needed data to the application server, for instance, and joining it there. First of all, moving unnecessary data incurs a cost. Second, joining rows in an application server costs more than it does in the database, not only because there are more rows but also because the application server is not designed for joins. For instance, if you need all undelivered orders for a certain customer, it would not be wise to move all the order information to the application server for further investigation. Of course, you should join the customer and the order in the database and only return the rows that belong to that customer (the join) and only the rows for undelivered orders (the WHERE part of the query).

Quite often people underestimate the power of existing skillsets. It is always fun to learn new things, new programming languages and techniques, but learning new things also incurs a cost. If you start learning a new programming language, no matter how good a programmer you are, it takes a while before you really are productive. And if you need to use your new skills for something really complicated, something that this programming language might not even be designed for, you will be required to expend a great deal of time and energy to complete your task. If you already have the skills for SQL and PL/SQL, why would you not take advantage of them? Remember SQL is the only language that can really access a relational database, and PL/SQL is the only programming language for Oracle databases invented for embedded SQL and that can be saved in the database.

There is no better place for business logic than the database. It is most likely well secured; there's no need to move unnecessary data anywhere (only the result set); it is designed for handling data; and you already have the right skillset. In fact, the more logic you have in the database, the better it performs and the easier it is to change to a new technology for implementing the user interface when needed. The database is not changed often, but, based on our experience, the user interface is. If the business logic lies in the user interface layer, it must be programmed (and tested) every time the technology is changed.

As mentioned earlier, SQL is the only language that can be used when accessing a relational database, and PL/SQL is its extension. PL/SQL can be executed as an anonymous script (for instance, @FindCustomer.sql), or it can be stored in the database. Both SQL and PL/SQL are executed inside the database. PL/SQL logic can be stored in a database as a standalone procedure, a standalone function, or as package holding procedures, functions, data structures, constants, and so on. When the PL/SQL logic is stored in the database, it can be called outside the database with a programming language that can connect to the database and perform SQL calls as well as call a stored PL/SQL unit. PL/SQL can also be stored in a database as a trigger. The trigger logic will be executed when the defined operation happens in the database. For instance, if a trigger has been defined that's launched after an insert to a table called CUSTOMER, it will automatically perform the business logic programmed into it every time a row is inserted in this table. Maybe the best part of PL/SQL is that it works the same way in any Oracle environment, if it compiles. PL/SQL is backward compatible, and the hardware or operating system used does not affect how PL/SQL works. If you program the business logic using SQL or PL/SQL once, it can be used forever, unless the business logic changes.

From a security aspect, the most secure way to implement business logic is in the database and in stored PL/SQL units. The best place to implement security is, in my opinion, the database using the database privileges. You might want to have two schemas in the database: one for the application tables and another for the business logic, which is the application programming interface (API) layer. The API schema would only hold the stored packages, procedures, and functions, and users only have privileges to those items. Only the stored PL/SQL would have privileges to the application tables, and therefore those tables are quite safe from any misuse. Since Oracle Database 12c, you are also able to define whitelists. This means that you can specifically define which PL/SQL units will have the privilege to call which PL/SQL units. When the list has been defined, there is no way anybody can access the application tables without permission—directly or using a stored PL/SQL unit. It is also possible to implement the third layer (schema) that only has access to the specifications of the business logic, not the code itself. Users having access to only the third layer would, for instance, know the table names, column names, or the business logic in the code. Using database schemas and privileges will definitely provide the best security for the application.

Designing a Database and Data Models

Designing a database is the most important action you can take to guarantee the quality of the data and the performance of the application. Data modeling is a process for analyzing, defining, and implementing the requirements into a data model. Generally the notations used include entity-relationship diagrams (ERDs) and data flow diagrams. When designing a database, you need to understand the target you're modeling for and not try to model everything. You must also fully understand the requirements to implement them correctly. If you use an agile development process, you will need a big picture of the database during requirements analysis, and during the conceptual design you specify the entities and attributes needed for that iteration.

The Design Process

In this author's opinion the best and most efficient way of modeling data is using a modeling tool. Especially if you are working within an agile system development process, you have no other choice but to use a tool. A personal favorite is Oracle SQL Developer Data Modeler (or just Data Modeler), which supports all the features needed and is free to use: you can just download and start using it. If you want to read more about database design and Data Modeler, see Heli Helskyaho's book *Oracle SQL Developer Data Modeler for Database Design Mastery* (Oracle Press, 2015).

The design process starts with requirements analysis. Then it's time for conceptual, logical, and physical database design before the designer gets the scripts (DDLs) for creating the database objects needed.

The relational database is based on relational theory, and there are many ways of modeling the same requirement. Although you can't always say that one is better than another, sometimes you can. The logic gives you guidance in finding and choosing one definition over another and reasons for that choice. The relational theory helps in implementing the logic in an ER model. Understanding the relational theory is a very valuable skill for a database designer. The designer should have at least an elementary awareness of basic logic to be able to rework the requirements into a more formal format and the courage to ask a lot of questions to be sure what the end user actually means. If you do not ask questions, you can never be sure you have understood the requirements correctly.

When you're designing the database, you'll find it valuable to start the work as soon as possible because when turning the requirements into a formal format, you'll understand that there are many questions you have not asked yet.

Requirements Analysis

During requirements analysis, the goal for a database designer is to find and analyze the requirements for the application and the database. The results of this process are the specifications of the user requirements. The work during requirements analysis involves gathering all the possible data available and formalizing it into a consistent format. The work mainly consists of interviews, meetings, reading documentation, and using any possible way to find the unwritten information. The requirements analysis phase is quite often mostly about listening and asking questions. The questions should not be limited to just data requirements but also address how the data will be used. And all this information should be documented. Most people will not tell you the same requirement twice, so make sure you listen the first time. A good tip from Daniel Linstedt (inventor of the Data Vault methodology) is to always record your sessions with end users. This helps guarantee better quality requirements and gives you the opportunity to listen to the requirements again. You might also understand them better later on in the process. Another important point that might be forgotten is that it is critical to verify the result with end users to be sure you have understood the requirements correctly.

Requirements analysis can also be used for defining project goals and for planning development cycles and increments in an agile system development method. A key outcome of requirements analysis is that the requirements also serve as a source for planning test cases; the business logic implemented should be equivalent to the one planned. Quite often, the requirements analysis also provides input for the project risk analysis. When defining requirements, it is valuable to determine which requirements are mandatory, which are optional, and which will be prioritized over others (ranking). There are at least three kinds of requirements: data, functional, and nonfunctional requirements. The better you understand all of these types, the better you can implement them in database design and in business logic.

The database designer should join the project in the early stages. Too often the designer joins the team during the conceptual design phase or during the logical database design phase. Many times the database designer does not even know there is a new project going on because everybody thinks he or she has nothing to do yet. During requirements analysis, the database designer should ask all the questions needed to find out what data this new system has (*data requirements*) and how it is used (*functional requirements*). Also, he or she should try to get all possible nonfunctional requirements for the database. Examples of nonfunctional requirements include security and performance requirements. Leaving the database designer out of this work is not very wise.

The documenting of the requirements analysis may vary depending on the processes your organization has and the tools you are using. Quite often the requirements analysis involves writing notes, but Data Modeler provides a logical entity relationship (ER) model, data flow diagrams (DFD), and transformation packages to formalize the documentation. Data Modeler also lets you document business information such as the responsible parties, contacts, phone numbers, e-mails, and so on. All models created during the requirements analysis in Data Modeler can be used as a basis for the design work when moving to the conceptual design phase. All the information added to Data Modeler can also easily be extracted from Data Modeler with built-in or custom reports. This is a good reason to have all the documentation in Data Modeler. Another good reason is that you will have all your documentation in one place, and you do not need to remember which disc and directory you saved your documents in.

Remember that in the requirements analysis phase the database designer does not try to model everything—just the main concepts and their relationships and behavior. Requirements analysis is important because it is during the design phase that you can see the whole picture and understand the scope for the design work. This author works mostly in agile projects, and therefore the other phases after this one involve looking at a specific iteration. This is also an important phase for a database designer because when the designer understands the scope, he or she can better comment on the content of the iterations from a database-design perspective.

Conceptual Database Design and Logical Model

Conceptual database design involves very much the same work for a database designer as requirements analysis, but the difference is that now the database designer must get all the information needed to really design the database. What's more, if the development methodology is agile, the scope is limited. You should start the modeling with the entity relationship (ER) model and data flow diagrams (DFDs) you created during requirements analysis. If you do not have anything from requirements analysis, you must start from scratch. At best that means more work; it might even mean you don't have enough information to make the right modeling decisions. Now all the entities and attributes you need should be added to the ER diagram and you should understand the data flows. The main concern in conceptual design is the data and how it should be saved and retrieved. Also, all possible business logic should be implemented in the data model. The result of conceptual database design is a conceptual schema and process models, and the main tools are the ER model and the DFDs.

Quite often the problem in conceptual database design, just like in requirements analysis, is that there is not enough material or information. The database designer must ask a lot of questions and demand answers. It is usually easier for the end users to provide brief answers, but the result will not be good if their answers are not complete. Another big problem is silent information: people do not always state everything because they assume everybody already knows it. And, as we all know, spoken language is not always exact, which also might cause misunderstandings. During the conceptual design phase, you should use the same methods as in the requirements analysis phase and record your meetings and interviews.

Conceptual database design is one of the most important phases in database design. In conceptual database design, you define all the entities, their attributes, and the relationships between entities. An *entity* is a logical object from the business scope—for instance, a customer or a bank account. *Attributes* are properties that define and specify that entity—for instance, first name, last name, date of birth, and account number. Each of these attributes has a data type and length. They can be mandatory or optional, and they might have default values, a list of allowable values, or defined ranges. A default value could be, for instance, the current day for the order date. A list of allowable values for an address might include the delivery address and invoicing address, and the range for an order amount could be 0–1000000. An attribute can also be designed as a sensitive attribute, in which case you can define redaction and/or masking rules for it. You can read more about these features in Chapter 13.

You should also define *relationships,* which describe how entities are related to other entities. A relationship can be mandatory or optional, and it has cardinality, such as 1:1, 1:m, or n:m. *Cardinality* means, for example, that for one customer there can be just one order (1:1) or several orders (1:m), or that one order can have several products and that one product can be in several orders (n:m). A relationship can also be *identifying,* which means that the primary key of the parent table is part of the primary key of the child table. These kind of entities are called *weak entities*—they always need another entity to define their existence. For instance, an order line would be nothing without an order. The same entity can participate in a relationship several times in different roles; for instance, an employee can be both an employee and a supervisor, and both an employee and a supervisor are employees. A relationship can also have its own attributes. For example, a relationship between the Customers and Orders entities might have an attribute of Date of Purchase.

Another important item to define is the primary key. For each entity, you specify one primary key that uniquely identifies each entity instance. In other words, this means that there cannot be two rows with the same primary key in a table. All attributes that are part of the primary key are mandatory; they cannot be nulls. The attributes for the primary key should be identifying, stable, and not undergo any changes in value. A primary key can be a natural key, meaning that it consists of one or more entity attributes. A natural key truly identifies that entity, especially for the business. Also, the primary key can be a surrogate key when it consists of one attribute (usually a numeric attribute) that has no meaning to the entity itself or the business, but it separates each entity from the others. You can also define one or more additional unique identifiers as unique constraints or unique keys, if needed. All of this should be defined in the conceptual design. If you decide to have a surrogate key as the primary key, be sure to define a unique key as well to ensure that there are no logical duplicate rows in the table.

Defining the primary key is one of the most important decisions to be made during conceptual database design. As mentioned earlier, when selecting the primary key, you have two choices: a natural key or a surrogate key. Which one is better? The only correct answer to any question about modeling issues is, "It depends." A natural key is usually more efficient: sometimes you can eliminate a join because the child table already has this valuable information, sometimes the query optimizer works more efficiently, and so on. However, finding a natural primary key is not always possible (although in many cases this indicates that there is something wrong with the model). In many cases the problem in finding a natural primary key is simply that designers are too cautious to set attributes to "not null" and therefore are only able to define those attributes as unique keys. As you'll remember, all the attributes in a primary key must be mandatory and therefore cannot have null values.

The business may not be understood well enough to know what really identifies the entity. One of the main concerns in designing the database is the data quality. To get good quality data, you must understand what you are modeling and you must be able to set as many attributes to "not null" as possible and to find all possible constraints. A surrogate primary key does not stop users from inserting logical duplicates in the database, but a natural key does. Also, the index for a surrogate primary key is not often used because queries are not performed based on a surrogate attribute. On the other hand, quite often the best solution for data that comes from another system and is not controlled by your organization is a surrogate key because you can never be sure whether the data you have considered as unique will change. This is often the case with data warehousing databases. Therefore, there is no single answer to the question. If you want to have a surrogate key, make sure you define at least one unique key as well.

For a database designer, it is also important to understand how the data behaves and flows, and that can be documented using DFDs. Each data flow should be investigated and documented to be understood.

During database design, it is very important to be consistent with your modeling solutions as well as with your naming conventions. It's also wise to define abbreviations for the words used and to be consistent in using them. For instance, if you decide to use "no" for a shorter way of saying "number," then always use that. For example, do not call one attribute "Customernumber" and another one "Orderno." Also, if you decide to use the plural form of words, do not call one entity "Customer" and another entity "Orders." Always use names that are correct and really describe what the entity is supposed to be—to both you as an IT professional as well to the business. For instance, if an entity is meant to be DiscountPercentage, do not call it "Percentage" or "Discount." Naming entities and attributes incorrectly will cause a lot of confusion and will be a big risk to the data quality.

When you are done with the conceptual design, you will have ER diagrams and DFDs to continue on to logical database design.

Logical Database Design and Relational Model

Logical database design mainly involves transforming the conceptual model into a logical data model, which in Data Modeler is called the *relational model*. The result of logical design is a relational database schema: a set of relational schemas and their constraints. In other words, you will have tables and foreign keys.

The logical database design starts with the ER model that was created during the conceptual design phase. If the ER diagram is complete after conceptual design, you can start transforming it right away. In most cases, the model is not complete: you need to add attributes, define the data types, and so on. And especially now, you might start thinking about whether the entities and relationships are modeled using the relational theory, and you must make decisions regarding the more difficult modeling issues. This is the point where you must know how this database will be used; otherwise, you might make some wrong decisions.

If you made the conceptual design with Data Modeler, the logical database design will be easy: you simply click the Engineering to Relational Model button, and your tables and foreign keys are created automatically. If the conceptual design was done with another tool or without a tool, the first step is to insert all the data into Data Modeler to be able to use the functionalities Data Modeler provides for the transformation and more.

The transformation itself is quite simple: an entity will become a table, an attribute will become a column, and a relationship will become a foreign key. For a 1:m relationship, the primary key column(s) of the parent table will be added to the child table for the foreign key, and in a 1:1 relationship those will be added to the table on the mandatory side of the relationship. In both cases, if the relationship is identifying, the new foreign key column will be also added to the primary key of the child table. If the relationship has a cardinality of m:n, a new table will be created to resolve the m:n cardinality and a new column (or columns) based on the primary key attribute(s) in each table on the relationship will be created. A primary key for the new table is created based on those columns. Also, new 1:m relationships are created for both tables involved.

If a relationship has its own attributes, some tools will create a new table with all original relationships and attributes from that relationship. However, Data Modeler does not do that unless the relationship is m:n. In the case of a 1:m relationship, Data Modeler adds the attribute as a column to the child table and creates a dependent column constraint for it. If you do not want the column to be added to the child table, do not create that attribute for the relationship, but rather for the entity to which you want it to belong. This might mean that you need to create a new entity.

If an attribute is *multivalued*—for example, a phone number (home number, office number, cell phone)—you can create a user-defined data type (collection) and use that for the data type for the attribute, or you can either split the attribute into several attributes in the entity or create a new entity for the multivalued attribute. Usually a new entity is recommended because it is more flexible. But as stated earlier, it depends. Sometimes you need to limit the values to a certain amount, and then it is better to use that number of attributes in the original entity. For instance, the business logic might define that a person is allowed to have no more than three phone numbers.

If an attribute is *composite* (structured)—for instance, an address (StreetName, Number, City, ZIP, Country)—you can create a user-defined data type (structured) and use that for the attribute, or you can either split the attribute into several attributes in the entity or create a new entity (or entities) for the composite attribute. Usually a new entity is recommended because it is more flexible, and you might also find additional attributes for the entity (AddressType, AddressValidUntil, and so on).

After the transformation, you will have the relational model: tables, columns, and foreign keys. There will also be primary keys, unique keys, and other constraints. The relational model is still on a logical level: you have not decided yet what technology will be used. That decision will be made when creating the physical model.

Physical Design

Until this phase, everything has been quite generic in the sense of the relational database management system (RDBMS) type and its version. Now it's time to decide what technology will be selected because all the RDBMSs have their own properties for database objects and might have their own physical objects to be designed. A lot of work is also involved in the physical database design, and some of the decisions must be made with the end users (for example, user and role definitions) and some even with the company board (for example, backup strategy and definitions for sensitive data).

In the physical database design phase, you design physical database elements related to the selected technology (tablespaces, data files, and so on) and add physical properties to database objects. You estimate the space needed for the database, plan disks and disk groups, and decide which database objects to put on which disk. You must plan the backup and recovery strategies and decide how to document the database changes. There are two kinds of changes in a database: changes in database objects and changes in the RDBMS. Changes in database objects involve, for instance, adding tables or columns and removing indexes. Changes in the RDBMS involve documenting actions such as which patch was run on the database and when. You also need to decide who will document what and where. In addition, you design the database schemas, database users, roles, and privileges. You define the indexes needed, other than just indexes for primary keys and foreign keys. You design the physical database so that you can create the database as planned. The generation of Data Definition Language (DDL) is mainly based on a physical model. The outcomes from physical database design are the DDLs needed to create the database.

The Data Definition Language is for creating database objects. To be able to create the objects designed, you need to get the DDLs for them. If you are not using a tool that generates them automatically, you simply must write them manually. At this point, you're likely convinced that you need to use a tool for designing—getting the DDLs generated automatically alone is a big enough reason for that. The syntax of a DDL depends on the technology chosen. A standard for SQL is generally used, but most of the RDBMSs have their own dialect of it. Therefore, the DDLs might look a bit different depending on the technology. After creating the DDL, you simply connect to the database using the schema owner credential and execute the DDL. Now the database design is a reality for other team members too.

Introduction to Oracle SQL Developer Data Modeler

Oracle SQL Developer Data Modeler (or just Data Modeler) is a tool for designing and documenting databases. It can be used for Oracle databases as well as Microsoft SQL Server and IBM DB2 databases, or actually for any database that uses standard SQL. The tool is available as a standalone product, but there is also a version that is integrated into Oracle SQL Developer. The user can decide which one of these two is the best to use. In general, the standalone version is for database designing and the integrated version is for viewing designs other people have created.

Installing the tool is very simple: you just go to the Oracle website, download the right version of the tool, extract the .zip file, and start using the tool. Data Modeler is a free to use, and support is provided by Oracle if the customer has a database support contract.

General Things About Data Modeler

In Data Modeler, a single design is called a *design*. A design consists of one logical model and, optionally, one or more relational models that are based on that logical model as well as one or more physical models that are based on one relational model. There can also be multidimensional models, data types models, process models, domains, business information, and more. Figure 2-1 shows what Data Modeler looks like. Every element is an XML file, and these files are saved in directories that are automatically created by Data Modeler.

On the left side of Figure 2-1 you can find the Browser. The Browser is a directory of all the objects in a design. You can navigate to any of the objects with your mouse, and by right-clicking the object you can see the actions allowed for this particular object type. In the middle of the screen you can find the Start Page, which is very useful when you start using the tool. The Start Page has links to different kinds of documentation, tutorials, videos, online demonstrations, the OTN forum, and so on. If, for some reason, the Start Page disappears, you can make it visible again by selecting Start Page from the Help menu. And if any of the other panes disappear, you can make them visible by selecting the pane needed from the View menu.

The Navigator on the right side of the screen shows the whole diagram and lets you navigate to the part of the diagram you want. This is especially handy when you are working on a very large diagram. Below the Start Page you find the Messages – Log pane, which shows all activity in the tool. Anything to do with version control can be found under the Team menu. The Versions pane shows the content of Subversion directory, and the Pending Changes pane shows the

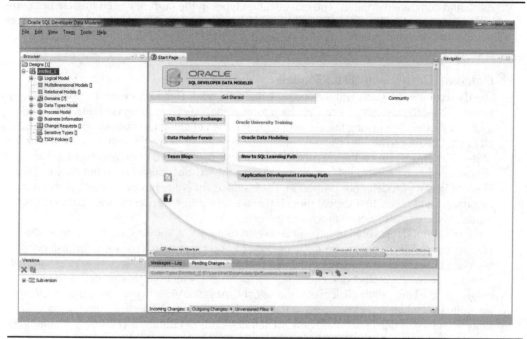

FIGURE 2-1. *Data Modeler*

Incoming Changes, Outgoing Changes, and Unversioned Files tabs. If you do not like the way these screens are arranged, you can simply drag and drop them in a different location on your monitor to support your way of working better. For instance this author prefers having the Navigator between the Browser and the working canvas.

Data Modeler does not save changes automatically. Remember to use the Save or Save As functionality under the File menu frequently enough to save any changes. You can open a design saved earlier using the Open functionality from File menu or by using the Recent Designs functionality from the same menu.

Preferences and Design Properties

Data Modeler is tuned by changing the preferences and design properties. Changing these will make the tool look and work differently. Before starting to use the tool in production, you should define some preferences and design properties. These can be changed afterward, but they only take effect at the moment of change. Also, if many other people are using the tool, it might be confusing to change the preferences and properties too often. Preferences can be found in the Tools menu, and design properties can be changed from the Browser by right-clicking the design name and selecting Properties. The difference between preferences and design properties is that preferences are valid in one installation of a Data Modeler, whereas the design properties are valid in one design. Since version 4.1, design properties can be defined as global design settings, which can be done by selecting Use Global Design Level Settings. If you select this option, the design properties will be modified to use the values in the global designs file. This file includes classification types, default fonts and colors, default line widths and colors, naming standard rules, and compare mappings. The classification types in the current design that are not currently included in the global designs file will be added automatically to the global designs file. Both settings and design properties can be exported and then imported to another computer or to another design.

Database Design with Data Modeler

The database design starts with designing a logical model. That is done on a canvas, as shown in Figure 2-2. At the top left you can see icon toolbar that has an icon for each element for designing a logical model. By clicking the element icon and then clicking the canvas, you can create this element. On the canvas you can also right-click any object to see the actions allowed for that object. The arrow sign on the very left will stop creating this kind of object, and you can either choose another type of object or start working on the existing elements on the canvas. Every element in Data Modeler has properties. For instance, an entity has properties such as name, short name, and synonyms. In a logical model, you define entities, attributes, and relationships. In Data Modeler, you can also define notes and pictures.

If the ER model is very large, you can create subviews. A subview contains the entities you choose and can be named to describe its content. You can create a subview, for instance, by selecting the entities wanted, right-clicking one of the entities, and selecting Create SubView from Selected, or you can select one entity, right-click, select Select Neighbors, define the level of neighbors, and then right-click again and select Create SubView from Selected. Any changes to an entity in a subview will be saved to the main logical model as well. A subview only contains links to entities; it does not create new implementations of entities. If you delete an entity by

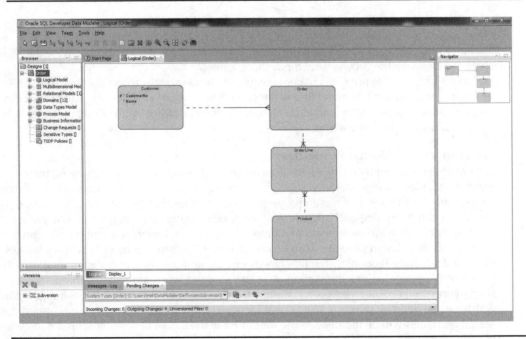

FIGURE 2-2. *A logical model*

right-clicking it and selecting Delete Object, the entity will be deleted completely. If you delete it by right-clicking and selecting Delete View, the entity will only be deleted from the subview.

The next step is to create a relational model based on the logical model, which can be done by clicking the Engineer to Relational Model icon on the toolbar for the logical model (the symbol for this icon is a double-arrow pointing to the right). You can then choose what you want to do on the Engineer to Relation Model screen and click Engineer. The relational model will then be created. You might be happy with it like that, or you might want to work with it before moving to the next phase. Whenever you change the logical model, remember to engineer those changes to the relational model using this same button.

The physical database design continues on from the relational model created in the logical database design. One relational model can have zero to as many physical models as needed. The physical model will be defined by its RDBMS site. An RDBMS site is an alias associated with an RDBMS type (Oracle 12c, Oracle 11g, SQL Server 2008, and so on) supported by Data Modeler. When creating a physical model, you must know what technology your database will be (Oracle, SQL Server, or DB2) and which version. To be able to design the physical model, you need a good understanding of the RDBMS site selected to be able to make the right decisions. All the properties for the physical model depend on the chosen technology. When you are ready with the relational model, it is time to create the physical model, which you can do by right-clicking Physical Model in Browser and selecting New.

When you have created a physical model, you should define the properties for the physical implementation of the database objects. Physical models do not have graphical presentations or diagrams, but only a browser to create, edit, and remove elements. After you have done that, you are ready to generate the DDLs (the SQL scripts for creating your database objects). DDLs can be created from the File menu under Export and DDL File. Then just execute these DDLs to your database to create the objects.

As with any naming standards, it would be valuable to agree on naming standards for physical objects such as tablespaces and data files. These cannot be documented as naming standards in Data Modeler, but for consistency it would be valuable to have a standard.

When the physical model has been created, all the updates to the relational model will be automatically implemented to the physical model (new tables or columns, for instance). In Preferences under Data Modeler | Model | Physical, you can define default values for different technologies. You can define the default user or default tablespace for a new table, for example. When you start Data Modeler, the default for physical models is to not open them automatically. The reason for this is performance: there can be hundreds of tables, tablespaces, and such in a physical model, and each of these is in its own XML file. If the tool needs to find and link all those files when opening, it might take quite a long time to open. You can define the physical model to be opened automatically by selecting a physical model when opening a design. Alternatively, you can go to Physical Models in the Browser, right-click the physical model, and select Open. The physical model will be opened.

Generating DDL scripts with Data Modeler is quite simple, and you can do it over and over again to find the right settings and preferences to get the right kinds of scripts. The more difficult task is deciding what kind of DDL files you want. Do you want a version of a whole database at a certain time in just one file, or do you want a file per object or something else? Where do you plan to keep the files and who will have access to them? What are you going to do with these files? Do you need a file for creating a whole test database of a particular version? Maybe you also need a file for creating the latest version of the CUSTOMER table for production? Before creating the DDL files, you must decide what they are for so you know what you need. Do you need different versions of DDLs for production and testing? How do they differentiate? Where do you keep the DDLs? Before the DDLs are executed in the database, they must be reviewed, and there should be a documented process for that as well. There should also be a clear understanding of who executes the DDLs in the database, as well as when and how this person documents what has been executed.

The DDLs are based on a relational model and one of its possibly many physical models. If you do not have a physical model open, only a relational model is used and the DDLs will be general without any physical parameters. You might want to use this, for instance, when creating objects for the test database where you have defined the defaults for tablespaces and users or for creating an object that does not need physical parameters of its own.

Comparing and Documenting Existing Databases

Comparing different versions of a design (or a design and database) to each other can sometimes be very valuable. When you can compare things, you gain a better understanding of what you have and what you do not have, which leads to better quality. Data Modeler has very good comparison functionalities.

In Data Modeler you can compare two designs to each other. There are two ways of doing this: via File | Import | Data Modeler Design or via Tools | Compare/Merge Models. The difference between these two methods is that File | Import | Data Modeler Design compares everything in the two designs, whereas Tools | Compare/Merge Models only compares relational and physical models, but it can also generate the ALTER DDLs for changing the database to be the same as the design.

A design and a database can be compared in four ways:

- Synchronize Model with Data Dictionary
- Synchronize Data Dictionary with Model
- File | Import | DDL File
- File | Import | Data Dictionary

The Synchronize Model with Data Dictionary and Synchronize Data Dictionary with Model options are generally used when the relational model is open and the designer wants to know how it differs from the database. The difference between these two options is that with Synchronize Model with Data Dictionary the target to be changed is the model, whereas with Synchronize Data Dictionary with Model, it is the database. File | Import | DDL File is generally used when the database designer has no access to the database but does have the DDLs for creating it. File | Import | Data Dictionary is used when the database designer has access to the database and wants to compare it to the design.

Plenty of preferences will affect these comparisons. By changing the preferences, you can change the results of the comparisons radically. Therefore, be sure to study the preferences carefully.

You can also use Data Modeler for documenting existing databases (Oracle, SQL Server, or DB2); in other words, you can reverse-engineer a database. You can do that using the data dictionary, existing DDL files, or the documentation you might have in another design tool (such as Oracle Designer or Erwin). You can also combine these items, for instance, by bringing some of the descriptions from another design tool and adding it all up with the information from the data dictionary. These features can be found under the File menu in the Import functionalities. Importing from DDL File and Importing from Data Dictionary are the same operations we use for comparisons; the only difference is that when comparing you import them to an existing relational model, whereas with reverse engineering, you import them to a new relational model.

When reverse engineering, you will have the relational and physical models created. If you want to start using Data Modeler for database design, as described earlier, you will need a logical model, which can also be generated for you automatically. Go to the canvas for the relational model. On the icon toolbar, you will find a double-arrow pointing to the left. This icon is titled Engineer to Logical, and by clicking it you tell Data Modeler to create the logical model for the relational model.

The Quality of a Database Design

Data Modeler has good support for improving the quality of your database design. You can use predefined design rules or create your own rules and rule sets. Design rules are used for automatically testing that the predefined rules for designing have been followed (for instance, there are no tables without columns, there are no attributes without a description, and so on). You can create glossaries based on the ER model or an existing glossary, and you can edit them both as much as you want. Glossaries can be used to automatically check whether the right terms are used, or they can just serve as documentation for users to know what terms are used. You can also define domains to make the data type settings for attributes more consistent. You might want to create a domain called Money (Number (15,2)) for any attributes that have anything to do with money, such as Price, DiscountedPrice, and Salary. Instead of defining Number(15,2) for all these attributes, you simply define them as domain Money.

You can compare designs and models to each other, and you can synchronize a model to a database, as well as the opposite, as explained earlier. As a result of synchronizing, you can either get your model updated to the same level with the database or get the ALTER DDLs to update your database to the same level as your model.

You can also define the table constraint templates in the design properties. You can, for instance, define how the surrogate primary keys will be named, how the surrogate primary key column will be named, or what the naming convention for foreign keys or foreign key columns will be. Also, integration with the Subversion version control tool brings better quality to the design work. When version control is enabled, even a database designer is allowed to make mistakes (you can always find a previous version of the design in which the error did not exist).

In Data Modeler, you can easily change the notation if somebody does not like the notation you are using. You can right-click the logical model canvas and select Notation, or you can select the notation from the View menu under Logical Diagram Notation.

Plenty of options are offered for adding more automatic operations to the work using Transformations or Table DDL Transformations. The difference between these two options is that Table DDL Transformations can be called when generating the DDL scripts, and it can be used, for instance, to generate DDLs for journaling tables and triggers automatically, whereas the Transformations option can be used to change the design elements automatically. Both these Transformations options can be found in the Tools menu and can be created using Java scripting.

Multiuser Environment and Version Control

Data Modeler offers integrated support for Subversion, a free-to-use version control tool. The version control integration enables both version control functionalities and a multiuser environment. As mentioned earlier, every element (entity, table, diagram, and so on) in Data Modeler has its own XML file, and each file is named by the object ID of the element. The integration with Subversion hides all the complexity of managing hundreds or thousands of files with strange and long names. In principle, it would be possible to use any version control tool for these files, but it definitely would not be wise.

To be able to use Subversion, you must first download and install it. Before starting to use it with Data Modeler, you need to consider how you want to use it. Should you have just one repository or several? What kind of directories should you have for a project? Trunk, branches, tags, or something else? How you want the user privileges to be created in Subversion dictates these decisions. Data Modeler does not control the privileges for the designs; Subversion does.

Subversion works via Copy-Modify-Merge. You copy the latest version from Subversion to your local working directory, edit it, and then save it to Subversion using Commit. When you save in Data Modeler, the changes are saved to your working directory. When you commit, the changes are saved to Subversion. The tools for version control can be found in the Team menu. The most important tool is the Pending Changes pane.

The information in Data Modeler can also be exported to Excel for editing and then imported back to the tool. The export is done by running an Excel format report using the Search tool, and the import is done by right-clicking either the logical, relational, or physical model in Browser and selecting Update Model with Previously Exported XLS (.xlsx) File. This functionality is quite useful, for instance, with end users who do not want to have access to Data Modeler but would like to add descriptions for entities and attributes.

Reporting

Reporting is one of the most important features in a design tool. There would be no point of collecting all the information in one place and then not being able to extract that information. The different needs for reporting have led to the different kinds of reports. In Data Modeler, you can find the reports under the File menu. A user can also print out a diagram by selecting that option from the File menu. Reports can be run on different output formats (HTML, PDF, RTF, XLS/XLSX) and they can be based on templates and configurations. Several report types are built into Data Modeler, and the user can create even more. A user can create *standard templates,* which are very simple but extremely easy to create and maintain, or *custom templates,* which are more complex but also very easy to create and maintain. The user can also define configurations, which means he or she can predefine which objects will be included in the report. A template might define that the report hold table names and column names, for example, whereas a configuration might define that all other tables but the ADDRESS table will be included in the report or that only those tables that are on subview_1 will be included in the report. The scope of a report can be those designs that are open, or it can be a separate reporting repository.

A *reporting repository* is a database schema with database objects for storing metadata and data about the Data Modeler designs. Designs can be added and removed from the repository using Data Modeler, and actually all the changes to the content must be done with Data Modeler using the export functionality. If you are using a reporting repository, you can also run reports written in SQL. In the datamodeler\datamodeler\reports\Reporting Schema diagrams directory, you can find the descriptions of the reporting repository, and by editing the file datamodeler\ datamodeler\reports\Reporting_Schema_Permissions.sql you get the SQL script for creating the schema owner for the reporting repository. The first time you export a design to the reporting repository, the reporting schema structure is created automatically. Remember to log in as the schema owner. You can find the exporting functionality from File | Export | To Reporting Schema.

You can also run reports through the Search option by clicking the Report button after a search. There are different ways of using Search. You can search inside an active model either by selecting View | Model Search, by clicking the Search icon on toolbar, or by right-clicking the Browser and selecting Search. When you search inside an active model, you must always select the level you are searching at—logical, relational, or physical—otherwise, the Reporting functionality is not possible. The model search can be done in two modes: simple and advanced.

In both modes you can define that the search be case sensitive, or you can use regular expressions as the search criteria. In advanced mode, you can search by any property the element type has. For instance, you can search for all attributes that have something in their Comment property. The search can also use negation (for example, all attributes that do *not* have something in their Comment property), and several properties can be combined using AND and OR operations. The search functionality is also very useful for reporting.

Summary

Understanding the requirements for business logic is vital, and implementing them correctly, in a right place, is equally vital. Some of the business logic can be implemented during the database design, but some, more complex logic cannot. It is extremely important to implement business logic in a way that takes at least into account maintainability, security, performance, and the existing skillsets people have. In my opinion, the best place for that is the database and stored PL/SQL units, which will be used as an API.

Database design helps guarantee the data quality and performance. If you make a mistake in designing the database, that mistake will live for a long time and cause a lot of problems. Database design is very systematic work and requires many skills. To make database design easier, you need a tool. Data Modeler is a good tool for database design, and it can also be used to document existing databases. In Data Modeler, when the modeling is done and the conceptual design is ready, you can use the Engineer to Relational Model button to generate the tables and their foreign keys automatically. A relational model can have as many physical models as needed. Data Modeler supports at least the Oracle, Microsoft SQL Server, and IBM DB2 relational database management systems (RDBMSs) for a physical model. A physical model is easy to create in Data Modeler—you just tell the tool which kind of physical model is needed. Using Data Modeler you can also easily generate the data definition scripts (DDLs) for creating the objects designed to go into a database—and even the ALTER DDLs for changing the object structures in the database. Data Modeler enables a multiuser environment and version control and also helps you improve the quality of your database design. Data Modeler is free to use and easy to install.

PART
II

Underutilized Advanced SQL Functionality

CHAPTER
3

Handling Advanced and Complex Data Sets

A *data set* is a collection of data. In a relational database, the data is saved in columns of the required data type. A column always belongs to one table. In an object-relational solution, the data is saved in an object. A data set can be saved data, inside or outside the database; it can be a data set used while performing a query; or it can be a query result of some form. Sometimes you need to make a decision how to save the data, sometimes getting the result might be complicated, and sometimes you need ways to handle the result set. The problem may arise because the data is big, because advanced features are used, or because the data is complex in some other way. The data can be complex, for instance, if the data type or the database structure is complex. This chapter introduces ways for saving data as well as for using the data. Note that some of the features introduced in this chapter require licensed options.

In this chapter we use mostly the EMP and DEPT tables for the examples:

```
SQL> desc Emp
 Name                                    Null?    Type
 --------------------------------------- -------- -----------------------
 EMPNO                                   NOT NULL NUMBER(4)
 ENAME                                            VARCHAR2(10)
 JOB                                              VARCHAR2(9)
 MGR                                              NUMBER(4)
 HIREDATE                                         DATE
 SAL                                              NUMBER(7,2)
 COMM                                             NUMBER(7,2)
 DEPTNO                                           NUMBER(2)


SQL> desc Dept
 Name                                    Null?    Type
 --------------------------------------- -------- -----------------------
 DEPTNO                                           NUMBER(2)
 DNAME                                            VARCHAR2(14)
 LOC                                              VARCHAR2(13)
```

Also, we will not get into the minute technical details concerning functionalities and features. The goal in this chapter is to introduce some features and techniques you might not be aware of. Knowing them might be useful when deciding how to implement a requirement. As an experienced developer, you can find all the details of a feature you find interesting on your own. We simply explain some basic concepts we think are vital to understand when you're making decisions on the right technical solution.

Some Tools for Designing the Database

The best way to guarantee the performance needed in a database is to define the performance requirements and then implement them as part of the database design. Designing the database well has a much bigger impact on the final result than anything you can do during the programming phase. That is why it is good to know about different options in database design.

Introduction to Tables

The two kinds of tables in Oracle Database are relational and object tables. There are different kinds of relational tables: heap-organized tables, index-organized tables, and external tables.

A table can be either permanent or temporary. For a permanent table, the table definition and the data persist as long as nobody deletes them. For a temporary table, the definition persists as long as nobody drops it, but the data exists only for the duration of a transaction or a session.

The data can be saved in a heap table, usually simply called a "table," inside the database, but there are other ways of saving it. The data can be saved in an external table, which is a structure saved outside the database that can be queried as if it were inside the database. The data can also be saved in an index-organized table or a temporary table, or it can be saved in a table that is partitioned to get better performance and maintainability. Alternatively, the data can be saved in a column of a special data type (for instance, a large object or a collection). Depending on the requirement, the right solution varies. It is good to know the possibilities in Oracle to be able to make the right decision.

All the different kinds of tables explained in this chapter can be designed using Oracle SQL Developer Data Modeler, and the DDLs can be automatically generated from the design.

External Table

A regular table in a database is a so-called *heap-organized table,* where the data is stored in an unorganized structure, in a heap, inside the database. A table is constructed on columns holding the data in a structured form. Another possibility to save the data is outside the database as an external table. If the data is saved in an external table, the database has no control over the existence of that data: somebody can, for instance, delete the file where the data exists without the database knowing about it. Since Oracle 10*g* it has been possible to write to external tables. In Oracle 9*i*, where this functionality was introduced, external tables were read-only structures. An external table is good when you have a flat file of data you want to upload to the database but for some reason you are not willing to create the staging table needed in the database, or if you want to load the data very quickly or the file is very large. The data in an external table can be easily queried using SQL, or it can be copied to a regular table using the INSERT INTO syntax and using SQL to transform the data on the way. Oracle uses both SQL*Loader (ORACLE_LOADER) and Datapump (ORACLE_DATAPUMP) access drivers to load and unload data. The data in an external table can, for instance, be compressed or encrypted in both reading and writing.

Another way of storing data outside the database is via a data type called BFILE, which is a Large Object (LOB) column stored outside the database. A column of the BFILE type stores only a locator, a pointer to a binary file on the server's file system. Using BFILE might be useful, for instance, if you have plenty of large pictures you do not want to be saved in the database. The downside of a BFILE is the same as with external tables: the database has no control over it; it can be removed totally from the system without the database knowing. We will talk about BFILEs later in this chapter.

Because an external table is an Oracle-specific feature in Data Modeler, you can define an external table only in the physical model of Oracle. There are two ways of doing this. If you have already designed a table in a relational model, you simply set its Organization property in Physical Model to EXTERNAL, and under the External Table Properties tab, you define the rest of the properties for it. Alternatively, if you have not defined the external table in a relational model, you select External Tables from the browser, right-click, and select New. Then you define the table properties. When generating the DDLs, note that the external tables are not found under the Tables tab but under the External Tables tab.

Index Organized Table (IOT)

As mentioned earlier, a regular relational table in a database is a heap-organized table, having data saved in a heap with no order. But there is another table structure called an *index-organized table,* which was introduced in Oracle Database 8.0. An index-organized table is sometimes more efficient because the data is stored in a b-tree index structure, ordered by a primary key: each leaf block in the index structure stores both the key and non-key columns (the actual data). Because the search only needs to find the location of key values to find all the data, the I/O operation of following the ROWID back to the table data is not needed, and the performance is much better for a search. As in any b-tree index, the rows will move when the data has been inserted (or changed) to keep the b-tree structured and balanced. Therefore, a row has no stable physical location, as rows in a heap table do, and the rows in an index-organized table will not have physical ROWIDs as heap table rows do. Instead, they have logical ROWIDs that will remain, despite the row moving between blocks constantly, as long as the primary key value for the row does not change. A logical ROWID consists of the primary key and a physical guess of a database block address where the row is likely to be found. You can use the logical ROWID as a column name in the SELECT part of a query or as part of the WHERE clause to access the rows. This is the fastest way to get data.

There is a data type in Oracle Database called Universal ROWID (UROWID) that holds any kind of ROWIDs: Oracle physical ROWIDs, Oracle logical ROWIDs, or a ROWID of another kind of database. If you are using ROWIDs in a heap table and you want to switch to an index-organized table, you have to change to UROWIDs in application development. Knowing this, it might be wise to use UROWIDs throughout your application development to avoid changes in ROWID. Although probably not something you need to worry about, it's still good to know that if you use columns of the UROWID data type, the value of the **compatible** initialization parameter must be set to 8.1 or higher, because UROWID was introduced in Oracle 8*i*.

An index-organized table performs much better in SELECT queries if only the primary key is used in accessing the data, not only because the primary key is efficient but also because the data is clustered in primary key order. Quite often the solution for a performance problem with a heap table is adding non-key columns to an index to avoid table access (having all the columns needed in the index), and an index-organized table does exactly that. On the other hand, changes to the data are also faster because only the index structure must be updated, not the table, and less storage space is needed because the primary key data is not saved twice: in the table itself and in the index structure. Index-organized tables are definitely useful if all the access to the data is through the primary key or its leading columns. If a table has only primary key column(s) and maybe one or two other columns, an index-organized table might be a good solution.

If you want to access an index-organized table efficiently without using the primary key or its leading columns, you might want to create a secondary index. This has been supported since Oracle Database 8*i*. A secondary index for an index-organized table consists of the indexed column(s) and a logical ROWID, holding the primary key columns and the physical guess of a database block address. There is something you should understand about secondary indexes: Because of the index-organized table's nature as an index, the index entries are moved when the data is inserted, deleted, or modified. Depending on the change, this can cause splits and the data ends in a different block than before. The secondary index is not automatically updated when a block split on the index-organized table occurs, so the secondary index should be maintained frequently. During an index scan on a secondary index, Oracle attempts first to use the guess of its physical location to access the block. If the location is still correct, the data wanted is found quickly and the query is performed. But if the location has changed since the last guess was updated, Oracle uses the primary key value, which is part of the logical ROWID, to perform a unique scan. As you can imagine, this is not the most efficient way for accessing the data, but it still works. Also, when defining a secondary index (or indexes), we are using more storage than without it; now we must store the primary key columns again, first in the index-organized table and then in the secondary index. The bigger the primary key is or the more we define secondary indexes, the more storage that's used and the less we are saving space with the solution using an index-organized table.

Quite often people say that they cannot define a natural primary key because most of the columns of the table would be in that primary key and they would waste a lot of valuable storage. So instead of a natural primary key they define a surrogate primary key, and hopefully at least a unique constraint for the natural primary key. An index-organized table might be the right solution in some of those cases. When using an index-organized table, you will save some storage because the key columns are not saved in both the table and the index. Also, some additional storage will be saved because no space for ROWIDs is needed. But if you do not access the data mostly using the primary key or its leading columns and need to create a secondary index (or several of them), it is possible that an index-organized table is not the best solution.

Because an index-organized table is an index structure, you can reorganize it or its table partition without rebuilding its secondary indexes, and you can do this online. The secondary index still stays usable and valid. The physical guess of the row changes, but the primary key remains, so the secondary index still works. The effect on the physical guess depends on the defined block split. If it has been defined as 50-50, it is very likely that rows will move and the physical guess will change. If it has been defined as 90-10, the impact on secondary indexes is minimized. Reorganizing is usually done to recover space or to improve performance. Also, secondary indexes can be rebuilt online. Being able to do maintenance online and without affecting other database objects is a great advantage.

 NOTE
An index-organized table cannot contain virtual columns.

Because an index-organized table is an Oracle-specific feature in Data Modeler, you can define a table to be "index organized" only in the physical model of Oracle. Set its Organization property in Physical Model to INDEX, and under the IOT Properties tab define the rest of the properties for it. When generating the DDLs, note that the external tables are not found under the Tables tab but rather under the External Tables tab.

Object Table

As we all know, Oracle Database is a relational database, not an object-oriented database. Object-oriented databases were introduced in the 1990s, and at the time were said to be superior to relational databases. For some reason they were not, and relational databases are still going strong. Object-oriented database systems have some features that have been implemented into some relational database systems (for instance, object tables). Some people call the RDBMS with object-oriented features an *object-relational database.*

Object tables combine the good features of both relational and object-oriented databases. In an object table, each row represents an object. An object identifier (OID) is a technical solution for giving the object its unique identity. An OID identifies a row object in object tables, and the object stays the same even though its attribute values might change. If you have a white chair that you paint red, it's still the same chair; its identity remains. In Oracle, an object table is based on an object type, which is a user-defined type with a name, attributes, and methods. Object types make it possible to model real-world entities such as customers and vehicles as objects in the database. In this section, we talk about the object table and its attributes, but the object also includes encapsulated methods (how the object behaves).

Let's look at a simple example of a customer object. A customer can be either a person or a company. First, we need to create the types using the Data Types Model in Data Modeler. In this case, we have three types: supertype Customer_Type and subtypes Person_Type and Company_Type:

```
CREATE OR REPLACE TYPE Customer_Type
AS
  OBJECT
  (
    Name VARCHAR2 (100 CHAR)) NOT FINAL;
  /

CREATE OR REPLACE TYPE Company_Type UNDER Customer_Type (CompanyID VARCHAR2
(11),
 ContactName VARCHAR2 (100)) FINAL;
/

CREATE OR REPLACE TYPE Person_Type UNDER Customer_Type (SSN VARCHAR2 (9)) FINAL;
 /
```

Note the NOT FINAL at the end of the CREATE clause for the supertype. It allows us to create subtypes of the supertype that has been defined in the database. If you define it as FINAL, you will not be able to create subtypes. If you want to change or drop the types, you must start with the subtypes because you cannot do anything to the supertype as long as subtypes refer to it. A type cannot be removed either if it is referred to by a table. The table must be dropped or altered first. If, for some reason, you cannot follow the right order in dropping types, you can use a parameter for dropping called **force**, which will drop the type.

After we have created the types, we can create the object tables based on these types. We want to define a table called PERSON_CUSTOMER and a table called COMPANY_CUSTOMER. To do that, we need to define the property "Based on Structured Type" for the entity or table as the corresponding type:

```
CREATE TABLE Person_Customer OF Person_Type ;
CREATE TABLE Company_Customer OF Company_Type ;
```

An object table can be seen as a multicolumn table in which each attribute of the object type occupies a column, thus allowing you to perform relational operations. In our example, the PERSON_CUSTOMER table will have all the attributes from the supertype Customer_Type and all the attributes from Person_Type as its columns. The same way, COMPANY_CUSTOMER will inherit its attributes from Customer_Type and get the attributes from Company_Type.

```
Desc Person_Customer
  NAME       VARCHAR2(100)
  SSN        VARCHAR2(9)

Desc Company_Customer
  NAME            VARCHAR2(100)
  COMPANYID       VARCHAR2(11)
  CONTACTNAME     VARCHAR2(100)
```

Note that Data Modeler automatically adds the OID for the entity after it has been defined and gives it a data type of REF Customer. There are two types of object identifiers: system-generated OID and primary-key-based OID. The system-generated identifier is created automatically by Oracle Database by default, unless you choose the primary-key-based option in the CREATE TABLE clause. The OID column is a hidden column without any access via it to the data. In Data Modeler, you can choose the primary-key-based OID by selecting the checkbox Object Identifier Is PK Property in the General Properties tab for an object table. Use Engineer to Relational Model functionality to create the tables and constraints. You might want to insert an object in the table:

```
INSERT INTO Company_Customer
VALUES (Company_Type('Company A','123456789', 'Betty Smith'));
```

And you might want to query its content:

```
SELECT * FROM Company_Customer;
1, Company A, 123456789, Betty Smith
```

Company A is an implementation of a Company_Customer object. But even though its name changes to Company B, it still is the same company:

```
UPDATE Company_Customer c
SET c.name = 'Company B'
where c.companyid = '123456789';

select * from Company_Customer;
1, Company B, 123456789, Betty Smith
```

As mentioned earlier, an object table can be seen as a multicolumn table in which each attribute of the object supertype Customer_Type and its subtypes Person_Type and Company_Type are columns, allowing you to perform relational operations. Alternatively, it can be seen as a single-column table in which each row is an object of a defined type, allowing you to perform object-oriented operations. If you want to access the objects in an object table, you cannot directly access the OID, but you can use a REF to access implementation of OIDs, as shown here:

```
select REF(c) from Company_Customer c where c.companyid = '123456789';
```

REF takes as its argument a correlation variable (a table alias, in our example, named **c**) associated with an object table (in our example, COMPANY_CUSTOMER) or an object view, and it returns the REF value for the object instance. A REF is a logical pointer or reference to an object instance, and it is an Oracle Database built-in data type. The REF can be used to access, examine, or update the object, as shown here:

```
SELECT VALUE(c) FROM Company_Customer c
WHERE c.CONTACTNAME = 'Betty Smith';

HELI.COMPANY_TYPE('Company B','123456789','Betty Smith')
```

You can save data in an object table as a row object, or you can use a relational table and save the object in its column as a column object. If the object has a meaning in the outside world, use an object table; if the object only has meaning in the scope of the implementation of a relational table entity, use a column.

Temporary Table

All the table types described earlier are permanent tables, where the data stays saved in nonvolatile storage until somebody deletes it permanently. There is another kind of table type for data: a temporary table. The data in these tables is saved only temporarily, and the data is deleted automatically either after the transaction or session. The definition of a temporary table is saved permanently, and it remains until somebody drops the table. Because temporary tables are temporal in nature, they do not cause redo log writing, which means that backup and recovery for the data in a temporary table is not available in case of a system failure. The definition of a temporary table is visible to all sessions, but the data is only visible to the session that inserts the data into the table, and each session can only modify its own data. Locks are not needed in temporary tables because each session has its own data, and a truncate operation will only affect the data owned by this session.

A temporary table is meant to be used when you need to temporarily store a set of rows to be processed against other tables or temporary tables. Temporary tables might also be a good solution if you need to use the result set for several other queries that cannot be combined (for instance, when you need to update several tables using the data in a temporary table). Do not use temporary tables to split a query into smaller queries, however; it will be less efficient than the original query because Oracle Database is specialized in performing queries in a database and will do them as efficiently as possible.

Temporary tables work the best when they are filled once and not updated during the processing; therefore, defining the data flow process is very important when using temporary tables. If populating a temporary table and using it in a query is slower than a regular query or another alternative solution, it might not be a good solution.

A temporary table is created using a CREATE GLOBAL TEMPORARY TABLE statement. At the end of the CREATE statement is the ON COMMIT clause, which indicates when the data is deleted or the table is truncated. If it is set to **delete rows**, the data is deleted after COMMIT, meaning that the temporality is transaction-wide. If it is set to **preserve rows**, the table content will be truncated after the session closes, or if the user defines **truncate table** before closing the session. This parameter defines the temporality session-wide. If a temporary table has been defined transaction-wide, it only allows one transaction per session to use it at a time. If there are several transactions using the same temporary table, each transaction can use the table only as soon as the previous one stops using it.

You can also create indexes on temporary tables. This can sometimes be the main reason for selecting a temporary table as a solution. Let's say you need an index that you cannot, for some reason, add to the original table, but it would be very useful for this particular processing. In this case, using a temporary table with an index might be a good solution. These indexes are also temporal, following the same rules on data persistency and deleting data as the table they have been created for. Temporary tables, unlike permanent tables, and their indexes do not allocate any segments when they are created. Segments are allocated only when the first row has been inserted into a temporary table. The segments are dropped either at the end of the transaction or the end of the session, depending on the temporary table definitions. If other transactions or sessions are using the same temporary table, the segments containing their data will remain until the end of the transaction or session. You can also create triggers on temporary tables or views that access temporary tables or both temporary and permanent tables. You can use export/import or replication utilities for temporary table definitions, but you cannot use them for the temporary table data.

When a temporary table is created, the tablespace attached to the temporary table is the default temporary tablespace of the user who creates the temporary table. The default temporary tablespace for a user has been defined in the CREATE USER ... DEFAULT TABLESPACE clause while creating the user account. You can define another temporary tablespace to be attached to global temporary tables by using the TABLESPACE clause of CREATE GLOBAL TEMPORARY TABLE. This might be a wise way to conserve space used by temporary tables over other actions in the database, and to let you define the configuration of this tablespace for temporary tables to meet the criteria for actions performed using temporary tables.

The data in a global temporary table is written in a temporary tablespace and therefore does not create redo logs. But when a data manipulating operation (DML) is performed in a global temporary table, a regular undo tablespace is used, and an undo tablespace is always protected by redo. Therefore, global temporary tables do generate both undo and redo. The amount of undo is about the same as for a regular table, but the amount of redo is a bit less, so we could say that using a global temporary table instead of a regular table improves performance by reducing redo generation. By selecting the right strategy for manipulating data, you are able to reduce the amount of undo and therefore the amount of redo as well. For instance, a simple process of insert, report, truncate would be quite efficient, whereas updates and deletes generate a lot of undo information, and undo generates redos.

NOTE
The database must be open and in a read-write mode to enable writing to the undo tablespace. Because of that behavior, a global temporary table, using an undo tablespace, can't be used in read-only databases or physical standby databases.

Oracle Database 12c (12.1) introduced the possibility of defining a temporary undo for a global temporary table. This feature allows global temporary tables to write the undo to the temporary tablespace. Because of that change in architecture, there is no need for undo to generate redos, and global temporary tables can be used in read-only databases or physical standby databases. The default for undo is still the traditional undo tablespace. To define it to be a temporary undo, you simply enable it on either the session or system level using the **temp_undo_enabled** parameter. To enable it in the session level, use **alter session set temp_undo_enabled = true**. And to disable it in the session level, use **alter session set temp_undo_enabled = false**. At the system level, you enable it using **alter system set temp_undo_enabled = true**. And you disable it using **alter system set temp_undo_enabled = false**. Note that you cannot change the undo strategy while you are operating on global temporary table data and have written any undo using either of those two strategies. Any attempts to change will be ignored. For read-only databases, such as physical standby databases, the temporary undo is the default, as you can understand after our discussion of undo and redo in this chapter, and using the **temp_undo_enabled** parameter in a standby database is ignored. As you might already know, the undo can be monitored using the V$UNDOSTAT view. Oracle Database 12c introduced a new view called V$TEMPUNDOSTAT for monitoring temporary undos.

NOTE
Oracle Database 12c (12.1) introduced the concept of a temporary undo. This feature allows the undo segments for global temporary tables to be stored in the temporary tablespace without causing redo logs. The temporary undo functionality enables the use of global temporary tables in read-only databases as well as physical standby databases. The temporary undo functionality is available only if the **compatible** *parameter for the database is set to 12.0.0 or higher.*

A global temporary table has only one set of statistics, and all sessions use the same set no matter if the table contains different data in different sessions. In Oracle Database 12c Release 1, session-private statistics for a global table were introduced. Each session will have a different set of statistics, and queries issued against the global temporary table use the statistics from that session.

Because a global temporary table is an Oracle-specific feature in Data Modeler, you can define a temporary table only in the physical model of Oracle. Set its Temporary property to "Yes (Delete Rows)" to delete ON COMMIT or to "Yes (Preserve Rows)" to preserve the rows ON COMMIT.

Table Cluster

Table clustering is a technique and a specific structure in a database where data related to one another is brought together so that data can be found more efficiently. This technique is often not the best solution available, but it is good to know just in case you run into an instance where it is. In my more than 20-year work history, I only recall one case where table clustering was the solution.

A table cluster is a cluster structure where the related data from two or more tables is clustered in same data blocks because the related data is often queried together and usually joined together. The data in these tables is often needed at the same time. When tables are clustered together, the related rows of different tables are stored in the same data blocks to speed up the queries. A single data block can contain rows from several tables. The cluster key is the column or columns the clustered tables have in common and is generally used to join them. The cluster key value is the value of the cluster key column(s) for a set of rows, and all data that contains the same cluster key value is physically stored together. Each cluster key value is stored only once in the cluster and once in the cluster index, no matter how many rows of different tables contain the same value.

The joins on these clustered tables use less disk I/O, and the access time improves because fewer blocks need to be read. Also, the tables and their indexes require less storage space because the cluster key value is not stored repeatedly for each row. Clustering tables might not be a good solution if the data in the tables is often updated or truncated or if indexes are not used but the data access is mainly via a full table scan. In these cases, the benefits of clustering tables are lost.

There are two different types of table clusters in Oracle Database: index clusters and hash clusters. An indexed cluster uses a b-tree index on the cluster key to locate the data. The index associates the cluster key value with the database block address of the block containing the data. A cluster index must be created before any rows can be inserted into tables in the cluster. First you create the cluster, then the index on cluster key, and finally you create the tables in the cluster. Then you are ready to add rows in the indexed cluster. The rows are stored in a heap, clustered together by the clustering key, and they are accessed using the index. When a new row is inserted into a cluster table, Oracle first checks whether the cluster key already exists. If it does, the row will be inserted in the same block. If it cannot be found, a new block will be allocated for the new value. Of course, the access speed is the same as it would be for a heap table for a single row, but because of the cluster, the access speed is much faster for several rows using the same cluster key.

Instead of being an index cluster, a table cluster can be a hash cluster. In a hash cluster, there is no separate index, but a hash function is used to find or store a row in a table cluster. The hash function defines the data block holding the data. A hash function is applied to the key value of the row, and the resulting hash value is used to define the data block in the cluster where this row belongs. Rows with the same hash value are stored together in the same block. A hash cluster may be a good solution if the hash key column is queried frequently with equality conditions, either with = or IN list predicates, since the hash key value points directly to the disk area that stores the row. With equality conditions, a hash cluster can be more efficient than an index cluster. A hash cluster is not good with range predicates (such as < and >, LIKE, and BETWEEN); an index cluster will handle them better. If you are using hash clustering, it would be beneficial if you could reasonably guess the number of hash keys and the size of the data stored with each key value to be able to define a hash function that spreads the data equally on the disc and to estimate the space needed. Oracle must reserve space for a hash cluster up front, and if that guess is very wrong, the effect on performance can be bad. If the space allocated is too small, not all rows with the same hash value will fit in a single block, and Oracle must chain them. If the hash key is chained, any access on that hash value will read at least two data blocks instead of just one. If the space allocated is too large, there might be performance problems with full table scans.

NOTE
To use clustering, you need to know the requirements and have the skills to set up a cluster correctly. A cluster is more difficult to manage, and it takes up more space than a regular table. Do not create clusters for fun; be sure this is the right solution for the requirement before implementing one. If you want to design a cluster using Data Modeler, you can do so in the Physical Model under Clusters. Simply right-click and select New. Then define the cluster properties.

Views and Materialized Views

One way to make life easier is to prepare queries and reuse them, which is the same principle we have for procedures and packages, but this time using a view. A view is a logical representation of a table, or a combination of tables or other views; in other words, it allows you to predefine a query. Note that views can be created on external tables and temporary tables as well. A view is a database object based on a query and executed when called, so the result set is always current. You can query a view just like a table, and with some limitations you can also update, insert into, and delete from views. Of course, all these actions are performed on the table the view is built on top of. Be sure to check the restrictions for the Oracle Database version you are using. In general, the restrictions are that you can only use data manipulation (DML) on rows that are identified in the base table, and the table should be a so-called key-preserved table. In general, that means you should have all the primary key columns involved in your DML. If the view is a join view, all the key columns of the table are involved in the result of the join to have all the keys and key columns preserved through a join. And it is quite clear that if the query of a view contains **set**, **distinct**, a **group by**, or any aggregate functions, DMLs are not possible because a row cannot be identified any more.

You can create views using the CREATE VIEW statement, where you define the name for the view and the query. If the query you define for a view will join tables or views, this view is called a *join view*. CREATE OR REPLACE VIEW will create a new view if the view does not exist, and it replaces an existing one with the new one if it already exists. REPLACE is very useful because you can use it to change the definition of an existing view, and all the previously granted privileges on it remain. A materialized view dependent on the replaced view will be marked **unusable**, and you need to refresh it. You can use **force** to create a view that is dependent on objects that do not exist, and you can also use **editioning** to create editioning views. An editioning view contains all the rows from only one table and shows all or some of its columns. A typical use case for an editioning view is to isolate an application from DDL changes to the base table. You can read more about editioning in Chapter 5.

You can also define whether or not a column in a view is visible. That can be done using the VISIBLE | INVISIBLE clause. By default, all view columns are VISIBLE, even though the column might have been specified INVISIBLE in the base table. We will talk more about invisible columns later in this chapter. The constraints defined for the base tables of a view apply also for the view, but in Oracle Database you can also define constraints specifically on a view. A constraint can be, for instance, a check constraint that makes sure the DML operation follows the rules defined in a subquery for the view definition. For example, if the table consists of all the rows, but using the view you are only allowed to see certain rows (let's say, **where company_id=1**), then using a WITH CHECK OPTION CONSTRAINT, you cannot add a row where the **company_id=2**. You can also define a READ ONLY constraint for a view to make it a read-only view, where no inserts, updates, or deletes are allowed to the base tables using the view. Alternatively, the constraint can also be a primary key, a foreign key, or a unique key constraint, but these are mainly for the Oracle Optimizer to help it find the best execution plan. You can define them at the view level using the OUT_OF_LINE_CONSTRAINT clause or as part of column or attribute specification using the INLINE_CONSTRAINT clause. Views can be defined as object type views using the **object_view_clause** or XMLType views using the **XMLtype_view_clause.**

A new procedure called **dbms_utility.expand_sql_text** was introduced in Oracle Database 12*c*. This procedure takes a query that references views as input and returns a query with the identical meaning that references only tables. This can be very helpful in the analysis of SQL using views. A good use for it might be when you need to solve performance issues or fix the application logic.

A materialized view is a view, but the result of its query is saved in a database and refreshed automatically as defined on creation of the materialized view. A materialized view was called a *snapshot* in previous Oracle Database versions; that name might explain the term to some readers better. Materialized views can be used for replication from one database to another—for instance, in distributed environments or if you want to share just part of the data to a mobile environment. Alternatively, materialized views can be used for saving query results to speed up the queries (for example, creating summarized data). Materialized views also have some restrictions, depending on the Oracle Database version. Therefore, be sure to check which kind of limitations your version has.

Use the CREATE MATERIALIZED VIEW statement to create a materialized view. In the FROM clause of the query, you can define tables, views, and other materialized views to be used in this materialized view. These objects are called *master tables* in replication or *detail tables* in data warehousing. I use the term *base tables* because these tables (or other database objects) are the base of the query for the materialized view. Here is a simple example of a materialized view on the EMP table:

```
CREATE MATERIALIZED VIEW mv_emp AS SELECT * FROM Emp;
```

The materialized view can be created based on a primary key or a ROWID. You can specify WITH PRIMARY KEY to create a primary key materialized view, which is the default and recommended way of creating one. If you have defined the materialized view based on the primary key, you are able to reorganize the base table without affecting the materialized view, for instance. In a materialized view based on a primary key, the base table must contain a valid primary key constraint that is enabled, and the materialized view query must be defined to use all of the primary key columns directly.

Obviously, object views cannot be created using a primary key. Just like object tables, object views, and XMLType views, they do not have column names specified for them, and Oracle Database defines a system-generated OBJECT_ID column for them. You can use this column name in queries and to create object views with the WITH OBJECT IDENTIFIER clause. The object view clause lets you specify the attributes used in the view, and the other branch of the object view clause lets you specify a superview for a view using UNDER. Note that you must create the subview in the same schema as the superview.

Using **XMLType_view_clause** you can create an XMLType view, which displays data from an XMLSchema table of type XMLType. The XMLSchema table must be created before you can create an XMLType view.

ROWID materialized views are the only possibility if the base table has no primary key or if the materialized view does not include all the primary key columns of the base table. There are quite a few limitations for a ROWID materialized view. A ROWID materialized view must be based on a single table, and it cannot contain distinct or aggregate functions, GROUP BY or CONNECT BY clauses, subqueries, or set operations. You can specify WITH ROWID to create a ROWID materialized view. Note that the incremental fast refresh does not work on ROWID materialized views after a base table has been reorganized until a complete refresh has been performed.

You can define the materialized view to be built (using BUILD clause options) as either IMMEDIATE or DEFERRED. If DEFERRED has been chosen, the materialized view is populated on the first requested refresh. Usually IMMEDIATE is used because the materialized view should be created, but DEFERRED is very useful if you have several materialized views that are dependent on each other, maybe nested materialized views or hierarchical materialized views. In such cases, if you create the materialized views using BUILD DEFERRED and then use one of the refresh procedures in the DBMS_MVIEW package to refresh all the materialized views, Oracle Database computes the dependencies and refreshes the materialized views in the right order.

If the data on base tables of a materialized view is modified, then the data in the materialized view must also be updated. The refreshing operation for a materialized view is defined using the CREATE_MV_REFRESH clause. Using it, you can schedule the times, the method, and the mode for refreshing the materialized view, meaning that the data in it will be refreshed.

An important thing to define is the timing of refreshing for the materialized view. The NEVER REFRESH clause will prevent the materialized view from being refreshed at all and by any means. DML operations are allowed, and to reverse NEVER REFRESH use an ALTER MATERIALIZED VIEW … REFRESH statement. The ON COMMIT clause will refresh the materialized view whenever the database commits a transaction on the base table of the materialized view. Note that this clause may increase the time taken to complete the commit in the base table, because the refresh operation is treated as a part of the commit process. You cannot use ON COMMIT with materialized views containing object types or Oracle-supplied types, nor can you use it with materialized views with remote tables. The ON DEMAND clause allows the materialized view to be refreshed only when the user manually launches a refresh through either the DBMS_MVIEW or DBMS_SYNC_REFRESH package. The DBMS_MVIEW package contains the APIs for refreshing a materialized view: DBMS_MVIEW.REFRESH, DBMS_MVIEW.REFRESH_ALL_MVIEWS, and DBMS_MVIEW.REFRESH_DEPENDENT. The DBMS_SYNC_REFRESH package contains the APIs for synchronous refresh, which was introduced in Oracle Database 12c Release 1. Note that you cannot specify both ON COMMIT and ON DEMAND; you can only specify one of them at a time. With the START WITH clause, you can define the first automatic refresh time using a datetime expression. And with the NEXT clause, you can define a datetime expression for calculating the interval between automatic refreshes. Both datetime expressions must point to a time in the future. If you do not define the START WITH value, then the first automatic refresh time will be calculated based on the creation time of the materialized view. If you define a START WITH value but do not define the NEXT value, the database refreshes the materialized view only once. If you do not define either the START WITH or the NEXT value, or you do not define anything in the CREATE_MV_REFRESH clause, the database does not refresh the materialized view automatically. If you specify ON COMMIT, there will be no point in defining either START WITH or NEXT. Similarly, if you specify START WITH and NEXT, there's no point in defining ON COMMIT.

The refresh method can be incremental or complete. It can be performed in-place or, since Oracle Database 12c Release 1, out-of-place. There are three basic types of refresh operations: complete refresh, fast refresh (log-based incremental), and partition change tracking (PCT) refresh. Oracle Database 12c Release 1 introduced a new refresh option, out-of-place refresh, as well as a new refresh method based on that one, called synchronous refresh. Not all the refresh methods are available for all materialized views; use the package DBMS_MVIEW.EXPLAIN_MVIEW to determine the ones available for your materialized view.

Specify **fast** to use the incremental log-based refresh method. Materialized view logs can be created to capture all changes to the base table since the last refresh. This information allows a fast refresh, which only needs to apply the changes rather than a complete refresh of the materialized view. The materialized view log is a database object that resides in the same database and schema as its base table. Each materialized view log is associated with a single base table. The changes for DML changes are stored in the materialized view log associated with the base table, and the changes made by direct-path INSERT operations are stored in the direct loader log. Note that the CREATE statement with REFRESH FAST will fail if the materialized view logs have not been created for the base tables. The direct loader log will be created automatically by Oracle Database when a direct-path INSERT takes place, so those logs do not need to be created. Materialized views cannot use fast refresh if the defining query contains either an analytic or the **XMLTable** function.

The PCT refresh method can be used if the modified base tables are partitioned and the modified base table partitions can be used to identify the affected partitions in the materialized view. In the case of partition maintenance operations on the base tables, this is the only incremental refresh method that can be used.

Each of these refresh methods can be performed in-place, and the refresh statements are executed directly on the materialized view. Since Oracle Database 12c Release 1 there has been another way to do this: using an out-of-place refresh. The out-of-place refresh creates one or more outside tables, executes the refresh statements on those tables, and then switches the materialized view or affected materialized view partitions with them. The benefit of the out-of-place refresh is that it enables high availability for a materialized view during refresh. That is important, especially if the refresh operation takes a long time to finish. Out-of-place refresh has all the restrictions that apply when using the corresponding in-place refresh and some additional restrictions (for instance, LOB columns are not permitted). Out-of-place refresh requires additional storage for the outside tables and indexes for the duration of the refresh. The global index will be affected by the partition exchange in an out-of-place PCT refresh, causing some overhead. If global indexes are defined on the materialized view base table, Oracle disables the global indexes before doing the partition exchange and rebuilds the global indexes after it.

A new refresh method, called a synchronous refresh, was introduced in Oracle Database 12c Release 1. The idea is to refresh both the materialized view and its base table(s) simultaneously to achieve as much high availability as possible with the freshest data possible. This method is especially aimed at data warehousing environments where the loading of incremental data is tightly controlled. The method is based on the out-of-place mechanism and needs temporary space for the operation. The user does not modify the contents of the base tables directly but instead using the APIs provided by the synchronous refresh package. This package applies the changes to the base tables and materialized views at the same time to ensure their consistency. A set of tables and the materialized views can be defined to be always in sync.

If you specify **complete**, the complete refresh method is used. If **complete** is defined, then Oracle Database performs a complete refresh even if a fast refresh is possible. If you specify **force**, Oracle Database will perform a fast refresh if it is possible. If it is not possible, a complete refresh is performed. If you do not specify a refresh method (**fast**, **complete**, or **force**), then **force** is the default.

In Data Modeler, you can create a view already on the Entity-Relationship Diagram but note that it is not an actual view but an entity view. A view is a database object can be defined in the Relational Model using the Query Builder or the Table to View Wizard that can be found on the Tools menu. In case you want to design an object view, select the structured type for its Based on Structured Type property.

You can design a materialized view object by designing a table and in Relational Model selecting the Materialized Query Table checkbox in the General Properties tab for the table. Then, in Materialized Query, you can define the query for the materialized table using Query Builder. Note that when the DDLs are generated, the materialized view is not found under Tables but under Materialized Views. If you have selected the On Prebuild Table property for the materialized view, the table for it will be created first and then a materialized view on top of it (**create materialized view … on prebuilt table**). If you have not selected that property, then just the materialized view is created. You can find the materialized view in Physical Model Browser under Materialized Views and define its physical properties.

Introduction to Data Types

Each value Oracle Database uses must have a data type specified, whether the element is a column in a table, an argument, or a variable in program code. A data type is either scalar or non-scalar. A scalar type contains an atomic value (for instance, Salary is 3000). A non-scalar data type contains a set of values (for instance, a PostalCode collection). A data type defines the domain of the element and how Oracle will treat that element. For instance, the data type for Salary (NUMBER(8,2)) specifies that the salary is numeric, it can only contain numeric information, the maximum amount for Salary is 999999.99, the functions for numeric information are available, and so on. A data type can be one of these categories:

- An Oracle built-in data type
- An ANSI, DB2, or SQL/DS data type
- A user-defined type
- An Oracle-supplied type

Oracle built-in data types are character, numeric, long/long raw, datetime, large object (LOB), and ROWID. We talked about ROWIDs in the section "Index-Organized Table (IOT)," earlier in this chapter. We will talk about LOBs later in this section; all the other data types are quite straightforward. Oracle has several built-in data types for string, numeric, and date types of data. It is important to choose the right data type for a column. There is no point in selecting VARCHAR2 for a column that will hold information about money; even though it could save that type of data, it would not work correctly. A comparison operation would give the wrong results, and using the column would be quite strange, not to mention the effect on programmers who misunderstand the meaning of the column and therefore waste their time for no reason.

NOTE
The Boolean data type is supported in PL/SQL but it is not supported in Oracle Database.

When you're creating tables, the ANSI, DB2, and SQL/DS data types can be used as well. Both DB2 and SQL/DS are products from IBM. Oracle recognizes the ANSI or IBM data type by its name and converts the data type to the equivalent Oracle data type.

User-defined types are data types users can define themselves using the tools Oracle provides. We will talk about user-defined data types later in this section.

The Oracle-supplied types are user-defined types that Oracle has defined using the same tools we can use for defining types. Oracle-supplied types are as follows:

- Any types
- XML types
- URI types
- Spatial types
- Media types
- JSON

Sometimes the best solution for a requirement is not a new table but a column of a complex type, especially if the data is semistructured or unstructured. For example, a column can be of type Large Objects (LOB) or Extended Markup Language (XML), or it can be of a data type defined by a programmer (the so-called user-defined data type). In this section, we will look a bit more closely at some of the complex data types.

Large Objects (LOBs)

The LOB data type is very useful with completely unstructured data because that kind of data cannot be saved in traditional database structures, and in LOB you can save anything. The problem with unstructured data is, of course, that a computer is not able to analyze data that has no structure. LOBs can be used very well with semi-structured data like JSON and XML. But, of course, it all depends on the data, its format, and content. A LOB is a scalar data type representing a large scalar value of binary or character data. Due to their large size, LOBs are subject to some restrictions that do not affect other scalar types. LOBs can be defined as columns of a table or attributes of an object type. You can use LOBs to create user-defined data types or store other data types as LOBs.

The four different LOB types are Character Large Object (CLOB), National Character Set Large Object (NCLOB), Binary Large Object (BLOB), and External Binary File (BFILE). CLOB is used for large strings (text) or documents that use only the database character set. NCLOB is like CLOB, but it also supports documents using the National Character Set and characters of varying widths. BLOB stores any kind of data in binary format. BLOBs are typically used for images, audio, and video. BFILE is similar to BLOB but different from all the other LOB types because it is stored outside the database, cannot participate in transactions, cannot be recovered, and is not updatable. BFILEs are quite ideal for storing static data (for instance, images). Make sure that the external file exists and that Oracle processes have operating system read permissions on the file; otherwise, the file is not accessible by the database. Any kind of data that can be saved in an operating system file can be stored in a BFILE, and if needed it can be loaded to the database in the correct LOB type format. For example, you can store character data of food recipes in a BFILE, and when you are ready you can load the BFILE data into a CLOB or NCLOB, specifying the character set for loading.

Each LOB instance has a locator and a value. For internal LOBs (LOBs in the database), the LOB column stores a locator to the LOB value. A BFILE column stores a BFILE locator (the directory name and the filename), which serves as a pointer to a binary file on the server file system. You can change the filename and path of a BFILE without affecting the base table by using the **bfilename** function. In both cases, a locator is stored in the table row of any initialized LOB column as a pointer to the data. A LOB instance with a locator and a value exists in a cell, and the techniques you use when accessing a cell in a LOB column differ depending on its state. A cell in a LOB column can be in one of these states:

- **NULL**   The cell is created but holds no locator or value.
- **Empty**   A LOB instance with a locator exists in the cell, but it has no value. The length of the LOB is zero.
- **Populated**   A LOB instance with a locator exists in the cell and has a value.

Before Oracle Database 11g, only one kind of LOB storage type was supported. In Oracle Database 11g, SecureFiles LOB storage was introduced, and the original storage type was given the name BasicFiles LOB storage. In Oracle Database 11g, the BasicFiles LOB storage is the default, but in Oracle 12c the SecureFile LOB is defined as the default. BasicFiles LOB storage must be defined for LOB storage in tablespaces that are not managed with Automatic Segment Space Management (ASSM). SecureFiles LOB storage supports compression, deduplication, and encryption. The best would be to enable those when creating the table (in the CREATE TABLE statement) because if you do it later (using the ALTER TABLE statement), all SecureFiles LOB data in the table must be read, modified, and written back. Depending on the parameters set on the ALTER clause, this operation can cause the database to lock the table for the length of the operation. In the CREATE TABLE statement, you can define which LOB storage will be used: **basicfile** specifies BasicFiles LOB storage, and **securefile** specifies SecureFiles LOB storage.

A LOB column is created using either the CREATE TABLE or ALTER TABLE ADD statement, and its parameters can be modified using the ALTER TABLE MODIFY statement. Besides the storage definition (**basicfile/securefile**) option, you have some more options you can specify. Let's look at a couple of them. Using **chunk**, you define the size of data used when handling the LOB data. It is used when saving the data as well as when accessing or modifying it. It is good for it to be a multiple of the block size. The **chunk** value cannot be changed after it has been defined. The data can be defined to be saved in-line, to the table, or out-of-line to its own location. If the data is less than approximately 4000 bytes, it is by default stored in-line; otherwise, it's stored out-of-line. Using the **disable storage in row** parameter, you can define all the data, despite its size, to be stored out-of-line. If the data is stored out-of-line, the importance of defining the right size of a **chunk** gets bigger: no matter what the size of the data is, the database always allocates a size defined in the **chunk** or a multiple of it for the data. Even though the data would be very small in size, the size of a **chunk** is allocated. It is very important to define as good a **chunk** value as possible for performance and storage optimization.

If **enable storage in row** is defined, smaller data is stored in-line and bigger data out-of-line. In some cases, **disable storage in row** is a better choice. For instance, you might want to store all the LOB data in a separate tablespace to have control over the space used by it. It might also be a better choice if you are performing a lot of base table processing (for instance, full table scans), because the LOB column and its data, if saved in-line, increases the size of a row and may affect the performance.

For LOBs, you can specify logging options:

- **logging**   Specifies the redo log file to be updated based on changes in the LOB.

- **nologging**   No redo is created, and recovery is not possible.

- **filesystem_like_logging**   Only valid for SecureFiles. The system only logs the metadata. **filesystem_like_logging** ensures that data is completely recoverable (an instance recovery) after a server failure.

The buffer cache parameter has three values, defined next:

- **cache**   LOB pages will be placed in the buffer cache for faster access.

- **nocache**   LOB values are not brought into the buffer cache.

- **cache reads**   LOB values are brought into the buffer cache only during a read operation, but not during write operations.

If you have **cache** defined, it does not matter what you chose for **logging** because caching demands logging, and that is done automatically by the database. When creating a table, you can specify a different tablespace and other storage characteristics for a LOB column using the STORAGE clause. If you have several LOB columns in a table, it might be useful to define them in all separate tablespaces to reduce device contention.

When a LOB column is defined, an index for it is automatically created. The LOB index is an internal structure that a user may not drop or rebuild. What you can do with the latest versions of Oracle Database is define it a name. If you specify a tablespace for the LOB data, that will be used for both data and index. If you do not specify it, the tablespace of the table will be used for both the LOB data and index.

Internal LOBs use copy semantics to ensure a unique LOB instance to each table cell or variable containing a LOB. Copy semantics means that both the LOB locator and value are logically copied during insert, update, or assignment operations. External LOBs instead use reference semantics copying only the LOB locator while inserting; updates are not allowed to external LOBs.

If you want to be sure that nobody will change the content of the row containing a LOB while you are selecting from it, you can use FOR UPDATE clause with your SELECT clause. That will lock the row until you end the transaction. The LOB APIs include operations that enable you to explicitly open and close a LOB instance. You can open any type of LOB for a read-only mode to ensure nobody will change the locator or the data while you are operating with it. When closing the LOB you allow others to change it again. You can also define LOBs in a database to be in a read-write mode to defer any index maintenance until you close the LOB. This might be useful if you have an extensible index on the LOB column that you do not want the database to maintain every time you write to the LOB. If you open a LOB, you must also close it at some point later in the session.

To access and modify the LOB values there are two different ways to do it: use the Data Interface for LOBs or use the LOB Locator. Both of these methods demand that the locator exists.

LOB instances that are NULL do not have a locator, so to be able to use the PL/SQL **dbms_lob.read** procedure or any other way of handling LOBs using a locator, you must initialize the LOB instance to provide it a locator. To initialize an internal LOB use an INSERT/UPDATE statement with the function **empty_blob** for BLOBs, or **empty_clob** for CLOBs and NCLOBs to initialize it as empty. Valid places where empty LOB locators may be used include the VALUES clause of an INSERT statement and the SET clause of an UPDATE statement. To initialize an external LOB (BFILE column), use the **bfilename** function.

When you're accessing the LOB data in program code, most of the rules and semantics you have learned about accessing a VARCHAR2 data type apply. You can use concatenation, some of the comparison functions, character functions, and some of the conversion functions with LOBs. Note that a LOB for relatively large-size operations might last a while. Aggregation or Unicode functions are not supported for LOBs. Some of the functions convert the CLOB to VARCHAR2. Only the first 4KB of the CLOB are converted in the SQL environment and used in the operation; in the PL/SQL environment, the amount of converted data is the first 32KB. LOBs cannot be used to join tables in SELECTs with DISTINCT, GROUP BY, or ORDER BY. Note that the binary comparison of the character data is performed irrespective of the **nls_comp** and **nls_sort** parameter settings. In PL/SQL, you can define a large enough VARCHAR2 variable and use a SELECT...INTO structure to assign a value to it from a database table column of CLOB or NCLOB.

A BFILE can be accessed using OCI (Oracle Call Interface), PL/SQL (DBMS_LOB package), precompilers (Pro*C/C++, Pro*COBOL), or Java (JDBC). BFILEs are initialized and managed with a DIRECTORY object, which is an alias for the full path name to the operating system file. Together with a BFILENAME object, they initialize the BFILE locator. You can use INSERT to set the BFILE column to point to an existing file on the disk and UPDATE to change the reference target. Let's create a table called EMP_PHOTOS that will have an Empno column and a BFILE-type column for photos:

```
CREATE TABLE Emp_photos (
Empno NUMBER NOT NULL,
Photo BFILE);
```

Next, we insert a photo in that table:

```
INSERT INTO Emp_photos VALUES
(1, BFILENAME('C:\\Users\helhel\Heli', 'launch0.jpg'));
```

We can also define the directory, and then we can use that to refer to when inserting another photo to the table:

```
CREATE OR REPLACE DIRECTORY photo_dir AS 'C:\\Users\helhel\Heli';

INSERT INTO Emp_photos VALUES
(2, BFILENAME('photo_dir', 'launch1.jpg'));

SELECT * FROM Emp_Photos;
EMPNO       PHOTO
1           bfilename('C:\\Users\helhel\Heli','launch0.jpg')
2           bfilename('photo_dir','launch1.jpg')
```

Next, we want to update the photo of employee number 1:

```
UPDATE Emp_photos
SET Photo = BFILENAME('photo_dir', 'launch2.jpg')
WHERE Empno = 1;

SELECT * FROM Emp_Photos;
EMPNO       PHOTO
1           bfilename('photo_dir','launch2.jpg')
2           bfilename('photo_dir','launch1.jpg')
```

For SecureFiles, there are three payable features: Advanced LOB Compression, Advanced LOB Deduplication, and SecureFiles Encryption. Advanced LOB Compression analyzes and compresses SecureFiles LOB data to save disk space and to improve performance. To be able to use this compression, you must have a license for the Oracle Advanced Compression option. Advanced LOB Deduplication automatically detects duplicate LOB data within a LOB column or partition and saves space by storing only one copy of the data. To be able to use this feature, you must have a license for the Oracle Advanced Compression option. SecureFiles Encryption encrypts data using Transparent Data Encryption (TDE). To be able to use this functionality, you must have a license for the Oracle Advanced Security option.

XMLType

Extensible Markup Language (XML) is a standard syntax developed by the World Wide Web Consortium (W3C) for structured and semistructured data. It is used both for exchanging and saving the data. The XML syntax and standards include the description of the data, the XML schema, and the data itself. Many organizations have defined their own standards for XML schemas and data exchange using those schemas. Because of the fact that the document includes both the description of the data and the data itself, XML is readable for both the human eye and a computer program.

As mentioned earlier in this chapter, XML data can be saved in a LOB-type column, but there is another possibility too: the XMLType. The Oracle-supplied type XMLType was introduced in Oracle Database 9*i* Release 1. It can be used to store and query XML data in the database and can represent an XML document instance in SQL. You can use XMLType, for example, as a data type for a column in a table or a view or as a parameter, a return value, or a variable in PL/SQL code. XMLType is an abstract data type, and XMLType tables and columns can be kept either as binary XML storage or object-relational storage. Binary XML storage is the default storage model for Oracle XML DB in Oracle Database 12*c*. It is compact and XML schema aware, but also allows documents that are not XML schema based to be handled, and it provides efficient partial updating and streamable query evaluation. The object-relational storage of XML documents is based on decomposing the document content into a set of SQL objects. It provides the best performance for highly structured data with a known and fixed set of queries.

XMLType has member functions for accessing the XML data using XPath (XML Path Language) expressions, a standard developed by the W3C committee for navigating through nodes (elements, attributes, text, namespaces, processing-instructions, comments, and document nodes) in XML documents. There are also functionalities for XMLType in the application programming interfaces (APIs) provided in PL/SQL and Java. For PL/SQL, there are three APIs for XMLType: the PL/SQL Document Object Model (DOM) API (package DBMS_XMLDOM), the PL/SQL XML

Parser API (package DBMS_XMLPARSER), and the PL/SQL XSLT Processor API (package DBMS_ XSLPROCESSOR).

Oracle XML DB is a set of Oracle Database technologies related to working with XML data in Oracle Database; it is both an XMLType framework and an Oracle XML DB Repository and has techniques to handle XML data. It was introduced in Oracle Database 9.2. In Oracle Database 12.1.0.1, Oracle XML DB is a mandatory component of Oracle Database. It is automatically installed when you create a database or upgrade an existing database to 12c. You cannot uninstall it. Oracle XML DB makes it possible to work with XML data as if it were relational data and with relational data as if it were XML data. This way, you can have all the good features of both worlds. For instance, using XMLType views, you can wrap the existing relational or object-relational data into XML format and view it as if it were XML without changing the applications or the saved data. To be able to do that, you must, of course, define the XML schema and the mapping. You can register a schema using the DBMS_XMLSCHEMA package. The subprograms generateSchema and generateSchemas in the package DBMS_XMLSCHEMA are deprecated in Oracle Database 12.1 without any replacements or workarounds. XMLType tables and views can be indexed for better performance. You can index XML data using XMLIndex and supplement XMLIndex with Oracle Text CONTEXT indexes. Note that in Oracle Database 12c, function-based indexes are deprecated.

XQuery is a query and functional programming language for collections of structured or unstructured data. It was developed by W3C. Oracle XML DB supports XQuery Update. All Oracle SQL functions for updating XML data are deprecated in Oracle Database 12.1, and using XQuery Update is recommended. Working with XMLType is strongly reliant on the version of Oracle Database you are working with. In this section, we mainly talk about Oracle Database 12c.

When XMLType was introduced, the storage data type for it was CLOB. In Oracle Database 11.1, a new storage type called Binary XML was introduced, and in Oracle Database 11.2.0.2 it was defined as the default for XMLType. Binary XML understands XML schemas, but it can also be used with XML data without the XML schema. In Oracle Database 12.1, CLOB storage of XMLType is deprecated and using binary XML storage of XMLType is recommended. Moving from CLOB to binary XML has been made very easy. To do this, you can use CREATE TABLE AS SELECT… from CLOB to binary XML, for instance. The data type behind binary XML is internally CLOB, though.

To create a table called XMLemp of XMLType, you use the following syntax:

```
CREATE TABLE XMLemp OF XMLType;
```

And to create a table with a column (Information) of XMLType, you can use syntax like the following and even define the storage parameters to each XMLType column individually:

```
CREATE TABLE Emp_XML
(empno NUMBER(10) PRIMARY KEY, Ename VARCHAR2(10), Information XMLType)
XMLType COLUMN Information
STORE AS BINARY XML (
TABLESPACE emp_tablespace
STORAGE (INITIAL 4096 NEXT 4096)
CHUNK 4096 NOCACHE LOGGING
);
```

Oracle XML DB provides several SQL functions that are defined in the SQL/XML standard, which is a part of SQL specifications. There are two kinds of functions: those for generating XML data from the result of a SQL query and those to query and update XML content in SQL operations.

These functions use XQuery or XPath expressions. You can insert data into the Oracle XML DB using SQL, PL/SQL, Java, C, SQL*Loader, or the DBMS_XDB_REPOS package, and you can query or update it with SQL using **XMLCast**, **XMLQuery**, and **XMLExists** functions. You can generate XML data from relational data using functions provided by Oracle. Oracle Database 12.1 has introduced a new PL/SQL package called DBMS_XDB_CONFIG. With this change, all Oracle XML DB configuration functions, procedures, and constants have been moved from the package DBMS_XDB to DBMS_XDB_CONFIG and deprecated for the package DBMS_XDB. The package DBMS_XMLSTORE can be used to insert, update, or delete data from XML documents that are stored object-relationally. You can use the XMLType method **transform()** to transform the XMLType instance to the form defined in the XSLT stylesheet. The stylesheet can be an XMLType instance or a VARCHAR2 string literal. You can check whether the XML data in the XMLType is valid for its schema definition using the SQL function **XMLIsValid** or the XMLType method **IsSchemaValid()**. You can concatenate two or more XMLType instances as one using the SQL/XML standard function **XMLConcat**.

XMLOptimizationCheck was introduced in Oracle Database 11.2.0.2. If you set that mode on (**SET XMLOptimizationCheck ON**) for XQuery optimization, the execution plan is automatically checked for XQuery optimization, and diagnostic information is written to the trace file. XMLOptimizationCheck brings a potential problem to your attention immediately, and it might be wise to turn it on permanently. Before this release of Oracle Database, you were able to obtain XQuery optimization information by directly manipulating event 19201.

JSON

Oracle Database 12c also supports the JSON (JavaScript Object Notation) data type. XML has been found sometimes to be too heavy of a solution because of the relatively large data (metadata and the actual data) that must be moved and saved. JSON is found to be a bit lighter and it is easier to change the schema. JavaScript is a very popular programming language in web development, and JSON can represent JavaScript object literals, which makes JSON a popular data-interchange language.

Oracle Database enforces that JSON stored in the database conforms to the JSON rules and can be queried using a PATH-based notation. There are also new operators that allow JSON PATH-based queries to be integrated into SQL operations. To define a table with a JSON-type column, you define it as a CLOB column with the CHECK constraint IS JSON or IS JSON STRICT:

```
CREATE TABLE Emp_JSON
(empno          NUMBER (10) NOT NULL,
Ename           VARCHAR2(10),
Emp_document CLOB
CONSTRAINT ensure_json CHECK (Emp_document IS JSON));
```

You can insert data into the table:

```
INSERT INTO Emp_JSON
VALUES (
1, 'Pirkko',
'{"Address" : "Kotikatu",
"HouseNo" : 7,
"City" : "Helsinki",
"Country" : "Finland"}'
);
```

And here's how to query the JSON data:

```
SELECT emp.Emp_document.Address FROM Emp_JSON emp;
Kotikatu
```

NOTE
The names in JSON are case-sensitive. For instance, if you would query:

```
SELECT emp.Emp_document.address FROM Emp_JSON emp;
```

The result of the query would be NULL since **emp.Emp_document .address** *is not the same as* **emp.Emp_document.Address**.

URI Data Types

The URI (Uniform Resource Identifier) data type, a generalized kind of URL data type, was introduced in Oracle Database 9*i*. It can reference any document or a specific part of a document. URI can be used to create table columns that point to data either inside or outside the database. The UriType is an abstract object type, and HTTPURITYPE, XDBURITYPE, and DBURITYPE are subtypes of it. You can also define your own subtypes of the UriType to handle different URL protocols. The UriType provides a set of functions to work with. Instances of UriType cannot be created directly; instead, you create columns of this type and store subtype instances in it. You will also be able to query the database columns using functions provided by the supertype UriType: **getblob**, **getclob**, **getcontenttype**, **getexternalurl**, **geturl**, and **getxml**. All these functions return data of the data type mentioned in the function name located in the address specified in the URI column. The subtypes also provide their own functions for their protocols.

Oracle also provides a UriFactory package. Using the UriFactory, you can invent a new protocol and define a subtype of the UriType to handle that protocol and then register it with UriFactory. After that, any factory method would generate the new subtype instance if it sees the prefix defined for the new subtype.

REF

The REF data type is used with objects. As we discussed earlier in this chapter in the section "Object Table," each object has an object identifier (OID) that uniquely identifies the object and enables you to reference it. REF is the data type for the reference; REFs use object identifiers (OIDs) to point to objects. A REF data type is a container for an object identifier, and a REF value is a pointer to objects. A REF contains three elements: the OID of the object referenced, the OID of the table or view containing the object referenced, and the ROWID hint. In the section on object tables, we briefly talked about using REFs.

Let's create a table called CUSTOMER with a column called Address_ref of type REF of Address_Type (collections and the array used in Address_Type definition are introduced in the section on user-defined types):

```
CREATE OR REPLACE TYPE PostalCode_Collection
IS
TABLE OF VARCHAR2 (6);

CREATE OR REPLACE TYPE Address_Type
```

```
AS
  OBJECT
  (
    StreetName VARCHAR2 (100) ,
    HouseNo    NUMBER (5) ,
    PostalCode PostalCode_Collection ,
    City City_Collection ,
    State State_Array ,
    Country Country_Collection );

CREATE TABLE Customer
  (
    CustomerID NUMBER (16) NOT NULL ,
    Name       VARCHAR2 (100 CHAR) ,
    Address_ref REF Address_Type
  );

DESC Customer
Name            Null      Type
-----------     --------  --------------------
CUSTOMERID  NOT NULL NUMBER(16)
NAME                     VARCHAR2(100 CHAR)
ADDRESS_REF              REF OF ADDRESS_TYPE
```

A REF value can point to an existing object or to an object that does not exist. When a REF value points to a nonexistent object, the REF is said to be *dangling*. You can use the condition **is [not] dangling** to determine whether or not a REF is dangling. **is dangling** will return TRUE if the reference is dangling and FALSE if it is not dangling. **is not dangling** will work the opposite: TRUE for not dangling and FALSE for dangling. Note that a dangling REF is different from a null REF. For example, let's look at the COMPANY_CUSTOMER example introduced in the section on object tables and select only those REFs that are not dangling or only those rows from the CUSTOMER table that have a reference to existing addresses:

```
select REF(c) from Company_Customer c where REF(c) IS NOT DANGLING;
Select Address_ref from Customer where Address_ref IS NOT DANGLING;
```

Just like with relational tables, you can define referential integrity constraints on REF columns to ensure that there is a row object for the REF.

You can specify a *scoped REF* when declaring a column type, collection element, or object type attribute of type REF. A scoped REF limits the references to a specified object table. Scoped REFs do not ensure that the referenced row object exists; they only ensure that the referenced object table exists. The ROWID hints are ignored in scoped REFs; therefore, using them might slow down the performance but saves storage space.

Let's create a simple example. First, we create a simple object type for the address (**Address_Type**), then we create an object table based on that type (ADDRESS_TAB), and finally we create a table (CUSTOMER) having a column (Address_ref) type of **Address_Type** that's scoped on the ADDRESS_TAB table:

```
CREATE OR REPLACE TYPE Address_Type
AS
```

```
OBJECT
(
StreetName VARCHAR2 (100) ,
HouseNo    NUMBER (5) );

CREATE TABLE Address_Tab of Address_Type;
DROP TABLE Customer;
CREATE TABLE Customer
(
CustomerID NUMBER (16) NOT NULL ,
Name       VARCHAR2 (100 CHAR) ,
Address_ref REF Address_Type SCOPE IS Address_Tab
);
```

You can change a REF to point to another object of the same object type hierarchy or assign it a null. REFs are an easy mechanism for navigating between objects.

User-Defined Types

In addition to those data types, Oracle allows a user to define his or her own data types, the so-called *user-defined types*. There are two kinds of user-defined types: object types and collection types. User-defined types are schema objects.

An *object type* is a user-defined data type, including the composite data structure (including collections) with functions and procedures to manipulate the data. The data structure can be built with scalar data types, collections, or other object types. You can read more about collections later in this chapter. The data elements within the data structure are called *attributes*. The functions and procedures of the object type are called *methods*.

In this example, we use the terminology used in Data Modeler because we use Data Modeler to create the types. *Collection* means a nested table, a collection without a set number of elements; and *array* means a collection with a set number of elements. Let's create a data type called Address that consists of the following attributes: StreetName, HouseNo, PostalCode, City, State, and Country. StreetName might be VARCHAR2(100) and HouseNo might be NUMBER(4,0), but the rest of the attributes might be lists of values, collections, or arrays. States will be an array because we know the exact number of states, but we do not know how many postal codes, cities, and countries there will be, so we will define them as collections. These types can be designed in the Data Types Model in Data Modeler using Distinct Types and Collection Types. You define the data types for the collection or array first as Distinct Types, and for the Collection Types you define the collections and arrays using the Distinct Types defined. For instance, for PostalCode_Type (Distinct Type), you might specify it as VARCHAR2 (6), and for a PostalCode_Collection (Collection Type), you might define it to be a collection of distinct types of PostalCode_Type. So first we must define the types for the collection—PostalCode_Collection, Country_Collection, City_Collection, and PostalCode_Type—and then we will define the collections and arrays for postal code, city, state, and country. The collections would look something like this:

```
CREATE OR REPLACE TYPE PostalCode_Collection
IS
TABLE OF VARCHAR2 (6);

CREATE OR REPLACE TYPE Country_Collection
IS
```

```
TABLE OF VARCHAR2 (30);

CREATE OR REPLACE TYPE City_Collection
IS
TABLE OF VARCHAR2 (30);
```

And the State_Array would look something like this:

```
CREATE OR REPLACE TYPE State_Array IS VARRAY ( 50 )
OF VARCHAR2 (100) ;
```

After we have defined the data types needed, we are ready to define a structured type using these data types in its structure. A structured type called Address includes attributes StreetName, HouseNo, PostalCode, City, State, and Country. We use the data types defined earlier, PostalCode_Collection, City_Collection, State_Array, and Country_Collection, to define the data types for PostalCode, City, State, and Country. In Data Modeler, this is done as a Structured Type in Data Types Model. If we have methods for Address we want to define, now is a good time for that too, but we will leave that for the section on SQL and PL/SQL. The DDL for creating the Address data type would look something like this:

```
CREATE OR REPLACE TYPE Address
AS
  OBJECT
  (
    StreetName VARCHAR2 (100) ,
    HouseNo    NUMBER (5) ,
    PostalCode PostalCode_Collection ,
    City City_Collection ,
    State State_Array ,
    Country Country_Collection );
```

Now we have the data type Address defined and we can design a table with a column of that data type. Let's create table CUSTOMER1 with a column of that type:

```
CREATE TABLE Customer1
  (
    CustomerID NUMBER (16) NOT NULL ,
    Name       VARCHAR2 (100 CHAR) ,
    AddressTable Address
  )
NESTED TABLE AddressTable.PostalCode STORE AS PostalCode
NESTED TABLE AddressTable.City STORE AS City
NESTED TABLE AddressTable.Country STORE AS Country ;
ALTER TABLE Customer ADD CONSTRAINT Customer_PK PRIMARY KEY ( CustomerID ) ;
```

After this example, it's easier to explain what *collection types* are. They are types such as the PostalCode and State types we just defined in our example. We could define the same table without the object type by just using these collections:

```
CREATE TABLE Customer2
  (
    CustomerID NUMBER (16) NOT NULL ,
```

```
  Name          VARCHAR2 (100 CHAR) ,
  StreetName VARCHAR2 (100 CHAR) ,
  HouseNo       NUMBER (5) ,
  PostalCode PostalCode_Collection ,
  City City_Collection ,
  State State_Array ,
  Country Country_Collection
)
  NESTED TABLE PostalCode  STORE AS PostalCode
NESTED TABLE City  STORE AS City
NESTED TABLE Country STORE AS Country ;
ALTER TABLE Customer ADD CONSTRAINT Customer_PK PRIMARY KEY ( CustomerID ) ;
```

Nested tables, as well as other collections, can be defined in PL/SQL, and we will talk about those in the section on collections later in the chapter, but they can also be defined in the database as a data type for a column, as shown in that example.

If you use Data Modeler to design the user-defined data types, there are some things that are good to know. There are four kinds of user-defined data types in Data Modeler: Distinct Types, Structured Types, Collection Types, and Logical Types.

Logical Types are not actual data types; they are names that can be associated with native types of the selected RDBMS Type (Oracle 12c, SQL Server 2008, and so on) and then defined as a data type for attributes or domains. To create a new Logical Type or to edit an existing one, go to Types Administration, which can be found under the Tools menu. To create a new one, define a User Defined Native Type for the selected RDBMS Type on the User Defined Native Types tab. Then click Save. Then go to the Logical Types to Native Types tab and click Add. Enter a name for the new Logical Type and select the Native Type you just created for the RDBMS Type. Click Save. Now this new Logical Type with the Native Type settings can be seen in the list on the Logical Types to Native Types tab. And it can be selected as a data type for an attribute or a domain. I have used this, for example, with a new Microsoft SQL Server version that had new data types that Data Modeler did not support yet. I defined those data types as Logical Types and was able to use them in designing.

Distinct, Structured, and Collection Types can be defined and managed under the Data Types Model in the browser. Both logical and relational models can use definitions from the Data Types Model to specify the data type for attributes and columns. Certain structured types can also be used to define an entity or a table. A Data Types Model can be built manually, or you can import one from the Oracle Designer repository. Import functionality can be found under the File menu.

To create a distinct type or a collection type, go to Browser, select the data type, and right-click. Fill in the information needed. For a new Distinct Type, you need to define the name and select the logical data type from the list of values. You can also define the size. Do not forget to comment and document your Distinct Type. After you have created the Distinct Type, it will be available on the data type list for an attribute or column. Remember to select the data type Distinct when defining the data type for an attribute or a column. To create a new Collection Type, you must define the name and set the collection to be either an array or collection. For an array, you must define the maximum number of elements in the array; for a collection, you do not have this element to be defined. You should also define the data type for your array or collection. The data type can be Domain, Logical, Distinct, Collection, or Structured. You should also define Max Size as a **string** parameter. Also, do not forget to comment and document your Collection Type. After you have created the Collection Type, it will be available as a data type for an attribute or column. Remember to select the data type Collection when assigning a data type to an attribute.

Structured Type is a user-defined data type that has attributes and methods; in other words, it is an object type. Attributes can be of type Logical, Distinct, Structured, or Collection. A Structured Type can also be defined as a supertype to another Structured Type. An entity can be defined based on a Structured Type. To create a new Structured Type, go to Data Types Model in the browser, right-click and select Show; or on SubViews (under Data Types Model in the browser), right-click and select New SubView. Then design the Structured Type using icons on the toolbar. Only Structured Type objects are represented graphically on the Data Types Diagram, which consists of Structured Types, reference links, embedded structure links, collections of reference links, collections of embedded structure links, and notes.

From the properties of a data type, you can see on the Used In tab whether (and where) this data type is used.

Invisible Columns

The concept of invisible columns was introduced in Oracle Database 12c. An invisible column is a table column that cannot be seen using SELECT * FROM, for instance, or using the DESCRIBE command. An invisible column can be set visible for the DESCRIBE command in SQL*Plus with the SET COLINVISIBLE ON command. An invisible column cannot be seen with the %ROWTYPE attribute in PL/SQL variable declarations either. An invisible column must be explicitly specified in queries to get its values in the result set. The most typical use case for invisible columns is probably when you need to add a column to a table without affecting existing applications, and maybe make the column visible when the whole application is ready for the change. A documented feature is that when an invisible column is changed to visible, the column will be shown as the last column of the table. That is a fact you might want to take advantage of if you need to change the column order for some reason.

Invisible columns were created to make modifying legacy code easier. You can add columns in the table without affecting existing code. You will have time to change the program code and define the column as visible when all the refactoring work is done. You can define a column as visible while creating the table (CREATE TABLE) or you can modify it to be invisible using the ALTER TABLE statement. Let's create a table, called EMP_INVISIBLE, where the Ename column is invisible:

```
CREATE TABLE EMP_invisible
(EMPNO NUMBER(4) NOT NULL,
ENAME VARCHAR2(10) INVISIBLE,
JOB VARCHAR2(9),
MGR NUMBER(4),
HIREDATE DATE,
SAL NUMBER(7,2),
COMM NUMBER(7,2),
DEPTNO NUMBER(2)
)
/
```

When inserting rows in a table that has invisible columns, make sure to define the column names if you want to insert a value in the invisible column too. If you don't, you will get an "ORA-00913: too many values" error. If you do not want to insert a value in the invisible column, and if it is either nullable or has a DEFAULT clause value, you can do INSERTs without column lists. In this example, we want to add a value to the invisible column too, so we must define all the columns in the INSERT clause:

```
INSERT INTO EMP_invisible
(EMPNO, ENAME, JOB, MGR, HIREDATE, SAL, COMM, DEPTNO)
VALUES
(1, 'Tim', 'CEO','', TO_DATE( '10.3.2010', 'DD.MM.YYYY'),5000,1000,20);
```

Here's what happens when we try to do the same without defining the columns:

```
INSERT INTO EMP_invisible
VALUES
(2,'Sam','Manager','1',TO_DATE('10.7.2012','DD.MM.YYYY'),3000,1500,20);
```

SQL Error: ORA-00913: too many values

Instead, if we do not define the columns and do not try to add a value to the invisible column (ENAME), inserting works, as shown here:

```
INSERT INTO EMP_invisible
VALUES
(2,'Manager','1', TO_DATE( '10.7.2012', 'DD.MM.YYYY' ),3000,1500,20);

SELECT EMPNO,ENAME,JOB,MGR,HIREDATE,SAL,COMM,DEPTNO
from EMP_invisible;
```

EMPNO	ENAME	JOB	MGR	HIREDATE	SAL	COMM	DEPTNO
1	Tim	CEO	\<null>	10.03.2010	5000	1000	20
2	\<null>	Manager	1	10.07.2012	3000	1500	20

Invisible columns let you add a column(s) to a table without affecting existing applications that use SELECT *, SELECT with a column list, INSERT without listing the columns, or INSERT with a list of columns not including the new invisible column(s), while the new and fixed program code fully uses the invisible column(s).

As mentioned earlier, changing an invisible column to visible always moves it to the last column of the table, as shown here:

```
ALTER TABLE EMP_invisible
MODIFY ENAME VISIBLE;

DESC EMP_invisible
```

Name	Null	Type
EMPNO	NOT NULL	NUMBER(4)
JOB		VARCHAR2(9)
MGR		NUMBER(4)
HIREDATE		DATE
SAL		NUMBER(7,2)
COMM		NUMBER(7,2)
DEPTNO		NUMBER(2)
ENAME		VARCHAR2(10)

Check constraints can be defined for invisible columns as well as indexes, and Oracle optimized does use those indexes. Also, table partitioning based on invisible columns is supported.

Virtual Columns

A virtual column is like any other column in a database except that its data is not saved to disk; the data is always derived when queried. If you define an index for the column, that is very similar to a function-based index. Virtual columns can be used like regular columns, except that they cannot be manipulated by DML, which makes sense because Oracle Database is looking after the data automatically. Virtual columns are not supported for index-organized, external, object, cluster, and temporary tables.

A virtual column is defined using the following syntax:

```
column_name [datatype] [GENERATED ALWAYS] AS (expression) [VIRTUAL]
```

The only mandatory parameter is **expression**, but for clarity it might be wise to use the **generated always** and **virtual** keywords too. If the data type is omitted, it is determined based on the result of the expression. In the virtual column definition, if you refer to a column (or columns), it must be defined in the same table, and if you use a function, that function must be deterministic, always returning the same result for the same query. The output of the expression must be a scalar value; for instance, user-defined types and LOBs are not supported.

Let's look at an example based on the EMP table. We want to see in the TOTAL_SALARY column how much this person is estimated to earn total per year (note that this is just an example). The total salary is based on both salary and commission. The salary will be paid 12 times a year, and the commission only once.

```
CREATE TABLE EMP_Virtual
(EMPNO NUMBER(4) NOT NULL,
ENAME VARCHAR2(10),
JOB VARCHAR2(9),
MGR NUMBER(4),
HIREDATE DATE,
SAL NUMBER(7,2),
COMM NUMBER(7,2),
DEPTNO NUMBER(2),
TOTAL_SALARY NUMBER GENERATED ALWAYS AS(12*SAL+COMM) VIRTUAL
);
```

Note that the function used for the virtual column must be deterministic, always returning the same value irrespective of when you call it or how many times you call it. Because of that, sysdate cannot be used with virtual columns. Otherwise, it would be a perfect solution for counting a person's age or the number of years a person has been working for a company. If you still want to use it for that, one option is to define a function that will return the number of years. A function could look something like this:

```
CREATE or REPLACE FUNCTION Work_in_years (hiredate IN date)
RETURN NUMBER DETERMINISTIC
is
work_years number (2,0);
BEGIN
```

```
work_years := trunc(months_between(hiredate, sysdate)/12);
RETURN work_years;
End;
```

Note that we have declared this function to be deterministic, so we are cheating a bit. If we had not done that, this would not work. Now we can create the table, like this:

```
CREATE TABLE EMP_Virtual2
(EMPNO NUMBER(4) NOT NULL,
ENAME VARCHAR2(10),
JOB VARCHAR2(9),
MGR NUMBER(4),
HIREDATE DATE,
SAL NUMBER(7,2),
COMM NUMBER(7,2),
DEPTNO NUMBER(2),
LENGTH_OF_CAREER NUMBER GENERATED ALWAYS AS (Work_in_years(hiredate)) VIRTUAL);
```

Now we have a virtual column called LENGTH_OF_CAREER that will be derived from the difference between sysdate and the date this person was hired every time that information is queried. This is not correct because the function is not really deterministic, and it will change every day. Not only will a change in the value in the table column affect it, but also time. But it works, and Oracle does update the value every time you query for it. In this case, it works because the column is only for display purposes, not for filtering queries, and it is not indexed. Besides, the interval for the change in data per employee is one year.

If you need to add a virtual column but without interfering with existing applications, you might want to create the virtual column as an invisible column. Let's add the Total_salary column as an invisible column:

```
CREATE TABLE EMP_Virt_Inv
(EMPNO NUMBER(4) NOT NULL,
ENAME VARCHAR2(10),
JOB VARCHAR2(9),
MGR NUMBER(4),
HIREDATE DATE,
SAL NUMBER(7,2),
COMM NUMBER(7,2),
DEPTNO NUMBER(2),
TOTAL_SALARY NUMBER INVISIBLE GENERATED ALWAYS AS(12*SAL+COMM) VIRTUAL
);
```

A virtual column can be used with partitioning, but a virtual column used as the partitioning column cannot use calls to a PL/SQL function. If a virtual column is defined using a deterministic user-defined function, it cannot be used as a partitioning key column—which is good, because programmers can be very creative, as I just proved, and using this kind of trick solution as a basis for partitioning might not end well.

Attribute Clustering

Attribute clustering was introduced in Oracle Database 12.1.0.2. It is a table property that defines how rows should be ordered and saved together based on values on one or multiple columns.

Having related data close to each other can significantly reduce the data processed and thus lead to better performance. Clustering can be done simply by ordering on specified columns or by using a function that permits multidimensional clustering (interleaved clustering). Attribute clustering was invented to improve the performance of zone maps, Exadata storage indexes, and in-memory min/max pruning, but it can be used also without those features. If you use attribute clustering with a partitioned table, it applies to all the table's partitions.

As mentioned earlier, table clusters store rows in a specialized cluster storage structure that must be specified in a certain order. Attribute clustering does not use any specific clustering structure; it simply orders rows within a table and saves related rows physically close to each other.

Attribute clustering can be defined for a single table, but it can also be defined for related tables using their join columns. The latter is called *join attribute clustering* and is very useful, for instance, in star schemas on data warehouse databases where one or more dimension tables can be clustered to the fact table, and then you can cluster the fact table by dimension hierarchy columns. To be able to use attribute clustering, the tables involved should be connected through a primary key–foreign key relationship. Foreign keys do not have to be enforced though.

The attribute clustering can be done in one of two ways: attribute clustering with linear ordering or with interleaved ordering. In both cases, you can cluster data based on a single table or by joining multiple tables (join attribute clustering). The default for attribute clustering is *linear ordering,* which stores the data based on the order of specified columns.

Linear ordering can be defined on a single table or multiple tables that are connected through a primary key–foreign key relationship. Linear attribute clustering can be defined for a table when you're creating it or when modifying it using **ADD CLUSTERING BY LINEAR ORDER (column list)** at the end of a CREATE TABLE or ALTER TABLE clause. Because attribute clustering is a property of the table, when it is added, existing rows are not re-ordered, but they can be ordered using MOVE. Let's assume that queries to table EMP are conducted using either Empno or a combination of Empno and Deptno. First, we alter table EMP to support these queries with linear attribute clustering and then we move the table to get the rows that exist in this table to be ordered:

```
ALTER TABLE Emp
ADD CLUSTERING BY LINEAR ORDER (Empno, Deptno);
ALTER TABLE Emp MOVE;
```

Now we want to cluster table EMP knowing that it will be joined often with the DEPT table and queried using **Emp.Empno** and possibly combined with **Dept.Loc**. This linear attribute cluster would support that requirement:

```
CREATE TABLE Emp_Cluster (
EMPNO NUMBER(4) NOT NULL,
ENAME VARCHAR2(10),
JOB VARCHAR2(9),
MGR NUMBER(4),
HIREDATE DATE,
SAL NUMBER(7,2),
COMM NUMBER(7,2),
DEPTNO NUMBER(2))
CLUSTERING
Emp_Cluster JOIN Dept ON (Emp_Cluster.Deptno = Dept.Deptno)
BY LINEAR ORDER (Empno, Loc);
```

Attribute clustering based on the linear order of columns works best if most of the queries have the clustering attributes or its leading columns in the WHERE clause and the clustering columns have a reasonable level of cardinality.

Interleaved ordering uses a multidimensional clustering technique based on z-order curve fitting, a mathematic function that maps multidimensional data points (multiple column attribute values) to one dimensional point (a single one-dimensional value) while still preserving the multidimensional locality of the data points (column values). The z-value of a point is calculated by interleaving the binary representations of its coordinate values. Interleaved ordering is especially good in a data warehouse with dimensional hierarchies of star schemas. A typical example would be a Sales table. Let's assume that the data is accessed mostly on time_id or product_id, or both time_id and product_id.

```
CREATE TABLE Scott.sales (
product_id         NUMBER(16) NOT NULL,
customer_id          NUMBER(16) NOT NULL,
time_id        DATE NOT NULL,
quantity_sold  NUMBER(10) NOT NULL,
amount_sold    NUMBER(15,2) NOT NULL
)
CLUSTERING
BY INTERLEAVED ORDER (time_id, product_id);
```

Using interleaved join attribute clustering is most common in data warehousing environments where the star schema fact table is clustered based on columns from its dimension tables. The columns from a dimension table usually contain a hierarchy, such as a product category and subcategory. For this reason, join attribute clustering for star schemas is referred to as *hierarchical clustering*. Interleaved clustering is most beneficial for queries with varying predicates on multiple columns, which is also very common in data warehouse environments. Clustering columns can be individual columns or placed together into column groups. Each individual column or column group will be used to constitute one of the multidimensional data points in the cluster. Queries benefit from I/O pruning when they specify columns from multiple tables in a nonprefix order, so the order of the columns is not as important as it is with linear ordering. Grouped columns are marked with (), and must follow the dimensional hierarchy from the coarsest to the finest level of granularity—for example, **(product_category, product_subcategory)**. Let's assume that the data is accessed on any of these predicates or combination of predicates: **time_id**, **product_category**, **(product_category and product_subcategory)**, **(time_id and product_category)**, or **(time_id and prod_category and prod_subcategory)**. The supportive attribute clustering for that might look as follows:

```
CREATE TABLE Scott.Sales_Clust (
product_id         NUMBER(16) NOT NULL,
customer_id          NUMBER(16) NOT NULL,
time_id        DATE NOT NULL,
quantity_sold  NUMBER(10) NOT NULL,
amount_sold    NUMBER(15,2) NOT NULL
)
CLUSTERING
sales_Clust JOIN products ON (sales_Clust.product_id = products.product_id)
BY INTERLEAVED ORDER ((time_id), (product_category, product_subcategory));
```

If you want to check whether or not the clustering is on, you can do so by querying the Clustering column in the DBA_TABLES view:

```
SELECT TABLE_NAME, CLUSTERING FROM DBA_TABLES WHERE OWNER='Scott';

TABLE_NAME          CLUSTERING
-----------         ------------
EMP_Clust              YES
DEPT                   NO
BONUS                  NO
SALGRADE               NO
```

There are some special views for attribute clustering. DBA_CLUSTERING_TABLES, for instance, tells whether the clustering is in linear or interleaved ordering. If you want to drop attribute clustering for the EMP table, you simply use ALTER TABLE with a **drop clustering** parameter:

```
ALTER TABLE emp DROP CLUSTERING;
```

Partitioning

Partitioning involves dividing a table, index, or index-organized table into smaller pieces, called *partitions*. Each partition has its own name and can also have its own storage definitions. A table can be partitioned for performance reasons to minimize the data accessed, to make maintaining the data and database structures easier, and/or to provide better availability for data. Partitioning is an option for Oracle Database and must be purchased to use.

The partitioning feature was first introduced in Oracle Database 8.0, and it's one of those features Oracle has improved in every release. Partitioning divides tables and indexes into smaller pieces (partitions) using a partitioning key. These partitions can be defined and managed either as a whole or separately. There are three different partition strategies: range, list, and hash. Partitioning can be single or composite—*single* meaning that only one strategy is applied, and *composite* meaning that a combination of two of those strategies is used. In Oracle Database 12*c*, some extensions were introduced: interval partitioning, reference partitioning, and virtual column-based partitioning. Three different kinds of indexes can be used when partitioning: a local index, a global partitioned index, and a global nonpartitioned index. It has been often said that partitioning does not affect applications and program code. That might be true, but it is possible that it does have an effect: you might need to add columns to have a partitioning key that really serves the purpose of partitioning.

If you have a lot of rows in a table and maybe a lot of requirements for management and performance, partitioning might be the solution. The first decision to make is defining the partitioning key and the partitioning strategy or data distribution method. The classic method is range partitioning. For instance, if there are plenty of orders in a database, you might want to partition them using the purchase date as a partitioning key. Each order will be saved in the partition it belongs to based on the partitioning key. The first partition can be open-ended and take all the order dates before the first one, and a new partition can be added automatically every day. The database knows exactly in which partition it has which information, and queries can be performed directly in the right partition, not the whole table. This provides better performance if you want to find an order using the order date, and it makes removing orders of a certain date easier: just drop that partition. For instance, dropping a partition of January is easier than deleting all the January rows. Range partitioning is often used as well when a "rolling window" is needed. For instance, you might want to have an element that shows orders for today and the past three days. That can easily be implemented using range partitioning and one day per partition.

Another method for partitioning is list partitioning. With list partitioning, you define a list of values for the partitioning key to specify which values will go to which partition. For instance, we have 12 months in a fiscal year and we want to have four partitions, one for each quarter: January, February, and March would go in partition one; April, May, and June would go in the second partition; and so on. If the data has rows that do not fit any of those criteria (a mistake in the data in this case), we can define a special partition called DEFAULT that will hold all the rows that do not fit the defined partitions. One more strategy is hash partitioning. With hash partitioning, we use an internal hash key to define the value for a partitioning key and use that to locate the data in the right partition. As you might have realized already, partitioning does not provide the logical connection between the data and the location in the database but rather provides a balance of data between the partitions. You can use one of these partitioning methods (single partitioning), or you can combine two of them (composite partitioning). You might, for instance, first partition per month using range partitioning and then partition by the quarter list using list partitioning.

Hash partitioning does not offer a logical mapping between the data and a certain partition as the other two mechanisms do. Hash partitioning simply divides the data as equally as possible to different partitions using an internal hash algorithm.

Composite partitioned tables are partitions that have subpartitions within them. So first you partition the table using one of the strategies just explained, and then you use another strategy to partition those partitions. Maybe you would like to partition by gender (male/female) using range partitioning and then by type of a cloth (socks, coats, dresses, and so on) using list partitioning. Composite partition is only supported for heap tables.

Partitioning is not supported for temporary or external tables. It is probably not needed with temporary tables, but sometimes it is needed with external tables. Before the partitioning feature was introduced, a thing called a *partition view* was used, which is simply a view built on several tables (partitions). For instance, if you have tables called JANUARY_2015_SALES, FEBRUARY_2015_SALES, and so on, you might want to build a partition view for Sales of 2015, as follows:

```
CREATE VIEW Sales_2015 AS
SELECT *
FROM January_2015_Sales
WHERE ...
UNION ALL
SELECT *
FROM February_2015_Sales
WHERE ...
UNION ALL
...etc...
```

Note that all these tables must have the same columns, data types, and so on; therefore, the UNION ALL construction works.

This solution does not bring the performance benefits that partitioning might bring by finding the right partition(s) and only reading that, but it allows you to build "rolling windows," for instance, create views automatically (if the naming standard is stable), or create a kind of partitioning for external tables. This is also a solution that can be used without a separate partitioning option.

Zone Maps

Zone maps are a new index-type structure in Oracle Database that can be built for a table to improve its performance. Zone maps are based on a concept of a zone, a range of contiguous blocks within a table. A zone map stores the min and max values of selected columns for each zone of a table, and using that technique it enables the pruning of disk access, skipping the blocks that will not satisfy the predicates on table columns. When a SQL statement contains predicates on columns defined in the zone map, the database compares these values to the min and max values for each zone to determine which zones of blocks to read or to skip during the table scan. Zone maps are physical objects, quite similar to materialized views, and can be refreshed, controlled, and maintained.

The two kinds of zone maps are basic zone maps and join zone maps. A basic zone map is defined for a single table, whereas a join zone map is defined on a table that has an outer join to one or more other tables. You can define at most one basic zone map on a table or for a partitioned table to cover all partitions and sub-partitions. The join zone map maintains the min and max values of some columns (for instance, in a star schema, the values of columns from the dimension tables for zones of the fact table); in the other tables, these join conditions are common in master-detail relationships and especially in data warehousing environments in star schemas between fact and dimension tables.

Unlike indexes, zone maps are not actively managed during DML operations. Depending on the zone map refresh property, the zone map is either updated or not during a DML operation, so be careful when defining the properties. The default refresh property is **refresh on load data movement**, which means the zone map in part becomes stale after DML operations.

Zone maps do not take up much space; a b-tree index entry would need space per referenced row of the table, whereas a zone map only needs space for one entry per zone of the table. Zone maps may or may not be used as part of the attribute clustering capabilities we talked about earlier in this chapter, but combining these two might provide a great improvement to performance. Using zone maps requires both the partitioning option and either Exadata or SuperCluster machines.

Constraints

Constraints are very important in designing databases to keep the data automatically in good shape. You are also able to define different kinds of constraints in addition to the regular primary key, foreign key, and NOT NULL. You can define, for instance, table-level constraints, column-level constraints, and existence-dependency constraints using Data Modeler. Table-level constraints are typically primary, unique, or foreign key constraints, and they affect the whole table.

A column-level constraint only affects one column in a table. An example of a column-level constraint would be a list of values or a list of ranges. A typical example is NOT NULL, but also several CHECK constraints can be defined for a column. A list of values is simply a list of allowable values. For instance, for the column Months, the allowable values would be ('January', 'February', and so on), or for the column MonthNumbers the range would be 1–12.

The existence dependency is very useful in a situation where you have one table (let's say CUSTOMER) that has two (or more) different types of data. One of them has certain mandatory columns, and the other one has other mandatory columns. In this example, customers can be either companies ("C") or persons ("P"). A discriminator column (Customer_TYPE) will divide the rows of the table to be either companies or persons. Data Modeler creates that column automatically as well as the existence-dependency constraint. This constraint is a check constraint that watches for the following: if Customer_TYPE is "C" then Company_ID cannot be NULL but SSN and PersonInfo must be NULL, and if Customer_TYPE is "P" then CompanyID and CompanyInfo must be NULL and both SSN and PersonInfo cannot be NULL. Data Modeler automatically creates the logic for the existence of either a person or a company. A design like this is created in the Entity-Relationship Diagram using the arc symbol.

In Oracle Database 12 Release 1, a new feature for the DEFAULT clause was introduced: you can define a default for a NOT NULL column for insertion. If a NULL is inserted into a NOT NULL column with this definition, the default value is automatically inserted instead. This will hopefully help database designers to design more NOT NULL columns for tables.

Another interesting new feature in Oracle Database 12.1 is the identity column. An identity column will replace the surrogate primary key system used with sequences and triggers. Now you simply create the column with an IDENTITY definition, and Oracle Database will automatically look after inserting a unique value to the column. Here is an example of creating a table with an identity column:

```
CREATE TABLE Emp_identity (
Empno        NUMBER GENERATED ALWAYS AS IDENTITY,
Ename        VARCHAR2(10));
```

NOTE
You must have the create sequence privilege to be able to create an identity column.

When you insert rows into the table, you do not insert any values into the identity column:

```
INSERT INTO Emp_identity (Ename) VALUES ('Tim');
```

If you try to add a value to the identity column, you will get an error message:

```
ORA-32795: cannot insert into a generated always identity column
```

Let's see if the column has been filled automatically:

```
SELECT * FROM Emp_identity;
```

```
EMPNO        ENAME
1            Tim
```

Some Tools for Implementing Requirements with SQL and PL/SQL

The most powerful tool for implementing performance requirements is the database design, but sometimes the toolset available for database design is not enough, the implementation is not good enough, or a requirement has changed. Therefore, other ways to implement a requirement are needed, and some of them are introduced in this section.

One problem from a performance perspective with the tools we talked about earlier is that the data is always saved on disk (except a view), and that is definitely not the fastest solution. Using SQL and PL/SQL, we have some tools that allow us to speed up the processing by not saving anything to disk during the processing. Another problem is that the database might have been designed a long time ago, and there is no way for you to influence those design decisions any more. Therefore, what you have left is to make your solutions on the program code level.

All the SQL we use when communicating with the database needs a cursor to be able to function. A *cursor* is a pointer to the context area where the query result is saved. Implicit cursors are created by Oracle Database, whereas explicit cursors are created by the programmer. A *variable* can be declared and referenced in PL/SQL, and it is bound to a data type or data structure: either scalar (single) or composite. A scalar variable, for instance, could be of type NUMBER or VARCHAR2 and declared as Empno NUMBER. You can also initialize a variable with a value (for instance, **COUNTER := 1**). If you do not initialize a variable, it is automatically initialized to NULL. Knowing that, make sure to assign a variable a value before referencing it. You can also declare a *constant*, which is a variable with an unchangeable value. A constant is declared like variables, but add the word CONSTANT before the data type of a constant and define the value: for example, **minimum_age CONSTANT NUMBER := 18**. A constant must be initialized in its declaration.

NOTE
The names of constants, variables, and parameters are not case-sensitive.

In PL/SQL, you can define two kinds of composite structures: records and collections. A *record* is like a row in a table, whereas a *collection* is like a column in a table. You can pass a composite variable to subprograms as parameters, or you can work with internal components of a composite variable individually. The components for those composite variables can be either scalar or composite. A *record* is a composite structure that consists of fields that can each have a different data type. To create a record variable, you define a RECORD type and then create a variable of that type, or you can use %ROWTYPE or %TYPE. You can access each field of a record variable by its name: **variable_name.field_name**. A *collection* has elements that always have the same data type as the other elements in that collection. You can access each element of a collection variable by its unique index: **variable_name(index)**. There are three types of collections: associative array, nested table, and VARRAY (variable-sized array). To create a collection variable, you define a collection type and then create a variable of that type or use %TYPE. You can create a collection of records and a record that contains collections. You can use table functions or pipelined table functions, or you can parallelize the queries.

In this section we do not go through exception handling. We trust that you are an experienced developer and, as such, understand the importance of exception handling.

Cursors

Every time a SQL clause is performed against a relational database, a cursor is used. A cursor is a pointer to the context area where the query result is saved. There are two kinds of cursors: implicit and explicit. *Implicit* cursors are automatically created by Oracle whenever a SQL statement is executed if there is no explicit cursor for the statement. Implicit cursors and the information in them cannot be controlled by the programmer. Explicit cursors are cursors that a programmer has defined to have more control over a cursor and the context area. An explicit cursor is defined in the declaration section of a PL/SQL block and allows you to name the cursor, which is why explicit cursors are also called *named cursors.* When you have named the cursor, you can access its work area and information as well as process the rows of the query individually. A cursor is used for fetching rows returned by a query to a *variable,* which can be used in a program for many purposes, such as calculating or updating the database. The number of cursors is limited by the amount of memory, and the value of the initialization parameter **open_cursors** defines the maximum number of cursors open per session.

A SQL cursor has attributes, such as %FOUND, %NOTFOUND, %ROWCOUNT, and %ISOPEN. It can also have additional attributes for the use of the FORALL statement, such as %BULK_ROWCOUNT and %BULK_EXCEPTIONS. When you want to refer to one of these attributes with an implicit cursor, you can use **DBMS_OUTPUT.put_line** to echo the value of the attribute. And with explicit cursors, you can simply attach the attribute to the cursor name (for instance, **HelisCursor%ROWCOUNT**). This example would return the number of records fetched from HelisCursor at the moment. %FOUND and %NOTFOUND can be used to find out whether or not the most recent FETCH returned rows. %ISOPEN returns TRUE if the cursor is open; otherwise, it returns FALSE. Both %BULK_ROWCOUNT and %BULK_EXCEPTION are attributes for bulk operations with the FORALL statement. %BULK_ROWCOUNT returns the number of rows processed by each DML execution, whereas %BULK_EXCEPTION returns exception information each DML execution might have raised. The values of cursor attributes always refer to the most recently executed SQL statement. If you want to save an attribute value for later use, assign it to a variable. This applies to both implicit and explicit cursors.

NOTE
Cursor attributes can be used with procedural code (PL/SQL) but not in SQL statements.

An implicit cursor (SQL cursor) is opened automatically by the database to process each SQL statement that is not associated with an explicit cursor. A typical example of an implicit cursor is a DML operation inside PL/SQL code (**DELETE FROM Emp;**) or defining a record and then performing a query on that record. For example, we could first define a record called **emp_ename_rec** that will hold all the names of employees having salary > 1000 in an implicit cursor (note that this is just an example to show the syntax; it will run into an error if the query returns more than one row):

```
DECLARE
emp_ename_rec emp.ename%TYPE;
BEGIN
SELECT ename
INTO emp_ename_rec
FROM emp
WHERE sal > 1000;
END;
```

An explicit cursor is more complicated than an implicit cursor because you need to construct and manage it yourself; however, it has some benefits that make all the trouble worthwhile. When declaring an explicit cursor, you define it, give it a name, and associate it with a query. Then you can either use operations such as OPEN, FETCH, and CLOSE with the cursor or use it with a FOR LOOP statement. You cannot assign a value to an explicit cursor, use it in an expression, or use it as a subprogram parameter or host variable. This is where cursor variables are needed. A cursor variable is not limited to one query; it can process one cursor result at the time, and then it is free to process the next one. A cursor variable can accept whole queries as parameters. Let's create a simple procedure that accepts a number (**no**) as the input parameter and uses that in a cursor as a parameter to limit the values returned:

```
CREATE OR REPLACE PROCEDURE NameForEmp (no IN NUMBER)
IS
CURSOR emp_name IS SELECT ename FROM emp WHERE empno = no;
BEGIN
for i in emp_name LOOP
DBMS_OUTPUT.PUT_LINE(i.ename);
END LOOP;
END;
/
```

You can refer to an explicit cursor or cursor variable by its name. Typically the process for using explicit cursors is as follows:

- Declare variables for storing the column values of a returned row in the DECLARE section of your PL/SQL code.

- Declare the cursor using the syntax **CURSOR cursor_name IS SELECT_statement**.

- Open a cursor using the syntax **OPEN cursor_name**.

- Fetch the rows from the cursor and store the values in the variables using the syntax **FETCH cursor_name INTO variable [,variable …]**.

- Close the cursor using the syntax **CLOSE cursor_name**.

An explicit cursor can be called without a parameter, as shown here:

```
CURSOR Emp_cur IS
SELECT Ename FROM Emp;
```

Or it can be called with a parameter:

```
CURSOR Emp_cur (Emp_no_in NUMBER(4)) IS
SELECT Ename FROM Emp
WHERE Emp_no = Emp_no_in;
```

You could use a cursor for defining a collection. Declare a cursor (**c1**), declare a collection (NameSet) of that type, and declare a variable for the collection:

```
DECLARE
   CURSOR c1 IS
     SELECT ename, job, hiredate
     FROM emp;
TYPE NameSet IS TABLE OF c1%ROWTYPE;
HighSalaryNames  NameSet;
```

Typically, cursors are used with a FOR LOOP:

```
...FOR r in c1 LOOP...
...FOR c1 IN (SELECT * FROM emp) LOOP...
...SELECT * BULK COLLECT INTO emp_nt FROM emp...
```

Cursor variables of the REF CURSOR type are pointers to a cursor. Any program that has access to that cursor variable can open, fetch from, and close this cursor. The syntax for creating a REF cursor is as follows:

```
TYPE type_name IS REF CURSOR [ RETURN return_type ]
```

Declare a type of REF CURSOR (**Cursor_Ref_Type**) and a cursor variable for that type (**crv**). Open the ref cursor variable, fetch it to a collection, and then close it:

```
TYPE Cursor_Ref_Type is REF CURSOR;
crv cursor_ref_type;
OPEN crv FOR
SELECT ename, job, hiredate FROM emp WHERE sal > 4000
ORDER BY hiredate;
FETCH crv BULK COLLECT INTO …;
CLOSE crv;
```

A constrained cursor (a strong cursor) has a specific return type that must match the data types of the columns in the query, whereas an unconstrained cursor (weak cursor) has no return type. An unconstrained cursor can be used to run any query.

Records

A record in PL/SQL is like the row of a table in a database: it's a composite structure that has no value itself, but its elements (fields) have their data types and values just like columns in a relational table. Using records in your PL/SQL code will make the code easier to write and easier to read. Instead of defining hundreds of variables, you define records, and you will be able to operate with the whole data set. To be able to work with records in the code, you need a record variable.

You can create a record variable in three different ways:

- Define a RECORD type and then create a variable of that type.
- Use %ROWTYPE.
- Use %TYPE.

If you define the RECORD type in a PL/SQL block, this type is a local type: it is only available in the block. If you define the RECORD type in a package specification, it is a public item and can be referenced from outside the package (**package_name.type_name**). RECORD types cannot be created at the schema level. Note that a RECORD type defined in a package specification is incompatible with an identically defined local RECORD type. If you declared the record variable using the RECORD type, you can also specify a different initial value for it when defining the type. You can create a RECORD type by using either %ROWTYPE or %TYPE. In this example, we create a RECORD type called **Emp_type** and assign it for a variable called **rec1**:

```
TYPE Emp_rec_type is RECORD Emp%ROWTYPE;
rec1 Emp_rec_type;
```

If you create a record variable based on the EMP table using %ROWTYPE and there are changes to the structure of the EMP table, this record variable does not need to be changed. This way of declaring a record variable creates a record variable that has all the columns of a database table as fields. If you use %ROWTYPE to declare a record variable, it is similar to the table row in our sample table EMP:

```
l_rec_Emp Emp%ROWTYPE;
```

Note that a feature called an invisible column (introduced in Oracle Database 12.1) can cause problems with record variables defined using %ROWTYPE, because they are not seen by it. We talked about invisible columns earlier in this chapter.

You can declare a record based on a database table (or a view), some of its columns based on a cursor, or you can define it completely yourself. To declare a record type or a record variable based on some of the columns of a table, use the %TYPE attribute. If you define a record type or record variable using %TYPE, you can define it for individual columns of a table (in our example, columns Empno and Ename in the EMP table). In this example, we create a RECORD type called **Emp_rec** that has two fields: ename and empno, both based on columns in the table EMP. Then we define a variable (**rec1**) of type **Emp_rec**. We select the first row on table EMP in the record variable and print it out.

```
DECLARE
TYPE Emp_rec IS RECORD (ename emp.ename%TYPE, empno emp.empno%TYPE);
rec1 Emp_rec;
BEGIN
    SELECT ename, empno INTO rec1 FROM emp WHERE ROWNUM < 2;
    DBMS_OUTPUT.PUT_LINE('Employee #' || rec1.empno || ' = ' || rec1.ename);
END;
```

Note the **ROWNUM < 2**. This is because a record can only handle one row at the time. If the result set is more than one row, a record is not able to handle it and you will get an error message. To be able to manage result sets of more than one row, you can either use a cursor or a collection, possibly combined with a record.

You can also define the record type fields yourself. In this method, each field, its name, and data type have been defined explicitly by you. This gives you a great deal of freedom to declare almost anything, including defining another record as a field. However, the downside is that it is more work, and any changes to the table structures in the database might cause changes to this record as well. The definition of the record might turn out to be very complicated and hard to understand and maintain. When declaring a record yourself, you first declare the record type, using the TYPE…RECORD statement, and then define the record fields. To define a field, specify its name, the data type, and, if needed, the NOT NULL constraint with its initial value. By default, the initial value of a field is NULL. The data type can either be manually defined using the logical data types, programmer-defined subtypes, PL/SQL cursor type, REF CURSOR, or automatically defined using the data types defined for the database table column (%TYPE and %ROWTYPE). Here's how to declare a programmer-defined record for the EMP table where the record will consist of the columns Empno, Ename, and Deptno; and the data types for Empno and Deptno are defined manually; and the data type for Ename is defined based on the data type of the table column:

```
DECLARE
TYPE emp_dept_rt IS RECORD (
Empno NUMBER(4),
Ename emp.ename%TYPE,
Deptno NUMBER(2));
Emp_dept  emp_dept_rt;
```

Note that each name for a field in a record must be unique. In a declaration you can define a default value for a field using either DEFAULT or := syntax. A programmer-defined record should not be used in this kind of simple situation when the record is based on a single table; the other two ways work much better for that. It should be used in more complex situations when the record is based on several tables or views, or the record has nothing to do with a table or a cursor.

If you do not want to define a record type, you can simply create a record variable either using %ROWTYPE or %TYPE. %ROWTYPE declares a record variable that represents a full set of columns in a database table or view. Let's create a record variable called **Emp_rec** using %ROWTYPE:

```
DECLARE
Emp_rec      EMP%ROWTYPE;
```

%TYPE declares a record variable of the same type as a previously declared record variable. In our example, we first create a record variable of the row type of the EMP table and then another record variable (**Emp2_rec**) of the same type:

```
DECLARE
Emp_rec      EMP%ROWTYPE;
Emp2_rec     Emp_rec%TYPE;
```

You can access each field of a record variable using its name: **variable_name.field_name**. The initial value of each field is NULL. The variable does not inherit the initial value of the referenced item, even though %TYPE or %ROWTYPE is used.

To declare a record type based on cursor, use the %ROWTYPE attribute with an explicit cursor or cursor variable, with each field representing a column in a table. Here's how to declare a record type based on a cursor on the EMP table:

```
CURSOR emp_cur IS SELECT ename, empno FROM EMP;
TYPE Emp_rec IS RECORD emp_cur%ROWTYPE;
```

To declare a record variable based on a cursor, use the %ROWTYPE attribute with an explicit cursor or cursor variable:

```
CURSOR emp_cur IS SELECT ename, empno FROM EMP;
Emp_rec emp_cur%ROWTYPE;
```

If you want your life to be easier, only create table-based records when possible. When doing so, you only need to declare the record variable—no single variables for each field of the record. Also, the structure of that record will automatically adapt the changes in the table with each compilation. Also, when appropriate, pass the record as a parameter rather than individual variables. It will require less typing (with fewer typos) and no changes are needed when the table structure changes. Using table-based records will give you a good base for stable code.

Regardless of how you define the record variables, working with them is the same. As mentioned earlier, you can either work on the record level or you can work on individual fields of the record. A record-level operation always sees the data as a whole row of data, not individual fields of it. Operations you can do on a record level are in general those that see the data on that level, similar to operations on a table instead of a column. For instance, you can copy the content of a record to another record, you can return a record, you can define and pass a record as an argument in a parameter list, you can assign NULL to a record, or since Oracle Database 9*i*

Release 2, you can insert a row in a database table using a record. However, you cannot compare two records to each other because that would mean you are actually comparing all the fields with each other. Remember, the record itself has no value; only the fields do. If you remember that a record is like a table and a field is like a column, it can be quite easy to understand what can be done and what cannot be done on a record level.

When working on the field level, you are able to work on individual data values. To access a field, use a dot notation of **schema_name.package_name.record_name.field_name**, where only the **record_name** and **field_name** are mandatory. Others should be defined if needed. You can set a value to a field using the **:=** notation. To compare whether two records are the same, you must compare all their fields with each other, just like you would do to compare whether the content of two tables is the same.

Collections

A collection in Oracle could be described as a single-dimensional array structure, or a list. There are three different kinds of collections: associative array, nested table, and VARRAY (variable-sized array). In a collection, a value is referenced by its row number. Collections are relatively easy to use and more efficient than using a table or a temporary table because everything is done using cache, without saving data to disk. You can also use the bulk operations FORALL and BULK COLLECT combined with collections to get better performance.

A collection is *bounded* if there are predefined limits, upper and/or lower, for the numbers of rows in it. If there are no limits, the collection is *unbounded*. A collection is *dense* if all rows are defined and have a value. In this context, NULL is considered to be a value too. A collection is *sparse* (undense) if there are gaps between elements in a collection. If a collection is sparse, the rows can be ordered in it using a primary key or another key that would improve the performance when working with lookups.

A collection type defined in a PL/SQL block is a local type and available only in the block. A collection type defined in a package specification is a public item and can be referenced outside the package (**package_name.type_name**). A collection type defined at the schema level is a stand-alone type and can be created with the CREATE TYPE statement. A schema-level collection type is stored in the database until you drop it. Note that a collection type defined in a package specification is incompatible with an identically defined local or stand-alone collection type.

A collection consists of elements of the same type; it could be seen as a column of a table. A collection has only one dimension, but if needed you can also create multidimensional collections simply by defining a collection whose elements are collections. You can declare collections as parameters of functions or procedures and pass them to stored subprograms, or you can specify a collection type in the RETURN clause of a function specification.

Associative Arrays

For associative arrays (which used to be called PL/SQL tables and index-by tables before Oracle 9*i* Release 2), the number of elements is unspecified; they are arrays without upper bounds (unbounded) so that they can extend as much as needed. They are sets of *key-value pairs*. Each key is unique and is used to locate the corresponding value pair in the array. It is absolutely vital that the key is unique because when you are assigning a value to an associative array using a key, the value is either added (if it is a new key value) or updated (if the key value already exists). Usually a primary key of a table is the easiest key to use for an associative array. Values for the key can be either an integer or a string because an associative array is indexed using either BINARY_INTEGER or VARCHAR2. Other data types, which can be converted to these, can be used for the index, but they will definitely cause more bad than good, so I would advise that you not use them. Indexes are stored in sort order, and for strings the order can be defined using the parameters **nls_sort** and **nls_comp**. If you change the value of either parameter after populating an associative array indexed by string, then the collection methods **first**, **last**, **next**, and **prior** (described later in this section) might return unexpected values or raise exceptions because the order has been changed on the fly. Changing the values is better to do before populating the associative array. I work in a European environment where dates are treated differently than in the United States. The character set includes Scandinavian letters, for instance, so I have learned that playing with data types and NLS_ parameters will eventually cause a lot of trouble.

An associative array is sparse. Because it is unbounded and sparse and uses an index based on the primary key for searches, an associative array is like a simple database table, but without using the disk space and network operations required for database tables. The nature of an associative array is temporary, but it can be made persistent for the length of a database session by declaring the type in a package and assigning the values in a package body. The most efficient way to pass collections is to use associative arrays with the FORALL statement or BULK COLLECT clause. DML operations or declarations at the schema level are not allowed with associative arrays because of their nature as temporary elements. Nested tables and VARRAYs can be stored as a data type of a database column, whereas associative arrays cannot.

Let's look at a very simple example of an associative array. First, we declare a type (**emp_sal**) for an associative array indexed by string (in our example, that is going to be the employee name, which in real life is silly because several employees might have the same name, but this is just a simple example). We then define an associative array variable called **Employee_salary** of type **emp_sal**. Next, we add values to our array: names and salaries. When we realize Brendan's salary is too low, we raise it. Finally, we print out all the names and their salaries. Note that whatever we do here happens only in the computer cache, and nothing is saved in the database.

```
DECLARE
TYPE emp_sal IS TABLE OF NUMBER(6) INDEX BY VARCHAR2(12);
Employee_salary emp_sal;
i   VARCHAR2(12);
BEGIN
Employee_salary ('Heli')   := 2000;
Employee_salary ('Martin') := 5000;
Employee_salary ('Brendan') := 3000;
Employee_salary ('Brendan') := 5000;
i := Employee_salary.FIRST;
WHILE i IS NOT NULL LOOP
DBMS_Output.PUT_LINE('Salary of ' || i || ' is ' || Employee_salary (i));
i := Employee_salary.NEXT(i);
END LOOP;
END;
```

Here's the result:

```
Salary of Brendan is 5000
Salary of Heli is 2000
Salary of Martin is 5000
```

Associative arrays are very useful with data sets of arbitrary size when the volume of data is unknown. The index values in associative arrays are flexible and allow both numeric and string values. The index structure enables efficient searching of an individual element without knowing its position. Associative arrays are for temporal use but are quite easy to use.

Nested Tables

A nested table stores an unspecified number of rows in no particular order. The order and subscripts for a nested table are not preserved in the database when the nested table is saved in a database and retrieved from there. PL/SQL gives each row in a nested table a consecutive index, starting at 1, while retrieving data. Using these indexes, you can access the individual rows of the nested table variable. The syntax is **variable_name(index)**. You must initialize a nested table, either by making it empty or by assigning a non-NULL value to it.

An associative array is initialized when the value is inserted into it. As mentioned earlier, if the unique value already exists, it's updated, if it does not exist yet, it's inserted. But nested tables and VARRAYs are different. To initialize a nested table or VARRAY, you use a constructor. A constructor is a system-defined function with the same name as the collection type and is used to construct a collection with the elements passed to it. You must explicitly call a constructor for each nested table and VARRAY variable. A simple example for a nested table would be as follows:

```
DECLARE
TYPE enames_tab IS TABLE OF VARCHAR2(10);
emp_names enames_tab;
BEGIN
emp_names := enames_tab('Arup','Brendan','Heli','Martin','Alex');END;
```

You can also combine the constructor in the collection declaration:

```
DECLARE
TYPE enames_tab IS TABLE OF VARCHAR2(10);
emp_names enames_tab := enames_tab('Arup','Brendan','Heli','Martin','Alex');
BEGIN
NULL;
END;
```

If you call a constructor without arguments, you get an empty but non-null collection. Here's an example:

```
emp_names enames_tab := enames_tab();
```

As mentioned, a nested table is unbounded but is also dense. Nested tables can get sparse because elements can be deleted after creation. Nested tables can be defined in PL/SQL, but they can also be defined in a database—for instance, as a column allowing some DML operations to the data. Let's create a simple example of a nested table. First, we create the type (**Employees**). Then we define a variable of that type (**Enames**) and the initial values for the nested table variable. To be able to see the content of the nested table variable, let's define a procedure that prints out values in the nested table (PRINT_ENAMES). We call the procedure to print out the initial values, then we update the value of the fourth element and print out the content of the nested table at that time. To assign a value to a scalar element of a collection variable, reference the element as **collection_variable_name(index)** and assign it a value—in our example, **enames(4) := 'Sam';**. Then we use the same nested table for another purpose—as a list of author names—and give it totally new content by initializing it again.

```
DECLARE
TYPE Employees IS TABLE OF VARCHAR2(10);
Enames Employees := Employees('Heli', 'Tim', 'Tom', 'Pirkko');
PROCEDURE print_enames (heading VARCHAR2) IS
BEGIN
DBMS_OUTPUT.PUT_LINE(heading);
FOR i IN enames.FIRST .. enames.LAST LOOP
DBMS_OUTPUT.PUT_LINE(enames(i));
END LOOP;
DBMS_OUTPUT.PUT_LINE('***');
END;
BEGIN
print_enames('Initial Values:');
enames(4) := 'Sam';
print_enames('Updated Values:');
enames := Employees('Arup', 'Brendan', 'Heli', 'Martin', 'Alex');
print_enames('Authors:');
END;
```

Here's the result:

```
Initial Values:
Heli
Tim
Tom
Pirkko
***
Updated Values:
Heli
Tim
Tom
Sam
***
Authors:
Arup
Brendan
Heli
Martin
Alex
***
```

There are two SET operators that can be used with nested tables to assign a value to a variable of the nested table type: SQL MULTISET and SQL SET. The SQL MULTISET operators can be used for two nested tables that have elements of the same data types to perform SET operations. MULTISET EXCEPT takes two nested tables and returns a nested table whose elements are in the first nested table but not in the second nested table. MULTISET INTERSECT takes two nested tables and returns a nested table whose values are common in both input nested tables. MULTISET UNION takes two nested tables and returns a nested table whose values are in both input nested tables.

Let's test the MULTISET UNION with the same example. Now we will have two nested table variables: Enames and Authors. Both of the nested tables are initialized in the declaration, and the third nested table, Union_emp (the result set of MULTISET UNION), is initialized to empty. First, we print out the MULTISET UNION of the nested tables Enames and Authors. Then we update the fourth element of Enames to "Sam" and print out the new MULTISET UNION.

```
DECLARE
TYPE Employees IS TABLE OF VARCHAR2(10);
Enames Employees := Employees('Heli', 'Tim', 'Tom', 'Pirkko');
Authors Employees := Employees('Arup', 'Brendan', 'Heli', 'Martin', 'Alex');
Union_emp Employees:= Employees();
PROCEDURE print_enames (heading VARCHAR2) IS
BEGIN
DBMS_OUTPUT.PUT_LINE(heading);
Union_emp:= Enames MULTISET UNION Authors;
FOR i IN Union_emp.FIRST .. Union_emp.LAST LOOP
DBMS_OUTPUT.PUT_LINE(union_emp(i));
END LOOP;
DBMS_OUTPUT.PUT_LINE('***');
END;
BEGIN
print_enames('Union Initial:');
enames(4) := 'Sam';
print_enames('Union Updated:');
END;
```

Here's the result:

```
Union Initial:
Heli
Tim
Tom
Pirkko
Arup
Brendan
Heli
Martin
Alex
***
Union Updated:
Heli
Tim
Tom
Sam
Arup
Brendan
Heli
Martin
Alex
***
```

Let's try the same example with MULTISET INTERSECT. First we print the MULTISET INTERSECT of the nested tables Enames and Authors, and then we update the fourth element in Enames to "Brendan" and print out the MULTISET INTERSECT again:

```
DECLARE
TYPE Employees IS TABLE OF VARCHAR2(10);
Enames Employees := Employees('Heli', 'Tim', 'Tom', 'Pirkko');
Authors Employees := Employees('Arup', 'Brendan', 'Heli', 'Martin', 'Alex');
Union_emp Employees:= Employees();
PROCEDURE print_enames (heading VARCHAR2) IS
BEGIN
DBMS_OUTPUT.PUT_LINE(heading);
Union_emp:= Enames MULTISET INTERSECT Authors;
FOR i IN Union_emp.FIRST .. Union_emp.LAST LOOP
DBMS_OUTPUT.PUT_LINE(union_emp(i));
END LOOP;
DBMS_OUTPUT.PUT_LINE('***');
END;
BEGIN
print_enames('Intersect Initial:');
enames(4) := 'Brendan';
print_enames('Intersect Updated:');
END;
```

Here's the result:

```
Intersect Initial:
Heli
***
Intersect Updated:
Heli
Brendan
***
```

Let's see how the **set** function works. We will use the same example, but now we have two nested tables: Enames for the employee list and Enames_uni for the list of unique employee names.

```
DECLARE
TYPE Employees IS TABLE OF VARCHAR2(10);
Enames Employees := Employees('Heli', 'Tim', 'Tom', 'Pirkko', 'Tim');
Enames_uni Employees := Employees();
PROCEDURE print_enames (heading VARCHAR2) IS
BEGIN
DBMS_OUTPUT.PUT_LINE(heading);
Enames_uni := SET (Enames);
FOR i IN enames_Uni.FIRST .. enames_Uni.LAST LOOP
DBMS_OUTPUT.PUT_LINE(enames(i));
END LOOP;
DBMS_OUTPUT.PUT_LINE('***');
END;
```

```
BEGIN
print_enames('Initial Unique Values:');
enames(4) := 'Sam';
print_enames('Updated Unique Values:');
END;
```

Here's the result:

```
Initial Unique Values:
Heli
Tim
Tom
Pirkko
***
Updated Unique Values:
Heli
Tim
Tom
Sam
***
```

You can use **is a set** conditions to test whether the nested table only includes unique elements. The condition returns TRUE if the nested table is a set (no duplicates or a size of zero) and returns FALSE otherwise. The condition returns NULL if the nested table is NULL.

You can use the **is [not] empty** condition to test whether the nested table is empty. The **is empty** condition returns TRUE if the collection is empty and returns FALSE if it is not empty. The **is not empty** condition returns TRUE if the collection is not empty and FALSE if it is empty. If the nested table is NULL, it is not considered to be empty or not empty.

A **member** condition tests whether an element is a member of a nested table. The return value is TRUE if the expression is equal to a member of the specified collection and FALSE if not. The return value is NULL if the expression is NULL or if the nested table is empty.

You can compare the two nested table variables for equality or inequality with the relational operators equal (=) and not equal (<>, !=), if those nested table variables are of the same nested table type, and the type does not have elements of a record type. Two nested table variables are equal if they have the same set of elements, in any order.

A nested table is useful when you do not know the number of elements in advance and you need to update or delete individual elements in the collection.

VARRAYs

A VARRAY collection is very similar to a nested table, but unlike a nested table, it must have an upper bound declared; a VARRAY is bounded. Also, when you retrieve or store a VARRAY, the order of elements is preserved. A VARRAY cannot be sparse because individual elements cannot be deleted to cause the dense structure to become sparse. VARRAYs can be used both in PL/SQL and in the database. When stored in the database, VARRAYs keep their ordering and subscripts. An uninitialized VARRAY variable is a null collection and must be initialized either by making it empty or by assigning a non-NULL value to it. Oracle arrays are called VARRAYs because they are of variable size, meaning that they do not allocate space when declared, only when used.

The lower bound of an index in a VARRAY is 1 and the upper bound is the current number of elements in it. The upper bound changes when you add and remove elements, but it cannot exceed the maximum number of elements defined. The Oracle Database stores a VARRAY variable as a single object. If the size of a VARRAY variable is less than 4 KB, it is saved inside the table of which it is a column; if it's larger than 4KB, it is saved in the same tablespace with the table, but outside the table. A VARRAY might be the solution if you know the maximum number of elements and usually access the elements sequentially. If the number of elements is very large, a VARRAY might not be the best solution because all elements are stored and retrieved at the same time, and a large set might cause performance issues.

Let's test using the same simple example we tested with nested tables. Now we must know the number of elements beforehand, and we define the VARRAY type Employees as five VARCHAR2(10) elements:

```
DECLARE
TYPE Employees IS VARRAY(5) OF VARCHAR2(10);
Enames Employees := Employees('Heli', 'Tim', 'Tom', 'Pirkko');
PROCEDURE print_enames (heading VARCHAR2) IS
BEGIN
DBMS_OUTPUT.PUT_LINE(heading);
FOR i IN enames.FIRST .. enames.LAST LOOP
DBMS_OUTPUT.PUT_LINE(enames(i));
END LOOP;
DBMS_OUTPUT.PUT_LINE('***');
END;
BEGIN
print_enames('Initial Values:');
enames(4) := 'Sam';
print_enames('Updated Values:');
enames := Employees('Arup', 'Brendan', 'Heli', 'Martin', 'Alex');
print_enames('Authors:');
END;
```

Here's the result:

```
Initial Values:
Heli
Tim
Tom
Pirkko
***
Updated Values:
Heli
Tim
Tom
Sam
***
Authors:
Arup
Brendan
Heli
Martin
Alex
***
```

Collection Methods

PL/SQL offers some built-in functions and procedures for collections, called *collection methods*. These methods are for getting information about the content of a collection and to modify it. The functions for obtaining information about the content of a collection are **count**, **exists**, **first**, **last**, **limit**, **prior**, and **next**. The procedures for modifying the content of a collection are **delete**, **extend**, and **trim**. Even though they are functions and procedures, they are referred to as methods because the syntax for using them is different from regular functions and procedures. The way to call them is to use the so-called member method syntax. For example, to call the function **last** for a collection named EMP_COL, we would use **emp_col.LAST**. The names of these methods tell you quite well what they do, so we won't go into any more detail. Here are just a few examples:

- The **trim** method can be used to remove elements from the end of a nested table or VARRAY. **trim** removes the last element of the collection, and **trim(n)** removes the last *n* elements. If you try to remove more elements from the collection than possible, you will get the exception **subscript_beyond_count**.

- **delete** deletes all the elements from the collection, **delete(n)** deletes the element with index *n*, **delete(m,n)** deletes elements with indexes between *m* and *n*, which *m<=n*.

- **extend** adds one NULL element to the collection. **extend(n)** adds *n* NULL elements, and **extend(n,i)** adds *n* copies of the element with index *i* to the collection.

- **limit** is actually only valid with VARRAYs. It returns the maximum number of elements for a collection. If the collection does not have a maximum value, it returns NULL.

- The **last**, **limit**, and **extend** methods can be used, for instance, to limit the number of elements in a VARRAY collection:

```
IF emp_list.LAST < emp_list.LIMIT
THEN emp_list.EXTEND;
END IF;
```

Bulk Processing

When running a SELECT INTO or DML statement, the PL/SQL engine sends the statement to the SQL engine, which runs it and returns the result to the PL/SQL engine. Bulk SQL minimizes the performance overhead of the communication between PL/SQL and SQL because the calls are fewer than in single-row processing. You can process in bulk using the FORALL statement and the BULK COLLECT clause. The FORALL statement sends statements from PL/SQL to SQL in batches, and the BULK COLLECT clause returns results from SQL to PL/SQL in batches.

Using FORALL is simple; you replace the FOR with FORALL and do not need a LOOP:

```
...FOR i IN enames.FIRST..depts.LAST LOOP...
...FORALL i IN enames.FIRST..depts.LAST...
```

The SQL%BULK_ROWCOUNT cursor attribute gives granular information about the rows affected by each iteration of the FORALL statement. It is like an associative array whose *i*th element is the number of rows affected by the *i*th DML statement in the most recently completed FORALL statement. The data type of the element is INTEGER.

Using BULK COLLECT means that instead of using a cursor and a LOOP, you add BULK COLLECT INTO with a collection variable. And instead of processing a row in a cursor at the time, you process them all at once.

```
...FOR c1 IN (SELECT * FROM emp) LOOP...
...SELECT * BULK COLLECT INTO emp_nt FROM emp...
```

Let's see an example of BULK COLLECT FETCH using two collections (names and sals) to fetch to. First, we define the types for the collections and then the variables for them. We also define a cursor (**c1**). The procedure **print_results** will print out the content of collection variables. We open the cursor and fetch its content to collection variables (names and sals) using the FETCH BULK COLLECT INTO clause. Then we close the cursor and call the **print_result** procedure to be able to see the content of the collection variables.

```
DECLARE
TYPE NameList IS TABLE OF emp.ename%TYPE;
TYPE SalList IS TABLE OF emp.sal%TYPE;
CURSOR c1 IS
SELECT ename, sal
FROM emp
WHERE sal > 1000
ORDER BY ename;
names   NameList;
sals    SalList;
PROCEDURE print_results IS
BEGIN
IF names IS NULL OR names.COUNT = 0 THEN
DBMS_OUTPUT.PUT_LINE('No results.');
ELSE
DBMS_OUTPUT.PUT_LINE('Result: ');
FOR i IN names.FIRST .. names.LAST
LOOP
DBMS_OUTPUT.PUT_LINE('  Employee ' || names(i) || ': $' || sals(i));
END LOOP;
END IF;
END;
BEGIN
OPEN c1;
FETCH c1 BULK COLLECT INTO names, sals;
CLOSE c1;
print_results();
END;
```

Alternatively, we can do the same FETCH BULK COLLECT using a record instead of a collection. We open the cursor and fetch its content to a record variable (recs) using the FETCH BULK COLLECT INTO clause. Then we close the cursor, and using the FOR LOOP, print out the content of the record variable.

```
DECLARE
CURSOR c1 IS
SELECT ename, sal FROM emp WHERE sal > 1000 ORDER BY ename;
TYPE RecList IS TABLE OF c1%ROWTYPE;
recs RecList;
BEGIN
OPEN c1;
```

```
FETCH c1 BULK COLLECT INTO recs;
CLOSE c1;
FOR i IN recs.FIRST .. recs.LAST
LOOP
DBMS_OUTPUT.PUT_LINE ('  Employee ' || recs(i).ename || ': $' || recs(i).sal
);
END LOOP;
END;
```

Here is the result:

```
Employee Heli: $3000
Employee Sue: $2500
Employee Tim: $3000
Employee Tom: $2000
```

The BULK COLLECT statement might return a very large number of rows, causing a large collection, and because everything happens in memory, this can cause problems. You can use any of these to limit the number of rows and the collection size: the ROWNUM pseudocolumn, SAMPLE clause, or FETCH FIRST clause. That would look something like this:

```
SELECT ename BULK COLLECT INTO emp_nt FROM emp WHERE ROWNUM <= 50;
SELECT ename BULK COLLECT INTO emp_nt FROM emp  SAMPLE (10);
SELECT ename BULK COLLECT INTO emp_nt FROM emp FETCH FIRST 50 ROWS ONLY;
```

You can also use **limit** to limit the number of rows processed at a time. Let's see the same example used earlier. First, we define the types for the collections and then the variables for them. We also declare a cursor (c1) and a variable (**v_limit**) to be used as our integer value for **limit**. The procedure **print_results** will print out the content of the collection variables. We open the cursor, and using the **loop** we fetch its content into collection variables (names and sals) using the FETCH BULK COLLECT INTO clause and **limit** with the variable **v_limit**. Then we call the procedure **print_result** to print the content at that moment. After the loop we close the cursor.

```
DECLARE
TYPE NameList IS TABLE OF emp.ename%TYPE;
TYPE SalList IS TABLE OF emp.sal%TYPE;
CURSOR c1 IS
SELECT ename, sal FROM emp WHERE sal > 1000 ORDER BY ename;
names   NameList;
sals    SalList;
v_limit PLS_INTEGER := 2;
PROCEDURE print_results IS
BEGIN
IF names IS NULL OR names.COUNT = 0 THEN
DBMS_OUTPUT.PUT_LINE('No results.');
ELSE
DBMS_OUTPUT.PUT_LINE('Result: ');
FOR i IN names.FIRST .. names.LAST
LOOP
DBMS_OUTPUT.PUT_LINE('  Employee ' || names(i) || ': $' || sals(i));
END LOOP;
```

```
END IF;
END;
BEGIN
DBMS_OUTPUT.PUT_LINE ('--- Using BULK COLLECT and LIMIT to process ' ||
v_limit || ' rows at a time ---');
OPEN c1;
LOOP
FETCH c1 BULK COLLECT INTO names, sals LIMIT v_limit;
EXIT WHEN names.COUNT = 0;
print_results();
END LOOP;
CLOSE c1;
END;
--- Using BULK COLLECT and LIMIT to process 2 rows at a time ---
Result:
  Employee Heli: $3000
  Employee Sue: $2500
Result:
  Employee Tim: $3000
  Employee Tom: $2000
```

Multidimensional Collection

Although a collection has only one dimension, you can declare a multidimensional collection with a collection whose elements are collections. As you'll remember, an associative array type is defined as follows:

```
TYPE emp_sal IS TABLE OF NUMBER(6) INDEX BY VARCHAR2(12);
```

A nested table type is defined as follows:

```
TYPE enames_tab IS TABLE OF VARCHAR2(10);
```

And a VARRAY type is defined as follows:

```
TYPE Employees IS VARRAY(5) OF VARCHAR2(10);
```

You can, for instance, declare an associative array type (AA_Type1) and an associative array type whose elements are of the type of the first associative array type (AA_Type2). Then declare variables for both (V_AA1, V_AA2):

```
DECLARE
TYPE AA_Type1 IS TABLE OF INTEGER INDEX BY PLS_INTEGER;
TYPE AA_Type2 IS TABLE OF AA_Type1 INDEX BY PLS_INTEGER;
V_AA1 AA_Type1;
V_AA2 AA_Type2;
```

As you learned before, you can reference the elements in variable V_AA1 with the element number. For instance, the third element would be V_AA1(3). Because V_AA2 is of type AA_Type2, which is multidimensional (two dimensions), you can refer it with two coordinates—the one in associative array of type AA_Type1 and the other in associative array of type AA_Type2.

For example, you can set a value of the whole associative array variable V_AA1 to the second coordinate of V_AA2:

```
V_AA2(23) := V_AA1;
```

The 23rd element of V_AA2 would have the whole content of V_AA1 as its value, and one of these values could be referred to as

```
V_AA2(23)(3)
```

which is the 23rd element in V_AA2 and its 3rd element.

The same way, we can define multilevel nested tables:

```
DECLARE
TYPE NT_Type1 IS TABLE OF VARCHAR2(20);
TYPE NT_Type2 IS TABLE OF NT_Type1;
V_NT1 NT_Type1 := NT_Type1('One', 'Two');
V_NT2 NT_Type2 := NT_Type2(V_NT1);
```

And, of course, the same goes for a VARRAY or any combination of collections. Let's look at a multilevel VARRAY a bit more carefully. Let's define a type of VARRAY (**VAR_Type1**) and another type of VARRAY whose elements are VARRAYs (**VAR_Type1**) and the corresponding variables (**v_Var1**, **v_Var2**) and then define values for them. Using DBMS.OUTPUT, we can see what value the multidimensional variable **v_Var2** has for the coordinate (2,3):

```
DECLARE
TYPE VAR_Type1 IS VARRAY(10) OF INTEGER;
TYPE VAR_Type2 IS VARRAY(10) OF VAR_Type1;
v_Var1 VAR_Type1 := VAR_Type1 (7,9,11);
v_Var2 VAR_Type2 := VAR_Type2 (VAR_Type1(7,9,24), v_Var1, VAR_Type1(6,8),
v_Var1);
i INTEGER;
BEGIN
i := v_Var2(3)(2);
DBMS_OUTPUT.PUT_LINE(' v_Var2(3)(2) = ' || i);
END;
/
Result:
v_Var2(3)(2) = 8
```

In our example, v_Var2 has the values (1)(1)=7, (1)(2)=9, (1)(3)=24, (2)(1)=7, (2)(2)=9, (2)(3)=11, (3)(1)=6, (3)(2)=8, (4)(1)=7, (4)(2)=9, and (4)(3)=11.

Let's extend the multidimensional variable, add new values on the fifth position, and see the value for (5,2):

```
DECLARE
TYPE VAR_Type1 IS VARRAY(10) OF INTEGER;
TYPE VAR_Type2 IS VARRAY(10) OF VAR_Type1;
v_Var1 VAR_Type1 := VAR_Type1 (1,2,3);
v_Var2 VAR_Type2 := VAR_Type2 (v_Var1, VAR_Type1(7,9,24), VAR_Type1(6,8),
v_Var1);
i INTEGER;
```

```
BEGIN
v_Var2.EXTEND;
v_Var2(5) := VAR_Type1(36, 38);
i := v_Var2(5)(2);
DBMS_OUTPUT.PUT_LINE(' v_Var2(5)(2) = ' || i);
END;
/
Result:
v_Var2(5)(2) = 38
```

Parallel Query

Parallel execution is sometimes needed for large-scale data processing. Parallel execution uses multiple processes to perform a single task. Sufficient resource availability is the most important prerequisite for scalable parallel execution. The Oracle Database provides a parallel execution engine that can parallelize queries as well as DDLs and DMLs. Parallel execution for queries and DDL statements is enabled by default. For DML statements, you need to enable this at the session level with an ALTER SESSION statement:

```
ALTER SESSION ENABLE PARALLEL DML;
```

Degree of parallelism (DOP) is for dividing the data work in chunks so that it can be processed at the same time. At the architectural level are two possible ways to make parallelism possible: a shared-everything architecture and a shared-nothing architecture. In a shared-nothing system, called a *massively parallel processing (MPP) system,* the system is physically divided into individual parallel processing units, and each unit has its own CPU cores and its own storage component. If you're using the shared-nothing architecture, everything must be designed well when setting up the system. Oracle Database uses the shared-everything architecture in parallelism. The shared-everything architecture allows more flexibility for the implementation of the parallel processing. Using Oracle Partitioning, though, Oracle Database can offer the same parallel processing capabilities as a shared-nothing system.

When a SQL statement is executed, it is decomposed into individual steps, which can be seen as separate lines in an execution plan. If the statement is executed in parallel, as many of the individual steps as possible are parallelized. That can be seen in the execution plan.

For the processing, we need one query coordinator (QC) and several parallel execution (PX) servers. The actual user process is the QC of a parallel SQL operation, and it distributes the work to the PX servers. The PX servers are those processes that perform work in parallel on behalf of the initiating session. Sets of PX servers work in pairs: one set is producing rows (producer) and one set is consuming the rows (consumer), which is the reason for always having an even number of PX servers. If there is some work that needs to be done to get the results from PX servers together, QC will do that work (for example, by using a SUM operation at the end of the processing).

You can give Oracle Database a full control over parallelism using the Automatic Degree of Parallelism (Auto DOP) framework, or you can control the parallelism manually. With Auto DOP, the database automatically decides whether or not a statement should execute in parallel and how to do it. Auto DOP uses the estimated elapsed time and **parallel_min_time_threshold** parameter to decide whether it runs the statement serially or in parallel. Using the **parallel_ degree_limit** parameter (whose default value is CPU), you can control the DOP. The Auto DOP optimizer will compare its ideal DOP with **parallel_degree_limit** and take the lower value.

If the initialization parameter **parallel_degree_policy** is set to MANUAL, Auto DOP is disabled and the user has full control over the usage of parallel execution in the system. Parallelism can be defined at the session, statement, or object level. You can either use the default DOP or define specific fixed values for the DOP. The default uses initialization parameters **parallel_threads_per_cpu** and **cpu_count** to define what to do. The default DOP can be set to a table (**ALTER TABLE emp PARALLEL**) or a statement (**SELECT /*+ parallel(default) */ COUNT(*) FROM emp**) or use the object-level hint (**SELECT /*+ parallel(emp, default) */ COUNT(*) FROM emp**). If you want to have full control over parallelism, you use Fixed Degree of Parallelism (FDOP). The FDOP can be set to a table (**ALTER TABLE emp PARALLEL 8**) or a statement (**SELECT /*+ parallel(8) */ COUNT(*) FROM emp**) or use the object-level hint (**SELECT /*+ parallel(emp, 8) */ COUNT(*) FROM emp**). Because we need both producer and consumer, the number of allocated PX servers can be twice the requested DOPs. The initializing parameter **parallel_max_servers** defines the maximum number of PX server processes in the pool. If all of the processes in the pool are allocated or the number of free PX servers is too small, new operations requiring parallelism are executed serially or with a downgraded DOP. That will obviously affect the performance.

For example, one way to insert rows in a table is using the CREATE TABLE… AS SELECT clause. This syntax lets you take rows wanted from one table and add them to another table. The rows can be all the rows in the original table or just some rows. If you use this mechanism to insert rows into a table, you can utilize parallel execution if needed. The **CREATE TABLE tablename PARALLEL NOLOGGING AS SELECT…** statement consists of two parts: a data definition (DDL) part (CREATE) and a query part (SELECT). Oracle Database can parallelize both parts of the statement.

Table Functions and Pipelined Table Functions

A table function produces a collection of rows, which can be used in SQL like a database table. The parameter for TABLE does not need to be a collection; it can also be a function that returns a collection, or it can be a REF cursor. The syntax looks like this (note the word TABLE):

```
SELECT columns FROM TABLE (collection);
```

Because the table function behaves in SQL just like a database table, you can join it with a database table, another table function, or a view. You can use GROUP BY, ORDER BY, and all the other features you usually use with SQL queries. Since Oracle Database 12.1, table functions have been able to consume associative arrays that are indexed by integer (not only VARCHAR). Both nested tables and VARRAYs are also supported. You can parallelize the execution of a table function as well as stream the returned rows directly to the next process. The rows can also be returned iteratively as they are produced (*pipelined*) instead of all rows being processed before anything is returned. Pipelining the processing demands less memory because there is no need to materialize the entire collection to the cache as a whole. Chaining pipelined table functions is an efficient way to perform multiple transformations on data (for instance, in a data warehousing environment). The pipelining can be done either using the interface approach or the PL/SQL approach. The approach used to implement pipelined table functions does not affect the way they are used in SQL statements, so you are free to choose the one you like more.

You might want to use a table function, for instance, when you need to merge data that is session specific with data from tables in a database, programmatically construct a data set to be passed as rows and columns to the host environment, create a parameterized view, improve the performance of parallelized queries using pipelined table functions, or reduce consumption of the Process Global Area using pipelined table functions. Table functions are especially useful in data warehouse environments. Instead of using a staging area and its tables during the ETL loading process to load data from external tables into the warehouse tables, you can use table functions. These are often referred to as *transformation pipelines,* where using pipelined table functions, tables, views, and so on, the data is moved (and transformed) from the source to the target. From a high level it would look something like this:

```
INSERT INTO Target
SELECT * FROM (Transformation_pipelined_function(SELECT * FROM Source));
```

Let's first look at the regular table function and how that can be used. We want to create a query that will use the rows from a collection (a nested table in our case). First, we must create the object type:

```
CREATE OR REPLACE TYPE Emp_ot AS OBJECT
(empno    NUMBER,
ename     VARCHAR2 (10));
```

Then we create a nested table based on that type:

```
CREATE OR REPLACE TYPE emp_nt
IS TABLE OF emp_ot;
```

We created both the types at the schema level so that they can be used anywhere in the code. Next, we create a function that will populate the nested table:

```
CREATE OR REPLACE FUNCTION Emp_function_to_populate RETURN emp_nt IS
l_return emp_nt := emp_nt (emp_ot (1, 'Tim'),
                    emp_ot (2, 'Tom'),
                    emp_ot (3, 'Pirkko'));
BEGIN
RETURN l_return;
END;
```

Now let's try to query a function by returning a collection using a table function:

```
SELECT empno, ename
FROM TABLE (Emp_function_to_populate ())
ORDER BY empno
/
EMPNO        ENAME
--------------------------------
1            Tim
2            Tom
3            Pirkko
```

As mentioned earlier, there are two approaches for implementing pipelined table functions: the interface approach and the PL/SQL approach. The interface approach can be used with PL/SQL, C/C++, and Java. The PL/SQL approach can only be used with PL/SQL. It is simpler to implement and requires only one PL/SQL function.

To declare a pipelined table function, use the PIPELINED keyword. The return type of a pipelined table function must be a collection type, either a nested table or a VARRAY. Regardless of the way the pipelined table functions are implemented, they are used in SQL statements in exactly the same way. A pipelined table function is declared using the PIPELINED clause and PIPE

ROW to push the function and return the rows as soon as they are produced. The PIPE ROW statement may be used only in the body of pipelined table functions. A pipelined table function must have a RETURN statement that does not return a value to be able to transfer the control back to the consumer. That empty RETURN statement ensures that the next fetch gets a NO_DATA_ FOUND exception. If a pipelined table function creates more data than is needed for the process querying it, the pipelined table function execution stops and raises the NO_DATA_NEEDED exception.

It is also possible to execute pipelined table functions in parallel. To be able to do that, first include the PARALLEL_ENABLE clause and then include the PARTITION BY clause. A parallelized pipelined table function would look something like this:

```
CREATE OR REPLACE FUNCTION f_pipelined(cur cursor_pkg.strong_refcur_t)
RETURN emp_nt PIPELINED PARALLEL_ENABLE (PARTITION cur BY ANY) IS
empno                 NUMBER(10);
ename                 VARCHAR2(10);
...
BEGIN
LOOP
FETCH cur INTO empno, ename,...;
EXIT WHEN cur%NOTFOUND;
IF ... THEN
PIPE ROW (emp_nt(empno, ename, ...));
END IF;
END LOOP;
CLOSE cur;
RETURN;
END;
```

Summary

To be able to handle advanced and complex data sets, one must first understand the requirements and then the tools available for implementing those requirements. Oracle Database offers a large variety of features and functionalities, but they are of no use if you are not aware of them. It is very important to understand what tools are available and when to use which.

In the Oracle Database, you can define different kinds of tables. There are two kinds of table categories in the Oracle Database: relational and object tables. There are different kinds of relational tables: heap-organized table, index-organized table, and external table. A table can be either permanent or temporary. Tables can also be clustered. In addition to tables, you have views and materialized views. Views can be used to add one more layer on top of the tables for security reasons, or maybe just to make complex queries easier to build if the complex part is already done in the query of the view. Materialized views are often used for summarized data or for replicating data.

Each value the Oracle Database uses must have a data type specified, whether the element is a column in a table or an argument or a variable in program code. A data type is either scalar or non-scalar. Oracle Database offers several data types and also the possibility to create your own user-defined data types.

Invisible columns can be used when adding new columns to the database and some time is needed before the legacy code is changed to use the new column. Alternatively, they can be used to change the logical order of the columns in a table if that is needed for some reason. Virtual columns are not saved on the disk; the value is always derived from other data when needed. Attribute clustering and partitioning can be used to achieve better performance. Partitioning also enables easier maintenance of the data structures; you can, for instance, drop a whole partition when it is no longer needed instead of deleting thousands of rows from a table.

The Oracle Database also offers several different kinds of constraints at the table and column level. Constraints help you keep the data clean and of good quality.

Every time a SQL clause is performed against a relational database, a cursor is used, so a cursor is an important concept in both SQL and PL/SQL. A cursor is a pointer to the context area where the query result is saved.

A record and a collection are composite structures that can be used in PL/SQL code. A record is like a single row in a database table, whereas a collection is like a column in a database table. There are three different kinds of collections in Oracle: associative arrays, nested tables, and VARRAYs. You can use bulk loading for collections. Even though a record and a collection are one-dimensional, you can build multidimensional structures by combining these elements (for instance, you can create a type of VARRAY that has elements of type VARRAY).

In some cases, you can get better performance for your queries using parallel query execution, table functions, or pipelined table functions.

CHAPTER
4

Regular Expressions

S upport for regular expressions was added to the Oracle Database to expand on single- and multiple-character wildcard searches to allow for more complicated search patterns. This greatly enhances searching capabilities; however, writing regular expressions can prove quite tricky. Sometimes it requires a different way of thinking. This chapter discusses the regular expression functions in Oracle.

With the arrival of Oracle Database 12*c*, pattern matching got another boost with the introduction of **match_recognize**. This functionality will be briefly explained toward the end of the chapter.

Also in Oracle Database 12*c*, it is possible to redact data. This functionality can also use regular expressions to mask data. Some built-in regular expressions are defined as standard methods to mask credit card numbers, passport data, salary information, and maybe even your (real) birthday. It is possible to define your own masking patterns, but in order to do that you need to understand how regular expressions work and how they can help you achieve the set goal. To learn more about data redaction, see Chapter 13.

To follow along with the examples in this chapter, download the sources from the Oracle Press website (http://community.oraclepressbooks.com/downloads.html).

Basic Search and Escape Possibilities

When you don't know the exact spelling, Oracle Database allows you to search using wildcard notation. Traditionally this functionality has been limited to zero or more character wildcards. An underscore (_) wildcard allows for searches with a single unknown character, whereas a percentage sign (%) allows for searches with zero or more unknown characters. To see the effect of the underscore and percentage sign in action, we'll use a simple single table with some sample data:

```
create table t
(name varchar2(25));
insert into t (name) values ('BLAKE');
insert into t (name) values ('BLOKE');
insert into t (name) values ('BLEAKE');
insert into t (name) values ('BLKE');
insert into t (name) values ('JAKESBLAKE');
insert into t (name) values ('BLAKESJAKE');
insert into t (name) values ('BL_KE');
insert into t (name) values ('BL%KE');

commit;
```

The sample data contains a number of names. Note the last two entries; these contain special characters used to define wildcards in Oracle.

The simplest form of searching for a pattern is to provide the exact series of characters you are looking for, like in the following equality search:

```
select name
  from t
 where name = 'BLAKE'
/
NAME
-------------------------
BLAKE
```

There is only one entry in the table that exactly matches the series of characters in the WHERE clause.

Using the equality search with the underscore or the percentage sign has no effect; it is treated as having no special meaning:

```
select name
  from t
 where name = 'BL_KE'
/

NAME
------------------------
BL_KE

select name
  from t
 where name = 'BL%KE'
/

NAME
------------------------
BL%KE
```

As you can see, the exact matches are returned and the underscore and percentage sign have no special meaning.

When the LIKE operator is used, the wildcard characters are not required; it is still possible to specify the exact series of characters you are looking for:

```
select name
  from t
 where name like 'BLAKE'
/

NAME
------------------------
BLAKE
```

However, when we use a LIKE operator instead of the equality search, the meaning of the wildcard characters becomes apparent:

```
select name
  from t
 where name like 'BL_KE'
/

NAME
------------------------
BLAKE
BLOKE
BL_KE
BL%KE
```

As you can see in this result set, all names are returned that start with *BL,* followed by any single character, and end with *KE.* The meaning of the underscore in this example is to use at least one and at most one character.

When the percentage sign is used as a wildcard, however, the result set is totally different. The percentage sign as a wildcard means zero or more characters, as shown here:

```
select name
  from t
 where name like 'BL%KE'
/

NAME
------------------------
BLAKE
BLOKE
BLEAKE
BLKE
BL_KE
BL%KE
BLAKESJAKE
```

But what if you want to search for a name that contains one of these special characters and there is a need for using a wildcard? In this case, you can "escape" the character using special syntax.

To search for a name in the table that contains an underscore, you need to escape the wildcard by using the ESCAPE keyword in the query, like so:

```
select name
  from t
 where name like 'BL\_KE' ESCAPE '\';

NAME
------------------------
BL_KE
```

Using the backslash as the escape character is not required, even though it is used frequently. In the following example, the double quotation mark character is used, and the results will be similar to the previous SQL statement:

```
select name
  from t
 where name like 'BL"_KE' ESCAPE '"';
```

REGEXP Functions

Starting with Oracle Database 10g, regular expressions are supported; these functions can be identified by the prefix **regexp**. The following functions are available:

- **regexp_like**
- **regexp_substr**

- **regexp_instr**
- **regexp_replace**
- **regexp_count**

The last function, **regexp_count**, was introduced with Oracle Database 11*g*.

All of these regular expression functions can be used in SQL as well as PL/SQL. Their names express what these functions do. They are comparable to the nonregular expression counterpart. The nonregular expression **replace** has a regular expression counterpart called **regexp_replace**, for example.

Depending on which regular expression function is used, the number of arguments will vary; in general, the first argument is the source string and the second argument is the regular expression pattern.

With regular expressions, you can use a number of metacharacters to describe the pattern you are looking for. A full list, including a short description of each metacharacter, is provided in Table 4-1.

Character	Description
^	Matches the beginning of a string. If used with a **match_parameter** of "m", it matches the start of a line anywhere within the expression. The meaning inside a bracket expression is different: see [^] in this table.
$	Matches the end of a string. If used with a **match_parameter** of "m", it matches the end of a line anywhere within the expression.
*	Matches zero or more occurrences.
+	Matches one or more occurrences.
?	Matches zero or one occurrence.
.	Matches any character except NULL.
|	Used like an XOR to specify more than one alternative.
[]	Used to specify a matching list where you are trying to match any one of the characters in the list.
[^]	Used to specify a nonmatching list, where you are trying to match any character except for the ones in the list.
()	Used to group expressions as a subexpression.
{m}	Matches *m* times.
{m,}	Matches at least *m* times.
{m, n}	Matches at least *m* times, but no more than *n* times.
\n	*n* is a number between 1 and 9. Matches the *n*th subexpression found in a bracket expression.
[..]	Matches one collation element that can be more than one character.
[::]	Matches character classes.
[==]	Matches equivalence classes.

TABLE 4-1. *Metacharacters*

Previously you saw that the underscore character will match exactly one character. Within the pattern for a regular expression, matching any character is done using the period (**.**) character.

To demonstrate the powerful searching capabilities of regular expressions, we'll use a table containing information about theme parks. The structure of the table is as follows:

```
create table theme_parks
(id          number
,name        varchar2(50)
,description clob
);
```

In the description attribute of the THEME_PARKS table is a summary of the parks, including the addresses and telephone numbers.

The theme parks in the table are all located in Florida, and the telephone numbers follow the North American Numbering Plan (NANP). The North American Numbering Plan is a closed telephone numbering plan in which all telephone numbers contain ten digits. The first three digits indicate the area code, and the last seven indicate the subscriber number. When a telephone number is written down, a hyphen is used to make it easier to read; however, periods can also be used as the separator. Sometimes the area code is enclosed in parentheses.

The pattern that we could write to extract the telephone number from the description column might look like the following:

```
...-...-....
```

Each period could be replaced by any character. The pattern reads as follows: three characters, followed by a hyphen, another three characters, another hyphen, and finally four characters.

NOTE
The sample data that is used throughout this chapter can be downloaded from the Oracle Press website: http://community .oraclepressbooks.com/downloads.html.

To extract the telephone number from the description column, we will use the **regexp_substr** regular expression, which performs a functionality similar to the common SQL function **substr**:

```
select id
      ,name
      ,regexp_substr (description, '...-...-....') phone
  from theme_parks;
```

```
        ID NAME                            PHONE
---------- ------------------------------- -------------
         1 Aquatica Orlando                407-351-3600
         2 Epcot
         3 Islands of Adventure            : 1-800-407-
         4 LEGOLAND Florida                877-350-5346
         5 Disney's Magic Kingdom
         6 Discovery Cove                  877-557-7404
         7 Universal Studios Florida       407-363-8000
         8 Disney's Animal Kingdom         407-939-5277
```

```
 9 SeaWorld Orlando          888-800-5447
10 Disney's Hollywood Studios  407-939-5277
```

```
10 rows selected.
```

For a first attempt to extract the telephone numbers, the results are not bad. As you can tell from this output, some of the phone numbers were extracted correctly and some weren't (such as Epcot, Islands of Adventure, and Disney's Magic Kingdom). Of course, there is also a possibility that there is no telephone number in the description, which would explain the NULL in the output.

Let's examine the cases where the telephone numbers weren't extracted correctly, starting with Islands of Adventure:

```
3 Islands of Adventure        : 1-800-407-
```

To determine what is going, let's inspect the data in the table.

The last part of the description is the actual address where the theme park is located. For the Islands of Adventure, the address part is repeated here:

```
6000 Universal Blvd.
Orlando, FL 32819
Region: Orlando
Phone: (407) 363-8000
Toll-Free: 1-800-407-4275
```

As you can tell from this information, there are actually two telephone numbers listed: a regular telephone number and a toll-free one. Both telephone numbers don't exactly match the pattern we were looking for. The first one uses parentheses around the area code, and the second one includes the country code before the area code, separated by a hyphen.

Because we are searching for three characters followed by a hyphen at the beginning of the pattern, there was a match on the string starting with the colon after the words Toll-Free. To prevent a false positive like this one, we could be more specific and only search for numbers with hyphens as delimiters.

Using square brackets, we can specify a matching list. This is called a *bracket expression,* and you specify a range of values that you want to match. To only search for numbers between 0 and 9, we would write the search pattern as follows:

```
[0123456789]
```

Be careful when specifying a range like this because it is easy to skip a number; therefore, it is easier and safer to specify a range, like so:

```
[0-9]
```

NOTE
There is yet another way to indicate that only numbers need to be matched: character classes. *Character classes provide a more generic way to indicate certain characters, which is especially useful when the expression needs to work across different languages and character sets. The next section is devoted to the topic of character classes.*

Within a bracket expression, you can specify any range of characters you want, such as lowercase from *A* through *Z*:

```
[a-z]
```

Or uppercase from *A* through *Z*:

```
[A-Z]
```

Or both:

```
[a-zA-Z]
```

in which case you'll get all letters, both uppercase and lowercase.

Returning to our previous example, the bracket expression clarifies that only numbers are to be included in the search pattern. We could replace each metacharacter period in the original search pattern with a range bracket expression, making the search pattern look as follows:

```
[0-9][0-9][0-9]-[0-9][0-9][0-9]-[0-9][0-9][0-9][0-9]
```

Even though this expression will only search for digits separated by hyphens (the delimiter hyphens appear outside the bracket expression), it is very hard to read.

With a regular expression you can also indicate how often a metacharacter should occur in the pattern. This is indicated by placing the number of repetition inside curly brackets, which is called an *interval qualifier:*

```
[0-9]{3}
```

This expression indicates that the number between 0 and 9 should match three times. It is also possible to indicate that the metacharacter should be at least three characters, which can be done as follows:

```
[0-9]{3,}
```

Note the comma in the interval qualifier. When you want to create a more flexible pattern, such as "at least three but no more than five," the interval qualifier would be

```
[0-9]{3, 5}
```

Because we are looking for telephone numbers, the pattern will be this:

```
[0-9]{3}-[0-9]{3}-[0-9]{4}
```

```
select id
      ,name
      ,regexp_substr (description
                  ,'[0-9]{3}-[0-9]{3}-[0-9]{4}') phone
   from theme_parks;

      ID NAME                            PHONE
---------- ---------------------------- ------------------------
       1 Aquatica Orlando                407-351-3600
```

```
 2 Epcot
 3 Islands of Adventure        800-407-4275
 4 LEGOLAND Florida            877-350-5346
 5 Disney's Magic Kingdom
 6 Discovery Cove              877-557-7404
 7 Universal Studios Florida   407-363-8000
 8 Disney's Animal Kingdom     407-939-5277
 9 SeaWorld Orlando            888-800-5447
10 Disney's Hollywood Studios  407-939-5277
```

10 rows selected.

Notice that the phone number for Islands of Adventure is matched based on the pattern we specified without the country code. The false-positive match we had previously is now resolved.

Let's examine the telephone number of Epcot. The actual address where Epcot is located is also in the description field. Only that part of the description is repeated here:

```
200 Epcot Center Drive
Lake Buena Vista, FL 32821
Region: Disney Area
Phone: 407 939 5277
Toll-Free: 800 647 7900
```

Obviously there are two telephone numbers in this text, and for humans this is easy to see. Both of these telephone numbers don't match the pattern we are looking for. There are no hyphens to separate the area code from the subscription number, not even for the toll-free number.

Now, if only there was a way to specify that we want either a hyphen or a space as the delimiter—turns out that there is functionality for doing exactly that. Using the pipe character, we can separate the alternate delimiters. To choose whether the separator should be a hyphen or a space, we specify the following:

```
(-| )
```

For the whole telephone number, with either a hyphen or a space as separator, the search pattern will be as follows:

```
[0-9]{3}(-| )[0-9]{3}(-| )[0-9]{4}
```

And here are the results from the query:

```
select id
      ,name
      ,regexp_substr (description
                ,'[0-9]{3}(-| )[0-9]{3}(-| )[0-9]{4}') phone
  from theme_parks;

        ID NAME                        PHONE
---------- --------------------------- -------------------------
         1 Aquatica Orlando            407-351-3600
         2 Epcot                       407 939 5277
         3 Islands of Adventure        800-407-4275
```

```
 4  LEGOLAND Florida                877-350-5346
 5  Disney's Magic Kingdom
 6  Discovery Cove                  877-557-7404
 7  Universal Studios Florida       407-363-8000
 8  Disney's Animal Kingdom         407-939-5277
 9  SeaWorld Orlando                888-800-5447
10  Disney's Hollywood Studios      407-939-5277
```

Now a telephone number is shown for Epcot as well. The only one missing is the telephone number for Disney's Magic Kingdom. The address as it appears in the description column shows that the telephone numbers are not separated by a hyphen or space, but by a period:

```
1180 Seven Seas Drive
Lake Buena Vista, FL 32830
Region: Disney Area
Phone: 407.939.5277
Toll-Free: 800.647.7900
```

The period metacharacter has special meaning in a regular expression—it matches any character. Therefore, in order to use it, the period needs to be escaped. To escape metacharacters in an expression, we'll use the backslash character. Here is the alteration that can be used to match a hyphen or a space or a period:

```
(-| |\.)
```

In the unlikely event that there is a telephone number that has two of the delimiter characters in the sequence, that number will not be matched. Alterations work as an exclusive OR (XOR).

The complete query to find telephone numbers for all theme parks contains quite a long pattern to match the different notations:

```
select id
     ,name
     ,regexp_substr (description
           , '[0-9]{3}(-| |\.)[0-9]{3}(-| |\.)[0-9]{4}') phone
  from theme_parks;

        ID NAME                           PHONE
---------- ------------------------------ ------------------------
         1 Aquatica Orlando               407-351-3600
         2 Epcot                          407 939 5277
         3 Islands of Adventure           800-407-4275
         4 LEGOLAND Florida               877-350-5346
         5 Disney's Magic Kingdom         407.939.5277
         6 Discovery Cove                 877-557-7404
         7 Universal Studios Florida      407-363-8000
         8 Disney's Animal Kingdom        407-939-5277
         9 SeaWorld Orlando               888-800-5447
        10 Disney's Hollywood Studios     407-939-5277

10 rows selected.
```

TIP
When you encounter a long regular expression and want to know why it matches certain results or when you are trying to debug the search pattern, read the expression out loud using normal words for its meaning, such as "exactly three characters in the range from zero through nine followed by either a hyphen, space, or period." Most likely, the mistake will pop right out.

Character Classes

Instead of searching for particular characters, sometimes you need to search for a particular class of characters. For instance, to find whitespace in a string of separate words, you need to search for spaces or tabs. Because it is easy to overlook a certain character, causing the search expression not to work as expected, you can also match on character classes. Character classes are especially important when you need to write expressions that work across languages and character sets.

In the previous section we were always on the lookout for numbers that would make up a telephone number. To match the area code of the telephone number, the following expression was used:

```
[0-9]{3}
```

Using character classes to match the area code, the expression would become this:

```
[[:digit:]]{3}
```

The character class indicates that only digits can match the pattern. Different languages can have different symbols for writing numbers, like in Hebrew or Bengali, but character classes can match all of them.

Character classes are only supported in bracket expressions. It is not possible to refer to the character class outside the square brackets. The names of the character classes are case sensitive, and they should appear in lowercase. When a capital is used in the name of the character class, an exception is raised:

```
select regexp_substr ('number 1'
                     ,'[[:DIGIT:]]'
                     )
  from dual;
                     ,'[[:DIGIT:]]'
                      *
ERROR at line 2:
ORA-12729: invalid character class in regular expression
```

Of course, there are many character classes, not just for numbers. Table 4-2 lists the different character classes along with a short description of each.

Greediness and Negating the Expression

So far the expressions have matched what we are looking for, such as the telephone number. Sometimes—and maybe more than you might expect—you need to create an expression that *excludes* characters in order to find what you are looking for.

Character Class	Description
[:alnum:]	Alphanumeric characters
[:alpha:]	Alphabetic characters
[:blank:]	Blank space characters
[:cntrl:]	Control characters
[:digit:]	Numeric digits
[:graph:]	Any of the following character classes: [:punct:], [:upper:], [:lower:], [:digit:]
[:lower:]	Lowercase alphabetic characters
[:print:]	Printable characters
[:punct:]	Punctuation characters
[:space:]	Nonprinting space characters, such as carriage return, newline, vertical tab, horizontal tab, and form feed
[:upper:]	Uppercase alphabetic characters
[:xdigit:]	Hexadecimal characters

TABLE 4-2.   *Character Classes*

When you want to extract the first word from the description in the THEME_PARKS table, you might first create an expression such as the following:

```
.+[[:space:]]
```

This expression means "any character, one or more occurrences, followed by a space character (from the character class)."

Let's put this expression to the test and inspect the results:

```
select regexp_substr (description, '.+[[:space:]]') first_word
  from theme_parks
 where id = 4;


FIRST_WORD
------------------------------------------------------------------
LEGOLAND Florida, the largest LEGOLAND park in the world ...
```

What happened there? Instead of giving us just the first word, the complete description is returned. (Note that the description in this output is clipped for brevity.)

The reason behind this phenomenon is what is commonly known as "greediness." A regular expression will attempt to match as much as possible; the search engine doesn't stop after it finds the first match.

To extract the first word from the description, we need to approach the expression differently. Instead of saying "we want all characters followed by a space," we write the expression the other way around: "look for as many characters as possible, as long as they are not a space."

In order to achieve this, we need to negate the bracket expression. This can be done with the caret character (^). Because the caret character appears in the bracket expression, it negates all characters within the expression. Inside a bracket expression metacharacters can have different meanings; outside the bracket expression the caret character signals the beginning of a string or newline.

To negate a character class, we place the caret in the bracket expression before the character class name:

```
[^[:space:]]
```

Now instead of matching on a range of characters, or character class in this case, all characters that are not in the specified character class are matched. In this example, we are looking for all characters that are not spaces—and lo and behold, only the first word is returned:

```
select regexp_substr (description, '[^[:space:]]*') first_word
  from theme_parks
 where id = 4;


FIRST_WORD
---------------------------
LEGOLAND
```

Notice that the asterisk metacharacter appears outside the bracket expression because we want to search for as many "nonspace" characters as possible to make up the first word. When the asterisk metacharacter is placed inside the bracket expression, the meaning of the regular expression changes, and only the first letter is returned because the meaning of the asterisk metacharacter is lost. The expression now reads "find me a character that is not a space or an asterisk." Because there is no interval qualifier after the bracket expression, only one character will be matched:

```
select regexp_substr (description, '[^[:space:]*]') first_word
  from theme_parks
 where id = 4;


FIRST_WORD
---------------------------
L
```

Backreferences

Extracting the data can be quite challenging; humans tend to make up new formats as time passes. A good example of this is the telephone numbers we extracted from the description column of the THEME_PARKS table.

Formatting output to create a consistent look can be of great benefit to the end users because it is easier on the eyes.

TIP
Instead of formatting the data when extracting it from the database, it is considered a best practice to prevent users from entering all kinds of variations. Regular expressions can also be used in check constraints, thus only allowing a certain format that can be entered and dispelling the need to write complicated regular expressions to extract data.

A *backreference* is a numbered reference to the text matching a previous subexpression. A *subexpression* is a logical group enclosed by parentheses.

You can refer to each of the subexpressions with a backslash followed by the number of the occurrence in the string. The numbered references are in the form **\1 \2 \3** and so on.

Although this sounds complicated, it is not as hard as it seems. Let's take a look at an example using the name in the THEME_PARKS table:

```
select regexp_replace (name, '(.)', '\1 ') name
   from theme_parks
;

NAME
----------------------------------------------------
A q u a t i c a   O r l a n d o
E p c o t
I s l a n d s   o f   A d v e n t u r e
L E G O L A N D   F l o r i d a
D i s n e y ' s   M a g i c   K i n g d o m
D i s c o v e r y   C o v e
U n i v e r s a l   S t u d i o s   F l o r i d a
D i s n e y ' s   A n i m a l   K i n g d o m
S e a W o r l d   O r l a n d o
D i s n e y ' s   H o l l y w o o d   S t u d i o s
```

For this example, the **regexp_replace** function is used to reformat the name. The regular expression is very straightforward: any character. Because the expression is enclosed in parentheses, it is a subexpression. There is only one subexpression, so this is subexpression number one and can be referenced as **\1**.

The third argument for **regexp_replace** is the replacement string. Here we reference the numbered subexpression. Instead of repeating the regular expression—which by the way is not possible—we simply refer to its number. In this example, we want any character, followed by a space, thus creating the names as shown previously. It is possible to reference the numbered subexpression multiple times:

```
select regexp_replace (name, '(.)', '\1 \1 ') name
   from theme_parks
 where id = 6;

NAME
----------------------------------------------------
D D i i s s c c o o v v e e r r y y   C C o o v v e e
```

In a previous section the telephone numbers from the descriptions in the THEME_PARKS table were extracted with some trouble because the formats were different. To create order in this chaos, backreferences can be used to nicely format the telephone numbers.

After extracting the telephone number from the description (using a previously described method) with the **regexp_substr** function, we can use **regexp_replace** to format the telephone number the way we want it.

Each part of the regular expression contained in parentheses is a subexpression that can be referenced by number as a backreference.

The second argument to the **regexp_replace** function creates the subexpression for each part of the telephone number. Because alterations are also included in parentheses, these become subexpressions as well.

To format the telephone number with hyphens as delimiters, the third argument of the **regexp_replace** function uses the backreferences with hyphens between them. Note that the first, third, and fifth subexpressions are used to format the data, whereas the alterations (also subexpressions) are not used to create the new telephone format:

```
select id
     , name
     , regexp_replace (
         regexp_substr (description
             , '([0-9]{3})(-| |\.)([0-9]{3})(-| |\.)([0-9]{4})'
             )
         , '([0-9]{3})(-| |\.)([0-9]{3})(-| |\.)([0-9]{4})'
         , '\1-\3-\5'
         )   phone
  from theme_parks;
        ID NAME                              PHONE
---------- ------------------------------    ------------------------
         1 Aquatica Orlando                  407-351-3600
         2 Epcot                             407-939-5277
         3 Islands of Adventure              800-407-4275
         4 LEGOLAND Florida                  877-350-5346
         5 Disney's Magic Kingdom            407-939-5277
         6 Discovery Cove                    877-557-7404
         7 Universal Studios Florida         407-363-8000
         8 Disney's Animal Kingdom           407-939-5277
         9 SeaWorld Orlando                  888-800-5447
        10 Disney's Hollywood Studios        407-939-5277
```

Check Constraints

To prevent users from entering data in all different formats, a check constraint can help. When all users enter data in the proper predefined format, searching for certain values is predictable and most likely results in better performance. Wildcard searches using regular expressions can be quite resource intensive.

Obviously a correct data model will help a great deal to prevent users from entering data in multiple formats and abusing other attributes to store data, such as the address and telephone numbers in the description field.

When the data model is normalized, the telephone number is stored in a separate attribute; a check constraint will prevent formats other than the one agreed upon from being entered. When you need to define regular expressions as check constraints, keep in mind that you're not the first one to do this. Search the Internet for the regular expression you need and, if necessary, make changes to suit the requirements.

Telephone numbers, e-mail addresses, website addresses, Social Security numbers, postal codes—all of these are very common patterns for which plenty of examples can be found.

Real-World Examples

A common scenario where regular expressions become very useful is when the data model allows for storing data in places where it doesn't belong, such as storing the address in the description field.

Searching for names, especially with different ways of spelling them, is also a common use case for regular expressions. If you're looking for "Steven" or "Stephen" (because you're not sure how his name is spelled), a regular expression can easily solve your problem. An alteration might be sufficient to find the Steven (or Stephen) you are looking for:

```
with t as
(select 'Steven' as name from dual union all
 select 'Stephen' from dual union all
 select 'Stephven' from dual union all
 select 'Stevphen' from dual
)
select name
  from t
 where regexp_like (name, 'Ste(v|ph)en');
```

Breaking Up a Delimited String

Sometimes it is necessary to break up strings that are stored in the database, even though the better solution would probably be to normalize the data model. For this example, we will create a table with a single column holding the denormalized data:

```
create table test
(str varchar2(500));
insert into test
values ('ABC,DEF,GHI,JKL,MNO');

commit;
```

The objective is to get each value from the comma-delimited string out of the str column on a separate row. Because we want to get part of a string, the natural choice would be to use the **regexp_substr** function.

We are looking for a pattern that matches all characters except the delimiter (in this case, the comma). Here is the pattern we will use:

```
[^,]+
```

This pattern translates to "don't match the comma, one or more times."

When this pattern is placed in the **regexp_substr** function, we get the following results:

```
select regexp_substr (str, '[^,]+') split
   from test;

SPLIT
------------------------
ABC


1 row selected.
```

Only the first value of our delimited string is returned because of the default values for the other arguments of the **regexp_substr** function. When you want to get the second value from the delimited string, the fourth argument should be used. The third argument defines where the search for the pattern should start, which defaults to the first character. The fourth argument is where the occurrence should be returned, which defaults to the first occurrence.

```
select regexp_substr (str, '[^,]+', 1, 2) split
   from test;
SPLIT
------------------------
DEF


1 row selected.
```

The requirement is to get each of the values on a separate row, not just get a specific value from the delimited string. To achieve this, rows need to be generated. But how many rows need to be generated? In our example, it is five rows, because there are five values in the delimited string:

```
select regexp_substr (str, '[^,]+', 1, rownum) split
   from test
 connect by level <= 5;
SPLIT
------------------------
ABC
DEF
GHI
JKL
MNO


5 rows selected.
```

This is not very dynamic—what if there are six or seven values in the delimited string? Then we would have to alter the query to get the correct results.

We could take advantage of a function that counts the number of occurrences in a string using the same pattern we used before. The function we are referring to is, of course, **regexp_count**. Thinking about it a little more, we could just count the number of commas in the column. In this case, there are four commas in the row; add one to that for the last value, and you have the number of individual values in the row:

```
select regexp_substr (str, '[^,]+', 1, rownum) split
  from test
  connect by level <= regexp_count (str, ',') + 1;


SPLIT
------------------------
ABC
DEF
GHI
JKL
MNO


5 rows selected.
```

Now the query results are dynamic, based on the number of values in the delimited string.

It is quite uncommon for a table to contain only one row, so let's add another row to our table:

```
insert into test
values ('123,456,789');
commit;
```

We then run the same query to break up the delimited strings in each of the rows:

```
select regexp_substr (str, '[^,]+', 1, rownum) split
  from test
  connect by level <= regexp_count (str, ',') + 1;
SPLIT
------------------------
ABC
DEF
GHI
JKL
MNO
<.. 25 NULL records, removed from output for brevity ..>
30 rows selected.
```

This is not the result that we are after: 30 records are returned, and most of them are NULL. The second row we added to the table isn't even shown in the result set as individual values.

The trick is to generate extra rows for each record in the table. This is done in the CROSS JOIN in the following query, which generates a Cartesian product:

```
select regexp_substr (str, '[^,]+', 1, rn) split
  from test
  cross
  join (select rownum rn
          from (select max (regexp_count (str, ',') + 1) mx
                  from test
               )
```

```
        connect by level <= mx
        )
where regexp_substr (str, '[^,]+', 1, rn) is not null;
SPLIT
------------------------
ABC
123
DEF
456
GHI
789
JKL
MNO

8 rows selected.
```

In Oracle Database 12c, you can take advantage of the new LATERAL join syntax. With the LATERAL clause, you create an inline view that can reference values from the table you are joining to:

```
select split
    from test
        ,lateral (select regexp_substr (str, '[^,]+', 1, rownum) split
                    from dual
                 connect by level <= regexp_count(str, ',') + 1);
SPLIT
------------------------
ABC
DEF
GHI
JKL
MNO
123
456
789

8 rows selected.
```

Sorting by the Numeric Part of a String

Sometimes you run into a situation where you need to sort data based on the numeric part of a string. Of course, it is always better to store data in the correct data type so that sorting can be done properly. The data used for this example is listed next:

```
select term
    from payment_terms;

TERM
---------------
Period 0.5 days
Period 1.0 days
```

```
Period 1.5 days
Period 10 days
Period 2.0 days
Period 2.5 days
Period 3.0 days
Period 3.5 days
Period 4.0 days
Period 4.5 days
Period 5.0 days
Period 5.5 days
Period 6.0 days
Period 6.5 days
Period 7.0 days
Period 7.5 days
Period 8.0 days
Period 8.5 days
Period 9.0 days
Period 9.5 days

20 rows selected.
```

In the table, payment terms are shown as a string. The how and why of storing data like this are beyond the scope of this discussion. Undoubtedly you have seen data stored like this in your own environment.

When this data is sorted, string-based sorting is performed. Most end users don't expect data sorted like this, where 10 is followed by 2—after all, 10 is (numerically) greater than 2. To sort correctly (the way end users expect it), a regular expression can prove valuable.

Extracting the numeric part of the string can be achieved by eliminating all other characters from the string. Replacing all nonnumeric characters with NULL will effectively remove them from the string. To do this, we use the following expression:

```
[^[:digit:]]
```

The expression reads "match all characters that are *not* from the character class digits." The caret (^) inside the bracket expression indicates that all characters listed should not be matched. However, this does not solve the problem. Let's examine this in detail and use the expression in the SELECT clause and see the effect:

```
select term
      ,regexp_replace (term, '[^[:digit:]]') num
   from payment_terms;

TERM             NUM
---------------- --------
Period 0.5 days  05
Period 1.0 days  10
Period 1.5 days  15
Period 10 days   10
Period 2.0 days  20
Period 2.5 days  25
```

```
Period 3.0 days 30
Period 3.5 days 35
Period 4.0 days 40
Period 4.5 days 45
Period 5.0 days 50
Period 5.5 days 55
Period 6.0 days 60
Period 6.5 days 65
Period 7.0 days 70
Period 7.5 days 75
Period 8.0 days 80
Period 8.5 days 85
Period 9.0 days 90
Period 9.5 days 95

20 rows selected.
```

Not only are the characters removed from the string, but the delimiter is also removed. There is no distinction between 1.0 days and 10 days any longer. Also notice that the extracted part is still not a number. To generate the output shown, SQL*Plus is used. This tool aligns numbers on the right side of the column. As you can tell from this output, the column is left-aligned, indicating that the extracted part is still a string.

Besides the numeric values from the string, the delimiter also needs to be spared. The following expression solves this:

```
[^[:digit:].]
```

Now the expression reads "match all characters that are not from the matching class digits or are a period." Because the period is in between the square brackets, it loses its special meaning; it is no longer a metacharacter:

```
select term
      ,regexp_replace (term, '[^[:digit:].]') num
  from payment_terms;

TERM             NUM
---------------- -----
Period 0.5 days  0.5
Period 1.0 days  1.0
Period 1.5 days  1.5
Period 10 days   10
Period 2.0 days  2.0
Period 2.5 days  2.5
Period 3.0 days  3.0
Period 3.5 days  3.5
Period 4.0 days  4.0
Period 4.5 days  4.5
Period 5.0 days  5.0
Period 5.5 days  5.5
Period 6.0 days  6.0
Period 6.5 days  6.5
```

```
Period 7.0 days 7.0
Period 7.5 days 7.5
Period 8.0 days 8.0
Period 8.5 days 8.5
Period 9.0 days 9.0
Period 9.5 days 9.5

20 rows selected.
```

Now the complete number, including the delimiter, is extracted from the string and can be used to sort the data. Simply convert the extracted data, which is still a string, to a number, and the data sorts as the end user would expect it to:

```
order by to_number (
          regexp_replace (term, '[^[:digit:].]')
         ,'999G999G999D999999'
         ,'NLS_NUMERIC_CHARACTERS='''.,'''
         )
```

The solution presented here can even be used in a virtual column, eliminating the complex expression from the ORDER BY clause.

The following statement adds a virtual column to the table that extracts the numeric part of the string. You can easily sort the data using this virtual column.

```
alter table payment_terms
add sort_column generated always
as (to_number (
          regexp_replace (term, '[^[:digit:].]')
         ,'999G999G999D999999'
         ,'NLS_NUMERIC_CHARACTERS='''.,'''
         ));
```

Pattern Matching: MATCH_RECOGNIZE

Oracle Database 12c introduces a new pattern-matching capability to search for patterns in a set of data. In this section, this new capability is explored using sample data based on the amount of precipitation that has fallen in the month of August.

For this example, the following table is used, which holds data for each day in August along with the amount of rain that has fallen:

```
create table weather
(dt    date  not null
,rain number not null
);
```

The table is loaded with sample data, and the contents are shown here:

```
select dt
      ,rain
  from weather
 order by dt;
```

```
DT              RAIN
---------    ----------
01-AUG-16          14
02-AUG-16           0
03-AUG-16          19
04-AUG-16           6
05-AUG-16          20
06-AUG-16           1
07-AUG-16          17
08-AUG-16          17
09-AUG-16          14
10-AUG-16          18
11-AUG-16           9
12-AUG-16           4
13-AUG-16          17
14-AUG-16          16
15-AUG-16           5
16-AUG-16           5
17-AUG-16          10
18-AUG-16           5
19-AUG-16          14
20-AUG-16          19
21-AUG-16          15
22-AUG-16          12
23-AUG-16          18
24-AUG-16           2
25-AUG-16           5
26-AUG-16           4
27-AUG-16          15
28-AUG-16           7
29-AUG-16           0
30-AUG-16          12
31-AUG-16          11
```

As you can see in the data, some days it doesn't rain, whereas other days it rains without stopping. Let's start to analyze some of this data.

The syntax for the **match_recognize** clause is something that might take some getting used to. Let's take a look at an example to start with. First, let's find out if the weather got better or worse as the dates went by:

```
select dt
      ,rain
      ,trend
  from weather
  match_recognize (
  order by dt
  measures classifier() as trend
  all rows per match
  pattern (better* worse* same*)
  define better as better.rain < prev (rain)
```

```
              ,worse   as worse.rain > prev (rain)
              ,same    as same.rain = prev (rain));

DT                  RAIN  TREND
---------   ----------  ---------
01-AUG-16           14
02-AUG-16            0  BETTER
03-AUG-16           19  WORSE
04-AUG-16            6  BETTER
05-AUG-16           20  WORSE
06-AUG-16            1  BETTER
07-AUG-16           17  WORSE
08-AUG-16           17  SAME
09-AUG-16           14  BETTER
10-AUG-16           18  WORSE
11-AUG-16            9  BETTER
12-AUG-16            4  BETTER
13-AUG-16           17  WORSE
14-AUG-16           16  BETTER
15-AUG-16            5  BETTER
16-AUG-16            5  SAME
17-AUG-16           10  WORSE
18-AUG-16            5  BETTER
19-AUG-16           14  WORSE
20-AUG-16           19  WORSE
21-AUG-16           15  BETTER
22-AUG-16           12  BETTER
23-AUG-16           18  WORSE
24-AUG-16            2  BETTER
25-AUG-16            5  WORSE
26-AUG-16            4  BETTER
27-AUG-16           15  WORSE
28-AUG-16            7  BETTER
29-AUG-16            0  BETTER
30-AUG-16           12  WORSE
31-AUG-16           11  BETTER
```

To determine whether the weather got better or worse, we need to define what makes a "better" day and what makes a "worse" day, or if the amount of rain stays the same from one day to the next. The definition of this classification is done in the **define** section. A "better" day is defined by the expression

```
better as better.rain < prev (rain)
```

When the rain for a certain day is less than the previous day, it gets the label "BETTER." When the rain is more than the previous day, it gets the label "WORSE." The expression in the **define** clause is as follows:

```
worse as worse.rain > prev (rain)
```

The last expression in the **define** clause signals days where the rain is the same from one day to the next. The expression is very straightforward:

```
same as same.rain = prev (rain)
```

Because the expressions in the **define** clause refer to the previous value, the **order by** is of importance. Because we want to compare the days based on calendar days, the obvious sorting is on the day in chronological order. The **order by** is the first expression in the **match_recognize** clause.

Since we only want to see whether the rain was getting better or worse, we only specify the **classifier()** function. This function allows us to identify which row maps to variables defined in the **define** section. There are other functions like that, such as the **match_number()** function.

The pattern we are looking for is defined in the **pattern** clause:

```
pattern (better* worse* same*)
```

The pattern states "zero or more iterations of 'better,' followed by zero or more iterations of 'worse,' followed by zero or more iterations of the 'same' amount of rain."

The data in our sample table starts with August 1st. Because there is no previous amount of rain to compare this day with, it doesn't get a classifier—it doesn't match any of the definitions. The amount of rain on August 2nd is less than August 1st, so this row gets the classifier "BETTER," and so on.

These results can also be achieved by using analytic functions, especially the **lag** function, which compares the current value with the previous record:

```
select dt
      ,rain
      ,case
       when rain < lag (rain) over (order by dt)
       then 'Better'
       when rain > lag (rain) over (order by dt)
       then 'Worse'
       when rain = lag (rain) over (order by dt)
       then 'Same'
       end trend
from weather;
```

The **match_recognize** clause really shows off its power when you use regular expressions to search for patterns in your data.

The following example searches for dry periods in August: one or more days when no rain fell, or at least not as much rain, is considered the start of a dry period. To get the **match_recognize** clause to work, we need to define what makes a "wet" day and what makes a "dry" day. In this example, a dry day is defined as follows:

```
dry as dry.rain <= 10
```

It is considered to be a dry day when there is less than 10 units of rain (probably millimeters—the table doesn't provide the unit of measurement).

The definition for a wet day is when the amount of rain is greater than 10:

```
wet as wet.rain > 10
```

What we are looking for is a period of at least two dry consecutive days. The pattern that describes this requirement is defined as follows:

```
wet dry{2,} wet*
```

This reads as "at least two or more dry days in a row, preceded by a wet day, and followed by zero or more wet days." The complete query with the results is shown here:

```
select *
  from weather
 match_recognize (
    order by dt
    measures
      first (wet.dt) as first_wetday
     ,dry.dt as dryday
     ,last (wet.dt) as last_wetday
    one row per match
    pattern (wet dry{2,} wet*)
    define wet as wet.rain > 10
          ,dry as dry.rain <= 10
  );
FIRST_WET DRYDAY    LAST_WETD
--------- --------- ---------
10-AUG-16 12-AUG-16 14-AUG-16
23-AUG-16 26-AUG-16 27-AUG-16
```

These results indicate that the first wet day started on August 10th and the last wet day ended on August 14th, with a number of dry days in between. Inspecting the data in the table reveals that this is indeed the case:

```
10-AUG-16        18 Worse
11-AUG-16         9 Better
12-AUG-16         4 Better
13-AUG-16        17 Worse
14-AUG-16        16 Better
```

The second dry spell in August started with the first wet day on August 23rd and ended with the last wet day on August 27th, with some dry days in between:

```
23-AUG-16        18 Worse
24-AUG-16         2 Better
25-AUG-16         5 Worse
26-AUG-16         4 Better
27-AUG-16        15 Worse
```

You might wonder why the period between August 27th and August 30th isn't included in the results returned by the **match_recognize** query:

```
27-AUG-16        15 Worse
28-AUG-16         7 Better
29-AUG-16         0 Better
30-AUG-16        12 Worse
```

It seems that there were two dry days with a wet day on each end. The pattern to identify the dry period states

```
dry{2,}
```

which means *at least* two dry days. Because there were exactly two dry days in between the two wet days, this period doesn't qualify as a dry period.

Summary

This chapter discussed searching for patterns in your data—from the simplest form, using only single- or multiple-character wildcards, to more complex forms using regular expressions. Using the description from various theme parks in Florida, we extracted the telephone numbers. When the data model is not normalized properly and storing data in a denormalized format is allowed, regular expressions help make sense of the data and create a uniform output. However, this is by no means a substitute for creating a proper data model. Implementing check constraints using regular expressions will ensure that the data entered is in a proper format.

At the end of the chapter, you were given a brief introduction to the **match_recognize** clause.

CHAPTER
5

Edition-Based Redefinition

Oracle Database 11*g* introduced edition-based redefinition (EBR), a new concept in the Oracle Database that is available for all editions of the database at no extra cost. Over the years a number of technologies have been used to reduce the downtime of the Oracle Database. The one thing that could keep users working uninterrupted was the actual database application they were using. Upgrading the database application always required downtime; it was simply not possible to replace PL/SQL objects that were in use.

The whole purpose of edition-based redefinition is to have zero downtime. However, the concept of edition-based redefinition has to be clear, and you need to prepare for it. This chapter introduces you to the concepts behind edition-based redefinition and shows you code samples to get you started.

Planned Downtime

Basically there are two kinds of downtime: planned and unplanned. Unplanned downtime occurs unexpectedly, and preparing for the unexpected is very hard to do. There are measures you can take to reduce unplanned downtime, but completely eliminating it is almost impossible.

Planned downtime is known about ahead of time, and Oracle offers a number of features you can have in place to reduce the amount of planned downtime required. Hardware failures can be protected by physical and/or logical standby databases, as well as Oracle Real Application Clusters (RAC). To upgrade the database software itself, you don't have to take down the database. When you have a logical standby and streams, it is possible to keep the database up and running while it's being upgraded. Indexes can be rebuilt online and tables can be redefined online, so neither of these has to be a reason to experience downtime.

The last piece of the puzzle is the downtime caused by custom applications. There has been no way to replace PL/SQL at run time without being noticed by the users. There can only be one version of a certain PL/SQL object. When you replace a PL/SQL object, that object must be locked and can't be executed, thus disrupting the regular business process. PL/SQL objects that depend on the object being replaced can become invalid and might require recompilation.

This last piece of the puzzle—being able to upgrade your custom application and to prevent additional downtime—is solved by edition-based redefinition. With edition-based redefinition, you can create PL/SQL changes in the privacy of an edition. Then, when the custom application is updated, it can be released to the users. Newly connecting users will use the new application objects, while the users who were using the application during the upgrade can continue to work as if nothing happened. When the last of the users has disconnected from the pre-upgraded application, that application can be retired and only the post-upgraded application will be available for use.

Terminology Used

Edition-based redefinition uses certain terminology that will be referred to throughout this chapter. Table 5-1 details the most commonly used definitions. This table can act as a quick reference.

Term	Explanation
Edition	Name identifying a nonschema object type to extend the standard naming resolution. Editionable objects are identified by edition, schema, and object name.
Editioning view	A special kind of view that acts as an abstraction layer for the underlying table. Because the editioning view exists in a certain edition, it reflects the current implementation of the underlying table. There are certain restrictions for the editioning view.
Editionable object	Schema objects that are editionable. These include Synonym, View, and all PL/SQL object types.
Noneditionable object	All schema objects that are not editionable. These include tables, database links, and materialized views.
Cross-edition trigger	Special kind of trigger that can cross the boundaries of editions.
NE on E prohibition	Noneditionable objects cannot depend on editionable objects.

TABLE 5-1. *Definitions Related to EBR*

The Concept

The purpose of edition-based redefinition is very straightforward: zero downtime patching and upgrading. When you have the luxury of taking downtime, by all means do so. It will be a lot easier for all parties involved.

There is a distinction between a patch and an upgrade: In an ideal situation, all the requirements for a program are implemented in the actual program, and the program implements exactly the written specification. When the program doesn't implement what the requirement specifies, a patch needs to be applied to correct the situation in order to bring the implementation and the specification together. The patch should bring the program up to par with the requirement of the functionality. An upgrade comes into play when the requirements change after the program is created. From this moment on, we will not make this distinction anymore. When the text says "upgrade," a patch is also implied, and vice versa.

Of course, the database is not the only part of the application that is involved when you want to achieve zero-downtime upgrades. The method used to set up the connection to the database will determine to which version of the database application the connection needs to be set up. This can be done by a load balancer or traffic director. Sessions that are in flight (that is, connected to the pre-upgrade application) will connect through one application server, whereas sessions that set up a new connection will use another application server and connect to the post-upgrade application.

Zero downtime needs to be designed deliberately in the Oracle Database and the application server, as well as in the client application. Obtaining zero downtime means that the application should be available to the users at all times. This is a big challenge: users of the pre-upgrade application don't want to stop what they are doing to allow for a new application being deployed. Users wanting to use the post-upgrade application don't want to wait until the users of the pre-upgrade application are done with their work so that they can finally connect to the application. Both applications (the pre- and post-upgrade versions) need to be active at the same time so they can accommodate the users using the pre-upgrade application as well as establish new connections to the post-upgrade application (we call this a *hot rollover*).

Deploying a new application while the old application is in use can be easy for certain types of applications, so deploying new source files might be sufficient. When a database is involved, however, this proves to be a lot harder. Therefore, some elementary questions need to be answered.

First of all, how can you make changes to an application when someone is using the application? Making changes to an application usually involves many objects that are modified, but you can't modify them one after the other. That would leave the application in an invalid state. On top of that, it is simply not possible to compile database code when someone is using it. All objects need to be changed at the same time, but that might interrupt the pre-upgrade application. It is possible to take a complete copy of the database with the pre-upgrade database application and make the changes needed to get to the post-upgrade state—this solves the first issue. Another option is to copy the database schema and make changes in this new schema. Both of these options allow you to change objects privately and prepare for the post-upgrade situation.

Now the following question arises: how can you keep data in sync between two applications, the pre-upgrade application and post-upgrade application? You can imagine that this is not an easy task to do. The original database objects are still in use and data can be entered and altered. There must be a mechanism to allow data changes to propagate between the pre- and post-upgrade application. When the data is shared between the pre-upgrade and post-upgrade application, the issue of synchronization is trivial. The pre-upgrade application will have access to the data that is created or changed by the post-upgrade application. The post-upgrade application will have access to the pre-upgrade application. The same is true for all objects that contain data, such as materialized views and indexes.

Upgrading an application might change data structures, so how do you define a different data representation for each application when the data is common to both the pre-upgrade and post-upgrade application? Transactions performed in the pre-upgrade application must be reflected in the post-upgrade application. The reverse is also true during the hot rollover period: changes in the post-upgrade application must also be reflected in the pre-upgrade application.

All three of the challenges with a zero-downtime requirement are met by edition-based redefinition. The mechanism to solve the three challenges are as follows:

- Changes are made in the privacy of a new edition.
- Different projections of the common tables are achieved by using an editioning view.
- The cross-edition trigger will keep data changes in sync between different editions during the hot rollover period.

Besides these structures introduced with edition-based redefinition, there are also two supporting features of the Oracle Database. The first supporting feature is nonblocking DDL. When you make changes to a table, such as adding a column, this is done in a nonblocking fashion. Current transactions on the table will not prohibit this change.

The other feature is fine-grained dependency tracking. When you have a package that refers to a certain table, there is a dependency between the two. Changing the table, like adding a column, would invalidate the package in the past. This is no longer the case. The dependency nowadays is more fine grained. Because there is no reference to the new column in the package, the package will not become invalid. The same holds true for adding new subprograms to a package specification; dependents will not become invalid.

Implementing edition-based redefinition is not as trivial as flipping a switch. The preparation phase of edition-based redefinition is very important and might require changing the existing database design and database source code.

Within the Oracle Database there are objects that hold data, such as tables, materialized views, and indexes, and there are code objects, such as all the PL/SQL objects. As a rule of thumb: data objects cannot be editionable and code objects can be editionable.

It is possible that you have a table where one of the columns is based on a user-defined type (such as an Object Type). Because the user-defined type is editionable and the table is not editionable, you can get into a situation that is not easily solved. Which user-defined type should be used when there are multiple versions across editions for the table definition? This predicament is called the *NE on E prohibition*. A noneditionable object cannot depend on an editionable object.

In Oracle Database 12.1, there is a possibility to work around this NE on E prohibition. Instead of having the complete schema being edition enabled, you can exempt objects from ever becoming editionable. In the example of the user-defined type in the table, you would want to define the user-defined type from ever becoming editionable, and thus you will not encounter the NE on E prohibition. In a later section this NE on E prohibition is examined in more detail.

Also starting with Oracle Database 12.1, materialized views and virtual columns can have extra metadata that provides information about the evaluation edition. Having this extra metadata is only relevant when the materialized view or virtual column uses a PL/SQL function call that is editionable. This metadata needs to be explicitly set by issuing CREATE and ALTER statements.

In versions prior to 12.1, public synonyms could not be edition enabled because that would violate the NE on E prohibition. From version 12.1 onward, the Oracle-maintained user called PUBLIC is edition enabled, but all existing public synonyms are marked as noneditioned. Creating new public synonyms can be editioned.

During the hot rollover period, you can also test the post-upgrade application in the privacy of the new edition. When you have to test DML in the post-upgrade application, make sure that you use fake data. With fake data, the actual data is not affected by the edition-based redefinition exercise and can be easily identified and removed once the tests are completed. The alternative is to test only in a read-only mode in order to prevent a removal of the edition leading to remnant data. In case something goes wrong, or the functionality is not living up to the specifications, you can keep going forward in the privacy of the post-upgrade edition. The objective is to create a post-upgrade application, and this can only be achieved when mistakes are corrected.

When the hot rollover period is completed, touch testing has been done, and there are no existing connections using the pre-upgrade application, the pre-upgrade edition can be retired. Preventing users from connecting to the pre-upgrade application might be the first step. The cross-edition triggers, used to keep the data in sync between the pre- and post-upgrade applications, are no longer needed. Objects in the pre-upgrade edition can be dropped, and eventually the unused columns can be removed from the table.

If, for whatever reason, the edition-based redefinition exercise fails and the edition must be removed, the edition can be dropped by a single statement. Keep in mind, though, that changes to the table are not reversed when an edition is dropped from the database. Also, changes to the data are not reversed and should be removed as well to return to the pre-upgraded version.

Preparation: Enable Editions

To prepare for the upcoming change, we need to take a number of steps. There are some simple steps required to prepare for the last downtime ever needed to upgrade the application. Every Oracle Database version, starting with 11gR2, has a default edition called ORA$BASE. Even when you don't intend on using edition-based redefinition, the ORA$BASE edition will always be there.

To make use of edition-based redefinition, the database schema needs to be enabled to make use of editions, as shown next. This is a one-time action and is irreversible. The fact that it is irreversible doesn't mean you must use edition-based redefinition; it is simply a necessary step to take on the road to reduced downtime.

```
alter user scott enable editions
```

As you can see in the following code sample, it is not possible to disable editions for a database schema. Enabling editions for a user is a one-way street.

```
alter user scott disable editions
                  *
ERROR at line 1:
ORA-00922: missing or invalid option
```

In versions prior to Oracle Database 12.1, the whole schema would be edition enabled. Starting with Oracle Database 12.1, it is possible to mark certain objects as noneditionable that normally would be editionable.

NE on E Prohibition

It is not possible for noneditionable objects to depend on editionable objects. This is called the *NE on E prohibition*. Prior to Oracle Database 12.1, when you wanted to edition-enable a schema, you would have to resolve this issue. For example, when you have a user-defined type that is used in a table definition, you violate the NE on E prohibition. A user-defined type is editionable, whereas a table can never be editionable. When you needed to adhere to the zero-downtime requirement prior to version 12.1, inevitably you would need to change your schema design.

Starting with Oracle Database 12.1, it is possible to define objects by explicitly setting these as noneditionable. This is only possible prior to edition-enabling the schema. Once an object is set as noneditionable and the schema is edition enabled, the status is fixed and can't be altered. Attempting to do so will result in the following exception:

```
ORA-38825: The EDITIONABLE property of an editioned object cannot be altered.
```

To demonstrate the NE on E prohibition, a new user (appropriately called NEONE) is created:

```
create user neone identified by neone
/
grant connect, create table, create type to neone
/
alter user neone quota unlimited on users
/
```

When connected as this user, first some user-defined types are created to hold a list of phone numbers:

```
conn neone/neone@pdborcl

create type phone_number_ot as object
(type_name varchar2(10)
,phone_number varchar2(20)
)
/


create type phone_numbers_tt as table of phone_number_ot
/
```

With the user-defined types in place, a database table is created where the user-defined type is the data type for the phone_numbers column:

```
create table emps
(empno number
,phone_numbers phone_numbers_tt
)
 nested table phone_numbers store as phone_numbers_nt
/
```

When an attempt is made to edition-enable the NEONE user, done by SYS, an exception is raised:

```
alter user neone enable editions
/
ERROR at line 1:
ORA-38819: user NEONE owns one or more objects whose type is editionable
and that have noneditioned dependent objects
```

Before the NEONE user can be edition enabled, the user-defined types will need to be noneditionable. This can be done by altering the user-defined types:

```
alter type phone_numbers_tt noneditionable
/
alter type phone_number_ot noneditionable
/
```

The user-defined types are now specified as noneditionable, meaning they can never be editionable. Now the road is cleared to edition-enable the NEONE schema. When changes are needed in a future edition of the user-defined types, they will need to be done in a similar fashion as other table columns.

When the schema is already edition enabled and you want to include a user-defined type as a column in a table definition, the user-defined types will need to be noneditionable. The syntax to create user-defined types supports this. User SCOTT was edition enabled in the previous section of this chapter. When an attempt is made to create the same table as in the previous example with the user-defined objects, an exception is raised:

```
conn scott/tiger@pdborcl

create type phone_number_ot as object
(type_name varchar2(10)
,phone_number varchar2(20)
)
/

Type created.

create type phone_numbers_tt as table of phone_number_ot
/

Type created.

create table emps
(empno number
,phone_numbers phone_numbers_tt
)
 nested table phone_numbers store as phone_numbers_nt
/

create table emps
*
ERROR at line 1:
ORA-38818: illegal reference to editioned object SCOTT.PHONE_NUMBER_OT
```

As you can see in this code sample, creating a table based on an editionable user-defined type is not allowed.

Because SCOTT is already edition enabled, the types can't be altered to be noneditionable:

```
alter type phone_numbers_tt noneditionable
/

*
ERROR at line 1:
ORA-38825: The EDITIONABLE property of an editioned object cannot be altered.
```

To be able to create the table based on user-defined types, you would have to re-create the user-defined types with noneditionable specified, as shown in the next example:

```
drop type phone_numbers_tt
/
Type dropped.

drop type phone_number_ot
/
Type dropped.
```

```
create or replace
 noneditionable type phone_number_ot as object
(type_name varchar2(10)
,phone_number varchar2(20)
)
/
Type created.

create or replace
 noneditionable type phone_numbers_tt as table of phone_number_ot
/
Type created.

create table emps
(empno number
,phone_numbers phone_numbers_tt
)
 nested table phone_numbers store as phone_numbers_nt
/
Table created.
```

Creating a New Edition

Because user SCOTT is edition enabled, we can create an extra edition. There is a hierarchical relationship between editions, where an edition always has a parent. The only exception here is ORA$BASE, or when this edition is eventually removed, the next edition in the hierarchy—the so-called *root edition*.

In order to create a new edition, the system privilege CREATE ANY EDITION is needed:

```
grant create any edition to scott
```

Before you can create an edition, you will also need the USE privilege on the edition that will be used as the parent edition. An edition is always created as the child of another edition. When you create an edition, the USE object privilege is automatically granted.

The USE privilege can also be granted separately, as shown in this code sample:

```
grant use on edition <edition_name> to <user>
```

Here, <edition_name> and <user> need to be replaced with the name of the edition and the user to whom you want to grant the privilege.

In order to remove a root or leaf edition, the DROP ANY EDITION system privilege is needed:

```
grant drop any edition to scott
```

While you are connected to a database, it is possible to change the edition by using an ALTER statement like in the next example, where <edition_name> should be changed to the edition you want to change to:

```
alter session set edition = <edition_name>
```

Keep in mind that it is not possible to change the edition when you have an open transaction. When attempting to change your edition when you haven't closed your transaction with either a COMMIT or ROLLBACK, an error is raised, as can be seen in this code sample:

```
alter session set edition = r2

ERROR:
ORA-38814: ALTER SESSION SET EDITION must be first statement of transaction
```

Complexity Levels

Using edition-based redefinition involves several levels of complexity. The lowest level is where only PL/SQL objects are changed between editions. The next level up is where table structures change between editions, and there is no need to keep multiple editions available at the same time because all users move to the post-upgrade edition at a specified time in the future. The most complex level is where you do have table structure changes and the users need to access multiple editions at the same time, thus keeping data in sync between multiple editions.

In the next few sections, we cover each of these levels, beginning with the easiest level: changing only PL/SQL objects between editions.

Replacing PL/SQL Code

All the following code samples will use SCOTT connected through SQL*Plus to an Oracle Database 12*c*.

Now that all the necessary privileges are in place and the user is edition enabled, we can start with the first real (albeit contrived) example. For the following example we will create a PL/SQL procedure and demonstrate that it's possible to have the same name with different functionality in a different edition.

To determine the edition of your current database session, use the following query:

```
select sys_context('userenv'
                   ,'current_edition_name'
                   ) "Current_Edition"
  from dual
/

Current_Edition
---------------
ORA$BASE
```

TIP
*When you use SQL*Plus, you can also enter **SHOW EDITION** to reveal the current edition.*

While in this edition (ORA$BASE), we will create a procedure called **hello**:

```
create or replace
procedure hello
is
begin
   dbms_output.put_line ('Hello World');
end hello;
/
```

This extremely simple procedure will output the text "Hello World" when executed, but only if SERVEROUTPUT is turned on:

```
begin
   hello;
end;
/
Hello World
```

With the introduction of edition-based redefinition, the data dictionary was extended with a number of views to reflect the edition as well. These dictionary views have the extension AE, believed to mean *All Editions*. One of these views is USER_OBJECTS_AE. When we inspect this data dictionary for our newly created procedure **hello**, we can see that it exists in ORA$BASE:

```
select object_name
      ,object_type
      ,edition_name
  from user_objects_ae
 where object_name = 'HELLO'
/

OBJECT_NAME         OBJECT_TYPE      EDITION_NAME
----------------    --------------   ------------------------------
HELLO               PROCEDURE        ORA$BASE
```

TIP
If you are querying the USER_OBJECTS_AE data dictionary and the EDITION_NAME column shows up empty, the user is not edition enabled.

Next, we will create a new edition named R1:

```
create edition r1 as child of ora$base
```

Although it is not strictly necessary to specify the AS CHILD OF clause, it's a good practice to be explicit in your code.

Just because we created the edition, it doesn't mean that we switched over to use it. To change the current edition to the newly created one, we need to issue an ALTER SESSION statement:

```
alter session set edition = r1
/

select sys_context('userenv'
                   ,'current_edition_name'
                   ) "Current_Edition"
    from dual
/

Current_Edition
---------------
R1
```

As you can see in the preceding query, the current edition is R1. It is also possible to connect to a specific edition when we log in using SQL*Plus, as shown in the following code snippet:

```
conn scott/tiger@pdborcl edition=r1
```

When we try to execute in the R1 edition of the procedure **hello**, we get the following results:

```
begin
    hello;
end;
/
Hello World
```

How is this possible? The procedure **hello** is inherited from ORA$BASE and can, therefore, be executed in the R1 edition. All editionable objects are inherited by a child edition. All PL/SQL objects are editionable objects as well as synonyms and views.

We introduced a new edition so that we can make improvements to the **hello** procedure. To do this, we will use a very familiar method to enhance the procedure with a CREATE OR REPLACE. The replacement of the procedure happens in the privacy of the R1 edition, leaving the original procedure valid. Users who are connected to the ORA$BASE edition are unaffected by this new version of the **hello** procedure.

```
create or replace
procedure hello
is
begin
    dbms_output.put_line ('Hello Universe');
end hello;
/
```

The procedure **hello** is replaced in the current edition R1, which is reflected in the data dictionary USER_OBJECTS_AE. The USER_OBJECTS_AE data dictionary view is similar to the USER_OBJECTS data dictionary view, with the exception that it will show objects across all editions:

```
select object_name
      ,object_type
      ,edition_name
  from user_objects_ae
 where object_name = 'HELLO'
/

OBJECT_NAME        OBJECT_TYPE      EDITION_NAME
----------------   --------------   -------------
HELLO              PROCEDURE        ORA$BASE
HELLO              PROCEDURE        R1
```

As you can see from this output, there are two procedures called **hello**: one that exists in ORA$BASE and one in R1. Depending on your current edition, when the correct procedure is executed, the result will be either "Hello World" or "Hello Universe."

It is also possible that a procedure is no longer needed in the post-upgrade edition. Removing the obsolete procedure is done by issuing a DROP statement. While in edition R1, issue the following statement to remove the **hello** procedure from this edition (keep in mind that a procedure with the same name still exists in ORA$BASE):

```
drop procedure hello
```

Inspecting the USER_OBJECTS_AE data dictionary view, after dropping the procedure, we see the following results:

```
select object_name
      ,object_type
      ,edition_name
  from user_objects_ae
 where object_name = 'HELLO'
/

OBJECT_NAME        OBJECT_TYPE      EDITION_NAME
----------------   --------------   ----------------------------------
HELLO              PROCEDURE        ORA$BASE
HELLO              NON-EXISTENT     R1
```

As you can see in this output, there are two references to an object with the name HELLO: one in ORA$BASE and one in R1. Notice that the object in ORA$BASE is a PROCEDURE and the object in R1 is NON-EXISTENT.

Once removed from a certain edition, the object will no longer be inherited by the next child edition. In a similar fashion, it is also possible to change a procedure into a function using a combination of DROP (for the procedure previously issued) and CREATE (for the function), as shown here:

```
create or replace
function hello
    return varchar2
is
begin
```

```
      return 'Hello Galaxy';
end hello;
/
```

This will yield the following results in USER_OBJECTS_AE:

```
select object_name
      ,object_type
      ,edition_name
  from user_objects_ae
 where object_name = 'HELLO'
/
```

```
OBJECT_NAME          OBJECT_TYPE       EDITION_NAME
----------------     ---------------   ------------------------------
HELLO                PROCEDURE         ORA$BASE
HELLO                FUNCTION          R1
```

Now that all new PL/SQL objects are in place, the new edition will need to be made available to the users and the old edition will need to be made unavailable. How to do all this is covered in the next sections describing how to retire old editions.

Changing Table Structures

Sometimes you need to change the structure of a table when you progress to the next version of your application. It is important to understand that a table cannot be editionable; it is not possible to have multiple versions of the same table. Adding columns to a table can be done without invalidating existing source code because of fine-grained dependency tracking. Also, thanks to nonblocking DDL, no sessions are hindered by this exercise.

There needs to be a different representation in the various editions in order to expose the newly added columns. Edition-based redefinition introduces the concept of an editioning view. As the name implies, it is a view, but a special kind of view. It acts as an abstraction layer for the underlying table. Because the editioning view is editionable, it can (and most likely will) have a different structure for each edition.

Because of the abstraction layer, data is still stored in a single place. The underlying table holds the data and will be a single point of truth. Indexes and constraints remain on the table.

Introducing editioning views will require some downtime for the first (and last) edition-based redefinition implementation. Keep in mind that some features you use on your tables might need to be rerouted to the editioning views, such as privileges, triggers, and virtual private databases (VPDs).

Suppose there is a table-level trigger named EMP_BIR whose purpose is to populate the EMPNO column in the EMP table, using the sequence EMPSEQ. Keep this script handy; you will need it when the editioning view is in place.

```
create sequence empseq
/

create or replace trigger emp_bir
before insert on emp
for each row
```

```
begin
    :new.empno := empseq.nextval;
end emp_bir;
/
```

We have six common steps to take when introducing the editioning views during the edition-based redefinition exercise:

1. Rename the tables.
2. Create the editioning view.
3. Reroute privileges to the editioning view.
4. Re-create triggers on the editioning view.
5. Recompile the PL/SQL.
6. Reapply the virtual private database policies.

We want the editioning view to be the abstraction layer between the actual table and the application. The application most likely references the actual table in various places throughout the source code. Changing the name of the actual table in the source code to the editioning view can be a quite daunting and error-prone task. Naming the editioning view the same as the actual table would have the least impact on the application. However, it is not possible to use the same name for the actual table and the editioning view. By first renaming the table and creating an editioning view with the same name as the original table, we can solve this predicament.

The table shouldn't be accessed directly in the application anymore, and creating a table name that is distinguishable from the regular table names should help prevent that. For example, the following naming convention introduces a special character (in this case, an underscore) and is case-sensitive:

```
alter table emp rename to "_emp"
```

Now the table cannot be selected from unless the table name appears in quotes, as shown. Because this is not a common convention for table names (using special characters and being case-sensitive), it signals to developers that this table is special.

Step 1 is complete: the table has been renamed. The next step is to create an editioning view with the same name as the original table:

```
create editioning view emp
as
select empno
      ,ename
      ,job
      ,mgr
      ,hiredate
      ,sal
      ,comm
      ,deptno
  from "_emp"
/
```

There are some restrictions to defining an editioning view. For instance, the editioning view can only be based on a single table and can't contain aggregates or expressions.

Any privileges (such as SELECT and INSERT) granted to other schemas need to be reissued. When these grants are scripted, you can use the same scripts to do this. Because the editioning view takes the name from the original table, the privileges are granted on the editioning view instead.

All table-level triggers originally on the table now can be re-created on the editioning view. Having the original scripts to create the table-level triggers will be beneficial once again. Run these scripts, and the table-level triggers are created on the editioning view. This is also a difference with a regular view, because on a regular view it is not possible to have table-type triggers. As with the privileges, the same scripts can be used to re-create the triggers.

After we rename the table, the trigger will remain on the table:

```
select trigger_name
      ,table_name
  from user_triggers
/

TRIGGER_NAME                   TABLE_NAME
------------------------------ ------------------------------
EMP_BIR                                _emp
```

To attach the trigger to the editioning view, the trigger needs to be dropped (as shown next) because it is not possible to have two objects with the same name in an edition:

```
drop trigger emp_bir
/

Trigger dropped.
```

After the editioning view is created, the trigger can be re-created with the same script as before:

```
create or replace trigger emp_bir
before insert on emp
for each row
begin
    :new.empno := empseq.nextval;
end emp_bir;
/

Trigger created.

select trigger_name
      ,table_name
  from user_triggers
/

TRIGGER_NAME                   TABLE_NAME
------------------------------ ------------------------------
EMP_BIR                        EMP
```

TIP

Having the table-level triggers scripted will make the re-creation of the triggers on the editioning views trivially easy. The same is true for the virtual private database policy scripts.

Because of the renaming of the table, the PL/SQL objects that refer to the table will be invalidated. Recompiling the PL/SQL will resolve this, and the PL/SQL code will now refer to the editioning view instead of the actual table.

When you use virtual private database (VPD) functionality (see Chapter 16), the policies need to be reapplied to the editioning view. Run the scripts that you created for the table, and the virtual private database policy will be in place on the editioning view.

Now all the components are in place and no more downtime is required to perform an application upgrade. Creating new functionality can be done in an isolated edition without affecting the existing application.

Let's suppose a new requirement for the application is that a phone number should be added to the employee data. The first thing we need to do to alter the "_emp" table is to include a column for the phone number:

```
alter table "_emp"
add (
     phone_number varchar2(10)
)
```

Adding a column to a table used to invalidate the PL/SQL objects referencing the table. With the introduction of fine-grained dependency tracking in Oracle 11*g*, this is no longer the case. The actual columns used in the PL/SQL code can invalidate the source code. Because there is no reference to the newly added column in any of the PL/SQL code, no code is invalidated.

In the privacy of the new edition, we can include this new column to the editioning view without invalidating the existing application:

```
create edition r2 as child of r1
/

Edition created.

alter session set edition = r2
/

Session altered.

create or replace
editioning view emp
as
select empno
      ,ename
      ,job
      ,mgr
      ,hiredate
      ,sal
      ,comm
```

```
        ,deptno
        ,phone_number
   from "_emp"
/

View created.

select empno
        ,ename
        ,phone_number
   from emp
/

     EMPNO ENAME       PHONE_NUMB
---------- ---------- ----------
      7369 SMITH
      7499 ALLEN
      7521 WARD
      7566 JONES
      7654 MARTIN
      7698 BLAKE
      7782 CLARK
      7788 SCOTT
      7839 KING
      7844 TURNER
      7876 ADAMS
      7900 JAMES
      7902 FORD
      7934 MILLER

14 rows selected.
```

As you can see in the query results, the phone number exists in the edition named R2. When we switch our session back to edition R1, the phone number column doesn't exist:

```
alter session set edition = r1
/

Session altered.

desc emp
 Name               Null?     Type
 ---------------- -------- --------------------------
 EMPNO                       NUMBER(4)
 ENAME                       VARCHAR2(10)
 JOB                         VARCHAR2(9)
 MGR                         NUMBER(4)
 HIREDATE                    DATE
 SAL                         NUMBER(7,2)
 COMM                        NUMBER(7,2)
 DEPTNO                      NUMBER(2)
```

Because the phone number doesn't exist in the ORA$BASE or R1 edition, there is no data that needs to be migrated from the pre-upgrade edition to the post-upgrade edition. Users of the R2 edition and application will maintain the phone number. Users of the ORA$BASE or R1 application will have no notion of the phone number.

Keeping the Data in Sync Between Editions

Things will be more complex when a column needs to be altered in some way from one edition to the next. Therefore, let's take a look at a slightly more complex example. The application uses ENAME to maintain an employee's name. Here is the new requirement we will implement:

> "ENAME must be split into FIRST_NAME and LAST_NAME, and the new LAST_NAME column must be increased in size to hold 25 characters. The original ENAME contains the same value as the new LAST_NAME column."

Adding the columns to the table is the easy part, as is modifying the editioning view to reflect the first and last name as well as omitting the ENAME column. Because the table is not editionable, it doesn't matter which edition is the current edition, although common sense dictates that you shouldn't perform DDL in older editions.

You might be tempted to alter the existing ENAME to be able to hold 25 characters and act as the newly required LAST_NAME column, which is trivially easy to do. This would impact the existing application because the source code will become invalid and cause (some) downtime. The whole objective of edition-based redefinition is to have zero downtime, so changing the width of the column is not acceptable.

```
alter table "_emp"
add (
    first_name varchar2 (10)
   ,last_name varchar2 (25)
   )
/


Table altered.

create edition r3 as child of r2
/

Edition created.

alter session set edition = r3
/

Session altered.

create or replace
editioning view emp
as
select empno
      ,first_name
      ,last_name
```

```
       ,job
       ,mgr
       ,hiredate
       ,sal
       ,comm
       ,deptno
       ,phone_number
   from "_emp"
/
```

```
View created.
```

At this point the LAST_NAME column doesn't contain any data. For the new situation, it should get the same values as ENAME in the original table. This can be accomplished with a straightforward UPDATE statement. However, a massive update might disrupt normal business because of the locking that occurs with the update.

If the users of the application will only use the latest version (edition R2 in this example), doing a massive update might be good enough. From that point forward, the users will only have to deal with FIRST_NAME and LAST_NAME, and ENAME is no longer maintained because there is no need to do so.

A better method than a straightforward UPDATE statement is utilizing DBMS_PARALLEL_ EXECUTE to minimize the time it takes to complete the task. This might especially be useful when you are dealing with a lot of data. There are other methods to synchronize the data between the ENAME and LAST_NAME columns during the transition phase of going from one edition to the next. These are described in the next sections.

During a time period when both editions need to be available to the users (the so-called hot rollover period), there needs to be a mechanism to keep the ENAME and LAST_NAME columns in sync. Users of the older application (R2) will only see and manipulate ENAME, whereas the users of the newer application (R3) will only deal with FIRST_NAME and LAST_NAME.

There is a mechanism that does just that. Because the data needs to be kept in sync across editions, the method to use is the cross-edition trigger. Let's take a look at a code sample. Cross-edition triggers are placed on the base table (in our case, "_emp"). The triggers can be created similar to either conventional table triggers (statement and row) or compound triggers. Just like ordinary table triggers, the cross-edition trigger is editionable and will need to be created in the new edition (R3).

```
create or replace trigger EMP_R2_R3_Fwd_Xed
before insert or update on "_emp"
for each row
forward crossedition
disable
begin
    :new.last_name := :new.ename;
end EMP_R2_R3_Fwd_Xed;
/
```

```
Trigger created.
```

As you can see, in the second line of code the trigger is created on the underlying table, not the editioning view. After specifying that the trigger needs to fire for each row, the **forward crossedition** signals that this trigger should fire whenever DML is executed in a parent edition (either edition R2, R1, or ORA$BASE).

As a best practice, the trigger is created in a disabled mode (on the fifth line). Only when the trigger is valid should it be enabled. The logic to keep LAST_NAME (R2) in sync with ENAME (R2) is very straightforward. The LAST_NAME column is filled with the same value as the ENAME column.

The next step is to enable the trigger so that it can fire when appropriate and the data in the latest edition (R3) is updated by the users of the older edition (R2):

```
alter trigger EMP_R2_R3_Fwd_Xed enable
/

Trigger altered.
```

To verify the correct behavior, an UPDATE statement is executed:

```
alter session set edition = R1
/

Session altered.

update emp
   set ename = 'Widlake'
 where ename = 'MARTIN'
/

1 row updated.

commit
/

Commit complete.

alter session set edition = R3
/

Session altered.

select empno
      ,first_name
      ,last_name
  from emp
 where empno = 7654
/

     EMPNO FIRST_NAME LAST_NAME
---------- ---------- ------------------------
      7654            Widlake
```

Invalid Cross-Edition Triggers

As mentioned earlier, creating cross-edition triggers in a disabled mode is a best practice. The reason is that when the trigger is created and turns out to be invalid, users of older editions (such as R1 and ORA$BASE) will immediately run into the following exception when trying to do DML:

```
update emp
       *
ERROR at line 1:
ORA-04098: trigger 'SCOTT.EMP_R2_R3_FWD_XED' is invalid and failed re-validation
```

When the cross-edition trigger is created in a disabled mode, this exception will not occur, not even if the trigger is invalid.

Only records that are touched (inserted or updated) by the users of the older edition will get the LAST_NAME set by the trigger, and records that are not touched will not have the LAST_NAME column set in the new edition.

One possibility of getting the data in sync between the two editions is to go back to the old edition and perform an update on the editioning view, thereby triggering the forward cross-edition trigger and thus filling in the LAST_NAME column in the new edition. The downside of this method is that you need to switch editions when you are installing the new software. This can be confusing and error prone.

Another method, while staying in the same (new) edition, is to trigger the forward cross-edition trigger by updating the underlying table in a special way. Note that cross-edition triggers don't fire when you update the underlying table. With DBMS_SQL you can trigger the cross-edition trigger when updating the underlying table. The parse procedure within the DBMS_SQL package contains an argument called **apply_crossedition_trigger**, which allows you to pass in the name of the cross-edition trigger that needs to fire in order to sync the data.

```
declare
   c number := dbms_sql.open_cursor();
   x number;
begin
   dbms_sql.parse
      (c => c
      ,language_flag => dbms_sql.native
      ,statement => 'UPDATE "_emp"
                            SET EMPNO = EMPNO'
      ,apply_crossedition_trigger => 'EMP_R2_R3_Fwd_Xed'
      );
   x := dbms_sql.execute(c);
   dbms_sql.close_cursor(c);
   commit;
end;
/
```

The statement that is passed in to DBMS_SQL is a bogus update statement against the underlying table. The name of the cross-edition trigger is provided for the **apply_crossedition_trigger** argument that needs to be applied. Triggering the cross-edition trigger will synchronize the data between the old and new editions.

When data is entered using the upgraded version of the application, and there are still users using the pre-upgrade version, the ENAME column is maintained. Similar to the forward cross-edition triggers method, there is also a so-called reverse cross-edition trigger. This will transform the entered FIRST_NAME column into the ENAME column.

```
create or replace trigger EMP_R3_R2_Rve_Xed
before insert or update of last_name on "_emp"
for each row
reverse crossedition
disable
begin
   if length (:new.last_name) > 10
   then
      raise_application_error (-20000
        ,'During the hot rollover it is not possible to enter more'||
        ' than ten (10) characters for the Last Name'
        );
   else
      :new.ename := :new.last_name;
   end if;
end EMP_R3_R2_Rve_Xed;
/

Trigger created.
```

The reverse cross-edition trigger is also created against the underlying table, just like the forward cross-edition trigger. Including the phrase **reverse crossedition** signals that the trigger should fire when changes are made in the latest edition. This trigger, similar to the forward cross-edition trigger, is created in a disabled state. The transformation of the LAST_NAME column into the ENAME column is done in the executable section of the trigger, keeping in mind that the length of the columns is different. During the hot rollover period, both the pre- and post-upgrade applications must contain valid data that the user entered. Because of the size limitation in the pre-upgrade edition, the size must be checked in the cross-edition trigger. It might be tempting to alter the entered data, such as using SUBSTR to get the first ten characters, and save that as the ENAME, but that is not what the user entered and the data belongs to the user.

When the trigger is valid, it is switched to an enabled state:

```
alter trigger EMP_R3_R2_Rve_Xed enable
/

Trigger altered.
```

Cross-Edition Triggers Don't Always Fire

Updating the underlying base table does not activate the cross-edition triggers. In this code sample, the cross-edition triggers are in place but have no effect:

```
update "_emp"
   set empno = empno
/

14 rows updated.

commit;

Commit complete.

select empno
      ,first_name
      ,last_name
  from emp
/
     EMPNO FIRST_NAME LAST_NAME
---------- ---------- --------------------------
      7369
      7499
      7521
      7566
      7654
      7698
      7782
      7788
      7839
      7844
      7876
      7900
      7902
      7934

14 rows selected.
```

To verify the correct behavior, INSERT, UPDATE, and MERGE operations are executed in the following code:

```
insert into emp
   (first_name, last_name)
values
   ('Heli', 'Helskyaho')
/
```

```
1 row created.

update emp
   set first_name ='Arup'
      ,last_name = 'Nanda'
 where empno = 7839
/

1 row updated.

merge into emp e
using (select 8888    empno
             ,'Brendan' first_name
             ,'Tierney' last_name
         from dual
      ) new_emp
on (e.empno = new_emp.empno)
when not matched
then
   insert
      (empno
      ,first_name
      ,last_name)
   values
      (new_emp.empno
      ,new_emp.first_name
      ,new_emp.last_name)
/

1 row merged.

commit
/
Commit complete.
```

Attempting to enter a last name that exceeds the ten-character limit will raise an exception, as expected:

```
insert into emp
   (last_name)
values
   ('This name is too long');
insert into emp
            *
ERROR at line 1:
ORA-20000: During the hot rollover it is not possible to enter more than
ten (10) characters for the Last Name
ORA-06512: at "SCOTT.EMP_R3_R2_RVE_XED", line 4
ORA-04088: error during execution of trigger 'SCOTT.EMP_R3_R2_RVE_XED'
```

With both the forward cross-edition and reverse cross-edition triggers in place (both are in the latest edition and defined on the table), data is kept in sync between the pre-upgrade and post-upgrade editions:

```
alter session set edition = R2
/


Session altered.

select empno
      ,ename
  from emp
 where empno in (7654, 7839, 1, 2)
/

     EMPNO ENAME
---------- ----------
         1 Helskyaho
         2 Tierney
      7654 Widlake
      7839 Nanda



alter session set edition = r3
/

Session altered.

select empno
      ,first_name
      ,last_name
  from emp
 where empno in (7654, 7839, 1, 2)
/


     EMPNO FIRST_NAME LAST_NAME
---------- ---------- -------------------------
         1 Heli       Helskyaho
         2 Brendan    Tierney
      7654            Widlake
      7839 Arup       Nanda
```

In the query results, notice that employee 7654 doesn't have a FIRST_NAME. This can be explained by the fact that this employee's data was changed in the pre-update edition. This pre-update edition is unaware of the existence of a FIRST_NAME. There is no way that the pre-update edition can provide a value for this column, and therefore this column remains NULL.

With Oracle 12c, there is a third method to synchronize the data between the pre-upgrade and post-upgrade version. The built-in package DBMS_EDITIONS_UTILITIES contains a procedure called **set_null_column_values_to_expr**. With this procedure you can provide an expression used to transform the data. Only rows that are NULL are set with the expression. The expression is invoked when an update or query is performed.

To demonstrate its usage, we'll start by making a copy of the "_emp" table and call it EMP_COPY:

```
create table emp_copy
as
select *
  from "_emp"
/

Table created.
```

The next step for this demonstration is to clear the LAST_NAME column and set it to NULL:

```
update emp_copy
    set last_name = null
/

16 rows updated.

commit
/

Commit complete.
```

Now we can use the procedure **set_null_column_values_to_expr** from the built-in package DBMS_EDITIONS_UTILITIES, as follows:

```
declare
    expr constant varchar2(30) := 'LOWER (ENAME)';
begin
    dbms_editions_utilities.set_null_column_values_to_expr
        (table_name   => 'EMP_COPY'
        ,column_name  => 'last_name'
        ,expression   => expr);
end;
/
PL/SQL procedure successfully completed.
```

Notice that this utility is used on the table, not an editioning view. This utility does not replace the cross-edition triggers, and it only has a purpose during the transformation phase of the upgrade.

When the data is inspected, you can see that the expression is applied and that the values in the LAST_NAME column are lowercase when compared to the values in the ENAME column:

```
select ename
      ,last_name
  from emp_copy
/
```

```
ENAME      LAST_NAME
---------- ----------
SMITH      smith
ALLEN      allen
WARD       ward
JONES      jones
Widlake    widlake
BLAKE      blake
CLARK      clark
SCOTT      scott
Nanda      nanda
TURNER     turner
ADAMS      adams
JAMES      james
FORD       ford
MILLER     miller
Helskyaho  helskyaho
Tierney    tierney

16 rows selected.
```

To clean up this demonstration, the EMP_COPY table can be dropped:

```
drop table emp_copy purge
/

Table dropped.
```

After this step, all data in the new edition is in sync with the data in the old edition. And because of the forward cross-edition trigger, the ENAME column is kept in sync with the LAST_NAME column.

The built-in package DBMS_EDITIONS_UTILITIES contains another useful procedure: **set_editioning_views_read_only**. With this procedure, you can change all editioning views that depend on a certain table to **read only**, which is very useful when you want to prevent changes made in a post-upgrade edition before the cross-edition triggers are in place. After the necessary cross-edition triggers are in place, the same procedure can be used to make the editioning view **read write** again.

```
select view_name
      ,read_only
      ,edition_name
  from all_views_ae
 where owner = user
/

VIEW_NAME          R EDITION_NAME
------------------ - ------------
EMP                N R1
EMP                N R2
EMP                N R3
```

In the previous output, the **read_only** property of the editioning views is set to N, meaning that the editioning views are in read-write mode.

```
begin
    dbms_editions_utilities.set_editioning_views_read_only (
        table_name => '_emp'
       ,owner      => user
       ,read_only  => true);
end;
/

PL/SQL procedure successfully completed.
```

By specifying TRUE for the **read_only** argument, we set all the editioning views that depend on the "_emp" table to read only, thus preventing DML on them:

```
select view_name
      ,read_only
      ,edition_name
  from all_views_ae
 where owner = user
/

VIEW_NAME                       R EDITION_NAME
------------------------------- - -----------------------------
EMP                             Y R1
EMP                             Y R2
EMP                             Y R3
```

The output shows Y for the **read_only** property of the editioning views, regardless of the edition where they occur. To make the editioning views available in read-write mode, pass in FALSE for the **read_only** argument:

```
begin
    dbms_editions_utilities.set_editioning_views_read_only (
        table_name => '_emp'
       ,owner      => user
       ,read_only  => false);
end;
/

PL/SQL procedure successfully completed.
```

Lost Update

When we are performing transformations of data from a pre-upgrade to a post-upgrade situation, it is vital that all transactions being performed by other sessions are completed. Because of the way Oracle works with its multiversioned read consistency model, this can be quite a challenge. During the transformation phase of an upgrade, we don't want to lose updates done by other sessions.

The built-in package DBMS_UTILITY contains a function that signals when all transactions are either committed or rolled back. The name of the function is **wait_on_pending_dml**.

To demonstrate the way it works, two database sessions are needed. In one of the sessions a table is created that will be used for the experiment:

```
create table s
    (x number)
/

Table created.
```

In this session, the following PL/SQL block is executed. This block will insert a value in the table, and to slow things down a call to **dbms_lock.sleep** is performed:

```
begin
    for i in 1..100 loop
        insert into s (x)
        values (dbms_random.value);
        dbms_lock.sleep(.1);
    end loop;
    commit;
end;
/

PL/SQL procedure successfully completed.
```

Finally, a commit is done to release the locks on the table.

While that PL/SQL block is running, the following code is executed in another database session:

```
declare
    l_bool boolean;
    l_scn number;
begin
    l_scn := timestamp_to_scn (systimestamp);
    l_bool := dbms_utility.wait_on_pending_dml
                (tables => 's'
                ,timeout => null
                ,scn => l_scn);
    dbms_output.put_line( 'scn:  ' || l_scn );
    dbms_output.put_line( 'now we start to do our thing' );
    l_scn := timestamp_to_scn (systimestamp);
    dbms_output.put_line( 'scn:  ' || l_scn );
end;
/
```

At the start of execution, the System Change Number (SCN) is stored in a local variable. Next, the call to the DBMS_UTILITY package is made, telling the execution to hold until all pending transactions are done. When calling the **wait_on_pending_dml** function, it is possible to specify multiple tables. It is also possible to set a timeout specifying the number of seconds to wait; when you don't specify a particular value, it will wait indefinitely. The last argument when calling the **wait_on_pending_dml** function specifies the SCN to which transactions must have begun to be considered relevant for this request.

For demonstration purposes, DBMS_OUTPUT is used instead of some real actions. To see that the SCN has changed from the beginning of the PL/SQL block compared to when it finishes, the code determines the SCN once again.

At first this PL/SQL block will hang, waiting for the other session to complete. When it completes, you might see a result similar to the following:

```
scn:  13737474
now we start to do our thing
scn:  13737485
```

Notice that the SCN has changed during the execution of the PL/SQL block.

Retiring the Old Edition

After the application has been upgraded and everything is working as expected, the old version of the application is no longer needed. When the old version of the application is still accessible to the users, there is a chance it might still be used. Obviously, there are reasons why this shouldn't be allowed. The old version of the application should be retired in such a way that it is no longer available to the users.

Although it is very uncommon to have multiple editions running side by side for extended periods of time, you can do this. However, the transition period between upgrading the application and retiring the old application is usually kept as short as possible.

To prevent new sessions from being set up and connecting to the old edition, simply revoke the USE privilege for every user and role in the database. In the following full example, the USE privilege is granted to database user ALEX and then this privilege is revoked. When user ALEX wants to connect to the edition from which the USE privilege is revoked, an exception is raised, and it is not possible to set up a database session, thus preventing the user from accessing the retired edition.

```
conn sys/oracle@pdborcl as sysdba

create user alex identified by alex
/
grant connect to alex
/

grant use on edition r1 to alex
/

Grant succeeded.
```

Granting the USE privilege enables user ALEX to use the edition. The following connection is made using SQL*Plus, and the edition is specified in the connect string:

```
conn alex/alex@pdborcl edition = R1
```

On a similar note, privileges that can be granted can also be revoked. This is shown in the following code:

```
conn sys/oracle@pdborcl as sysdba

revoke use on edition r1 from alex
/

Revoke succeeded.
```

Now that the USE privilege is revoked from the user ALEX, it is not possible to create a connection to the database using the R1 edition. Connecting to the ORA$BASE edition, however, is still possible.

```
conn alex/alex@pdborcl edition = ora$base

Connected.

conn alex/alex@pdborcl edition = r1
ERROR:
ORA-38802: edition does not exist


Warning: You are no longer connected to ORACLE.
```

Revoking the USE privilege prevents users from connecting to the edition, effectively retiring it.

To Drop or Not to Drop?

Editions can be dropped when it concerns a root edition or a leaf edition. It is not possible to drop an edition, however, when it has a child edition.

When you are deploying the post-upgrade application in the privacy of the new edition and things don't go as planned (for example, certain objects are invalid), it might be tempting to drop this edition and start from scratch. But why would you do that? You can continue in this edition and fix whatever needs to be fixed. Dropping the edition could leave artifacts behind, such as changes to the underlying table. There might be valid reasons for reverting back to a previous edition, but keep in mind that these artifacts could be left behind. The same holds true for any changes made to the data.

To revert back to a previous edition, we can remove the child edition by dropping it. This can be done by any user who has the DROP ANY EDITION privilege:

```
drop edition r3 cascade
/

Edition dropped.
```

With the CASCADE specified in the DROP statement, objects that are created in this edition will also be dropped.

```
drop edition r3
/
drop edition r3
*
ERROR at line 1:
ORA-38811: need CASCADE option to drop edition that has actual objects
```

If an edition is still in use by a session, an exception is raised, as shown in the following code:

```
drop edition r3 cascade
/
drop edition r3 cascade
            *
ERROR at line 1:
ORA-38805: edition is in use
```

This method is ideal when it is needed to reverse an upgrade.

It is possible to remove a retired edition as well, although this is not necessary. Having multiple retired editions doesn't interfere with performance because references are resolved at compile time. It is advisable that you remove all the objects from the pre-upgrade edition as they are no longer needed, as well as the cross-edition triggers from the post-upgrade edition. This is just a matter of good housekeeping.

Changing the Default Edition

If you are running at least Oracle Database 11*g*R2, you have the default ORA$BASE edition. When a connection is set up and the edition is not specified, the default edition will be used. Changing the edition for a session will require an ALTER SESSION command (as seen many times in the chapter so far).

By issuing the following command, you can change the default edition. For this to work, you will need the ALTER DATABASE privilege, as well as the USE object privilege WITH GRANT OPTION on the specified edition. Typically the DBA will take care of this.

```
alter database default edition = r1
/

Database altered.
```

The default edition for the entire database is immediately changed. All object privileges from the edition are revoked from all users, except SYS. At the same time, the USE privilege is granted to PUBLIC.

When you are logged in as a normal user (not SYS), you can see this behavior. When querying ALL_EDITIONS, you can still see ORA$BASE with the usable indicator of YES.

Attempting to change your session to the ORA$BASE edition will produce an exception stating that the edition doesn't exist:

```
select edition_name
      ,parent_edition_name
      ,usable
  from all_editions
/
```

```
EDITION_NAME                     PARENT_EDITION_NAME              USA
------------------------------   ------------------------------   ---
ORA$BASE                                                          YES
R3                               R2                               YES
R1                               ORA$BASE                         YES
R2                               R1                               YES


alter session set edition = ora$base
/
ERROR:
ORA-38802: edition does not exist
```

Connecting as SYS can alter its session to an edition to ORA$BASE, and even make it the default edition again:

```
conn sys/oracle@pdborcl as sysdba
Connected.

show edition

EDITION
-----------------------------
R1

alter session set edition = ora$base
/

Session altered.

alter database default edition = ora$base
/

Database altered.
```

SQL Developer and EBR

Oracle SQL Developer is a free integrated development environment (IDE) that allows you to develop database applications. Many other IDEs are commercially available, and each one has its own strengths and weaknesses.

SQL Developer boasts support for the latest features of the Oracle database, and new features that are added to SQL and PL/SQL are quickly supported in the tool. Commercial tools will always lag behind.

When connected to Oracle Database 11g or higher, you'll see several folders related to edition-based redefinition. Currently it is not possible to specify which edition the connection needs to use. This was verified on Version 4.1.1.19.

In Figure 5-1, the SQL Developer navigator is shown with the EBR-specific folders highlighted. The folders specifically related to edition-based redefinition are Editioning Views, Crossedition Triggers, and Editions.

Right-clicking the folders reveals the functionality that can be performed. The only actions that can currently (SQL Developer Version 4.1.1.19) be performed with editioning views and

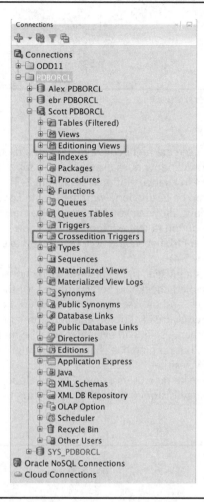

FIGURE 5-1.   *SQL Developer navigator*

cross-edition triggers are refresh, clear filter, and apply filter. Editioning views and cross-edition triggers are visible in the folder and can be edited.

Right-clicking the folder Editions reveals more functionality:

- Open
- Set Current Edition
- Create Edition
- Drop Edition

In the Editions folder, there will always be at least one edition. Clicking Open in the context menu will show details about the edition, such as name, parent edition, comments, and whether it is usable.

FIGURE 5-2. *Edition hierarchy*

In Figure 5-2, you can see the hierarchy of the editions used throughout this chapter.

The Set Current Edition window does exactly what it says: it sets the edition similar to the ALTER SESSION statement to change editions (see Figure 5-3).

Creating an edition can be easily done with the Create Edition option in the context menu. This opens a modal window, allowing you to enter the name for the edition you want to create. After you click the Apply button, a leaf edition to the edition on which you invoked the context menu is created. If you want to inspect the SQL before you execute it, click the SQL tab in the modal window (see Figure 5-4).

To edition-enable existing users, right-click the user, choose Edit User from the context menu, and check the Edition Enabled checkbox. See Figure 5-5 for the modal window that will be opened. Apply the changes, and the user is edition enabled. Keep in mind that the checkbox is not disabled when the user is already edition enabled. It might appear that you can uncheck the checkbox and apply the changes—it will even give you the message "Successfully processed SQL command" as a response, but nothing has changed. You might recall from earlier that edition-enabling a user is a one-way street.

It is also possible to create new users using SQL Developer and edition-enable them at the same time. The methodology is similar to editing an existing user.

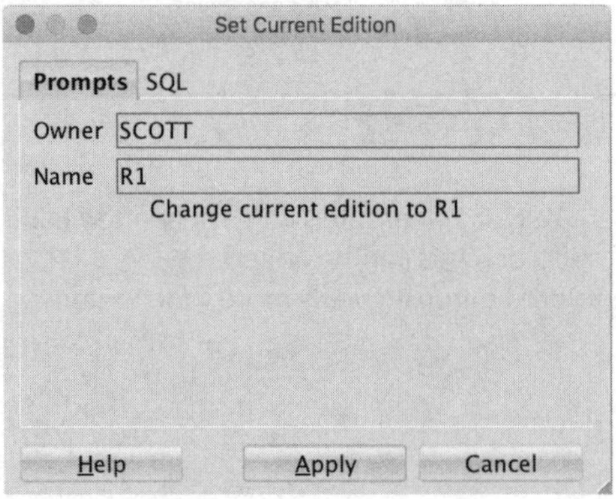

FIGURE 5-3. *Changing the current edition*

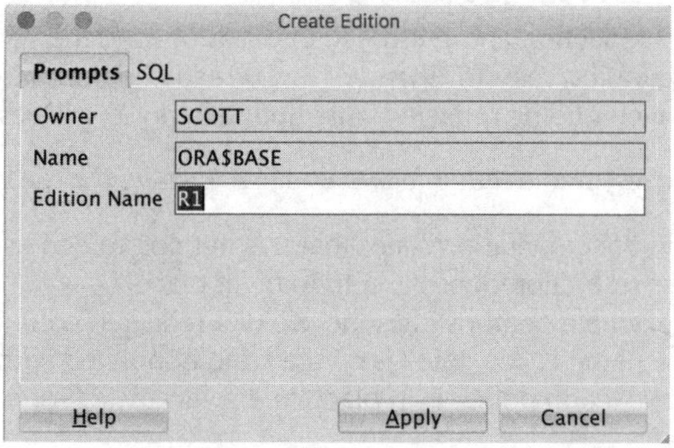

FIGURE 5-4. *Create Edition dialog*

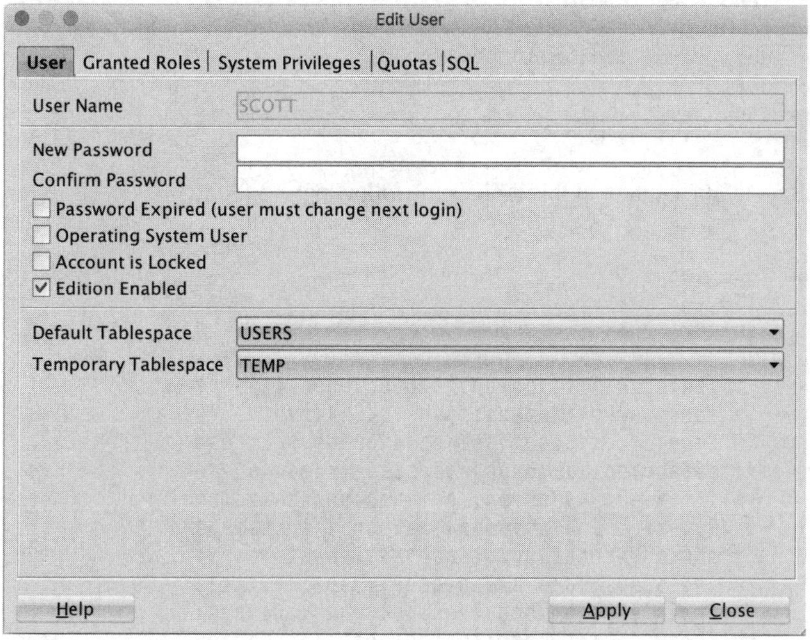

FIGURE 5-5. *Edit User window*

EBR and DBMS_REDACT

A full description of redaction and DBMS_REDACT is beyond the scope of this chapter. For a full description of these topics, refer to Chapter 13. Currently edition-based redefinition does not support editioning views being redacted. Attempting to do so will result in the following:

```
ORA-28061: This object cannot have a data redaction policy defined on it.
```

Even though the documentation states that it is not possible to use redacted columns in an editioning view, this restriction doesn't seem to be in place.

The following example demonstrates the use of a redacted column in an editioning view. A two-column table named "_cc_info" is created and populated with random numeric data for the CC column. A redaction policy is in place to display an "X" for each number.

```
create table "_cc_info"
(id number primary key
,cc varchar2(40))
/
```

Populate the table with some sample data:

```
insert into "_cc_info"
select rownum
       ,dbms_random.value(10000, 20000)
  from dual
 connect by level <= 10
/
```

Currently the content of this table is the following:

```
select *
  from "_cc_info"
/
        ID CC
---------- ----------------------------------------
         1 11875.7413173700680728205803909284385697
         2 16249.9662446058231634737545844229270079
         3 16993.4407700507756142394702309896413894
         4 19380.1501137402864895035535444864400766
         5 11913.5726493557341380137924652356236181
         6 17962.7101747457650349924900319106533948
         7 15943.7840001509186556978211256520456239
         8 19035.5514564876905888596747993129711433
         9 15396.5659809290034788653467547401472234
        10 18577.2155452575615231791283814064970397

10 rows selected.
```

Apply a redaction policy to the table to mask the CC column:

```
begin
    dbms_redact.add_policy
        (object_schema  => user
        ,object_name    => '"_cc_info"'
        ,policy_name    => 'Hide Creditcard'
        ,expression     => '1=1'
        ,column_name    => 'CC'
        ,function_type  => dbms_redact.regexp
        ,regexp_pattern => dbms_redact.re_pattern_any_digit
        ,regexp_replace_string => 'X'
        );
end;
/
PL/SQL procedure successfully completed.
```

Querying the table shows the following:

```
select *
  from "_cc_info"
/

        ID CC
---------- ----------------------------------------
         1 XXXXX.XXXXXXXXXXXXXXXXXXXXXXXXXXXXXXXXXXX
         2 XXXXX.XXXXXXXXXXXXXXXXXXXXXXXXXXXXXXXXXXX
         3 XXXXX.XXXXXXXXXXXXXXXXXXXXXXXXXXXXXXXXXXX
         4 XXXXX.XXXXXXXXXXXXXXXXXXXXXXXXXXXXXXXXXXX
         5 XXXXX.XXXXXXXXXXXXXXXXXXXXXXXXXXXXXXXXXXX
         6 XXXXX.XXXXXXXXXXXXXXXXXXXXXXXXXXXXXXXXXXX
         7 XXXXX.XXXXXXXXXXXXXXXXXXXXXXXXXXXXXXXXXXX
         8 XXXXX.XXXXXXXXXXXXXXXXXXXXXXXXXXXXXXXXXXX
         9 XXXXX.XXXXXXXXXXXXXXXXXXXXXXXXXXXXXXXXXXX
        10 XXXXX.XXXXXXXXXXXXXXXXXXXXXXXXXXXXXXXXXXX

10 rows selected.
```

Now that the redaction policy is in place, let's create an editioning view using the table:

```
create editioning view cc_info
as
select *
  from "_cc_info"
/

View created.
```

The editioning view is created and can be queried:

```
select *
  from cc_info
/

       ID CC
---------- ----------------------------------------
        1 XXXXX.XXXXXXXXXXXXXXXXXXXXXXXXXXXXXXXXXXXX
        2 XXXXX.XXXXXXXXXXXXXXXXXXXXXXXXXXXXXXXXXXXX
        3 XXXXX.XXXXXXXXXXXXXXXXXXXXXXXXXXXXXXXXXXXX
        4 XXXXX.XXXXXXXXXXXXXXXXXXXXXXXXXXXXXXXXXXXX
        5 XXXXX.XXXXXXXXXXXXXXXXXXXXXXXXXXXXXXXXXXXX
        6 XXXXX.XXXXXXXXXXXXXXXXXXXXXXXXXXXXXXXXXXXX
        7 XXXXX.XXXXXXXXXXXXXXXXXXXXXXXXXXXXXXXXXXXX
        8 XXXXX.XXXXXXXXXXXXXXXXXXXXXXXXXXXXXXXXXXXX
        9 XXXXX.XXXXXXXXXXXXXXXXXXXXXXXXXXXXXXXXXXXX
       10 XXXXX.XXXXXXXXXXXXXXXXXXXXXXXXXXXXXXXXXXXX

10 rows selected.
```

Performing DML using the editioning view works as expected:

```
update cc_info
   set cc = 1234
 where id= 3
/

1 row updated.

select *
  from cc_info
 where id = 3
/

       ID CC
---------- ----------------------------------------
        3 XXXX
```

According to the documentation, edition-based redefinition and DBMS_REDACT don't mix. Experimenting with both seems to work. Because this behavior is not documented, be cautious implementing it.

Summary

In this chapter a solution is outlined to reduce, and maybe even eliminate completely, planned downtime. Until Oracle Database release 11gR2, planned downtime was incurred when you upgraded your custom application. Edition-based redefinition solves this planned downtime issue.

Deploying an upgraded application in the privacy of an edition is key. When the upgrade is completed, users are switched over to the post-upgrade application without experiencing downtime.

You can use several levels of complexity, depending on your needs. These range from simply replacing PL/SQL objects in different editions to creating multiple editioning views with cross-edition triggers to keep data synchronized across editions. The method for retiring old editions was discussed as well.

Finally, SQL Developer is shown to have somewhat-limited support for edition-based redefinition. The combination of data redaction and edition-based redefinition is explored, however, and found to be working even though the documentation says otherwise.

PART
III

Essential Everyday
Advanced PL/SQL

CHAPTER
6

Running PL/SQL from SQL

I t is natural to think about running SQL from PL/SQL—after all, PL/SQL was created to provide a procedural language within (and alongside) the Oracle RDBMS, in order to be able to enhance SQL with all of the looping, logical, and exception-handling constructs of a traditional programming language. However, PL/SQL also allows you to extend the capabilities of SQL within Oracle. As a programmer, you are able to create your own functions that can be called from SQL, almost as if they are part of the SQL language. This allows you to extend the capabilities of SQL with all the benefits of PL/SQL. For example, you can do the following:

- Write code to carry out a specific, repeated task once in a compartmentalized manner.
- Call the code from any SQL DML statement you wish.
- Store the new code and business logic within the database where it is used (and backed up).
- Use all the features of PL/SQL you are familiar with.

In this chapter we first discuss the differences and, just as importantly, the similarities between PL/SQL and SQL standard functions, how Oracle implements the standard PL/SQL functions, and how we as programmers can extend SQL by creating our own functions. We, of course, give you examples of creating your own PL/SQL functions and using them within SQL.

Several aspects of creating your own PL/SQL functions are often overlooked. You need to be aware of the potential impact that calling PL/SQL functions from SQL can have on the point-in-time integrity of your application and why ensuring that your new functions are deterministic is important. We also highlight the performance impact caused by calling PL/SQL from SQL due to context switching, as well as methods for reducing this impact. This includes two new features introduced with 12c. We also cover methods for improving performance by caching values returned by functions, especially with the relatively new 11g function results cache.

SQL and PL/SQL Functions

Before diving into how you extend SQL with user-defined PL/SQL functions, let's cover what standard SQL and PL/SQL functions actually are.

We use SQL functions all the time within our SQL queries and other DML, often to modify the values we are selecting out of tables or inserting into them, but we can use SQL functions anywhere in a SQL statement where a value or expression is valid. When you use commands such as INSTR, TRIM, UPPER, and SUBSTR, these are all functions built into the SQL language. The following code shows an old script for looking at tablespace contents and listing SYS/SYSTEM objects first; it uses SQL functions in the SELECT, WHERE, and ORDER_BY sections:

```
select ds.tablespace_name                        ts_name
      ,ds.owner                                   owner
      ,rtrim(ds.segment_name
          ||' '||ds.partition_name)               segment_name
      ,substr(ds.segment_type,1,7)                typ
      ,to_char(ds.extents,'999')                  exts
      ,to_char(ds.bytes/1024,'99,999,999')        size_k
      ,to_char(do.created,'YYYY-MM-DD')           cre_date
      ,to_char(do.last_ddl_time,'MM-DD HH24:MI:SS') last_mod
```

```
from sys.dba_segments ds
    ,sys.dba_objects  do
where ds.tablespace_name             like upper(nvl('&ts_name','whoops')||'%')
and    do.object_name                = ds.segment_name
and    do.owner                      = ds.owner
and    nvl(ds.partition_name,'X~') = NVL(do.subobject_name,'X~')
order by 1, decode(owner,'SYS'    ,'AAAAAA'
                         ,'SYSTEM','AAAAAB'
                         ,ds.owner)
        ,3
```

Nearly all functions available in SQL are also built into the PL/SQL language, and that can lead to a little confusion over what's a SQL function and what's a PL/SQL function. Here is how we think of it: If we reference a function within the SQL statement and we do not have to say which package it is in, it is a native SQL function. If we have to state the package it is in (that is, *PACKAGE.NAME,* examples being **dbms_lock.sleep** and **dbms_utility.get_hash_value**), then it is a PL/SQL function. If a function is used outside of a SQL statement in PL/SQL, then obviously it is a PL/SQL function.

Most non-aggregate SQL functions are also available in PL/SQL and work in exactly the same way. This allows you to use the functions in a PL/SQL declaration or expression just as you do in a section of a SQL statement, without resorting to what we used to do in the dark ages—use a dummy select from DUAL to get them. In PL/SQL, you would not do the following:

```
select upper(substr(variable,3,8)) into :v1 from dual
```

Instead, you would simply write this:

```
v1:= upper(substr(variable,3,8)
```

It is still not uncommon to stumble across people doing this:

```
select sysdate into v_date from dual
```

This is odd because you have been able to say **v_date :=sysdate** for two decades. If you ever use the FROM DUAL method for simple SQL functions or for getting sysdate, systimestamp, user, and so on… just don't. It's inefficient (as you will see soon) and almost always unnecessary.

When you use a "standard" function in PL/SQL (**to_char, substr, decode, least, greatest**, and so on) that is not contained within a SQL statement, you are actually using a PL/SQL built-in function. These functions are all defined in the SYS-owned package STANDARD, which, along with DBMS_STANDARD, is created when you create a database. These functions contain much of the basic functionality of PL/SQL.

STANDARD and DBMS_STANDARD

The SYS-owned PL/SQL packages STANDARD and DBMS_STANDARD contain a considerable number of procedures and functions that most people assume are in some way coded into the PL/SQL language itself, at a low level and in a way that cannot be examined. Well, anyone with access to the database can actually use **describe** on these two packages from SQL*Plus and, for STANDARD, look at the package text via **all_source** (you should also be able to do this with whatever PL/SQL development GUI you use). Unlike many other built-in PL/SQL packages, the code is not wrapped and hidden from prying eyes. The following code uses **desc sys.standard** from an account that only has CONNECT and RESOURCE privileges (note that only parts of the output are shown):

```
describe sys.standard
FUNCTION  SYS$DSINTERVALSUBTRACT RETURNS INTERVAL DAY TO SECOND
 Argument Name                    Type                    In/Out Default?
 ------------------------------   ---------------------   ------ --------
 LEFT                             TIMESTAMP               IN
 RIGHT                            TIMESTAMP               IN
FUNCTION  SYS$DSINTERVALSUBTRACT RETURNS INTERVAL DAY TO SECOND
...
FUNCTION ADD_MONTHS RETURNS DATE
 Argument Name                    Type                    In/Out Default?
 ------------------------------   ---------------------   ------ --------
 LEFT                             DATE                    IN
 RIGHT                            NUMBER                  IN
...
FUNCTION ASCII RETURNS NUMBER(38)
 Argument Name                    Type                    In/Out Default?
 ------------------------------   ---------------------   ------ --------
 CH                               VARCHAR2                IN
...
FUNCTION SQRT RETURNS BINARY_DOUBLE
 Argument Name                    Type                    In/Out Default?
 ------------------------------   ---------------------   ------ --------
 D                                BINARY_DOUBLE           IN
...
FUNCTION SUBSTR RETURNS VARCHAR2
 Argument Name                    Type                    In/Out Default?
 ------------------------------   ---------------------   ------ --------
 STR1                             VARCHAR2                IN
 POS                              BINARY_INTEGER          IN
 LEN                              BINARY_INTEGER          IN     DEFAULT
...
FUNCTION SYSDATE RETURNS DATE
FUNCTION SYSTIMESTAMP RETURNS TIMESTAMP WITH TIME ZONE
FUNCTION SYS_AT_TIME_ZONE RETURNS TIME WITH TIME ZONE
 Argument Name                    Type                    In/Out Default?
 ------------------------------   ---------------------   ------ --------
 T                                TIME WITH TIME ZONE     IN
 I                                VARCHAR2                IN
```

Even SYSDATE is a PL/SQL function defined in the SYS.STANDARD package. DBMS_STANDARD contains a lot less than STANDARD, but it does include the definitions of a lot of the data types we assume are just part of PL/SQL. Part of this is shown here:

```
package STANDARD AUTHID CURRENT_USER is        -- careful on this line
                                               -- SED edit occurs!

  /********** Types and subtypes, do not reorder **********/
  type BOOLEAN is (FALSE, TRUE);
```

```
type DATE is DATE_BASE;

type NUMBER is NUMBER_BASE;
subtype FLOAT is NUMBER; -- NUMBER(126)
subtype REAL is FLOAT; -- FLOAT(63)
subtype "DOUBLE PRECISION" is FLOAT;
subtype INTEGER is NUMBER(38,0);
subtype INT is INTEGER;
subtype SMALLINT is NUMBER(38,0);
subtype DECIMAL is NUMBER(38,0);
subtype NUMERIC is DECIMAL;
subtype DEC is DECIMAL;
```

The procedures **commit, savepoint, rollback_nr, rollback_sv,** and **commit_cm** can be found in the DBMS_STANDARD package. These are not the SQL commands but rather the procedures used from within PL/SQL. You won't find a package body for DBMS_STANDARD because, we believe, all entries in the package specification are types or functions/procedures that lead to C functions, via the ADA-like pragma directive. (If you did not know, PL/SQL is based on the ADA language.) The following shows one of these procedure specification stubs in the DBMS_STANDARD package specification, pointing to a C program:

```
procedure commit;
pragma interface (C, commit);
```

There is no procedure code for **commit** written in PL/SQL in an associated package body. The procedure **commit** is written in C and is not available to us to view.

However, there is a package body for SYS.STANDARD, and it is interesting to have a look at it. In the following code (a small section from that package body), you can see that SYSDATE is actually a call to a C function to get the system clock time; if it fails, it resorts to using the old SELECT SYSDATE FROM DUAL method. (Oracle does not resort back to that fallback on any modern system; it's a last-ditch save if you are running on some really old or obscure hardware.)

```
function pessdt return DATE;
  pragma interface (c,pessdt);

-- Bug 1287775: back to calling ICD.
-- Special: if the ICD raises ICD_UNABLE_TO_COMPUTE, that means we should do
-- the old 'SELECT SYSDATE FROM DUAL;' thing.  This allows us to do the
-- SELECT from PL/SQL rather than having to do it from C (within the ICD.)
function sysdate return date is
  d date;
begin
  d := pessdt;
  return d;
exception
  when ICD_UNABLE_TO_COMPUTE then
    select sysdate into d from sys.dual;
    return d;
end;
```

One thing that is special about SYS.STANDARD and SYS.DBMS_STANDARD is that there is no need to include the package name when referencing any of the procedures, functions, or types they hold. If Oracle sees a locally qualified object reference (a procedure, function, or type that lacks a code block, package, or stored procedure/function portion to the name), then Oracle looks for a local object defined in the current block and then the parent PL/SQL block(s). If it does not find it there, Oracle looks for the object in SYS.STANDARD and SYS.DBMS_STANDARD. This does open the possibility for you to create your own local version of, say, SYSDATE:

```
-- show_date_override
declare
sysdate varchar2(20) := '31-DEC-4713BC';
begin
declare
out_text varchar2(100);
begin
  select to_char(sysdate) into out_text from dual;
  dbms_output.put_line (out_text);
end;
end;
/

@show_date_override
31-DEC-4713BC
```

Here, not only do we create a local variable called SYSDATE that overrides the built-in variable, but we set it to a different data type so that we can give it a value that is not even allowed in Oracle—Oracle DATE values cannot be before 01-JAN-4712BC.

Note that although replacing built-in variables with your own is possible, *it is a very unwise thing to do*. Just because something is possible does not mean it is sensible to do it. Debugging code where standard PL/SQL variables have been overridden could be very tricky. If you turn on compilation warnings (see Chapter 7 for more information on compilation warnings), you will see the error code PLW-05004 if you ever define something with the same name as an object in the STANDARD package.

As stated earlier, most functions available in SQL are also available in PL/SQL, which greatly aids reusing code snippets using these functions between the two languages. A list of SQL functions not available in PL/SQL can be found in the 12c Database PL/SQL Language Reference Guide, "PL/SQL Language Fundamentals." Up to version 12.1.0.2, this includes a small number of single-row (scalar) SQL functions that are not available in PL/SQL—namely, **nvl2**, **decode**, and **width_bucket**. They have simply not been included in SYS.STANDARD or SYS.DBMS_STANDARD. It is not difficult to code around at least the first two of these missing functions, but although it is usually the case that you can take an expression containing scalar functions used in a SQL statement and simply drop it into PL/SQL, it is a little annoying that you cannot do this when any of these three have been used. For example, the SQL function construct in:

```
SELECT NVL(SUBSTR(POST_CODE,1,INSTR(POST_CODE,' ',1)-1),'UNKNOWN') from table
```

can be copied and used directly in PL/SQL:

```
v_region:= NVL(SUBSTR(v_postcode) ,1,INSTR(v_postcode),' ',1)-1),'UNKNOWN');
```

but this cannot be done with any expression using **decode**, **nvl2**, or **width_bucket**.

We won't go any further into SYS.STANDARD and SYS.DBMS_STANDARD here. However, you now know that you can look at them and see many interesting things that you probably did not think were so exposed or available.

Do Not Attempt in Any Way to Alter SYS.STANDARD or DBMS_STANDARD
You have just seen that SYS.STANDARD and SYS.DBMS_STANDARD are stored PL/SQL. You might wonder if you can alter them or add anything to them. Do not be tempted to try this. These packages are core to how PL/SQL works, and if you touch them in any way, more than likely things will go horribly wrong. Further, Oracle Corporation will likely refuse to help you sort it out. Feel free to look at these packages, but do not touch them.

Simplifying Nested SQL Functions with PL/SQL

You probably know that you can use multiple SQL functions together, nest functions within functions (within functions (within functions (within functions))), and achieve relatively complex results. As an example, here we have a simple table called PERSON that we use in training courses. The code to create and populate this table with as much data as you like is available on the book's website (http://community.oraclepressbooks.com/downloads.html).

```
Name                                     Null?     Type
---------------------------------------- --------  ---------------
PERS_ID                                  NOT NULL  NUMBER(8)
SURNAME                                  NOT NULL  VARCHAR2(30)
FIRST_FORENAME                           NOT NULL  VARCHAR2(30)
SECOND_FORENAME                                    VARCHAR2(30)
PERS_TITLE                                         VARCHAR2(10)
SEX_IND                                  NOT NULL  CHAR(1)
DOB                                                DATE
ADDR_ID                                            NUMBER(8)
STAFF_IND                                          CHAR(1)
LAST_CONTACT_ID                                    NUMBER(8)
PERS_COMMENT                                       VARCHAR2(2000)
```

This table has four columns holding parts of a person's name: SURNAME, FIRST_FORENAME, SECOND FORENAME, and PERS_TITLE. These values are held in all-uppercase format.

```
PERS_TITLE FIRST_FORENAME  SECOND_FORENAME SURNAME
---------- --------------- --------------- ---------------
MR         LENNY           TOBY            THOMAS
MRS        VALERIE         AMANDA          WILLIAMS
MRS        SOPHIE          KATE            SINGH
MRS        AMBER           VICTORIA        MAHOUD
MR         LEWIS                           HUGHES
MRS        AMELIA          NICKIE          JONES
MR         DECLAN          JONATHAN        HALL
MR         SAMUEL          ASHFAQ          PREFECT
MR         JOHN                            WEBBER
MR         JAMES           STEVEN          SMITH)
```

With textual data, you'll often want to store it as all uppercase to simplify searching. Oracle is case sensitive when it applies WHERE clauses—in other words, WIDLAKE does not equal Widlake does not equal widlake.

If we do a case-insensitive search such as

```
where upper(SURNAME)=upper(search_string))
```

This invalidates the use of indexes on the SURNAME column unless we create a function-based index to match the search function. We have little control over how text is capitalized when we allow data to be entered manually in mixed case, so in general practice we don't allow mixed case. We store most user-entered textual information in uppercase. However, when we produce letters or e-mails to people, we want their names in the traditional style of the first letter of the surname and first forename being in uppercase with the rest in lowercase and (depending on geographic locality) the initials of the middle name. This can quite easily be done by nesting standard functions, such as this:

```
--ch6_t1
select pers_title title,    first_forename    ,second_forename    , surname
      ,substr(pers_title,1,1)||lower(substr(pers_title,2))||' '
      ||substr(first_forename,1,1)||lower(substr(first_forename,2))||' '
      ||nvl2(second_forename,substr(second_forename,1,1)||' ',null)
      ||substr(surname,1,1)||lower(substr(surname,2))        Display_Name
from person
where pers_id > 100100
and rownum < 10
```

TITLE	first_fn	secon_fn	SURNAME	DISPLAY_NAME
MR	HARRISON	RICHARD	HARRIS	Mr Harrison R Harris
MRS	ANNEKA	RACHAEL	HARRIS	Mrs Anneka R Harris
MRS	NICKIE	ALISON	ELWIG	Mrs Nickie A Elwig
MASTER	JAMES	DENZIL	ELWIG	Master James D Elwig
MR	JEFF		GARCIA	Mr Jeff Garcia
MRS	SARAH	GILLIAN	GARCIA	Mrs Sarah G Garcia
MASTER	MOHAMMAD	EWAN	GARCIA	Master Mohammad E Garcia
MISS	JODIE	MELISSA	GARCIA	Miss Jodie M Garcia
MRS	AMELIA	MARIA	ORPINGTON-SMYTH	Mrs Amelia M Orpington-smyth

Creating the SQL expression of nested functions to manipulate the text in this way is not difficult, but it can take a few goes to get it right, and deciphering the code can take a minute. If we are only doing this once, we would be best doing it directly in the SQL statement. However, we might need to do this sort of processing in several places in our application. We can cut and paste the code as needed, but if we need to change the code in any way, we now have the problem of duplicating that change in all the places in the application where we have pasted the code! If you look at the previous example carefully, you'll see that we do not properly handle the hyphenated surname "Orpington-Smyth," and some of you are probably wondering why we handled initial capping words manually when Oracle provides a function to do this. Not everyone knows all the SQL functions available or they might have just taken code off the Internet without reviewing it (an increasingly common but very poor programming habit), so here is an improved version:

```
-- ch6_t2
select pers_title title,     first_forename    ,second_forename    , surname
       ,initcap(pers_title)||' '
         ||initcap(first_forename)||' '
         ||nvl2(second_forename,substr(second_forename,1,1)||' ',null)
         ||initcap(surname)       Display_Name
from person
where pers_id > 100100
and rownum < 10

TITLE    first_fn   secon_fn   SURNAME    DISPLAY_NAME
-------  ---------  ---------  ---------  ---------------------------
MR       HARRISON   RICHARD    HARRIS     Mr Harrison R Harris
MRS      ANNEKA     RACHAEL    HARRIS     Mrs Anneka R Harris
MRS      NICKIE     ALISON     ELWIG      Mrs Nickie A Elwig
MASTER   JAMES      DENZIL     ELWIG      Master James D Elwig
MR       JEFF                  GARCIA     Mr Jeff Garcia
...
MRS      AMELIA     MARIA      ORPINGTON- Mrs Amelia M Orpington-Smyth
                               SMYTH
```

Code Simplification with Functions

If the preceding chunk of function-based code is in just one SQL statement, that is fine. If it's not, though, we now have to find all the other occurrences of the code in the source code repository and apply the same changes. Not only that, but we have to test all those changed pieces of code (there is nothing as dangerous as an "innocuous" cut-and-paste change you do *not* test) and put all the changes through your change control process.

Wouldn't it be great if we could compartmentalize and control what is fast becoming a complex piece of code? To have it in one place where we can extend the logic to handle new issues? One of the greatest powers of PL/SQL is that it allows you to create your own functions and call them from within any SQL statement, *just as if they were one of the built-in functions*. This feature has been available for a very long time (since Oracle 7.3 in a basic way), but it is still underused at some sites. And where it is used, the considerations we go into later on in this chapter are often overlooked.

In the following code, we create a new stored function called **disp_name**, which takes in the four parts of a name and returns a VARCHAR2 holding the display name:

```
create or replace
function disp_name (p_sn      in varchar2
                   ,p_fn1     in varchar2
                   ,p_fn2     in varchar2   :=null
                   ,p_title   in varchar2   :=null)
return varchar2
is
v_return      varchar2(1000);
begin
  -- NVL2 and DECODE not available in PL/SQL (still true in 12.1)
  v_return := case when p_title is null then ''
                   else p_title||' '
              end
```

```
            ||initcap(p_fn1)||' '
            ||case when p_fn2 is null then ''
                   else p_fn2||' '
                end
            ||initcap(p_sn);
return v_return;
end disp_name;
```

The code is slightly different from what we had before. We allow for PERS_TITLE to be null because elsewhere in our application the title of the person is not always available. A central function has to be able to handle all the slight nuances between the different places it is going to be called from, which can make it a little more complex. We also use the CASE statement to detect if certain values are NULL and then pad the resulting output string differently. As mentioned in the section on STANDARD and DBMS_STANDARD, **nvl2** is one of the small number of single-row SQL functions that PL/SQL lacks. We could have created temporary variables and used simple IF...THEN...ELSE statements to do the same thing:

```
-- code fragment only!!!
v_title        varchar2(15);
v_fn2          varchar2(30);
...
begin
  -- NVL2 and DECODE not available in PL/SQL (still true in 12)
  if p_title is null then
    v_title :='';
  else
    v_title :=initcap (p_title)||' ';
  end if;
```

As a result of our new stored PL/SQL function, our code to select the display_name is now much simpler, and the name of the function helps document what we are doing in our SQL SELECT statement:

```
select pers_title title        ,first_forename
       ,second_forename        ,surname
       ,disp_name(p_sn =>surname        ,p_fn1  =>first_forename
                 ,p_fn2=>second_forename  ,p_title=>pers_title)   display_name
from person
where pers_id > 100100
and    rownum  < 10
```

TITLE	first_fn	secon_fn	SURNAME	DISPLAY_NAME
MR	HARRISON	RICHARD	HARRIS	Mr Harrison R Harris
MRS	ANNEKA	RACHAEL	HARRIS	Mrs Anneka R Harris
MRS	NICKIE	ALISON	ELWIG	Mrs Nickie A Elwig
MASTER	JAMES	DENZIL	ELWIG	Master James D Elwig
MR	JEFF		GARCIA	Mr Jeff Garcia
MRS	SARAH	GILLIAN	GARCIA	Mrs Sarah G Garcia
MASTER	MOHAMMAD	EWAN	GARCIA	Master Mohammad E Garcia
MISS	JODIE	MELISSA	GARCIA	Miss Jodie M Garcia
MRS	AMELIA	MARIA	ORPINGTON-SMYTH	Mrs Amelia M Orpington-Smyth

Centralizing Code with PL/SQL Packages and Extending SQL

You can create a stand-alone stored function as we did previously, but it is much better to have a central package to hold all the new functions you might want to create, at least for a functional area, so that you can manage and release all the code for that area in one object. You are certainly familiar with Oracle's built-in packages, such as DBMS_STATS, DBMS_SCHEDULER, UTL_FILE, and so on. Some people think there is something special about the built-in packages—that Oracle somehow embeds them into PL/SQL in a way not available to us. Many of these packages are wrapped, and internally some of them call C code or Java, but in essence they are no different from the packages we create ourselves.

Let's create a package called STR_UTIL and within it use our **disp_name** function to format names. This is based on a package of that same name that I often create for projects I am involved in. It includes several functions for handling textual information. One in particular is called **piece**.

What is the **piece** function? It is just a nice example of how you can bring something you like from another language or some data manipulation you find you do over and over again and make it available from Oracle's SQL language. Before I got involved with Oracle technology a couple of decades ago, I worked with a language called MUMPS, which, among other things, had a lot of functionality around managing string data. One of the main commands was $PIECE, which would extract a section of a string as delimited by another character or characters. For example,

```
$PIECE("ERIC~THE~RED",3,"~")
```

would return RED. I really missed this functionality in SQL, and as soon as I learned about adding my own PL/SQL functions, I added them. Since then, whenever I have to deal with overloaded columns (where more than one piece of information is stored in a column using delimiters) or have to handle a lot of text, I've created the **piece** function for that project.

The whole code for the STR_UTIL package is available from the book's website (http://community.oraclepressbooks.com/downloads.html), but this code shows some of the key fragments from CRE_STR_UTIL:

```
-- cre_str_util.sql;
-- package to consolidate implementing string handling functions
create or replace package str_util as
...
function piece (p_string in varchar2      ,p_start     in number
              ,p_end    in number:= null ,p_delimiter in varchar2 := ',')
return varchar2;
function disp_name (p_sn   in out varchar2      ,p_fn1     in varchar2
                  ,p_fn2  in     varchar2 :=null ,p_title  in varchar2 :=null)
return varchar2;
end str_util;

create or replace package body str_util as
...
function piece (p_string in varchar2      ,p_start     in number
              ,p_end    in number := null ,p_delimiter in varchar2 := ',')
return varchar2
is
v_string    varchar2(2000) := p_string;
v_start     number:= floor(abs(p_start)); v_end       number:= floor(abs(p_end));
```

```
v_delimiter varchar2(20)    := p_delimiter;
v_return    varchar2(2000) := null;
v_dlen      number          := length(v_delimiter);
v_from      number;                    v_to         number;
begin
-- parameter checking simplified for this demo
if v_string is null or v_start is null or v_delimiter is null then
  null;
else -- all parameters make sense.
   if v_start <2 then       -- ie want first part
     v_from :=1;            -- ensure v_from is 1
     v_start :=1;           -- Start at beginning of string
   else
     v_from := instr(v_string,v_delimiter,1,v_start-1)+v_dlen;
   end if;
   if v_end is null then
     v_end := v_start;
   end if;
   v_to := instr(v_string,v_delimiter,1,v_end) -1;
   if v_to = -1 then
     v_to := length(v_string);
   end if;
   v_return := substr(v_string  ,v_from  , (v_to-v_from)+1);
end if;
return v_return;
end piece;
--
function disp_name (p_sn  in out varchar2             ,p_fn1      in varchar2
                    ,p_fn2 in     varchar2  :=null  ,p_title   in varchar2  :=null)
return varchar2
is
v_return      varchar2(1000);
begin
   -- NVL2 and DECODE not available in PL/SQL (still true in 12)
   v_return := case when p_title is null then ''    else initcap(p_title)||' '  end
             ||initcap(p_fn1)||' '
             ||case when p_fn2 is null then ''     else substr(p_fn2,1,1)||' '  end
             ||initcap(p_sn);
return v_return;
end disp_name;
...
end str_util;
```

It makes sense to create a package for each business or processing area within your system holding the functions specific to that area, but things like **piece** are generic to almost any system. I personally create functions to extract numbers out of strings, automatically increment the numeric component within a string, create an alias for a string based on the leading letter or letters of the words in the string, and things like that. I then use these generic functions throughout the more task-specific code I develop.

Maintenance Benefits of PL/SQL Functions

Because you are only writing the function once, you can afford to spend a little extra time making it check that the parameters passed in are valid and that exceptions are handled in a sensible way. One approach is to make functions pass back a NULL if the inputs do not make sense rather than an error, but you might decide that this is not how you would like it to work and you want to raise an error. You can also afford to take some time making the code efficient. After all, you could be calling these functions millions of times in a single SELECT statement. For example, think carefully about the order of checks with any IF...THEN...ELSE and CASE statements as Oracle stops when it finds the first match. You may wish to consider native compilation of the functions.

A real benefit of using PL/SQL functions is that you have defined the action of that code in a simple way. You have stated the name of the function and the number and data types of all the input values as well as the data type of the output value—that is the specification of the function. You can change the code within the function in any way you like so long as the input parameters and return value keep the same data types and names. Even if the function ends up being called from a hundred different places in your application code (and something as generic as the **piece** function could), so long as the definition of the function remains the same, any code calling it will keep working and will not need retesting, unlike if you were changing the code locally to each place it is being used. Obviously, you need to ensure the changed function gives the same return value for the given input values for that to be true.

Another advantage of putting such shared code in a function is that when new features of PL/SQL are introduced with new versions, you can review your central functions and use these new features where applicable. You only have to apply the changes to the one place to get the benefit of the changes throughout your application. If we had no central **piece** function but had actually written the same (or, more likely, only *similar*) code in several parts of the application, even if we knew there was an improvement we could use, it would be a larger task to change the code in all those places, and we would therefore be less likely to do so. Extending your SQL with PL/SQL functions means you have a small code set that is worth investing time and effort into improving with each new version of PL/SQL. My **piece** function is very old, and the version I have included in this chapter uses NUMBER data types internally. Swapping to PLS_INTEGER would be a little more efficient, and if I am using Oracle Database 11*g* or later, I should be looking into using SIMPLE_INTEGER data types and native compilation. So long as I do not change the function specification and ensure I produce the same return values for a given set of input values, I can safely update my central function code and get the performance gain across my application.

Coming back to our **disp_name** function, you can probably imagine other issues that could arise, such as how to handle capitalizing McDonald or the fact that the Dutch "van" (as in Vincent van Gogh) is not capitalized. We could embed rules with checks for such sections to the name and handle them that way, or we could create a table with exceptions that can be checked for. (If you decide on the latter, you now have SQL calling PL/SQL that calls SQL, and some new issues arise that we will cover in the next section of this chapter.) An initially very simple function is quickly becoming complex and needs more thought, which is what always tends to happen in reality. By having the one occurrence of this code in a single stored function, you only have to solve and code up the solution once and then maintain it in a single place. The encapsulation of your business logic in one place, stored within the database it is acting upon, is one of the key advantages to using PL/SQL for your business logic.

User-defined PL/SQL Functions Have Been Available for a Long Time
Oracle actually added the ability to create your own functions in PL/SQL way back in Version 2.1, which came with Oracle 7.1, although there were initially more limitations on what was possible. I started using my own user-defined PL/SQL functions in 1995, but it was not until Oracle started adding more and more functionality via the built-in packages that it became a more common practice. Again, the first handful of built-in packages arrived with Version 2.1 (DBMS_OUTPUT, DBMS_LOCK, and DBMS_SQL among them; Version 2.3 introduced UTL_FILE), but the number increased substantially through Oracle Version 8.0 (when the PL/SQL version number was synchronized with the database version number) until the present.

PL/SQL Function Considerations

As we have seen, creating user-defined PL/SQL functions for use in SQL is easy, and they integrate with your SQL statements as if they were either built into the language or were provided by Oracle as part of the built-in packages. There are some further considerations, though, with respect to reliability, performance, and database consistency.

Parameters, Purity Levels, and Deterministic

This section covers some considerations when creating functions to be used within SQL DML statements, which we group into the following areas: function parameters, code purity, and deterministic functions.

Function Parameters

Do we need to tell you that you cannot use OUT or IN OUT parameters for a PL/SQL function called by SQL? After all, you generally should not use OUT or IN OUT parameters for functions in any case, even though you can—it is a bad practice. But for functions being called by SQL, you would be trying to alter literals or columns passed in as parameters to the function—and that would be illogical. All parameters for functions called from SQL have to be IN parameters. If you *do* create a function that has "out" arguments and you call it from SQL, you will get an error such as "ORA-06572: Function DISP_NAME has out arguments."

Changing Data and Purity

The concept of purity for functions that are intended to be called from SQL is an important one. Actually, I'd go further and say it is vital. *Purity* refers to the ability of the function to influence or be influenced by other things going on elsewhere in the database.

It should also be self-evident that one thing you do *not* want to do within a user-defined PL/SQL function is alter the contents of any database tables. If you were able to do so, you could have a SELECT statement or a PL/SQL expression that uses the function and alters stored data. Again, this would nearly always be illogical, and Oracle prevents you from doing this.

As an example of having a function that alters table data, we will alter the **disp_name** function to include a SQL INSERT statement just prior to returning the value. We will use a table that we created for tracking and testing the use of PL/SQL functions, EXEC_FUNC_TRACK:

```
-- Table to track function execution activity
create table exec_func_track
(function_name      varchar2(30) not null
,exec_timestamp     timestamp    not null
,extra_info         varchar2(100)
)
```

```
begin
   v_return := case when p_title is null then ''    else initcap(p_title)||' '  end
            ||initcap(p_fn1)||' '
            ||case when p_fn2 is null then ''       else substr(p_fn2,1,1)||' ' end
            ||initcap(p_sn);
insert into exec_func_track (function_name,exec_timestamp)
values ('DISP_NAME',SYSTIMESTAMP);
return v_return;
```

You can re-create the function with this INSERT statement embedded in it with no problems. There is nothing preventing a function doing DML; the package-creation statement will not give you an error. However, when you issue a SELECT statement that uses the function, an error is given:

```
       str_util.disp_name(p_sn =>surname              ,p_fn1  =>first_forename
         *
ERROR at line 2:
ORA-14551: cannot perform a DML operation inside a query
ORA-06512: at "MDW.STR_UTIL", line 224
ORA-06512: at line 1
```

At this juncture, you are possibly thinking we can use the pragma RESTRICT_REFERENCES to check for the purity of a package function or procedure at compilation time to ensure such errors do not occur. A pragma is a compile-time directive, an order to Oracle to check or enforce something about the PL/SQL code when it is stored in the database with the CREATE or REPLACE command; when you create or replace your PL/SQL stored code, the compiler will be influenced by any pragmas that are present and, depending on the type of pragma, either alter the pcode it creates (*pcode* is semi-parsed code and is what Oracle actually executes when it runs stored PL/SQL code) or does not create the stored code at all and gives an error. Pragmas are stated in the declaration section for the function and before the first BEGIN. Though they can occur anywhere in the declaration section, they are often stated as the first line of the declaration section, directly after the RETURN clause, for the sake of clarity.

To state purity, we *previously* used the RESTRICT_REFERENCES pragma, which states some rules about what the function (or procedure) does. For a function that was to be called from SQL, you had to state as a minimum that the function code did not write any database states (that is, it did not change the contents of any database tables). This was done with

```
pragma restrict_references (WNDS);
```

where WNDS stands for "Writes No Database State." If the compiler detected that the code broke these rules, it was not compiled. You may still come across code that includes these statements; here is an example of one:

```
function num_inc(p_text in varchar2,p_incr in number)
return varchar2;
pragma restrict_references (num_inc,wnds,rnds,wnps,rnps);
```

However, as of Oracle Version 11.1g, the RESTRICT_REFERENCES pragma is deprecated and Oracle does not support its continued use. If you compile your code with PL/SQL compilation warnings turned on, you will get a warning about the use of RESTRICT_REFERENCES:

```
PLW-05019: the language element near keyword RESTRICT_REFERENCES is deprecated
beginning with version 11.2
```

TIP
PL/SQL compile-time warnings (sometimes called compilation warnings) provide an excellent way of checking your code for deprecated features, common mistakes, or potential performance problems. You can check code for compile-time warnings as you create or replace stored PL/SQL or check existing stored code. I highly recommend that you use compile-time warnings. This feature is explained further in Chapter 7.

A pure function will not depend on anything that can change in the database (table data) or in the session (for example, package variables), and that was what the pragma RESTRICT_REFERENCES was all about. You used it to state rules about what that function did with respect to reading any data from the database or writing to or changing anything in the database, and similarly did not read or alter package variables. This is because doing any of these things could have unexpected consequences. As mentioned earlier, it would make no sense to have a function change data in the database because then a simple SELECT statement could change data. If you are reading data from the database (and we will return to this topic), then the result of the function will depend on the data in the database. At that point, you cannot be sure what the function is going to do, and in some situations that is a real problem. Similarly, if you change package variables for your session, how is that going to impact the other activity carried out by your session? You have no control over when someone will use the function and therefore have limited or no control over the impact from packaged variables or table data being changed.

Deterministic

A pure function is *deterministic*—the return value is always the same for a given input to the function, and the result is determined solely by the input values to the function. Our **disp_name** function is deterministic because the result is totally dependent on the input values and only the input values. The **piece** function is also deterministic. The old pragma method of stating the purity of the function could only ever be partially verified and as such became redundant. What does this mean? Well, look at this function:

```
package body pkg1 is
  c1 constant pls_integer not null := to_char(sysdate, 'J');
  function f1 return integer is
  begin
    return c1;
  end f1;
end pkg1;
```

This function does not read from or alter any table data or package functions; it could be stated as fully pure in the old method—and yet it is not deterministic. The result will change every day.

What we used to indicate with RESTRICT_REFERENCES is not what we actually want to tell the database about our function. We want to tell the database when the function is *deterministic* and therefore safe to use for creating function-based indexes or when the function can have its values cached (we discuss function caching later in this chapter in "PL/SQL Results Caching"). We do that with the DETERMINISTIC keyword within the function:

```
function disp_name (p_sn      in varchar2
                   ,p_fn1     in varchar2
                   ,p_fn2     in varchar2 :=null
                   ,p_title   in varchar2 :=null)
return varchar2 DETERMINISTIC;
```

With this command we are telling Oracle that it can trust us that the function is deterministic. *Oracle does not ensure it is deterministic*—it can't. It is up to us, the programmers, to ensure that it is. We should only state that a function is deterministic if we are absolutely sure it is—and it would be madness to do so if we were not sure. A function has to be deterministic to allow certain activities (for example, for it to be usable in the creation of a function-based index and for function results caching). As an example, let's create a function to generate the year in which someone becomes an adult (we will chose 18 because it's the common age used in Europe for various legal and social rules) and then create a function-based index on it:

```
function year_adult (p_dob   in date)
return integer deterministic
is
begin
  return to_number(to_char(p_dob,'YYYY'))+18;
end year_adult;

select count(*) from person where str_util.year_adult(dob)=2010;
  COUNT(*)
----------
       396
-------------------------------------------------------------------------------
| Id  | Operation            | Name        | Rows  | Bytes  | Cost  | Time      |
-------------------------------------------------------------------------------
|   0 | SELECT STATEMENT     |             |     1 |      8 |   776 | 00:00:01  |
|   1 |   SORT AGGREGATE     |             |     1 |      8 |       |           |
|*  2 |    INDEX FAST FULL SCAN| PERS_SNFFDOB |  5691 |  45528 |   776 | 00:00:01  |
-------------------------------------------------------------------------------
--  Note the INDEX FAST FULL SCAN and cost of 776

create index pers_adult_yr on person (str_util.year_adult(DOB));
Index created.

select count(*) from person where str_util.year_adult(dob)=2010;
  COUNT(*)
----------
       396
-------------------------------------------------------------------------------
| Id  | Operation          | Name          | Rows  | Bytes  | Cost  | Time      |
-------------------------------------------------------------------------------
|   0 | SELECT STATEMENT   |               |     1 |     13 |    16 | 00:00:01  |
|   1 |   SORT AGGREGATE   |               |     1 |     13 |       |           |
|*  2 |    INDEX RANGE SCAN| PERS_ADULT_YR |  5691 |  73983 |    16 | 00:00:01  |
-------------------------------------------------------------------------------
```

```
-- we built an index of the results from the deterministic function STR_UTIL.YEAR_ADULT
-- Oracle uses this new index, INDEX_RANGE_SCAN and the cost of the statement has
-- dropped to 16 from 776
```

If you try to use a function that is not marked as deterministic, you get the following error:

```
ORA-30553: The function is not deterministic
```

Just a quick word of warning: If you alter the user-defined function, it does not invalidate the function-based index. If you do not remember to rebuild the index, the values it contains will be based on the old version of the function. To demonstrate this (and to show that Oracle does not validate that your function is not deterministic), let's alter the **year_adult** function to be based on SYSDATE, select some data, and then drop and rebuild the index. As you can see, we get a different result:

```
function year_adult (p_dob    in date)
return integer deterministic
is
begin
  return to_number(to_char(sysdate,'YYYY'))+18;
end year_adult;
@cre_str_util
Package created.
Package body created.

-- make sure I now get a the same value for different values passed into the func
select str_util.year_adult(sysdate-1000)
      ,str_util.year_adult(sysdate-10000)
from dual;
STR_UTIL.YEAR_ADULT(SYSDATE-1000) STR_UTIL.YEAR_ADULT(SYSDATE-10000)
--------------------------------- ----------------------------------
                             2033                               2033
-- I still get 396 rows for my test select
select count(*) from person where str_util.year_adult(dob)=2010;
  COUNT(*)
----------
       396

--drop and recreate the index
drop index pers_adult_yr;
Index dropped.

create index pers_adult_yr on person (str_util.year_adult(DOB));
Index created.

-- re do my select having only rebuilt my function-based index and I find no rows
select count(*) from person where str_util.year_adult(dob)=2010;
  COUNT(*)
----------
         0
```

Side-stepping Restrictions on Functions Called from SQL with Autonomous Transactions

As mentioned before at the start of this section, no DML is allowed by a PL/SQL function that is called from SQL. You may have thought at the time that this is not strictly true because there is a way to work around this limitation, which is to use an autonomous transaction. An autonomous transaction effectively runs in its own private session and does not affect the parent session. You mark a procedure to run as an autonomous transaction with a pragma in the declaration section. The following code shows a procedure that inserts a record into a table to document that the function was called and is designated to run as an autonomous transaction. It is called from within a simple function (in the STR_UTIL package) to illustrate the fact that the function was called:

```
procedure func_track (p_vc1 in varchar2)
is
pragma autonomous_transaction;
begin
  insert into exec_func_track (function_name,exec_timestamp)
  values (p_vc1,SYSTIMESTAMP);
  commit;
end func_track;

function get_ts (p_vc1 in varchar2)
return timestamp
is
begin
  func_track('get_ts');
  return systimestamp;
end get_ts;

select surname,str_util.get_ts(pers_id) from person where rownum < 4;

SURNAME                         STR_UTIL.GET_TS(PERS_ID)
------------------------------- -----------------------------------------------
WALKER                          19-OCT-15 10.29.09.447000000
WALKER                          19-OCT-15 10.29.09.475000000
PATEL                           19-OCT-15 10.29.09.480000000
3 rows selected.

select * from exec_func_track where exec_timestamp > systimestamp -(1/144)

FUNCTION_NAME                   EXEC_TIMESTAMP
------------------------------- -----------------------------------------------
get_ts                          19-OCT-15 10.29.09.447000
get_ts                          19-OCT-15 10.29.09.475000
get_ts                          19-OCT-15 10.29.09.480000
3 rows selected.
```

As you can see, we can still run our function and get information written to the database. But just because you *can* do something does not mean you should. This use of an autonomous transaction to circumvent the rules is usually a terrible idea for several reasons:

- The impact on the performance of your function will be considerable. As a test, we altered the code to select 1000 records, and it took four seconds, even with output suppressed. That is a very long time to perform 1000 simple SELECT operations! The same code without the autonomous transaction and INSERT statement took under 0.02 seconds. What will happen if you select a million records?

- If more than one session is using the function at the same time, contention on that logging table is highly likely.

- You cannot roll back the autonomous changes you've made. In this example, we are using a SELECT, but what if you are running an UPDATE, INSERT, or DELETE using the function and want to roll it back? You will roll back the parent statement, but not anything done by the autonomous transaction.

- Our example is doing something that you could consider "stand-alone," not connected to the original query—but what if you used this method to alter business data?

- As we will see later, you do not have control over when a function fires. You have no real control over what your under-the-covers DML will actually do.

About the only valid reason to use autonomous transactions within a function designed to be called from SQL that we can think of is to investigate how your user-defined function is behaving. Even so, we would not normally create records in the database to do this. We would create a package-level variable for each function and, within our autonomous transaction, rather than insert a database record to track the activity of the function, we would increment the package-level variable as a counter. That would be a much lighter task, but we would still not do it in a production system—and it is still circumventing the very sensible purity concept.

Context Switching Overhead

Two processing engines run in Oracle: SQL and PL/SQL. (There is also a Java engine but this book does not cover Java.) Why are there two distinct engines? Because SQL and PL/SQL are utterly different languages, even though they mesh together very well. PL/SQL is a standard, procedural, third-generation language. It is designed along the same lines as ADA. A PL/SQL program is parsed into byte-code (actually called *pcode)* and executed, utilizing loops, expression evaluations, and logic checks in the same way as most programming languages. SQL is very, very different. It is a fourth-generation language, and you in effect ask the engine to do something, and the engine works out how to do it. You can think of it as a one-shot language because each command is a distinct task, and Oracle decides how to satisfy that task. As was covered in Chapter 1, using PL/SQL is a brilliant way to add procedural control over SQL, and it keeps all the activity within the Oracle environment. However, it is a separate language.

Context switching is not unique to Oracle when moving between SQL and PL/SQL. A context switch is generally required when you move from any programming language to another. It is a fairly CPU- and memory-intensive process because the first programming engine halts what it is doing, saves its state, and passes information over to the second programming engine.

The Impact of Context Switching on SQL Calling PL/SQL Functions

When PL/SQL issues a SQL command, there is a context switch from the PL/SQL engine to the SQL engine. This involves a nontrivial amount of CPU and memory processing as control and information are moved from one engine to the other. Similarly, when you call a PL/SQL function from within SQL, there is a context switch and a similar overhead. Generally, calling SQL from PL/SQL involves less overhead—and if you are doing things right, the total workload being done by the PL/SQL code is small and is the controlling portion of the task. The bulk of the work (that is, the manipulation of data) is being done by the SQL, and the context switches are few. But the context switch caused by SQL calling PL/SQL functions can be much more significant because it is often being done for *every row processed*. Each time there is a context switch from SQL to PL/SQL, a PL/SQL virtual machine is initiated to run the PL/SQL code.

As an example, we've rewritten the display-name code to have two versions. One is done using the PL/SQL function (and incurs the context switch overhead) and one with pure SQL. (Note that the **case** function is available in SQL; it is not restricted to PL/SQL.) One hundred thousand rows are processed by both, and we select back the average display name length and the count of records.

```
select /*mdw_1a */ avg(length(
      str_util.disp_name(p_sn =>surname              ,p_fn1  =>first_forename
                        ,p_fn2=>second_forename    ,p_title=>pers_title)
          )        )    avg_name_length
        ,count(*)
from person
where pers_id > 100100
and rownum < 100000
/
--
--
Select /*mdw_1b */ avg(length(
      case when pers_title is null then ''
                 else initcap(pers_title)||' '
          end
         ||initcap(first_forename)||' '
         ||case when second_forename is null then ''
                 else substr(second_forename,1,1)||' '
          end
         ||initcap(surname)
          )        )    avg_name_length
        ,count(*)
from person
where pers_id > 100100
and rownum < 100000
```

Because we are going to compare performance, we should say a little about how we test. When we compare the performance of similar SQL statements, we put both versions in a single script and execute the script several times. Depending on your test platform and what other activity is occurring on your hardware (this can include the network, shared storage, and any client machine activity as well as the database server), the performance (especially the elapsed time) of each statement can vary. If the difference between the two versions is significant—say, more than

25 percent and nontrivial compared to the clock speed we are measuring with (so more than 0.05 seconds for SQL*Plus timing)—we repeat any test four times and ignore the first run. We ignore the first run because it is skewed by parsing time, recursive SQL, and data being cached—unless those are aspects we are interested in. If the difference in elapsed time between the two versions is less than 10 percent, we will repeat the tests several times—for example, six, eight, or ten times—so we can average over all but the first test runs to help rule out random fluctuations. If the pattern is still not obvious, then it is nearly always not worth worrying about! For tuning exercises, you are often dealing with performance differences in orders of magnitude rather than percentages. Of course, we pay attention to figures such as consistent gets, physical reads, and redo bytes, but it is often easier to use elapsed run time as a surrogate for "improved performance" and then pay more attention to the specific statistics once we feel we have a solution.

As you will see over the next few pages, for judging the impact of context switching, the usual metrics you might look at are not going to help, so the crude "elapsed time" metric is very useful.

NOTE
You may also notice we include a comment in the code consisting of the author's initials and a few characters. This is to help me identify the code variations in the SGA and any graphical performance tools being used.

The next example shows the output and statistics for the scripts. The output for the two statements run with autotrace on shows that the SELECT output is the same, the explain plans are the same (as is indicated by the plan hash values being identical), and the statistics for consistent gets and such are the same—and yet the version with the PL/SQL function takes 0.71 seconds compared to 0.11 seconds for the native SQL version. That's almost seven times longer and is the only difference.

```
AVG_NAME_LENGTH    COUNT(*)
--------------- ----------
     18.6638366       99999


Elapsed: 00:00:00.71

Execution Plan
----------------------------------------------------------
Plan hash value: 3553163410
--------------------------------------------------------------------------
| Id  | Operation                            | Name    | Rows  | Bytes | Cost |
--------------------------------------------------------------------------
|   0 | SELECT STATEMENT                     |         |     1 |    31 | 7790|
|   1 |  SORT AGGREGATE                      |         |     1 |    31 |     |
|*  2 |   COUNT STOPKEY                      |         |       |       |     |
|   3 |    TABLE ACCESS BY INDEX ROWID BATCHED| PERSON  |  100K|  3027K| 7790|
|*  4 |     INDEX RANGE SCAN                 | PERS_PK |       |       |  216|
--------------------------------------------------------------------------

Statistics
----------------------------------------------------------
       7637  consistent gets
          0  physical reads
          0  redo size
```

```
AVG_NAME_LENGTH    COUNT(*)
--------------- ----------
    18.6638366      99999
Elapsed: 00:00:00.11


Execution Plan
----------------------------------------------------------
Plan hash value: 3553163410

--------------------------------------------------------------------------------
| Id  | Operation                            | Name    | Rows  | Bytes | Cost |
--------------------------------------------------------------------------------
|   0 | SELECT STATEMENT                     |         |     1 |    31 | 7790|
|   1 |  SORT AGGREGATE                      |         |     1 |    31 |     |
|*  2 |   COUNT STOPKEY                      |         |       |       |     |
|   3 |    TABLE ACCESS BY INDEX ROWID BATCHED| PERSON  |  100K | 3027K | 7790|
|*  4 |     INDEX RANGE SCAN                 | PERS_PK |       |       |  216|
--------------------------------------------------------------------------------

Statistics
----------------------------------------------------------
     7637  consistent gets
        0  physical reads
```

You may feel that an extra 0.6 seconds for 100,000 rows is not a significant overhead, but it is close to six times the total run time of the native SQL version. Also, data volumes in many systems vastly exceed 100,000 records. Context switching for every row in a 100-million-row query is going to be a considerable overhead—scaling up our test figures for 100,000 records to 100 million, the elapsed time would be 2 minutes for the version with no PL/SQL function and close to 12 minutes for the version with the PL/SQL function.

However, note the number of consistent gets and physical reads. We are doing no physical reads in our test—partly because we run the code several times so that execution times are consistent. If your SQL statements are incurring physical I/O, even if it is only a few percent of the consistent gets, this will probably have a much larger impact on your execution time than the context switching caused by one function. It is all relative. Context switching has an impact on performance but not as significant an impact as physical I/O.

> ### CAUTION: Select Columns in Tests to Ensure Your Plan Does Not Change
> A common mistake made by people testing SELECT code is to replace all the columns being selected by a statement with a **count(*)** to reduce the output. The Optimizer is smart enough to work out if the rows in a table are actually needed to satisfy the query or if the query can be satisfied via an index only. Using only the index is likely to be the case with **count(*)**. To ensure your test code still visits the tables, use group functions on columns that are not indexed. Your first test should be that your reduced output version has the same explain plan as the original SELECT. Then you can start tuning the code.

Detecting Context Switching

You may be concerned that you cannot "see" the context switches. The plans are the same, the statistics are the same, and the estimated costs are the same. Unfortunately, there is no easily visible metric for showing how many context switches have occurred for a session (or for the system or statement) in, for example, V$SESSTAT, such as there are consistent_gets, commit cleanouts, DB block changes, free buffer requested, and 1150 other things. You just have to know that it happens. However, you can detect some of its impact. If we select our session CPU from V$MYSTAT or V$SESSTAT (where it is recorded in hundredths of a second) before we start a re-execution of the test script and after each statement, we see the following:

```
select n.name statname,s.value
from v$mystat s,v$statname n
where n.statistic#=s.statistic#
and n.name = 'CPU used by this session'

1/100th seconds: 546

-- PL/SQL calling code
AVG_NAME_LENGTH    COUNT(*)
--------------- ----------
     18.6638366       99999
Elapsed: 00:00:00.90

cpu in 1/100th seconds: 626

-- Native SQL code
AVG_NAME_LENGTH    COUNT(*)
--------------- ----------
     18.6638366       99999
Elapsed: 00:00:00.14

cpu in 1/100th seconds: 638
```

The version of the code that context switches due to the PL/SQL call has caused the session to accumulate 80 centiseconds of CPU (626 – 546 = 80), whereas the native SQL version has caused the session to accrue only 12 centiseconds of CPU (638 – 626 = 12). That extra CPU was burned doing the context switching. Further, we can go and find the code in V$SQL and check out the statistics for the statement there (this is why I include the comments **/*mdw_1a*/** and **/*mdw_1b*/** in the SQL, so I can find the code in V$SQL easily!):

```
select sql_id
      ,plan_hash_value      plan_hashv
      ,parse_calls          prse
      ,executions           excs
      ,buffer_gets          buffs
      ,disk_reads           discs
      ,cpu_time             cpu_t
      ,plsql_exec_time      plsql_exec
      ,rows_processed       rws
      ,substr(sql_text,1,80) sql_txt
from v$sql
where upper(sql_text) like upper('%'||nvl('&sql_txt','whoops')||'%')

SQL_ID        PLAN_HASHV PRSE  EXCS      BUFFS DISCS     CPU_T PLSQL_EXEC   RWS
------------- ---------- ----- ----- --------- ----- --------- ---------- ------
```

```
SQL_TXT
--------------------------------------------------------------------------------
c855h1h4jyb0v 3553163410     5     5      38198    0   4156250    2444823       5
select /*mdw_1a */ avg(length(        str_util.disp_name(p_sn =>surname

0mf8xzdma5cnu 3553163410     5     5      38198    0    609375          0       5
select /*mdw_1b */ avg(length(        case when pers_title is null then ''
```

Note that the script, when run from SQL*Plus or SQL Developer, will prompt for a value for SQL_TXT to search on—enter **mdw_1a**.

The code labeled with **/*mdw_1a */** is our version with the call to our PL/SQL function, and **/* mdw_1b */** is our native SQL version. Note that the SQL_IDs are different for the two statements (the code *is* different), but the **plan_hash_value (3553163410)** is identical—the same plan is used. Parses, executions, buffer gets, disk gets metrics are all the same. But the first statement, our context-switching friend, shows a significantly higher CPU_TIME and PLSQL_EXEC_TIME (which is something else we select). Both are shown in microseconds (that is, millionths of a second).

If PLSQL_EXEC_TIME has a value for a SQL DML statement (SELECT.INSERT,UPDATE/MERGE/DELETE), then PL/SQL is being invoked and context switching is occurring.

As an aside, note that reading session CPU and other elapsed-time information from different sources can show some small discrepancies. If you look back at the information we extracted from V$SQL, you can see we have executed the test script five times, and the CPU times per execution (83 centiseconds and 12 centiseconds, respectively, once the math is done) are comparable to the session CPU times we saw of 80 and 12 centiseconds. But be warned that the two will often not match up exactly. Oracle is very, very good at instrumenting its activity (see Chapter 7), and the statistics against the SQL statements seem to be very accurate. However, CPU time can fail to be recorded against a session in V$SESSTAT when the CPU expenditure is small. It is recorded in hundredths of a second, and if the CPU activity of a statement or action is less than this, it can be missed. Sometimes we do more than just run the test code between getting the values for session CPU, for example, if we have autotrace turned on in our session that has to do a tiny bit of CPU to gather and show that information and it is included in the figures. On the other hand, elapsed time seems to sometimes round down a little—it has a value one or two hundredths below the CPU time for the actual SQL statement executed.

The point is that either method is accurate enough to give a good indication of CPU effort. We learned many years ago not to worry about such tiny differences between the two.

One way you can see context switching occurring is to enable DBMS_TRACE. This shows the PL/SQL activity for a session. You can find full details of setting up and using PL/SQL tracing in Chapter 7, which includes creating the table PLSQL_TRACE_EVENTS with a public synonym and relevant grants. If you cannot see this table with the Oracle user you are using or the DBMS_TRACE package, check out the "DBMS_TRACE" in Chapter 7.

Because we only want to trace specific stored PL/SQL, we enable PL/SQL debugging for the session. Within SQL*Plus, we alter the session like so:

```
alter session set PLSQL_DEBUG=true;
```

We then recompile the package STR_UTIL. When we recompile the stored PL/SQL, having set PLSQL_DEBUG to true, the code is marked such that when we run it again, diagnostic information is stored, depending on what level we have set with the DBMS_TRACE.SET_PLSQL_TRACE package. In this example, we set it to 4 because we want to limit the output. If we set it to 2, it will only trace the stored PL/SQL we compiled with debug mode, but it would be more verbose about each such call. We set the trace level in SQL*Plus with this command:

```
exec dbms_trace.set_plsql_trace(4)
```

We then run the code, which selects nine records from PERSON and calls STR_UTIL.DISP_NAME for each record, and we then pull out the trace information from PLSQL_TRACE_EVENTS for the latest session. As you can see, the PL/SQL Virtual Machine is started and stopped nine times in this example:

```
select pers_title title          ,first_forename
       ,second_forename          ,surname
       ,disp_name(p_sn =>surname          ,p_fn1 =>first_forename
                 ,p_fn2=>second_forename  ,p_title=>pers_title)  display_name
from person
where pers_id > 100100
and   rownum  < 10

SELECT e.runid,
       e.event_seq,
       TO_CHAR(e.event_time, 'HH24:MI:SS') AS event_time,
       e.event_unit,
       e.event_unit_kind,
       e.event_comment
FROM   plsql_trace_events e
where  e.runid = (select max(runid) from plsql_trace_runs)
ORDER BY e.runid, e.event_seq
```

run id	event seq	EVENT_TI	EVENT_UNIT	EVENT_UNIT_KIND	proc line	EVENT_COMMENT
8	1	13:56:26				PL/SQL Trace Tool started
8	2	13:56:26				Trace flags changed
8	3	13:56:26				PL/SQL Virtual Machine stopped
8	4	13:56:44	<anonymous>	ANONYMOUS BLOCK		PL/SQL Virtual Machine started
8	5	13:56:44				PL/SQL Virtual Machine stopped
8	6	13:56:45	<anonymous>	ANONYMOUS BLOCK		PL/SQL Virtual Machine started
8	7	13:56:45				PL/SQL Virtual Machine stopped
8	8	13:56:45	<anonymous>	ANONYMOUS BLOCK		PL/SQL Virtual Machine started
8	9	13:56:45				PL/SQL Virtual Machine stopped
8	10	13:56:45	<anonymous>	ANONYMOUS BLOCK		PL/SQL Virtual Machine started
8	11	13:56:45				PL/SQL Virtual Machine stopped
8	12	13:56:45	<anonymous>	ANONYMOUS BLOCK		PL/SQL Virtual Machine started
8	13	13:56:45				PL/SQL Virtual Machine stopped
8	14	13:56:45	<anonymous>	ANONYMOUS BLOCK		PL/SQL Virtual Machine started
8	15	13:56:45				PL/SQL Virtual Machine stopped
8	16	13:56:45	<anonymous>	ANONYMOUS BLOCK		PL/SQL Virtual Machine started
8	17	13:56:45				PL/SQL Virtual Machine stopped
8	18	13:56:45	<anonymous>	ANONYMOUS BLOCK		PL/SQL Virtual Machine started
8	19	13:56:45				PL/SQL Virtual Machine stopped
8	20	13:56:45	<anonymous>	ANONYMOUS BLOCK		PL/SQL Virtual Machine started
8	21	13:56:45				PL/SQL Virtual Machine stopped

If we ran the code with **dbms_trace.set_plsql_trace(2)**, we would also see details of the activity from the debug-enabled package. Let's alter the session with **exec dbms_trace.set_plsql_trace(2)** and run the code again. Here is just an extract because it is more verbose, even for our very simple function:

```
run event                                               proc
 id   seq EVENT_TI EVENT_UNIT  EVENT_UNIT_KIND  line EVENT_COMMENT
 ---  ----- -------- ----------- --------------- ----- ------------------------------
  8    42 14:38:10 DBMS_TRACE  PACKAGE BODY       81 Return from procedure call
  8    43 14:38:10 DBMS_TRACE  PACKAGE BODY        1 Return from procedure call
  8    44 14:38:10                                   PL/SQL Virtual Machine stopped
  8    45 14:38:13 <anonymous> ANONYMOUS BLOCK       PL/SQL Virtual Machine started
  8    46 14:38:13 <anonymous> ANONYMOUS BLOCK   208 Procedure Call
  8    47 14:38:13 STR_UTIL    PACKAGE BODY          PL/SQL Internal Call
  8    48 14:38:13 STR_UTIL    PACKAGE BODY          PL/SQL Internal Call
  8    49 14:38:13 STR_UTIL    PACKAGE BODY          PL/SQL Internal Call
  8    50 14:38:13 STR_UTIL    PACKAGE BODY        1 Return from procedure call
  8    51 14:38:13                                   PL/SQL Virtual Machine stopped
  8    52 14:38:14 <anonymous> ANONYMOUS BLOCK       PL/SQL Virtual Machine started
  8    53 14:38:14 <anonymous> ANONYMOUS BLOCK   208 Procedure Call
  8    54 14:38:14 STR_UTIL    PACKAGE BODY          PL/SQL Internal Call
  8    55 14:38:14 STR_UTIL    PACKAGE BODY          PL/SQL Internal Call
  8    56 14:38:14 STR_UTIL    PACKAGE BODY          PL/SQL Internal Call
  8    57 14:38:14 STR_UTIL    PACKAGE BODY        1 Return from procedure call
  8    58 14:38:14                                         PL/SQL Virtual Machine stopped
```

A big drawback with DBMS_TRACE is similar to what we had with our autonomous transaction that recorded when a function is called—namely, that a lot of information is potentially created per row selected when we trace PL/SQL being called from SQL and it is persisted into the database. The performance impact of this activity is significant. However, a small test like this shows the constant starting and stopping of the PL/SQL Virtual Machine due to the context switches.

You might be wondering about using a 10046 trace to see the function firing—in our case, you will not see this. The 10046 trace is a SQL trace. It shows any SQL the function fires but will *not* show the pure PL/SQL and will give no indication of context switching directly.

For much of the rest of this chapter, we won't keep showing the PL/SQL debug information to prove context switching is occurring for the reasons outlined previously; its impact is too high. Instead, we will rely on changes to elapsed time and the V$SQL columns for CPU and PLSQL_EXEC_TIME to act as surrogates for occurrences (and the impact) of context switching.

Context Switching Overhead Is Cumulative

The impact of context switching also occurs with the PL/SQL built-in packages Oracle provides. In this next example, we alter the code so that one version invokes the **dbms_random.value** function and gets an average of that, and the native SQL does the same on another column in the table:

```
-- use the below to get the session CPU before and after each statement
select n.name statname,s.value
from v$mystat s,v$statname n
where n.statistic#=s.statistic#
and n.name = 'CPU used by this session'

-- and this for the statement CPU/PLSQL_EXEC information for the statements
select /* ignorethis!!! */
 sql_id
,plan_hash_value  plan_hashv
```

```
,cpu_time          cpu_t
,plsql_exec_time plsql_exec
,substr(sql_text,1,40) sql_txt
from v$sql
where upper(sql_text) like upper('%mdw_2%')
and sql_text not like '%/* ignorethis!!! */%'

--
select /*mdw_2a */
        avg(dbms_random.value) avg_rdm
       ,avg(addr_id)
       ,count(*)
from person
where pers_id > 100100
and rownum < 100000

select /*mdw_2b */
        avg(pers_id)
       ,avg(addr_id)
       ,count(*)
from person
where pers_id > 100100
and rownum < 100000

-- Times are converted into seconds
code       elapsed    sess_cpu   v$sga cpu   v$sga plsql_exec
mdw_2a     0.82       0.83       0.83        0.63
mdw_2b     0.03       0.04       0.04        0
```

Again, the explain plans and execution costs are identical, but the first statement takes 0.82 seconds and the session accumulates 83 centiseconds of CPU to run, and the second statement takes 0.03 seconds and accumulates 4 centiseconds of CPU. Checking V$SGA for the two statements shows almost identical values to the session CPU time for each statement, and only the version with the function call to DBMS_RANDOM accumulates PLSQL_EXEC_TIME— of 0.63 seconds.

We can take a few lessons away from this:

- Even simple native SQL functions take a little bit of time. Removing all that initial capping and casing has more than halved the run time and CPU of the native SQL version (mdw_2b) compared to mdw_1a, which ran in 0.11 seconds.

- The context switching overhead is still there for built-in PL/SQL packages. (As we have said before, they really aren't very different from the PL/SQL packages we can write.)

- **dbms_random** is a slightly more demanding function than our **disp_name** function—even though it is provided by Oracle (and we suspect that, at its heart, it uses some C code).

So we have seen the impact of context switching and how to get some insight into this impact. What happens if we call more than one PL/SQL function? Do we get several context switches and an escalating impact? In the following code, we have three examples. First, we have one PL/SQL function call to DBMS_RANDOM. In the second, we also have a call to our

str_util.disp_name function. Finally, we also add a call to **str_util.piece**. Thus we have an increasing number of calls to PL/SQL.

```
--Version 1:
select /*mdw_4a */
        avg(dbms_random.value) avg_rdm
       ,avg(addr_id)
       ,count(*)
from person where pers_id > 100100 and rownum < 100000

--version 2:
select /*mdw_4b */
        avg(dbms_random.value) avg_rdm
       ,avg(length(str_util.disp_name
                    (p_sn =>surname              ,p_fn1  =>first_forename
                    ,p_fn2=>second_forename    ,p_title=>pers_title)
            ) ) disp_name_len
       ,avg(addr_id)
       ,count(*)
from person where pers_id > 100100 and rownum < 100000

--version 3
select /*mdw_4c */
        avg(dbms_random.value) avg_rdm
       ,avg(length(str_util.disp_name
                    (p_sn =>surname              ,p_fn1  =>first_forename
                    ,p_fn2=>second_forename    ,p_title=>pers_title)
            ) ) disp_name_len
       ,avg(length(str_util.piece(surname,2,'A'))) col3
       ,avg(addr_id)
       ,count(*)
from person where pers_id > 100100 and rownum < 100000
```

We actually extended this code to five and seven different function calls, but we do not show the code here to save space. The execution times and session CPU times are listed in the following table:

Number of Distinct PL/SQL Calls	Execution Time	Session CPU Centiseconds
1	0.84	85
2	1.71	174
3	2.74	278
5	4.49	447
7	6.34	635

As you can see, as more functions are called, the impact is cumulative—in other words, *there is a context switch for each function for each row.* Nothing clever is going on where Oracle realizes there are several calls to PL/SQL per row and does one context switch for each row and then runs them all. Logically, it would seem possible for the Oracle Database to do a single context switch to process all PL/SQL functions for each row processed (because, being simple column selects, they would not impact which rows are fetched or any table joins), but this logic is obviously not built into the SQL engine. It might not be built in for a good reason, of course—we are only looking at a simple test here.

However, if we have exactly the same function structure multiple times in the same select list (that is, the same function name *and* the same actual parameters—not different parameters that give the same result), then the Optimizer will realize we want the same thing and only execute the function with those parameters once. In the following example, we have two extended versions of the code—one that now has five different PL/SQL functions and one that has three different functions and two repeats of one of them:

```
select /*mdw_5b */
        avg(dbms_random.value) avg_rdm
       ,avg(length(str_util.disp_name(p_sn =>surname    ,p_fn1  =>first_forename
         ,p_fn2=>second_forename    ,p_title=>pers_title)        ) ) DNL
       ,avg(length(str_util.piece(surname,2,'A'))) col3
       ,avg(length(str_util.piece(surname,2,'E'))) col4
       ,avg(length(str_util.piece(surname,2,'I'))) col5
       ,avg(addr_id)
       ,count(*)
from person
where pers_id > 100100
and    rownum  < 100000


    AVG_RDM       DNL  COL3  COL4  COL5 AVG(ADDR_ID)   COUNT(*)
----------- ----------- ----- ----- ----- ------------ ----------
  .50065199 18.6638366     3     2     3    503047.01     99999
Elapsed: 00:00:04.81

select /*mdw_5c */
        avg(dbms_random.value) avg_rdm
       ,avg(length(str_util.disp_name(p_sn =>surname          ,p_fn1  =>first_forename
         ,p_fn2=>second_forename    ,p_title=>pers_title)        ) ) DNL
       ,avg(length(str_util.piece(surname,2,'A'))) col3
       ,avg(length(str_util.piece(surname,2,'A'))) col4
       ,avg(length(str_util.piece(surname,2,'A'))) col5
       ,avg(addr_id)
       ,count(*)
from person
where pers_id > 100100
and    rownum  < 100000


    AVG_RDM       DNL  COL3  COL4  COL5 AVG(ADDR_ID)   COUNT(*)
----------- ----------- ----- ----- ----- ------------ ----------
  .50061023 18.6638366     3     3     3    503047.01     99999
Elapsed: 00:00:03.10
```

The elapsed time for five different PL/SQL function calls is 4.81 seconds, which is very similar to our previous test for five calls, and 3.10 seconds for three different calls and two duplicates, which is pretty much the same amount of time as three distinct PL/SQL calls. Interestingly, we did not have any of the functions set as DETERMINISTIC at the time this example was run (see later in this chapter for details on what DETERMINISTIC does). It appears that Oracle is treating PL/SQL function calls as deterministic within the context of each row *if they have the same parameters*.

Context Switching and When Oracle Calls PL/SQL Functions Used in SQL

The usual assumption is that Oracle executes a function each time an expression is evaluated and that an expression in the SELECT list is evaluated for each row processed. This is actually not always the case.

Let's explore this with calls to DBMS_RANDOM. If we have several references to DBMS_RANDOM, does Oracle generate several different values? Look at this:

```
-- grouped average over the data set
select avg(dbms_random.value) avg_dbrav1,avg(dbms_random.value) avg_dbrav2
     ,avg(addr_id) avg_addr_id
from person
where pers_id >100100 and rownum < 100000
/


AVG_DBRAV1 AVG_DBRAV2 AVG_ADDR_ID
---------- ---------- -----------
.501492222 .501492222    503047.01

-- data for specific rows
select dbms_random.value  dbrav1    ,dbms_random.value dbrav2
     ,addr_id
from person
where pers_id >100100 and rownum < 6

    DBRAV1     DBRAV2    ADDR_ID
---------- ---------- ---------
.114702105 .980702155    437456
.686506432 .780837409    437456
.706921245 .503403527    344386
.375036806 .396850327    344386
.650248679 .724716967    213623
```

With **dbms_random.value** contained in group functions, we get identical values for the two columns selected. Oracle recognizes that it is the same definition of a function being called and does it only once (this is not as a result of the same seed value being used for *two threads of random number generation*—it simply doesn't work like that). For the second example, where we are selecting individual rows, Oracle generates distinct values for each **dbms_random.value** call, even though they are the same. Is this a bug?

It is not. *Oracle does not guarantee how often or when a PL/SQL function is called within a SQL statement*. It never has and probably never will.

This does highlight a key consideration with using functions, especially in places such as WHERE clauses and ORDER BY. When Oracle parses your SQL statements, it can rewrite them internally to a logically identical format. This is partly why Oracle does not guarantee when and how often functions are executed. As we have seen, if a function is called with the same inputs (in the case of **dbms_random.value** there are no inputs) in the same row, Oracle treats them as identical and may decide to execute it only once. Is this important? It is, and we will explain why by first describing what, at first, seems to be an unconnected, but quite well-known, issue.

Consider the following SQL statement. We want to pull out a few records from our people for a given range of date of birth (DOB):

```
select surname, first_forename,dob
from person
where dob between to_date ('01-JAN-1970','DD-MON-YYYY')
         and      to_date ('04-JAN-1970','DD-MON-YYYY')
```

If we have no ORDER BY, the data may *or may not* be ordered by DOB—it depends on how Oracle satisfies the plan. In all likelihood, if there is an index on DOB, the data will be identified by a range scan of the index and come back in DOB order. People used to rely on this in their code logic (and occasionally still do). However, they then have problems in their application when Oracle suddenly returns the data unordered (the plan changes, parallel query is invoked, all sorts of things can cause this to happen). Oracle does not guarantee the data set to be ordered unless you state an ORDER BY clause. When this loss of implicit order started to happen a lot with Versions 8 and 9, people felt aggrieved because they had tested and tested and tested their code and it "just worked" for years; they had seen their data being implicitly ordered. Sadly, sometimes empirical testing and a history of an assumed side effect working is not enough. You also need to understand the rules by which Oracle processes your data.

Now let's change the code so it is ordered by a **dbms_random.value**. This is something that people occasionally want to do, especially when creating test data:

```
select surname, first_forename,dob
from person
where dob between to_date ('01-JAN-1970','DD-MON-YYYY')
         and      to_date ('04-JAN-1970','DD-MON-YYYY')
-- To force the random order?
order by dbms_random.value
```

What will this code do? Will DBMS_RANDOM.VALUE be evaluated once and the values ordered by a static value? In that case the Optimizer might spot this and save itself the effort, remove the ORDER BY, and give us the data in DOB order still. Or it might evaluate it for every row and give us a randomized data set as we requested. *There is no guarantee*. When people write a statement like the previous one, in their minds they know what the aim is. But if you think about it, the SQL statement is ambiguous.

This next example is taken from the excellent "Ask Tom" website. The original question asked why this seemingly inconsistent query returned a row (see https://asktom.oracle.com/pls/asktom/ f?p=100:11:0::::P11_QUESTION_ID:3181424400346795479 for the original discussion):

```
select * from dual where dbms_random.value = dbms_random.value and
not ( dbms_random.value = dbms_random.value );

DUM
---
X

1 row selected.
```

In 10*g* it did not return a row. In 11 it did.

Tom replied to reiterate that you cannot rely on when or how many times the SQL will call your function and that the previous statement could be rewritten logically in various ways:

```
select …
from t
where f() = f()

-- or

with data as (select f() F from dual)
select …
from t,data
where F=F
```

When it comes down to it, the original question about which response to **order by dbms_random.value** is correct is an interesting thought experiment—but it makes little sense. You are asking for data where **unknown=unknown** and **unknown!=unknown**. And, as you now know, you cannot even be sure how many distinct unknowns there are. You are on very questionable ground when using a nondeterministic PL/SQL function in SQL.

This question of how often a function is fired is far less of an issue when you use a deterministic function; the function makes use of selected values and is in relation to real data. If we have calls to **dbms_random** or any other function where we pass in real column values, the function will be executed with those column values. Because the input values come from the rows being processed, the function has to be fired with those values—that is, per row.

This also gives us a solution for ensuring we get a distinct value from **dbms_random.value**. We can create our own function that takes in a parameter and all it does is execute **dbms_random.value** and pass back the value. If we call that function with a value that will never be the same, to ensure no caching goes on (even if someone does later change the function to be labeled DETERMINISTIC), we will get an execution per row processed. We could use the **rowid** from one of the tables or a unique column as the variable passed in.

Reducing the Impact of Context Switching

With Oracle Database 12.1, two new features were introduced that may be of use in reducing the impact of context switching. The first involves using the WITH clause (often referred to—inaccurately—as *subquery factoring,* but that may change now with the new usages of the WITH clause) to define the function text that you use within the main query, rather than defining it in a stored PL/SQL function or package. The other involves using the new pragma UDF command to label a stored function as a user-defined function.

Local Functions Declared in a WITH Clause   PL/SQL functions can now be embedded in a SQL statement natively using the WITH clause. In the next example, we embed our **disp_name** function into the SQL statement in this way:

```
with
  function l_disp_name(p_sn        in varchar2
                      ,p_fn1       in varchar2
                      ,p_fn2       in varchar2    :=null
                      ,p_title     in varchar2    :=null)
return varchar2
is
```

```
v_return       varchar2(1000);
begin
  v_return := case when p_title is null then ''
                   else initcap(p_title)||' '
              end
            ||initcap(p_fn1)||' '
            ||case when p_fn2 is null then ''
                   else substr(p_fn2,1,1)||' '
              end
            ||initcap(p_sn);
return v_return;
end l_disp_name;
select /*mdw_7a */
       avg(length(l_disp_name(p_sn =>surname              ,p_fn1  =>first_forename
          ,p_fn2=>second_forename   ,p_title=>pers_title)          ) ) disp_name_len
      ,avg(addr_id)
      ,count(*)
from person
where pers_id > 100100
and rownum < 100000
```

When executed and compared to similar code that uses our **str_util.disp_code** function, a significant speed improvement is seen—from the usual 0.8 seconds we are used to coming down to 0.23 seconds.

Checking PLSQL_EXEC_TIME shows that the version with the local WITH clause is not accumulating time in the PL/SQL engine. The other SQL_ID is for the version calling the stored function:

```
select /* ignorethis!!! */
 sql_id
,plan_hash_value  plan_hashv
,parse_calls      prse
,executions       excs
,buffer_gets      buffs
,disk_reads       discs
,cpu_time         cpu_t
,plsql_exec_time  plsql_exec
,rows_processed   rws
,substr(sql_text,1,80) sql_txt
from v$sql
where upper(sql_text) like upper('%'||nvl('&sql_txt','whoops')||'%')
and sql_text not like '%/* ignorethis!!! */%'
order by (greatest(buffer_gets,1)/greatest(rows_processed,1)) desc
```

SQL_ID	PLAN_HASHV	PRSE	EXCS	BUFFS	DISCS	CPU_T	PLSQL_EXEC	RWS
SQL_TXT								
0h2ctbt00kkkv	3553163410	3	3	22922	0	718750	0	3
with function l_disp_name(p_sn in varchar2 ,p_fn1								
bpkx9avbb9why	3553163410	3	3	22922	0	2296875	1338889	3
select /*mdw_7a */ avg(length(str_util.disp_name(p_sn =>surname								

The conversion of the stored PL/SQL function to one stated in the WITH clause reduces the impact of calling PL/SQL from SQL, but, of course, this goes against the idea of centralizing and encapsulating the code. Therefore, you should use stored PL/SQL functions for situations where performance is not the key issue (such as data input screens and small-volume reports) or the overhead is acceptable, and only use the WITH structure for code that processes very large volumes of data where performance is crucial and the context switching overhead is going to extend the duration of the code beyond what is acceptable.

How does Oracle manage to reduce the overhead via the WITH clause? How is the context switch overhead reduced? It is not by removing the actual context switching. If you enable DBMS_TRACE for your session and run code that includes a PL/SQL function WITH clause (remember to reduce the number of records you fetch!), you will still see calls to start and stop the PL/SQL Virtual Machine.

```
with
    function l_disp_name(p_sn      in varchar2
                        ,p_fn1     in varchar2
                        ,p_fn2     in varchar2   :=null
                        ,p_title   in varchar2   :=null)
return varchar2
is
v_return      varchar2(1000);
... our usual function code
end l_disp_name;
select /*mdw_7b */
        avg(length(l_disp_name(p_sn =>surname        ,p_fn1  =>first_forename
          ,p_fn2=>second_forename  ,p_title=>pers_title) ) ) disp_name_len
        ,avg(addr_id)
        ,count(*)
from person
where pers_id > 100100
and rownum < 6
```

```
    run event
    id   seq EVENT_TI EVENT_UNIT    EVENT_UNIT_KIND     EVENT_COMMENT
----- ----- -------- ------------- ------------------  ------------------------------
    7     7 18:06:49 <anonymous>   ANONYMOUS BLOCK     PL/SQL Virtual Machine started
    7     8 18:06:49 <anonymous>   ANONYMOUS BLOCK     PL/SQL Internal Call
    7     9 18:06:49 <anonymous>   ANONYMOUS BLOCK     PL/SQL Internal Call
    7    10 18:06:49 <anonymous>   ANONYMOUS BLOCK     PL/SQL Internal Call
    7    11 18:06:49                                   PL/SQL Virtual Machine stopped
... 3 more repeats of stating the PL/SQL vm, 3 calls and stopping it
    7    52 18:06:49 <anonymous>   ANONYMOUS BLOCK     PL/SQL Virtual Machine started
    7    53 18:06:49 <anonymous>   ANONYMOUS BLOCK     PL/SQL Internal Call
    7    54 18:06:49 <anonymous>   ANONYMOUS BLOCK     PL/SQL Internal Call
    7    55 18:06:49 <anonymous>   ANONYMOUS BLOCK     PL/SQL Internal Call
    7    56 18:06:49                                   PL/SQL Virtual Machine stopped
```

We've trimmed the output from the query on PLSQL_TRACE_EVENTS, but our code has one column based on our factored function and selects five records. There are five calls to start and stop the PL/SQL Virtual Machine. The same number of such events is seen if we have code that calls the stored version of the PL/SQL function. So how is the impact reduced? It is a little beyond the scope of this book, but if you trace the process at the OS level, it seems that compared to calling the function, when using the WITH clause the code stack (the C calls made) is reduced and changes are made to how data is passed between SQL and PL/SQL.

If you decide to use the WITH clause to make your PL/SQL function local and more efficient, you could use a view to implement the functionality and build the complex function into that view. This means you still have one place to manage that complexity. If you can implement this with only the standard SQL functions, you will avoid the context switching completely, of course.

You can declare more than one function using the WITH clause, just as you can declare more than one subquery. You simply put a comma between each function declaration. Thus, you can use this feature to put several PL/SQL functions into your SQL statement.

Issues with Embedding Functions in WITH clauses   There are a couple of things to be aware of when using functions in the WITH clause. First, notice the use of the semicolon in the function text, as shown in the following:

```
with
    function l_disp_name(p_sn        in varchar2
...
is
v_return       varchar2(1000);
begin
...
                ||initcap(p_sn);
return v_return;
end l_disp_name;
```

This semicolon can cause issues with client tools and GUIs, especially those that predate Oracle Database 12c as they are interpreted as end-of-SQL-statement characters. In SQL*Plus, you will need to use the block terminator (/) to end statements, and in other tools/versions you might need to change the SQL terminator. In 12c SQL*Plus, the following shows that ; on a new line is ignored, so you have to use the / block terminator:

```
ora12> with function sal_inc(i in number) return number is
    2  begin
    3  return i+1234;
    4  end;
    5  select ename,sal,sal_inc(sal) from emp
    6  where sal>2000
    7  ;
    8
    9  /

ENAME            SAL SAL_INC(SAL)
---------- ---------- ------------
JONES           2975         4209
BLAKE           2850         4084
...
```

PL/SQL in Oracle Version 12.1 does not recognize functions embedded in SQL using the WITH clause and an error is given, as shown in the following:

```
create procedure embed_with_demo
as
begin
  for v_rec in (with function sal_inc(i in number) return number is
                begin
                return i+1234;
                end;
                select ename,sal,sal_inc(sal) new_sal from emp
                where sal>2000) loop
    dbms_output.put_line(v_rec.ename||' sal:'||v_rec.sal||' new_sal:'||v_rec.new_sal);
  end loop;
end embed_with_demo;
/
LINE/COL ERROR
-------- --------------------------------------------------------------------
4/17    PL/SQL: SQL Statement ignored
4/31    PL/SQL: ORA-00905: missing keyword
6/30    PLS-00103: Encountered the symbol ";" when expecting one of the
        following:
        loop
```

You can work around this by using dynamic SQL (see Chapter 8 for details on using dynamic SQL).

Finally, if you wish to use functions within WITH clauses in SQL subqueries, you have to "warn" Oracle that you are doing so with a hint, namely **+ with_plsql**:

```
select * from
(with function sal_inc(i in number) return number is
begin
return i+1234;
end;
select ename,sal,sal_inc(sal) from emp) emp_high
where sal>2000
/

(with function sal_inc(i in number) return number is
 *
ERROR at line 2:
ORA-32034: unsupported use of WITH clause

select /*+ with_plsql */ * from
(with function sal_inc(i in number) return number is
begin
return i+1234;
end;
select ename,sal,sal_inc(sal) from emp) emp_high
where sal>2000
/

ENAME          SAL SAL_INC(SAL)
---------- ---------- ------------
JONES         2975         4209
BLAKE         2850         4084
...
```

Pragma UDF　Another feature new to 12c is the pragma UDF (user-defined function), which tells the compiler that this function is intended to mostly be called from SQL. The manual entry for this pragma is not exactly verbose in explaining what it does:

> "The **UDF** pragma tells the compiler that the PL/SQL unit is a **user-defined function** that is used primarily in SQL statements, *which might improve its performance.*"

Note the italics (which are mine). It *might improve its performance,* but there's no detail as to what it does. You designate a function as being UDF with a simple PRAGMA UDF command in the declaration section of the function. If you state it in the first line of the declaration section, it is nice and clear. The impact on performance is similar to using a function local to the SQL statement via the WITH clause, as shown in the prior section of this chapter. Tests show PRAGMA UDF to be slightly more advantageous than the WITH clause with respect to performance, but the margins are very small. Using the WITH function, the execution time for this specific test dropped to around 0.21 seconds, averaged over several runs on our test system. Using PRAGMA UDF, this drops to around 0.18 seconds on average. In our experience, the performance benefit of PRAGMA UDF is generally a few percentages better than using WITH, but sometimes WITH wins out.

```
function disp_name_udf (p_sn       in varchar2
                       ,p_fn1      in varchar2
                       ,p_fn2      in varchar2
                       ,p_title    in varchar2  ) return varchar2 is
PRAGMA UDF;
v_return       varchar2(1000);
begin
...

-- str_util.disp_name form
Elapsed: 00:00:00.74

-- str_util.disp_name_UDF form
Elapsed: 00:00:00.18
```

An advantage of PRAGMA UDF over the WITH clause is that it is a very simple change and does not have to be applied directly to SQL statements. You can still keep your function code as stored functions or packages. A disadvantage is that it can slightly slow down the use of the function from other PL/SQL code. Therefore, you should only mark functions with PRAGMA UDF that you really do predominantly call them from SQL.

Another drawback with PRAGMA UDF is that in 12.1c it is sensitive to the data types you are using. If you are sharp eyed, you will have noticed in the specification for the **disp_name_udf** function that our default values for **p_fn2** and **p_title** have been removed. On our 12.1.0.2 test system, PRAGMA UDF does not benefit functions that have parameter defaults. Further, functions that take in DATE data type parameters or return the DATE data type do not benefit from PRAGMA UDF. No errors are given; you simply won't see an improvement in performance. I suggest you test any functions you alter to use PRAGMA UDF to ensure you actually see a benefit, especially if you use data types other than NUMBER and VARCHAR2.

The way that PRAGAMA UDF reduces the impact is similar to that of the WITH clause in that if the process is traced at a C level, then certain function calls are avoided, though different ones from those with the WITH clause.

Loss of Point-in-Time View

Oracle is an ACID-compliant database: atomicity, consistency, isolation, and durability are enforceable. As part of isolation, Oracle preserves a point-in-time view of the data during the execution of any SQL statement. If you issue a statement such as

```
select * from person where modified_datetime<=sysdate
```

and it takes several seconds or minutes to run, Oracle will ensure that any rows created or modifications made to existing rows during that time are not seen by your query. Your view of the database will be preserved at the very point in time—in fact, to the value of the System Change Number—when your query started. Even if a new row is created while your SELECT is running with modified_datetime set in the past, it will not be seen. This is called *read consistency*.

Furthermore, if you reference SYSDATE (or SYSTIMESTAMP or anything derived from these pseudo-columns) several times in your query, the same value for SYSDATE will be used for each and every reference.

However, *point-in-time consistency can be compromised with PL/SQL functions*. We've created a very simple function that returns SYSTIMESTAMP, and we use it in a very, very simple SELECT statement. You're probably thinking, especially given what we said earlier about using SYSDATE and SYSTIMESTAMP directly in a SQL statement, that all values returned from the function will be for the very point in time our SQL statement was executed. Take a look at this example:

```
function get_ts (p_vc1 in varchar2)
return timestamp
is
b number;
begin
  -- the time-waste loop is needed as systimestamp via the system clock ticks too
  -- slow for two calls on same row to come up with a different result.
  for a in 1..10000 loop
    b:=sqrt(a);
  end loop;
  return systimestamp;
end get_ts;


select systimestamp, str_util.get_ts('A'), str_util.get_ts('B')
from dual;

SYSTIMESTAMP                 STR_UTIL.GET_TS('A')               STR_UTIL.GET_TS('B')
---------------------------- ---------------------------------- ----------------------
11-OCT-15 16.24.15.3330 +01:00 11-OCT-15 16.24.15.4870 11-OCT-15 16.24.15.6430
Elapsed: 00:00:00.31
```

Here we are selecting one row—just one row—and yet we get three different values for TIMESTAMP! Time moves on. Note that we added the loop to the function to do some work (it calculates all square roots from 1 to 10,000) just to simulate some activity. Also, if the function just returns SYSTIMESTAMP, because SYSTIMESTAMP is derived from the system clock in thousandths of a second (this is a limit of the OS clock on my machine), we might not see the SYSTIMESTAMP increase.

This happens when the PL/SQL function is fired, each time control is passed to the PL/SQL Virtual Machine, and *the code runs as a distinct action*—at a different time and SCN. We have just broken the integrity of the RDBMS, specifically the preservation of a point-in-time view.

This issue is more insidious than many realize. As an example, consider the following code that selects records with a high salary from the EMP standard demonstration table and compares the salary to the president, called KING:

```
with function king_sal(i in number) return number is
v_rtn number;
begin
  select sal into v_rtn from emp where ename='KING';
  dbms_lock.sleep(3);
  return v_rtn;
end;
select ename,sal,king_sal(rownum) King_sal
from emp
where sal >2000

-- output
ENAME            SAL   KING_SAL
----------  ----------  ----------
JONES           2975       5000
BLAKE           2850       5000
CLARK           2450       5000
SCOTT           3000       3900
KING            5000       2800
FORD            3000       1700

6 rows selected.
```

How can that be? The function is simply selecting the salary for KING—and you can see that KING has a salary of 5000 (fifth record selected). The **dbms_lock.sleep** in the function is just there to allow enough time for us to do something *in a second session,* which is

```
update emp set sal=sal-1100 where ename='KING';
1 row updated.
commit;
```

Our query on EMP keeps a point-in-time view so it sees KING's salary as it was at the very point the query started running. But functions are run in their own subsession and any SQL sees the database as it is *at the time the function executes.* In a second session, we ran that update to reduce KING's salary a couple of times, and the function sees the impact of that change—even when the function is defined as part of the SQL statement using the WITH statement. It is, of course, no different when the function is in a stored procedure.

Now consider a business report running on a database that has no SLEEP commands but takes several minutes to run. You have a function in the report that gets the profit that an item you sell has made in the last week. You used a function to get the information because it is a fairly complex thing to calculate—has the price varied? Do you take into account returns and special offers? Plus, you use the same code when you display information on an individual item in your stock management application, so you want a single stored function to do this task.

Each time the function is called it will calculate the profit at different times. Orders are coming in all the time, and your distinct function calls will see those new orders coming in as the report runs. You may decide because this is just a report that you can accept that lack of consistency—but you need to know that this issue exists. What if the function is collecting stock price points via a SELECT against a constantly updating table or even an external source? You might not be able to accept the lack of read consistency.

You have a few possible solutions to this problem:

■ **Option 1:** Pull the function code into the SQL of the report. This might not be acceptable if the function is used in many different SQL statements because you then have the issue of maintaining them all. It might also not be possible because the function code is too complex to easily include in the SQL.

■ **Option 2:** Write a view that includes the function code. Depending on the function, this may not be possible or is possible but unacceptably complex or performs poorly, as in option 1, but it would keep the complex code in one place. Also, you would need to change code to look at the new view.

■ **Option 3:** Make the tables that underlie the function read-only such that you control when updates to it occur. This sounds simple, but how do you ensure that code you are protecting from the read inconsistency issue is not running at the times you make the table read-write to update it?

■ **Option 4:** Use the SERIALIZABLE transaction model or set the transaction as read-only (which you will need to repeat for each transaction and limit what the transaction can do). Both are restrictive solutions and may require extra code to handle failures to serialize access.

■ **Option 5:** You could use DBMS_FLASHBACK to fix the view your session has of the database to a specific time before the code is run. That's a pretty strongly engineered solution and only worth considering for solving very specific and high-business-impact problems.

■ **Option 6:** Accept the risk to your read consistency.

Several of these solutions—namely, Options 3, 4, and 5—will not stop the issue with TIMESTAMP from occurring. They can help you preserve your point-in-time consistency but will have considerable impact on the rest of your application.

My preference would be Option 1 or 2 for replacing simple functions or targeting specific long-running or critical reports, and Option 3 if you can control when you reference or when slowly changing dimension data is altered. Option 6 would work if the function is only used for online, informational purposes.

That last option may surprise you, but you have to ask yourself what it is you are trying to achieve for the business and whether the benefits of the centralized, modular code outweigh the occasional inclusion of later data in a query. If you are getting summarized sales figures over thousands of items to get a feel for how the business day is going, inclusion of a handful of extra items is probably unimportant and is insignificant. After all, simply running the report one minute later will probably show a larger difference in numbers than that caused by the loss of a point-in-time view as a result of calling SQL via PL/SQL functions from SQL.

However, checking the state of accounts as a set of transactions is recorded cannot go wrong, and thus losing your point-in-time view is not acceptable.

The important thing is that the issues from the point-in-time view being lost for SQL-called-from-PL/SQL-called-from-SQL are considered—and the solution should be chosen with the limitations in mind. After all, how much code is out there suffering from this issue and is not even noticed? Some of this code should be fixed as it will be (silently) impacting the business, but some of it will have no real impact.

A common use of PL/SQL functions is to replace simple lookup joins in order to expand a code (such as a status code or a country ID). If this lookup involves collecting information from a table, you may well hit this point-in-time issue. I discuss this issue next.

PL/SQL Results Caching

The fastest way to do something is to not do it. If you have a PL/SQL function that is doing the same thing over and over again—say, calculating a value for the same inputs or repeatedly looking up details for a small set of reference values—you could save time by running it once per input value(s), caching the result, and using that result the next time the same inputs are fed to the function. Let's look at a new example to show this, based on having an ACTIVITY table that holds a foreign key to a COUNTRY table where the full name is held for that table. Scripts to create and populate these tables can be found on the website.

```
DESC ACTIVITY
 Name                                               Null?    Type
 -------------------------------------------------- -------- ---------------
 ID                                                 NOT NULL NUMBER
 COUNTRY_ID                                                  NUMBER(3)
 R2                                                         NUMBER(2)
 NUM1                                                       NUMBER(4)
 NUM2                                                       NUMBER(3)
 VC1                                                        VARCHAR2(10)
 VC_R1                                                      VARCHAR2(20)
 V_PAD                                                      VARCHAR2(1000)

DESC COUNTRY
 Name                                               Null?    Type
 -------------------------------------------------- -------- ---------------
 ID                                                 NOT NULL NUMBER(3)
 NAME                                               NOT NULL VARCHAR2(40)
 EU_IND                                             NOT NULL VARCHAR2(1)
 SHORT_NAME                                         NOT NULL VARCHAR2(6)
 COUN_COMMENT                                                VARCHAR2(1000)

SELECT * FROM COUNTRY WHERE ROWNUM < 7
        ID NAME                                     E SHORT_ COUN_COMMENT
---------- ---------------------------------------- - ------ ------------
         1 United Kingdom                           Y UK
         2 United States of America                 N USA
         3 India                                    N IND
         4 Bangladesh                               N BAN
         5 Russia                                   N RUS
         6 Austria                                  Y AUS
```

You may think that a simple lookup in a table for a reference value—say, expanding a country code into its full name—is going to be efficient because the data block(s) for the COUNTRY table are cached in the SGA. This is certainly more efficient than going to disk, but there is still a cost to getting the numeric code from the parent table, finding it in the relevant index on the COUNTRY.ID column, and then finding the block in the COUNTRY table and extracting the relevant column. (You can simplify this by having a concatenated index on both the ID and NAME columns so that once the index has been visited, all the data is there, thus saving the trip to the COUNTRY table. However, that is not really relevant here.)

Caching with DETERMINISTIC

The way our test tables have been created and populated matches a lot of real-world situations. We have a reference or lookup table that holds tens or hundreds (or even thousands) of values that are constantly referenced in a fact table. Each row in the lookup table is used by hundreds, thousands, or even millions of records in the fact table—it is the perfect example of normalizing reference data that RDBMSs are intended for. We have 32 different COUNTRY records and 10 million ACTIVITY records. We will be looking up the same country code in the COUNTRY table a lot of times. Therefore, we'll create a simple function to do this lookup for us:

```
CREATE OR REPLACE FUNCTION get_country(p_id IN number) RETURN varchar2 IS
v_rtn country.name%type;
BEGIN
  Select /*mdw_18a*/ name into v_rtn
  from country where id=p_id;
  RETURN v_rtn;
END;

select get_country(13) from dual;
GET_COUNTRY(13)
-------------------------------------------
Estonia

select get_country(1) from dual;
GET_COUNTRY(1)
-------------------------------------------
United Kingdom

select get_country(33) from dual;
GET_COUNTRY(33)
-------------------------------------------

1 row selected.
```

With that last SELECT, you may have noticed something that is often overlooked. The function did not find any data (we have country records from 1 to 32), but rather than raise a NO_DATA_FOUND error, it simply returned NULL. If we want to handle no data being found by our function, we need to capture that exception within the function code.

Now we will write two different SQL statements—one that does the lookup via the standard table join and one that uses the function to get the expanded name for the country. Which will be faster?

```
select max(ac.id),co.name co_name,max(ac.vc1)
from activity ac, country co
where co.id          =ac.country_id
and    ac.id         between 50000 and 50000+1000000
and    mod(ac.id,100)=0
group by co.name
/
MAX(AC.ID) CO_NAME                              MAX(AC.VC1
---------- ------------------------------------ ----------
   1032000 Denmark                              XQQQQQQQQQ
   1040000 Poland                               WQQQQQQQQQ
   1050000 Croatia                              XGGGGGGGGG
...
32 rows selected.
Elapsed: 00:00:00.21


Execution Plan
----------------------------------------------------------
Plan hash value: 4061328850

-------------------------------------------------------------------------------
| Id  | Operation                              | Name     | Rows  | Bytes | Cost )|
-------------------------------------------------------------------------------
|   0 | SELECT STATEMENT                       |          |    32 |  1056 |  2541)|
|   1 |  HASH GROUP BY                         |          |    32 |  1056 |  2541)|
|*  2 |   HASH JOIN                            |          | 10000 |  322K |  2540)|
|   3 |    TABLE ACCESS FULL                   | COUNTRY  |    32 |   416 |     3)|
|   4 |    TABLE ACCESS BY INDEX ROWID BATCHED | ACTIVITY | 10000 |  195K |  2537)|
|*  5 |     INDEX RANGE SCAN                   | ACTI_PK  | 10000 |       |  2169)|
-------------------------------------------------------------------------------
Statistics
----------------------------------------------------------
          0  recursive calls

select max(ac.id),get_country(ac.country_id) co_name,max(ac.vc1)
from activity ac
where ac.id          between 50000 and 50000+1000000
and    mod(ac.id,100)=0
group by get_country(ac.country_id)

MAX(AC.ID) CO_NAME                              MAX(AC.VC1
---------- ------------------------------------ ----------
   1032000 Denmark                              XQQQQQQQQQ
   1040000 Poland                               WQQQQQQQQQ
   1050000 Croatia                              XGGGGGGGGG
...
32 rows selected.
Elapsed: 00:00:00.46
```

```
Execution Plan
------------------------------------------------------------
Plan hash value: 614599487

------------------------------------------------------------------------------
| Id  | Operation                            | Name     | Rows  | Bytes | Cost |
------------------------------------------------------------------------------
|   0 | SELECT STATEMENT                     |          |    32 |   640 | 2538|
|   1 |  HASH GROUP BY                       |          |    32 |   640 | 2538|
|   2 |   TABLE ACCESS BY INDEX ROWID BATCHED| ACTIVITY | 10000 |  195K | 2537|
|*  3 |    INDEX RANGE SCAN                  | ACTI_PK  | 10000 |       | 2169|
------------------------------------------------------------------------------

Statistics
------------------------------------------------------------
       10002  recursive calls
```

The function version took twice as long (0.46 seconds compared to 0.21), so it is slower. This should come as no surprise. In general, it is faster to do something in SQL alone if it can be done in SQL. However, the difference in performance is not as great as you may have expected. You might also note that the full SQL version does not keep repeatedly looking up the country codes. It looks them up *once* and then hashes them together with the data collected from the ACTIVITY table. SQL has a lot of optimizations in it to aid repeated lookups.

Something I want to highlight is exemplified by the previous code. For the second version of the code, which uses a PL/SQL function to resolve the country code lookup, the explain plan for that SQL no longer shows the access to the COUNTRY table you see in the first (table-join) version because it is being done as recursive calls. This often confuses people; database activity that is carried out via PL/SQL functions is, as we have discussed earlier, carried out as distinct and separate transactions (thus the potential for losing point-in-time consistency—don't forget about that). As such, this causes the activity and thus the steps to drop out of the explain plan for the statement because it is now being done under a different SQL ID. The following shows the SQL code for the lookup in the SGA (as shown in V$SQL) after we have run the code:

```
SQL_ID        PLAN_HASHV  PRSE   EXCS   BUFFS DISCS   CPU_T PLSQL_EXEC    RWS
------------  ----------  -----  -----  ----- -----   -----  ----------  ------
SQL_TXT
------------------------------------------------------------------------------
bncf9q7qu0r01 2256147665      1  10022  20044     0   62500           0  10022
SELECT NAME FROM COUNTRY WHERE ID=:B1
```

You can see SQL ID **bncf9q7qu0r01**, which is the SQL statement run by our **get_country** function. It has been executed 10,022 times: 20 times for another test we do not show the details for and 10,002 times recursively for our test code. We fetch 10,002 records from ACTIVITY, so we have to expand the code 10,002 times, which means 10,002 calls to the function and its SQL.

Tracking down SQL that is fired via PL/SQL functions is not as easy as for standard SQL because the PL/SQL engine pre-parses the SQL and, as part of this, puts all the command words in uppercase, removes the INTO section, and removes comments. You can see this if you compare the SQL text in the data we extracted from the SGA against the SQL in the example code.

We have seen (and used) this method of employing PL/SQL functions to look up reference data to improve SQL performance in the past. Our example is a straight foreign-key lookup to a second table; this method will not improve performance in this scenario (as it stands at present). What if the lookup is more complex than a simple visit to a child table via a foreign key lookup?

Perhaps it has to go through an intermediate table, has more complex logic, or is only needed for some of the rows found, where, for example, the code value in the ACTIVITY table being expanded is often NULL. It sometimes used to be the case that a function to carry out the specific lookup that is only fired for each row selected by the driving query was more efficient than the plan that the CBO came up with to follow the joins through two or three tables to the data needed—especially if you could use some logic to only resolve the lookup for certain situations. This was often the case when you needed the "foreign key" lookup to be to more than one table (some values were held in one table, some in another). The function could detect this difference and go only to the required table. The equivalent SQL would need to use an outer join to all the child tables and use DECODE or some other logic to concatenate several NULL outer-join lookups into the one value.

Improvements in the capabilities of SQL, including the use of subquery factoring, have reduced the impact of this improvement, but the replacement of a complex lookup with a PL/SQL function, especially one over several tables where outer joins are involved, can still give a performance boost.

In any case, we have our simple example where a normal table join is faster. What if we use the new Oracle Database 12c pragma UDF feature? In this case (on our test system), it does not help, at least not enough to be detectable above the natural variation of multiple executions of the code (so, in reality, not enough to care about). However, we have not told Oracle that our function is deterministic. It is not, strictly speaking, deterministic—if someone updates the COUNTRY table, then any in-flight SQL that uses the function will potentially be impacted by the change because no point-in-time view is persisted for PL/SQL function calls (sorry to keep mentioning this, but you really do need to be aware of this—if only so you can decide when to *relatively safely* ignore it). In the real world, new countries are rarely ratified by the United Nations, so the data will not change very often. You would probably deem a change to a generally static table like this as coming under a code release. Therefore, let's mark the function as deterministic and see what happens. We do this simply by adding the keyword DETERMINISTIC after the RETURN clause (in both the package specification and body if it is a packaged function):

```
CREATE OR REPLACE FUNCTION get_country(p_id IN number) RETURN varchar2
DETERMINISTIC   IS
v_rtn country.name%type;
BEGIN
  begin
    select name into v_rtn
    from country where id=p_id;
  exception
    when no_data_found then v_rtn :='Unknown!';
  end;
  RETURN v_rtn;
END;
/

select max(ac.id),get_country(ac.country_id) co_name,max(ac.vc1)
from activity ac
where ac.id         between 50000 and 50000+1000000
and    mod(ac.id,100)=0
group by get_country(ac.country_id)
```

```
MAX(AC.ID) CO_NAME                              MAX(AC.VC1
---------- ------------------------------      ----------
   1032000 Denmark                             XQQQQQQQQQ
   1040000 Poland                              WQQQQQQQQQ
...
    965000 Netherlands                         XUUUUUUUUU
32 rows selected.
Elapsed: 00:00:00.29
```

I ran this code several times and confirmed 0.29 seconds was the average value. Why do we see an improvement? Because Oracle takes us at our word that the function is deterministic, and, as suggested at the start of this section, *it saves time by caching the results for a given set of input values, and if it sees the same input values again, rather than executing the code again, it returns the cached value.*

The DETERMINISTIC option has been available since the Oracle 10*g* Database and replaced the use of the pragma RESTRICT REFERENCES, which was deprecated with Oracle Database 11.1*g*.

A word of warning concerning the DETERMINISTIC flag: Oracle will do this caching optimization within a single SQL statement execution utilizing this function—it does not persist the cache between executions. If we run the code once and then run the code again, or another SQL statement using the same function, the cached values will not be used from our initial SQL statement. Caching is only done within the confines of a single SQL statement. It will also not be used for PL/SQL calls to the function.

Another word of warning: if the underlying lookup table has any level of update activity on it (or even delete activity on it), we have lied to Oracle about our function being deterministic, and even though we will not notice because *no error will occur,* we will almost certainly be getting situations and odd queries where a lookup changes as our code runs. We will be getting wrong results. We'll just never notice it. That is why we have stressed how PL/SQL functions called from SQL can compromise point-in-time read consistency. We can imagine scenarios where a report grouped by the lookup value will give a result where two values for the same lookup appear in the result and you have no way to control which rows are summed under which lookup value.

An important consideration with stating that a function is deterministic is, how many different input values to the function will your SQL statement provide? If your code will select 1000 rows and there will be 999 different input values to the function, any DETERMINISTIC-derived caching based on input values will not help you. In fact, chances are, as Oracle has to do something internally (determine if your input values have been seen before), you may notice a negative performance impact. If for 1000 rows you provide only two input values, the DETERMINISTIC-derived caching will reap even larger benefits than shown here, but this is *only* within a single SQL statement.

Function Result Cache

From Oracle Database 11*g* onward, the function result cache has been available. It is very, very simple to use and supersedes the old method of package-based caching we touch on later in this chapter. When you turn on the function result cache, Oracle stores the input values for that function and the output values, similar to how it does within a single SQL execution when the function is labeled as deterministic. The big advantage of the function result cache is that *the list of known input values and their return values is maintained across not only SQL statements but also sessions.* The Oracle Database 11.2*g* improves on this and shares the cache between RAC nodes also.

A key benefit is that you (or Oracle, depending on the version) identify which tables the function is dependent on. Then, when any changes are committed to the underlying table(s), the cache is cleared and future calls to the function repopulate the cache. This avoids the point-in-time issues we keep mentioning. Also, as a consequence of this, using a function cache on a function based on tables that change often is not going to gain you any benefit because the cache will be constantly thrown away—but in that situation you also need to be questioning trying to cache such dynamic data. You could argue that any reference data set that only adds values should still be cached (and in fact the cache should not be invalidated by adding values), but maybe we are getting a little esoteric now.

You don't need to code anything to use the function result cache as you do with the older package-based caching; you simply declare the cache and dependencies in the function. Also, the cache is used whenever you use the function, not just when you call it from SQL.

This code shows the format for the function declaration for Oracle Database 11.1*g*:

```
CREATE OR REPLACE FUNCTION get_country(p_id IN number) RETURN varchar2
RESULT_CACHE RELIES_ON (COUNTRY) IS
v_rtn country.name%type;
BEGIN
  begin
    select name into v_rtn
    from country where id=p_id;
  exception
    when no_data_found then v_rtn :='Unknown!';
  end;
  RETURN v_rtn;
END;
/

-- to indicate that the function relies on more than one table or view...
CREATE OR REPLACE FUNCTION get_country(p_id IN number) RETURN varchar2
RESULT_CACHE RELIES_ON (COUNTRY,DEPARTMENT,COUN_HIST_VW) IS
v_rtn country.name%type;
BEGIN
```

With Oracle Database 11.1*g*, it is up to you to state all the tables and views that the result cache function relies on. You do not need to state the tables that any view is based on; Oracle will work that out from the view definition. If the function is in a package, the RELIES ON clause must appear (and be the same) in both the package specification and body.

From Oracle Database 11.2*g* onward, the RELIES ON clause is deprecated and *should not be used*. Oracle will infer what tables the function relies on for itself. In fact, it appears that the clause is ignored because stating a nonexistent table does not result in an error. Note that you do not have to state that the function is DETERMINISTIC. It is assumed that it is deterministic, with the corollary that alterations to the tables used by the function will change the results of the function and cause the existing cache to be invalidated and cleared. Implementing the feature is as easy as this:

```
CREATE OR REPLACE FUNCTION get_country(p_id IN number) RETURN varchar2
deterministic IS
v_rtn country.name%type;
```

```
-- becomes
CREATE OR REPLACE FUNCTION get_country(p_id IN number) RETURN varchar2
RESULT_CACHE IS
v_rtn country.name%type;
```

If we now re-run the tests from earlier, we can see how the result cache aids our very simple SQL lookup:

```
-- using the function now marked with RESULTS_CACHE
select max(ac.id),get_country(ac.country_id) co_name,max(ac.vc1)
from activity ac
where ac.id          between 50000 and 50000+1000000
and    mod(ac.id,100)=0
group by get_country(ac.country_id)

MAX(AC.ID) CO_NAME                              MAX(AC.VC1
---------- ----------------------------------- ----------
   1032000 Denmark                             XQQQQQQQQQ
   1040000 Poland                              WQQQQQQQQQ
...
    965000 Netherlands                         XUUUUUUUUU

32 rows selected.
Elapsed: 00:00:00.22
```

The performance of the function with result cache is improved, dropping to 0.22 seconds. This is superior to using DETERMINISTIC, where the run time was 0.29 seconds, as well as to not using DETERMINISTIC or caching, which took 0.49 seconds.

The PL/SQL result cache is a really nice feature of Oracle and replaces and improves upon the old method of using a package to cache your function values.

We'll demonstrate the caching of values by altering our function to issue a DBMS_OUPUT line each time it is fired (something you should only ever do in small-scale testing) and then select our 20 records again to see the results. We'll then issue the statement again. Finally, we'll update the COUNTRY table in a second session and re-run the SQL.

```
CREATE OR REPLACE FUNCTION get_country(p_id IN number) RETURN varchar2
RESULT_CACHE IS
v_rtn country.name%type;
BEGIN
  begin
    select name into v_rtn
    from country where id=p_id;
  exception
    when no_data_found then v_rtn :='Unknown!';
  end;
  dbms_output.put_line ('called with input '||p_id);
  RETURN v_rtn;
END;

select ac.id,get_country(ac.country_id) co_name,ac.vc1
from activity ac
where ac.id between 50000 and 50000+10000
and    mod(ac.id,500)=0
```

```
        ID CO_NAME                          VC1
---------- ------------------------------ ----------
     56500 India                          JHHHHHHHHH
     57000 India                          JHHHHHHHHH
     58000 Russia                         KIIIIIIIII
     57500 Russia                         KIIIIIIIII
     59000 Denmark                        LJJJJJJJJJ
     58500 Denmark                        LJJJJJJJJJ
...
21 rows selected.
called with input 15
called with input 13
called with input 21
called with input 17
called with input 18
called with input 27
called with input 3
called with input 5
called with input 12
called with input 28
Elapsed: 00:00:00.01
-- NOTE only 10 DBMS_OUTPUT lines for 21 rows and each one is for a unique input value


/
        ID CO_NAME                          VC1
---------- ------------------------------ ----------
     50000 France                         CAAAAAAAAA
     50500 Estonia                        DBBBBBBBBB
     51000 Estonia                        DBBBBBBBBB
...
21 rows selected.

Elapsed: 00:00:00.01
-- NOTE No output from DBMS_OUTPUT as all those values are cached already
-- {from second session}
UPDATE COUNTRY SET COUN_COMMENT='The Land of Apple Pie'
where id=2

1 row updated.
ora122> commit;
-- back to original session
/
        ID CO_NAME                          VC1
---------- ------------------------------ ----------
     50000 France                         CAAAAAAAAA
     50500 Estonia                        DBBBBBBBBB
     51000 Estonia                        DBBBBBBBBB
     51500 Latvia                         ECCCCCCCCC
...
21 rows selected.

called with input 15
called with input 13
called with input 21
called with input 17
```

```
called with input 18
called with input 27
called with input 3
called with input 5
called with input 12
called with input 28
Elapsed: 00:00:00.01
```

This example contains quite a bit of information. In the first SELECT statement after the **updates** function text, you can see that although we select 21 records out of the database and they all have their country names expanded, only ten lines are produced by the **dbms_output** in the function. If you check the lines, there is only one for each distinct ID seen. The function was only fired once per unique input value. The next time we select the same records, there are no messages from the function via **dbms_output** because the function is never fired—all the values are cached already. Finally, from the second session we alter a record in the source COUNTRY table. We are not altering one of the records that has already been seen by the function (we modify the record for ID 2, USA), but it invalidates the function result cache in any case. Then, when we return to the original session and run the query again, we see the same ten messages because the cache is repopulated.

You might imagine that the Oracle Database could check whether the alteration to the table is actually on any of the cached records (via, say, the primary key) and only invalidate the cache if it holds a value derived from that row or only invalidate cached values related to changed rows— but with just a minute's thought you can probably come up with issues with that. For now, it is a simple total invalidation, and simple is fast and reliable. Maybe future versions will be smarter.

We mentioned earlier that you should not apply the function result cache to functions that use tables that change often, as you will see a performance degrade for such functions. Like any performance improvement tool, it should be used with some consideration for each case where it is applied and not simply implemented against all functions blindly. Sadly, this has been seen on occasion. If you suspect that the function result cache has been applied to functions where it is not beneficial (or you simply want to check that it is helpful), then you can look at the information in V$RESULT_CACHE_OBJECTS, which holds statistics on each function result cache.

The function result cache was introduced by Oracle to address a specific issue. Some applications built on top of Oracle (think corporate financial and business applications) had complex list-of-value lookups that were inefficient. Constantly linking to these reference tables via an inefficient path was a major and chronic cost to the application. To work around this, people coded up solutions based on packaged-based caching.

Packaged-Based Caching

Prior to Oracle Database 11g (and after, if people did not know of or have opportunity to swap to the new feature of the function result cache), a common technique to reduce the impact of complex list-of-value record lookups was to write a package-based cache. We could provide example code for this but (a) there are plenty of good examples out there on the Web and (b) it is an outdated way of achieving results caching. This book is about getting the best out of PL/SQL and is written with Oracle Database 12c and the future in mind. You can find plenty of examples of code to do this on the Web. However, for the sake of completeness and so that you can understand the principle should you come across this technique in use, we will explain the principle and why it has issues.

You create a package-level variable that contains a table type variable based on your lookup table(s). You then take one of two routes:

- **Option A:** Populate the table type variable with all the values the first time a session touches the package, via the package-level execution unit (the optional section of code you can place in a package after all the variable, exception, function, and procedure definitions).

- **Option B:** Write a function that takes in the ID, checks the table type for the value, and returns it if it has been seen before. If it has not been seen, you collect the value, put it in the table type variable, and *then* return the value.

Option A has a high upfront cost the first time the function is called, but after that all lookups are answered immediately. Option B is slower overall but has no high first-call cost and only caches the values you use.

Both options have some significant drawbacks. The first is that each session holds its own set of values. If you have a lot of values, you end up with all sessions that use the function holding their own copy of the lookup table in the PGA (Process Global Area, the memory area that exists just for a single session). That can be a significant chunk of memory for each session—and for each package-based cache you create in that session. If you create such cache-based function lookups for several objects (say, country, department, customer, and item code) and every session connected to the database has its own copy, you better have a lot of memory on the server that is not allocated to the SGA! Second, if there are any changes to the underlying tables, your function is blind to them—unless you add code to cope with the scenario, and that will involve some control tables you constantly have to check. Therefore, you now might have a potential latch contention point. The issues covered earlier about the point-in-time view of PL/SQL functions called by SQL are nothing compared to the potential for errors with this method. Finally, the cache only lasts as long as the session does. If your application creates a session, does work, and then logs out, you would be constantly building up your private session's cache only to lose it.

If you have static lookup tables (for example, read-only tables or tablespaces), long-lasting sessions, and enough memory to allow caching of these values for each session in its PGA, then, okay, it might be fine. However, the function result cache introduced in Oracle Database 11*g* addresses all these issues and is built into the Oracle code base. It would be a real shame not to use it.

Correct Implementation for the DISP_NAME Functionality

Much of this chapter has used the concept of the function **disp_name** to convert a set of name elements into a display name that can be used when we are communicating with the person. Although this is a useful device to explain the aspect of calling PL/SQL functions from SQL, we want to finish with a short section on how you could better implement this functionality, which still includes using the function.

At the start of the chapter, we evolved the **disp_name** function to the point where it capitalized sections of the name and allowed for sections of the name to be blank. However, we did not address the aspect of nonstandard initial capping of names that was mentioned and other exceptions. Because people are sensitive about errors in how their names are written, this does need to be addressed.

First of all, we, of course, don't store the person's title (Mr., Mrs., Dr., Madam, and so on) in the PERSON table, but instead have a code that references a lookup table. Therefore, our **disp_ name** function needs to resolve that lookup.

Second, we should implement an exceptions table for the SURNAME field where we could check for exceptions to standard initial capping, such as "McDonald," "van," "de Souse," and so on. The function code would check whether the surname matches an entry in the table; if so, we would use the form stated there. If there is no entry, we would simply initial cap the surname.

Finally, the result of the **disp_name** function would be persisted in a new column, DISPLAY_ NAME, in the PERSON table. When a PERSON record is created or any of the driving fields are changed, the **disp_name** function would be called and the results put in the DISPLAY_NAME column. The application would allow for this field to be updated so that if the function still comes up with the wrong result, and a customer complains that her name is being capitalized incorrectly, it can be corrected.

One reason to persist the name in a new column is to allow for corrections to what is produced by the function; the other is to avoid calling the function over and over again whenever a display name is needed.

Our function is now quite a complex piece of code that uses two reference tables and could have other logic built into it (forenames that are initialized differently, handling complex surnames, and so on). One of the key tenets of programming languages is to take a complex algorithm and hide the complexity behind a simple, static interface. That complexity exists in only one location; it can be altered without changing the interface, and the programmers not concerned with that functionality need never worry about it. The business logic is compartmentalized. A PL/SQL stored program gives us that compartmentalization.

The PL/SQL function described would be used to initially populate the DISPLAY_NAME and would also be used if that column was NULL for a record.

Although employing user-defined PL/SQL functions is a powerful tool and can enhance your Oracle SQL, if you are generating (generally) static information, you should not repeatedly create it on the fly but rather persist it in a column in a manner similar to what's described here.

Summary

Oracle has provided almost all the scalar functions available in SQL in PL/SQL, and we can use them directly in our PL/SQL code. We can even examine these functions in the SYS.STANDARD and SYS.DBMS_STANDARD packages.

Oracle has constantly extended the capabilities of the Oracle Database by providing built-in packages holding new functions, and we as programmers can further extend the capabilities of our Oracle Database and Oracle SQL by creating our own functions that encapsulate business or data-processing logic. By doing this with PL/SQL, we keep the business logic within the database, so it is always present and is backed up with the database.

These user-defined functions work exactly the same as the built-in functions provided by Oracle. They can be called from SQL statements in exactly the same way as all SQL functions and built-in PL/SQL functions.

However, there is a cost associated in calling PL/SQL functions from SQL (that is, context switching). This cost is cumulative with each distinct function call used. Although this cost is important, especially for large data volumes or microsecond-critical response times, in the greater scheme of things the cost is probably less than that of poorly written SQL or SQL that incurs physical I/O. We need to be aware of it but not be paranoid.

More of an issue is the fact that PL/SQL functions execute outside the point-in-time consistency rules that SQL operates in. As programmers, we are responsible for ensuring that such functions are pure and thus deterministic or that we acknowledge and allow for the loss of that point-in-time consistency. Although we can bend these rules using autonomous transactions or wrongly labeling user-defined functions as deterministic, we now understand the issues involved. It is usually a poor decision to bend these rules.

Any use of PL/SQL functions from SQL that are not deterministic, including issuing their own SQL or looking at pseudo-columns such as SYSDATE or **dbms_random** functions, can have an impact on point-in-time consistency that we need to be aware of. We then can decide what is acceptable from a business perspective and document that choice. It is important to keep in mind that Oracle never guarantees when and how often PL/SQL functions used in SQL will be fired.

Both Oracle Database 11*g* and Oracle Database 12*c* add new functionality in caching PL/SQL results to aid performance and replace the old methods of session-level caches that have been created with package-level collections.

Oracle Database 12*c* introduces two new features—local functions defined within WITH clauses and pragma UDF—to reduce the impact of context switching between SQL and PL/SQL, both with considerable success.

CHAPTER
7

Instrumenting and Profiling PL/SQL

W e've all been there. Someone comes up to you in an agitated state: "The system is
running slow!"

What—all of it? Very occasionally they do mean that, but usually it means that a
certain thing critical to the business is taking too long to run. Less often, but usually with even
more agitation, someone will come up and say "The X function is broken!"

In such situations the problem needs to be fixed and it needs to be fixed as quickly as possible.
Usually a few questions will reveal the part of the application that is the issue (let's say it is the daily
batch load that ran in 2 hours rather than 20 minutes). But where *is* the problem exactly?

Usually the first place people look is to the whole—instance monitoring, the screens showing
the overall workload of the database. Often there is no clear cause. Sometimes there is something
"odd" visible at the system level (for example, unusual levels of contention or buffer gets), but as
often as not that turns out to be a red herring—either that odd thing happens all the time or it is
an unrelated issue. Therefore, all you know is that there is something wrong with the daily batch
load and you are *guessing* **what it is from system-wide metrics.** You can spend hours checking
out these oddities only to find that they have nothing to do with the issue that has been raised—
the one someone important in the business is very agitated about.

This is a very common situation—and there is no need for it! All you need is some information
about where and when the problem is occurring. This could be as simple as knowing when exactly
the batch load started and when it started and ended on other days—so you can at least compare
the system activity between those exact periods for any differences. Occasionally this will highlight
that the code is not running more slowly but maybe it started running later—the problem was with
an earlier task. Or that it has started later and is now running at a time when the instance is really
busy, whereas it normally runs during a quiet time. A surprising number of times it turns out that
the database finished the job just fine but for some reason the information has not gotten to the
user. A very common situation is that something *is* wrong—but not in the part of the process the
database does. For some reason, the database is often blamed for any problem, and you have to
show that, actually, the problem is outside the database (it's usually the network).

The worrying thing is that, in our experience, even that simple information about run starts
and run durations is often lacking—or the information is only available for the last run or last
few runs.

Let's say you have the start times and durations and, yes, there is a problem. That helps, but
you are still guessing as to what the problem is. What you *really* want is some information about
the steps the batch process is doing, how long those steps are taking, and some general indication
of the data being processed so that you know *where* the problem is.

As an example, let's say the batch processing does something like this:

1. Initiation (gather any rules, start and end times, and reference data needed).

2. Collect data type A.

3. Collect data type B.

4. Pre-process data type B.

5. Collate and process data types A and B.

6. Place the results into the target tables.

7. Clean up and end the process.

You'll often be in a situation where you don't know any of this information, so having this overall flow of the batch-load process recorded somewhere is a significant gain. What you would ideally like to have for the slow batch run is this:

1. Initiation	5 seconds
2. Collect data type A	3 minutes, 1 million records
3. Collect data type B	1 minute, 200,000 records
4. Pre-process data type B	**103 minutes**
5. Collate and process A and B	10 minutes
6. Place the results into the target tables	2 minutes, 1.7 million records
7. Clean up and end the process	10 seconds

With this information, there is no point in looking for the source of the slow processing in any part of the code except step 4—it is taking up the vast majority of the time.

There may be a "slow" nested-loop SQL statement collecting the data for step 2 that could be improved—and that is the sort of thing that will be highlighted by looking system-wide for "problems." You could spend a couple hours improving step 2 to make it 100 times faster, reducing the run time from 3 minutes to a few seconds, but this will only reduce the run time from 120 minutes to 117 minutes. You need to know where the real issue is for this batch job and concentrate on step 4.

In an ideal world, you would also have the following information from a prior "good" run:

1. Initiation	6 seconds
2. Collect data type A	4 minutes, 1.1 million records
3. Collect data type B	**1 minute, 15,000 records**
4. Pre-process data type B	8 minutes
5. Collate and process A and B	3 minutes
6. Place the results into the target tables	2 minutes, 1.7 million records
7. Clean up and end the process	10 seconds

Now you can see that, yes, step 4 was a lot faster in the prior run—but step 3, which *took the same amount of time for both runs,* is now finding a lot more data to process than in this prior run. You may or may not be able to improve step 4, but you might have a bug in step 3, or maybe the data being received and processed has changed. You now know where to go and concentrate your efforts. You can pass this information back to development, or you can look at the code yourself; the key thing is *you are no longer guessing.* The batch run took longer because step 3, which collects data type B, collected a significantly larger volume of data.

This is an example of *instrumentation*—recording what is going on within the code. Without it, solving problems is like finding your way in the dark. Actually, no. Without it, solving problems is like finding your way in a snowstorm. There is a lot of light and information, but you can't see any detail and you can't make sense of it! With instrumentation you can *profile* your code—that is, see what the work pattern and distribution is.

Many developers instrument their code when they first write it so that they can see what it is doing and help debug the application as it builds up. Debugging code is a vital skill for all developers and most DBAs. But then some developers remove the instrumentation before releasing the code, following the mantras that (a) production code should not contain anything that is not required for the actual application and (b) for performance reasons any unnecessary overhead must be removed.

But as you saw in our example, you still need the instrumentation to solve production issues. We would argue that instrumentation is not an optional part of your code, maybe to be removed by conditional compilation (which could easily result in you releasing something you did not fully test). Instead, it is a mandatory element of good production code. You cannot solve problems if you do not know where to look, and you cannot judge the scale of the impact without having a profile of the activity.

SQL and RDBMS Instrumentation

The Oracle RDBMS itself is heavily instrumented. Every time it does "something," such as performing a consistent block get or obtaining a latch, the activity is recorded via the wait interface—the CPU waits for the event to complete. This is the basis of all the performance information that some of us use to solve SQL and database performance issues. The graphical information that OEM and other monitoring tools use to allow you to see the real-time activity of the database is built on this low-level instrumentation. It is *because* the Oracle RDBMS is so well instrumented that we can understand what it is doing and solve most of the SQL and database design problems we encounter. However, this built-in instrumentation is not particularly helpful for PL/SQL code because PL/SQL is a different language and runs in a different engine (see Chapter 6, and the section "Context Switching Overhead" in particular, for more details on that). However, this chapter is all about adding your own instrumentation, profiling your code, and helping you simplify fixing performance and other issues with your PL/SQL code.

Instrumentation Overhead

As mentioned earlier, some people are concerned about the overhead of instrumentation. After all, if you are recording extra information and have code to do so, this will slow down your application, right? Also, the extra code is something more to test that could go wrong.

In our experience, these concerns are misplaced. You can over instrument your code and slow it down—we will cover that concern and show you how to avoid it. The ways of instrumenting and profiling your code we cover are either very simple or use built-in and well-tested Oracle features, so things are very unlikely to go wrong.

As for slowing down the application, the impact of instrumentation is usually less than 1 percent, but it allows you to solve performance problems that are an overhead that's hundreds of times greater. It also allows you to see problems that are building, before they become critical. If you look back at our earlier example, if step 3 did not suddenly start finding more data and the volume increased slowly over time, instrumentation and profiling would give you the chance to detect that before it became a problem. We would say that the "overhead" of instrumentation is actually a negative number. As a whole system, your applications will run slower without proper instrumentation, and that negative impact will increase over time.

A few years ago, Tom Kyte made this exact point in his blog. You can see his original post at http://tkyte.blogspot.co.uk/2009/02/couple-of-links-and-advert.html, but here's part of it:

> One time, while presenting [on instrumentation] someone raised their hand and innocently asked: *What is the overhead of this, what performance impact will this have on my system?*
>
> I paused for a second, thought about it, and said: *Probably at least negative 10 percent or less* (meaning more—like negative 1000%, more negative).
>
> The audience now paused and we sort of looked at each other and then I explained. *The addition of this instrumentation/repository will allow your database to perform better than it currently is—any "overhead" of the additional instrumentation is more than offset by the gain in performance.*

Instrumentation Is Built In by the Developer but Sometimes Seen Only by the DBA

A couple of years ago there was a discussion on one of our blogs that could be given the general title "All Good PL/SQL Developers Should Use DBMS_APPLICATION_INFO." DBMS_APPLICATION_INFO is one of the main tools for instrumenting PL/SQL. The conversation went on for several weeks, including many comments on the posts. The general consensus from many experts was that, yes, you could be a very good PL/SQL programmer without using DBMS_APPLICATION_INFO—but you had to be doing *something* to instrument your code.

Part of the issue is that often developers have no access to the production system, so they see little benefit in putting in instrumentation they will not see once the code is completed, tested, and released. They may even remove their "testing instrumentation" before putting the code under source control. The DBAs or analysts who do have access to the system are responsible for spotting and/or resolving production issues. They have little or no knowledge of the code and probably no authority/access to change it. The DBAs would love the code to be instrumented. This is partly why I personally have never signed up to the DBA/developer divide—we are all part of the same logical team. If the developer puts in instrumentation, the DBA uses it and feeds the information back to the developer, who can then look at exactly the spot in the code where the problem is being manifested. They won't be guessing because they know where the problem is.

Instrumentation for Debugging

As briefly mentioned earlier, the other time you instrument your code is to help debug it. The two types of instrumentation (profiling and debugging) are related but have a different focus. In the previous examples, you are looking to profile your code in a lightweight manner in order to spot performance trends and resolve issues. When you are debugging code, especially as you are developing it, you often need go into a lot more detail and you don't care much about performance—*while you are debugging*. You also want immediate feedback, which is why DBMS_OUTPUT and GUI debugging tools are the best options. If you add instrumentation to help debug your code, you probably want to remove some (but not all!) of it for the final testing and production release. As we cover later in this chapter, it is possible to leave the extra instrumentation in place without it impacting your production code.

Obviously, if the results from running your code are wrong, you need to work out why and fix it. However, if your code produces the right result, but either in a time that is not acceptable to the business or in a way that requires too many resources (CPU, memory, I/O), then your code is still not acceptable; it is still "broken" and you need to look at making it run more efficiently.

In our experience, profiling code is almost impossible without instrumentation, and debugging code is considerably more difficult without a profile and almost impossible without instrumentation. In fact, profiling is often little more than looking at the instrumentation information. This is why in this chapter we concentrate on showing you several ways of instrumenting and profiling your PL/SQL code and getting the most out of each method.

The Difference Between Instrumentation, Profiling, and Debugging

Instrumentation is at the core of profiling and debugging. It involves the recording of metrics and information with respect to the progress of your code and the activities that have occurred (for example, what activities are carried out, at what time, and the volume of data processed). It may also include more specific information such as control data and certain variables.

Profiling involves the use of the information gathered via the instrumentation to understand how control flows through the code, where time and resources are being spent, and which areas may benefit from further consideration and tuning effort. Profiling is key to performance tuning.

Debugging involves identifying why your code is not doing what you intended it to do. It is usually not about performance; it is about the correct thing being done. Although debugging is a key programming skill, in this chapter we concentrate on profiling and instrumentation.

Instrumentation

In its simplest form, instrumentation is marking when things happen. You mark when a section of code is executed, when a distinct function is called, or when a certain point in the program is reached. Often you will also record other information at that point, such as the value of variables, the values passed into the function, or the number of iterations of a loop. You are recording the ongoing location and state as your code progresses.

If you do not preserve this information, it can only be seen "on the fly" as transient information. Such transient information is useful if you are constantly monitoring your code, but it's far more powerful if you save the information for later analysis. This analysis can be as soon as something goes wrong when the code is run; within a few minutes, hours, or days if some problem is later suspected; or even days, weeks, or months if you are tracking changes in performance or activity over time.

One of the reasons that the Oracle RDBMS overtook many of its rival RDBMS offerings, and continues to be a popular choice, is that it is very well instrumented. Oracle records many hundreds of the individual actions it can take, such as performing a consistent get, waiting on a physical I/O, and obtaining a lock on a record. Oracle records all of these as the various wait events that are recorded against the SQL statement, the session, and also for the database as a whole. This is the information that is used by the Oracle Enterprise Manager's (OEM) performance pages, SQL Monitor, and third-party tools such as Toad and even statspack for showing what the database is doing and historical average performance. This data is held in dictionary objects such as VSQL, VSESSTAT, and V$SYSSTAT. If you have the diagnostics and tuning pack license, you can look at the Active Session History and Active Workload Repository information where this instrumentation information is persisted.

This data is often called *performance data,* but this isn't what it really is. It is activity information, which you then use to derive performance information. Dozens of books and articles have been written about SQL and Oracle RDBMS tuning using this internal instrumentation to profile the SQL and RDBMS. Therefore, we are not going to cover this topic in this chapter.

With PL/SQL things are different. The SQL it runs is instrumented as described earlier, but the PL/SQL code itself has very little in the way of instrumentation turned on, especially automatically. You have to add your own instrumentation. This is reasonable because Oracle is not writing your code—you are. *Therefore, it is up to you to decide what information you want to record and when to record it.* There is no way for you to turn on automated instrumentation for actual PL/SQL commands (for example, to record each time a loop command is run), and the built-in packages do not have instrumentation coded into them (at least, not that we normal users can get at!). However, if instrumentation was built into these by Oracle, then Oracle would have to decide how it was done and to what level. You also cannot expect Oracle to instrument the built-in PL/SQL when in fact it is their proprietary code.

What Oracle does provide is a whole suite of ways you can instrument your code:

- The most common method, and in many ways the least capable, is to output messages as the code progresses with DBMS_OUTPUT.

- You can use DBMS_APPLICATION_INFO to record where your code is in real time, and this information is exposed in many Oracle and third-party tools such as OEM, PL/SQL Developer, and Toad. You can even put information into the dictionary view V$SESSION_LONGOPS via this package.

- You can store information in the database in your own tables. This is probably the most powerful and flexible method of instrumenting your code, but also the one with which you have to take the most care.

All of these methods have their advantages and disadvantages, which we will cover in detail. You can also use a mixture of these techniques, and we will pull all of them together to describe a simple, lightweight, and easy-to-implement approach to instrumenting your code.

Profiling

Profiling is predominantly about performance rather than correctness. You want to know where time is being spent so you can reduce it.

To profile PL/SQL, you have two main options—add your own instrumentation or use one of Oracle's profiling tools. If you add your own instrumentation, then analyzing it to study the code profile is almost just a case of how good your programming skills are. However, simple techniques give you the majority of the benefit.

The second option is to use one of Oracle's profiling tools. You may not be able to add instrumentation to your code, but Oracle provides three tools for profiling your PL/SQL automatically, two of which have been around for a while—DBMS_TRACE and DBMS_PROFILER—but both of which tend to be underutilized.

The third tool is the PL/SQL Hierarchical Profiler that came in with Oracle 11.1. This is something like a mixture of DBMS_TRACE/DBMS_PROFILER and the 10046 trace tool, and it is implemented via the package DBMS_HPROF.

We will review all three tools and what their various strengths and weaknesses are.

Debugging

Debugging is traditionally seen as working out why your code is going wrong or why you are getting the wrong outcome. There is some crossover with performance tuning, where although the result is correct, it is not in a time frame that satisfies the business need (which may be user perception—for example, no one wants to wait five seconds for a web page to respond, even though there is nothing intrinsically wrong with such a wait). However, performance is generally covered under profiling.

Although this chapter is not intended to cover debugging, because instrumenting is such a key aspect of debugging, the sections on that topic are highly relevant to debugging, so there is some mention of it throughout this chapter.

Generally speaking, bugs come down to a logical errors, where we have not appreciated the outcome of our looping constructs or simply have done things in the wrong order. Variables are "scope sensitive," and if they are not named sensibly, you may be referring to the wrong version of a variable. Instrumenting your code greatly helps in solving bugs, but you cannot beat stepping through your code and watching the variables change in order to spot what is going wrong.

Sample Tables Used

For some of the examples in this chapter, we will use the standard Oracle HR and SALES example schemas. These schemas are generally created for you when you create a test database using the Database Configuration Assistant, download and install Oracle from OTN, or download one of the prebuilt virtual environments. The accounts are locked initially, but your DBA (which could well be you if you are using your own personal test system!) can easily unlock them. If the schemas are missing, they can easily be created (refer to "Database Sample Schemas" in the Application Development section of the official online Oracle documentation).

For other examples, we use the same PERSON, PERSON_NAME, and ADDRESS tables and PNA_MAINT package used extensively in Chapter 6. Code to create these is available from the book's website, and the version specific to this chapter has the extra code that's covered in this chapter.

Instrumentation of PL/SQL

We will now look at the main methods of instrumenting PL/SQL. DBMS_OUTPUT is the most common tool used, but is in fact a poor tool to use in isolation for instrumenting production code. Logging tables allow a far more superior method of instrumenting PL/SQL, and a lot can be achieved with a very simple approach. Finally, the real-time activity of your PL/SQL can be instrumented and monitored via the DBMS_APPLICATION_INFO package.

We will discuss the strengths and weaknesses of each in turn. It is possible, of course, to use all three methods together, and this is what we find produces the best overall solution.

DBMS_OUTPUT

DBMS_OUTPUT was the first "tool" used for instrumenting (and thus profiling and debugging) PL/SQL and is still the most popular method used today. We have used DBMS_OUTPUT throughout this book to show what is going on within PL/SQL. In fact, the Oracle V12.1 Database PL/SQL Packages and Types Reference describes DBMS_OUTPUT thus (our italics):

The DBMS_OUTPUT package enables you to send messages from stored procedures, packages, and triggers. *The package is especially useful for displaying PL/SQL debugging information.*

And yet, DBMS_OUPUT was not really designed to communicate with the end user! It was designed as a temporary in-memory stack for holding data, and its ability to feed information back to us is almost just a happy accident.

DBMS_OUTPUT is appealing because it is such a simple and easy way of adding instrumentation to your code, and it would be surprising if you have not already used it yourself. As a quick example, though, the following code is run against the HR.COUNTRIES table:

```
--ch7_t1
begin
  dbms_output.put_line('started');
  for c in
    (select country_name,country_id from countries
    where country_name like'U%')
  loop
    dbms_output.put_line ('found country '||c.country_name);
  end loop;
  dbms_output.put_line('our code finished');
end;


@ch7_t1
started
found country United Kingdom
found country United States of America
our code finished
```

Disadvantages of DBMS_OUTPUT

As the use of DBMS_OUTPUT for instrumenting, profiling, and debugging PL/SQL code is ubiquitous, we are going to go into some detail about DBMS_OUTPUT, especially because most people use it without giving a second thought to how it works and its limitations.

One disadvantage is that it has to be enabled to work. Within SQL*Plus, you have to use

```
set serveroutput on
```

to enable the output to be displayed in your SQL*Plus session, or you can turn it on in your development tool. Figure 7-1 shows how to do this in SQL Developer. An annoyance of DBMS_OUTPUT is forgetting to turn it on when running some code you want DBMS_OUPUT from. This is especially true when you are testing some code that takes a long time to run. You set it running, come back an hour later, and the code has finished—and there is no output. You cannot get the output by any other method, so you have to run the code a second time. (Probably all of us have done this at some point.)

There is a second way to enable the display of DBMS_OUTPUT messages in SQL Developer, and that is to simply issue the SQL*Plus-style command **set serveroutput on** in the worksheet directly—but that results in the output being shown on the Script Output tab and not the DBMS_OUTPUT tab, which seems a little confusing to us (see Figure 7-2).

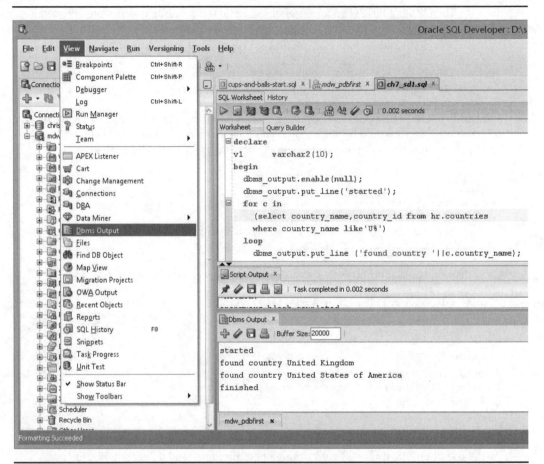

FIGURE 7-1. *Turning on DBMS_OUTPUT in SQL Developer*

DBMS_OUTPUT and a Client's Pain: Part I

A few years ago one of the authors was working at a client site, and the client needed to produce a governmental regulatory report in a hurry…like yesterday. A developer was assigned to put together some PL/SQL to create this report and used DBMS_OUTPUT to write out the information. The PL/SQL did the job, but it was slow—it was doing a lot of work, and the code was written in a hurry. There was no time to tune it, and management was already extremely anxious to get the report out and felt no delay was possible.

From the run time on development we knew it would take several hours for the code to run to completion on the production database. Therefore, it was kicked off to run overnight with someone tasked to monitor it and let management know when the report completed. It ran almost all night, and when it finished all we got was the "PL/SQL procedure successfully completed" message. No report.

Yes, the person who ran it had forgotten to **set serveroutput on**. It was a very stressful experience for all involved.

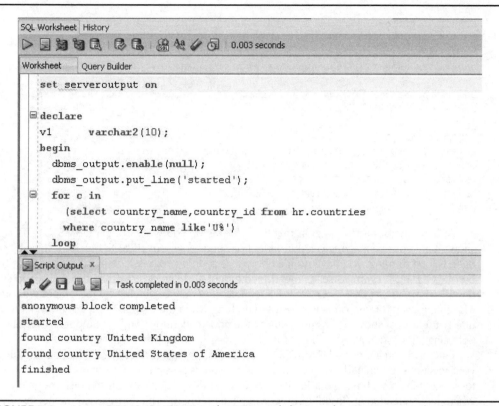

FIGURE 7-2. *Using DBMS_OUTPUT in the SQL worksheet and Script Output tab of SQL Developer*

DBMS_OUPUT is very easy to use, but there are some serious drawbacks to it. Early versions of Oracle, before version 10gR2, had some awkward limits on line and buffer size, limiting the size of a single line to 255 bytes and the whole buffer to 1 million bytes (with a default of 20,000 bytes when you enable it without stating the buffer size). Since Oracle 10gR2, a single line can be 32KB and the size of the buffer is unlimited—and this is what it is set to by default when you enable DBMS_OUTPUT from SQL* Plus without stating a size (**set serveroutput on**).

It should be noted that having a buffer of "unlimited" is not really unlimited. This is a memory stack, and it takes up space in your session's PGA on the database server. If it grows too large, it could cause memory shortages on the server and will eventually crash your session!

In later versions you can still set a maximum size, but we struggle to see why you would do that unless it is to force your PL/SQL code to fail if too much output is produced. In the following example, we set the buffer to a very low 2000 bytes just to demonstrate the error:

```
mdw2> set serveroutput on size 2000
--DBMS_O_Overflow
begin
for i in 1..100 loop
  dbms_output.put_line (lpad('a',100,'a'));
end loop;
```

```
end;
@DBMS_O_Overflow

aaaaaaaaaaaaaaaaaaaaaaaaaaaaaaaaaaaaaaaaaaaaaaaaaaaaaaaaaaaaaaaaaaaaaaaaaaaaaaaaaaaa
aaaaaaaaaaaaaaaaaaaaaaaaaaaaaaaaaaaaaaaaaaaaaaaaaaaaaaaaaaaaaaaaaaaaaaaaaaaaaaaaaaaa
...
aaaaaaaaaaaaaaaaaaaaaaaaaaaaaaaaaaaaaaaaaaaaaaaaaaaaaaaaaaaaaaaaaaaaaaaaaaaaaaaaaaaa
begin
*
ERROR at line 1:
ORA-20000: ORU-10027: buffer overflow, limit of 2000 bytes
ORA-06512: at "SYS.DBMS_OUTPUT", line 32
ORA-06512: at "SYS.DBMS_OUTPUT", line 97
ORA-06512: at "SYS.DBMS_OUTPUT", line 112
ORA-06512: at line 3
```

Another major disadvantage is that the information you write out via DBMS_OUTPUT is not shown until your package, procedure, function, or anonymous PL/SQL block finishes. If your code is long running, you have no idea how that code is progressing via information put out by DBMS_OUTPUT. Even worse, as mentioned earlier and demonstrated by the real-world situation described in the first DBMS_OUTPUT anecdote, you may be relying on the output without realizing it is not turned on—until you see nothing when the code completes. DBMS_OUTPUT is utterly useless for showing progress during the code execution. And no output is given if you are not using a tool such as SQL*Plus, SQL Developer, or some other interactive tool.

Further, if you are using DBMS_OUTPUT for instrumentation and leave the code running, if your session is terminated (for example, your network is set up to close connections that are inactive for longer than a set time), your PL/SQL code will finish its work (because no stop signal is sent when the connection is closed) but you will have no output. That has caused me personally several issues over the years; I have been running some data-processing code, instrumented with DBMS_OUTPUT, and upon coming back to the machine found that the session has been terminated. The data-processing code has run—and there is no information from the instrumentation as to how it went, if there were any issues, or how much data was created! Sometimes I have been able to work it all out from the processed data; sometimes I have had to undo that chunk of work and do it again.

DBMS_OUTPUT and a Client's Pain: Part II

Quite a few years back I was working at a client site (as a DBA) that was moving to a new version of its billing system, the core of which was written in PL/SQL. Part of the billing system was new functionality, where all customers could now log onto their account via the Web and look at their account details. This had been publicized to the customers extensively.

The weekend of the "Big Release" arrived, and the code was pushed out to production. Everything went well until the nightly batch ran—and failed with the following error:

```
ORA-20000: ORU-10027: buffer overflow, limit of 1000000 bytes
```

The batch was processing accounts, and any anomalies were being fed out using DBMS_OUTPUT. The new code had been tested extensively before release—but on a much smaller data set. On the production system, the number of anomalies being raised was as expected for the production system—but it pushed DBMS_OUTPUT beyond its fixed limit (back then) of 1 million characters. The anomaly data was vital! It was processed outside the database by an existing and arcane piece of software, and it had to be produced. However, DBMS_OUTPUT could not handle the data volume.

Pulling the release would have been a major task at this point—and potentially very embarrassing to the client. Thankfully, despite the very questionable use of DBMS_OUTPUT for this task, all of the anomaly logging went through one central PL/SQL package.

I was able to step in and write (in the middle of the night, with a lot of very stressed senior managers wanting updates on the progress every five minutes) a temporary fix to the package to push the data out to the file via UTL_FILE.

The fix worked, the day (well, night) was saved, and the client was able to go live with the new application.

DBMS_OUTPUT Is Really a FIFO Memory Stack

The reason for all these issues is that DBMS_OUTPUT is not really a communication tool! *It is a memory stack for temporarily holding textual information.* The information goes into an area of memory in your session's Private Global Area (PGA); if you put a lot of information in there, you will increase the size of your PGA. You will want to be mindful of this if you ever decide to use the UNLIMITED buffer option and put millions of lines into DBMS_OUTPUT, especially if it is code that many sessions will run at the same time. You could end up using a lot of memory on the server.

We are all familiar with **dbms_output.put_line('*text*')**. This actually puts **text** as a *distinct line* into the stack. There are two other procedures for populating the stack:

- **dbms_output.put('*text*')** puts **text** onto the current line in the stack but without a line feed.
- **dbms_output.new_line** puts an end-of-line character onto the current line in the stack so the next input will be to a new line.

Actually, **put_line** just internally calls **put** followed by **new_line** (you will see evidence of this in the later sections on profiling PL/SQL code).

There are two procedures for retrieving text from the stack:

- **dbms_output.get_line(*varchar2, integer*)** returns a single line in the **varchar2** variable and a status indicator in the **integer** variable (0 means a line was returned; 1 means no line was returned).
- **dbms_output.get_lines(*chararr, integer*)** returns **integer** lines in the **chararr** array—an object type called DBMSOUTPUT_LINESARRAY, which is a table of varchar2(32767) indexed by a BINARY_INTEGER. The **out** value of **integer** is the actual number of lines returned.

The DBMS_OUTPUT commands for putting information onto the stack or taking it off have no effect if the stack is not enabled. You enable/disable it within PL/SQL with the **dbms_output .enable(*integer*)** and **dbms_output.disable** procedures. Here, *integer* is the number of bytes that can be placed on the stack, and it defaults to 20,000. If you state *integer* as NULL, then the buffer is unlimited. When you **set serveroutput on** and **off** in SQL*Plus, these procedures are called for you, with *integer* by default being NULL. If you want to use DBMS_OUTPUT as a stack, your code needs to call **dbms_output.enable** before you use the stack in any way.

The DBMS_OUPUT stack is a FIFO (first in, first out) stack. Therefore, data is returned from the stack in the order it was pushed onto it. To demonstrate this, we'll create a table and sequence into which we can put the information we retrieve from DBMS_OUTPUT, in the order we get it:

```
create table dbou_test
(id number,line number,text varchar2(4000));

create sequence dbte_seq cache 10;
```

Now we will alter our earlier test code to get our data out of the stack and insert it into the table:

```
declare
lines1      integer :=10;
do_arr      dbms_output.chararr;
begin
  dbms_output.put_line('started');
  for c in
    (select country_name,country_id from countries
    where country_name like'U%')
  loop
    dbms_output.put_line ('found country '||c.country_name);
  end loop;
  -- I now get out several lines of stored DBMS_OUTPUT data.
  dbms_output.get_lines(do_arr,lines1);
  -- and insert the lines, in order, into my temporary table.
  for i in 1..lines1 loop
    insert into dbou_test(id,line,text)
    values (dbte_seq.nextval,i,do_arr(i));
  end loop;
  dbms_output.put_line('our code finished');
end;
```

Now when we run our code with **serveroutput on**, we only see the last DBMS_OUTPUT line, the one saying "finished," because we have popped the rest of the data off the stack, as can be seen by querying the table, where we see the rest of the original output:

```
@ch7_t2
Our code finished
PL/SQL procedure successfully completed.

select * from dbou_test order by id
        ID      LINE TEXT
---------- ---------- ----------------------------------------
```

```
1               1 started
2               2 found country United Kingdom
3               3 found country United States of America
```

```
3 rows selected.
```

As you can see, the lines came off the DBMS_OUTPUT stack in the order we put them in.

At this point you are probably thinking that the stack is added to via PUT… commands and taken from via GET… commands, and that if we use PUT_LINE for ten lines and use GET_LINES to retrieve three lines, then seven lines will remain in the stack. *However, this isn't the case.*

As soon as you use a GET_LINE or GET_LINES command, the next PUT or PUT_LINES command *clears the stack* before more information is added. We make only one alteration to our code: we change the variable **lines1** to be **2**, so we will only **GET_LINES (do_arr,2)** records off the stack. This would leave **found country United States of America** in the stack. However, our next **dbms_output.put_line('finished');** clears the stack first, so the only output to our session when the code has completed is the line "Finished," and we have only inserted two lines into our test table:

```
declare
lines1        integer :=2;
do_arr        dbms_output.chararr;
begin
  dbms_output.put_line('started');
  for c in
    (select country_name,country_id from countries
    where country_name like'U%')
  loop
    dbms_output.put_line ('found country '||c.country_name);
  end loop;
  -- I now get out several lines of stored DBMS_OUTPUT data.
  dbms_output.get_lines(do_arr,lines1);
  -- and insert the lines, in order, into my temporary table.
  for i in 1..lines1 loop
    insert into dbou_test(id,line,text)
    values (dbte_seq.nextval,i,do_arr(i));
  end loop;
  dbms_output.put_line('our code finished');
end;

@ch7_t2
Our code finished
PL/SQL procedure successfully completed.

select * from dbou_test where id>3 -- to ignore my first test
order by id;

        ID      LINE TEXT
---------- ---------- ------------------------------------------
         4         1 started
         5         2 found country United Kingdom

2 rows selected.
```

We effectively lost the line **found country United States of America**.

The only reason that we can use DBMS_OUTPUT for instrumenting our PL/SQL code is because Oracle bolted on a bit of code to SQL*Plus to perform **dbms_output.get_lines** after running any PL/SQL (if **serveroutput** is **on**). It then echoes the result of GET_LINES in our session. GUI development tools basically do the same thing. This also explains the occasional oddity you might see where you run code that uses **dbms_output.put_line** but forget to **set serveroutput on**. Then, when you do set it to **on** and run your code, you see output from prior runs as well. You will only see this if you, somewhere, use the **dbms_output.enable** procedure too.

Therefore, DBMS_OUTPUT is really a memory stack to hold textual information. Its use as an instrumenting tool is almost accidental and is a result of a secondary decision by Oracle to add code to SQL*Plus to enable the stack for you and then check for any contents in the stack after running any PL/SQL. If you were to use it as a stack within a PL/SQL routine, you would probably mess up any attempt to use it for instrumentation—though in practice we never see anyone using it as a stack (apart from myself, once, a long time ago). In fact, because it is used so extensively for instrumenting and debugging, it is probably very dangerous to use it as a stack now!

Given these issues with DBMS_OUTPUT, you might expect us to now tell you to not use it for instrumenting your code. But that would be disingenuous of us. We use it all the time; it is so easy to use, and it generally does the job. However, we tend to use it only for throwaway code, quick tasks, or debugging code when we can add our DBMS_OUTPUT lines and then remove them all once we have finished fixing the code. If we want to instrument any code that is going to become production code or be used for a serious task, we instrument with the two methods we cover after DBMS_OUTPUT: logging tables and DBMS_APPLICATION_INFO.

Hints for Using DBMS_OUTPUT to Instrument Code

This section provides some hints on how to best use DBMS_OUPUT (and instrumentation in general).

Timestamp Information   In the previous example, our instrumentation is simple labels of where we are in the code. Although this is useful, we can (and should) do so much more. We cannot instrument how long things take without timings. Therefore, unless we are simply adding a label to see if a piece of code was reached, we add a timestamp to the text:

```
dbms_output.put_line(TO_CHAR(SYSTIMESTAMP,'YY-MM-DD HH24:MI:SS.FF3')|| ' started');
```

```
16-01-08 14:24:34.783 started
```

We use SYSTIMESTAMP because the accuracy of SYSDATE to the second is too crude. If the change between two lines of instrumentation is from 15:25:01 to 15:25:02, then that step could have taken almost no time but occurred right at the end of 15:25:01, or it could have taken almost two seconds, running from 15:25:01.01 to 15:25:02.99. Also, a lot of PL/SQL code can be processed in two seconds, so we could potentially get a lot of instrumentation lines with the same time.

With timestamps, we limit the partial second output to three decimal places (the **.FF3** at the end of the format string) because that is as accurate as SYSTIMESTAMP gets on our test box, and when profiling PL/SQL code, we don't generally care about anything programmatically that is quicker than one-thousandth of a second. On most platforms, you should get SYSTIMESTAMP to six decimal places if you want that level of accuracy.

Apart from the "start line," we do not tend to output the date if we are just using DBMS_OUTPUT for our instrumentation, and we don't tend to repeat what program we are running. This is because

DBMS_OUTPUT instrumentation is "immediate" instrumentation; we are running something interactively and seeing the output at the end. Alternatively, we have a little wrapper to spool the output to a different file each time we run it, and that file will have the program name and the date/time it ran in the name of the spool file. We want to keep our output compact so it is easier to read and understand (in a human context). We also tend to left-justify sections of our output to aid scanning it—but that is because our native languages are left-justified. If your native language is right-justified, you may want to justify sections of the DBMS_OUTPUT that way.

We altered our code to do a little more work (in an admittedly silly way) with better instrumentation. (Note, you need execute privilege on DBMS_LOCK for the SLEEP command):

```
-- ch7_t4.sql
v_count1      integer;
lines1        integer :=2;  do_arr      dbms_output.chararr;
begin
  dbms_output.put_line(TO_CHAR(SYSTIMESTAMP,'YY-MM-DD HH24:MI:SS.FF3')||
                       ' started ');
  for l_c in
    (select country_name,country_id from countries where country_name
like'U%')
  loop
    dbms_output.put_line(TO_CHAR(SYSTIMESTAMP,'HH24:MI:SS.FF3')||
     rpad(' processing country ',25,' ')||l_c.country_name);
    v_count1 :=0;
    for l_d in (select dept.department_id,dept.department_name
                from departments dept, locations loca
                where loca.location_id = dept.location_id
                and   loca.country_id = l_c.country_id
                order by dept.department_name)
    loop
      v_count1 :=v_count1+1;
      dbms_output.put_line(TO_CHAR(SYSTIMESTAMP,'HH24:MI:SS.FF3')||
       rpad(' processing department ',30,' ')||l_d.department_name);
      sys.dbms_lock.sleep(dbms_random.value(1,5)); -- to fake some processing;
    end loop;
    dbms_output.put_line(TO_CHAR(SYSTIMESTAMP,'HH24:MI:SS.FF3')||
    rpad(' No dept processed ',32,' ')||v_count1);
  end loop;
  dbms_output.put_line(TO_CHAR(SYSTIMESTAMP,' HH24:MI:SS.FF3')|| ' finished');
end;

@ch7_t4
16-01-08 17:22:21.016 started
17:22:21.016 processing country        United Kingdom
17:22:21.037 processing department     Human Resources
17:22:22.213 processing department     Sales
17:22:23.513 No dept processed         2
17:22:23.513 processing country        United States of America
...
17:23:08.911 processing department     Operations
17:23:10.501 processing department     Payroll
```

```
17:23:11.952 processing department      Purchasing
17:23:16.712 processing department      Recruiting
17:23:17.092 processing department      Retail Sales
17:23:20.632 processing department      Shareholder Services
17:23:22.213 processing department      Shipping
17:23:23.103 processing department      Treasury
17:23:24.674 No dept processed          23
17:23:25.674 finished
```

```
PL/SQL procedure successfully completed.
```

Let's look at a few things about this code. First, the code is now quite bulky—about a third of the code is there to instrument it. We're not happy about having to do all that typing, and all those added lines confuses the code. (We'll address that in a page or two.) Second, we've added a counter called **v_count1**, which is highlighted in bold in the preceding code. This is there just to allow us to keep track of how many records have been processed and feed it back. Third, we can now see that there are a lot more departments for the U.S. than the U.K., and one department (that is, Purchasing in the United States) took a lot longer to process than other departments. If we had issues with the performance of the code, we can now go and look at that department. (In this case, it is just random due to the time-wasting SLEEP statement.)

But because we have the timings, we now know where the code is spending time. Usually it will be a section of code that is taking time, rather than one iteration in a loop, but you get the idea. Having timings is invaluable to understanding where time is spent in the code.

Limit Instrumentation Information and Wrap DBMS_OUTPUT to Preserve Clarity
We trimmed the output of our instrumentation in the preceding example, taking out several lines to save space—and that is an important consideration. A key to good code instrumentation is *providing enough information to be useful without producing a flood of information that can swamp out important detail.* Remember, the instrumentation is taking up space (in this case, in a memory stack in your PGA), and if we are processing, say, 10,000 line items for a sales report, we do not want to instrument that each and every line item has been processed—we can't sensibly examine 10,000 lines of output. For instrumentation to keep its clarity, we have to avoid creating too much information. However, we may want an indication of general progress. We can have a happy medium. Remember our counter **v_count1**? Something we often do is output instrumentation for every *n*th record processed, or for only every *n*th loop—and we use a **mod** function on the counter. For example, **mod (v_count1,10)=0** will only be true for values of 0, 10, 20, 30, and so on (that is, every tenth loop).

Here's a small alteration we made to our code and the corresponding output:

```
    if mod(v_count1,5)=1 then
        dbms_output.put_line(TO_CHAR(SYSTIMESTAMP,'HH24:MI:SS.FF3')||
        rpad(' got to department ',30,' ')||l_d.department_name);
    end if;
```

```
@ch7_t4
16-01-08 18:05:04.418 started
18:05:04.418 processing country     United Kingdom
18:05:04.418 got to department          Human Resources
18:05:11.330 No dept processed          2
```

```
18:05:11.330 processing country    United States of America
18:05:11.330 got to department        Accounting
18:05:27.002 got to department        Control And Credit
18:05:46.734 got to department        IT
18:05:57.576 got to department        Operations
18:06:13.589 got to department        Shareholder Services
18:06:21.841 No dept processed        23
18:06:21.841 finished

PL/SQL procedure successfully completed.
```

Now we see every fifth department only. The output is much cleaner and easier to examine. When we are bulk-processing hundreds of thousands of records, we may well use **mod(v_count1,10000)** or something similar. In fact, we sometimes use a variable for the **mod** function so we can change what percentage of records we feed back:

```
mod(v_counter,v_check)=0
```

Our instrumentation is now taking up about 30 percent of the code, and we have to keep typing the same sort of things over and over again, like

```
dbms_output.put_line(to_char(systimestamp,'HH24:MI:SS.FF3')||...
```

We can address this by using a little procedure to replace those repeated elements. This is a very simple wrapper procedure to call **dbms_output.put_line** and append SYSTIMESTAMP to it:

```
procedure pl (v_text in varchar2) is
begin
  dbms_output.put_line(to_char(systimestamp,'HH24:MI:SS.FF3 :')||v_text);
end pl;

procedure test1 is
begin
  pl('started code');
  -- do stuff
  pl('ended code');
end test1;

17:36:28.824 :started code
17:36:28.824 :ended code
```

Using this wrapper, we reduce how much typing we do and also the "clutter" in our instrumented code (if you want to try these two procedures out stand-alone, just add "create or replace" before the procedure definitions).

Performance Overhead of DBMS_OUTPUT   DBMS_OUTPUT does not incur much of a performance overhead itself, other than memory usage (which can be an issue if you go mad with it). This is because it is simply information going into a private memory construct. There isn't even any need for Oracle to control who is accessing the information because the only access is via your session. This lack of visibility from other sessions is also a drawback of DBMS_OUTPUT—no other process, not even the SYS user, has access to the stack and thus the messages on it. No one else can see what is in your DBMS_OUTPUT stack.

As a quick demonstration of how light DBMS_OUTPUT is, we created a simple procedure to read through a section of a table called PERSON (the scripts to create this table and populate it can be found on the website, and the table is used extensively in Chapter 6). We use DBMS_OUTPUT to feed back the names of the people processed.

```
-- ch7_t5.sql
-- The impact (or not) of dbms_output.
set term off
spool ch7_t5.lst
declare
v_count1    integer;
v_text      varchar2(4000);
v_pad       varchar2(1001) := rpad('A',1000,'A');
begin
  dbms_output.put_line(TO_CHAR(SYSTIMESTAMP,'YY-MM-DD HH24:MI:SS.FF3')
                       || ' started ');
  v_count1 :=0;
  for l_c in
    (select surname,first_forename from person
     where  dob between to_date('01-JAN-1961','DD-MON-YYYY')
               and      to_date('01-JAN-1971','DD-MON-YYYY')
    )
  loop
    v_count1 :=v_count1+1;
    v_text :=  rpad(' processing person ',25,' ')||l_c.surname
                  ||' '||l_c.first_forename||v_pad;
    dbms_output.put_line(TO_CHAR(SYSTIMESTAMP,'HH24:MI:SS.FF3')||v_text);
  end loop;
  dbms_output.put_line(TO_CHAR(SYSTIMESTAMP,' HH24:MI:SS.FF3')
                       || ' finished and processed '||v_count1);
end;
/
spool off
set term on
```

If we run the code with the DBMS_OUTPUT lines commented out or without having enabled DBMS_OUTPUT, it takes about 0.210 seconds. The code processes about 60,380 records. We then enable DBMS_OUTPUT with **set serveroutput on**, and we also spool the output to a file and use **set term off** to remove the overhead of throwing the output to the screen and scrolling—it simply gets pushed into the spool file. The elapsed time jumps to 14.2 seconds, and the output file is 63MB in size. However, if we examine the output file, the time from the start and end line is as follows:

```
16-01-11 19:24:48.337 started
19:24:48.349 processing person      ADAMS
AALIYAHAAAAAAAAAAAAAAAAAAAAAAAAAAAAAAAAAAAAAAA
19:24:48.349 processing person      ADAMS
AALIYAHAAAAAAAAAAAAAAAAAAAAAAAAAAAAAAAAAAAAAAA
...
19:24:48.637 processing person      YOUNG
```

```
WENDYAAAAAAAAAAAAAAAAAAAAAAAAAAAAAAAAAAAAAAAAAAAAAA
19:24:48.637 processing person      YOUNG
WENDYAAAAAAAAAAAAAAAAAAAAAAAAAAAAAAAAAAAAAAAAAAAAAA
19:24:48.637 finished and processed 60368

PL/SQL procedure successfully completed.
Elapsed: 00:00:14.18
```

This shows that *the code* took 0.300 seconds to run, compared to 0.21 seconds with no DBMS_OUPUT—a whole .09 seconds to push out 60,368 lines of output, each just over 1KB in size. All of the extra elapsed time was our session fetching back the DBMS_OUTPUT data. We can corroborate this if we tune our SQL*Plus session's network communication by altering the default array size from 15 to 100 records (so fewer round trips are needed to pull the **dbms_output .getlines** data to our session). The elapsed time drops to 3.68 seconds, but the difference between the start and end lines of the output remains at 0.300 seconds.

We also pulled out the PGA information from our session before we ran the code, after we had run it without DBMS_OUTPUT enabled and then after running it with DBMS_OUTPUT enabled. (Note that to run the script to get your PGA information, you need access to V$ tables. The easiest way is to be granted the system privilege SELECT ANY DICTIONARY).

```
-- chk_my_pga
select vses.username||':'||vsst.sid||','||vses.serial# username
, vstt.name
, vsst.value value
from v$sesstat vsst
, v$statname vstt
, v$session vses
where vstt.statistic# = vsst.statistic#
and vsst.sid = vses.sid
and vstt.name in ('session pga memory','session pga memory max')
and vsst.sid = sys_context('userenv','sid')

ora122> @chk_my_pga

USERNAME             NAME                                  VALUE
-------------------  -----------------------------------   ----------
MDW:299,48902        session pga memory                    967,160
                     session pga memory max              2,491,544

@ch7_t5
-- took 0.21 seconds
@chk_my_pga

USERNAME             NAME                                  VALUE
-------------------  -----------------------------------   ----------
MDW:299,48902        session pga memory                    967,160
                     session pga memory max              2,491,544

set serveroutput on
@ch7_t5
```

```
-- took 14.2 seconds, but all but 0.3 seconds was my session fetching the data
@chk_my_pga
```

```
USERNAME                NAME                               VALUE
-------------------     ------------------------------     ----------
MDW:299,48902           session pga memory                 71,680,504
                        session pga memory max             71,74,6040
```

Oracle allocated 2.4MB of PGA to our session when it was initiated. Running our code with no DBMS_OUPUT had no impact on the PGA size (there was no sort or hash processing in the SQL, so no PGA was needed for that sort of thing). However, enabling DBMS_OUPUT pushed it up to about 65MB. Our output file was 61MB or so.

If you are passing a lot of information back to your session, especially if it is directly to your screen and not a spooled file, *that* can be slow. In other words, it is not DBMS_OUTPUT that is slow but rather the passing of data back to your session in small arrays. If you are going to produce a lot of DBMS_OUTPUT information, increase your client buffer size. Also, in SQL*Plus, spool this output to a file and use **set termout off**. You may in fact be better not using DBMS_OUTPUT and instead recording the information in table, perhaps via a temporary table (so you are not writing out millions of single rows to a permanent table that incurs redo generation).

The takeaway message is, especially when you are using DBMS_OUTPUT as your instrumentation, to add only what instrumentation you need and use sampling to keep the noise down. So long as your development environment/rules do not prevent it, adding more instrumentation to your code later (if you need it) is easy.

Logging Tables

Using DBMS_OUPUT is fine for instrumenting code while you debug it or for a script you run by hand on an occasional basis, but it is a poor method for anything that is run regularly or does something substantial, such as splitting off new partitions and/or archiving old data, running regular data loads, or performing data transformations. For these tasks you want a permanent record of the steps in your code and how long they took, for two reasons:

- You can investigate an issue after the fact.
- You can trend the performance of not only the whole process, but also the steps within it over time, to give you a heads-up of future performance problems.

You could write out information to an operating system file using UTL_FILE, but you are working in a database—so use the database to log your database activity! Write your activity to a log table.

Common Issues with Log Tables

Over the years we have created log tables for many applications and processes, and they all tend to be very similar. We record the steps in the application, the time of each step, any input values or control variables of particular interest, and any errors that occur via the EXCEPTIONS sections of the code.

One common mistake (which we have been guilty of a few times) is to create a separate log table for each application. This is usually done because when you are writing the PL/SQL and designing supporting tables to control a process, it is easiest to just create your own new table(s). But that means for each process you need to track down the right log table to look at to solve an issue.

Another common mistake is to try and record the elapsed time for each step in the log table. This makes it (slightly) simpler to look at the log data and spot the long-running steps—but you spend a lot more time coding the logic to keep track of the elapsed time in your application code and, critically, debugging it.

The final issue, especially when you have a dedicated log table for each process, is adding further columns to the log table to record specific variables that are pertinent to that process, such as PERSON_ID or ACCOUNT_ID. If you do have a generic log table that is used for the logging of several applications, you often get placeholder "variable" columns in the log table, such as NUMBER_1, NUMBER_2, and so on, or VARCHAR_1, VARCHAR_2, and so on. You then need to work out for each application how it is using those placeholder columns.

A Standard Log Table Layout

Over the years, a standard table layout has evolved out of our experiences. When we are developing systems or utilities for clients, we create a table like the one shown here:

```
create table PLSQL_LOG
(process_name     varchar2(30) not null
,start_timestamp timestamp(6) not null
,log_timestamp   timestamp(6) not null
,status          varchar2(1)  not null
,log_level       number(1)    not null
,log_text        varchar2(4000)
,error_code      varchar2(10)
)
```

PROCESS_NAME is the unique name of the process or application—for example, PARTITION_MAINTENANCE or BATCH_ACCOUNT_CLOSE. (This column is used in the set of tables for controlling automated processes in Chapter 9).

START_TIMESTAMP is the start time for this execution of the process. Along with PROCESS_NAME, it uniquely identifies the actual run of that process and also gives us a column we can use to get the elapsed time from the start of the run to the current entry in the log.

STATUS is the state of the process at the time of this log entry being created: it could be **I** for initiating or **R** for running, or it might indicate a special sort of execution such as a **(C)ontinuation** or **(R)ecovery run**. It is generally set to **E** for error for information written out by exception clauses.

LOG_LEVEL indicates the level of logging with which the code was run. We'll discuss this further later in the chapter, but for now know that it is very useful to be able to turn the level of logging up and down (a larger number means more logging). The level is higher when we start with a new process or are hitting problems, and it is lower once things calm down.

ERROR_CODE is there to record any Oracle errors. These errors may not actually stop the process/application from running, but if they do occur, we record them in the log table, too, so that all the details are in once place.

That leaves LOG_TIMESTAMP and LOG_TEXT, which hold the details of the log entry. Experience has led us to no longer making any attempt to hold specific variables or values in extra columns on the table—it has never saved us any time or effort in the long run, especially with a central log table used for several processes. In fact, it just confuses the use of the log table over time. What we do is put extra details in the LOG_TEXT column as delimited information so that we can parse it out if we need to (with a user-defined function that we create called **piece**, which was discussed in Chapter 6 and is included in the sample package code on the website). Thus, we might have the following entry in the LOG_TEXT column:

```
Processing department*60*Haematology
```

We could use **str_util.piece(log_text,3,'*')** to get "Haematology" out of that log entry. On those occasions when we want to analyze the variables stored in the log data, we find this adequate and a lot simpler than having some (or lots!) of extra columns in the log table for variables we *might* want to hold for *certain* applications using the log table.

We have a number of SQL scripts we run against the PLSQL_LOG table to show the information we commonly want, an example of which we will look at here, but more examples are in the section "Using the PLSQL_LOG Table."

We ran the **pna_maint.pop_addr_batch** procedure to create some new data in the ADDRESS table (the code is available from the book's website) and then ran the following query soon afterward:

```
--chk_pllo.sql
col process_name form a16
col start_timestamp form a19 trunc
col log_level       form 99 head 11
col log_text        form a50 word wrap
col error_code      form a5 head err
break on start_timestamp nodup
select process_name
     ,start_timestamp
     ,substr(log_timestamp,10,13) log_ts
     ,log_level
     ,log_text
from plsql_log
where log_timestamp >systimestamp -0.01
order by process_name, log_timestamp
```

PROCESS_NAME	START_TIMESTAMP	LOG_TS	11	LOG_TEXT
POP_ADDR_BATCH	24-JAN-16 21.26.12	21.26.12.449	5	started at 16-01-24 21:26:12.449
POP_ADDR_BATCH	24-JAN-16 21.26.12	21.26.12.449	5	towns 1 to 69 roads 1 to 81 types 1 to 74
POP_ADDR_BATCH	24-JAN-16 21.26.12	21.26.14.605	5	intermediate commit at 50000 addresses
POP_ADDR_BATCH	24-JAN-16 21.26.12	21.26.16.752	5	intermediate commit at 100000 addresses
POP_ADDR_BATCH	24-JAN-16 21.26.12	21.26.18.947	5	intermediate commit at 150000 addresses
...				
POP_ADDR_BATCH	24-JAN-16 21.26.12	21.26.53.434	5	intermediate commit at 950000 addresses
POP_ADDR_BATCH	24-JAN-16 21.26.12	21.26.55.580	5	intermediate commit at 1000000 addresses
POP_ADDR_BATCH	24-JAN-16 21.26.12	21.26.55.587	5	elapsed is 0 00:00:43.138000000
POP_ADDR_BATCH	24-JAN-16 21.26.12	21.26.55.587	5	ended at 16-01-24 21.26.55.587

The script simply pulls out the logging data since SYSDATE-0.01, which is about 14 minutes. We often want to see what has happened in the last few minutes.

We'll now stray briefly into the other major topic of this chapter—profiling—and review the output. It is easy to understand the log output without actually knowing anything about the

PL/SQL—and it should be. If it is not easy to understand, you probably need to alter the text of the logging. Something that populates addresses, either in or by batch, started on the 24th of January at 21:26.12.449. It processed data based on 1–69 towns, 1–81 roads, and 1–74 road types. Chunks of 5000 addresses were processed; by just looking at adjacent lines in the output, we can see that the first 5000 took 2.1 seconds and the last 5000 also took 2.1 seconds—in other words, the processing was done at a steady rate. The whole job took 43.138 seconds (the next-to-last line of the output). We could have calculated the total elapsed time by looking at the raw data for the start and end entries, but it may stretch over a page. We could use a bit of simple SQL to get the total elapsed time (and usually we do, see the section "Using the PL/SQL_LOG Table"), but because we have the START_TIMESTAMP available for each log entry, it is very simple to visually work this out—though subtracting times in your head takes more effort than you'd think.

One slight issue with our PLSQL_LOG table is that if we create a unique or primary key constraint on PROCESS_NAME, START_TIMESTAMP, or LOG_TIMESTAMP, we occasionally get ORA-00001 Unique Constraint violations. If you look at the last two rows in the example output, you will see that they both have the same PROCESS_NAME and START_TIMESTAMP (of course) but also the same LOG_TIMESTAMP. Therefore, these two records would violate a primary key on those columns. This is because we have instrumented two points that occur in less than one tick of the system clock—remember, the system clock runs in thousands of a second on Windows platforms, for example, and we know a lot of people have test Oracle systems on their own Windows PCs and laptops. Quite a few lines of PL/SQL code can be executed in that time. On Linux (even on Linux VMs running on Windows!) the system clock, and therefore SYSTIMESTAMP, is reported to six decimal places, which makes this problem evaporate. (If you know you will never use your instrumenting code on Windows or any other platform that reports SYSTIMESTAMP to only three decimal places, you could save the timestamp to six decimal places and add the unique constraint).

We could add a new column to the audit table that is populated from a sequence and include that in the primary key, but we want our instrumentation to be as light as possible—and I personally feel that using a sequence is incompatible with this aim, especially because we might have several automated systems instrumented, potentially running on RAC, and access to sequences has to be coordinated.

We could add code to hold the timestamp last used when writing to PLSQL_LOG and check against that the next time the procedure is called; if the current SYSTIMESTAMP is the same or earlier than the last used value, we add one millisecond to it. Again, this is a complexity we would rather do without.

The other option is to have a nonunique index on those columns (to support the querying to the log table) and not have a primary key on the instrumentation table. Despite my usual position of questioning any permanent table on a production system without a primary key, I'm actually happy with this solution in this case, so this is what we'll do.

The write_log Procedure

The following is our procedure for logging information to PLSQL_LOG, taken from the package PNA_MAINT:

```
procedure write_log(v_log_text   in varchar2
                    ,v_status     in varchar2  :=''
                    ,v_error_code in  varchar2 :=''
                    )
--autonomous transaction so immediately observable and isolated from calling code
```

```
is
pragma autonomous_transaction;
v_timestamp        timestamp :=systimestamp;
begin
   if pv_log_level>=5 then
   dbms_output.put_line (pv_process_name||' log '||pv_log_level||' - '
                         ||to_char(v_timestamp,'HH24:MI:SS.FF3 :')||v_log_text);
   end if;
   INSERT INTO plsql_log(process_name
                        ,start_timestamp
                        ,log_timestamp
                        ,status
                        ,log_level
                        ,log_text
                        ,error_code)
   values (pv_process_name
          ,pv_executed_timestamp
          ,v_timestamp
          ,nvl(v_status,'I')
          ,pv_log_level
          ,v_log_text
          ,v_error_code
          );
   commit;
end write_log;
```

The code is simple, but the key is that it is executed as an *autonomous transaction,* achieved by the inclusion of the first line in the declaration section **pragma autonomous_transaction**, which is highlighted in bold. (Pragmas have to appear in the declaration section, but do not have to be the first line [or lines]. We put any PRAGMA statements right after the package or procedure specification for clarity.) This means that, with respect to saving data to the database, the code will be executed within its own transaction. Any COMMITs or ROLLBACKs in the procedure will not have any impact on changes carried out by the calling transaction. This procedure will write a record to PLSQL_LOG and commit it. This will *not* commit any outstanding transactions in the calling code.

The results of using an autonomous transaction are as follows:

- The record written to PLSQL_LOG will be seen immediately by any other session looking at PLSQL_LOG after the commit.

- The commit of the PLSQL_LOG record will not cause any data created thus far by the calling procedure to be committed.

- Any subsequent rollback by the calling procedure will not roll back this autonomous transaction, thus preserving the instrumentation in the event of any error, abort, or similar occurrence.

A great boon to using a logging table and autonomous transactions over DBMS_OUPUT is that you can see any logging and progress *during the execution of the parent code.* Unlike with DBMS_OUTPUT, you do not need to wait for the application to finish to see the output. Also, you can monitor the application's progress from another session. This might give you the information you need to decide whether you need to abort the application if it is reported as still running after its usual completion time.

Also, note the code highlighted in bold italic font. If the LOG_LEVEL is 5 or above, this writes whatever would go to PLSQL_LOG to DBMS_OUTPUT too. Therefore, if we are running the code via an interactive session, by setting the log level to 5 or above, we get the output to our screen as well. This is very useful when debugging code.

Finally, note the PV_ variables in the INSERT statement, which are highlighted in italic font. These are package-level variables that we set within the body of our code. You might feel these would be better supplied as parameters to the **write_log** procedure, and we would not argue too strongly against that. But we don't like typing the same bits of text several times. Within a given procedure in our code, we would pass the same PROCESS_NAME, START_TIMESTAMP, and LOG_LEVEL with each call to **write_log** if they were input parameters, so we use package-level variables instead. This is simpler, involves less code, and reduces the impact of the instrumentation on the look of the code. But you do need to set those package-level variables in each procedure.

We have the same few lines of code at the start of each procedure to set up the package variables, including one that makes the initial call to **write_log** to say the procedure has started:

```
pv_process_name         :='POP_SOURCE';
pv_log_level            := p_log_level;
pv_executed_timestamp := systimestamp;
write_log ('started at '||to_char(pv_executed_timestamp,'YY-MM-DD
HH24:MI:SS.FF3'));
```

This use of package variables is why we have a **write_log** procedure in any significant package we write. If we had it in a central package, we would have little option but to pass in the PROCESS_NAME, EXECUTED_TIMESTAMP, and LOG_LEVEL each time we wanted to write out to the log table. Using package-level variables in a central "logging package" that is called from other packages that maintain those central logging package variables is possible—but also complex (as this sentence itself probably shows) and very error prone. With a local version and the use of local package variables (which hold values we usually want to use elsewhere in our main procedure anyway), we keep the call and thus the code and typing simple.

The following is the code for the procedure **pop_addr_batch** in the package PNA_MAINT, which produced the output we looked at earlier in the section "A Standard Log Table Layout." We have removed some of the code so as not to take up too much space (the full code is available online). What we want to show is how, using our package variables and **write_log** procedure, the instrumentation is simple; it is obvious to anyone new looking at the code what it is doing, and it is not a huge burden to add.

```
procedure pop_addr_batch(p_rows      in pls_integer :=1000000
                          ,p_log_level in pls_integer :=5) is
v_tona_min      pls_integer;
-- declaration code trimmed
v_num_addr       pls_integer;
begin
  pv_process_name         :='POP_ADDR_BATCH';
  pv_log_level            := p_log_level;
  pv_executed_timestamp := systimestamp;
  write_log ('started at '||to_char(pv_executed_timestamp,'YY-MM-DD
HH24:MI:SS.FF3'));
```

```
select min(tona_id),max(tona_id) into v_tona_min,v_tona_max from town_name;
select min(rona_id),max(rona_id) into v_rona_min,v_rona_max from road_name;
select min(roty_id),max(roty_id) into v_roty_min,v_roty_max from road_type;
write_log ('towns '||to_char(v_tona_min)||' to '||to_char(v_tona_max)
         ||'  roads '||to_char(v_rona_min)||' to '||to_char(v_rona_max)
         ||'  types '||to_char(v_roty_min)||' to '||to_char(v_roty_max) );
-- Now create as many addresses as asked (default 1 million)
v_count :=0;
loop_count :=0;
while v_count < p_rows loop
  -- trimmed code
  forall idx in indices of addr_array
  insert into address (addr_id
    -- trimmed code
  v_count:=v_count+v_chunk_size;
  loop_count:=loop_count+1;
  if mod(loop_count,10)=0 then
    commit;
    write_log ('intermediate commit at '||v_count||' addresses');
  end if;
end loop; -- main p_rows insert
write_log ('ended at '||to_char(systimestamp,'YY-MM-DD HH24:MI:SS.FF3'));
write_log ('elapsed is '||substr(systimestamp-pv_executed_timestamp,10,20));
commit;
end pop_addr_batch;
```

The bold text is either the actual instrumentation code or code we had to add to assist with the instrumentation. The unedited procedure is about 100 lines long, and the code added to instrument it is 12 lines long. For that "overhead" we get information on when the procedure starts, the reference data it uses, progress summary information as it creates data, when it finishes, and the elapsed time. This 12 percent overhead is much more than you get with most real code because the first 4 and the last 2 lines of those 12 lines are "fixed," and any extra instrumentation will be simple lines like the following:

```
write_log('processing code-chunk name');
```

A secondary benefit of instrumentation, especially when it is "clean" like this, is that it also helps document your code. You may find, like we do, that you comment less because any comment and the line of instrumentation say almost the same thing.

You will remember from the section on DBMS_OUTPUT that we suggest you don't over-instrument—you want to see progress as you process data in a loop, but not every single loop, because that is too much detail. In the code for this instrumentation, we process 1 million addresses in chunks of 5000 rows (5000 rows because we get no further performance increase with chunk sizes of more than a thousand and we don't want to use too much memory). However, we don't want 200 rows of instrumentation showing our progress at one-fifth of a second intervals. Therefore, we use our "modulus of the loop count" trick to trim down the output:

```
if mod(loop_count,10)=0 then...
```

We would also not usually put two lines of instrumentation out at the same time, as we do with the last two lines. We would merge them into one line, but we wanted to show the issue with primary key/timestamp.

Levels of Logging

For anything but a simple application, it is very useful to have levels of logging. The higher the level, the more that is logged. The intention is that when a new application (say, an incremental data load application that processes data received since the last run) is being developed, it is helpful to have considerable detail in the logging—a lot of information is stored in the log table and also written out via DBMS_OUTPUT.

When the code is initially implemented in production, you want a fairly high level of logging but probably not the DBMS_OUTPUT. If issues occur, it would be beneficial to be able to step up the logging without any need for any code changes; you just change a value in a procedure call. Releasing new code should always be done via a controlled process.

Once the application is bedded in, you still want instrumentation but probably not to the same level of detail. You do not want to land yourself with a new task of constantly archiving off instrumentation data!

We handle this by having the LOG_LEVEL column in PLSQL_LOG and package variables to hold the LOG_LEVEL, which you will have seen in the examples already. Either we have an **in** parameter in the procedure specification for the application so we can set the level when we call the code (as we do for **pna_maint.pop_addr_batch**) or we have a column in a control table to state the level, which is read as part of the initiation of the job execution. Or we have both! Therefore, to increase or decrease the log level, we simply alter the value held in the control table, or, if we are able to manually call the procedure, we use the value we pass in at call time.

Level 0 is the base level of instrumentation, where we have simple calls to **write_log** within the body of the application code:

```
write_log('identifying the range to process with limits of '||pv_process_range
          ||' rows and '||pv_max_window||' days','I');
```

This instrumentation is always on; it cannot be turned off. It is the bare minimum of information we want to be preserved no matter what.

Levels above this alter what calls are made to **write_log**, and this is implemented with simple if-then-else logic based on the log level:

```
if pv_log_level>=1 then
   write_log('Following record skipped, invalid trade_ID
             '||lv_gst_data(batch_loop).sdtrxtra_creation_ts,'I');
end if;
...
if pv_log_level>=3 then
  write_log('Finished identifying the range ','I',NULL);
end if;
```

A log level of 1 will cause just the first of the preceding instrumentation lines to be written out; a level of 3 or more will cause both to be written out. This is how we implement the various levels of logging. In practice, we tend to use levels of 1, 3, 5, and 7. This allows us to introduce further intermediate levels of instrumentation later with the even numbers—say, if there is some section of the code that is only invoked under certain circumstances.

As you saw earlier in the discussion of the **write_log** procedure, a log level of 5 (or above) is special in that it will result in any information being written to the table PLSQL_LOG to also be written out with DBMS_OUTPUT. As you saw in the discussion on DBMS_OUPUT, this can still be suppressed by not enabling DBMS_OUTPUT for your session, so you can have level 5 (and above) logging without DBMS_OUPUT activity if you want.

Logging Level Nearly Killed Our Project

A couple of years back, a client was using an Oracle tool to load real-time data into a new data warehouse system on Exadata. We were not processing very large volumes of data yet—about 100MB a day. But our redo generation was huge—several hundred gigabytes! This was causing us backup issues, and we knew the data volumes we were processing would increase significantly. We had a problem.

We quickly worked out that the problem was the load tool. We were using it in a slightly unusual way, doing thousands of very small loads each hour. Each load was logged, and the log table held several CLOB columns. What's more, the tool was updating nearly all the columns (including the CLOBs) for each log entry as it progressed. All this was generating huge levels of redo. Effectively, the same data was written many, many times. It was a crazy way to do the logging.

We turned down the tool's logging because there was an option to do this, but it did not seem to help. So we turned it right down to its lowest level—and it still did not help! In fact, it got worse. By now we were processing maybe a couple hundred megabytes a day—and daily redo generation had exceeded a terabyte. This was now potentially a disaster.

It turned out that with that version of the data-loading tool, turning down logging did not reduce what was written; it just turned up how much was *deleted after it had all been written*. Deleting stuff only creates more redo!

We eventually solved the problem by altering how we used the tool in that project, and the tool itself was soon modified by Oracle to remove the issue. But it did reinforce in my mind the dangers of over instrumenting. We still chuckle about the lunacy of "reducing logging" by simply deleting more of the huge volumes being written and (mostly pointlessly) repeatedly updated.

Logging More Than PL/SQL and SQL

In these examples, we are only recording PL/SQL or SQL activity in PLSQL_LOG. But there is nothing to stop you recording activity from other parts of your computer systems in PLSQL_LOG. In fact, you have a lot to gain. If you have an application written in Java, Python, Ruby, or whatever that is doing work outside of the database (for example, collating and preparsing files) and then using the database as the data store, you can benefit from recording all the stages of the whole application in one place.

The PLSQL_LOG table is a good choice for this central log of the whole process, only some of which is within the Oracle database, for several reasons:

■ The logging information is persisted in something that is already backed up.

■ The Oracle database is required for part of the process and therefore will be available—or else the process will fail anyway!

- You can analyze and report on the logging for the whole end-to-end process using simple SQL queries.
- All the auditing and security aspects of Oracle can be applied to the PLSQL_LOG table.

DBMS_APPLICATION_INFO

DBMS_APPLICATION_INFO is one of our favorite instrumenting tools in PL/SQL. In fact, it is simply one of my personal top-ten PL/SQL features. This is a fantastic, simple, built-in PL/SQL package that Oracle has provided since Oracle 8*i* to allow you to instrument your code in a very easy and yet powerful way. It allows you to populate three values held against your session: MODULE, ACTION, and CLIENT_INFO.

```
ora122> desc v$session
 Name                                      Null?    Type
 ----------------------------------------- -------- ------------------------
 SADDR                                              RAW(8)
 SID                                                NUMBER
 USERNAME                                           VARCHAR2(30)
 ...
 MODULE                                             VARCHAR2(64)
 MODULE_HASH                                        NUMBER
 ACTION                                             VARCHAR2(64)
 ACTION_HASH                                        NUMBER
 CLIENT_INFO                                        VARCHAR2(64)
```

Setting and Viewing MODULE, ACTION, and CLIENT_INFO

MODULE, ACTION, and CLIENT_INFO are VARCHAR2 columns (ignore the lengths of these columns as specified in V$SESSION; we will see later that the usable size of these columns is different). MODULE_HASH and ACTION_HASH are set to numeric representations of the text held in MODULE and ACTION, respectively, and the number is the same for identical text between versions 11 and 12 of Oracle. They are used internally by Oracle and hardly ever looked at by normal database users.

It is incredibly easy to use the DBMS_APPLICATION_INFO built-in package to set these columns via the procedures **set_module(module_name,action_name)**, **set_action(action_name)**, and **set_client_info(client_info)**. The values set are held in memory, and there is no inserting or updating of any table rows, so it is incredibly quick and lightweight. The following are simple examples of setting these values:

```
-- I am logged in as user MDW
exec dbms_application_info.set_module('APPLICATION_NAME','BIT RUNNING')
PL/SQL procedure successfully completed.

exec dbms_application_info.set_client_info('A place to hold more detail')
PL/SQL procedure successfully completed.

select sid,username,module,action,client_info from v$session
where type != 'BACKGROUND'
```

```
   SID USERNAME   MODULE               ACTION               CLIENT_INFO
------ ---------- -------------------- -------------------- ---------------------------
     3 MDW        APPLICATION_NAME     BIT RUNNING          A place to hold more detail
     9 MDW2       SQL*Plus
   185 HR         SALARY RUN           INITIATING
   302 MDW2       SQL Developer
   419 SH         SALES MONTHLY        PROCESSING RETURNS
```

As you can see, we set values for these three columns that indicate what we and most other people use them for: MODULE indicates the overall application or process that is running, ACTION indicates the step within that module, and CLIENT_INFO is for extra information. By looking at the preceding output, we see that there is something running as user HR that suggests it is initiating the salary run, and user SH is running "sales monthly" and is currently "processing returns," which we could assume is a report or end-of-month batch.

> **The V$SESSION Columns Are Larger Than the Allowed Values**
> The three columns MODULE, ACTION, and CLIENT_INFO are VARCHAR2(64) columns, but DBMS_APPLICATION_INFO itself truncates MODULE to 48 bytes, ACTION to 32 bytes, and CLIENT_INFO to 64 bytes. This is true for all versions from Oracle 8*i* through 12*c*.

Because the value you want to be held for ACTION changes as the code progresses, you do not have to call SET_MODULE and repeatedly specify the same MODULE name and the new ACTION; the procedure SET_ACTION sets only the ACTION column in V$SESSION:

```
exec dbms_application_info.set_action('COLLECTING_CUST_DATA')
```

```
select sid,username,module,action,client_info from v$session
where type != 'BACKGROUND'
```

```
   SID USERNAME   MODULE               ACTION               CLIENT_INFO
------ ---------- -------------------- -------------------- ---------------------------
     3 MDW        APPLICATION_NAME     COLLECTING_CUST_DATA A place to hold more detail
     9 MDW2       SQL*Plus
   185 HR         SALARY RUN           INITIATING
   302 MDW2       SQL Developer
   419 SH         SALES MONTHLY        PROCESSING RETURNS
```

You can also see that SQL*Plus and SQL Developer set the MODULE for any of their sessions accordingly, and this hints at part of why DBMS_APPLICATION_INFO is so useful. Those V$SESSION columns are used by many of the Oracle tools, internal activities, and even third-party software. If you pull out all values for MODULE from V$SESSION, you are likely to see MMON_SLAVE, DBMS_SCHEDULER, KTSJ, Streams, and others. Further, Oracle's performance and monitoring tools, such as Enterprise Manager and its performance screens, are predesigned to use those columns.

DBMS_APPLICATION_INFO is used predominantly for real-time instrumentation, for seeing what the session is currently doing. When you set the various values, Oracle does not remember the previous values and the information is not, by default, persisted—just like all the wait and other information in V$SESSION. However, just as with much of the session and wait information, if you have access to the Automatic Workload Repository (AWR) via the OEM Oracle Diagnostics Pack (an extra-cost option), this information *is* preserved, and this includes MODULE and ACTION information. This is the information shown in the following OEM screens.

Figure 7-3 shows a sample screenshot from Enterprise Manager Database Express, which is the simplified management tool Oracle supplies with Windows-based Oracle installs. This, like the full OEM, is designed to show you the module and action of sessions, as well as view performance information based on these columns. The main performance information at the top and middle of the screen is the "classic" mountain range of wait types. However, rather than showing the SQL statements where most of the work is occurring, we show the modules and actions, allowing you to see which of your PL/SQL applications are contributing to the workload (MODULE) and even which sections (ACTION).

You can even change the main graphs to show not the recent history of wait events, but the recent history of modules (or actions), as shown in Figure 7-4.

You have access to the MODULE, ACTION, and CLIENT_INFO information in V$SESSION with no license restriction, so you can run any SQL queries against them that you like. Many monitoring tools show this information.

Figure 7-5 is from the SQL Developer real-time session-monitoring screen, which, as you can see, also shows you the MODULE, ACTION, and CLIENT_INFO information for sessions and allows you to order and filter the session screens by them.

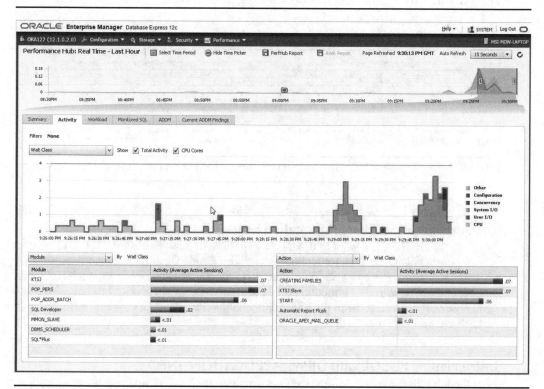

FIGURE 7-3. *All of Oracle's performance-monitoring tools support investigating by module and action.*

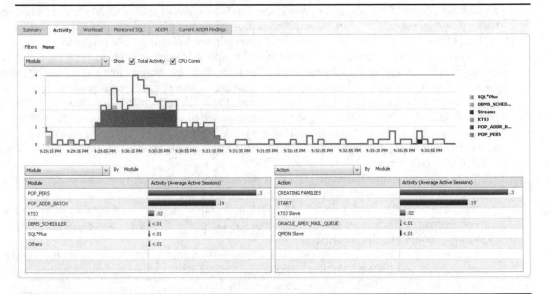

FIGURE 7-4. *Recent history of module workload as seen in OEM Database Express*

SID	SERIAL	Username	Seconds in Wait	Command	...	OS User	Status	Module	Action	RESOUR...	CLIENT_INFO
3	36162	MDW	(null)	(null)	M...	MSI-MDW...	inactive	APPLICATION_NAME	BIT RUNNING	OTHER ...	An place to hold...
9	2902	MDW2	(null)	(null)	M...	MSI-MDW...	inactive	SQL*Plus	(null)	OTHER ...	(null)
185	40757	HR	(null)	(null)	M...	MSI-MDW...	inactive	SALARY RUN	INITIATING	OTHER ...	(null)
302	8750	MDW2	0	SELECT	M...	mwidl_000	active	SQL Developer	(null)	OTHER ...	(null)
361	10828	SYS	(null)	ALT USER	M...	MSI-MDW...	inactive	sqlplus.exe	(null)	OTHER ...	(null)
419	981	SH	(null)	(null)	M...	MSI-MDW...	inactive	SALES MONTHLY	PROCESSING RETURNS	OTHER ...	(null)

FIGURE 7-5. *SQL Developer's session-monitoring screen shows module, action, and client info.*

Gather the V$SESSION Information Yourself

As we discussed, if you want to use the Automatic Workload Repository, you also need the extra-cost Diagnostics Pack (often bought with the Tuning Pack). However, there is nothing stopping you from writing your own code that will periodically persist the V$SESSION data in your own table. This is something we have done when a client does not have the extra license but we need some of the V$SESSION data to investigate a problem. Also, some free tools are available that do this.

Instrumenting PL/SQL with DBMS_APPLICATION_INFO

Even though DBMS_APPLICATION_INFO is simple to use, it gives an immediate indication of what your system is doing in a way that is exposed in many tools and ways. We have used it several times to help identify applications that are taking up considerable resources as well as where in an application that time is being spent, just by looking at the real-time performance-monitoring screens. But this can only be helpful if it is used, and many PL/SQL developers do not use it, perhaps because they don't monitor their production systems (as was suggested at the beginning of this chapter). Because adding to the code is so easy and lightweight, we would strongly encourage any PL/SQL developers who do not use DBMS_APPLICATION_INFO to start doing so.

We use DBMS_APPLICATION_INFO as a broad-brush indicator of activity. If we are looking at V$SESSION or a performance-monitoring tool to see what is currently running on your system and using resources, we do not want too complex a picture. It is enough that we can see how many sessions are running a certain module and get a feel for which modules are using the most resources. We do not want to be making the ACTION column too specific to a task. If we want detail about a given processes, we have more detailed instrumentation in the PLSQL_LOG table—what we want to see interactively on a monitoring screen is the general progress. Has it finished initiating? If the code loads data to temporary tables, processes it, and then pushes it out to the destination tables, all we want to see is which of the three stages it is at.

For simple applications/packages, just set the MODULE (and possibly the ACTION) once, at the very start. If the code is doing a lot of work or is going to run for a while (more than a minute or two generally), we'll also set the ACTION at key points in the code.

In the following code, which should run in just a couple of seconds, we just set the MODULE and ACTION at the start:

```
procedure trunc_tabs(p_log_also in varchar2 :='N') is
-- Note sequences are not reset (and should not matter)
begin
  dbms_application_info.set_module(module_name => 'TRUNC_TABS',action_name =>'START');
```

The following is taken from a real package developed for a client to bulk-process data (altered slightly to preserve client's confidentiality). MODULE is set by a package-level variable that is in fact a constant. All the code within this package is set with the session MODULE value set to XYZ_DATA_TRANSFORMATION. It sets the ACTION before each major step of the processing, usually done by a specific procedure in the code:

```
create or replace package body        xyz_data_transformation
pc_module                    varchar2(48) :='XYZ_DATA_TRANSFORMATION';
pv_action                    varchar2(32);
...
Procedure load_data_x
begin
    pv_action :='INCREMENT_DATA_X';
    DBMS_APPLICATION_INFO.SET_MODULE(pc_module,pv_ACTION);
...
    if v_recovery_fl=Y then
      pv_action :='INC_RECO_DATA_X';
    end if;
...
  dbms_application_info.set_module(null,null)
end load_data_x;
--
Procedure load_data_Y
```

```
Begin
    pv_action :='INCREMENT_DATA_Y';
    DBMS_APPLICATION_INFO.SET_MODULE(pc_module,pv_ACTION);
...
  dbms_application_info.set_module(null,null)
end load_data_y;
```

Why did we set up two package variables and use them within DBMS_APPLICATION_INFO? For three reasons. The first is the aforementioned "fixed" value. If we did not create a package-level "constant" variable, we would have to code the name of the package in several places—and mistakes could easily happen. The second reason is that we could use the variables for other instrumentation. The third reason is that DBMS_APPLICATION_INFO will accept strings longer than the maximum length it will set the columns in V$SESSION to, and we needed to know when developing the code that we would not have any of the values trimmed in that way. Therefore, we set up two VARCHAR2 variables, defined as the maximum size that would be used, that the **set_module** and **set_action** procedures would trim the values down to. Here's a quick demonstration of that trimming:

```
-- dbms_application_info silently trims text that is too long
BEGIN
 dbms_application_info.set_module
   ('123456789A123456789B123456789C123456789D123456789E123456789F123456789G'
   ,'123456789A123456789B123456789C123456789D123456789E123456789F123456789G');
end;
PL/SQL procedure successfully completed.

select module,action from v$session where sid=sys_context('USERENV','SID')

MODULE
----------------------------------------------------------------
ACTION
----------------------------------------------------------------
123456789A123456789B123456789C123456789D12345678
123456789A123456789B123456789C12
```

There is one other thing to notice from our real-world example. The code sets MODULE and ACTION to null at the end of each procedure. This is because none of the developers in that particular environment had used DBMS_APPLICATION_INFO before our code introduced it. The DBAs were aware of it and were happy that our code (and all future code) would be using it, so they could see how much of the database resources were being used by the new application via OEM. Because we had no control over how the client would use the code in the future, we did not want the sessions running the new application to be left marked with the application's module name and last action because any further work done by that session would then be confused with this particular application. One issue with DBMS_APPLICATION_INFO is that you have to maintain the values sensibly via your code (that is, ensure MODULE and ACTION are set and cleared as needed).

Another approach to managing MODULE and ACTION session settings is to decide to add DBMS_APPLICATION_INFO instrumentation to all of your major PL/SQL packages so that MODULE and ACTION are set whenever you do something significant; this way, you do not need to clear it when you finally exit the PL/SQL code. The big drawback of this is that even though the intention is that all significant code will set MODULE and ACTION, reality falls short of this. Again, we can leave sessions wrongly marked once the code has finished.

The previous situation is common and can result in the use of DBMS_APPLICATION_INFO being a little messy. Also, if you have several PL/SQL procedures calling a central package and you want to instrument that central package, you really need to be controlled in how you set and unset MODULE and ACTION. That package will set your ACTION and MODULE, and you always need to remember to reset them in your calling code again after the call to the central code.

There is a simple and easy alternative. DBMS_APPLICATION_INFO can read as well as set the various values it controls, *so you can read the values at the start of a central package (or any PL/SQL you instrument in this way) and reset them to their initial state at the end of your code.* As an example, we run the following in one session (which happens to have a SID of 4) and check the values for MODULE and ACTION from a second session:

```
--dbin2
declare
v_init_module    varchar2(48);
v_init_action    varchar2(32);
begin
  dbms_application_info.read_module(v_init_module,v_init_action);
  dbms_application_info.set_module('MY_MODULE','INITIATION');
  dbms_lock.sleep (5);
  dbms_application_info.set_action('PROCESSING');
  dbms_lock.sleep (20);
  dbms_application_info.set_module(v_init_module,v_init_action);
end;
/

-- from our first session
select to_char(sysdate,'hh24:mi:ss') time ,sys_context('USERENV','SID') sid
from dual;
TIME        SID
-------- ----
12:59:10    4

exec dbms_application_info.set_module('BI REPORTING',NULL);

@dbin2

-- from the second session you run the below several times
select to_char(sysdate,'hh24:mi:ss') time, sid, username, module, action
from v$session
where sid =4

TIME       SID USERNAME  MODULE               ACTION
-------- ---- --------- -------------------- --------------------
12:59:05    4 MDW2      BI REPORTING
...
12:59:13    4 MDW2      MY_MODULE            INITIATION
...
12:59:18    4 MDW2      MY_MODULE            PROCESSING
...
12:59:31    4 MDW2      MY_MODULE            PROCESSING
...
12:59:35    4 MDW2      BI REPORTING
```

As you can see, before the code is run in the first session, MODULE is BI_REPORTING and ACTION is NULL. ACTION and MODULE are set as the code runs, and after the code finishes, session 4 has the same MODULE and ACTION it started with. Preserving the session's MODULE and ACTION at the start of central PL/SQL code and setting the columns back to these preserved values is a simple and effective way to implement DBMS_APPLICATION_INFO.

We have not mentioned CLIENT_INFO much yet. Although this column in V$SESSION is also populated by DBMS_APPLICATION_INFO, via SET_CLIENT_INFO and read via READ_CLIENT_INFO, it is not used by the Oracle monitoring tools nearly as much as the other two columns—and perhaps as a result of this it is less used in general. It works in just the same way and can hold a longer string, at 64 bytes. Sometimes we use it to hold data to indicate the progress of a long-running step, such as in the following code snippet (again from a real-world example):

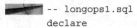

```
dbms_application_info.set_client_info(pv_process_name||' Savepoint. Processed: '
                        ||TO_CHAR(pv_rows_processed||' of '||pv_process_range));
```

```
SID MODULE              ACTION           CLIENT_INFO
----- ------------------ ---------------- ---------------------------------------
  248 TR_TRADE_LOAD      XYZ_UPDATE       Savepoint. Processed: 100000 of 570000
...
  248 TR_TRADE_LOAD      XYZ_UPDATE       Savepoint. Processed: 200000 of 570000
...
  248 TR_TRADE_LOAD      XYZ_UPDATE       Savepoint. Processed: 300000 of 570000
...
  248 TR_TRADE_LOAD      XYZ_UPDATE       Savepoint. Processed: 300000 of 570000
...
  248 TR_TRADE_LOAD      XYZ_UPDATE       Savepoint. Processed: 500000 of 570000
...
  248 TR_TRADE_LOAD      XYZ_UPDATE       Savepoint. Processed: 570135 of 570000
...
```

We use CLIENT_INFO in this way because it is simple and we have scripts to look at MODULE and ACTION, so it is simple to include CLIENT_INFO as well.

V$SESSION_LONGOPS and DBMS_APPLICATION_INFO

DBMS_APPLICATION_INFO also includes a procedure to create entries in V$SESSION_LONGOPS, which usually holds information about long-running SQL statements and an estimate of how long they are going to take to complete. Therefore, it could be seen as the "correct" place to hold such progress information. We'll quickly show you how to put your own information into $SESSION_LONGOPS, which is a little more complex than just setting MODULE, ACTION, or CLIENT_INFO.

You need a "hook" to populate a row in V$SESSION_LONGOPS, which you get by setting a **binary_integer** variable to

```
DBMS_APPLICATION_INFO.SET_SESSION_LONGOPS_NOHINT
```

(I have no idea why it has this somewhat odd name). When you call SET_SESSION_LONGOPS the first time, you pass in this variable for the parameter **rindex**, which is an IN OUT parameter. The value passed back is what you now use to maintain the entry in V$SESSION_LONGOPS.

```
-- longops1.sql
declare
```

```
v_rindex  binary_integer;
v_slno    binary_integer;
v_module  varchar2(48) :='ORDER DAILY BATCH';
v_action  varchar2(32) :='NEW CUSTOMERS';
v_count   binary_integer;
begin
  -- this sets v_rindex to a placeholder value;
  v_rindex := dbms_application_info.set_session_longops_nohint;
  dbms_output.put_line ('initial v_rindex value is '||v_rindex);
  -- slno is used internally for repeat calls to set_session_longops- leave alone
  -- nb - you need some way of estimating how far through the task you are!
  dbms_application_info.set_session_longops
    (rindex        => v_rindex              -- used to id your entry in v$session_longops
    ,slno          => v_slno                -- used by the package to track "stuff"
    ,op_name       => v_module||'-'||v_action -- what you want to call it
    ,target        => 1234                  -- numeric ID of your target
    ,target_desc   => 'BATCH_LOAD_TABLE'    -- text of your target
    ,context       => 42                    -- any number you want
    ,sofar         => 1                     -- what has been done
    ,totalwork     => 10                    --   out of this many
    ,units         => 'beans');             --     in these units
  dbms_output.put_line ('v_rindex value is '||v_rindex||' slno value is '
                        ||v_slno);
  --
end;

mdw2> @longops1
initial v_rindex value is -1
v_rindex value is 489  slno value is 1241


PL/SQL procedure successfully completed.

select sid||'-'||serial# sid_ser    ,opname    ,target  ,sql_id
     ,start_time  ,last_update_time  ,elapsed_seconds      ,time_remaining
     ,sofar          ,totalwork          ,units      ,message
from V$SESSION_LONGOPS
where target=1234
```

SID_SER	OPNAME	TARGET	SQL_ID
-----------	--------------------------------	--------------------	------------

START_TIME	LAST_UPD	elapsed	to_go	SOFAR	TOTALWORK	UNITS
--------------	--------------	--------	--------	----------	----------	--------

```
MESSAGE
--------------------------------------------------------------------------------
4-27517    ORDER DAILY BATCH-NEW CUSTOMERS  1234                3v52udfqgs5ct
31-01 17:12:43 31-01 17:12:43    0       0         1      10 beans
ORDER DAILY BATCH-NEW CUSTOMERS: BATCH_LOAD_TABLE 1234: 1 out of 10 beans done
```

When you initially set the variable **v_rindex** with **dbms_application_info.set_session_longops_hint**, it is set to –1 (on Oracle 11 and 12 at least). In fact, you can just set your variable initially to –1 and it will work, but this would be bad practice because you do not know how this built-in

package variable may be changed by Oracle in the future. The values passed back out of
set_session_longops for RINDEX and SLNO appear to increment by 1 each time we manually
create a new entry. After calling the procedure to create an entry in V$SESSION_LONGOPS, we
pull out some of the columns from V$SESSION_LONGOPS so that you can see what has been
populated—namely, OPNAME, TARGET SOFAR, TOTALWORK, UNITS, and MESSAGE.

Now let's look at an example where we do some work and increment the values for SOFAR
and TOTALWORK. Once we have initiated our row in V$SESSION_LONGOPS, we just use the
values of RINDEX and SLNO to update the entry. You do not need to pass in all the values each
time, *but be warned*—if you pass in only SOFAR and not TOTALWORK too, *you get odd behavior.*
TOTALWORK gets set to the default of 0, no value for TIME_REMAINING is calculated, and the
MESSAGE lines state something like

```
OBJECT MAINT-ALTERED OBJECTS: ALL_OBJECTS 35: 11 out of 0 Letters done
```

The following code demonstrates updating V$SESSION_LONGOPS as work progresses:

```
-- longops2.sql
declare
v_rindex  binary_integer;
v_slno    binary_integer;
v_module  varchar2(48) :='OBJECT MAINT';
v_action  varchar2(32) :='ALTERED OBJECTS';
v_count   binary_integer;
begin
  -- this sets v_lops to a placeholder value;
  v_rindex := dbms_application_info.set_session_longops_nohint;
  dbms_output.put_line ('initial v_rindex value is '||v_rindex);
  dbms_application_info.set_session_longops
    (rindex  => v_rindex ,slno        => v_slno ,op_name    => v_module||'-'||v_action
    ,target  => 36        ,target_desc => 'ALL_OBJECTS',context=> 12
    ,sofar   => 0          ,totalwork  => 26                ,units => 'Letters');
  dbms_output.put_line ('v_rindex value is '||v_rindex||'  slno value is '||v_slno);
  for a in 1..26 loop
    select count(*) into v_count
    from all_objects where object_name like (chr(64+a)||'%');
    dbms_lock.sleep(2);
    dbms_application_info.set_session_longops
    (rindex  => v_rindex ,slno        => v_slno
    ,sofar   => a ,totalwork=> 26);
    dbms_output.put_line ('v_rindex value is '||v_rindex||'  slno value is '||v_slno);
  end loop;
end;

-- output
@longops2
initial v_rindex value is -1
v_rindex value is 498   slno value is 1248
v_rindex value is 498   slno value is 1248
...
v_rindex value is 498   slno value is 1248
v_rindex value is 0  slno value is 0
```

```
PL/SQL procedure successfully completed.

-- looking at the relevant V$SESSION_LONGOPS row from another session
-- where TARGET =36

SID_SER     OPNAME                            TARGET              SQL_ID
----------- -------------------------------   --------------------  -------------
START_TIME    LAST_UPD      elapsed   to_go      SOFAR  TOTALWORK UNITS
------------- ------------- --------- -------- ---------- ---------- --------
MESSAGE
---------------------------------------------------------------------------------
4-27517      OBJECT MAINT-ALTERED OBJECTS      36                  as0ys6vrsj9ra
31-01 18:27:49 31-01 18:27:49    0                   0          26 Letters
OBJECT MAINT-ALTERED OBJECTS: ALL_OBJECTS 36: 0 out of 26 Letters done

4-27517      OBJECT MAINT-ALTERED OBJECTS      36                  as0ys6vrsj9ra
31-01 18:27:49 31-01 18:27:53    4        48        2          26 Letters
OBJECT MAINT-ALTERED OBJECTS: ALL_OBJECTS 36: 2 out of 26 Letters done

4-27517      OBJECT MAINT-ALTERED OBJECTS      36                  as0ys6vrsj9ra
31-01 18:27:49 31-01 18:27:59   10        42        5          26 Letters
OBJECT MAINT-ALTERED OBJECTS: ALL_OBJECTS 36: 5 out of 26 Letters done
-- skipped several lines of output
4-27517      OBJECT MAINT-ALTERED OBJECTS      36                  as0ys6vrsj9ra
31-01 18:27:49 31-01 18:28:40   51         2       25          26 Letters
OBJECT MAINT-ALTERED OBJECTS: ALL_OBJECTS 36: 25 out of 26 Letters done

4-27517      OBJECT MAINT-ALTERED OBJECTS      36                  as0ys6vrsj9ra
31-01 18:27:49 31-01 18:28:42   53         0       26          26 Letters

OBJECT MAINT-ALTERED OBJECTS: ALL_OBJECTS 36: 26 out of 26 Letters done
```

We can see that not only are our columns for SOFAR and TOTALWORK being populated, but Oracle keeps track of ELAPSED_SECONDS and makes a calculated estimate at TIME_REMAINING (our script calls these "elapsed" and "to go" to save space). If we do not include TOTALWORK in our update statements, Oracle does not re-estimate TIME_REMAINING for us. We presume this is because we could be updating the TOTALWORK value as our code progresses also, so **set_session_longops** just expects us to keep providing the value. The package seems happy to remember the other values (OP_NAME, TARGET, CONTEXT, and UNITS) that we initially passed in.

Using V$SESSION_LONGOPS Yourself Can Confuse Others
Just a final word of warning on putting your own information into V$SESSION_LONGOPS—if you are not the only person monitoring the database(s) in which this code runs, you better mention what you are doing to the people who *are* monitoring it. It is not uncommon for V$SESSION_LONGOPS to be looked at with the specific aim of spotting long-running SQL, such as long-duration queries, stats-gathering statements, table copies, and index rebuilds. Many people will not be expecting user-defined information to start appearing there, or even be aware that this is possible. On a couple of occasions I've seen this cause a bit of a panic!

SQL*Plus SET APPINFO and SYS_CONTEXT

We have just two final things to cover about DBMS_APPLICATION_INFO.

In SQL*Plus you can **set appinfo on** or **set appinfo** *text*. The latter form sets MODULE to *text*. Both forms result in MODULE being set to the name of any script you execute with @ or @@— *during the execution of the script*. Once it completes, the entry reverts back to any default of *text* you set. (As you have seen, SQL*Plus sets this value to "SQL*Plus" for you behind the scenes if you do nothing to APPINFO—if you **set appinfo off** for a session and then run a script, the session's MODULE becomes blank.)

Setting **appinfo on** can be useful for instrumenting and monitoring the running of scripts from SQL*Plus:

```
set appinfo 'ORDERS_BATCH'
select module,module_hash from v$session where type !='BACKGROUND'

  SID MODULE
----- -------------------------------------------------------------
    8 ORDERS_BATCH
    9 01@ eric1.sql
  189 01@ D:\sqlwork\sqlutils\chk_mac.sql
  190 01@<k\sqlutils\verlongnameofscriptfortesting.sql
```

You can see that our session (SID 8) is now marked with ORDERS_BATCH. Also, where we have **set appinfo on** for three other sessions, you can see the last SQL script they executed. One was in the working directory (SID 9), and the final two were in one of the directories in my SQLPATH. Note that the contents of MODULE are still trimmed to 48 characters—but it is the start of the string that is trimmed (see SID 190, where "D:\sqlwor" has been trimmed). If you explicitly state the directory of the SQL script, that also shows up in MODULE. And remember, if you **set appinfo** *text*, you see *text* in the module when the session is not running a script.

You cannot set ACTION or MODULE via **set appinfo**.

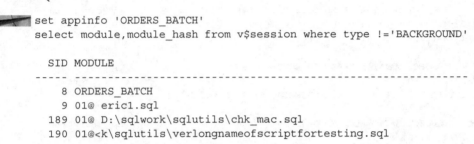

NOTE
For Oracle Forms users, Oracle Forms sets the MODULE name for you since version 11.1. Oracle warns you that although you can change the value within a form using DBMS_APPLICATION_INFO, this is not supported because the change was intended for new OEM features that use MODULE.

You can access the values for MODULE, ACTION, and CLIENT INFO for your session via SYS_CONTEXT:

```
BEGIN
    dbms_application_info.set_module('ORDERS BATCH','NEW ORDERS');
    dbms_application_info.set_client_info('processed 572 new orders');
    dbms_lock.sleep(1);
    dbms_output.put_line('Module      : '||sys_context('userenv','module'));
    dbms_output.put_line('Action      : '||sys_context('userenv','action'));
    dbms_output.put_line('Client info : '||sys_context('userenv','client_info'));
end;
```

```
-- output
Module      : ORDERS BATCH
Action      : NEW ORDERS
Client info : processed 572 new orders
```

SYS_CONTEXT information is held in memory and therefore is a slightly more efficient way of getting the MODULE, ACTION, and CLIENT INFO information than querying V$SESSION for your current SID. However, if you are setting these values to provide high-level instrumentation, as suggested, you shouldn't really need to check it all the time, so the performance difference is not significant. Use whichever method suits you.

Overview of Instrumentation Options

We have covered three main options for instrumenting your code: DBMS_OUTPUT, DBMS_APPLICATION_INFO, and logging tables.

DBMS_OUPUT has the advantage that it is very easy to use and almost everyone who does any PL/SQL programming knows how to use **dbms_ouput.put_line**. You can put out whatever information you wish to. However, the information is transient and easily lost, and you cannot see it until the PL/SQL code finishes running. No other session can see it. You can make DBMS_OUTPUT a little easier to live with by creating a wrapper procedure for it. The impact on performance is low unless you over instrument, in which case you waste memory and the time to fetch the data back to your session grows. On older versions of Oracle, you could generate errors with large volumes. It is probably the tool of choice for debugging as you develop your code.

DBMS_APPLICATION_INFO is very, very lightweight, the information is used across the Oracle tool set, and it is simple to use. Furthermore, the information is seen by other sessions immediately. However, it can only show a small amount of information, and that information is transient. You are very unlikely to adversely impact performance or any other aspect of your database with it. It is ideal for real-time monitoring of your production PL/SQL.

Log tables need to be set up and a small amount of code written to make use of the data. But the data is persisted, can be seen immediately, and can be queried to profile your code in any way you can come up with using SQL. Log tables provide for long-term monitoring and are the most flexible in allowing you to instrument exactly what you want. They potentially have the largest impact on your system performance if you overinstrument. Using log tables is the ideal choice for instrumenting production code.

Of course, you can use all three options in conjunction, as was demonstrated. You can use DBMS_APPLICATION_INFO for broad-brush real-time monitoring of information, as well as a procedure that logs to a table and, optionally, to DBMS_OUTPUT, controlled by a simple LOG_LEVEL parameter.

Instrumentation Packages

A few packages/utilities are available for instrumenting your PL/SQL code, and these are usually free. They generally automate the population of a logging table and/or provide wrappers for DBMS_OUTPUT or DBMS_APPLICATION_INFO. However, we provide code for you to do these things in this chapter! We are not going to review any of these packages other than to mention one, Instrumentation Library for Oracle, or ILO. This is produced by Method-R, a very well-known and respected company in the aspect of Oracle Performance. At the time of writing, ILO is at version 2.3, and you can download it for free from SourceForge: http://sourceforge.net/projects/ilo/.

The code has not been altered much in the last few years—it does not need to because it works fine as it is. The authors of ILO occasionally get requests to persist the data in log tables, but they feel that would involve specifying the tables and how they are used, which could be client-specific. Taking the code and adding your own persistence to tables is easily done.

The package simplifies the calling of DBMS_APPLICATION_INFO and DBMS_SESSION to record the progress of code and allow the DBA to identify and monitor the code as it runs. It also aids in the creation of Oracle trace files and placing extra information in them and the alert log, which is what helps make it one of the better instrumentation packages. Trace files are not covered in this book. Although producing, analyzing, and reading trace files is an important skill for performance tuning, it is amply covered in many other books, web articles, and blogs. Performance tuning is probably *the* most written-about Oracle skill!

Once the required user is created and the package and such are installed, using the package is very simple. You just include calls at the very beginning of any procedure or function you wish to instrument, at the exit points (just before the terminal END and in EXCEPTION clauses), and at any key points in the code where you want to change the ACTION name:

```
create or replace PROCEDURE ORDERS_BATCH(
    P_date        varchar2,
    P_department pls_integer) is
begin
    ilo_task.begin_task(module => 'ORDERS_BATCH', action => 'NEW_ORDERS');
    select ord_id,status,cust_id...
    ...
    ...  -- lots of code
    ...
    ilo_task.end_task;
exception
when others
then
    dbms_output.put_line('Exception thrown');
    ilo_task.end_task(error_num =>SQLCODE);
end;
```

As stated earlier, we are not going to cover this tool in detail; just know that it and other packages are available. If you think ILO could be useful to you, go to SourceForge and follow the links to the documentation and code.

Profiling

Once you have instrumented your code, then profiling it is almost a side effect of that instrumentation. After all, that was probably the main reason for having that instrumentation in place in the production code. However, there are other tools you can use to profile your PL/SQL when there is no instrumentation in place—namely DBMS_TRACE, DBMS_PROFILER, and DBMS_HPROF, which we will come to later.

Drawbacks of Profiling Production Code with DBMS_OUPUT

If your instrumentation is via DBMS_OUTPUT, then profiling the code is probably going to be a manual process of looking at the output and simply reading it. Here is the output from another run of our address-populating procedure **pna_maint.pop_addr_batch**:

```
POP_ADDR_BATCH log 5 - 12:18:19.603 :started at 16-02-03 12:18:19.603
POP_ADDR_BATCH log 5 - 12:18:19.603 :towns 1 to 69  roads 1 to 81  types 1 to 74
POP_ADDR_BATCH log 5 - 12:18:24.603 :intermediate commit at 100000 addresses
POP_ADDR_BATCH log 5 - 12:18:30.296 :intermediate commit at 200000 addresses
POP_ADDR_BATCH log 5 - 12:18:36.726 :intermediate commit at 300000 addresses
POP_ADDR_BATCH log 5 - 12:18:44.043 :intermediate commit at 400000 addresses
POP_ADDR_BATCH log 5 - 12:18:52.136 :intermediate commit at 500000 addresses
POP_ADDR_BATCH log 5 - 12:19:00.998 :intermediate commit at 600000 addresses
POP_ADDR_BATCH log 5 - 12:19:10.734 :intermediate commit at 700000 addresses
POP_ADDR_BATCH log 5 - 12:19:21.321 :intermediate commit at 800000 addresses
POP_ADDR_BATCH log 5 - 12:19:32.590 :intermediate commit at 900000 addresses
POP_ADDR_BATCH log 5 - 12:19:44.694 :intermediate commit at 1000000 addresses
POP_ADDR_BATCH log 5 - 12:19:44.694 :ended at 16-02-03 12:19:44.694
POP_ADDR_BATCH log 5 - 12:19:44.694 :elapsed is 0 00:01:25.091000000
```

If you look at the output, you may notice that each intermediate commit is taking longer. The code is slowing down as it works through the data set. We could have made it easier to see by having the change in time between each step, but that would have involved more complex instrumentation code. So with the DBMS_OUTPUT code, we just have to look at the output. (However, we hasten to stress that this is much, much better than having no instrumentation!)

You can also see from the last line that the elapsed time is over a minute, 1:25.091. You may remember from before that it took 43.138 seconds. Actually, you probably *don't* remember that, as it was back about 20 pages. We are actually making a point here about why the use of DBMS_OUTPUT is just fine when we are working on debugging code (because we repeatedly run it and can remember or check our notes of the last few run times) but is inadequate for monitoring production code. You probably won't remember the run time from a few days ago, if you actually looked at it. If you go as far as to spool out and preserve the output of DBMS_OUTPUT for production batch code, you will have to go and find it.

On that topic, if you have spooled the output to a set of files, you could process it with all sorts of tools, but you will in effect be writing a small program to do it. In the past we have written shell scripts or used awk (or both) to process OS-based log files, or even pulled the information into Microsoft Excel and done some work on it there. But these are all crude ways of doing the task compared to using a log table and SQL.

Using the PLSQL_LOG Table

When we have put our logging information into a table like PLSQL_LOG, we can modify how we see that data with SQL, of course. We will look at some examples in the following pages.

The same information we saw displayed with DBMS_OUTPUT in the previous section was also inserted into our PLSQL_LOG table, so let's look at that. How long is the run taking over the last few days? Our instrumentation for that code includes a final entry giving the elapsed time, so we can pull out just those entries for the last few days:

```
select process_name,start_timestamp,log_text
from plsql_log
where process_name='POP_ADDR_BATCH'
and  log_text like '%elapsed%'
and start_timestamp > systimestamp -5
order by 2
```

```
PROCESS_NAME     START_TIMESTAMP          LOG_TEXT
---------------  -----------------------  -------------------------------
POP_ADDR_BATCH   23-JAN-16 20.59.48.926   elapsed is 0 00:00:42.037000000
POP_ADDR_BATCH   24-JAN-16 21.26.12.449   elapsed is 0 00:00:43.138000000
POP_ADDR_BATCH   25-JAN-16 20.52.56.916   elapsed is 0 00:00:44.089000000
...
```

If we want to know the elapsed time per section, we use a very simply analytical function. We also use a subquery to find the latest run for the given process name, so we see the information for the latest run, which is a common requirement:

```
select  process_name,start_timestamp
      ,to_char(log_timestamp,'HH24:MI:SS.FF3') log_timestmap
      ,log_level,log_text
      ,substr(log_timestamp - lag(log_timestamp,1)
                        over (order by log_timestamp),12,12) as elapsed
from plsql_log
where process_name='POP_ADDR_BATCH'
and start_timestamp = (select max(start_timestamp) from plsql_log
                   where process_name = 'POP_ADDR_BATCH')
order by log_timestamp
```

PROCESS_NAME	START DATE	LOG TIMESTAMP	LOG LEV	LOG_TEXT	ELAPSED
POP_ADDR_BATCH	03-FEB-16	12:18:19.603	5	started at 16-02-03 12:18:19.603	
		12:18:19.603	5	towns 1 to 69 roads 1 to 81 types 1 to 74	00:00:00.000
		12:18:24.603	5	intermediate commit at 100000 addresses	00:00:05.000
		12:18:30.296	5	intermediate commit at 200000 addresses	00:00:05.693
		12:18:36.726	5	intermediate commit at 300000 addresses	00:00:06.430
		12:18:44.043	5	intermediate commit at 400000 addresses	00:00:07.317
		12:18:52.136	5	intermediate commit at 500000 addresses	00:00:08.093
		12:19:00.998	5	intermediate commit at 600000 addresses	00:00:08.862
		12:19:10.734	5	intermediate commit at 700000 addresses	00:00:09.736
		12:19:21.321	5	intermediate commit at 800000 addresses	00:00:10.587
		12:19:32.590	5	intermediate commit at 900000 addresses	00:00:11.269
		12:19:44.694	5	intermediate commit at 1000000 addresses	00:00:12.104
		12:19:44.694	5	ended at 16-02-03 12:19:44.694	00:00:00.000
		12:19:44.694	5	elapsed is 0 00:01:25.091000000	00:00:00.000

Another common requirement is to get the latest instrumentation to see what is happening on the system. We can do this with a simple WHERE clause to look back for a short period in time. The following example shows all the logging information for the last 15 minutes:

```
AND  start_timestamp > sysdate-(1/(24*4))
```

To look back a specific period of time, you subtract a fraction from the current SYSDATE. Use x/24 to look back x hours, x/(24*60) to look back x minutes, and x/(24*60*60) to look back x seconds. Here we look back 30 minutes:

```
select  process_name, to_char(start_timestamp,'DD-MM-YY HH24:MI:SS') Start_Date
      ,to_char(log_timestamp,'HH24:MI:SS.FF3') log_ts
```

```
        ,log_text
        ,substr(log_timestamp - start_timestamp,12,12) as elapsed
from plsql_log
where process_name='POP_ADDR_BATCH'
and start_timestamp > sysdate-(30/(24*60)) -- 30 minutes
and log_text like 'end%'
order by log_timestamp desc


PROCESS_NAME   START_DATE        LOG_TS        LOG_TEXT                       ELAPSED
-------------- ----------------- ------------- ------------------------------ -----------
POP_ADDR_BATCH 20-02-16 15:41:06 15:41:55.560 ended at 16-02-20 15:41:55.560 00:00:48.934
```

In the POP_ADDR_BATCH example, our instrumentation includes a final "Elapsed" entry, but in practice we do not need such an entry in our instrumentation because it is derived information and it is easy to extract from the log data in PLSQL_BATCH. We just extract the "start" and "end" entries and use a lag analytical function, as shown here:

```
select  process_name,start_timestamp
       ,to_char(log_timestamp,'HH24:MI:SS.FF3') log_timestmap
       ,log_level,log_text
       ,substr(log_timestamp - lag(log_timestamp,1)
                   over (partition by start_timestamp order by log_timestamp)
                   ,12,12) as elapsed
from plsql_log
where process_name='POP_ADDR_BATCH'
and (log_text like 'start%' or log_text like 'end%')
and start_timestamp > sysdate -3
order by log_timestamp
                START    LOG         LOG
PROCESS_NAME    DATE     TIMESTAMP   LEV LOG_TEXT
ELAPSED
-------------- ---------- ----------- --- ---------------------------------------- ------------

POP_ADDR_BATCH 01-FEB-16 11:43:27.824  5 started at 16-02-01 11:43:27.824
                         11:44:27.708  5 ended at 16-02-01 11:44:27.708        00:00:59.884
               02-FEB-16 11:46:34.370  5 started at 16-02-02 11:46:34.370
                         11:57:27.841  5 ended at 16-02-02 11:57:27.841        00:00:53.471
               03-FEB-16 12:18:19.603  5 started at 16-02-03 12:18:19.603
                         12:19:44.694  5 ended at 16-02-03 12:19:44.694        00:01:25.091
               03-FEB-16 16:03:36.964  5 started at 16-02-03 16:03:36.964
                         16:06:08.590  5 ended at 16-02-03 16:06:08.590        00:02:31.626
```

Looking at the elapsed time over the last few runs, we can see that the problem has been getting worse over time. It would be easy enough to write some SQL, a daily check, to see if the elapsed times of anything being logged to PLSQL_LOG were getting significantly worse over time or were, say, more than 50 percent slower than the last run.

As covered earlier in our discussion of instrumentation, one benefit of the PLSQL_LOG table and using autonomous transactions to populate the table is that we can see the progress of the code while it is still running. If someone comes and asks us why the "population of addresses batch" is taking so long, we can look at our PLSQL_LOG table or the MODULE information in the OEM performance screen and almost certainly identify that the "addresses batch" is probably POP_ADDR_BATCH. Because progress information is being written to PLSQL_LOG, we can immediately see what it has done and what it is doing now. Figure 7-6 is a screenshot from SQL Developer (filling in for any GUI database-monitoring tool you like to use) taken during a run of the POP_ADDR_BATCH code.

We can see that the code started (and when), that it has passed some setup stage, and that it is progressing with intermediate commits. And we can see each batch getting slower than the previous one (if this was a real issue, the elapsed time for each batch is likely to be minutes rather than seconds, but you get the idea). We now have information; we are not guessing. The code *is* running, it is not stuck, and we can see what steps have completed and that each batch is slower than the previous one for the same number of records. We can now start asking the question, What could cause this specific behavior? We can also pull up the code for the package and look for the LOG_TEXT in the code. We can now provide feedback to the user and decide if we have a problem that needs to be addressed. If there is a problem and you are the DBA, you now have vital information that you can pass back to the development team to help them look into the issue. Everyone wins.

We could show you several more scripts for pulling data out of PLSQL_LOG, but you get the idea. When you put your instrumentation into a log table, the ways you can look at it are limited only by your imagination and time. The table should never get too large (given you do not overinstrument, as highlighted earlier in this chapter), but you might want to partition it by month or year, if only to make it easy to archive off old data if you should desire. Because you are persisting these run-time logs of your core code, you can track changes in performance over time. This has all sorts of unexpected benefits. One of them is that when management starts getting

```
    ▷ 🖫 🏂 🖫 🖫  🗗 🖫  🖴 ✎ ✐ ⓞ
Worksheet    Query Builder
   1 ▤ select process_name,start_timestamp
   2        ,to_char(log_timestamp,'HH24:MI:SS.FF3') log_timestmap
   3        ,log_text
   4        ,substr(log_timestamp - lag(log_timestamp,1)
   5                        over (order by log_timestamp),12,12) as elapsed
   6   from mdw2.plsql_log
   7   where process_name ='POP_ADDR_BATCH'
   8   AND    start_timestamp > sysdate-(1/(24*15))
   9   /
```

Autotrace ✕ ▷ Query... ✕

📌 🖨 🔁 🗈 SQL | All Rows Fetched: 7 in 0 seconds

	PROCESS_NAME	START_TIMESTAMP	LOG_TIMESTMAP	LOG_TEXT	ELAPSED
1	POP_ADDR_BATCH	03-02-2016 18.08.24	18:08:24.279	started at 16-02-03 18:08:24.279	(null)
2	POP_ADDR_BATCH	03-02-2016 18.08.24	18:08:24.279	towns 1 to 69 roads 1 to 81 types 1 to 74	00:00:00.000
3	POP_ADDR_BATCH	03-02-2016 18.08.24	18:08:32.433	intermediate commit at 100000 addresses	00:00:08.154
4	POP_ADDR_BATCH	03-02-2016 18.08.24	18:08:44.536	intermediate commit at 200000 addresses	00:00:12.103
5	POP_ADDR_BATCH	03-02-2016 18.09.00	18:09:00.674	intermediate commit at 300000 addresses	00:00:16.138
6	POP_ADDR_BATCH	03-02-2016 18.09.20	18:09:20.774	intermediate commit at 400000 addresses	00:00:20.100
7	POP_ADDR_BATCH	03-02-2016 18.09.44	18:09:44.989	intermediate commit at 500000 addresses	00:00:24.215

FIGURE 7-6. *Seeing the progress of POP_ADDR_BATCH in real time*

agitated that "X is taking too long" and the finger is inevitably pointed at the database, you have the information immediately at hand to show that either the code is taking the same amount of time as last year and the problem is elsewhere or that, yes, the problem is in the database, it started to get slower on day X in section B of the code, and you are currently looking into it.

A Real-World Example of the Power of Instrumentation

We will finish this section on the use of logging tables with a real-world example of when instrumentation held within a logging table made what would have been an extremely hard job into a manageable one.

I was hired by a client to help them with migrating their Oracle database from one version to another. The brief was very typical—they were replacing the server with a newer, more powerful one and migrating their database to the current version of Oracle to maintain support. They wanted to make no changes to the applications that used the database, no changes to the database structure, and no changes to any SQL or PL/SQL. They were hoping (and, in reality, *expecting*) the new database to "run faster," but the critical thing was that nothing, no SQL statement, no PL/SQL package, should run slower. Nothing.

It is an almost impossible aim: although most SQL will run just as fast or faster on a later version of Oracle, it is a different optimizer with different capabilities, and there are nearly always some situations where a new access path will help 95 percent of the time and hinder 5 percent of the time. Setting compatibility to the current version was deemed unacceptable—they wanted all the potential gains, but none of the losses.

Another typical part of the situation was that they were not really clear on the full flow of their applications and how things interacted. Staff move on, new parts of the application get bolted on to existing parts, and things have been tweaked to solve a prior issue. They were not even sure of the elapsed run times of many of the components—just the ones that regularly went wrong and had to be nursed. There was some documentation, but much of it was old or missing.

Thankfully, when the database and its applications had originally been created, they had been instrumented—and new code added afterward was also instrumented. The start and end time of each process—be it in shell script, Java, or PL/SQL—was recorded in a log table in the database. Not a lot else, though. There was nothing about data volumes or key parameters, but they had all the start and end times and success indicators going back over a year (they trimmed the data). There were also secondary tables that described the hierarchy of all the components.

Within a week or two, from that information we had worked out the flow of applications, identified those that ran in the database, and determined the average run times over recent months. We now had the profiles of the current system components and a clear view of where time was spent. Before this, the client knew they had the instrumentation data, but they had not generated these profiles and data flows. It would have been very difficult, if not impossible, to gain this information if we had no instrumentation.

We were now in a position to build and test the new system (such a short sentence covers what was actually a lot of work) and compare the run profiles—simply and easily due to the instrumentation—and fix those components that ran slower. Even though the final production system was not quite the same as the test system and the outage for the actual migration would alter the data being processed on the first day (more of it!), we were able to use the instrumentation and profiling to predict with considerable accuracy (within 6 percent for every step) the duration of the database components of the system post-migration, as well as to monitor progress in real time over that first 24 hours. Without that instrumentation, we would have had severe performance issues post-migration and may have missed some components to migrate.

Instrumentation and profiling are not an overhead. They are vital to running and maintaining a system professionally.

Profiling and Debugging Packages

Oracle provides several packages to help you profile PL/SQL without adding your own instrumentation. These are very useful when you have code that has not been instrumented but you need to look into issues with the code. The three main packages are DBMS_TRACE, DBMS_PROFILER, and DBMS_HPROF. We will look at all three and compare them.

We will also look at PLSQL_WARNINGS, which can be used to indicate potential issues with your PL/SQL. Strictly speaking, it is more of a debugging (or bug-avoidance) tool, but it fits in well with the profiling tools. Especially because, just like them, it offers valuable help for little effort and yet seems to be rarely used.

PL/SQL Warnings

PLSQL_WARNINGS is an Oracle initialization parameter that can be set at the instance or session level. When you enable PL/SQL warnings, whenever you compile any PL/SQL, Oracle will check it for some known issues, such as the use of reserved words or deprecated features, and either issue warnings and compile the PL/SQL code, or give an error and not compile the code. PLSQL_WARNINGS was introduced with Oracle 10.1 and by default is initially set to DISABLE:ALL, as shown here:

```
select name,value from v$parameter where name ='plsql_warnings';

NAME             VALUE
--------------   -----------------------------
plsql_warnings   DISABLE:ALL
```

You can enable it in your session with the ALTER SESSION command or the DBMS_WARNING package. The following uses ALTER SESSION to enable all compilation warnings:

```
alter session set plsql_warnings='enable:all'
Session altered.
```

It is used to control what warnings you see when you compile PL/SQL. It is very useful for identifying deprecated or suboptimal PL/SQL features and constructs. You actually have to recompile stored PL/SQL code for the warnings to be checked for. If any are found, you do not get the "Warning: Package created with compilation errors" message but rather SP2-0808:

```
ora122> @bad_code
SP2-0808: Package created with compilation warnings
```

In SQL*Plus, once you have been told that warnings were issued, you use SHOW ERRORS to display the actual list of errors. GUI PL/SQL development tools will handle this for you. Compilation warnings are mentioned in Chapter 6 with respect to using the deprecated PRAGMA RESTRICT REFERENCES, so let's use that as an example:

```
create or replace package bad_code authid definer as
function dummy1 (p_num in number)
return varchar2;
pragma restrict_references (dummy1,wnds);
```

```
end bad_code;

SP2-0808: Package created with compilation warnings

show errors
Errors for PACKAGE BAD_CODE:

LINE/COL ERROR
-------- ----------------------------------------------------------------------
4/8      PLW-05019: the language element near keyword RESTRICT_REFERENCES
         is deprecated beginning with version 11.2
```

The value you set PLSQL_WARNINGS to is composed of one or more *state* and *category* pairs. The possible states are as follows:

- **enable**   Turn on this category of warning or specific warning code(s).
- **disable**   Turn off this category of warning or specific warning code(s).
- **error**   Make this code an error (that is, do not compile the PL/SQL object).

Here are the possible categories:

- **severe**   Unexpected behavior or incorrect results might occur.
- **performance**   Will perform correctly but performance could be suboptimal, such as using implicit conversion or not using COPY for large parameters.
- **informational**   Other issues such as deprecated features or code is present that can never be called.
- **all**   All of the preceding three categories.

Setting the value to **enable:severe** will only give you warnings of that category. You can enable severe and performance warnings and disable informational warnings with the following:

```
alter session set plsql_warnings='enable:all,enable:performance,disable:informational'
Session altered.

show parameter plsql_warnings
NAME                                 TYPE        VALUE
------------------------------------ ----------- ------------------------------
plsql_warnings                       string      DISABLE:INFORMATIONAL, ENABLE:
                                                 PERFORMANCE, ENABLE:SEVERE
```

Note the use of the SQL*Plus SHOW PARAMETER command.

Oracle provides the DBMS_WARNING package to allow you to manage PLSQL_WARNINGS for both the session and system (privileges allowing), including setting specific error codes on and off. You can refer to the Oracle Database PL/SQL Packages and Types reference for full details, but the following demonstrates some of the functionality. We'll look at the code for setting PLSQL_ WARNINGS in various ways (so you can try it yourself) and the values for the parameter afterward.

```
declare
v_temp varchar2(1000);
```

```
BEGIN
  v_temp := dbms_warning.get_warning_setting_string;
  dbms_output.put_line('plsql warning string : '||v_temp);
  -- set plsql_warning to a certain string
  dbms_warning.set_warning_setting_string('ENABLE:SEVERE','SESSION');
  dbms_output.put_line('plsql warning string : '||dbms_warning.get_warning_setting_string);
  -- set one of the categories
  dbms_warning.add_warning_setting_cat('performance','enable','session');
  dbms_output.put_line('plsql warning string : '||dbms_warning.get_warning_setting_string);
  -- get the category for a number
  v_temp := dbms_warning.get_warning_setting_num(5005);
  dbms_output.put_line('warning code 5005 : '||v_temp);
  -- error if warning code 5005 occurs
  dbms_warning.add_warning_setting_num(5005,'error','session');
  dbms_output.put_line('warning code 5005 : '||dbms_warning.get_warning_setting_num(5005));
  dbms_output.put_line('plsql warning string : '||dbms_warning.get_warning_setting_string);
end;

-- output
-- different settings for the PLSQL_WARNING parameter
plsql warning string : DISABLE:INFORMATIONAL,DISABLE:PERFORMANCE,ENABLE:SEVERE
plsql warning string : DISABLE:INFORMATIONAL,ENABLE:PERFORMANCE,ENABLE:SEVERE
-- Showing the warning level for specific codes
warning code 5005 : ENABLE:  5005
warning code 5005 : ERROR:  5005
-- PLSQL_WARNINGS when you set specific actions for a given error code
plsql warning string : DISABLE:INFORMATIONAL,ENABLE:PERFORMANCE,ENABLE:SEVERE,ERROR:  5005
```

As you can see, the value for this parameter can get quite complex—but in reality most people just set all warnings on or off! However, if you turn on PL/SQL compilation warnings and keep seeing a specific warning you wish to ignore, you can turn it off. This is especially useful if you set it at the instance level (say, in your development environment). For example, let's say you do not want to keep seeing the PLW-07203 NOCOPY warning, so you want to exclude it. Here's how:

```
-- what are my plsql warnings
show parameter plsql_warnings

NAME                                 TYPE        VALUE
------------------------------------ ----------- --------------
plsql_warnings                       string      ENABLE:ALL

create or replace package body bad_code as
procedure dummy1 (p_vc in out varchar2) is
begin
  p_vc:=p_vc||'aaaaaaaaaaaaaaaaaaaaaaaaaaaaaaaaaaaaaaaaaaaaaa';
end dummy1;
end bad_code;

SP2-0810: Package Body created with compilation warnings
```

```
show errors
LINE/COL ERROR
-------- ----------------------------------------------------------------
2/19     PLW-07203: parameter 'P_VC' may benefit from use of the NOCOPY
         compiler hint

-- exclude that warning
exec dbms_warning.add_warning_setting_num(7203,'disable','session');
show parameter plsql_warnings
NAME                                 TYPE          VALUE
------------------------------------ ----------- ---------------------------
plsql_warnings                       string        ENABLE:ALL, DISABLE:  7203

--now it should compile with no warnings
alter package bad_code compile body;
Package body altered.

show errors
No errors.
```

You can see all the PLW error codes in the Database Error Messages manual (it makes for some interesting reading). You can get a feel for the sort of feedback you get with compilation warnings from the following examples. First, let's compile a package specification with some issues:

```
alter session set plsql_warnings='enable:all';
Session altered.

create or replace package bad_code as
function dummy1 (p_num in number
               ,p_vc  in out varchar2)
return varchar2;
pragma restrict_references (dummy1,wnds);
procedure dummy2 (p_num in number
               ,p_vc in out nocopy varchar2);
end bad_code;

SP2-0808: Package created with compilation warnings

ora122> show errors
Errors for PACKAGE BAD_CODE:

LINE/COL ERROR
-------- ----------------------------------------------------------------
1/1      PLW-05018: unit BAD_CODE omitted optional AUTHID clause; default
         value DEFINER used
3/18     PLW-07203: parameter 'P_VC' may benefit from use of the NOCOPY
         compiler hint
5/8      PLW-05019: the language element near keyword RESTRICT_REFERENCES
         is deprecated beginning with version 11.2
```

With SQL*Plus, SHOW ERRORS only shows the errors for the last command run, so now we will compile the body. Have a look at the code and try to predict what warnings you will see:

```
create or replace package body bad_code as
function dummy1 (p_num in number
                ,p_vc   in out varchar2)
return varchar2 is
v_vc      varchar2(1000);
systimestamp  number;
begin
  v_vc :=p_vc;
end;
--
procedure dummy2 (p_num in number
                 ,p_vc in out varchar2) is
v_num number;
cursor get_name is
select surname into p_vc
from person where pers_id=45678;
begin
  select count(*) into v_num from person
  where pers_id =p_vc;
end dummy2;
--
procedure dummy3 (p_num in number
                 ,p_vc in out varchar2) is
begin
  null;
end dummy3;
end bad_code;

SP2-0808: Package created with compilation warnings
ora122> show errors
Errors for PACKAGE BODY BAD_CODE:

LINE/COL ERROR
-------- ------------------------------------------------------------------
2/1      PLW-05005: subprogram DUMMY1 returns without value at line 9
3/18     PLW-07203: parameter 'P_VC' may benefit from use of the NOCOPY
         compiler hint
6/1      PLW-05004: identifier SYSTIMESTAMP is also declared in STANDARD
         or is a SQL builtin
12/19    PLW-05000: mismatch in NOCOPY qualification between specification
         and body
12/19    PLW-07203: parameter 'P_VC' may benefit from use of the NOCOPY
         compiler hint
14/1     PLW-06006: uncalled procedure "GET_NAME" is removed.
15/1     PLW-05016: INTO clause should not be specified here
19/18    PLW-07204: conversion away from column type may result in
         sub-optimal query plan
22/1     PLW-06006: uncalled procedure "DUMMY3" is removed.
23/19    PLW-07203: parameter 'P_VC' may benefit from use of the NOCOPY
         compiler hint
```

One thing you might expect to see but do not is our use of an IN OUT parameter on a function, which is generally a frowned-upon practice.

"PLW-05004 identifier X is also declared in STANDARD or is a SQL built in" is interesting because it highlights a point made in Chapter 6, which is that you can use object names in PL/SQL that people think would not be allowed (in this case, SYSTIMESTAMP). Don't do it!

"PLW-07204: conversion away from column type may result in sub-optimal query plan" is also interesting because it highlights a common performance error—using a variable of the wrong data type so that implicit data conversion occurs. This can stop indexes being used and seriously impacts SQL performance.

This demonstrates that you may well benefit from turning on compilation warnings in your development environment to highlight many of the common mistakes made. It does not catch everything, of course, but some help is better than none. If there are any specific warnings you don't want to have highlighted constantly, you now know how to suppress them.

DBMS_TRACE

DBMS_TRACE is a tool for showing what PL/SQL code your session is running. It has been around since Oracle 8*i*. As you would expect from a tool that has been around for so long, it gives you very simple output—the PL/SQL steps taken by your session for the traced activity.

Setup   First, you need to see if the package is installed. Any user should be able to use DESC on the package if it has been created normally. If you can't see the package, check by logging on as SYS, with the SYSDBA privileges or with the DBA role, and either use DESC on the package or look for it in DBA_OBJECTS:

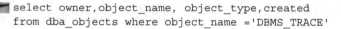

```
select owner,object_name, object_type,created
from dba_objects where object_name ='DBMS_TRACE'
```

OWNER	OBJECT_NAME	OBJECT_TYPE	CREATED
SYS	DBMS_TRACE	PACKAGE BODY	11-SEP-2014 09:04
SYS	DBMS_TRACE	PACKAGE	11-SEP-2014 09:00
PUBLIC	DBMS_TRACE	SYNONYM	11-SEP-2014 09:00

As you can probably guess by the CREATED_DATE, our Oracle 12.1.0.2 test system had the package there at creation time. If you do not have the package, you will need to have it installed as the SYS user. The scripts to run (in order) are as follows:

- **$ORACLE_HOME/RDBMS/ADMIN/dbmspbt.sql**   Creates the package specification.
- **$ORACLE_HOME/RDBMS/ADMIN/prvtpbt.plb**   Creates the package body, wrapped.

As always, looking at the package specification for Oracle's provided packages is interesting. In fact, the official documentation for DBMS_TRACE in the Database PL/SQL Packages and Types reference (from Oracle Database 12*c* all the way back to Oracle 9*i* at least!) says to look at dbmspbt.sql for a list of all the features you can trace.

The data from tracing is placed in the PLSQL_TRACE_EVENTS table, so you need to make sure that is there too. If it isn't, then run $ORACLE_HOME/RDBMS/ADMIN/tracetab.sql (again as SYS) to create the tables PLSQL_TRACE_RUNS and PLSQL_TRACE_EVENTS and the sequence PLSQL_TRACE_RUNNUMBER.

Fundamentals of DBMS_TRACE You can see the most recent DBMS_TRACE runs in the table PLSQL_TRACE_RUNS. The following code shows the trace runs during the last day:

```
select runid,run_date,run_owner
from plsql_trace_runs
where run_date > sysdate-1
order by runid desc
/
     RUNID RUN_DATE          RUN_OWNER
---------- ----------------- ----------------
        12 07-FEB-2016 14:14 MDW2
        11 06-FEB-2016 15:44 MDW2
```

> ## Most Columns in PLSQL_TRACE_RUNS Are Not Used
> PLSQL_TRACE_RUNS has several columns in it, but the only ones that seem to be used by DBMS_TRACE are RUNID, RUN_DATE, and RUN_OWNER. None of the others are populated, not even RUN_END when you stop tracing for your session.

You trace at a session level and you control whether tracing is on and what is actually traced via DBMS_TRACE.SET_PLSQL_TRACE. For example, DBMS_TRACE.SET_PLSQL_TRACE(1) will turn on tracing for all PL/SQL calls in your session. Here is a very simple example that only calls our **pna_maint.test1** procedure, which does little more than set DBMS_APPLICATION_INFO information. Note, we have **serveroutput on**, so we see any DBMS_OUTPUT lines.

```
-- turn on tracing of all PL/SQL in my session
exec dbms_trace.set_plsql_trace(1)
PL/SQL procedure successfully completed.

exec pna_maint.test1
15:16:38.044 :started code
15:16:38.060 :ended code
PL/SQL procedure successfully completed.

-- the below turns tracing off and ends the session.
exec dbms_trace.set_plsql_trace(16384)
PL/SQL procedure successfully completed.

-- test1 code
procedure test1 is
v_vc1 varchar2(100);
begin
  dbms_application_info.set_module(module_name => 'PNA_TEST'
                                  ,action_name =>'START');
  pl('started code');
  -- do stuff
  v_vc1 :=piece('eric*the*red',3,'*');
  pl('ended code');
```

```
dbms_application_info.set_module(module_name => 'PNA_TEST'
                                ,action_name =>'END');
end test1;
```

Figure 7-7 shows the contents of the PLSQL_TRACE_EVENTS table for our DBMS_TRACE run (a DBMS_TRACE "run" is from when you enable tracing until you either stop tracing or log out). We've swapped from using SQL*Plus to view the data to SQL Developer. This is because there can be a lot of information in DBMS_TRACE, and it is easier to look at it in a GUI tool that caches the results of queries and allows you to alter the size of the columns, scroll up and down, and so on. (You can view the information via SQL*Plus if you prefer.)

You can see the PL/SQL starting up as well as the PL/SQL virtual machine stopping and starting as the context switches between SQL and PL/SQL occur (see Chapter 6 for more details on context switching). Next, you can see our setting of the DBMS_TRACE level and then the calls to DBMS_OUTPUT, which is actually SQL*Plus checking for **serveroutput** after each PL/SQL statement. There is no sign of "our" code yet (we need to look further down). Figure 7-8 shows our actual code executing. This is one of the drawbacks of DBMS_TRACE—it can be very verbose.

In Figure 7-8, we have stepped forward to line 15 and see the PL/SQL virtual machine start and PNA_MAINT.TEST1 being called. Then we see several lines of output as DBMS_APPLICATION_INFO sets our MODULE and ACTION columns, which also exist in the PLSQL_TRACE_EVENTS table. We also see some information about what the Oracle built-in packages are doing.

Then from line 26, the procedure PL is called, which just assigns a value to a variable (the STANDARD calls) and then DBMS_OUTPUT (so we see lots of internal DBMS_OUTPUT activity)

```
Worksheet    Query Builder
13 ⊟ SELECT pte.runid rid,
14          pte.event_seq seq,
15          TO_CHAR(pte.event_time, 'DD-MM-YY HH24:MI:SS') AS event_time,
16          pte.event_unit_owner ownr ,
17          pte.event_unit,
18          pte.event_unit_kind eu_kind,
19          pte.event_line      e_line,
20          pte.proc_name       p_name,
21          pte.proc_line       p_line,
22          pte.event_comment,
23          pte.module,
24          pte.action
25  FROM    plsql_trace_events pte
26  where   pte.runid = (select max(runid) from plsql_trace_runs)
27  ORDER BY pte.runid, pte.event_seq
```

Script Output ✕ | ▷ Query Result ✕

SQL | Fetched 50 rows in 0.016 seconds

	RID	SEQ	EVENT_TIME	OWNR	EVENT_UNIT	EU_KIND	E_LINE	P_NAME	P_LINE	EVENT_COMMENT	MODULE	ACTION
1	16	1	07-02-16 15:24:25	(null)	(null)	(null)	(null)	(null)	(null)	PL/SQL Trace Tool started	(null)	(null)
2	16	2	07-02-16 15:24:25	(null)	(null)	(null)	(null)	(null)	(null)	Trace flags changed	(null)	(null)
3	16	3	07-02-16 15:24:25	SYS	DBMS_TRACE	PACKAGE BODY	21	(null)	75	Return from procedure call	(null)	(null)
4	16	4	07-02-16 15:24:25	SYS	DBMS_TRACE	PACKAGE BODY	76	(null)	81	Return from procedure call	(null)	(null)
5	16	5	07-02-16 15:24:25	SYS	DBMS_TRACE	PACKAGE BODY	81	(null)	1	Return from procedure call	(null)	(null)
6	16	6	07-02-16 15:24:25	(null)	(null)	(null)	(null)	(null)	(null)	PL/SQL Virtual Machine stopped	(null)	(null)
7	16	7	07-02-16 15:24:25	(null)	<anonymous>	ANONYMOUS B...	0	(null)	(null)	PL/SQL Virtual Machine started	(null)	(null)
8	16	8	07-02-16 15:24:25	(null)	<anonymous>	ANONYMOUS B...	1	(null)	180	Procedure Call	(null)	(null)
9	16	9	07-02-16 15:24:25	SYS	DBMS_OUTPUT	PACKAGE BODY	192	(null)	(null)	PL/SQL Internal Call	(null)	(null)
10	16	10	07-02-16 15:24:25	SYS	DBMS_OUTPUT	PACKAGE BODY	200	(null)	(null)	PL/SQL Internal Call	(null)	(null)
11	16	11	07-02-16 15:24:25	SYS	DBMS_OUTPUT	PACKAGE BODY	202	(null)	129	Procedure Call	(null)	(null)
12	16	12	07-02-16 15:24:25	SYS	DBMS_OUTPUT	PACKAGE BODY	133	(null)	202	Return from procedure call	(null)	(null)
13	16	13	07-02-16 15:24:25	SYS	DBMS_OUTPUT	PACKAGE BODY	205	(null)	1	Return from procedure call	(null)	(null)

FIGURE 7-7. *PLSQL_TRACE_EVENTS as seen in SQL Developer*

	RID	SEQ	EVENT_TIME	OWNR	EVENT_UNIT	EU_KIND	E_LINE	P_NAME	P_LINE	EVENT_COMMENT	MODULE	ACTION
15	16	15	07-02-16 15:24:26	(null)	<anonymous>	ANONYMOUS B...	0	(null)	(null)	PL/SQL Virtual Machine started	(null)	(null)
16	16	16	07-02-16 15:24:26	(null)	<anonymous>	ANONYMOUS B...	1	TEST1	142	Procedure Call	(null)	(null)
17	16	17	07-02-16 15:24:26	MDW2	PNA_MAINT	PACKAGE BODY	145	(null)	36	Procedure Call	(null)	(null)
18	16	18	07-02-16 15:24:26	SYS	DBMS_APPLICATION_INFO	PACKAGE BODY	38	(null)	(null)	PL/SQL Internal Call	(null)	(null)
19	16	19	07-02-16 15:24:26	SYS	DBMS_APPLICATION_INFO	PACKAGE BODY	38	(null)	(null)	PL/SQL Internal Call	(null)	(null)
20	16	20	07-02-16 15:24:26	SYS	DBMS_APPLICATION_INFO	PACKAGE BODY	38	(null)	(null)	PL/SQL Internal Call	(null)	(null)
21	16	21	07-02-16 15:24:26	SYS	DBMS_APPLICATION_INFO	PACKAGE BODY	38	(null)	(null)	PL/SQL Internal Call	(null)	(null)
22	16	22	07-02-16 15:24:26	SYS	DBMS_APPLICATION_INFO	PACKAGE BODY	38	(null)	(null)	PL/SQL Internal Call	(null)	(null)
23	16	23	07-02-16 15:24:26	SYS	DBMS_APPLICATION_INFO	PACKAGE BODY	38	(null)	(null)	PL/SQL Internal Call	(null)	(null)
24	16	24	07-02-16 15:24:26	SYS	DBMS_APPLICATION_INFO	PACKAGE BODY	38	(null)	(null)	PL/SQL Internal Call	(null)	(null)
25	16	25	07-02-16 15:24:26	SYS	DBMS_APPLICATION_INFO	PACKAGE BODY	40	TEST1	146	Return from procedure call	PNA_TEST	START
26	16	26	07-02-16 15:24:26	MDW2	PNA_MAINT	PACKAGE BODY	146	PL	105	Procedure Call	PNA_TEST	START
27	16	27	07-02-16 15:24:26	MDW2	PNA_MAINT	PACKAGE BODY	107	(null)	590	Procedure Call	PNA_TEST	START
28	16	28	07-02-16 15:24:26	SYS	STANDARD	PACKAGE BODY	593	(null)	(null)	PL/SQL Internal Call	PNA_TEST	START
29	16	29	07-02-16 15:24:26	SYS	STANDARD	PACKAGE BODY	599	PL	107	Return from procedure call	PNA_TEST	START
30	16	30	07-02-16 15:24:26	MDW2	PNA_MAINT	PACKAGE BODY	107	(null)	(null)	PL/SQL Internal Call	PNA_TEST	START
31	16	31	07-02-16 15:24:26	MDW2	PNA_MAINT	PACKAGE BODY	107	(null)	109	Procedure Call	PNA_TEST	START
32	16	32	07-02-16 15:24:26	SYS	DBMS_OUTPUT	PACKAGE BODY	112	(null)	77	Procedure Call	PNA_TEST	START
33	16	33	07-02-16 15:24:26	SYS	DBMS_OUTPUT	PACKAGE BODY	82	(null)	67	Procedure Call	PNA_TEST	START
34	16	34	07-02-16 15:24:26	SYS	DBMS_OUTPUT	PACKAGE BODY	69	(null)	(null)	PL/SQL Internal Call	PNA_TEST	START
35	16	35	07-02-16 15:24:26	SYS	DBMS_OUTPUT	PACKAGE BODY	75	(null)	88	Return from procedure call	PNA_TEST	START
36	16	36	07-02-16 15:24:26	SYS	DBMS_OUTPUT	PACKAGE BODY	107	(null)	113	Return from procedure call	PNA_TEST	START
37	16	37	07-02-16 15:24:26	SYS	DBMS_OUTPUT	PACKAGE BODY	113	(null)	117	Procedure Call	PNA_TEST	START
38	16	38	07-02-16 15:24:26	SYS	DBMS_OUTPUT	PACKAGE BODY	127	(null)	115	Return from procedure call	PNA_TEST	START
39	16	39	07-02-16 15:24:26	SYS	DBMS_OUTPUT	PACKAGE BODY	115	PL	108	Return from procedure call	PNA_TEST	START
40	16	40	07-02-16 15:24:26	MDW2	PNA_MAINT	PACKAGE BODY	108	TEST1	148	Return from procedure call	PNA_TEST	START
41	16	41	07-02-16 15:24:26	MDW2	PNA_MAINT	PACKAGE BODY	148	PIECE	94	Procedure Call	PNA_TEST	START
42	16	42	07-02-16 15:24:26	MDW2	PNA_MAINT	PACKAGE BODY	101	PIECE	42	Procedure Call	PNA_TEST	START
43	16	43	07-02-16 15:24:26	MDW2	PNA_MAINT	PACKAGE BODY	55	(null)	(null)	PL/SQL Internal Call	PNA_TEST	START
44	16	44	07-02-16 15:24:26	MDW2	PNA_MAINT	PACKAGE BODY	56	(null)	(null)	PL/SQL Internal Call	PNA_TEST	START

FIGURE 7-8. *The section of DBMS_TRACE where PNA_MAINT.TEST1 is executed*

until we return from that at line 40. Now we see the use of the **piece** function in the PNA_MAINT package. It is very interesting to see all this detail, but for general use it is too verbose. Thankfully, we can control what is traced via calls to DBMS_TRACE.

Controlling What DBMS_TRACE Traces   We called DBMS_TRACE with a value of 1, which means "trace all PL/SQL." If we called it with a value of 2, we would only trace stored PL/SQL that had been compiled with tracing turned on. Each "magic number" (2 to the power n) either alters what is traced or controls tracing itself. We have seen that 16384 stops tracing. Any code that controls tracing should be used in isolation, but other values can be combined by adding the numbers together. You probably realize each number equates to a position in a 2-byte, 16-bit pattern. The package also defines a named constant for each of these values and encourages you to use them. Doing so involves more typing, but the statements make more sense.

Table 7-1 shows the tracing control values with their package constant names. These controlling values should be used in isolation.

Table 7-2 shows the values that modify the scope of what will be traced, and they can be combined except for TRACE_ALL_ and TRACE_ENABLED_ pairs; for example, you cannot use TRACE_ALL_EXCEPTIONS and TRACE_ENABLED_EXCEPTIONS. Setting tracing for both of them (for example, using the value 12) will result in all exceptions being traced. We cover exactly what the difference is between ALL and ENABLED a little later.

If we want to trace all PL/SQL calls but ignore administrative events such as the PL/SQL virtual machine starting up and stopping, we can use

```
DBMS_TRACE.SET_PLSQL_TRACE(32769)
```

Name	Number	Action
TRACE_LIMIT	16	Controls how many records are preserved in PLSQL_TRACE_EVENTS. This is 8192 records + (up to 1000). See "Performance Impact and Data Volume from DBMS_TRACE."
TRACE_PAUSE	4096	Pauses tracing (does not end the tracing session).
TRACE_RESUME	8192	Resumes tracing.
TRACE_STOP	16384	Stops tracing, ending the session.

TABLE 7-1. *DBMS_TRACE Control Values*

which is 32768+1. However, it is clearer if we use the constants. We show this in the following and also turn off **serveroutput** before tracing PNA_MAINT.TEST1 again.

```
set serveroutput off
exec dbms_trace.set_plsql_trace(dbms_trace.trace_all_calls
                               +dbms_trace.no_trace_administrative)
PL/SQL procedure successfully completed.

exec pna_maint.test1
PL/SQL procedure successfully completed.
```

As you can see in Figure 7-9, there is now less "fluff" in the output—you do not see the PL/SQL virtual machine messages and you will notice the calls to DBMS_OUTPUT (line 12) from our

Name	Number	Action
TRACE_ALL_CALLS	1	Trace all PL/SQL calls and returns.
TRACE_ENABLED_CALLS	2	Trace only enabled calls and returns.
TRACE_ALL_EXCEPTIONS	4	Trace all exceptions.
TRACE_ENABLED_EXCEPTIONS	8	Trace enabled exceptions and handlers.
TRACE_ALL_SQL	32	Trace all SQL statements (*not* 10046 trace!).
TRACE_ENABLED_SQL	64	Trace SQL statements in enabled PL/SQL code.
TRACE_ALL_LINES	128	Trace each line executed.
TRACE_ENABLED_LINES	256	Trace each line in enabled PL/SQL code.
NO_TRACE_ADMISTRATIVE	32768	Do not trace virtual machine and trace tool lines.
NO_TRACE_HANDLED_EXCEPTIONS	65536	Do not trace handled exceptions.

TABLE 7-2. *DBMS_TRACE Scope Settings*

procedure PL comprise a single line of the trace output. If DBMS_OUTPUT is not enabled, the call to it still happens but immediately returns. We also removed the lines for DBMS_APPLICATION_INFO, but we did that by adding a WHERE clause to our SQL query (thus the jump from SEQ 5 to 14). This demonstrates that you can control what information you see from DBMS_TRACE, not just by modifying the scope, but also the information you query out of the table. However, our output is still quite verbose.

EVENT_LINE, PROC_LINE, and ALL_SOURCE

You may have noticed EVENT_LINE (E_LINE) and PROC_LINE (P_LINE) in the output. What are they? They are the lines in the stored code. EVENT_LINE is where the event takes place, and PROC_LINE is the target of the line. Therefore, if PNA_MAINT.PL is making a "Procedure Call" to DBMS_OUTPUT, then an EVENT_LINE of 107 is the line in PNA_MAINT that is executing, and a PROC_LINE of 109 is the line in DBMS_OUTPUT that control is passing to. At the end of the DBMS_OUTPUT activity you'll see a "Return from Procedure Call." An EVENT_LINE of 115 means that line 115 in DBMS_OUTPUT is being processed and it is going to PROC_LINE 108, which is the line in PNA_MAINT after the call to DBMS_OUTPUT. The PROCEDURE_NAME on that row is PL, but the next row shows the name of the package, PNA_MAINT. If you have access to the source code in ALL_SOURCE (which you won't for DBMS_OUTPUT but you will for your own code), you can link to that to see the actual lines.

You really might want all this detail, but usually you just want the output for your code or the code you are having issues with. You have two methods to narrow down the scope of your output. One is to use all those "_ENABLED" tracing options.

	RID	SEQ	EVENT_TIME	OWNR	EVENT_UNIT	EU_KIND	E_LINE	P_NAME	P_LINE	EVENT_COMMENT	MODULE	ACTION
1	20	1	07-02-16 17:34:00	SYS	DBMS_TRACE	PACKAGE BODY	21	(null)	75	Return from procedure call	(null)	(null)
2	20	2	07-02-16 17:34:00	SYS	DBMS_TRACE	PACKAGE BODY	76	(null)	81	Return from procedure call	(null)	(null)
3	20	3	07-02-16 17:34:00	SYS	DBMS_TRACE	PACKAGE BODY	81	(null)	1	Return from procedure call	(null)	(null)
4	20	4	07-02-16 17:34:22	(null)	<anonymous>	ANONYMOUS BLOCK	1	TEST1	142	Procedure Call	(null)	(null)
5	20	5	07-02-16 17:34:22	MDW2	PNA_MAINT	PACKAGE BODY	145	(null)	36	Procedure Call	(null)	(null)
6	20	14	07-02-16 17:34:22	MDW2	PNA_MAINT	PACKAGE BODY	146	PL	105	Procedure Call	PNA_TEST	START
7	20	15	07-02-16 17:34:22	MDW2	PNA_MAINT	PACKAGE BODY	107	(null)	590	Procedure Call	PNA_TEST	START
8	20	16	07-02-16 17:34:22	SYS	STANDARD	PACKAGE BODY	593	(null)	(null)	PL/SQL Internal Call	PNA_TEST	START
9	20	17	07-02-16 17:34:22	SYS	STANDARD	PACKAGE BODY	599	PL	107	Return from procedure call	PNA_TEST	START
10	20	18	07-02-16 17:34:22	MDW2	PNA_MAINT	PACKAGE BODY	107	(null)	(null)	PL/SQL Internal Call	PNA_TEST	START
11	20	19	07-02-16 17:34:22	MDW2	PNA_MAINT	PACKAGE BODY	107	(null)	109	Procedure Call	PNA_TEST	START
12	20	20	07-02-16 17:34:22	SYS	DBMS_OUTPUT	PACKAGE BODY	115	PL	108	Return from procedure call	PNA_TEST	START
13	20	21	07-02-16 17:34:22	MDW2	PNA_MAINT	PACKAGE BODY	108	TEST1	148	Return from procedure call	PNA_TEST	START
14	20	22	07-02-16 17:34:22	MDW2	PNA_MAINT	PACKAGE BODY	148	PIECE	94	Procedure Call	PNA_TEST	START
15	20	23	07-02-16 17:34:22	MDW2	PNA_MAINT	PACKAGE BODY	101	PIECE	42	Procedure Call	PNA_TEST	START
16	20	24	07-02-16 17:34:22	MDW2	PNA_MAINT	PACKAGE BODY	55	(null)	(null)	PL/SQL Internal Call	PNA_TEST	START
17	20	25	07-02-16 17:34:22	MDW2	PNA_MAINT	PACKAGE BODY	56	(null)	(null)	PL/SQL Internal Call	PNA_TEST	START
18	20	26	07-02-16 17:34:22	MDW2	PNA_MAINT	PACKAGE BODY	67	(null)	(null)	PL/SQL Internal Call	PNA_TEST	START
19	20	27	07-02-16 17:34:22	MDW2	PNA_MAINT	PACKAGE BODY	78	(null)	(null)	PL/SQL Internal Call	PNA_TEST	START
20	20	28	07-02-16 17:34:22	MDW2	PNA_MAINT	PACKAGE BODY	83	(null)	(null)	PL/SQL Internal Call	PNA_TEST	START
21	20	29	07-02-16 17:34:22	MDW2	PNA_MAINT	PACKAGE BODY	92	PIECE	101	Return from procedure call	PNA_TEST	START
22	20	30	07-02-16 17:34:22	MDW2	PNA_MAINT	PACKAGE BODY	103	TEST1	148	Return from procedure call	PNA_TEST	START
23	20	31	07-02-16 17:34:22	MDW2	PNA_MAINT	PACKAGE BODY	149	PL	105	Procedure Call	PNA_TEST	START

All Rows Fetched: 32 in 0.005 seconds

FIGURE 7-9. *DBMS_TRACE output with administrative messages removed*

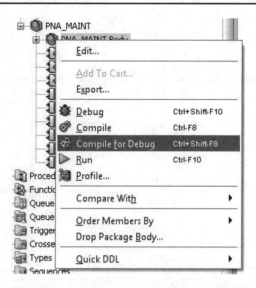

FIGURE 7-10. *In SQL Developer, we can select Compile for Debug to use DBMS_TRACE.*

When you only trace enabled PL/SQL, it is PL/SQL that has been compiled with DEBUG enabled. Note that this is not the same as running your PL/SQL in debug mode in a GUI PL/SQL development tool like SQL Developer. If you look at Figure 7-10, you will see we have two debug options. The top one is SQL Developer's debug tool, and the highlighted option is to compile with DEBUG enabled, which is what we are talking about here. You can do this in the GUI of your choice or recompile the stored PL/SQL manually, like so:

```
alter package pna_maint compile debug;
Package altered.
```

Now, if we stop and re-enable tracing in our session, but only debug ENABLED code, we will only debug the PNA_MAINT code and get a manageable volume of data. We trimmed the output slightly in Figure 7-11 (that is, we removed RUNID and EVENT_TIME) to allow the image to be larger. This way, the whole activity of calling PNA_MAINT.TEST1 can be seen on one screen. We have lost all the internal PL/SQL because that is not compiled with debug turned on, but we do see the calls to DBMS_APPLICATION_INFO still.

```
exec dbms_trace.set_plsql_trace(16384)
PL/SQL procedure successfully completed.

alter package pna_maint compile debug;
Package altered.

exec dbms_trace.set_plsql_trace(dbms_trace.trace_enabled_calls
                             +dbms_trace.no_trace_administrative)
PL/SQL procedure successfully completed.

exec pna_maint.test1
PL/SQL procedure successfully completed.
```

SEQ	OWNR	EVENT_UNIT	EU_KIND	E_LINE	P_NAME	P_LINE	EVENT_COMMENT	MODULE	ACTION
1	(null)	\<anonymous\>	ANONYMOUS BLOCK	1	PNA_MAINT	1	Package Body Elaborated	(null)	(null)
2	MDW2	PNA_MAINT	PACKAGE BODY	604	(null)	1	Return from procedure call	(null)	(null)
3	(null)	\<anonymous\>	ANONYMOUS BLOCK	1	TEST1	142	Procedure Call	(null)	(null)
4	MDW2	PNA_MAINT	PACKAGE BODY	145	(null)	36	Procedure Call	(null)	(null)
5	SYS	DBMS_APPLICATION_INFO	PACKAGE BODY	40	TEST1	146	Return from procedure call	PNA_TEST	START
6	MDW2	PNA_MAINT	PACKAGE BODY	146	PL	105	Procedure Call	PNA_TEST	START
7	MDW2	PNA_MAINT	PACKAGE BODY	107	(null)	590	Procedure Call	PNA_TEST	START
8	SYS	STANDARD	PACKAGE BODY	599	PL	107	Return from procedure call	PNA_TEST	START
9	MDW2	PNA_MAINT	PACKAGE BODY	107	(null)	(null)	PL/SQL Internal Call	PNA_TEST	START
10	MDW2	PNA_MAINT	PACKAGE BODY	107	(null)	109	Procedure Call	PNA_TEST	START
11	SYS	DBMS_OUTPUT	PACKAGE BODY	115	PL	108	Return from procedure call	PNA_TEST	START
12	MDW2	PNA_MAINT	PACKAGE BODY	108	TEST1	148	Return from procedure call	PNA_TEST	START
13	MDW2	PNA_MAINT	PACKAGE BODY	148	PIECE	94	Procedure Call	PNA_TEST	START
14	MDW2	PNA_MAINT	PACKAGE BODY	101	PIECE	42	Procedure Call	PNA_TEST	START
15	MDW2	PNA_MAINT	PACKAGE BODY	55	(null)	(null)	PL/SQL Internal Call	PNA_TEST	START
16	MDW2	PNA_MAINT	PACKAGE BODY	56	(null)	(null)	PL/SQL Internal Call	PNA_TEST	START
17	MDW2	PNA_MAINT	PACKAGE BODY	67	(null)	(null)	PL/SQL Internal Call	PNA_TEST	START
18	MDW2	PNA_MAINT	PACKAGE BODY	78	(null)	(null)	PL/SQL Internal Call	PNA_TEST	START
19	MDW2	PNA_MAINT	PACKAGE BODY	83	(null)	(null)	PL/SQL Internal Call	PNA_TEST	START
20	MDW2	PNA_MAINT	PACKAGE BODY	92	PIECE	101	Return from procedure call	PNA_TEST	START
21	MDW2	PNA_MAINT	PACKAGE BODY	103	TEST1	148	Return from procedure call	PNA_TEST	START
22	MDW2	PNA_MAINT	PACKAGE BODY	149	PL	105	Procedure Call	PNA_TEST	START
23	MDW2	PNA_MAINT	PACKAGE BODY	107	(null)	590	Procedure Call	PNA_TEST	START
24	SYS	STANDARD	PACKAGE BODY	599	PL	107	Return from procedure call	PNA_TEST	START
25	MDW2	PNA_MAINT	PACKAGE BODY	107	(null)	(null)	PL/SQL Internal Call	PNA_TEST	START
26	MDW2	PNA_MAINT	PACKAGE BODY	107	(null)	109	Procedure Call	PNA_TEST	START
27	SYS	DBMS_OUTPUT	PACKAGE BODY	115	PL	108	Return from procedure call	PNA_TEST	START
28	MDW2	PNA_MAINT	PACKAGE BODY	108	TEST1	150	Return from procedure call	PNA_TEST	START
29	MDW2	PNA_MAINT	PACKAGE BODY	150	(null)	36	Procedure Call	PNA_TEST	START
30	SYS	DBMS_APPLICATION_INFO	PACKAGE BODY	40	TEST1	151	Return from procedure call	(null)	(null)
31	MDW2	PNA_MAINT	PACKAGE BODY	151	(null)	1	Return from procedure call	(null)	(null)

FIGURE 7-11. *DBMS_TRACE output for only ENABLED PL/SQL code*

This is why there are pairs of options to turn on debugging for ALL and ENABLED code. You might want to see ALL exceptions (**trace_all_exceptions, 4**) but only trace ENABLED calls (**trace_enabled_calls, 2**). Thus, you would use the following:

```
exec dbms_trace.set_plsql_trace(dbms_trace.trace_all_exceptions
                              +dbms_trace.trace_enabled_calls)
```

You can alter your session with **alter session set plsql_debug=true** such that all code you subsequently create (or replace or compile) will be in debug mode. The intention is that you alter your session, recompile all your code under investigation, and then run the trace.

Note that PL/SQL code will stay compiled in debug mode until you recompile it not in debug mode. This can lead to issues when you next use DBMS_TRACE and see output for packages that you were not expecting.

Performance Impact and Data Volume from DBMS_TRACE A potentially major drawback of DBMS_TRACE is the volume of information it generates and the performance impact it has. The tracing of only enabled code and specific recompilation of only the code where you suspect (or preferably know) you have the problem may be enough to limit this volume. However, our POP_ADDR_BATCH code generates potentially millions of addresses, with lots of calls to

DBMS_RANDOM. If we trace a run of that code, even for only 100,000 addresses, the output will be huge. We won't show you the result, but we did do this. Without tracing, the code runs in about a minute. With tracing, after about an hour, we killed the session and truncated the data in PLSQL_TRACE_EVENTS.

Setting PLSQL_DEBUG=TRUE at the Session Level

Personally, I am not such a fan of **alter session set plsql_debug=true** because I feel you should be more targeted in what you put into debug mode, and by altering your session you could forget and compile things in debug mode you really do not want to. For example, you might want to debug stored procedure X, which is called once or twice by the larger master procedure Y. Therefore, you alter your session, recompile X, and get some debugging information. This leads you to then compile the master procedure Y to change something—but when you run your next test, you create huge volumes of tracing data and, as discussed earlier, the performance hit can mean you have to kill your session.

Be very careful of tracing code that is repeatedly called by loops, such as user-defined functions, or using ALL options to trace PL/SQL that does a lot of work. In such cases, the impact on performance is massive.

You can limit the volume of data kept in PLSQL_TRACE_EVENTS for a run using TRACE_LIMIT. When you set this option, it limits the output to 8192 + (up to 1000) lines. We set this up and ran the test code—but for only 10,000 addresses this time and at a reduced logging level—checking the number of entries in PLSQL_TRACE_EVENTS for the latest RUN_ID from another session:

```
select count(*) from plsql_trace_events
where runid=(select max(runid) from plsql_trace_runs);
9260

...
9316

...
9219

...
9244
```

The volume of data in the table is being limited, but the impact on the run time of the code is still considerable. With tracing it took 58 seconds to run. However, we never saw more than 9500 entries for the run in PLSQL_TRACE_EVENTS. When we ran the code with DBMS_TRACE disabled, it took 0.420 seconds. Thus, using DBMS_TRACE had a 100× impact on our code. It is, after all, recording every PL/SQL step and putting it into a table.

You can fine-tune the volume of data preserved in DBMS_TRACE for a session run with TRACE_LIMIT using event 10940. You set the event to level n, and the record limit is changed to $n \times 1024$.

```
alter session set events='10940 level 12'
Session altered.

exec dbms_trace.set_plsql_trace(1+16)
PL/SQL procedure successfully completed.
```

```
exec pna_maint.pop_addr_batch(10000)

-- in second session count the number of entries for latest trace session
-- it should be 12+1024 + up to 1000
select count(*) from plsql_trace_events
where runid=(select max(runid) from plsql_trace_runs)
count(*)
--------
13382
```

The key message here is that if you have code that is doing a lot of PL/SQL processing and you have an issue you want to trace, you probably want to be a lot more specific in what you trace. And you can be, *so long as you can change the code you are tracing* (often the access to change code is very limited, in which case you may want to look at using one of the other two profiling tools).

You can add calls to DBMS_TRACE to turn it on (and off) at specific points in the code. Via your instrumentation you should already know pretty much where the issue in the code is, so you can insert calls to turn on DBMS_TRACE around that area. In the following example, we add a few lines to the POP_ADDR_BATCH code to give it more instrumentation, but our code now takes almost 8 seconds to run rather than 0.45 seconds. We can get DBMS_TRACE information of just that area of the code. Note that we trace *all calls and all SQL* for this section.

```
dbms_trace.set_plsql_trace(dbms_trace.trace_all_calls
                          +dbms_trace.trace_all_SQL);
if pv_log_level >5 then
  chk_addr_count;
end if;
write_log ('ended at '||to_char(systimestamp,'YY-MM-DD HH24:MI:SS.FF3'));
write_log ('elapsed is '||substr(systimestamp-pv_executed_timestamp,10,20));
dbms_trace.set_plsql_trace(dbms_trace.trace_stop);
commit;
```

We then execute the code, and the elapsed time only increases by 0.1 seconds (not 54!), as we had limited the section of code for which DBMS_TRACE was enabled. The output of the trace (first 17 lines of 54) was:

SEQ	EVENT_TI	OWNR	EVENT_UNIT	E_LINE	P_NAME	P_LINE	EVENT_COMMENT
1	11:29:29						PL/SQL Trace Tool started
2	11:29:29						Trace flags changed
3	11:29:29	SYS	DBMS_TRACE	21		75	Return from procedure call
4	11:29:29	SYS	DBMS_TRACE	76		81	Return from procedure call
5	11:29:29	SYS	DBMS_TRACE	81	POP_ADDR_BATCH	565	Return from procedure call
6	11:29:29	MDW2	PNA_MAINT	566	*CHK_ADDR_COUNT*	496	Procedure Call
7	**11:29:29**	**MDW2**	**PNA_MAINT**	**499**			**SELECT COUNT(*) FROM ADDRESS**
8	**11:29:36**	**MDW2**	**PNA_MAINT**	**500**	**WRITE_LOG**	**110**	**Procedure Call**
9	11:29:36	MDW2	PNA_MAINT	118		590	Procedure Call
10	11:29:36	SYS	STANDARD	593			PL/SQL Internal Call
11	11:29:36	SYS	STANDARD	599	WRITE_LOG	118	Return from procedure call
12	11:29:36	MDW2	PNA_MAINT	121			PL/SQL Internal Call
13	11:29:36	MDW2	PNA_MAINT	121		109	Procedure Call

```
14 11:29:36 SYS    DBMS_OUTPUT    115 WRITE_LOG       121 Return from procedure call
15 11:29:36 MDW2   PNA_MAINT      124                     INSERT INTO PLSQL_LOG(PROCE
16 11:29:36 MDW2   PNA_MAINT      139                     COMMIT
17 11:29:36 MDW2   PNA_MAINT      140 CHK_ADDR_COUNT   501 Return from procedure call
```

The lines in bold are where the problem is—the time jumps by 7 seconds from SEQ 7 to 8. Because we included the trace option to show lines of SQL, we can see the statement that's causing the problem. It is in CHK_ADDR_COUNT. We are counting the rows in a large table, and there is no index to support it.

Don't forget that you can pause and restart tracing in the same run via **dbms_trace.set_plsql_trace(dbms_trace.trace_pause)** and **dbms_trace.set_plsql_trace(dbms_trace.trace_resume)**, so you can disable tracing around chunks of code that you know are fine and are doing a lot PL/SQL work—large loops or SQL statements that use PL/SQL functions (be they user defined or built in).

In summary, DBMS_TRACE can be turned on at the session level, for stored code compiled in debug mode, and the activity that is traced can be controlled. If you can alter code, you can target DBMS_TRACE accurately. But you almost certainly need to target DBMS_TRACE because the information it produces is a very detailed and therefore verbose. The performance impact of the tool is potentially very, very significant.

DBMS_PROFILER

DBMS_TRACE is a primarily a debugging tool; its output is verbose and its impact high. You use it once you have the profile of the issue from instrumentation to allow you to focus on the area of interest.

In comparison, DBMS_PROFILER is used to profile your PL/SQL code and see where time is being spent. Like DBMS_TRACE, this tool has been available for a long time (since Oracle 7). If you are using Oracle 11 or later, you should look at DBMS_HPROF, the hierarchical PL/SQL profiler.

Setup   First make sure the tool is available to you—see the start of the section for DBMS_TRACE, but look for the DBMS_PROFILER package. If you are using Oracle 10 or later, it would be surprising if it was not present. If it is indeed not present, run the following script as SYS:

```
$ORACLE_HOME/RDBMS/ADMIN/profload.sql
```

This runs the following two scripts in the same location and then verifies the install. If internal checks fail, it immediately removes the package and synonym.

- **DBMSPBP.SQL**   Creates the package specification
- **PRVTPBP.PLB**   Creates the package body and wrapper

Even if the package is already present, if you have access to the script DBMSPBP.SQL, it would be beneficial to read the comments there.

You will also need the PLSQL_PROFILER tables, created by the PROFTAB.SQL script in the same directory. Three tables are created:

- PLSQL_PROFILER_RUNS
- PLSQL_PROFILER_UNITS
- PLSQL_PROFILER_DATA

The script should be run in the schema from which you want to profile PL/SQL code (that is, who you will be logged in as when you run the profiler) or created in a central schema, with the relevant grants and synonyms created accordingly.

You May Only Profile Code You Have the Privilege to Create

The profiler will only collect data on code you have the privilege to create—that is, it is your code or you have privileges to compile it. You can also only profile code that is *not* natively compiled.

Starting and Stopping DBMS_Profiler   Using the profiler is very simple. You just start a profiling session by calling **dbms_profiler.start_profiler**, run the code you want, end the session, and then query the profiling data generated.

There are two procedures and two functions with the same name you can use to start profiling. The procedures will return an Oracle error if they fail, and the functions will return an error code. Other than that, they work the same.

With both the function and procedure, you can pass in two comments, both text columns, that are recorded in the underlying PSLQL_PROFILER_RUNS table. COMMENT defaults to SYSDATE at the time of calling, and COMMENT1 defaults to null. There is a version of both the function and procedure that returns the **runid** for the profiler session and one that does not:

```
DBMS_PROFILER.START_PROFILER(
    run_comment   IN VARCHAR2 := sysdate,
    run_comment1  IN VARCHAR2 :='',
    run_number    OUT BINARY_INTEGER)
  RETURN BINARY_INTEGER;

DBMS_PROFILER.START_PROFILER(
    run_comment IN VARCHAR2 := sysdate,
    run_comment1 IN VARCHAR2 :='')
RETURN BINARY_INTEGER;

DBMS_PROFILER.START_PROFILER(
    run_comment   IN VARCHAR2 := sysdate,
    run_comment1  IN VARCHAR2 :='',
    run_number    OUT BINARY_INTEGER);

DBMS_PROFILER.START_PROFILER(
    run_comment IN VARCHAR2 := sysdate,
    run_comment1 IN VARCHAR2 :='');
```

To stop the profiler, you use a single pair of an identically named function and procedure:

```
DBMS_PROFILER.STOP_PROFILER
  RETURN BINARY_INTEGER;

DBMS_PROFILER.STOP_PROFILER;
```

To start and stop the profiler, you can set a variable you populate with the procedure or select the function (for example, **from dual**):

```
--method using the procedure
var runno number
exec :runno := dbms_profiler.start_profiler('mdw '||sysdate)
PL/SQL procedure successfully completed.


-- execute some code
exec pna_maint.test1
PL/SQL procedure successfully completed.


exec :runno := dbms_profiler.stop_profiler
PL/SQL procedure successfully completed.


-- alternative method using the functions

select dbms_profiler.start_profiler('mdw '||sysdate) from dual;
DBMS_PROFILER.START_PROFILER('MDW'||SYSDATE)
--------------------------------------------
                                           0

exec pna_maint.test1
PL/SQL procedure successfully completed.


select dbms_profiler.stop_profiler from dual;
STOP_PROFILER
-------------
            0
```

If we look at PLSQL_PROFILER_RUNS, we can see the data for the two runs:

```
select runid,run_owner,run_date,run_comment,run_total_time
from plsql_profiler_runs
order by runid
```

RUNID	RUN_OWNE	RUN_DATE	RUN_COMMENT	RUN_TOTAL_TIME
1	MDW2	08-FEB-2016 17:27	mdw 08-FEB-2016 17:27	191,563,000,000
2	MDW2	08-FEB-2016 17:50	mdw 08-FEB-2016 17:50	40,032,000,000

The RUN_TOTAL_TIME is held in nanoseconds, but only to a precision of microseconds on our test platform. The session is recording everything, including recursive calls when a package, procedure, or function is run for the first time. You can see this earlier in RUN_TOTAL_TIMES. The code is doing exactly the same thing, but the first run has accrued more time. Therefore, you should run your code once without profiling before you profile it to avoid this one-off overhead.

Interpreting the DBMS_PROFILER Data   The data held in PLSQL_PROFILER_DATA and PLSQL_PROFILER_UNITS takes some effort to understand. Some GUI tools will process it for you, but SQL Developer, being a more recent tool, concentrates on the Hierarchical Profiler introduced with Oracle 11g.

PLSQL_PROFILER_UNITS holds a record for each unit of PL/SQL (anonymous block, package, procedure, or function) used in the session.

PLSQL_PROFILER_DATA holds a record for each line executed that summarizes the executions and time spent—but most hold 0 for the timing columns. These effectively do not contribute to the profile and should be ignored. This is, after all, a profiling tool, not a debugging tool. You are looking at where time was spent, not the detailed flow of the code.

The impact of the profiler is considerably less than that of DBMS_TRACE. After all, you are only collating data about each line of the code executed, not recording an entry every time a line is executed. As an example, we traced our PNA_MAINT.POP_ADDR_BATCH code twice: once for 10,000 addresses and once for 100,000 addresses. The two runs have the same number of steps and therefore entries in PLSQL_PROFILE_DATA:

```
select count(*),runid --count(*)
from plsql_profiler_data
where runid in (3,4)
group by runid
order by runid

count(*) runid
-------- -----
     396     3
     396     4
```

The elapsed run time for 100,000 addresses is 5.68 seconds, compared to 4.12 seconds without the profiler being active. The overhead for the 10,000-addresses run was a similar ratio: 0.591 seconds compared to 0.438 seconds. If we had DBMS_TRACE turned on, it would have been close to a full minute for the 10,000-addresses run.

As with DBMS_TRACE, the lines in PLSQL_PROFILER_DATA correspond to entries in ALL_SOURCE. The data is pretty verbose, so you probably only want lines that have a nonzero total time. In fact, you may well only want to report on lines that make up at least 0.1 percent of the workload. In the following example, we extract the timings for runid 3, considering only lines where the total time spent on that line is more than 0.01 percent of the execution time:

```
select ppu.runid,            ppu.unit_type,      ppu.unit_owner  owner,
       ppu.unit_name,        ppd.line# line,     ppd.total_occur execs,
       ppd.total_time tot_time,                  ltrim(also.text) line_text
from   plsql_profiler_units ppu
      ,plsql_profiler_data  ppd
      ,plsql_profiler_runs  ppr
      ,all_source           also
WHERE  ppr.runid         = 3
and    ppr.runid         = ppu.runid     and    ppu.runid     = ppd.runid
and    ppu.unit_number = ppd.unit_number and    ppu.unit_type = also.type
and    ppu.unit_name   = also.name       and    ppu.unit_owner = also.owner
and    also.line        = ppd.line#
and    ppd.total_time  >0  -- we are not interested in lines with no activity
and    ppd.total_time > (ppr.run_total_time/10000)
order by ppu.unit_number, ppd.line#;

id UNIT_TYPE  OWNER   UNIT_NAME   LINE   EXECS   TOT_TIME LINE_TEXT
```

```
-- ---------- ------- ---------- ----- ------- ----------- -----------------------------------------
3 PACKAGE BO MDW2    PNA_MAINT   110    14       61118 procedure write_log(v_log_text    in varc
3 PACKAGE BO MDW2    PNA_MAINT   121    14      104201 dbms_output.put_line (pv_process_name||'
3 PACKAGE BO MDW2    PNA_MAINT   124    14     1199319 INSERT INTO plsql_log(process_name
3 PACKAGE BO MDW2    PNA_MAINT   139    14      682319 commit;
3 PACKAGE BO MDW2    PNA_MAINT   510     1      104201 select min(tona_id),max(tona_id) into v_
3 PACKAGE BO MDW2    PNA_MAINT   511     1       68131 select min(rona_id),max(rona_id) into v_
3 PACKAGE BO MDW2    PNA_MAINT   512     1       60116 select min(roty_id),max(roty_id) into v_
3 PACKAGE BO MDW2    PNA_MAINT   520 10020      864672 for a in 1..v_chunk_size loop
3 PACKAGE BO MDW2    PNA_MAINT   521 10000     7439389 addr_array(a).tn := trunc(dbms_random.va
3 PACKAGE BO MDW2    PNA_MAINT   522 10000     6626817 addr_array(a).rn := trunc(dbms_random.va
3 PACKAGE BO MDW2    PNA_MAINT   523 10000     6861271 addr_array(a).rt := trunc(dbms_random.va
3 PACKAGE BO MDW2    PNA_MAINT   524 10000     8682794 addr_array(a).hn := case trunc(dbms_rand
3 PACKAGE BO MDW2    PNA_MAINT   525     0     2736292 when 0 then trunc(dbms_random.value(1,61
3 PACKAGE BO MDW2    PNA_MAINT   526     0     2487812 when 1 then trunc(dbms_random.value(1,12
3 PACKAGE BO MDW2    PNA_MAINT   527     0     3091980 when 2 then trunc(dbms_random.value(1,12
3 PACKAGE BO MDW2    PNA_MAINT   530 10000     6481536 addr_array(a).pcn := trunc(dbms_random.v
3 PACKAGE BO MDW2    PNA_MAINT   531 10000     4386484 addr_array(a).pcvc := dbms_random.string
3 PACKAGE BO MDW2    PNA_MAINT   533    40   157336328 forall idx in indices of addr_array
3 PACKAGE BO MDW2    PNA_MAINT   557    20       65125 if mod(loop_count,2)=0 then
3 PACKAGE BO MDW2    PNA_MAINT   559    10      604168 commit;
```

The output is ordered by line number, and with this being fairly simple code, we can "see" the flow of the program. However, although there is a logical thread to our code and PL/SQL is procedural, any complex code is not so ordered because of nested procedures and functions.

What is more important for us to know is where time is being spent, so we pull out the rows in descending order of elapsed time:

```
id UNIT_TYPE   OWNER UNIT_NAME   LINE   EXECS    TOT_TIME LINE_TEXT
-- ---------- ----- ---------- ----- ------- ----------- -----------------------------------------
3 PACKAGE BO MDW2    PNA_MAINT   533    40   157336328 forall idx in indices of addr_array
3 PACKAGE BO MDW2    PNA_MAINT   524 10000     8682794 addr_array(a).hn := case trunc(dbms_rand
3 PACKAGE BO MDW2    PNA_MAINT   521 10000     7439389 addr_array(a).tn := trunc(dbms_random.va
3 PACKAGE BO MDW2    PNA_MAINT   523 10000     6861271 addr_array(a).rt := trunc(dbms_random.va
3 PACKAGE BO MDW2    PNA_MAINT   522 10000     6626817 addr_array(a).rn := trunc(dbms_random.va
3 PACKAGE BO MDW2    PNA_MAINT   530 10000     6481536 addr_array(a).pcn := trunc(dbms_random.v
3 PACKAGE BO MDW2    PNA_MAINT   531 10000     4386484 addr_array(a).pcvc := dbms_random.string
3 PACKAGE BO MDW2    PNA_MAINT   527     0     3091980 when 2 then trunc(dbms_random.value(1,12
3 PACKAGE BO MDW2    PNA_MAINT   525     0     2736292 when 0 then trunc(dbms_random.value(1,61
3 PACKAGE BO MDW2    PNA_MAINT   526     0     2487812 when 1 then trunc(dbms_random.value(1,12
3 PACKAGE BO MDW2    PNA_MAINT   124    14     1199319 INSERT INTO plsql_log(process_name
3 PACKAGE BO MDW2    PNA_MAINT   520 10020      864672 for a in 1..v_chunk_size loop
```

If performance is an issue for this code, we will check out the top line: the FORALL statement is using up over 90 percent of the time.

Incidentally, earlier we said that SQL Developer does not have anything built into it for viewing DBMS_PROFILER information. Well, my friend and fellow co-author of this book, Alex Nuijten, wrote a report for SQL Developer to view DBMS_PROFILER data a few years back. You can find it at https://technology.amis.nl/2007/07/19/dbms_profiler-report-for-sql-developer/. Figure 7-12 shows a screenshot of it, showing data that's similar to our example.

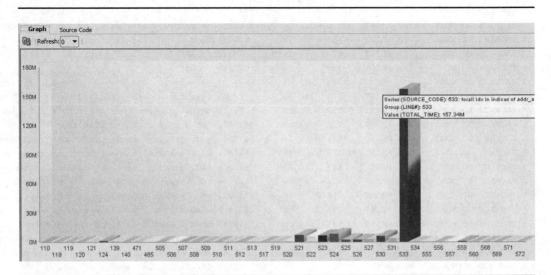

FIGURE 7-12. *Using a report in SQL Developer to visualize DBMS_PROFILER data*

DBMS_HPROF

If you have Oracle Version 11.1 or later, you can use the hierarchical profile introduced in that version. This is implemented with the package DBMS_PROFILER. Unlike DBMS_TRACE or DBMS_PROFILER, the hierarchical profiler is a little more complex in how it works. It uses files that are written to and read from the operating system, so it needs a directory (both at the OS level and an Oracle directory object) to work from. It is also a two-part process. You start and stop the collection of data to the file system files, and then you analyze the data and place the results in the hierarchical profiler tables. The benefit of this complexity is that you can analyze the raw data in many ways and, rather than just getting information for each part of the code you are analyzing, you can see how parts of the code relate to each other—that is, the hierarchy of it; not just how much time is spent in a procedure called **process_order**, but how often and from where it is called.

Also, a command-line tool called plshprof is available for processing the profile information into an HTML-formatted report, which we will cover in this section.

Setup   The DBMS_PROF package should be installed by default because it is created as part of the catalog build of the database. If for any reason it is missing, you can use the script $ORACLE_HOME/rdbms/admin/dbmshpro.sql to create it. However, you will have to grant access to the profiler package to any user who needs to use it:

```
grant execute on dbms_hprof to mdw2;
```

You will need to create a set of target tables for the processed data in the schema you will run the profiler from or else create them in a shared schema and create synonyms and grants accordingly. The script to create the tables is

```
$ORACLE_HOME/rdbms/admin/dbmshptab.sql
@?/rdbms/admin/dbmshptab.sql
```

NOTE
If you already had the tables and sequence, this script will drop them and re-create them, causing you to lose any existing data.

The tables created are

- DBMSHP_RUNS
- DBMSHP_FUNCTION_INFO
- DBMSHP_PARENT_CHILD_INFO

As with DBMS_TRACE and DBMS_PROFILER, if you have access, it is worth having a look at the creation script for the comments within it, such as the OWNER in DBMSHP_FUNCTION_INFO is the user who started the run. As you can see from the table names, Oracle sticks to its prior naming standards (joke!), but you can work out from the names what the three tables are for.

Finally, create a directory (as in an Oracle directory object) to use for the raw trace files and grant access to your user (of course, you need the OS directory to exist as well):

```
create directory plsql_hprof_dir as 'D:\sqlwork\p_hprof';
Directory created.

grant all on directory plsql_hprof_dir to mdw2;
Grant succeeded.
```

Fundamentals of DBMS_HPROF   We can now run the hierarchical profiler (hprof). We will do so initially using our PNA_MAINT.TEST1 code, as in prior examples. We stop and start hprof with calls to **dbms_hprof.start_profiling** and **dbms_hprof.stop_profiling**, respectively. For **start_profiling**, we pass in the directory and name of the file to create. The only other parameter option to pass in is MAX_DEPTH, which we will come to later in our discussion. **stop_profiling** has no parameters; it simply ceases profiling. Between starting and stopping the profiler, all PL/SQL activity is recorded to the specified file in the specified directory. Here is our first simple test:

```
--plhp1.sql
begin
  dbms_hprof.start_profiling (location => 'PLSQL_HPROF_DIR'
                             ,filename => 'mdw2'             );
  pna_maint.test1;
  dbms_hprof.stop_profiling;
end;
```

A 2KB file called mdw2 is created in our new directory. If you look at the raw file, it sort of makes sense—but this is not how you are intended to look at it. However, if you want more details on the structure of this file, they can be found in Chapter 13 of the Oracle 12c Database Development Guide, along with general details on the PL/SQL Hierarchical Profiler. Here is a section of the raw report:

```
P#V PLSHPROF Internal Version 1.0
P#! PL/SQL Timer Started
P#C PLSQL."MDW2"."PNA_MAINT"::11."__pkg_init"
P#X 8
```

```
P#R
P#C PLSQL."MDW2"."PNA_MAINT"::11."TEST1"#980980e97e42f8ec #142
P#X 43
P#C PLSQL."SYS"."DBMS_APPLICATION_INFO"::11."SET_MODULE"#963b7b52b7a7c411 #36
P#X 23
P#R
P#X 1
P#C PLSQL."MDW2"."PNA_MAINT"::11."PL"#c5dd7e95abfe7e9f #105
P#X 83
P#C PLSQL."SYS"."DBMS_OUTPUT"::11."PUT_LINE"#c5dd7e95abfe7e9f #109
```

Now we can analyze the file, which we do with the **dbms_hprof.analyze** procedure. We have to provide it with the LOCATION (directory) and FILENAME (the name of the file we stated when we started HPROF), and it makes sense to state a RUN_COMMENT. There are some other optional parameters we will cover later. The procedure passes back the **runid** it creates the data under. In the following example, we analyze our file, display the **runid**, and show what is recorded in DBMSHP_RUNS:

```
-- an_plhp1
declare
v_num pls_integer;
begin
  v_num := dbms_hprof.analyze(location => 'PLSQL_HPROF_DIR'
                             ,filename => 'mdw2'
                             ,run_comment =>'first test run');
  dbms_output.put_line('runno '||v_num);
end;

@an_plhp1
runno 1
PL/SQL procedure successfully completed.

select * from DBMSHP_RUNS
  RUNID RUN_TIMESTAMP               TOTAL_ELAPSED_TIME RUN_COMMENT
------- -------------------------- ------------------ ------------------
      1 09-FEB-16 15.36.59.468000                 213 first test run
```

We can query the data stored in the target tables DBMSHP_FUNCTION_INFO and DBMSHP_PARENT_CHILD_INFO directly, and for something as simple as TEST1, we can make pretty fair sense of the information. If we just look at the OWNER, MODULE, TYPE, FUNCTION, LINE#, and FUNCTION_ELAPSED_TIME, then the data is very similar to that obtained from DBMS_PROFILER, and it can also be linked in the same way to ALL_SOURCE via the object info and line number (see the earlier section on DBMS_PROFILER):

```
select runid       ,symbolid     ,owner      ,module
    ,type         ,function     ,line#
    ,function_elapsed_time f_elap
    ,subtree_elapsed_time st_elap
    ,calls
from dbmshp_function_info
where runid = &runid
```

```
order by symbolid
```

```
RUN
ID SYMBOLID OWNER   MODULE              TYPE          FUNCTION       LINE#   F_ELAP  ST_ELAP CALLS
--- -------- ------- ------------------- ------------- -------------- ------- ------- ------- -----
  1        1 MDW2    PNA_MAINT           PACKAGE BO    PIECE             94        2      14     1
  1        2 MDW2    PNA_MAINT           PACKAGE BO    PIECE             42       12      12     1
  1        3 MDW2    PNA_MAINT           PACKAGE BO    PL               105       93     111     2
  1        4 MDW2    PNA_MAINT           PACKAGE BO    TEST1            142       45     198     1
  1        5 MDW2    PNA_MAINT           PACKAGE BO    __pkg_init         0        8       8     1
  1        6 SYS     DBMS_APPLICATION_I  PACKAGE BO    SET_MODULE        36       28      28     2
  1        7 SYS     DBMS_HPROF          PACKAGE BO    STOP_PROFILING    63        0       0     1
  1        8 SYS     DBMS_OUTPUT         PACKAGE BO    NEW_LINE         117        3       3     3
  1        9 SYS     DBMS_OUTPUT         PACKAGE BO    PUT               77       18      18     3
  1       10 SYS     DBMS_OUTPUT         PACKAGE BO    PUT_LINE         109        4      25     3
```

The hierarchical information comes from DBMSHP_PARENT_CHILD_INFO:

```
select * from dbmshp_parent_child_info
 RUN
  ID PARENTSYMID CHILDSYMID SUBTREE_ELAPSED_TIME FUNCTION_ELAPSED_TIME CALLS
---- ----------- ---------- -------------------- --------------------- -----
   1           1          2                   12                    12     1
   1           3         10                   18                     3     2
   1           4          3                  111                    93     2
   1           4          6                   28                    28     2
   1           4          1                   14                     2     1
   1          10          9                   18                    18     3
   1          10          8                    3                     3     3
```

From here, we can work out that step 4 is our root step (it has the greatest subtree elapsed time and has no parents in the hierarchical view). We can write some SQL to draw the hierarchical picture for us:

```
select rpad('-',level*2,'-')||dfip.owner||':'||dfip.module||'.'||dfip.function||' '||dfip.line#
      ||' calls '||dfic.owner||':'||dfic.module||'.'||dfic.function||' '||dfic.line# hierarchy
     ,dpci.subtree_elapsed_time st_elap
     ,dpci.function_elapsed_time f_elap
     ,dpci.calls
from dbmshp_function_info     dfip
    ,dbmshp_function_info     dfic
    ,dbmshp_parent_child_info dpci
start with  dpci.runid      =1
     and dfip.runid      = dpci.runid
     and dfic.runid      = dpci.runid
     and dpci.childsymid  = dfic.symbolid
     and dpci.parentsymid = dfip.symbolid
     and dfip.symbolid   =4
connect by  dpci.runid          = prior dpci.runid
       and dfip.runid       = dpci.runid
       and dfic.runid       = dpci.runid
```

```
        and dpci.childsymid    = dfic.symbolid
        and dpci.parentsymid   = dfip.symbolid
        and prior dpci.childsymid = dpci.parentsymid
HIERARCHY                                                    ST_ELAP   F_ELAP CALLS
----------------------------------------------------------- --------- ------ -----
--MDW2:PNA_MAINT.TEST1 142  calls MDW2:PNA_MAINT.PIECE 94          14       2    1
----MDW2:PNA_MAINT.PIECE 94  calls MDW2:PNA_MAINT.PIECE 42         12      12    1
--MDW2:PNA_MAINT.TEST1 142  calls MDW2:PNA_MAINT.PL 105           111      93    2
----MDW2:PNA_MAINT.PL 105  calls SYS:DBMS_OUTPUT.PUT_LINE 109      18       3    2
------SYS:DBMS_OUTPUT.PUT_LINE 109  calls SYS:DBMS_OUTPUT.NEW_LINE 117   3   3    3
------SYS:DBMS_OUTPUT.PUT_LINE 109  calls SYS:DBMS_OUTPUT.PUT 77    18      18    3
--MDW2:PNA_MAINT.TEST1 142  calls SYS:DBMS_APPLICATION_INFO.SET_MODULE  28  28  2
```

Thus, we can see that the function **pna_maint.test1** calls **pna_maint.piece** once, that **pna_maint.test1** also calls **pna_maint.pl** twice, and in turn calls **dbms_output.put_line**—which itself calls the subprocedures **put** and **new_line**. Finally, **pna_maint.test1** calls **dbms_application_info** twice. The most time is taken in processing the PNA_MAINT.PL subtree.

Simple CONNECT BY Queries Will Error on More Complex Code

The SQL we use for querying the hierarchical data held in the target tables has quite complex START WITH and CONNECT BY clauses. Some of the code on the Web to perform similar queries uses a simpler form, but it causes "ORA-01436 connect by loop in user data" errors with most real-world profiles. We struggled at first to solve this, and then we pulled the SQL that SQL Developer uses out of the library cache and used that as a template. Why reinvent the wheel?

It is nice that we can get at the information directly, but even for this very basic example, it is not simple or clear what the data means.

Analyzing HPROF Data   We invoked the hierarchical profiler for our POP_ADDR_BATCH code, which was run to create 100,000 records. One thing to note is it took over 10 seconds, compared to just under 5 seconds with DBMS_PROFILER invoked, and 4 seconds with no profiling. Thus, the performance impact of DBMS_HPROF is noticeable but not onerous, as it can be with DBMS_TRACE. The file created in the directory was 270MB. If you use the hierarchical profiler for a lot of complex, looping code, you should be mindful of the volume of trace files you will produce—it can be considerable!

We analyzed the trace file with DBMS_HPROF.ANALYZE, which took 4 seconds. Only 23 rows are produced in DBMSHP_FUNCTION_INFO. We are not getting a record per executed line or even a record per line of PL/SQL processed (as we did with DBMS_PROFILER); instead, we are getting *a line per call to another PL/SQL code unit*. We pulled the profile out of the tables using the same query as before, but with a **runid** of 2 and a root **symbolid** of 1.

```
HIERARCHY                                                           ST_ELAP F_ELAP
CALLS
------------------------------------------------------------------- ------- ------
-------
:.__plsql_vm 0 to :.__anonymous_block 0                             4955097     70
2
```

```
--:.__anonymous_block 0 to MDW2:PNA_MAINT.POP_ADDR_BATCH 471                      4955027 364914
1
----MDW2:PNA_MAINT.POP_ADDR_BATCH 471 to MDW2:PNA_MAINT.WRITE_LOG 110                2431     518
14
------MDW2:PNA_MAINT.WRITE_LOG 110 to SYS:DBMS_OUTPUT.PUT_LINE 109                      6       6
14
------MDW2:PNA_MAINT.WRITE_LOG 110 to MDW2:PNA_MAINT.__static_sql_exec_line124 124   1216    1216
14
------MDW2:PNA_MAINT.WRITE_LOG 110 to MDW2:PNA_MAINT.__static_sql_exec_line139 139    691     691
14
----MDW2:PNA_MAINT.POP_ADDR_BATCH 471 to SYS:DBMS_APPLICATION_INFO.SET_MODULE 36       11      11
1
----MDW2:PNA_MAINT.POP_ADDR_BATCH 471 to SYS:DBMS_RANDOM.STRING 169              824459  194167
100000
------SYS:DBMS_RANDOM.STRING 169 to SYS:DBMS_RANDOM.VALUE 87                      630292  162358
200000
--------SYS:DBMS_RANDOM.VALUE 87 to SYS:DBMS_RANDOM.RECORD_RANDOM_NUMBER 67       863716  863716
800000
--------SYS:DBMS_RANDOM.VALUE 87 to SYS:DBMS_RANDOM.REPLAY_RANDOM_NUMBER 76       990093  990093
800000
--------SYS:DBMS_RANDOM.VALUE 87 to SYS:DBMS_RANDOM.SEED 16                          331     331
1
--------SYS:DBMS_RANDOM.VALUE 87 to SYS:STANDARD.__static_sql_exec_line180 180        39      39
1
----MDW2:PNA_MAINT.POP_ADDR_BATCH 471 to SYS:DBMS_RANDOM.VALUE 130              2119752  270973
600000
------SYS:DBMS_RANDOM.VALUE 130 to SYS:DBMS_RANDOM.VALUE 87                     1848779  462534
600000
--------SYS:DBMS_RANDOM.VALUE 87 to SYS:DBMS_RANDOM.RECORD_RANDOM_NUMBER 67       863716  863716
800000
--------SYS:DBMS_RANDOM.VALUE 87 to SYS:DBMS_RANDOM.REPLAY_RANDOM_NUMBER 76       990093  990093
800000
--------SYS:DBMS_RANDOM.VALUE 87 to SYS:DBMS_RANDOM.SEED 16                          331     331
1
--------SYS:DBMS_RANDOM.VALUE 87 to SYS:STANDARD.__static_sql_exec_line180 180        39      39
1
----MDW2:PNA_MAINT.POP_ADDR_BATCH 471 to SYS:DBMS_RANDOM.__pkg_init 0                   3       3
1
----MDW2:PNA_MAINT.POP_ADDR_BATCH 471 to MDW2:PNA_MAINT.__static_sql_exec_line510 510  83      83
1
----MDW2:PNA_MAINT.POP_ADDR_BATCH 471 to MDW2:PNA_MAINT.__static_sql_exec_line511 511  48      48
1
----MDW2:PNA_MAINT.POP_ADDR_BATCH 471 to MDW2:PNA_MAINT.__static_sql_exec_line512 512  41      41
1
----MDW2:PNA_MAINT.POP_ADDR_BATCH 471 to MDW2:PNA_MAINT.__static_sql_exec_line533 533 1642047 642047
100
----MDW2:PNA_MAINT.POP_ADDR_BATCH 471 to MDW2:PNA_MAINT.__static_sql_exec_line559 559  1223    1223
10
----MDW2:PNA_MAINT.POP_ADDR_BATCH 471 to MDW2:PNA_MAINT.__static_sql_exec_line571 571    15      15
1
--:.__anonymous_block 0 to SYS:DBMS_HPROF.STOP_PROFILING 63                             0       0
1
```

Here, we can see the overall structure of the code from the output, as well as what calls what and the time spent. This allows us to understand the flow of the code and focus on any performance issues. This is much clearer than either DBMS_TRACE or DBMS_PROFILER. The text of each line is not included here because it makes the output too messy, but it is simple to get the code by linking to ALL_SOURCE. We can see a lot of time (1642047) is spent on static SQL line 533, so we extracted the code to see what is happening there. In general, getting the text from one line above to ten or so lines after the line of interest is usually enough to let us know what is going on and certainly find the code in dev or a GUI tool:

```
select line,text from all_source where owner ='MDW2' and name='PNA_MAINT'
and type= 'PACKAGE BODY' and line between 532 and 543
      LINE TEXT
---------- -------------------------------------------------------------
       532    end loop;
       533    forall idx in indices of addr_array
       534    insert into address (addr_id
       535                        ,house_number
       536                        ,addr_line_1
       537                        ,addr_line_2
       538                        ,addr_line_3
       539                        ,addr_line_4
       540                        ,post_code)
       541    select addr_seq.nextval
       542          ,addr_array(idx).hn
       543          ,rona.road_name||' '||roty.road_type
```

You may remember that this step took most of the time in our example of using DBMS_ PROFILER, but now, even though it is still one of the slower steps, it is no longer the slowest. It is considerably faster. That's because we had altered the code and reduced the size of the ADDR_ ARRAY in the POP_ADDR_BATCH code for the much, much slower testing with DBMS_TRACE. Our tests with DBMS_PROFILER reminded us of this, so we increased the batch size before this test. Why did we leave this inconsistency in the text? Because it highlights a great use for the profilers (and instrumentation). *If you profile your code as you develop it, you will spot performance weak spots as you go and have the option to address them*. These profiler tools are not just for solving production problems; they are for qualifying your code as you develop it.

Even with our simple code, we soon hit several levels of hierarchy. For production code from applications that extensively use packages, you could easily get very deep nesting of code, which becomes confusing. You may wish to only look "so deep" into your code. For example, suppose you have the following hierarchy:

Procedure A
    Procedure B
        Procedure C
            Procedure E
                Procedure F

    Procedure Q
        Procedure R
        Procedure S

In this case, you may wish to look only two or three levels down into the code.
With HPROF, you can do this at the profiling stage by stating the MAX_DEPTH:

```
dbms_hprof.start_profiling (location => 'PLSQL_HPROF_DIR'
                           ,filename => 'mdw10'
                           ,max_depth=>3
                           );
-- analyze the code and you see:
```

HIERARCHY	ST_ELAP	F_ELAP	CALLS
MDW2:PNA_MAINT.POP_ADDR_BATCH 471 to MDW2:PNA_MAINT.WRITE_LOG 110	891	139	5
--MDW2:PNA_MAINT.WRITE_LOG 110 to SYS:DBMS_OUTPUT.PUT_LINE 109	1	1	5
--MDW2:PNA_MAINT.WRITE_LOG 110 to MDW2:PNA_MAINT.__static_sql_exec_line124 124	471	471	5
--MDW2:PNA_MAINT.WRITE_LOG 110 to MDW2:PNA_MAINT.__static_sql_exec_line139 139	280	280	5
MDW2:PNA_MAINT.POP_ADDR_BATCH 471 to SYS:DBMS_APPLICATION_INFO.SET_MODULE 36	12	12	1
MDW2:PNA_MAINT.POP_ADDR_BATCH 471 to SYS:DBMS_RANDOM.STRING 169	715877	175862	100000
--SYS:DBMS_RANDOM.STRING 169 to SYS:DBMS_RANDOM.VALUE 87	540015	540015	200000
MDW2:PNA_MAINT.POP_ADDR_BATCH 471 to SYS:DBMS_RANDOM.VALUE 130	1844353	266679	600000
--SYS:DBMS_RANDOM.VALUE 130 to SYS:DBMS_RANDOM.VALUE 87	1577674	1577674	600000
MDW2:PNA_MAINT.POP_ADDR_BATCH 471 to MDW2:PNA_MAINT.__static_sql_exec_line510 510	73	73	1
MDW2:PNA_MAINT.POP_ADDR_BATCH 471 to MDW2:PNA_MAINT.__static_sql_exec_line511 511	41	41	1
MDW2:PNA_MAINT.POP_ADDR_BATCH 471 to MDW2:PNA_MAINT.__static_sql_exec_line512 512	36	36	1
MDW2:PNA_MAINT.POP_ADDR_BATCH 471 to MDW2:PNA_MAINT.__static_sql_exec_line533 533	1532447	1532447	10
MDW2:PNA_MAINT.POP_ADDR_BATCH 471 to MDW2:PNA_MAINT.__static_sql_exec_line559 559	560	560	1
MDW2:PNA_MAINT.POP_ADDR_BATCH 471 to MDW2:PNA_MAINT.__static_sql_exec_line571 571	14	14	1

With a limit of 3, we see two levels into the output from our script, and although we see the calls to DBMS_RANDOM and DBMS_OUTPUT, the calls they make are now missing from the profile. Elapsed times for all the steps below them are merged into the value for the parent step at the lowest allowed level. Thus, we have simplified our profile.

More Advanced Analysis Using plshprof   As you have seen, you *can* use just SQL to look at the DBMS_HPROF data—but there are other, much better options. The first is plshprof. This is a command-line tool for producing HTML output from the raw trace data, which is a set of screens you can view in any browser. The following will take the HPROF *filename* and create a set of files in directory *destname* with names derived from *filename*:

```
plshprof –output destname filename
```

We create a new directory to hold the HTML files (D:\sqlwork\p_hprof\reports) and generate a new HPROF file (mdw8) of our POP_ADDR_BATCH code. From the command line, we then process the file as shown here:

```
D:\sqlwork\p_hprof\reports> plshprof -output mdw8 \sqlwork\p_hprof\mdw8
PLSHPROF: Oracle Database 12c Enterprise Edition Release 12.1.0.2.0 - 64bit Production
[20 symbols processed]
[Report written to 'mdw8.html']
```

This creates a set of HTML files in the directory specified, as you can see in Figure 7-13.

You simply click on the root file (*filename*.html), and this will show the front screen in your browser (see Figure 7-14).

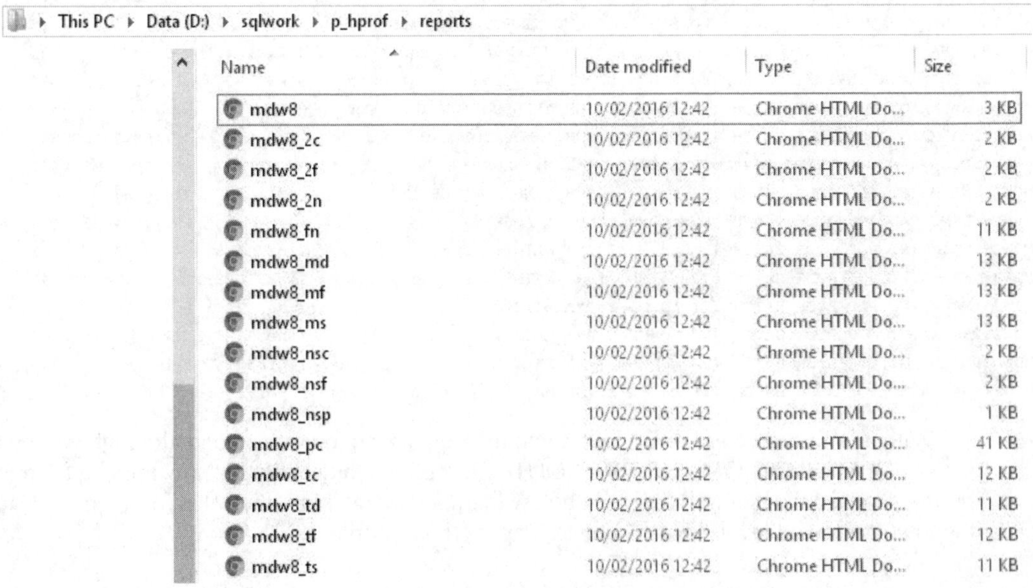

This PC ▸ Data (D:) ▸ sqlwork ▸ p_hprof ▸ reports

Name	Date modified	Type	Size
mdw8	10/02/2016 12:42	Chrome HTML Do...	3 KB
mdw8_2c	10/02/2016 12:42	Chrome HTML Do...	2 KB
mdw8_2f	10/02/2016 12:42	Chrome HTML Do...	2 KB
mdw8_2n	10/02/2016 12:42	Chrome HTML Do...	2 KB
mdw8_fn	10/02/2016 12:42	Chrome HTML Do...	11 KB
mdw8_md	10/02/2016 12:42	Chrome HTML Do...	13 KB
mdw8_mf	10/02/2016 12:42	Chrome HTML Do...	13 KB
mdw8_ms	10/02/2016 12:42	Chrome HTML Do...	13 KB
mdw8_nsc	10/02/2016 12:42	Chrome HTML Do...	2 KB
mdw8_nsf	10/02/2016 12:42	Chrome HTML Do...	2 KB
mdw8_nsp	10/02/2016 12:42	Chrome HTML Do...	1 KB
mdw8_pc	10/02/2016 12:42	Chrome HTML Do...	41 KB
mdw8_tc	10/02/2016 12:42	Chrome HTML Do...	12 KB
mdw8_td	10/02/2016 12:42	Chrome HTML Do...	11 KB
mdw8_tf	10/02/2016 12:42	Chrome HTML Do...	12 KB
mdw8_ts	10/02/2016 12:42	Chrome HTML Do...	11 KB

FIGURE 7-13.   *The HTML files generated by plshprof*

PL/SQL Elapsed Time (microsecs) Analysis

4874157 microsecs (elapsed time) & 3100204 function calls

The PL/SQL Hierarchical Profiler produces a collection of reports that present information derived from the profiler's output log in a variety of formats. The following reports have been found to be the most generally useful as starting points for browsing:

- Function Elapsed Time (microsecs) Data sorted by Total Subtree Elapsed Time (microsecs)
- Function Elapsed Time (microsecs) Data sorted by Total Function Elapsed Time (microsecs)

In addition, the following reports are also available:

- Function Elapsed Time (microsecs) Data sorted by Function Name
- Function Elapsed Time (microsecs) Data sorted by Total Descendants Elapsed Time (microsecs)
- Function Elapsed Time (microsecs) Data sorted by Total Function Call Count
- Function Elapsed Time (microsecs) Data sorted by Mean Subtree Elapsed Time (microsecs)
- Function Elapsed Time (microsecs) Data sorted by Mean Function Elapsed Time (microsecs)
- Function Elapsed Time (microsecs) Data sorted by Mean Descendants Elapsed Time (microsecs)
- Module Elapsed Time (microsecs) Data sorted by Total Function Elapsed Time (microsecs)
- Module Elapsed Time (microsecs) Data sorted by Module Name
- Module Elapsed Time (microsecs) Data sorted by Total Function Call Count
- Namespace Elapsed Time (microsecs) Data sorted by Total Function Elapsed Time (microsecs)
- Namespace Elapsed Time (microsecs) Data sorted by Namespace
- Namespace Elapsed Time (microsecs) Data sorted by Total Function Call Count
- Parents and Children Elapsed Time (microsecs) Data

FIGURE 7-14. *The main page from a plshprof analysis*

The top two links go to summaries of your profiled code; the first is ordered by which areas of code take up the most time (see Figure 7-15), and the second is ordered by the functions.

The final link, Parents and Children Elapsed (microsecs) Time Data, shows how each module (chunk of PL/SQL or static SQL statement) relates to its parent and children and is linked to by many of the other reports (this report is not shown).

Other pages show information by function, module, and namespace (see Figures 7-16 through 7-18). Module is, rather perversely, not the MODULE as set by DBMS_APPLICATION_ INFO, but the name of the stored function, procedure, or package.

One thing to note about plshprof is that the reports do not link back to ALL_SOURCE to show the actual lines of PL/SQL or SQL, which is a bit of a shame. This is because the database is not used to process the raw data—you are not stating in the tool which database or connection details to use, and you can shut down your database and still run plshprof.

NOTE
If you use the same output name for a plshprof analysis that has been used before, the previous files are wiped over.

Function Elapsed Time (microsecs) Data sorted by Function Name

4874157 microsecs (elapsed time) & 3100204 function calls

Subtree	Ind%	Function	Ind%	Descendants	Ind%	Calls	Ind%	Function Name
4874154	100%	368581	7.6%	4505573	92.4%	1	0.0%	MDW2.PNA_MAINT.POP_ADDR_BATCH (Line 471)
2732	0.1%	618	0.0%	2114	0.0%	14	0.0%	MDW2.PNA_MAINT.WRITE_LOG (Line 110)
15	0.0%	15	0.0%	0	0.0%	1	0.0%	SYS.DBMS_APPLICATION_INFO.SET_MODULE (Line 36)
0	0.0%	0	0.0%	0	0.0%	1	0.0%	SYS.DBMS_HPROF.STOP_PROFILING (Line 63)
9	0.0%	9	0.0%	0	0.0%	15	0.0%	SYS.DBMS_OUTPUT.NEW_LINE (Line 117)
65	0.0%	65	0.0%	0	0.0%	15	0.0%	SYS.DBMS_OUTPUT.PUT (Line 77)
87	0.0%	13	0.0%	74	0.0%	15	0.0%	SYS.DBMS_OUTPUT.PUT_LINE (Line 109)
851671	17.5%	851671	17.5%	0	0.0%	800000	25.8%	SYS.DBMS_RANDOM.RECORD_RANDOM_NUMBER (Line 67)
976475	20.0%	976475	20.0%	0	0.0%	800000	25.8%	SYS.DBMS_RANDOM.REPLAY_RANDOM_NUMBER (Line 76)
823089	16.9%	193817	4.0%	629272	12.9%	100000	3.2%	SYS.DBMS_RANDOM.STRING (Line 169)
2467137	50.6%	638991	13.1%	1828146	37.5%	800000	25.8%	SYS.DBMS_RANDOM.VALUE (Line 87)
2106650	43.2%	268785	5.5%	1837865	37.7%	600000	19.4%	SYS.DBMS_RANDOM.VALUE (Line 130)
1380	0.0%	1380	0.0%	0	0.0%	14	0.0%	MDW2.PNA_MAINT.__static_sql_exec_line124 (Line 124)
650	0.0%	650	0.0%	0	0.0%	14	0.0%	MDW2.PNA_MAINT.__static_sql_exec_line139 (Line 139)
102	0.0%	102	0.0%	0	0.0%	1	0.0%	MDW2.PNA_MAINT.__static_sql_exec_line510 (Line 510)
69	0.0%	69	0.0%	0	0.0%	1	0.0%	MDW2.PNA_MAINT.__static_sql_exec_line511 (Line 511)
56	0.0%	56	0.0%	0	0.0%	1	0.0%	MDW2.PNA_MAINT.__static_sql_exec_line512 (Line 512)
1571641	32.2%	1571641	32.2%	0	0.0%	100	0.0%	MDW2.PNA_MAINT.__static_sql_exec_line533 (Line 533)
1205	0.0%	1205	0.0%	0	0.0%	10	0.0%	MDW2.PNA_MAINT.__static_sql_exec_line559 (Line 559)
14	0.0%	14	0.0%	0	0.0%	1	0.0%	MDW2.PNA_MAINT.__static_sql_exec_line571 (Line 571)

FIGURE 7-15. *The "Function" reports show the time spent and calls in each function and their subtrees.*

The command-line tool plshprof offers a couple of other tricks, but the main one is the ability to compare two profiles. Of course, this only makes sense if the profiles are from very similar code! We altered the **pop_addr_bulk** procedure so that it does 100-row batches as opposed to 10,000-row batches, and we created a hierarchical trace file called mdw9 for it. We then use plshprof to analyze it compared with mdw8:

```
plshprof -output mdw89_diff \sqlwork\p_hprof\mdw8 \sqlwork\p_hprof\mdw9
PLSHPROF: Oracle Database 12c Enterprise Edition Release 12.1.0.2.0 - 64bit
Production
[23 symbols processed]
[Report written to 'mdw89_diff.html']
```

The front page of the HTML report now includes a summary (see Figure 7-19). As you can see, some things got faster and some got slower.

Function Elapsed Time (microsecs) Data sorted by Total Function Call Count

4874157 microsecs (elapsed time) & 3100204 function calls

Subtree	Ind%	Function	Ind%	Descendants	Ind%	Calls	Ind%	Cum%	Function Name
2467137	50.6%	638991	13.1%	1828146	37.5%	800000	25.8%	25.8%	SYS.DBMS_RANDOM.VALUE (Line 87)
976475	20.0%	976475	20.0%	0	0.0%	800000	25.8%	51.6%	SYS.DBMS_RANDOM.REPLAY_RANDOM_NUMBER (Line 76)
851671	17.5%	851671	17.5%	0	0.0%	800000	25.8%	77.4%	SYS.DBMS_RANDOM.RECORD_RANDOM_NUMBER (Line 67)
2106650	43.2%	268785	5.5%	1837865	37.7%	600000	19.4%	96.8%	SYS.DBMS_RANDOM.VALUE (Line 130)
823089	16.9%	193817	4.0%	629272	12.9%	100000	3.2%	100%	SYS.DBMS_RANDOM.STRING (Line 169)
1571641	32.2%	1571641	32.2%	0	0.0%	100	0.0%	100%	MDW2.PNA_MAINT.__static_sql_exec_line533 (Line 533)
87	0.0%	13	0.0%	74	0.0%	15	0.0%	100%	SYS.DBMS_OUTPUT.PUT_LINE (Line 109)
9	0.0%	9	0.0%	0	0.0%	15	0.0%	100%	SYS.DBMS_OUTPUT.NEW_LINE (Line 117)
65	0.0%	65	0.0%	0	0.0%	15	0.0%	100%	SYS.DBMS_OUTPUT.PUT (Line 77)
650	0.0%	650	0.0%	0	0.0%	14	0.0%	100%	MDW2.PNA_MAINT.__static_sql_exec_line139 (Line 139)
2732	0.1%	618	0.0%	2114	0.0%	14	0.0%	100%	MDW2.PNA_MAINT.WRITE_LOG (Line 110)
1380	0.0%	1380	0.0%	0	0.0%	14	0.0%	100%	MDW2.PNA_MAINT.__static_sql_exec_line124 (Line 124)
1205	0.0%	1205	0.0%	0	0.0%	10	0.0%	100%	MDW2.PNA_MAINT.__static_sql_exec_line559 (Line 559)
102	0.0%	102	0.0%	0	0.0%	1	0.0%	100%	MDW2.PNA_MAINT.__static_sql_exec_line510 (Line 510)
4874154	100%	368581	7.6%	4505573	92.4%	1	0.0%	100%	MDW2.PNA_MAINT.POP_ADDR_BATCH (Line 471)
56	0.0%	56	0.0%	0	0.0%	1	0.0%	100%	MDW2.PNA_MAINT.__static_sql_exec_line512 (Line 512)
69	0.0%	69	0.0%	0	0.0%	1	0.0%	100%	MDW2.PNA_MAINT.__static_sql_exec_line511 (Line 511)
15	0.0%	15	0.0%	0	0.0%	1	0.0%	100%	SYS.DBMS_APPLICATION_INFO.SET_MODULE (Line 36)
0	0.0%	0	0.0%	0	0.0%	1	0.0%	100%	SYS.DBMS_HPROF.STOP_PROFILING (Line 63)
14	0.0%	14	0.0%	0	0.0%	1	0.0%	100%	MDW2.PNA_MAINT.__static_sql_exec_line571 (Line 571)

FIGURE 7-16. *Function calls ordered by the name of the function. Note that this is ordered by OWNER and then by the function name, with SQL lines at the end.*

Module Elapsed Time (microsecs) Data sorted by Module Name

4874157 microsecs (elapsed time) & 3100204 function calls

Module	Ind%	Calls	Ind%	Module Name
1944316	39.9%	157	0.0%	MDW2.PNA_MAINT
15	0.0%	1	0.0%	SYS.DBMS_APPLICATION_INFO
0	0.0%	1	0.0%	SYS.DBMS_HPROF
87	0.0%	45	0.0%	SYS.DBMS_OUTPUT
2929739	60.1%	3100000	100%	SYS.DBMS_RANDOM

FIGURE 7-17. *The "Namespace" reports are good for highlighting how much time is spent in the SQL and PL/SQL, and how many calls are in each.*

Namespace Elapsed Time (microsecs) Data sorted by Total Function Elapsed Time (microsecs)

```
4874157 microsecs (elapsed time) & 3100204 function calls
```

Function	Ind%	Cum%	Calls	Ind%	Namespace
3299040	67.7%	67.7%	3100062	100%	PLSQL
1575117	32.3%	100%	142	0.0%	SQL

FIGURE 7-18. *The "Module" reports highlight the amount of time spent and number of calls within each unit of PL/SQL.*

PL/SQL Elapsed Time (microsecs) Analysis - Summary Page

This analysis finds a net **regression** of 1115473 microsecs (elapsed time) or **23%** (4874157 versus **5989630**).
Here is a summary of the 23 most important individual function regressions and improvements:

	Regressions: 1115475 microsecs (elapsed time)						Improvements: 2 microsecs (elapsed time)				
Function	**Rel%**	**Ind%**	**Calls**	**Rel%**	**Function Name**	**Function**	**Rel%**	**Ind%**	**Calls**	**Rel%**	**Function Name**
793458	+50.5%	71.1%	900	+900%	MDW2.PNA_MAINT._static_sql_exec_line533 (Line 533)						
193812	NA%	17.4%	90	+643%	MDW2.PNA_MAINT._static_sql_exec_line124 (Line 124)						
29617	+3.0%	2.7%	0		SYS.DBMS_RANDOM.REPLAY_RANDOM_NUMBER (Line 76)						
21022	+5.7%	1.9%	0		MDW2.PNA_MAINT.POP_ADDR_BATCH (Line 471)						
19944	NA%	1.8%	0		MDW2.PNA_MAINT._static_sql_exec_line510 (Line 510)						
13833	+1.6%	1.2%	0		SYS.DBMS_RANDOM.RECORD_RANDOM_NUMBER (Line 67)						
12873	+4.8%	1.2%	0		SYS.DBMS_RANDOM.VALUE (Line 130)						
7055	+3.6%	0.6%	0		SYS.DBMS_RANDOM.STRING (Line 169)						
5658	+0.9%	0.5%	0		SYS.DBMS_RANDOM.VALUE (Line 87)	**Function**	**Rel%**	**Ind%**	**Calls**	**Rel%**	**Function Name**
4660	+754%	0.4%	90	+643%	MDW2.PNA_MAINT.WRITE_LOG (Line 110)	-2	-14.3%	100%	0		MDW2.PNA_MAINT._static_sql_exec_line571 (Line 571)
4488	+372%	0.4%	90	+900%	MDW2.PNA_MAINT._static_sql_exec_line559 (Line 559)						
4471	+688%	0.4%	90	+643%	MDW2.PNA_MAINT._static_sql_exec_line139 (Line 139)						
1602	NA%	0.1%	0		MDW2.PNA_MAINT._static_sql_exec_line511 (Line 511)						
1445	NA%	0.1%	0		MDW2.PNA_MAINT._static_sql_exec_line512 (Line 512)						
646		0.1%	1		SYS.STANDARD._static_sql_exec_line180 (Line 180)#						
447		0.0%	1		SYS.DBMS_RANDOM.SEED (Line 16)#						
286	+440%	0.0%	90	+600%	SYS.DBMS_OUTPUT.PUT (Line 77)						
89	+685%	0.0%	90	+600%	SYS.DBMS_OUTPUT.PUT_LINE (Line 109)						
61	+678%	0.0%	90	+600%	SYS.DBMS_OUTPUT.NEW_LINE (Line 117)						
7		0.0%	1		SYS.DBMS_RANDOM.__pkg_init#						
1	+6.7%	0.0%	0		SYS.DBMS_APPLICATION_INFO.SET_MODULE (Line 36)						

FIGURE 7-19. *plshprof comparison analysis*

Elapsed Time (microsecs) Comparison for MDW2.PNA_MAINT.__static_sql_exec_line533 (Line 533) (71.1%

MDW2.PNA_MAINT.__static_sql_exec_line533 (Line 533)	First Trace	Ind%	Second Trace	Ind%	Diff	Diff%
Function Elapsed Time (microsecs)s	1571641	32.2%	2365099	39.5%	793458	+50.5%
Function Calls	100	0.0%	1000	0.0%	900	+900%
Mean Function Elapsed Time (microsecs)s	15716.4		2365.1		-13351.3	-85.0%

MDW2.PNA_MAINT.__static_sql_exec_line533 (Line 533)

Subtree	Function	Descendants	Calls	Function Name
793458	793458	0	900	MDW2.PNA_MAINT.__static_sql_exec_line533 (Line 533)
Parents:				
793458	793458	0	900	MDW2.PNA_MAINT.POP_ADDR_BATCH (Line 471)

FIGURE 7-20. *Detail of the step with the greatest difference, showing its parent*

Looking at the report, you can see that 23 things got worse and 1 got better—but most of the things that got worse either took very little time or were only worse by a little bit. This was probably impacted by the machine (a reasonably specified laptop) being a little busier during the run. The big hitter is static line 533 at the top of the summary report: it took twice as long and took up the largest section of time. Our logging and instrumenting calls jumped in numbers, and total cost rose (DBMS_OUTPUT and **write_log**) because the instrumentation is dependent on the number of batch runs we process, and with a smaller batch we have more runs.

We clicked on that top line to show the detail (see Figure 7-20). Reducing our batch size so that there are 1000 calls rather than 100 (processing the same total volume) makes the elapsed time increase by 50.5 percent.

More information can be found on plshprof in Chapter 13 of the Oracle 12*c* Database Development Guide.

HPROF and SQL Developer   Finally, you can generate and view hierarchical profiles from SQL Developer. Getting to generate a hierarchical profile is a little odd, and you need access to SYS (or the SYSDBA privileged account) the first time you do this in order to set up the tables, access, and the directory objects.

Navigate to a PL/SQL object in the CONNECTIONS tab, just as you would to see any information about it. In this case, we are going to our PNA_MAINT package. Right-click to get the object activity menu shown in Figure 7-21.

You will be presented with the Profile PL/SQL screen shown in Figure 7-22, where you select which actual procedure or function you want to test (oddly, it does not list those with no input parameters), put in a comment (top of the box) if you want one, and then *alter the PL/SQL block* to replace the NULL values it defaults to with the input parameters. Click OK. This part is highlighted in Figure 7-22. (You can also save these scripts and load old ones.) At this point, if you have never

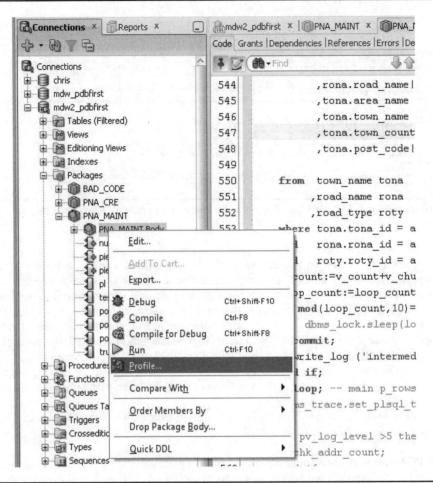

FIGURE 7-21. *Running the Hierarchical Profiler for an object in SQL Developer*

run this before in SQL Developer, you will be prompted to enter a directory to use (in this case, we used our previously created \sqlwork\hprof dir) and the SYS password. It then runs the profile.

The Profile PL/SQL dialog box will disappear, and nothing much will happen initially. Be patient; in a few seconds (or however long it takes to run profiler and then the analyzer if you have scripted it), control passes to the Profiles tab for that object and you see all the profiles run to date. This includes any you created manually.

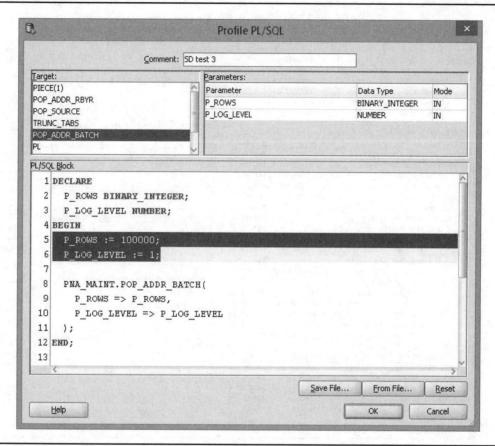

FIGURE 7-22. *Stating the parameters for the code to be profiled*

If you have created hierarchical profiles for any stored PL/SQL by other methods, you can find them in SQL Developer by going to the object and clicking the Profile tab (the one on the far right). You can see this in Figure 7-23.

For reasons that are not apparent, profiles created via SQL Developer can show up more than once in the list. It does not matter which one you highlight; the details remain the same, including the very nice graphical view shown in Figure 7-23, which you do not get from the HTML reports generated by plshprof.

Code	Grants	Dependencies	References	Errors	Details	Profiles

▼ Actions...

RUNID	Timestamp	Comment	Total Elapsed Time
7	10-feb-2016 04:57	SD test 3	4880641 μs
7	10-feb-2016 04:57	SD test 3	4880641 μs
6	09-feb-2016 10:45		4899491 μs
5	09-feb-2016 10:44	mdw5	4955101 μs
4	09-feb-2016 10:42	test4	409 μs
3	09-feb-2016 10:41	test3	1173 μs

Function Calls	Module	Namespace	Call Hierarchy

Callee	Elapsed	Aggregated	Calls#
MDW2.PNA_MAINT.POP_ADDR_BATCH	380518 μs	4880504	1
MDW2.PNA_MAINT.WRITE_LOG	120 μs	873	5
MDW2.PNA_MAINT.__static_sql_exec_line124	485 μs	485	5
MDW2.PNA_MAINT.__static_sql_exec_line139	268 μs	268	5
SYS.DBMS_APPLICATION_INFO.SET_MODULE	18 μs	18	1
SYS.DBMS_APPLICATION_INFO.__pkg_init	1 μs	1	1
SYS.DBMS_RANDOM.STRING	197950 μs	827564	100000
SYS.DBMS_RANDOM.VALUE	163430 μs	629614	200000
SYS.DBMS_RANDOM.RECORD_RANDOM_NUMBER	849807 μs	849807	800000
SYS.DBMS_RANDOM.REPLAY_RANDOM_NUMBER	987197 μs	987197	800000
SYS.DBMS_RANDOM.SEED	344 μs	344	1
SYS.STANDARD.__static_sql_exec_line180	53 μs	53	1
SYS.DBMS_RANDOM.VALUE	268794 μs	2111425	600000
SYS.DBMS_RANDOM.VALUE	471414 μs	1842631	600000
SYS.DBMS_RANDOM.RECORD_RANDOM_NUMBER	849807 μs	849807	800000
SYS.DBMS_RANDOM.REPLAY_RANDOM_NUMBER	987197 μs	987197	800000
SYS.DBMS_RANDOM.SEED	344 μs	344	1
SYS.STANDARD.__static_sql_exec_line180	53 μs	53	1
SYS.DBMS_RANDOM.__pkg_init	4 μs	4	1
MDW2.PNA_MAINT.__static_sql_exec_line510	91 μs	91	1
MDW2.PNA_MAINT.__static_sql_exec_line511	53 μs	53	1
MDW2.PNA_MAINT.__static_sql_exec_line512	48 μs	48	1
MDW2.PNA_MAINT.__static_sql_exec_line533	1559318 μs	1559318	10
MDW2.PNA_MAINT.__static_sql_exec_line559	576 μs	576	1
MDW2.PNA_MAINT.__static_sql_exec_line571	15 μs	15	1
MDW2.PNA_MAINT.__pkg_init	5 μs	5	1
SYS.DBMS_HPROF.STOP_PROFILING	0 μs	0	1

FIGURE 7-23. *The hierarchical view of the HPROF output in SQL Developer*

Overview of the Profiling Options

Now that we have discussed the three main PL/SQL profiling tools, Table 7-3 summarizes their main strengths and weaknesses.

DBMS_TRACE is more of a debugging tool than the other two tools, but it is simple to use. The information it produces is the most detailed. Its potential impact on the system is very high. Code changes are needed to limit its impact.

DBMS_HPROF is more complex to use, potentially gives the best profiling information, and has a fairly low impact on the system. Access to directories and even the OS are needed to get the most out of it.

DBMS_PROFILER is probably the simplest tool overall to use and has the least impact on performance. It does not need access to the code or the OS to use.

Tool	Advantages	Disadvantages
DBMS_TRACE	Very easy to set up, only needing access to one package and two tables. Fairly easy to use, although the calls to manage what is traced can be a little confusing. Output is very detailed and verbose (both an advantage and disadvantage, depending on what you want). Gives a lot of information and shows some things the other options do not (for example, the PL/SQL context switching).	Potentially large impact on performance. Potentially generates considerable data volumes. Needs access to change code to limit data volume and performance impact. Output is very detailed and verbose. Can be hard to see the woods for the trees. Lacks a hierarchical view. Data is not specifically shown in other Oracle tools.
DBMS_PROFILER	Very easy to set up, only needing access to one package and three tables. Very easy to use. Least run-time impact of all three options.	Lacks the detail available with DBMS_TRACE. Lacks a hierarchical view. Data is not specifically shown in other Oracle tools.
DBMS_HPROF	Shows hierarchical information. Level of detail (depth) is easily capped. Intermediate run-time impact. Data can be generated from and seen in other tools. A separate analysis tool is available.	More complex to set up, needing access to OS directories. More complex to use (involves a two-step process).

TABLE 7-3. *Overview of the Profiling Options*

Summary

Instrumenting your PL/SQL code is not just for debugging your code as you develop it—it is vital if you want to be able to investigate and solve production problems quickly. While DBMS_OUPUT is the most common method of instrumentation and is good for debugging PL/SQL during the writing stage, it is a poor choice for production instrumentation.

However, Oracle provides DBMS_APPLICATION_INFO for real-time monitoring, and all of the tools in the tool set have awareness of this feature built into them. The two can be combined with user-generated instrumentation saved to a log table via autonomous transactions to provide a lightweight, robust instrumenting solution for all your PL/SQL. This information can be used to profile your PL/SQL code to help solve production issues in a sensible and targeted manner, rather than guessing at root causes, as is sadly the norm without instrumentation.

Oracle provides several profiling tools you can use in different situations. DBMS_TRACE is more suited to debugging, DBMS_HPROF to profiling code and finding the most demanding activities, and DBMS_PROFILER is a happy medium between the two.

The profiling tools and PL/SQL compilation warnings can also be used during the development process to highlight potential issues with your code and show where there might be performance issues.

PL/SQL has been around for over 20 years, and the existing tools to instrument and profile it are still underutilized, which is a great shame because learning to use them will make you a better PL/SQL developer. They can help you identify where issues really are (and avoid guessing) and, overall, help you produce faster, more resilient PL/SQL applications.

CHAPTER

8

Dynamic SQL

I f you need to write a SQL statement but do not know all the elements of it, you might need dynamic SQL. With dynamic SQL, the actual SQL clause is built during the execution. For instance, dynamic SQL can be used when you do not know the columns in the SELECT part of the query or the table names in the FROM part of the query, or if the WHERE part of the query is unknown before run time. Dynamic SQL should be used *only* if you are not able to do what's needed using static SQL. Dynamic SQL can only be used in PL/SQL.

SQL injection is seen as a big security risk while using dynamic SQL. If you are not already familiar with SQL injection, we would advise you to become familiar with it before starting to use dynamic SQL. You can read more about SQL injection and code security in Chapter 15.

Dynamic SQL programs can handle changes in data definitions without the need to recompile, whereas static SQL cannot. The SQL statement typically depends on the input from a user or another program and is only known after that input during run time. Dynamic SQL also lets you execute Data Definition Language (DDL) statements and Session Control Language (SCL) statements, which are not supported in static SQL. Examples of DDL statements are CREATE, DROP, GRANT, and REVOKE, and examples of SCL statements are ALTER SESSION and SET ROLE.

Typical use cases for dynamic SQL could include daily, weekly, monthly, and yearly tables, which might be named TABLENAME_YYYYMMDD or use any other naming standard known beforehand. In these cases, the table might not exist when the dynamic SQL clause is written but the rule for the name exists. Dynamic SQL can be used in querying that table, but also in creating the table. Another example might be reusability: the same SQL statement can be used in several places with minor changes. Instead of writing several SQL clauses, just one dynamic SQL clause is written and used in many places.

Using dynamic SQL has its own risks. Because the SQL statement is built and compiled only during execution, it is possible that it won't compile, some privileges are missing, performance is poor, or even the result is wrong if the statement isn't built correctly.

PL/SQL provides two ways to write dynamic SQL: using native dynamic SQL and using the DBMS_SQL package. Native dynamic SQL is typically easier to read and write, and it usually performs faster than the equivalent code using the DBMS_SQL package. However, if you do not know the number of input and output parameters and their data types for the dynamic SQL statement, you must use the DBMS_SQL package instead. Also, if you want a stored subprogram to return a query result implicitly (not through an **out ref cursor** parameter), you must use the DBMS_SQL package because it would need the **dbms_sql.return_result** procedure. However, native dynamic SQL must be used instead of the DBMS_SQL package if the dynamic SQL statement retrieves rows into records, or if you need to use any of the SQL cursor attributes %FOUND, %ISOPEN, %NOTFOUND, or %ROWCOUNT after issuing a dynamic SQL statement of INSERT, UPDATE, DELETE, or MERGE. If you are using both the DBMS_SQL package and native dynamic SQL, you can switch between them using the **dbms_sql.to_refcursor** function and the **dbms_sql.to_cursor_number** function, which will be introduced later in this chapter.

Using Native Dynamic SQL

Most of the time, native dynamic SQL uses the EXECUTE IMMEDIATE statement to process dynamic SQL statements. But if the dynamic SQL statement is a SELECT statement that returns multiple rows, native dynamic SQL can be written using either an EXECUTE IMMEDIATE statement with the BULK COLLECT INTO clause or an OPEN FOR, FETCH, or CLOSE statement. Note that in native dynamic SQL INSERT, UPDATE, DELETE, MERGE, and single-row SELECT statements, the SQL cursor attributes work the same way they work with static SQL. You can read more about cursors in Chapter 3.

EXECUTE IMMEDIATE is the most common way of writing native dynamic SQL. It is easy to both read and write, and it usually performs better than the more complex identical solution using DBMS_SQL package.

If you are writing DDL or DML without bind variables, the simplest way of writing dynamic SQL (using the EXECUTE IMMEDIATE string) can be employed. You simply create a string variable that will hold the SQL clause:

```
V_String VARCHAR2(3000) := 'SELECT '||columnname||
' FROM '||tablename||' WHERE '||whereclause;
```

Using PL/SQL, you add the other elements of the SQL clause when you get them (probably using concatenation), and finally you have the whole SQL clause in your variable (V_String):

```
'SELECT ename FROM Emp WHERE empno = 7782'
```

Then you can execute the dynamic SQL clause:

```
EXECUTE IMMEDIATE V_String;
```

For example, suppose we want a procedure that creates a yearly SALES table. The procedure (**create_y_sales**) has the year as an input parameter:

```
CREATE OR REPLACE PROCEDURE Create_Y_Sales (V_Year NUMBER) IS
V_String VARCHAR2(2000);
V_Columns VARCHAR2(1000);
BEGIN
V_String := 'CREATE TABLE Sales_';
V_Columns := '(product_id NUMBER(16) NOT NULL,
customer_id NUMBER(16) NOT NULL,
time_id  DATE NOT NULL,
quantity_sold  NUMBER(10) NOT NULL,
amount_sold NUMBER(15,2) NOT NULL)';
V_String := V_String||To_Char(V_Year)||' '||V_Columns;
DBMS_OUTPUT.PUT_LINE(V_String);
EXECUTE IMMEDIATE V_String;
END;
/
```

NOTE
The SQL clause should not have a semicolon at the end because EXECUTE IMMEDIATE will automatically add it when the query is executed.

Let's call procedure **create_y_sales** with an input parameter of **2016**:

```
set serveroutput on
exec create_y_sales(2016);
```

Our example would generate a SQL clause like this:

```
CREATE TABLE Sales_2016
(product_id NUMBER(16) NOT NULL,
customer_id NUMBER(16) NOT NULL,
time_id  DATE NOT NULL,
quantity_sold  NUMBER(10) NOT NULL,
amount_sold NUMBER(15,2) NOT NULL)
```

Also, the table (SALES_2016) has been created:

```
DESC Sales_2016
Name            Null      Type
-------------   --------  -----------
PRODUCT_ID      NOT NULL  NUMBER(16)
CUSTOMER_ID     NOT NULL  NUMBER(16)
TIME_ID         NOT NULL  DATE
QUANTITY_SOLD   NOT NULL  NUMBER(10)
AMOUNT_SOLD     NOT NULL  NUMBER(15,2)
```

NOTE
*Dynamic DDL can also be performed using the **exec_ddl_statement**
procedure in the DBMS_UTILITY package—for example, **dbms_utility**
.exec_ddl_statement(v_string). However, we recommend using
EXECUTE IMMEDIATE because it is very easy to use, newer, and has
not been deprecated.*

If you are writing a query with a fixed number of expressions in the SELECT list, use the
following syntax:

```
EXECUTE IMMEDIATE v_string INTO
```

In this example, we query one column (ename) from the EMP table that has **empno = 7782**,
and we use INTO to assign the column value to a variable (**v_ename**). We couldn't do this if we
didn't know the number (and the data types) of the elements in the SELECT list.

```
DECLARE
v_ename emp.ename%TYPE;
BEGIN
EXECUTE IMMEDIATE 'SELECT ename FROM EMP WHERE EMPNO = 7782 ' INTO v_ename;
DBMS_OUTPUT.put_line(v_ename);
END;
/
Result:
CLARK
```

If the dynamic SQL statement is a SELECT statement that returns multiple rows, you can either
use the EXECUTE IMMEDIATE statement with the BULK COLLECT INTO clause or use the OPEN
FOR, FETCH, and CLOSE statements. If you use OPEN, FOR FETCH, and CLOSE, first use the

OPEN FOR statement to associate a cursor variable with the dynamic SQL statement, and then in the USING clause specify a bind variable for each placeholder in the dynamic SQL statement. The USING clause cannot contain the literal NULL because NULL is often a problem in relational databases and SQL, as discussed in Chapter 1. You can then use the FETCH statement to retrieve result set rows either one at a time (**into_clause**), several at a time (**bulk_collect_into_clause** and **define LIMIT numeric_expression**), or all at once (**omit LIMIT numeric_expression**). Finally, you use the CLOSE statement to close the cursor variable. In Chapter 3, we discussed cursors in more detail.

The EXECUTE IMMEDIATE statement with the BULK COLLECT INTO clause is much easier to use. Let's see the same example but now we use a nested table variable and use BULK COLLECT INTO to fetch the result of the query. Then we print out the name of the third element in that collection.

```
DECLARE
TYPE emp_nt_type IS TABLE OF emp%ROWTYPE;
v_emp_nt emp_nt_type;
BEGIN
EXECUTE IMMEDIATE 'SELECT * FROM EMP' BULK COLLECT INTO v_emp_nt;
DBMS_OUTPUT.put_line(v_emp_nt(3).ename);
END;
/
```

```
Result:
MILLER
```

If you are writing a query and you know the number of bind variables (the WHERE part of the SQL clause), use the syntax **EXECUTE IMMEDIATE v_string USING**. Here is the same example as the previous one, except that now we find the row with **empno = 7782** by using a placeholder (**:empno**) and, after the keyword USING, the value that will be assigned to the placeholder:

```
DECLARE
l_emp emp%ROWTYPE;
BEGIN
EXECUTE IMMEDIATE 'SELECT * FROM EMP WHERE EMPNO = :empno ' INTO l_emp USING 7782;
DBMS_OUTPUT.put_line(l_emp.ename);
END;
/
```

```
Result:
CLARK
```

If the dynamic SQL statement includes placeholders for bind variables, each placeholder must have a corresponding bind variable in the appropriate USING clause of the EXECUTE IMMEDIATE statement. If the dynamic SQL statement does not represent an anonymous PL/SQL block or a CALL statement, placeholders are associated with bind variables in the USING clause by *position*, not by name. To associate the same bind variable with each occurrence of that placeholder, you must repeat the bind variable. Here's an example:

```
EXECUTE IMMEDIATE V_SQL USING x, x, y, x
```

If the dynamic SQL statement represents an anonymous PL/SQL block or a CALL statement, the bind variable *name* is used to associate it with a placeholder, and there is no need to repeat the bind variable:

```
EXECUTE IMMEDIATE V_SQL USING x, y
```

Each unique placeholder name must have a corresponding bind variable in the USING clause.

Dynamic SQL supports all the SQL data types, but it does not support PL/SQL-specific types (for instance, BOOLEAN). The only exception is a PL/SQL record that can appear in the INTO clause.

To me personally, the most complex use of dynamic SQL was a case when end users were given a chance to create their own queries dynamically on an Oracle Forms user interface. We created a table that contained information about the tables and columns that were allowed (and possibly needed) to be used in the query. We had three variables on the PL/SQL code: **v_select**, **v_from**, and **v_where**. In the user interface, the user selected the tables and the columns he or she wanted to add to the query and then set the criteria for them. For instance, in the table CUSTOMER, the number of children must be > 0 and the customer must be interested in cooking. The end user was able to define several criteria and also define either "and" or "or" between all those different criteria, and the program created the SQL clause based on the user's selection. After that, the dynamic SQL clause was built based on the selection and the knowledge we had on the criteria table. In the criteria table, we had information on how tables should be joined in the **v_where** variable, for instance. Quite soon we realized that sometimes the queries were fast and sometimes they were extremely slow, and that was confusing to the end users. We then decided to add hints to queries to keep the response times about the same, and we added a new variable called **v_hint**. Also, that was during Oracle Database 8*i*, when the optimizer was not as good as it is today.

You can use this same technique for dynamic PL/SQL blocks. The block must be a valid anonymous block in order to be executed with EXECUTE IMMEDIATE. Note that the dynamic PL/SQL block must end with a semicolon (;). Otherwise, it's parsed as a SQL statement. As mentioned earlier, the placeholders are referenced by the bind variable names, so there is no need to mention those names more than once. When there is a clear pattern in the code, dynamic PL/SQL might be useful.

Regardless of what you use dynamic SQL for, make sure you are systematic in building the logic and test each phase of it. My advice is that you test it much more than you generally test your SQL. Test it as a whole, but also test each piece of the code separately. Usually it helps if you build static logic first and then convert it to dynamic. During development time, use DBMS_OUTPUT to pass out the generated dynamic SQL so that, when any issues arise, you can see the whole statement and potentially execute it.

Using the DBMS_SQL Package

The DBMS_SQL package has been part of the Oracle Database for a very long time, starting with Oracle Database release 7. Before the introduction of native dynamic SQL in release 8*i* of Oracle Database, it was the only way to execute SQL that was built at run time, as opposed to compile time. Most of the time native dynamic SQL will be sufficient, but in certain situations, DBMS_SQL is the only way to solve a problem. Returning implicit result sets to a client application is one such occasion.

Interacting with REF CURSORS is a lot easier than working with DBMS_SQL cursors. REF CURSORS can be opened for a SELECT statement, fetched from, and then closed when you are done. DBMS_SQL cursors need to be opened, variables bound, statements executed, and finally closed.

When you have worked with DBMS_SQL, you will recognize this. Oracle Database 11*g* enhanced the DBMS_SQL package with functionality that allows you to switch between a DBMS_SQL cursor and a REF CURSOR, and vice versa.

Returning a Result Set to the Client

Several client programming languages can consume result sets from the database and show their contents. In the past, the only option when dealing with an Oracle database was the REF CURSOR. The database programmer had to create an output argument with the data type REF CURSOR, or a function returning a REF CURSOR. This REF CURSOR could then be consumed by the client application. This type of result set is called an *explicit result set*. It is explicit because you know that when you interact with the procedure or function, there is a result set (that is, the REF CURSOR), and you can describe the structure of the result set.

Other databases have implemented what is called an *implicit result set*. When you are calling a program that returns an implicit result set, the number of result sets or the structure is not known until execution time.

Suppose there is a client application that interacts with a non-Oracle database and relies on the implicit result set. If the database would change to an Oracle Database, the client application would have to be rewritten so it can handle REF CURSORs. Therefore, instead of "just" replacing the database code, you would also have to change the client code.

To ease the migration to an Oracle Database, implicit result sets are supported in the DMBS_SQL package with release 12*c*. Returning an implicit result set from PL/SQL will ease the migration because now the client-side application does not have to be modified; it will already know how to handle the implicit result sets. When you introduce REF CURSORs, the client application will need to be rewritten in order to handle the explicit result sets.

NOTE
The following code snippets are executed using SQL*Plus 12. Previous releases of SQL*Plus can't handle implicit result sets. When you attempt to execute the code using an older release of SQL*Plus, the following exception is raised:
ORA-29481: Implicit results cannot be returned to client.

In the following example, a stand-alone procedure is created, which can return two implicit result sets—one for the department table (DEPT) and one for the employee table (EMP). The procedure accepts two arguments. The first argument is the department number that needs to be returned; this argument is mandatory. The second argument is a boolean indicating whether the employee data also needs to be returned.

```
create or replace
procedure show_dept_emps (p_deptno    in number
                         ,p_show_emps in boolean := true
                         )
is
   l_rc sys_refcursor;
begin
   open l_rc
   for
   select deptno
```

```
        ,dname
        ,loc
    from dept
   where deptno = p_deptno;
  dbms_sql.return_result(l_rc);
  if p_show_emps
  then
      open l_rc
      for
      select empno
            ,ename
            ,job
            ,sal
        from emp
       where deptno = p_deptno
      ;
      dbms_sql.return_result (l_rc);
   end if;
end show_dept_emps;
/
```

Because the **return_result** procedure is overloaded in the DBMS_SQL package, it is possible to use a REF CURSOR to open the initial cursor, as shown in the previous code sample. However, this can also be accomplished using **dbms_sql.open_cursor**.

A cursor that is opened using DBMS_SQL returns an integer that can be referenced when working with other DBMS_SQL procedures and functions.

Executing the previous procedure yields the following results:

```
begin
    show_dept_emps (p_deptno => 10);
end;
/
ResultSet #1
    DEPTNO DNAME            LOC
---------- -------------- -------------
        10 ACCOUNTING      NEW YORK

ResultSet #2
    EMPNO ENAME        JOB              SAL
---------- ---------- --------- ----------
      7782 CLARK       MANAGER         2450
      7839 KING        PRESIDENT       5000
      7934 MILLER      CLERK           1300
```

As you can see in the this output, two result sets are returned.

When the second argument is set to **false**, only the departmental information is returned, as shown in the following example:

```
begin
    show_dept_emps (p_deptno    => 10
                   ,p_show_emps => false
                   );
```

```
end;
/
ResultSet #1
    DEPTNO DNAME          LOC
---------- -------------- --------------
        10 ACCOUNTING     NEW YORK
```

Calling an Implicit Result Set from PL/SQL

The previous section discussed implicit result sets. Most of the time these procedures will be called from a client application. However, it is possible to call these procedures from PL/SQL as well. To illustrate this functionality, we will use the following procedure, which returns an implicit result set based on the DEPT table for a specific department number (deptno):

```
create or replace
procedure show_dept (p_deptno in number)
is
    l_rc sys_refcursor;
begin
    open l_rc
    for
    select deptno
         ,dname
         ,loc
      from dept
     where deptno = p_deptno;
    dbms_sql.return_result(l_rc);
end show_dept;
/
```

To call this procedure from PL/SQL and process the results from the implicit result set, we need the PL/SQL code to act as the client for the results. This can be done using the DBMS_SQL package when you open a cursor. The **open_cursor** function has an argument called **treat_as_client_for_results**, which defaults to FALSE.

The cursor is opened immediately after beginning the anonymous block, with the **treat_as_client_for_results** argument set to TRUE:

```
declare
   l_sql_cursor       integer;
   l_rows_processed   number;
   l_ref_cursor       sys_refcursor;
   l_deptno           number;
   l_dname            varchar2(20);
   l_loc              varchar2(20);
begin
   l_sql_cursor := dbms_sql.open_cursor
           (treat_as_client_for_results => true);
   dbms_sql.parse(c              => l_sql_cursor
               ,statement       => 'begin show_dept(:p_deptno); end;'
               ,language_flag => dbms_sql.native
               );
```

```
      dbms_sql.bind_variable (c      => l_sql_cursor
                             ,name  => 'p_deptno'
                             ,value => 10
                             );
      l_rows_processed := dbms_sql.execute (c => l_sql_cursor);
      dbms_sql.get_next_result (c  => l_sql_cursor
                               ,rc => l_ref_cursor
                               );
      fetch l_ref_cursor into l_deptno
                             ,l_dname
                             ,l_loc;
      dbms_output.put_line ('Department Number: '|| to_char (l_deptno));
      dbms_output.put_line ('Department Name   : '|| l_dname);
      dbms_output.put_line ('Location          : '|| l_loc);
      close l_ref_cursor;
      dbms_sql.close_cursor (c => l_sql_cursor);
end;
/
```

After the cursor has been opened, the parse phase is initiated using the statement to call the previously created procedure. A bind variable value is set using the **bind_variable** procedure, and the argument **p_deptno** is set to **10**.

Opening a cursor using the DBMS_SQL package will return an integer. This integer will need to be passed to the other procedures and functions when interacting with the cursor. Instead of having Oracle do all the work for you when you run a static SQL statement (such as opening, binding, and fetching), now you will need to take care of that.

Next, the execute phase is called in order to execute the anonymous block call to the procedure. The implicit result set is fetched by calling **get_next_result** (from the DBMS_SQL package). The implicit result set is placed in the **out** parameter, called **l_ref_cursor**.

Now that the implicit result set is retrieved from the procedure, you can process the REF_CURSOR the usual way. Fetch from the REF_CURSOR, and don't forget to close it after you're done with it.

Executing the previous anonymous block yields the following results (with SERVEROUTPUT on in SQL*Plus):

```
Department Number: 10
Department Name   : ACCOUNTING
Location          : NEW YORK
```

The DBMS_SQL.TO_REFCURSOR Function

Returning a REF CURSOR to a client application can create a very flexible application. The **dbms_sql.to_refcursor** function converts a SQL cursor number to a weak cursor variable, which can be used in native dynamic SQL statements. The following function will return a REF CURSOR with data from the EMPLOYEES table in the HR schema. The arguments allow the user to specify which departments should be returned as well as which columns should be returned.

```
create or replace
function emps (p_department_id in number
              ,p_cols          in varchar2
```

```
                 )
     return sys_refcursor
is
     l_sql      varchar2(32767);
     l_cursor   binary_integer;
     l_execute binary_integer;
begin
     l_sql := 'select '
               ||p_cols
               ||' from employees '
               ||'where department_id = :department_id';
     l_cursor := dbms_sql.open_cursor;
     dbms_sql.parse (c               => l_cursor
                    ,statement       => l_sql
                    ,language_flag => dbms_sql.native
                    );
     dbms_sql.bind_variable (c     => l_cursor
                            ,name  => 'department_id'
                            ,value => p_department_id
                            );
     l_execute := dbms_sql.execute (c => l_cursor);
     return dbms_sql.to_refcursor (cursor_number => l_cursor);
end emps;
/
```

After the declaration of all the necessary variables, the beginning of the executable section starts by building the SQL statement. The column names are passed in an argument; these are concatenated right after the SELECT keyword. The other argument passes in the **department_id** to be queried. This argument is not concatenated, of course, to prevent SQL injection.

The DBMS_SQL cursor is opened and parsed, and the incoming argument is used as a bind variable. Before the REF CURSOR can be returned, the DBMS_SQL cursor will need to be executed. Not executing the DBMS_SQL cursor will lead to an exception at run time:

```
ORA-01001: invalid cursor
```

The last part of the function is where the DBMS_SQL cursor is transformed into a REF CURSOR.

SQL*Plus knows how to handle a weakly typed REF CURSOR, and it's ideally suited to demonstrate the previous function. First, a variable of the REF CURSOR type needs to be declared:

```
var rc refcursor
```

Next, the function can be called using the declared RC variable:

```
begin
     :rc := emps (100, 'first_name, last_name, email');
end;
/

PL/SQL procedure successfully completed.
```

Now that the procedure has executed successfully, we can inspect the RC variable by using the PRINT command, which will show the contents of the REF CURSOR:

```
print rc

FIRST_NAME            LAST_NAME                 EMAIL
-------------------   ----------------------    -------------------------
Nancy                 Greenberg                 NGREENBE
Daniel                Faviet                    DFAVIET
John                  Chen                      JCHEN
Ismael                Sciarra                   ISCIARRA
Jose Manuel           Urman                     JMURMAN
Luis                  Popp                      LPOPP

6 rows selected.
```

Let's run the statement again, but this time with different arguments:

```
begin
    :rc := emps (30, 'last_name, phone_number');
end;

PL/SQL procedure successfully completed.

SQL> print

LAST_NAME                  PHONE_NUMBER
------------------------   --------------------
Raphaely                   515.127.4561
Khoo                       515.127.4562
Baida                      515.127.4563
Tobias                     515.127.4564
Himuro                     515.127.4565
Colmenares                 515.127.4566

6 rows selected.
```

The DBMS_SQL.TO_CURSOR_NUMBER Function

REF CURSORs are easier to work with than the DBMS_SQL cursor: simply construct your SQL statement, and you can fetch from the REF CURSOR. However, it is not possible to describe the columns that make up the SQL statement of the REF CURSOR. With DBMS_SQL you can describe the cursor. The **dbms_sql.to_cursor_number** function converts a REF CURSOR variable to a SQL cursor number, which can be passed to DBMS_SQL subprograms, thus making it easy to get a description of the structure of the SQL statement.

The anonymous block shown next declares local variables, as well as a few helper procedures, as wrappers for DBMS_OUTPUT, and it describes a record returned from the **dbms_sql.describe_columns3** procedure:

```
declare
    rc sys_refcursor;
    --
    l_cursorid         number;
    l_column_count     integer;
    l_describe_table dbms_sql.desc_tab3;
    --
    l_sql_stmt         varchar2(32767);
    --
    procedure p (p_text in varchar2)
    is
    begin
       dbms_output.put_line (p_text);
    end p;
    --
    procedure p (p_text1 in varchar2
                ,p_text2 in varchar2)
    is
    begin
       p (rpad (p_text1, 13)||': '||p_text2);
    end p;
    --
    procedure print_rec (p_rec in dbms_sql.desc_rec3)
    is
    begin
       p ('-------------------');
       p ('col_type', p_rec.col_type);
       p ('col_maxlen',p_rec.col_max_len);
       p ('col_name',p_rec.col_name);
       p ('col_precision',p_rec.col_precision);
       p ('col_scale',p_rec.col_scale);
       p ('type name',p_rec.col_type_name);
       p ('type name len',p_rec.col_type_name_len);
    end print_rec;
    --
begin
    open rc for 'select * from countries';
    l_cursorid := dbms_sql.to_cursor_number (rc);

    dbms_sql.describe_columns3 (c        => l_cursorid
                               ,col_cnt => l_column_count
                               ,desc_t  => l_describe_table
                               );

    for i in 1..l_describe_table.count
    loop
       print_rec (l_describe_table(i));
    end loop;

    dbms_sql.close_cursor( l_cursorid );

end;
```

In the executable section of the anonymous block, a REF CURSOR is opened for a query against the COUNTRIES table (it resides in the HR schema, which is a sample schema).

Next, the REF CURSOR is converted to a DBMS_SQL cursor with the **dbms_sql.to_cursor_number** function, which returns the unique ID for the created DBMS_SQL cursor.

DBMS_SQL has three procedures that allow you to describe the columns of the cursor: **describe_columns**, **describe_columns2**, and **describe_columns3**. The main difference between **describe_columns** and **describe_columns2** is the OUT arguments. The first procedure will return a collection of the DESC_REC record, whereas the latter returns a collection of DESC_REC2 records. One of the fields contains the name of the column, which in the DESC_REC record is limited to 32 characters, whereas the DESC_REC2 record can hold up to 32,767 characters. Because of the limitation of 32 characters, the DESC_REC record has been deprecated, thereby deprecating the DESC_TAB collection and the **describe_columns** procedure.

The **describe_columns3** procedure has two additional fields: **type name** and **col_type_name_len** for describing object types and nested table types. In this example, it is not strictly necessary to use the **describe_columns3** procedure because the **describe_columns2** will suffice.

After we get the description for the callout to the **descirbe_columns3** procedure, a helper procedure is used to print out each of the columns. The output from that procedure is listed here:

```
-------------------
col_type       : 96
col_maxlen     : 2
col_name       : COUNTRY_ID
col_precision: 0
col_scale      : 0
type name      :
type name len: 0
-------------------
col_type       : 1
col_maxlen     : 40
col_name       : COUNTRY_NAME
col_precision: 0
col_scale      : 0
type name      :
type name len: 0
-------------------
col_type       : 2
col_maxlen     : 22
col_name       : REGION_ID
col_precision: 0
col_scale      : -127
type name      :
type name len: 0

PL/SQL procedure successfully completed.
```

Finally, the cursor is closed. Note that the cursor that needs to be closed is of the DBMS_SQL cursor type, not the REF CURSOR type, simply because the REF CURSOR was converted to the DBMS_SQL cursor. As you can see from the previous output, it is trivial to transform a REF CURSOR to a DBMS_SQL cursor and investigate the structure of the cursor.

Summary

Dynamic SQL can be used when the elements of the query are only known during run time. There are two ways of performing dynamic SQL: using native dynamic SQL and using the DBMS_SQL package. Dynamic SQL should only be used as a last resort and when static SQL is not enough. With dynamic SQL, there are always risks related to performance, security, privileges, and events. Because dynamic SQL is compiled at run time, you might even encounter a situation where the statement might not even run at all because of compilation errors. Bottom line: use dynamic SQL with caution.

CHAPTER
9

PL/SQL for Automation and Administration

T his chapter is all about what PL/SQL has to offer to those of us who administer databases and automate tasks—and it offers us a lot. PL/SQL can help us have easier jobs with less drudgery, leaving us more time for the more interesting, complex parts of our working lives.

The lack of the acronym DBA in the chapter's title is significant. There is a lot here that we hope DBAs will find helpful, but much of it is also of use to PL/SQL developers. Writing tools and utilities in PL/SQL can make the life of a production DBA a lot easier, and a lot of traditionally DBA-type tasks can be achieved with PL/SQL built-ins. Many PL/SQL built-ins may be looked upon as being "DBA specific" but can be a boon to developers. We are going to cover three main topics with respect to using PL/SQL for database administration:

- Using PL/SQL for quick scripts and tasks
- Using PL/SQL to control administrative or batch tasks
- PL/SQL built-ins for database administration

The first section is a gentle start, more to indicate some real-world situations where PL/SQL has been a boon in the DBA role and highlight why we feel PL/SQL is an invaluable skill for DBAs as well as developers.

In the second section we describe an architecture used for automating batch and administrative tasks—the sort of thing both DBAs and developers are often asked to do. "Architecture" is a bit of a grand title to use for this because the set of tables and concepts we cover are all fairly simple, but they are the result of the lead author of this chapter having to do this sort of thing for 25 years and having devised a way of doing it that works, is pragmatic, and is pretty easy to perform. This discussion ties in well with Chapter 7.

In the final section of this chapter we describe and demonstrate some of the less-well-known PL/SQL built-ins that can help a DBA or server-side developer do their job more easily. With each version of Oracle, more and more packages are introduced and some of the existing ones are improved. We could spend several hundred pages covering a multitude of them, but we will limit ourselves to a selection that we personally have found helpful and/or that fill a common need but are not generally covered in depth in other sources.

The DBA/Developer Divisive Divide

The DBA/developer "divide" is a curious one. None of the authors of this book sign up to this traditional division between the two camps. All of us have been or are developers, and all of us are or have been database administrators or database designers.

Obviously there are people who are developers and there are people who are DBAs. Most large organizations have dedicated teams with these labels, and people are often hired as one or the other. But there really need not be such a divide, and certainly the antagonism you get between them (for example, "the DBAs won't let us developers do that" or "the developers messed it up again") is of no benefit. The terms *developer* and *DBA* are more like the opposite ends of the spectrum that is the database professional. What we are sure of is this: if Oracle is a database you work with, then PL/SQL is very beneficial at both ends of the spectrum.

PL/SQL and the DBA

A while back there was an article on one of our blogs titled "Do good DBAs need PL/SQL skills?" This was prompted by a discussion between members of the OakTable network and other Oracle experts. The general consensus was that you can be a very good production DBA without PL/SQL. In fact, installing Oracle, backup and recovery, user maintenance, and all the day-to-day tasks that take up most DBAs' time can be done without PL/SQL, especially with modern database management tools. But there is always a need to do tasks that a program can either simplify or even automate, and pretty much all DBAs know how to program in something—be it shell script, C, or Java. However, PL/SQL is the ideal language for an Oracle DBA for two main reasons:

- PL/SQL's sole purpose is to control SQL, to add the procedural element that SQL lacks. Unlike other programing languages, it is fully aware of and integrated with Oracle's SQL, recognizing all SQL data types and offering almost all the same functions as SQL.

- If there is an Oracle Database, then PL/SQL is always available—and with the exception of new versions introducing new features, it works the same in all Oracle Databases. Shell scripting comes in many flavors and what programming languages are available to you on a server vary from site to site, even sometimes from server to server. Most of us change employers at some point. Given that you still work with Oracle, PL/SQL will be there, whereas other languages and flavors of Unix/Linux may or may not be used at your new workplace.

The thing we all agreed on was that if you were a DBA and did not know PL/SQL, learning it would make you a better DBA. If you are a DBA reading this, then we are probably preaching to the choir, given that you are reading a book on SQL and PL/SQL! We hope this book helps.

The next section highlights how even some basic PL/SQL expertise can help in administering databases.

Simple Task-Specific PL/SQL Scripts

PL/SQL allows you to do some things with the database that are either harder to do with just SQL or are almost impossible. When you are administering databases, especially if you do not have access to OEM, Grid Control, or a similar administration tool (sometimes you don't have them, and sometimes the agent is down or not installed on a server and you need to do something to the database *now*), then sometimes SQL and PL/SQL are all you have at hand.

Access to the Data Dictionary Views

Most of the scripts in this section access data dictionary views. If you want to try the scripts, you will need access to these views. The simplest way to see them is to have the system privilege SELECT ANY DICTIONARY granted to your user. When I act as a DBA, this is a system privilege I am happy for developers to have—strictly speaking it allows some things to be seen that can compromise security, such as the code for functions used by VPD, but it does not allow anyone to see data. The more information that developers can see about the objects in the database, the better job they can do, which in turn allows them to learn the more "database-y" things.

Investigating LONGs with PL/SQL

This first example involves a perennial problem that will not go away—searching LONGs. LONG data types are not deprecated; however, the Oracle 12*c* Database SQL Language Reference states the following:

> Do not create tables with LONG columns. Use LOB columns (CLOB, NCLOB, BLOB) instead. LONG columns are supported only for backward compatibility.

And yet, there they are in the data dictionary tables. Even in Oracle 12*c*, there are lots of LONGs in the data dictionary. LONGs cannot appear in SQL built-in functions, expressions, or conditions. Therefore, the following fails with an error:

```
select owner,view_name,text
from dba_views where text like '%PERSON%'

from dba_views where text like '%PERSON%'
                 *
ERROR at line 2:
ORA-00932: inconsistent datatypes: expected CHAR got LONG
```

But you want to be able to search such structures at times. For example, suppose you know there is a view on the PERSON table that shows people who are legally children. This view has a slight issue, so you want to find it. You suspect you could look for "-16" (the number of years in age many countries use to define a child) in the view. What do you do? You use PL/SQL, as shown next. (Note that the PERSON table is a demonstration table created with code you can download for this chapter and is part of the same demonstration set of tables used in Chapters 6 and 7.)

```
-- this creates out test view we want to find
create or replace view pers_children
as select * from person
where dob > add_months(trunc(sysdate),12*-16)


-- show_vw_txt
set serveroutput on
declare
v_name varchar2(4000) :='&viewname';
v_search varchar2(100) :='&search_txt';
cursor get_vw_txt is
select vw.owner owner, vw.view_name name, vw.text_length textlen, vw.text text
from all_views vw
where vw.view_name     like upper(nvl(v_name,'%')||'%')
and    vw.text_length <32767; -- anything beyond 32K is silently truncated
                              -- don't show such long text as a 'warning'
v_text varchar2(32767);
v_where number;
begin
  v_name :=upper (v_name);
  v_search := upper(v_search);
  for vtr in get_vw_txt loop
    v_text := upper(vtr.text);      v_where := instr(v_text,v_search);
```

```
    if v_where !=0 then
      dbms_output.put_line('view '||vtr.owner||'.'||vtr.name||':** '
                            ||substr(v_text,greatest(0,v_where),80)||' **'  );
      dbms_output.put_line(vtr.text);
    end if;
  end loop;
end;


--
@show_vw_txt
Enter value for viewname: %
Enter value for search_txt: -16
view MDW9.PERS_CHILDREN:** -16) **
select
"PERS_ID","SURNAME","FIRST_FORENAME","SECOND_FORENAME","PERS_TITLE","SEX_IND"
,"DOB","ADDR_ID","STAFF_IND","LAST_CONTACT_
ID","PERS_COMMENT" from person
where dob > add_months(trunc(sysdate),12*-16)

PL/SQL procedure successfully completed.
```

Without PL/SQL, you would have struggled to find the view if the text you wanted was more than 4000 characters in (in which case the column TEXT_VC could be used). With PL/SQL you can work with LONGs, at least up to the first 32K of them, and that covers 99 percent of situations. Our code specifically ignores such large views, but the other option would be to raise an application error.

Complex SQL or Simple PL/SQL: Identifying SQL with Identical Execution Plans

The next example is a script to show different SQL statements with the same execution plan. This is often due to missing bind variables or "the same" code being written in several places. Although it is possible to perform this example in straight SQL, as the comments in the code say, "at that point I figured a simple PL/SQL query is better." The code is quite long but really is very simple:

```
-- show_same_plan.sql
-- pull out a set of statements where the plan is massively shared
-- (on the system this was built for, this is over 100 sql statements)
-- Use pl/sql as otherwise I would have to use an analytical function in the
-- inline query to limit the join back to v$sqlarea on... but at that point
-- I figure a simple PL/SQL query is better
accept match_size number def 99 prompt 'number of statements with same plan(99) '
accept samp_no number def 5 prompt 'number of example statements to show(5) '
accept samp_size number def 100 prompt 'number of chars of samples to show(100) '
declare
v_match_size number :=&match_size;   v_samp_no   number :=&samp_no;
v_samp_size  number :=&samp_size;   v_tot       number :=0;
cursor get_matches(p_size number) is
    select
```

```
           min(substr(first_load_time,4,16)) frst_load_time
        ,count(*)          occ      ,inst_id            inst_id
        ,plan_hash_value   p_hash   ,sum(parse_calls)   prse
        ,SUM(EXECUTIONS)   exec     ,sum(buffer_gets)   buffs
        ,sum(disk_reads)   discs    ,sum(rows_processed) rws
    from gv$sqlarea
    where parsing_schema_id !='0'
    group by plan_hash_value,inst_id
    having (count(*) > v_match_size        or
           sum(buffer_gets)>500000 and count(*)>greatest (v_match_size/2,5)  )
    order by inst_id asc,occ desc,buffs desc;
cursor get_tots is
select inst_id,count(*) r_count
from gv$sqlarea
group by inst_id;
cursor get_examples (p_hash     number        ,p_inst_id number
                    ,p_no       number        ,p_size    number) is
select substr(sql_text,1,p_size) found_text
from gv$sqlarea
where plan_hash_value =p_hash
and inst_id = p_inst_id        and rownum <= p_no;
v_inst_id number :=0;
begin
  v_match_size :=nvl(v_match_size,100);       v_samp_size  :=nvl(v_samp_size,5);
  v_samp_no    :=nvl(v_samp_no,200);
  dbms_output.put_line ('starting at '||to_char(sysdate,'hh24:mi:ss DD-MM-YY'));
  for tots_rec in get_tots loop
    dbms_output.put_line('Instance '||to_char(tots_rec.inst_id)
                   ||' total cursors '||to_char(tots_rec.r_count));
    v_tot:=v_tot+tots_rec.r_count;
  end loop;
  dbms_output.put_line('total for all instances '||to_char(v_tot));
  for mat_rec in get_matches (v_match_size) loop
    if v_inst_id != mat_rec.inst_id -- and it won't if v_inst_id is null at start
    then
      dbms_output.put_line (lpad('+',80,'+'));
    end if;
    dbms_output.put_line (lpad ('-',80,'-'));
    dbms_output.put_line (to_char(mat_rec.inst_id)||' - '
              ||to_char(mat_rec.p_hash)||' - '||mat_rec.frst_load_time);
    dbms_output.put_line (mat_rec.occ||' occurrences, ' ||mat_rec.prse ||' prse, '
               ||mat_rec.exec ||' executes, ' ||mat_rec.buffs||' buff gets, '
               ||mat_rec.discs||' disc, '      ||mat_rec.rws ||' rows');
    v_inst_id:=mat_rec.inst_id;
    for ex_rec in get_examples(mat_rec.p_hash   ,mat_rec.inst_id
                          ,v_samp_no           ,v_samp_size) loop
      dbms_output.put_line (ex_rec.found_text);
    end loop;
  end loop;
  dbms_output.put_line('ending');
end;
```

We ran this code on our test system just as a quick demonstration, having run some very similar SQL for it to find:

```
@show_same_plan
number of statements with same plan(99) 5
number of example statements to show(5) 3
number of chars of samples to show(100) 60
starting at 18:33:04 28-02-16
Instance 1 total cursors 1975
total for all instances 1975
++++++++++++++++++++++++++++++++++++++++++++++++++++++++++++++++++++++++++++++++
--------------------------------------------------------------------------------
1 - 2939684812 - 6-02-15/17:01:01
89 occurrences, 4039 prse, 4039 executes, 3368418 buff gets, 0 disc, 4039 rows
SELECT /* DS_SVC */ /*+ dynamic_sampling(0) no_sql_tune no_m
SELECT /* DS_SVC */ /*+ dynamic_sampling(0) no_sql_tune no_m
SELECT /* DS_SVC */ /*+ dynamic_sampling(0) no_sql_tune no_m
--------------------------------------------------------------------------------
1 - 1388734953 - 6-02-16/10:14:22
24 occurrences, 224 prse, 224 executes, 3775 buff gets, 90 disc, 224 rows
select sys_context('USERENV','SESSIONID') from dual
select dbms_utility.get_time         ,dbms_utility.get_time/10
SELECT DECODE('A','A','1','2') FROM DUAL
--------------------------------------------------------------------------------
1 - 1391249417 - 6-02-28/18:30:26
15 occurrences, 15 prse, 15 executes, 249 buff gets, 21 disc, 10 rows
select * from ADDRESS where ADDR_ID = 2365492
select * from ADDRESS where ADDR_ID = 2364792
select * from ADDRESS where ADDR_ID = 2166492
--------------------------------------------------------------------------------
1 - 1154882994 - 6-02-27/12:00:30
8 occurrences, 8 prse, 8 executes, 320367 buff gets, 294638 disc, 8 rows
select count(*) from person where surname LIKE 'JONE%'
select count(*) from person where surname LIKE 'DAS%'
select count(*) from person where surname LIKE 'NICH%'
ending
```

We see (as examples) some internal dynamic sampling code, selects from dual, and some repeated queries against PERSON and ADDRESS that could suggest bind variables are missing.

A Lightweight Tool for Gathering and Preserving Session Stats

This example is from a customer we were working with who had no OEM and no access to ASH (Active Session History) information (this was an old version of Oracle). However, we needed information about the total work that key sessions were doing and how this work was changing over a period of time and/or between sections of an application to help investigate performance issues. We created two tables—one to record when we took snapshots of the session statistics and the other to hold all the session statistics information at that time. Here are the tables:

```
-- cre_sesn
create table sesstat_snap_parent
(sesn_id        number(8) not null
```

```
,sid             number     not null
,snap_ts            timestamp not null
,sesn_comment    varchar2(1000)
, constraint ssp_pk primary key (sesn_id)  )
--
create table sesstat_snap
(sesn_id        number(8)        not null
,sid            number           not null
,statistic#     number
,stat_name      varchar2(64)
,stat_value     number
,snap_ts        timestamp
,snap_comment varchar2(1000)
,constraint sesn_pk primary key (sesn_id,statistic#)  )
--
create index sesn_idx1 on sesstat_snap(sesn_id,stat_name);
create sequence ssp_seq;
```

To populate the tables, we used a very simple PL/SQL package with some procedures to handle the data. Following is the code (slightly simplified from the original version to remove some of the procedures and create a more compact layout for the sake of space) that contains the key procedure to populate the data:

```
--cre_s_snap_pkg.sql
-- simple package to save the session stats.
create or replace package s_snap as
procedure my_snap (p_comment in varchar2);
-- public package variable
pv_me number;
end s_snap;
/
--
create or replace package body s_snap as
-- pv_me is set to your SID the first time you execute this package.
pv_int_test     varchar2(10);
pv_owner        all_tables.owner%type;
--
procedure my_snap (p_comment in varchar2) is
v_sesn_id number;
v_now timestamp;
begin
  select ssp_seq.nextval,systimestamp into v_sesn_id,v_now from dual;
  insert into  sesstat_snap
  ( sesn_id      ,sid      ,statistic#  ,stat_name ,stat_value   ,snap_ts )
  select v_sesn_id     ,vm.sid      ,vm.statistic#
        ,vs.name        ,vm.value   ,v_now
  from v$sesstat  vm      ,v$statname vs
  where vs.statistic#=vm.statistic#
  and vm.sid =pv_me;
  insert into sesstat_snap_parent
  ( sesn_id  ,sid     ,snap_ts  ,sesn_comment)
```

```
   values
   (v_sesn_id ,pv_me  ,v_now    ,p_comment);
   commit;
end;
--
begin
  pv_me :=sys_context('USERENV','SID');
end s_snap;
/
```

We inserted calls to this procedure at key points in the application code. You may be wondering why we have a package variable to get the session's SID rather than use the V$MYSTAT view. The reason is that the code originated on a site that did not have Oracle 10g. Also, selecting from V$MYSTAT takes a latch on the session state, and repeated calls to it can cause performance to suffer. We also had another procedure (not shown) that gathered the information for a stated session ID, and we had several collections running.

We could then look at the history of how various statistics (for example, consistent gets and DB block gets) were increasing. The following shows any statistics that had increased (we also had other, more complex scripts to use analytical functions over the last four or five snaps for a given SID):

```
select ss2.statistic#            stat#  ,ss2.stat_name       stat_name
       ,ss2.stat_value                  ,ss1.stat_value      prev_val
       ,ss2.stat_value-ss1.stat_value diff
from sesstat_snap ss1
   ,sesstat_snap ss2
where ss2.sesn_id=&last_sesn_id
and   ss1.sesn_id = ss2.sesn_id-1
and ss2.statistic#=ss1.statistic#
and (ss2.stat_value-ss1.stat_value)>1
order by ss1.stat_name
```

st#	STAT_NAME	STAT_VALUE	PREV_VAL	DIFF
1007	CCursor + sql area evicted	27	25	2
19	CPU used by this session	18105	18,100	5
18	CPU used when call started	18105	18,100	5
20	DB time	18706	18,694	12
...				
1091	bytes received via SQL*Net from client	24579	16,687	7,892
1090	bytes sent via SQL*Net to client	29611	20,855	8,756
...				
205	commit cleanouts	99114	99,067	47
206	commit cleanouts successfully completed	99109	99,063	46
511	commit txn count during cleanout	5368	5,353	15
132	consistent gets	8458847	8,458,396	451

This was simple to implement with PL/SQL but would have been hard to do with just SQL or using the admin GUI the customer had (a very simple affair; you could see some information, but there was no way to save it).

Even with OEM and ASH in place, this would be a useful way of preserving session stats for a process under investigation.

Handling Database Statistics Rapidly Becoming Stale

During the implementation of a brand-new application we knew that the data volumes in the key tables would explode from empty to holding thousands or hundreds of thousands of records in a small number of days, escalating to millions in anything from a week to a month, depending on the success of the application.

When data volumes in tables increase by an order of magnitude (from 10 records to 100, 100 to 1000, 100,000 to 1 million, that sort of thing) that is very often when execution plans that were performing well start performing very poorly—nested loops slow down at the square of the data volumes, if not worse. The fix is to re-gather object statistics for the larger volumes, allowing the optimizer to make better cost estimates and chose more optimal plans. Once the system had been live for a few weeks, the data volumes would be increasing *as a percentage* in a slow enough way for the automated stats job and our own stats gathering process designed for the very biggest, partitioned tables to handle smoothly.

We knew we would almost certainly hit severe performance problems due to the exploding data, but not *when*—we needed to do something for the time between go-live and the data volumes having built up and become stable.

The solution was simple. A job placed on the PL/SQL DBMS_SCHEDULER to run stats gathering on the key schema each hour for, initially, a week:

```
BEGIN
   DBMS_SCHEDULER.create_job (
      job_name        => 'stats_gather_performance',
      job_type        => 'PLSQL_BLOCK',
      job_action      => 'BEGIN dbms_stats.gather_schema_stats'||
                         '(ownname=>''KEY_SCHEMA'',no_invalidate=>FALSE); END;',
      start_date      => SYSTIMESTAMP,
      repeat_interval => 'freq=hourly; byminute=40; bysecond=0;',
      end_date        => sysdate+7,
      enabled         => TRUE,
      comments        => 'gather stats on this schema every hour until Mon 14th');
END;
/
```

That did the job. We had a couple of "exciting" moments on day 2 or 3 (I forget exactly) when key queries for the main application web pages slowed down, but this job kicked in and re-gathered stats before the code slowed down and got to the point where the response time to the users was unacceptable.

A Flexible Emergency Backup Script via PL/SQL

This is our final example for this section. It is from a few years back, but it exemplifies when some PL/SQL skills can really come in useful. We arrived onsite to carry out a performance review and consult on migrating a database to a new platform. However, within a few hours it became obvious that the customer had no valid backup of their database! They were performing a "full export" that failed every week and had other issues—for example, the export was actually doing schema-level exports, and new schemas with production data had been added in the years since this "backup" was first put in place. We needed a working backup ASAP, and we could not use RMAN at that juncture. To make matters worse, new tablespaces and data files were regularly being added to this system. Therefore, we needed to use the "manual" method of placing each tablespace in backup mode in turn and copying the relevant data files, plus doing a few other tasks. The following code was written in a couple of hours:

```
-- emergency backup
-- Below turns of most sql*plus formatting, column headings and number of rows
set feedback off pagesize 0 heading off verify off timi off
-- Below sets the linesize (must be longer than longest single dos command)
-- whitespace to be trimmed from the output.
set linesize 180 trimspool on
-- Set SQL*Plus user variables used in script
define dir = 'd:\ora_backup\backup'
define fil = '&dir\open_backup_commands.sql'
define spo = '&dir\open_backup_output.lst'
prompt *** Spooling to &fil
set serveroutput on
spool &fil
prompt spool &spo
-- All log files after the below one will be needed for recovery.
prompt alter system switch logfile;;
--PL/SQL script to dump out all files in non-temp tablespaces.
declare
  cursor get_ts is
   select tablespace_name
   from dba_tablespaces
   where contents !='TEMPORARY';
  cursor get_dbf (tn varchar2) is
    select file_name
    from   dba_data_files
    where tablespace_name = tn;
BEGIN
  FOR ct in get_ts loop
  -- put TS in backup mode, make a copy, then put TS back into normal mode
  -- more redo is generated for a tablespace in backup mode so do one at a time
    dbms_output.put_line ('alter tablespace '||ct.tablespace_name
                          || ' begin backup;');
    FOR cd IN get_dbf (ct.tablespace_name) LOOP
      dbms_output.put_line ('host copy '||cd.file_name||' &dir');
-- Below dbms_output must produce a line under the size of "linesize".
      dbms_output.put_line ('host zip -1 -q -T -u '||' &dir\'
        ||ct.tablespace_name||'.zip '||cd.file_name||'');
    END LOOP;
    dbms_output.put_line ('alter tablespace '||ct.tablespace_name
                          ||' end backup;');
  END LOOP;
END;
/
```

```
-- switch log files to give the smallest set needed to recover the database.
prompt alter system switch logfile;;
-- back up the controlfile to a readable version. Goes into the dump dir
prompt alter database backup controlfile to trace;;
-- Now put a binary copy in the backup location
select 'alter database backup controlfile to '''||'&dir'
        ||'\control'||to_char(sysdate,'YMMDD-hh24MI')||'.ora'';' from dual;
--
select 'create pfile=''D:\ora_backup\backup\initXYZ_'
        ||to_char(sysdate,'YMMDD-hh24MI')
        ||'.ora''','from spfile=''D:\ORACLE\PRODUCT\10.2.0\DB_1\DBS\SPFILEXYZ.ORA'';'
from dual;
prompt spool off
spool off;
```

This script did the job for the client; we created a backup and proved it by creating a copy of the database on a second server, opening it, and then verifying it was working. At its core, the code uses a PL/SQL program to create a SQL file to do the backup. And it worked for several months, during which time the customer added new tablespaces and data files. They then moved to RMAN and a much better backup strategy.

NOTE
Do not use the script yourself *to back up your databases without extensively reviewing and testing it. We recommend you use RMAN or some other modern method for carrying out your backups.*

Whether it is a simpler way of getting information out of the data dictionary, setting up a specific gathering of session performance information, a quick and simple scheduling of critical object statistics information gathering, or an emergency backup script, PL/SQL makes all these tasks easier.

Controlling Administrative and Batch Tasks with PL/SQL

There are a lot of administrative tasks that can take up a fair amount of time for a DBA, even on the latest version of Oracle. A classic example is maintaining table and index partitions. Even though Oracle 11*g* introduced interval partitioning with automatic partition creation, either the limits on it prevent you from using it, you have existing partitioned objects to maintain, or you want to extend/alter what Oracle does for you. We have seen many sites where someone has to manually create new partitions or move partition data around each week, month, or whenever someone remembers. Archiving off old data is a similar task in which, whether there are partitions or not, people regularly move data around manually.

These tasks involve a regular and predictable process or set of processes and are ideal for being automated—but often they are not automated because each week or month it takes less time to do the task by hand, so there's less motivation to write something to automate it. You *have* to split off the new partitions or archive off the data but you are really busy and can't afford more than the half a day to do it and check the results. Over the course of a year that is 6 days. You could maybe write an automated system in 6 days—and once the solution is there, if you use it for more than a year, you are saving time overall. Further, once the process is automated it is less likely to go wrong. How many times do we perform a manual task we have done half a dozen times but we get distracted, make a mistake, and then spend even more time sorting things out?

These tasks are in fact very similar to the regular data-loading tasks required for data warehouses (or data lakes, or whatever the current on-trend phrase is) and daily batch processing.

Automating these sorts of tasks consists of two parts:

- Writing the code to do the job (which is often surprisingly easy)
- Writing the controlling framework to run the job (which is often surprisingly more challenging)

A further frustration is that very often, if a task *is* automated, a new controlling framework is written each time. If you implement a flexible controlling framework, however, you do not need to do that—you can write it once and re-use it for all sorts of tasks. Now you are not just saving 6 days over the course of a year but maybe 3 or 4 times that.

Our intention here is to give you a framework for the second part of the task—the thing that keeps getting reinvented but is really the bit that stays the same. The design is based on many years of writing such frameworks and trying different flavors and approaches. There are generally two extremes of automating tasks: the "trying to throw a solution together in a day" and the "all-singing, all-dancing solution developed over a month (or more)." Oddly enough, the "in a day" solution invariably gets improved later on, and the "all singing, all dancing" version has parts that are never used—and so the same general solution is the final product in both cases.

This framework should allow you to code up the automation of one of these tasks in a couple of days, which should save you 4 days over the year. And because *it is a flexible solution that you can use for a whole range of automation tasks,* you can re-use it for all those tasks and save yourself even more time throughout the year.

The whole solution is based on four tables:

- **PROCESS_MASTER** Holds details of each task automated
- **PROCESS_RUN** One record per run of an automated task
- **PROCESS_LOG** Logging associated with an automated task
- **PROCESS_ERROR** Errors that occur during a run

The Test Code Is Available on the Website

In this next section on automating tasks we show extensive examples of code, but much of it is code fragments—there is not enough space to show complete code listings. However, all the code is in the PNA_MAINT package unless stated otherwise, which is available from the website, where you can also get the code to create all the test tables. We encourage you to download that code and run through the examples with it.

The Core Master-Detail Control Tables

At the core of the controlling framework are two tables: a Master table and a Runs table. Whenever we have attempted to create a quick, simple control framework with only one table, the second table comes along. When we have tried to create Master, Runs, and Run Parameters tables, the Run Parameters table has turned out to be a bit overly complex and eventually became mostly redundant.

We will start, quite sensibly, with the Master table, called PROCESS_MASTER. This table will hold one record for each process you are automating. The version shown here allows for the ability to halt (or abandon) a task and restart it, which may be beyond what you want for simple tasks, but is often a highly desirable ability for regular batch processing. (We can't count the number of times a simple task has morphed into a more regulated batch process.)

```
Create table process_master
(process_name            varchar2(30) not null -- Unique name of the utility or job
,last_executed_timestamp timestamp(6) not null -- when last run
,status                  varchar2(1)  not null -- running, finished etc
,log_level               number(1)    not null -- Level of logging
,abandon_fl              varchar(1)   not null -- Y to block runs or abandon current
--  controlling the processing window and processing
,process_range           number(12)         -- max number of records to process
,batch_size              number(5)          -- size of batch for array processing
,stage                   number (2)         -- skip to process point X on recovery
,max_window              number(3)          -- max size of processing window
,process_delay           number(6)          -- time in past to process up to
,last_id_num1            number             -- largest num of unique key processed
,last_id_num2            number             -- 2nd largest num of u key processed
,last_timestamp1         timestamp(6)       -- largest ts of the u key processed
-- used for restart functionality
,window_start_timestamp1 timestamp(6)       -- window start for reco or restart
,window_end_timestamp1   timestamp(6)       -- window end for recovery or restart
,window_start_id_num1    timestamp(6)       -- numeric start for recovery or restart
,window_end_id_num1      timestamp(6)       -- numeric end for recovery or restart
-- constraints
,constraint prma_abandon_fl check (abandon_fl in ('Y','N'))
,constraint prma_status check (status in ('C','I','R','A','E'))
                        -- Complete, In-progress, Recovery, Abandoned, Error
,constraint prma_pk primary key(process_name)
 )
```

The first columns in the table are the key ones for controlling any process, even a simple one that is set to run once a day and just does a fixed task with no reference to its previous executions. For example, to run a daily AWR report, here are the only mandatory columns:

- **PROCESS_NAME** This is the primary key on the table, and it is the name of the process we are automating. This might be PARTITION_SPLIT; it might be DAILY_CUST_LOAD. Choose something that makes reasonable sense because we will put this value into the MODULE column of V$SESSION via DBMS_APPLICATION_INFO, so we can see when

the code is running and the resources it takes. (See Chapter 7 for more details on DBMS_
APPLICATION_INFO.)

■ **LAST_EXECUTED_TIMESTAMP** This is a timestamp. It is also part of the primary key for
the PROCESS_RUN table, where it is used to identify each individual run of this process.
In the PROCESS_MASTER table, it indicates when the current run started or the last run
finished (whether it completed, errored, or was abandoned).

■ **STATUS** This is the current status of the job—C(omplete), I(n-progress), E(rror),
A(bandoned), or R(ecovery). Normally you should only see C or I.

■ **LOG_LEVEL** The default logging level for this process. In Chapter 7, we discuss turning
up and down the instrumentation for an automated task with LOG_LEVEL. The higher
this level is, the more logging/instrumentation information is recorded. This assists in
resolving issues.

The next set of columns has to do with controlling the data range that is processed and the
actual processing. These columns are not required for many database administration tasks:

■ **PROCESS_RANGE** This is the maximum number of records to process. Over the years,
this has proven to be very valuable to stop batch jobs trying to "bite too big a mouthful"
when they are restarted after some sort of processing gap as well as when taking on an
initial volume of data (for example, your typical data load of existing legacy data into a
new system).

When you process large volumes of data, there is a tipping point when some step (nearly
always a SQL statement) processes a volume of data where an order-by clause or a hash
join results in data spilling over from memory to the TEMP tablespace (that is, to disk).
At this point the process slows down markedly due to the extra I/O. If this then reaches
the point where "multipass sorts" or similar occur (that is, chunks of information are
repeatedly written to TEMP, read back, and written to TEMP again), then performance
nosedives. At this point it is actually more efficient, maybe counterintuitively, to process
a larger number of smaller chunks.

■ **BATCH_SIZE** Efficient processing of data via PL/SQL often requires the use of BULK
COLLECT and FORALL statements where data is processed in arrays (see Chapter 3 for
more information on collections, and Chapter 7 for a sample use of them in the demo
code PNA_MAINT.POP_ADDR). It is not strictly necessary, but we like to be able to
easily modify that batch size.

■ **ABANDON_FL** This column has two purposes. It can be used to stop any attempts to
run the process (either automated or by hand) or to abandon a running task. The latter
may be more control than you want, but we have found, especially if we have built in
the ability to restart a load after it has failed, that a controlled abandon is a nice feature
to have. Management (and the DBAs) like the idea that you can stop a job mid-flight in a
clean way (rather than killing the Oracle server process!).

■ **STAGE** Records the current or last completed stage by the process. It is required
information if you want to be able to restart a process that does more than one thing.

■ **MAX_WINDOW** Optional. This puts a cap on the largest range of time (in terms of
the data being processed) to process. An issue encountered a couple of times has been
when, similar to the PROCESS_RANGE parameter, a break in processing or data take-on

has resulted in trying to process a chunk of data that is either too large to be processed efficiently or takes longer than the processing interval for the job (for example, the job normally runs hourly but has been on hold for 2 days). This column would be set to 12 hours, so that the application would only try to process the first 12 hours of outstanding data, and then an hour later the next 12 hours of data, until it catches up.

- **PROCESSING_DELAY** When you are processing data that is coming in, you might have an issue with the data being spread over several tables and, at the very millisecond your processing starts, the latest logical record(s) exist in one table but further details have yet to be placed in other tables. This means you will process a partial record set. By only processing records received up to PROCESSING_DELAY seconds ago, you remove that issue.

- **LAST_ID_NUM1** This is the ID column of the primary key of the last record you processed. Your next run will consider all records with an ID greater than this. See later.

- **LAST_ID_NUM2** This is the second ID column of the last record you processed. Your next run will consider all records with a second ID column greater than this. See later.

- **LAST_TIMESTAMP1** This is the timestamp of the last record you processed. Your next run will process any records *after* this timestamp. See later.

The next four columns are only needed if you allow the recovery/restart of runs. It can be very difficult to recalculate the set of records you were processing in a run that failed or abandoned, especially if you are looking for "all records since the last run up to … (X records/Y timestamp/Z time ago)." By recording the window that was last processed, you can just use those limits again and the "last processed" information in the PROCESS_RUN table.

- WINDOW_START_TIMESTAMP1

- WINDOW_END_TIMESTAMP1

- WINDOW_START_ID_NUM1

- WINDOW_END_ID_NUM1

The PROCESS_RUN table is a child table of PROCESS_MASTER and will hold one record for each execution of the process. It is used to preserve the conditions for that run from the PROCESS_MASTER table and to record progress, and it can be used to check what has run, and when, and what the outcome was.

```
create table process_run
(process_name       varchar2(30) not null -- Unique name of the utility or job
,start_timestamp    timestamp(6) not null - When this run started
,status             varchar2(1)  not null -- Running, Finished etc
,log_level          number(1)    not null -- log level for this run
,process_range      number(12)        -- max no of recs this run should process
,batch_size         number(5)         -- the batch size used
,process_delay      number(6)         -- time in seconds to process up to
,max_window         number(3)         -- top size of window to process
-- below are tracking this run
,start_timestamp1   timestamp(6)      -- start ts of the unique key processed
,start_id_num1      number            -- start no of the unique key processed
```

```
,start_timestamp2    timestamp(6)     -- start 2nd ts of the unique key processed
,start_id_num2       number           -- start 2nd no of the unique key processed
,end_timestamp1      timestamp(6)     -- end ts of the unique key processed
,end_id_num1         number           -- end no of the unique key processed
,end_timestamp2      timestamp(6)     -- end 2nd ts of the unique key processed
,end_id_num2         number           -- end 2nd no of the unique key processed
,completed_timestamp timestamp(6)     -- so we can see how long each run took.
,records_processed   number           -- number of records this run processed
,records_skipped     number           -- number of records this run skipped
,records_errored     number           -- number of errors this run recorded
,constraint prru_status check (status in ('C','I','R','A','E'))
                     -- Complete, In-progress, Recovery, Abandoned, Error
,constraint prru_pk primary key(process_name,start_timestamp)
,constraint prru_prma_fk foreign key (process_name)
    references process_master(process_name)
 )
```

Many of the columns in PROCESS_RUN are the same as in PROCESS_MASTER. LAST_EXECUTED_TIMESTAMP becomes START_TIMESTAMP and, along with PROCESS_NAME, is the primary key for the PROCESS_RUN table. (A surrogate primary key column of a NUMBER is not generated from a sequence because it is not needed. If a table has a natural primary key, as it does in the case, don't confuse matters by introducing a meaningless number.)

STATUS is set to I (for In-progress) or R (for Recovery) during code execution and set to C (for Complete), A (for Abandoned), or E (for Error) as appropriate at the end of the run.

It is helpful to know what the control variables were for prior runs, so we preserve the values of PROCESS_RANGE, BATCH_SIZE, LOG_LEVEL, PROCESS_DELAY, and MAX_WINDOW that were in PROCESS_MASTER when this run occurred, if they were set.

Note that there is no ABANDON_FL. You only need one place to set the abandon flag, and that is in the master record. If the run is abandoned, that will be recorded in the STATUS column.

COMPLETED_TIMESTAMP, RECORDS_PROCESSED, RECORDS_SKIPPED, and RECORDS_ERRORED are self-explanatory. RECORDS_ERRORED can be more than one because a common approach with batch processing is to catch certain errors and record them but let the main processing continue. We would advise, though, that you always have a maximum number of errors you allow for a given run and you error the run at that point. Otherwise, you risk processing a large volume of data when there is some sort of fundamental issue with the data you are processing and you might miss it if the run does not error.

COMPLETED_TIMESTAMP could theoretically be found from the logging table entries for a run (which we come on to later) but it is such a common piece of information you want to see, especially when looking back over historical runs, that it is also recorded here.

The final columns, START_TIMESTAMP1, _TIMESTAMP2, _ID_NUM1, _ID_NUM2, and their END_ equivalents are all to do with the "processing window" and need a little more explaining later on in this chapter, along with the WINDOW_ columns on the RUN_MASTER table.

A Basic Example of Automating a Simple Task

Before we go any further, let's look at an example of automating a simple task. We will use a package called PNA_MAINT, which was introduced in Chapters 6 and 7 for creating test data in the tables PERSON, PERSON_NAME, and ADDRESS. This package is available in full from the website for the book.

We will add a new procedure called TEST_AUTO whose sole purpose is to demonstrate the automation of code. It does nothing "real"; it is just a simple example. First, we need to create a record for this task in PROCESS_MASTER:

```
insert into process_master( PROCESS_NAME  ,LAST_EXECUTED_TIMESTAMP
                           ,STATUS        ,LOG_LEVEL    ,ABANDON_FL)
values                     ('TEST_AUTO'   ,systimestamp
                           ,'C'           ,5            ,'N')
```

For a simple task we do not need the columns for tracking the last records processed and the processing window; we just need the basic information, as shown here. We set a value for LAST_EXECUTED_TIMESTAMP because the column is mandatory—in normal running we would always want to see when the latest run was.

Next, we need code to collect this PROCESS_MASTER record when the procedure is executed. We create a package-level record variable to hold this (and also one for PROCESS_RUN). You could create a set of scalar variables local to each procedure to hold only the columns you will use in automating that procedure, but then you would also need code to collect only those columns local to that procedure. For the sake of simpler, more easily maintained, and more portable code, we use package-level record variables and accept the tiny "cost" of collecting a few more columns than we strictly need.

In the following example we define the variables (in the declaration section of the package) and create a package-level procedure to get the PROCESS_MASTER information:

```
-- We need two rowtype variables to hold our control information
pv_prma_rec          process_master%rowtype;
pv_prru_rec          process_run%rowtype;

--
procedure get_prma (p_process_name in process_master.process_name%type
                   ,p_upd          in boolean :=true) is
Begin
   -- note how simple the code is to select the row into our rowtype variable
   select prma.* into pv_prma_rec
   from process_master prma
   where prma.process_name = upper(p_process_name);
   if p_upd then
      -- we update the record variable and then push the values to the table
      pv_prma_rec.status                :='I';
      pv_prma_rec.last_executed_timestamp :=pv_exec_ts;
      update process_master
      set status                =pv_prma_rec.status
         ,last_executed_timestamp=pv_prma_rec.last_executed_timestamp
      where   process_name = p_process_name;
   end if;
   commit;
exception
   when no_data_found then
      -- cannot write to process_log or process_error as have no run to link to!
      -- so write to plsql_log
      pv_log_level :=5;
      pv_process_name :=nvl(pv_process_name,p_process_name);
```

```
    write_log ('Failed to find record in PROCESS_MASTER for '||p_process_
name,'F','01403');
  raise;
end get_prma;
```

The code collects all columns from PROCESS_MASTER into PV_PRMA_REC. By default, it then updates the PROCESS_MASTER record setting STATUS "I" (for "In progress") and LAST_EXECUTED_TIMESTAMP to a package variable **pv_exec_ts**, which we set at the start of any procedure that can be called externally. Thus, when we get the control details of the process, we are also recording that our code is running.

If we wanted to simply get the current information for the process, we would call the procedure with **p_upd** passed in as FALSE. You'll see an example of that later on in this section.

Note that GET_PRMA is an *autonomous transaction*. We want to commit the changes we make to PROCESS_MASTER but not impact any outstanding DML from the calling code.

Next, we need to create a record in PROCESS_RUN for this run, using the following procedure to do this:

```
procedure ins_prru (p_prru_rec    in process_run%rowtype) is
pragma autonomous_transaction;
begin
  insert into process_run
  values p_prru_rec;
  commit;
exception
  when others then
    pv_err_msg:=dbms_utility.format_error_stack;
    pv_err_stack := dbms_utility.format_error_backtrace;
    write_log(pv_err_msg,'E',SQLCODE);
    write_log(pv_err_stack,'E',SQLCODE);
    raise;
end ins_prru;
```

This code is even simpler than GET_PRMA. We pass in a record variable whose declaration is anchored to the PROCESS_RUN table and just insert whatever values are there. Using a row type variable really does simplify the code—half of this sample code is the exception handling.

So we have our package variables, a procedure to collect the PROCESS_MASTER (and update it), and a procedure to create a new PROCESS_RUN. Any code that we automate needs to use these elements. Here we show the first half of the **test_auto** procedure:

```
1)  procedure test_auto is
2)  -- the most basic test of automating a task
3)  v_count pls_integer;
4)  begin
5)  pv_process_name        :='test_auto';
6)  pv_log_level           := 5;
7)  pv_exec_ts := systimestamp;
8)  pv_prma_rec:=null;
9)  pv_prru_rec:=null;
10) get_prma('TEST_AUTO');
11) pv_prru_rec.process_name        := pv_prma_rec.process_name;
12) pv_prru_rec.start_timestamp     := pv_prma_rec.last_executed_timestamp;
```

```
13) pv_prru_rec.status            := pv_prma_rec.status;
14) pv_prru_rec.log_level         := pv_prma_rec.log_level;
15) ins_prru(pv_prru_rec);
16) -- the work of the procedure now begins
17) select count(*) into v_count from person;
18) --
```

In lines 5–9, we set up the package variables to control the process, including blanking the two package row type variables, **pv_prma_rec** and **pv_prru_rec**. In line 10, we call our **get_prma** procedure to fetch the control information into **pv_prma_rec**. In lines 11–14, we duplicate the control data into the **pv_prru_rec** record variable, and in line 15 we use our INS_PRRU to record the actual run.

We have line 17 to simulate everything our process might do—gather stats, run performance reports, and check tablespace usage. In this case, we just count the number of PERSON records.

We also need to record when we have finished the task. We will create two more procedures— UPD_PRMA to update the PROCESS_MASTER table, and UPD_PRRU to update the PROCESS_RUN table:

```
procedure upd_prma (p_prma_rec in    process_master%rowtype
                        ,p_upd     in varchar2 :='CS') is
pragma autonomous_transaction;
begin
  if p_upd='CS' then -- complete simple
    update process_master
    set status              = p_prma_rec.status
      ,stage                = p_prma_rec.stage
      ,abandon_fl           = p_prma_rec.abandon_fl
    where  process_name            = p_prma_rec.process_name
    and    last_executed_timestamp = p_prma_rec.last_executed_timestamp;
-- trimmed
  end if;
  commit;
end upd_prma;
```

UPD_PRMA updates the PROCESS_MASTER, accepting a row type record based on the table and **p_upd** to indicate the type of update. It defaults to CS, which means Close Simple. For a process that needs no special control, we simply need to record the new STATUS, STAGE, and ABANDON_FL. Normally this would be C (for Complete), null, and N (for Not abandoned).

As more complex tasks are automated, we will need other update types (**p_upd** values) to include other columns. If no **p_upd** value is provided or one that is not known, we update all columns to the values passed in with the **p_prma_rec** variable (code not shown here). It is generally not good practice to update columns to their current value; it just needlessly generates redo. But when we are talking about a small number of records (one in this case), there is an argument that rather than have lots of complex permutations of what columns you update, you have "simple, average, everything." This approach is shown in the following UPD_PRRU code to update PROCESS_RUN:

```
procedure upd_prru (p_prru_rec    in process_run%rowtype
                        ,p_upd        in varchar2 :='CS') is
pragma autonomous_transaction;
```

```
begin
  if p_upd='CS' then -- complete simple
    update process_run
    set status                = p_prru_rec.status
       ,completed_timestamp   = p_prru_rec.completed_timestamp
       ,records_processed     = p_prru_rec.records_processed
    where  process_name       = p_prru_rec.process_name
    and    start_timestamp = p_prru_rec.start_timestamp;
  else -- upd all the values. Generally you should only upd all that need it
    update process_run
    set status                = p_prru_rec.status
       ,completed_timestamp   = p_prru_rec.completed_timestamp
       ,records_processed     = p_prru_rec.records_processed
       ,start_timestamp1      = p_prru_rec.start_timestamp1
       ,start_id_num1         = p_prru_rec.start_id_num1
       ,start_timestamp2      = p_prru_rec.start_timestamp2
       ,start_id_num2         = p_prru_rec.start_id_num2
       ,end_timestamp1        = p_prru_rec.end_timestamp1
       ,end_id_num1           = p_prru_rec.end_id_num1
       ,end_timestamp2        = p_prru_rec.end_timestamp2
       ,end_id_num2           = p_prru_rec.end_id_num2
       ,records_skipped       = p_prru_rec.records_skipped
       ,records_errored       = p_prru_rec.records_errored
    where  process_name       = p_prru_rec.process_name
    and    start_timestamp = p_prru_rec.start_timestamp;
  end if;
  commit;
exception
  when others then
    pv_err_msg:=dbms_utility.format_error_stack;
    pv_err_stack := dbms_utility.format_error_backtrace;
    write_plog(pv_err_msg,'E',SQLCODE);
    write_plog(pv_err_stack,'E',SQLCODE);
    write_error(pv_err_msg,sqlcode,'F');
    raise;
end upd_prru;
```

The intention with both procedures is that the main code maintains the record variables **pv_prma_rec** and **pv_prru_rec**, and these two procedures persist the data in the two tables. Without these record variables, we would need to maintain many "old-style" scalar variables.

Here is the second half of our very simple **test_auto** procedure, to record that the task has finished:

```
select count(*) into v_count from person;
dbms_lock.sleep(10);
pv_prru_rec.records_processed    :=v_count;
pv_prru_rec.status               :='C';
pv_prru_rec.completed_timestamp  :=systimestamp;
upd_prru(pv_prru_rec,'CS');
pv_prma_rec.status :='C';
pv_prma_rec.stage  :=null;
```

```
upd_prma(pv_prma_rec,'CS');
 write_plog ('ended at '||to_char(systimestamp,'YY-MM-DD HH24:MI:SS.FF3'));
end test_auto;
```

The DBMS_LOCK.SLEEP is just there so we can catch it in action. The rest of the code is simply setting columns in PV_PRRU_REC and PV_PRMA_REC and calling our two procedures to close out the task.

So we are ready to go. Before we run the code, we will check the PROCESS_MASTER. Afterward, we will check it again as well as the PROCESS_LOG table.

```
PROCESS_NAME      Last_Exec_Timestamp      STATUS  LOG_LEVEL ABANDON
---------------   ----------------------   ------  --------- -------
TEST_AUTO         09-MAR-16 12.26.38.713   C             5 N

Exec pna_maint.test_auto
PL/SQL procedure successfully completed.

PROCESS_NAME      Last_Exec_Timestamp      STATUS  LOG_LEVEL ABANDON
---------------   ----------------------   ------  --------- -------
TEST_AUTO         09-MAR-16 18.18.50.036   C             5 N

                                                            Recs    LOG
PROCESS_NAME   START_TIMESTAMP         STATUS COMPLETED_TIMESTAMP    procd   LEVEL
-------------  ----------------------  ------ ---------------------- ------  -----
TEST_AUTO      09-MAR-16 18.18.50.036  C      09-MAR-16 18.18.50.067 275424      5

--run again
Exec pna_maint.test_auto
PL/SQL procedure successfully completed.

PROCESS_NAME      Last_Exec_Timestamp      STATUS  LOG_LEVEL ABANDON
---------------   ----------------------   ------  --------- -------
TEST_AUTO         09-MAR-16 18.43.59.6790  C             5 N
PROCESS_NAME      START_TIMESTAMP         STATUS COMPLETED_TIMESTAMP    recs_procd
---------------   ----------------------  ------ ---------------------- ----------
TEST_AUTO         09-MAR-16 18.43.59.679  C      09-MAR-16 18.43.59.710     275424
TEST_AUTO         09-MAR-16 18.18.50.036  C      09-MAR-16 18.18.50.067     275424
```

We can see the details about the last run in PROCESS_MASTER updating and the PROCESS_RUN records being created for each run. We will run the code again and, in a second session, look at the PROCESS_MASTER and PROCESS_LOG tables "in flight":

```
-- session 1
Exec pna_maint.test_auto

-- session 2
PROCESS_NAME      Last_Exec_Timestamp      STATUS  LOG_LEVEL ABANDON
---------------   ----------------------   ------  --------- -------
TEST_AUTO         09-MAR-16 20.23.53.0670  I             5 N

                                                            RECS    LOG
PROCESS_NAME   START_TIMESTAMP         STATUS COMPLETED_TIMESTAMP    PROCD   LEVEL
```

TEST_AUTO	**09-MAR-16 20.23.53.067** I				5
TEST_AUTO	09-MAR-16 18.43.59.679 C		09-MAR-16 18.43.59.710	275424	5
TEST_AUTO	09-MAR-16 18.18.50.036 C		09-MAR-16 18.18.50.067	275424	5

As you can see, because the data in the control tables is maintained via autonomous transaction procedures, a second session can see the progress. In our very simple test case we just see the status is I (for In progress) in both tables. PROCESS_RUN has no COMPLETED_TIMESTAMP or RECORDS_PROCESSED. If we were using more of the control columns, we would, of course, also see them updating accordingly.

So we now have a control harness for simple tasks. We could take TEST_AUTO code we have created, duplicate it, and drop anything into the section where we have **select count(*) into v_ count from person**. As long as it can be executed with no other control requirements (so it can kick off gathering standard schema stats or run a report that needs no input parameters) the code will execute and everything will be logged. In fact, that is what we did in developing the rest of the sample code here. We copied TEST_AUTO, changed the line setting PV_PROCESS_NAME to our new process name, and created a record in PROCESS_MASTER. We then added whatever extra control mechanisms we needed.

The code on the website has a few extra things in it, such as instrumentation code (as covered in Chapter 7) and exception handling (which we cover more extensively in the rest of this chapter).

Let's move onto logging/instrumenting your automated code with PROCESS_LOG and PROCESS_ERROR.

Logging and Error Tables

The use of a logging table for instrumenting your code is covered extensively in Chapter 7 (where the table used is called PLSQL_LOG). The following is the logging table for our automated tasks:

```
create table process_log
(process_name     varchar2(30) not null
,start_timestamp timestamp(6) not null
,log_timestamp   timestamp(6) not null
,status          varchar2(1)  not null
,log_level       number(1)    not null
,log_text        varchar2(4000)
,error_code      varchar2(10)
,constraint prlo_prru_pk foreign key (process_name,start_timestamp)
          references   process_run( process_name,start_timestamp)
)
--
Create index polo_prna_stti_loti
on process_log(process_name,start_timestamp,log_timestamp)
```

You will note that PROCESS_LOG and START_TIMESTAMP are inherited from PROCESS_RUN. Every log entry links back to a process run and is enforced by the foreign key. Chapter 7 covers the use of this table extensively. To summarize, it is used to store the instrumentation information from your PL/SQL (and any other) code. The information can be seen as the code progresses as it is populated via an autonomous transaction procedure.

We do not see instrumenting your code as an overhead: it is vital to running and maintaining a system professionally. Although the PROCESS_MASTER/PROCESS_RUN tables described earlier can show you something about the progress of a single run (when it started, the step it is on, and so on) and the history of when it ran and how long it took, that outline information is not enough to help you investigate an issue when it occurs or to identify where in your code the issue can be found, or to track the changing profile of the code as data volumes change over time. That requires instrumentation.

The purpose of each column in PROCESS_LOG is fairly self-evident. Refer to Chapter 7 if you want further details.

The column LOG_LEVEL in PROCESS_MASTER can be used to determine how much information is logged. Certain activities, such as the starting and ending of a task, are written to PROCESS_LOG no matter what. However, instrumentation about key variables, where in the code you are, and the number of iterations of a loop are optional and are written out only if LOG_LEVEL is at or above a certain value. In this way you can control how much logging is done. Again, see Chapter 7 for more details.

PLSQL_LOG and PROCESS_LOG

The tables PLSQL_LOG and PROCESS_LOG are very similar. The difference is that PROCESS_LOG is a child table of PROCESS_RUN and a grandchild of PROCESS_MASTER, enforced in our example here by a foreign key to PROCESS_RUN. As such, only log entries for PL/SQL managed through these tables can be recorded in this table. Also, before an automated task has found its associated PROCESS_MASTER record and created an entry for that execution in PROCESS_RUN, you cannot put a record in PROCESS_LOG (or PROCESS_ERROR). You have the choice of removing the foreign key from PROCESS_LOG or recording instrumentation/errors for these early steps of the code into PLSQL_LOG.

For this reason you may want to have both tables. PLSQL_LOG is used to log code that is not being controlled via the PROCESS_MASTER/PROCESS_RUN tables.

The LOG_PROCESS table has a column named ERROR_CODE that you might decide is enough for you and that you will use the one table for both logging and errors. But we actually like to have a table that is dedicated to recording errors. Some errors you might be able to step by (for example, a data type mismatch when converting what should be a date in a number field into an actual date) and just record that they happened in the PROCESS_ERROR table. Others will be terminal to the program, and the error is recorded in the RUN_ERROR table via the relevant EXCEPTIONS handling code. In any case, if there are any errors, you know exactly where to go and look for them (and quickly find them!) should they be recorded in a PROCESS_ERROR table. The table should remain small:

```
create table process_error
  (process_name    varchar2(30) not null
  ,start_timestamp timestamp(6)    not null
  ,error_timestamp timestamp(6)    not null
  ,status          varchar2(1)  not null -- fatal or none-fatal
  ,error_text      varchar2(4000)        -- Error text and identifying values
  ,error_code      varchar2(10)          -- the oracle error code if applicable
  ,constraint prer_pk primary key (process_name,start_timestamp,error_timestamp)
  ,constraint prer_prru_pk foreign key (process_name,start_timestamp)
        references   process_run (process_name,start_timestamp)
  )
```

The table structure is very similar to PROCESS_LOG, with LOG_TEXT replaced with ERROR_TEXT, and we do not need the LOG_LEVEL column.

We, of course, create a central procedure to populate each of these tables, rather than coding an insert at each point where we want to write to them. They are autonomous transactions so that the information is immediately available to other sessions (so progress can be tracked) and have no impact on the committing and rolling back of data in the main program:

```
procedure write_plog(v_log_text    in varchar2
                    ,v_status      in varchar2 :=''
                    ,v_error_code  in varchar2 :=''   )
is
pragma autonomous_transaction;
v_timestamp      timestamp :=systimestamp;
begin
  if pv_log_level>=5 then
  dbms_output.put_line (pv_process_name||' log '||pv_log_level||' - '
                          ||to_char(v_timestamp,'HH24:MI:SS.FF3 :')||v_log_text);
  end if;
  INSERT INTO PROCESS_LOG(process_name  ,start_timestamp   ,log_timestamp
                  ,status         ,log_level      ,log_text      ,error_code)
  values (pv_process_name  ,pv_exec_ts         ,v_timestamp
         ,nvl(v_status,'I'),pv_log_level       ,v_log_text    ,v_error_code
          );
  commit;
end write_plog;
--
procedure write_error(v_error_text in varchar2
                    ,v_error_code in varchar2 :=''
                    ,v_status     in varchar2 :='' )
is
pragma autonomous_transaction;
v_timestamp      timestamp :=systimestamp;
begin
  if pv_log_level>=3 then
  dbms_output.put_line (pv_process_name||' log '||pv_log_level||' - '
                          ||to_char(v_timestamp,'HH24:MI:SS.FF3 :')||v_error_text);
  end if;
  INSERT INTO process_error(process_name  ,start_timestamp   ,error_timestamp
                          ,status         ,error_text      ,error_code)
  values (pv_process_name   ,pv_exec_ts    ,v_timestamp
         ,nvl(v_status,'E')   ,v_error_text ,v_error_code
          );
  commit;
  exception
  when others then
  dbms_output.put_line('CRITICAL the error handling subroutine write_error in '
                      ||pv_process_name||' failed');
  raise;
end write_error;
```

WRITE_ERROR has a simple exception handler to resort to a call to DBMS_OUTPUT if, for any reason, the procedure itself errors. Usually, once you have automated one or two tasks, this procedure is simple and reliable enough to never fail. But the backup of a call to DBMS_OUTPUT is worth the minimal effort to include.

You have already seen one or two examples of calling these procedures in our code (that is, UPD_PRMA and UPD_PRRU). WRITE_ERROR should be called from exception handlers and WRITE_PLOG at significant points throughout your code.

Our test code also includes the procedure WRITE_LOG (no P), and you will see that it's used in GET_PRMA and INS_PRRU. That's because, before you have the relevant PROCESS_RUN to relate a PROCESS_LOG record to, you can't write to it! WRITE_LOG writes to the stand-alone PLSQL_LOG table.

PROCESS_LOG and PROCESS_ERROR complete the four tables that are the basis of our controlling framework. We have also given examples of all the code needed to read from or write to these tables in order to automate simple tasks.

Automating a Simple Data-Processing Task

As a more realistic example of automating a task, we will add a new procedure to PNA_MAINT called POP_ADDR_H for creating a small set of ADDRESS records. First, we need to insert a row into PROCESS_MASTER for this new task:

```
insert into process_master
     ( PROCESS_NAME  ,LAST_EXECUTED_TIMESTAMP    ,PROCESS_RANGE
     ,STATUS         ,LOG_LEVEL     ,ABANDON_FL     ,BATCH_SIZE)
values                    ('POP_ADDR_H'  ,systimestamp          ,20000
                    ,'C'            ,5              ,'N'         ,5000)
```

We will use PROCESS_RANGE to hold the number of records to create each run (that is, 20,000 and a BATCH_SIZE of 5000). We will also use ABANDON_FL in our code.

We copy the code from TEST_AUTO but add in code to abort the task if the ABANDON_FL flag is set, and we use the PROCESS_RANGE and BATCH_SIZE information to control the task. For brevity, we do not show the SQL for creating the ADDRESS records (the full code can be found on the website.)

```
1)  procedure pop_addr_h is
2)  -- Define local variables
3)  begin
4)    pv_process_name :='POP_ADDR_H'; pv_log_level:=5; pv_exec_ts:= systimestamp;
5)    pv_prma_rec:=null;              pv_prru_rec:=null;
6)    get_prma(pv_process_name);
7)    pv_log_level            := pv_prma_rec.log_level;
8)    pv_prru_rec.process_name := pv_prma_rec.process_name;
9)    -- several other lines setting pv_prru_rec variables
10)   ins_prru(pv_prru_rec);
11)   write_plog ('started at '||to_char(pv_exec_ts,'YY-MM-DD HH24:MI:SS.FF3'));
12)   if pv_prma_rec.abandon_fl = 'Y' then
13)     write_plog('process set to Abandon so halted');
14)   else
15)     -- address processing code
```

```
16)     write_plog ('towns '||to_char(v_tona_min)||' to '||to_char(v_tona_max));
17)     while v_count < pv_prma_rec.process_range loop
18)       for a in 1..pv_prma_rec.batch_size loop
19)         --
20)         -- address processing code
21)         --
22)       end loop;
23)       v_count:=v_count+pv_prma_rec.batch_size;
24)       commit;
25)       write_plog ('intermediate commit at '||v_count||' addresses');
26)     end loop; -- main p_rows insert
27)     commit;
28)     pv_prru_rec.records_processed     :=v_count;
29)   end if; -- abandon_check
30)   if pv_prma_rec.abandon_fl='Y' then
31)     pv_prru_rec.status    :='A';     pv_prma_rec.status    :='A';
32)   else
33)     pv_prru_rec.status    :='C';     pv_prma_rec.status    :='C';
34)   end if;
35)   pv_prru_rec.completed_timestamp  :=systimestamp;
36)   upd_prru(pv_prru_rec,'CS');
37)   pv_prma_rec.stage  :=null;
38)   upd_prma(pv_prma_rec,'CS');
39)   write_plog ('ended at '||to_char(systimestamp,'YY-MM-DD HH24:MI:SS.FF3'));
40) exception
41)   when others then
42)     --
43)     --error logging code
44)     --
45)     --update the control tables to show it errored
46)   pv_prru_rec.status    :='E';     pv_prru_rec.completed_timestamp  :=systimestamp;
47)   upd_prru(pv_prru_rec,'CS');
48)   pv_prma_rec.status :='E';     pv_prma_rec.stage  :=null;   pv_prma_rec.abandon_fl :='Y';
49)   upd_prma(pv_prma_rec,'CS');
50)   raise;
51) end pop_addr_h;
```

The new code is shown in bold. Lines 4–10 are very similar to the start of the TEST_BATCH code, setting up the package-level row type variables, updating PROCESS_RUN, and creating the PROCESS_LOG record. Then in line 12 we test the ABANDON_FL record and, if it's set to 'Y', we skip all of the processing via an IF_THEN_END-IF construct. Why do we only do the test now? Because we want to record that the run occurred but was aborted. After the END_IF on line 29 we again use ABANDON_FL to check what status we should record in the control tables.

In lines 16 and 17 we use the PV_PRMA_REC.PROCESS_LIMIT and BATCH_SIZE columns to control the processing of our data.

Lines 45–49 we show the relevant section of the exception handler to update the control tables and write to the log and error table in the event of any errors occurring. When you automate your code, you need to update the control tables at all possible exit points from your code! If it is designed well, this will be just two places—the end of the normal code and the exception handler. You will notice several calls to WRITE_PLOG throughout the code to instrument what is going on.

We can manually call POP_ADDR_H and make sure everything is working okay. We show this next, with the records generated in PROCESS_MASTER, PROCESS_RUN, and PROCESS_LOG:

```
exec pna_maint.pop_addr_h
PL/SQL procedure successfully completed.
-- checking process_master, process_run and process_log for POP_ADDR_H
```

PROCESS_NAME	Last_Exec_Timestamp	STATUS	LOG_LEVEL	ABANDON	range	batch
POP_ADDR_H	10-MAR-16 17.51.46.118	C	5	N	20,000	5000

PROCESS_NAME	START_TS	ST	COMPLETED_TIMESTAMP	recs_procd	LL	RANGE	BATCH
POP_ADDR_H	10-MAR-16 17.51.46.118	C	10-MAR-16 17.51.46.978	20000	5	20,000	5000

PROCESS_NAME	START DATE	LOG TIMESTAMP	LL	LOG_TEXT	ELAPSED
POP_ADDR_H	10-MAR-16	17:51:46.118	5	started at 16-03-10 17:51:46.118	
		17:51:46.118	5	towns 1 to 69 roads 1 to 81 types 1 to 74	00:00:00.000
		17:51:46.337	5	intermediate commit at 5000 addresses	00:00:00.219
		17:51:46.540	5	intermediate commit at 10000 addresses	00:00:00.203
		17:51:46.743	5	intermediate commit at 15000 addresses	00:00:00.203
		17:51:46.978	5	intermediate commit at 20000 addresses	00:00:00.235
		17:51:46.978	5	ended at 16-03-10 17:51:46.978	00:00:00.000

We can set the process not to run by setting ABANDON_FL to 'Y' and then try to run the code:

```
update process_master set abandon_fl='Y'
where process_name='POP_ADDR_H';
COMMIT;

exec pna_maint.pop_addr_h
PL/SQL procedure successfully completed.
```

PROCESS_NAME	Last_Exec_Timestamp	STATUS	LL	ABANDON	RANGE	BATCH
POP_ADDR_H	10-MAR-16 18.12.49.981	A	5	Y	20,000	5000

PROCESS_NAME	START_TS	ST	COMPLETED_TIMESTAMP	recs_procd	LL	RANGE	BATCH
POP_ADDR_H	10-MAR-16 18.12.49.981	A	10-MAR-16 18.12.49.981	0	5	20,000	5000

PROCESS_NAME	START DATE	LOG TIMESTAMP	LL	LOG_TEXT	ELAPSED
POP_ADDR_H	10-MAR-16	18:12:49.981	5	started at 16-03-10 18:12:49.981	
		18:12:49.981	5	process set to Abandon so halted	00:00:00.000
		18:12:49.981	5	ended at 16-03-10 18:12:49.981	00:00:00.000

Note that the status in PROCESS_MASTER is set to A, as it is for the latest run in PROCESS_RUN (but we do record a run that was started and then abandoned), and the PROCESS_LOG confirms this.

Of course, the whole point of automating a task is to run it automatically! To do this, we can simply automate the task with DBMS_SCHEDULER:

```
BEGIN
   DBMS_SCHEDULER.create_job (
      job_name        => 'HOURLY_ADDRESS_ADD',
      job_type        => 'PLSQL_BLOCK',
      job_action      => 'BEGIN pna_maint.pop_addr_h'||  '; END;',
      start_date      => SYSTIMESTAMP,
      repeat_interval => 'freq=hourly; byminute=40; bysecond=0;',
      end_date        => sysdate+2,
      enabled         => TRUE,
      comments        => 'Should create 20k addresses every hour');
END;
```

We are scheduling it to run from now, every hour at 40 minutes past the hour, for 2 days. We actually did this, and after a few hours we checked the runs for that process (the most recent runs appear at the top):

```
PROCESS_NAME   START_TS                 ST COMPLETED_TIMESTAMP    recs_procd LL   RANGE  BATCH
-------------  -----------------------  -- ---------------------  ---------- --  ------- ------
POP_ADDR_H     10-MAR-16 20.40.03.929 I                                    0  5  40,000  10000
POP_ADDR_H     10-MAR-16 19.40.01.975 A  10-MAR-16 19.40.01.975            0  5  40,000  10000
POP_ADDR_H     10-MAR-16 18.40.00.825 A  10-MAR-16 18.40.00.825            0  5  40,000  10000
POP_ADDR_H     10-MAR-16 17.50.32.926 C  10-MAR-16 17.50.34.579        40000  5  40,000  10000
POP_ADDR_H     10-MAR-16 17.40.03.461 C  10-MAR-16 17.40.05.158        40000  5  40,000  10000
POP_ADDR_H     10-MAR-16 16.40.01.226 C  10-MAR-16 16.40.02.943        40000  5  40,000   4000
POP_ADDR_H     10-MAR-16 15.40.02.965 C  10-MAR-16 15.41.45.084        40000  5  40,000   4000
POP_ADDR_H     10-MAR-16 14.40.03.523 C  10-MAR-16 14.41.45.673        40000  5  40,000   4000
POP_ADDR_H     10-MAR-16 13.40.01.342 C  10-MAR-16 13.40.42.299        20000  5  20,000   5000
```

What happened at 14:40? The number of records processed jumped. This is because we altered the setting in PROCESS_MASTER to create more data with a slightly smaller batch size:

```
update process_master
   set process_range=40000,batch_size=4000
   where process_name = 'POP_ADDR_H'
```

Before 17:40 we altered the batch size to 10000 records.

Before 18:40 we had set ABANDON_FL to 'Y' to halt processing temporarily, and we left it set to that for a couple of hours. But before the latest run you see that at 20:40 we set ABANDON_FL back to 'N' and we caught the task "in flight," as can be seen by the contents of PROCESS_MASTER and PROCESS_RUN too:

```
PROCESS_NAME   Last_Exec_Timestamp     STATUS LL ABANDON   RANGE  BATCH
-------------  ----------------------  ------ -- -------  ------- ------
POP_ADDR_H     10-MAR-16 20.40.03.929 I        5 N         40,000  10000


               START        LOG
PROCESS_NAME   DATE     TIMESTAMP      LL LOG_TEXT                                          ELAPSED
------------   -------- ------------   -- ------------------------------------------------  ----------
POP_ADDR_H     10-MAR-16 20:40:03.929  5 started at 16-03-10 20:40:03.929
```

```
20:40:03.929  5 towns 1 to 69  roads 1 to 81  types 1 to 74  00:00:00.000
20:40:14.181  5 intermediate commit at 10000 addresses       00:00:10.252
20:40:24.415  5 intermediate commit at 20000 addresses       00:00:10.234
20:40:34.642  5 intermediate commit at 30000 addresses       00:00:10.227
```

Although our examples are of processing data, this level of automation and control is what we normally use for database administrative tasks such as splitting off new partitions or moving data from the production tables to archive tables. We do not show explicit examples of these because the actual code is quite verbose, especially for the full working versions. However, to give you a taste of doing so, we describe some parts of code to split off partitions in the following section.

Sample Code for Splitting Off Partitions

We do not have the space to cover all the code for automatically splitting off new partitions for tables, but we include some code here to give you an indication of how to automate such tasks. This is real code from a production system developed for a client (edited slightly to remove identifying names), so the code is *not* on the website.

Splitting off new partitions is actually more complex than it first seems. Doing so for one table is relatively easy because you (hopefully!) have a standard naming practice for the partitions, what tablespace they will go into, a fixed range, and the indexes are partitioned in the same way. However, to create a more generic solution, you need to be aware of factors such as global indexes and the fact that local index partitions might have names different from the related table partition (often it is when you try to automate something you find the mistakes made in the past) and the different types of partitioning. Therefore, you need a task-specific table to hold the details of each table you want to maintain the partitions for; something like this:

```
create table partition_control
   ( table_owner                 varchar2(30) not null,
     table_name                  varchar2(30) not null,
     partition_type              varchar2(30) not null,
     date_format                 varchar2(20),
     partition_prefix            varchar2(30),
     high_value                  varchar2(256),
     partition_range_in_days     number,
     create_number_of_partitions number,
     default_partition_name      varchar2(30),
     created_by                  varchar2(30),
     created_timestamp date,
     constraint paco_pk primary key (table_owner, table_name)   )
```

In your application code, you loop through the contents of this table and, for each row, you find the latest partition for the stated table and use that information to construct the name of the new partition to create and the new maximum value, like this:

```
when i.partition_range_in_days <30 then
lv_part_name_date:=to_char(lv_split_date,lv_date_format);
lv_split_date :=lv_split_date+i.partition_range_in_days;
lv_partition_name :=to_char(lv_split_date,lv_date_format);
when i.partition_range_in_days <32 then
-- month
lv_part_name_date:=to_char(lv_split_date,lv_date_format);
```

```
lv_split_date  :=add_months(lv_split_date,1);
lv_partition_name :=to_char(lv_split_date,lv_date_format);
else
lv_part_name_date:=to_char(lv_split_date,lv_date_format);
lv_split_date  :=lv_split_date+i.partition_range_in_days;
lv_partition_name :=to_char(lv_split_date,lv_date_format);
end case;
```

When it comes to doing the actual partition split you have to use dynamic SQL—you do not know what the split statement is until you generate it—and even if you did, you could not have it as SQL in the PL/SQL procedure because it would reference partitions that did not exist at compile time! This is a common "problem" with database administration tasks—you need to write code that either generates things that do not currently exist or works on objects that do not exist at compilation time. Chapter 8 covers dynamic SQL. Our sample code uses native dynamic SQL (that is, EXECUTE IMMEDIATE).

```
PROCEDURE split_range_partition
(i_table_owner              IN VARCHAR2
,i_table_name               IN VARCHAR2
,i_new_partition            IN VARCHAR2
,i_high_value               IN VARCHAR2 -- 'DD-MON-YYYY HH24:MI'
,i_split_partition          IN VARCHAR2
,i_override_tablespace      IN VARCHAR2
) IS
...
BEGIN
 write_plog(to_char(sysdate,'DD-MON-YY HH24:MI:SS')
                    || '    Split range     : ' || i_split_partition);
--
-- code to handle the target TS changing and a few other site-specific things
--
   lv_sql := 'ALTER TABLE '
          || i_table_owner || '.' || i_table_name
          || ' SPLIT PARTITION '  || i_split_partition
          || ' AT (  to_date('''  || i_high_value
          ||''',''DD-MON-YYYY HH24:MI'')  )'
          || ' INTO ( PARTITION '    || i_split_partition||lv_ts
          || ', PARTITION '    || i_new_partition || lv_ts
          || ')';
   write_plog(to_char(sysdate,'DD-MON-YY HH24:MI:SS')||' '||lv_sql);
   EXECUTE IMMEDIATE lv_sql;
```

As you can see, we are constructing a split statement partially derived from the name and max value data we previously constructed. We write this statement to PROCESS_LOG as well as execute it—whenever you generate dynamic SQL, you want to record what you generate in order to simplify problem resolution.

The whole code set to split off new partitions is verbose and complex. However, we can *develop it separately and then just drop it into the control framework*.

Let's move on to one of the main issues of automating tasks, which is controlling the processing of batch-load-type activities.

Automating a Task May Reveal Historical Mistakes

I have automated partition maintenance tasks for several clients, and half the time I discover odd things that happened in the past, such as tables with indexes on them owned by a user different from the table owner, indexes with local partitions that are in the wrong tablespace, and partitions with names that *should* indicate the partition key range but don't. I also see old partitions that "never got split," so they cover several months rather than just one. I see all sorts of things. I have even seen a partitioned table with a partitioned global index that just "looked" like it was locally partitioned.

The irony is that when you code up an automated task that perpetuates these historical mistakes, you can end up getting blamed for them. When you automate maintenance tasks, allow some time for spotting and working around these issues. Just keep in mind that Oracle often gives you the flexibility to do some very odd things!

The Processing Window

Like with our very simple example, some tasks you automate will just run with no consideration of what has happened before; there is no need to check what the process did in its last run and no need to identify a range of data to process. But for other automated tasks, such as data take-on, each execution has to know where the last load got to so it can continue from that point without losing data. Occasionally you can just check what's in the target table(s) and process from there, but in our experience we often find data is generated from more than one source (for example, from the batch and also from online input or updates), and so it is either hard or impossible to work out from the target tables where the batch got to. It is far safer and simpler to record it.

The first issue is that you have to be able to work out how the range of data to be processed is to be identified. It usually comes down to using an incrementing ID on a table (often generated via a sequence—in which case, see the following note about using sequence-sourced primary keys) or a date/timestamp, such as CREATED_TIMESTAMP or ORDERED_TIMESTAMP. If data you are processing can be modified later on, you might also have to consider a LAST_MODIFIED DATE/TIMESTAMP.

If more than one table holds the data to be processed (say, the classic ORDER and ORDER_LINES pair of tables), you will control the processing of the data via the ORDER table identifier, which is inherited by the child ORDER_LINES table.

Let's look at an example of simple batch processing. We create three new tables. CUSTOMER_ORDER and CUSTOMER_ORDER_LINE are highly simplified versions of these sorts of tables, and the third table, CUSTOMER_ORDER_SUMMARY, will be populated by our sample code (note that the Chapter 9 sample scripts create these tables for you).

```
create table customer_order
(id              number    not null
,created_dt      date      not null
,customer_id     number    not null
,address_id      number    not null
,status          varchar2(1)
,completed_dt    date
)

alter table customer_order
```

```
add constraint cuor_pk primary key (id,created_dt)

create table customer_order_line
(cuor_id        number    not null
,created_dt     date      not null
,line_no        number    not null
,product_code   number    not null
,unit_number    number
,unit_cost      number
)

alter table customer_order_line
add constraint col_pk primary key (cuor_id,line_no,created_dt)

create table customer_order_summary
(id             number    not null
,created_dt     date      not null
,customer_id    number    not null
,num_items      number    not null
,tot_value      number    not null
)

alter table customer_order_summary
add constraint cos_pk primary key (id,created_dt)
```

Processing by IDs Generated from Sequences

A lot of Oracle Databases are designed such that activity tables have a primary key (PK) on them that is generated from a sequence. Sometimes this is a good idea, and sometimes it is just poor design. If there is a natural primary key you can use, use it. However, we often encounter situations where the primary key is derived from an Oracle sequence. Therefore, these records will always be in order of the sequence, yes? No!

If you use RAC, unless you set NOCACHE and ORDER for the sequence (in which case you will probably have terrible performance with any active sequence), then each instance will get values from the sequence that are guaranteed unique *but not ordered*. In fact, if you use CACHE, they will certainly *not* be ordered.

Even with no RAC, all Oracle guarantees is that a sequence value will be unique. On a single-node instance the values will be generated in an ordered way—but how your application commits records using those values is out of Oracle's control. If you have three sessions creating records with a PK based on the sequence, they will get values in order depending on when they request them (sess1, sess2, sess3), but that does not guarantee that sess1 commits before sess2 before sess3.

As a result of this, if you process data up to the latest value seen in that column (for example, 12345) and then in the next run process all values above that prior highest value (12345+1) up to the new highest value—you could miss the odd record! In this example, it's record 12344, which just happened to be committed a second or so after record 12345.

Processing data with a time delay of 60 seconds, for example, can remove this out-of-order issue on single-node instances—but not when RAC is involved. If RAC is involved, you need to seriously think about and investigate how you order your data.

The copies of the tables created by the website scripts are partitioned on CREATED_DT, which is why we include it in the primary keys, but you can create them unpartitioned, as shown here. Using a procedure in our test package, **pna_maint.pop_cuor_col** (so you can see what it does), we created a few thousand CUSTOMER_ORDER records per day, going back a couple of months, and between one and ten CUSTOMER_ORDER_LINES per order. We want to batch-process the data and create a summary of each order in a third table, CUSTOMER_ORDER_SUMMARY.

Let's pretend that the data volumes are much larger, so we have to process the data in chunks. We can do this by processing by ranges of CREATED_DT. We also know we want to be able to interrupt the processing. To make this safe, *we have to process the data in order*. If it is not and the load is interrupted, we would not know which records in the range had been processed. Let's create our PROCESS_MASTER record:

```
insert into process_master
       ( PROCESS_NAME ,LAST_EXECUTED_TIMESTAMP     ,PROCESS_RANGE
       ,STATUS        ,LOG_LEVEL       ,ABANDON_FL   ,BATCH_SIZE
       ,MAX_WINDOW    ,PROCESS_DELAY,LAST_TIMESTAMP1 )
values ('SUMMARIZE_ORDERS'   ,systimestamp           ,50000
       ,'C'           ,5               ,'N'          ,5000
       ,12            ,10              ,TO_TIMESTAMP('01-01-2016','DD-MM-YYYY') )
```

We are stating a few new columns and using one in a slightly different way. PROCESS_RANGE is the maximum number of records processed per execution. MAX_WINDOW limits how many days of data we will consider—which can also limit how many records we process but also stops our processing code from considering too much of the data at one time. PROCESS_DELAY means we will not consider data created in the last 10 minutes once we are up to date. This is because our application is poorly designed, and CUSTOMER_ORDER_LINES is not committed with CUSTOMER_ORDERS and may be committed a few seconds later. This is not an uncommon real-world situation, and leaving a little time gap before processing data can often solve the problem. Finally, LAST_TIMESTAMP initially has to be set to a date earlier than our first record; otherwise, we will miss data.

The second key part is identifying the range of data to process. We know the start point—it is where the last run got to. We just need the end point, but it can be limited by several factors (such as PROCESS_DELAY, MAX_WINDOW, and PROCESS_RANGE). We do this with code like the following (all the code is in procedure **pna_maint.summarize_orders**):

```
with source_t as
   (select /*+ materialize */ created_dt
                            ,rownum r1
    from (select created_dt
          from   customer_order
          where created_dt> pv_prma_rec.last_timestamp1
          and    created_dt <= pv_prma_rec.last_timestamp1
                                +(interval '1' hour*pv_prma_rec.max_window)
          and    created_dt <= systimestamp
                                -(interval '1' minute*pv_prma_rec.process_delay)
          order by created_dt)
    where rownum <=pv_prma_rec.process_range
   )
   -- get the max row from the ordered and limited set.
```

```
select max(created_dt)
          ,max(r1)
into p_end_dt
    ,p_expected_rows
from source_t st;
```

The bold section finds all the rows we might want to process:

- Any record older than our last run, **last_timestamp1**
- Any record younger than our largest time range, **max_window**
- Any record younger then now minus our delay, **process_delay**

This data set then has to be ordered by **created_dt**—we have to process the data in order. Having got the ordered set of data, we then limit it further by PROCESS_RANGE (**where rownum <=pv_prma_rec.process_range**), and that is our ordered and limited set. All we need now is the maximum CREATED_DT from that set. We also get the number of rows (**max(r1)**) because it is a useful sanity check.

As a second example, let's consider processing a historical set of data that goes back a year; we want to process the data in chunks of 100,000 rows (about a day or so's worth of data). Hopefully you can see that finding the first chunk would involve scanning the whole year of data and ordering it—if we did not have the MAX_WINDOW limit. So in this case, we might set MAX_WINDOW to be a week. On one system we saw that lacked this MAX_WINDOW concept, it took about an hour to scan and sort that volume of data and about two minutes to process the data it actually wanted to process. Adding the MAX_WINDOW concept reduced the hour scan-and-sort to a few seconds.

Our application code will then use this range of dates to fetch the data, via a cursor:

```
cursor get_cos is
    select cuor.id, cuor.created_dt,cuor.customer_id
        ,sum(col.unit_number) num_items
        ,sum(col.unit_number*col.unit_cost) tot_value
    from customer_order cuor
        ,customer_order_line col
    where cuor.id =col.cuor_id
    and    cuor.created_dt = col.created_dt
    and    cuor.created_dt >    p_start_dt
    and    cuor.created_dt <=   p_end_dt
    group by cuor.id, cuor.created_dt,cuor.customer_id
    order by cuor.created_dt;
```

Variables P_START_DT and P_END_DT are the values we just calculated. Note that the cursor orders the data set. We preserve this data range in the PROCESS_MASTER.WINDOW_ columns and PROCESS_RUN.START/END columns so that we know what was processed and we can either sort out issues manually if there is a failure (probably deleting a partial data set) or build in recovery code to carry on from where we got to:

```
pv_prma_rec.window_start_timestamp1 := pv_prma_rec.last_timestamp1;
pv_prma_rec.window_end_timestamp1   := p_end_dt;
pv_prma_rec.stage                        :=1;
upd_prma(pv_prma_rec,'WU');
```

```
pv_prru_rec.start_timestamp1 := pv_prma_rec.last_timestamp1;
pv_prru_rec.end_timestamp1   := p_end_dt;
upd_prru(pv_prru_rec,'WU');
```

The final piece involves how the data is processed. In reality we could do what we did here with a simple SQL statement, but we are demonstrating the method. We open the cursor, start looping, and bulk-collect a set of records, as defined with PROCESS_MASTER.BATCH_SIZE, on each loop. We "process" those records and then bulk-insert them into our target table. At each iteration of the loop we commit the new data and update the control tables with the progress to date.

We quit the loop when we run out of data, and then we update the control tables as we did in our simpler example. Here is the code to perform that processing loop:

```
v_count :=0; v_loop_count :=0;
open get_cos;
loop
   fetch get_cos bulk collect
   into get_cos_array  limit pv_prma_rec.batch_size;
   exit when get_cos_array.count = 0;
   v_loop_count:=v_loop_count+1;
   v_last       := get_cos_array.count;
   v_count :=v_count+v_Last;
   for i in 1..v_last loop  -- process the data
      if get_cos_array(i).num_items >60 then
         get_cos_array(i).tot_value :=round(get_cos_array(i).tot_value*.9,2);
      end if;
   end loop;
   -- push date into the final table
   forall i in indices of get_cos_array
  -- it would actually be best practice to state the columns and array columns
   insert into customer_order_summary
   values
      get_cos_array(i);
   commit;
   -- now update where we are
   pv_prma_rec.last_timestamp1 :=get_cos_array(v_last).created_dt;
   upd_prma(pv_prma_rec,'CF');
   pv_prru_rec.records_processed :=v_count;
   upd_prru(pv_prru_rec,'CS');
end loop main_loop;
```

In reality, your processing would be more complex and may well include looping through data from several tables or complex data processing. All you do is build up the code steps to do this, make calls to UPD_PRRU and UPD_PRMA to record the progress, and add in whatever extra control logic you want.

We now have our code and test data. In the sample code for this chapter, it is the procedure **pna_maint.summarize_orders**. We ran the processing a few times and queried PROCESS_RUNS:

```
PROCESS_NAME
----------------
SUMMARIZE_ORDERS
```

```
START_TS                ST COMPLETED     recs_p WIN  RANGE   BATCH ROWS_FROM    ROWS_TO
--------------------    -- ------------  ------ ---  ------- ----- -----------  -----------
12-MAR-16 14.06.57.857  C  14:07:04.403  29870  72   40,000  5000 11-15:07:14  14-15:07:05
12-MAR-16 13.54.34.157  A  13:54:34.158         72   40,000  5000
12-MAR-16 13.52.53.115  A  13:52:53.115         72   40,000  5000
12-MAR-16 13.47.41.240  C  13:47:50.267  29868  72   40,000  5000 08-15:07:20  11-15:07:14
12-MAR-16 13.46.26.110  C  13:46:32.799  20000  72   20,000  5000 06-14:48:32  08-15:07:20
12-MAR-16 13.26.13.165  C  13:26:16.525  15000  48   15,000  5000 05-02:40:32  06-14:48:32
12-MAR-16 13.24.42.388  C  13:24:45.638  15000  48   15,000  5000 03-14:32:57  05-02:40:32
12-MAR-16 13.23.31.234  C  13:23:35.450   8000  24    8,000  2000 02-19:12:52  03-14:32:57
12-MAR-16 13.17.57.130  C  13:18:01.375   8000  24    8,000  2000 01-23:55:55  02-19:12:52
12-MAR-16 13.17.20.897  C  13:17:22.120   4967  12   50,000  5000 01-11:59:56  01-23:55:55
12-MAR-16 13.06.49.531  C  13:06:51.805   5034  12   50,000  5000 01-00:00:00  01-11:59:56
```

The rows are shown from latest to earliest. Reading from the bottom, you can see us altering PROCESS_RANGE (RANGE) and MAX_WINDOW (WIN) and how that impacts the number of RECORDS_PROCESSED (recs_p). You can see which range of data each run processed and that for two recent runs we had set the job to (A)bandon.

The following shows the population of our WINDOWS columns in PROCESS_MASTER and the LAST_TIMESTAMP1 increasing as data is processed and committed:

```
PROCESS_NAME     LAST_EXECUTED_TS        LAST_TIMESTAMP1    WINDOW_START       WINDOW_END
---------------  ---------------------   -----------------  -----------------  -----------------
SUMMARIZE_ORDERS 12-MAR-16 15.46.26.422  15-JAN-16 03.06.04 14-JAN-16 15.07.05 17-JAN-16 15.06.58
```

```
START_TS                LOG_TS        ST LL LOG_TEXT
--------------------    -----------   -- -- --------------------------------------------------------
12-MAR-16 15.46.26.422  15:46:26.422  I   5 started at 16-03-12 15:46:26.422
12-MAR-16 15.46.26.422  15:46:26.422  I   5 identifying the range of data to process, limited by 40000
12-MAR-16 15.46.26.422  15:46:26.562  I   5 would process up to 17-JAN-16 15:06:58 processing 29908
12-MAR-16 15.46.26.422  15:46:29.176  I   5 iteration 1 processing 5000
```

```
-- A little later as the processing progresses
```

```
PROCESS_NAME     LAST_EXECUTED_TS        LAST_TIMESTAMP1    WINDOW_START       WINDOW_END
---------------  ---------------------   -----------------  -----------------  -----------------
SUMMARIZE_ORDERS 12-MAR-16 15.46.26.422  15-JAN-16 14.58.28 14-JAN-16 15.07.05 17-JAN-16 15.06.58
```

```
START_TS                LOG_TS        ST LL LOG_TEXT
--------------------    -----------   -- -- --------------------------------------------------------
12-MAR-16 15.46.26.422  15:46:26.422  I   5 started at 16-03-12 15:46:26.422
12-MAR-16 15.46.26.422  15:46:26.422  I   5 identifying the range of data to process, limited by 40000
12-MAR-16 15.46.26.422  15:46:26.562  I   5 would process up to 17-JAN-16 15:06:58 processing 29908
12-MAR-16 15.46.26.422  15:46:29.176  I   5 iteration 1 processing 5000
12-MAR-16 15.46.26.422  15:46:39.204  I   5 iteration 2 processing 5000
```

This shows the information from PROCESS_MASTER and PROCESS_LOG for one of our runs as it progresses. In the top half we processed 1 iteration of 5000 records. In the lower half we processed two iterations. We preserved our processing window in the PROCESS_MASTER .WINDOW_ columns: 14-JAN-16 15.07.05 17-JAN-16 15.06.58. As we progress and commit data, the value in PROCESS_MASTER.LAST_TIMESTAMP1 increments from 15-JAN-16 03.06.04 to 15-JAN-16 14.58.28, showing that we are recording the latest record committed.

That's it. We process all the historical data, and once we are up to date, the same code will process any new data that comes in (with that important ten-minute delay). However, there is one final part, which is abandoning the code mid-flight and recovering after an error. We will get to that after we discuss a few considerations about the processing window.

Automated Processing Easing Cyclic Development

The sample code in this section is very, very close to a real system we developed for a client not long ago. Initially the client simply wanted to migrate X years' worth of data from an old application to a new system. Then they wanted to feed from the old system to the new system in near real time for Y months, so the initially simple control code needed to be far more complex. As development progressed, it became apparent that the mapping of data from old to new was still being "discussed" and that the structure of the data in the old system had altered over time—and no documentation now existed on how it had changed. Also, the testing team needed at least a full year of transformed data to test the loaded and transformed data to ensure it was in the new format, which had only been decided that day, and which we soon learned would change the next day.

Our initial version of the bulk conversion code could have used a simpler set of tables than these and no recovery or restart. However, we implemented these features "just in case."

Over the weeks we ended up having to reprocess hundreds of gigabytes of the same historic data over and over again, with regular failures as new "forgotten features" of the data were found. The ability for the control harness to chunk though the data, halt on error (or change of specification), and be restarted saved us a lot of time, effort, and pain. We would often run it overnight, fix any errors in the morning, and have the converted data ready in the afternoon—for the latest requirement changes to force us to do it all again.

Further Considerations of the Processing Window

In our template Process Control tables, we allow for numeric and timestamp processing windows. Our example uses timestamps (or rather dates), but we do not have WINDOW columns for VARCHAR2. That is because we do not see true VARCHAR2 columns being used for the data ranges (the only time we can remember ever having to process data on a range of VARCHAR2 values, it was actually a prefixed numeric where the prefix could be ignored).

In our experience, we have processed data where we identified the last record by a NUMBER column, a DATE/TIMESTAMP column, both a NUMBER and DATE/TIMESTAMP, and rarely by two NUMBER columns. Therefore, PROCESS_MASTER has LAST_ID_NUM1, LAST_ID_NUM2, and LAST_TIMESTAMP1 to cope with all these permutations. If you encounter anything beyond that, you will need to add another column. Again, the only time we have encountered a VARCHAR2 as the "last processed" column, it was really holding a numeric.

We have covered why you would want to limit the range of data you consider when processing historical data (for performance reasons) and also why the process delay is potentially useful (to avoid partial data sets or issues around sequences used as primary keys) to come up with the processing window.

Why do we preserve the current processing window information in the PROCESS_MASTER table in the WINDOW_ columns? For recovery purposes, which we will get to later. Recalculating the values can be troublesome (for example, your PROCESS_DELAY would have to be based on the time when you last correctly ran the code) and it is a step you can avoid simply by recording the window details. We record the START_ and END_ values in the PROCESS_RUN table so we know the data range that particular run processed.

But you may be wondering why there is only LAST_TIMESTAMP1 in the PROCESS_MASTER table when we have columns for START_TIMESTAMP2 and END_TIMESTAMP2 on PROCESS_ RUN. This is because of an issue we have run into a couple of times, where the columns needed to identify the data to process on are not indexed and are not in the partition key—and getting them indexed would be a major issue because the application was provided by a third party. There is a solution to this, however.

Let's consider an example. Our CUSTOMER_ORDER table has a CREATED_DT but also a COMPLETED_DT, as shown here:

```
create table customer_order
(id              number    not null
,created_dt      date      not null
,customer_id     number    not null
,address_id      number    not null
,status          varchar2(1)
,completed_dt    date
)
```

Our business rule is that we only process orders that are completed, and we identify the records to be processed by that column—everything from the last COMPLETED_DT processed to one day after that. Therefore, our cursor to identify the code to process would be something like this:

```
cursor get_cos is
   select cuor.id, cuor.created_dt,cuor.customer_id
       ,sum(col.unit_number) num_items
       ,sum(col.unit_number*col.unit_cost) tot_value
   from customer_order cuor
       ,customer_order_line col
   where cuor.id =col.cuor_id
   and   cuor.created_dt = col.created_dt
   and   cuor.completed_dt >  last_rows_processed_dt
   and   cuor.completed_dt <= last_rows_processed_dt+1
   group by cuor.id, cuor.created_dt,cuor.customer_id
```

However, there is no index on CUOR.COMPLETED_DATE, and the partitioning does not include this column. The performance of this statement could be terrible, scanning the whole table, especially when there are several years of data in the table.

However, we can use some logic to help us out. First, the COMPLETED_DT cannot be before the CREATED_DT. Second, we may know that there are business rules such as the orders are all completed (or cancelled) within a given timespan (say three days). We can check what the largest gap between CREATED_DT and COMPLETED_DT has ever been (in our case it is about two days). So being conservative, we double that. We can add new WHERE clauses to our code:

```
   and   cuor.completed_dt >  last_rows_processed_dt
   and   cuor.completed_dt <= last_rows_processed_dt+1
   and   cuor.created_dt > last_rows_processed_dt-4
   and   cuor_created_dt < last_rows_processed+1
```

The CREATED_DT is indexed, so the cursor will perform significantly better.

We have used this method many times, and not just in automated batch-processing code. However, we do want to record this "wider window" that helps our processing—thus the extra columns.

Abandon, Error, and Restart

The final areas we have not covered are abandoning a run in a controlled manner part way through and restarting after an error. The two are actually pretty much the same. In one you are opting to end the run; in the other, this occurs by accident. However, the result is the same.

The first thing to ask yourself when building in the ability to abandon a current run and allow it to restart after abandoning or erroring is, is it worth the effort? More specifically, is it worth *the extra testing effort?* When you allow a process to be interrupted and then continue, you have to generate ways to cause that interruption and ensure that the data generated on recovery is as it would be if there had been no interruption (see the next sidebar, "Testing of Automated Database Administration Processing"). That is a lot more effort than actually adding the code to do it. The more complex the actual processing being done, the more potential there is for errors to occur, and the more test scenarios you will need to "prove" your restart capability.

Adding in the ability to abandon a task is easy, as you have already seen. The RUN_MASTER .ABANDON_FL column is already there; all you need is to add a check against that flag at the start of the code and at intervals within the body of the code. If the task is very simple and does not run for long, you may decide that it is not worth being able to abandon a current run.

However, we are going to modify our test code to allow in-flight abandoning of the code. First, we need to add a check for the abandon flag and a smooth exit of the code. *This is best done after you have committed data and updated the control information*. In the following example, we add code to do this, as well as code in the final control data update to check for the process being abandoned and to change the STATUS recorded in PROCESS_MASTER and PROCESS_RUN:

```
        insert into customer_order_summary
        values
          get_cos_array(i);
        commit;
        -- now update where we are
        pv_prma_rec.last_timestamp1 :=get_cos_array(v_last).created_dt;
        upd_prma(pv_prma_rec,'CF');
        pv_prru_rec.records_processed :=v_count;
        upd_prru(pv_prru_rec,'CS');
        -- check for abandon
        select abandon_fl into pv_prma_rec.abandon_fl
        from  process_master where process_name=pv_prma_rec.process_name;
        exit when pv_prma_rec.abandon_fl='Y';
      end loop main_loop;
...
    if pv_prma_rec.abandon_fl='Y' then
      pv_prru_rec.status      :='A';   pv_prma_rec.status      :='A';
    else
      pv_prru_rec.status      :='C';   pv_prma_rec.status      :='C';
    end if;
    pv_prru_rec.completed_timestamp  :=systimestamp;
    upd_prru(pv_prru_rec,'CF');
```

With this in place, after each set of records is processed, a check is made of ABANDON_FL; if it is set, the code exits cleanly.

One other thing is needed. We need to tell the code that it is recovering from being abandoned (you *can* code in logic to do this automatically, but this method is easier). The process will not run again while the STATUS is A (for abandoned); we have seen that already. When we are ready to go again, we set the status to R (for recovery).

The code picks this up and, rather than calculate the processing window as normal, it collects the preserved values from the PROCESS_MASTER table:

```
get_prma(pv_process_name,false); -- Need to see if last run errored or is running
if pv_prma_rec.status = 'I' then -- want to simply stop - Altering PRMA or PRRU would
                                 -- mess up running version
  write_log('attempted to run whilst already running, so aborted');
  raise abort_run;
elsif pv_prma_rec.status in ('E','R') then
  null; -- we leave as error, record the run, skip processing and close as error.
else pv_prma_rec.status :='I';
end if;
pv_prma_rec.last_executed_timestamp :=pv_exec_ts;
upd_prma(pv_prma_rec,'SU');
...
  if pv_prma_rec.status ='R' then
    p_end_dt :=pv_prma_rec.window_end_timestamp1;
    p_expected_rows :=-1;
  else
    write_plog('identifying the range of data to process, limited by'
||pv_prma_rec.process_range||' rows' ||' and '||pv_prma_rec.max_window||' hours');
    with source_t as
      (select /*+ materialize */ created_dt
...
```

Note that we are no longer calling GET_PRMA so that it updates the PROCESS_MASTER record automatically; we have to get the information only (**get_prma(pv_prma_rec,false)**) and then do different things depending on the status.

With this new code in place we can now do a controlled abandon of the code and then perform a recovery run:

```
PROCESS_NAME     LAST_EXECUTED_TS       ST  LAST_TIMESTAMP1   WINDOW_START        WINDOW_END
---------------- ---------------------- --  ----------------- ------------------- ------------------
SUMMARIZE_ORDERS 12-MAR-16 17.28.16.044 I   11-FEB-16 03.07.35 10-FEB-16 15.05.52 13-FEB-16 15.05.41


START_TS               LOG_TS        ST LL LOG_TEXT
---------------------- ------------- -- -- -----------------------------------------------------------
12-MAR-16 17.28.16.044 17:28:16.044 I   5 started at 16-03-12 17:28:16.044
12-MAR-16 17.28.16.044 17:28:16.044 I   5 identifying the range of data to process, limited by 40000
12-MAR-16 17.28.16.044 17:28:16.153 I   5 would process up to 13-FEB-16 15:05:41 processing 30023
12-MAR-16 17.28.16.044 17:28:16.153 I   5  processing range 10-FEB-16 15:05:52 to 13-FEB-16 15:05:41
12-MAR-16 17.28.16.044 17:28:16.434 I   5 iteration 1 processing 5000

-- in second session
update process_master set abandon_fl='Y'
```

```
where process_name = 'SUMMARIZE_ORDERS'
commit;
```

```
PROCESS_NAME      LAST_EXECUTED_TS       ST  LAST_TIMESTAMP1     WINDOW_START        WINDOW_END
----------------  ---------------------  --  ------------------  ------------------  ------------------
SUMMARIZE_ORDERS  12-MAR-16 17.28.16.044  A  11-FEB-16 15.06.46  10-FEB-16 15.05.52  13-FEB-16 15.05.41
```

```
START_TS                LOG_TS        ST LL LOG_TEXT
---------------------   ------------  -- -- ------------------------------------------------------------
12-MAR-16 17.28.16.044  17:28:16.044  I   5 started at 16-03-12 17:28:16.044
12-MAR-16 17.28.16.044  17:28:16.044  I   5 identifying the range of data to process, limited by 40000
12-MAR-16 17.28.16.044  17:28:16.153  I   5 would process up to 13-FEB-16 15:05:41 processing 30023
12-MAR-16 17.28.16.044  17:28:16.153  I   5 processing range 10-FEB-16 15:05:52 to 13-FEB-16 15:05:41
12-MAR-16 17.28.16.044  17:28:16.434  I   5 iteration 1 processing 5000
12-MAR-16 17.28.16.044  17:28:26.472  I   5 ended at 16-03-12 17:28:26.472
```

The process stopped after completing the processing of 5,000 records—we can see the LAST_TIMESTAMP has moved on and that process log shows the run ending in a controlled manner. The run was forecast to process 30,023 records. If we try to run this process again, it will simply abort because ABANDON_FL is set to A in PROCESS_MASTER.

We update the PROCESS_MASTER to set ABANDON _FL back to N and update the STATUS to R so that a recovery run occurs:

```
update process_master
set ABANDON_FL='N'
   ,status = 'R'
where process_name = 'SUMMARIZE_ORDERS';
```

```
PROCESS_NAME      LAST_EXECUTED_TS       ST  LAST_TIMESTAMP1     WINDOW_START        WINDOW_END
----------------  ---------------------  --  ------------------  ------------------  ------------------
SUMMARIZE_ORDERS  12-MAR-16 17.29.07.079  C  13-FEB-16 15.05.41  11-FEB-16 03.07.35  13-FEB-16 15.05.41
```

```
START_TS                LOG_TS        ST LL LOG_TEXT
---------------------   ------------  -- -- ------------------------------------------------------------
12-MAR-16 17.29.07.079  17:29:07.079  I   5 started at 16-03-12 17:29:07.079
12-MAR-16 17.29.07.079  17:29:07.079  I   5 would process up to 13-FEB-16 15:05:41 processing -1
12-MAR-16 17.29.07.079  17:29:07.079  I   5 processing range 11-FEB-16 03:07:35 to 13-FEB-16 15:05:41
12-MAR-16 17.29.07.079  17:29:07.079  I   5 would process up to 13-FEB-16 15:05:41 processing -1
12-MAR-16 17.29.07.079  17:29:07.297  I   5 iteration 1 processing 5000
12-MAR-16 17.29.07.079  17:29:17.323  I   5 iteration 2 processing 5000
12-MAR-16 17.29.07.079  17:29:27.351  I   5 iteration 3 processing 5000
12-MAR-16 17.29.07.079  17:29:37.371  I   5 iteration 4 processing 5000
12-MAR-16 17.29.07.079  17:29:47.401  I   5 iteration 5 processing 5000
12-MAR-16 17.29.07.079  17:29:57.423  I   5 iteration 6 processing 23
12-MAR-16 17.29.07.079  17:30:07.445  I   5 ended at 16-03-12 17:30:07.445
```

The job continues where it left off and processes 5 lots of 5,000 records and then 23 lots—so with the 5,000 records from the aborted run, that is the 30,023 rows initially expected.

Finally, we need to enhance the code to recover after an error. We slightly alter the exception code to roll back any outstanding changes before updating the control tables. The changes we added before had already prepared the code to recover after a failure. We insert a record into the

CUSTOMER_PROCESS_SUMMARY table so that the next record would fail with a unique constraint error. When we run the code, it fails:

```
insert into customer_order_summary
SELECT ID,CREATED_DT,CUSTOMER_ID,20,200
FROM CUSTOMER_ORDER
WHERE ID= 501500


exec pna_maint.summarize_orders
```

```
PROCESS_NAME     LAST_EXECUTED_TS          ST  LAST_TIMESTAMP1     WINDOW_START        WINDOW_END
---------------- ---------------------- -- ------------------ ------------------ --------------------
SUMMARIZE_ORDERS 12-MAR-16 18.34.10.083 E  20-FEB-16 03.04.57  19-FEB-16 15.05.40  22-FEB-16 15.05.30


START_TS               LOG_TS         ST LL LOG_TEXT
---------------------- ------------ -- -- ---------------------------------------------------------------
12-MAR-16 18.34.10.083 18:34:10.083 I   5 identifying the range of data to process, limited by 40000
12-MAR-16 18.34.10.083 18:34:10.083 I   5 started at 16-03-12 18:34:10.083
12-MAR-16 18.34.10.083 18:34:10.208 I   5  processing range 19-FEB-16 15:05:40 to 22-FEB-16 15:05:30
12-MAR-16 18.34.10.083 18:34:10.208 I   5 would process up to 22-FEB-16 15:05:30 processing 29986
12-MAR-16 18.34.10.083 18:34:10.208 I   5 would process up to 22-FEB-16 15:05:30 processing 29986
12-MAR-16 18.34.10.083 18:34:12.913 I   5 iteration 1 processing 5000
12-MAR-16 18.34.10.083 18:34:22.936 I   5 iteration 2 processing 5000
12-MAR-16 18.34.10.083 18:34:22.967 E   5 ORA-00001: unique constraint (MDWCH9.COS_PK) violated
12-MAR-16 18.34.10.083 18:34:22.967 E   5 ORA-06512: at "MDWCH9.PNA_MAINT", line 1595
```

We fix the error (by deleting the extra row we had added), set the PROCESS_MASTER.STATUS to R, and run the code again:

```
PROCESS_NAME     LAST_EXECUTED_TS          ST  LAST_TIMESTAMP1     WINDOW_START        WINDOW_END
---------------- ---------------------- -- ------------------ ------------------ --------------------
SUMMARIZE_ORDERS 12-MAR-16 18.38.51.306 C  22-FEB-16 15.05.30  19-FEB-16 15.05.40 22-FEB-16
15.05.30


START_TS               LOG_TS         ST LL LOG_TEXT
---------------------- ------------ -- -- ---------------------------------------------------------------
12-MAR-16 18.38.51.306 18:38:51.306 I   5  processing range 20-FEB-16 03:04:57 to 22-FEB-16 15:05:30
12-MAR-16 18.38.51.306 18:38:51.306 I   5 would process up to 22-FEB-16 15:05:30 processing -1
12-MAR-16 18.38.51.306 18:38:51.306 I   5 would process up to 22-FEB-16 15:05:30 processing -1
12-MAR-16 18.38.51.306 18:38:51.306 I   5 started at 16-03-12 18:38:51.306
12-MAR-16 18.38.51.306 18:38:53.884 I   5 iteration 1 processing 5000
12-MAR-16 18.38.51.306 18:39:03.916 I   5 iteration 2 processing 5000
12-MAR-16 18.38.51.306 18:39:13.948 I   5 iteration 3 processing 5000
12-MAR-16 18.38.51.306 18:39:23.979 I   5 iteration 4 processing 5000
12-MAR-16 18.38.51.306 18:39:34.011 I   5 iteration 5 processing 4986
12-MAR-16 18.38.51.306 18:39:44.043 I   5 ended at 16-03-12 18:39:44.043
```

As you can see, the code simply picked up where it left off and completed the next run. The total number of records processed by the failed and recovery runs combined matches the expected number of 29,986 records.

Testing of Automated Database Administration Processing

In the main code we describe the requirement to design a process such that it can be restarted—and that testing such code is the main difficulty. With database administration tasks, the potential to do damage with automated tasks is far higher than with data processing or application tasks. This is not to belittle data processing and application tasks or to suggest they do not need proper testing. However, there is a significant difference between making a mistake that damages data, which may or may not be fixable, and making a mistake in an automated archiving process where data is actually deleted rather than moved (or too much data is deleted). That will probably require a database recovery.

When you are automating database administration tasks that alter anything, be sure to test especially thoroughly! Once or twice early on in my career, I did not test such code well enough. The results were...painful—for both myself and the wider team.

Lack of Schedule Information in the Tables

You may be wondering why the RUN_MASTER table has no information about the scheduling of the process. This is because there are many ways to schedule automated tasks—with a dedicated scheduling application, with the Oracle scheduler (DBMS_SCHEDULER) as we have used in earlier examples, or even with cron—and most sites have a standard method of scheduling tasks.

In these cases, there is no need to hold scheduling information in the master table—when an application runs, the first thing it will do is collect its control information from the master table.

If you have no scheduling solution that can be used for Oracle tasks at your site, we would suggest you investigate the Oracle scheduler (DBMS_SCHEDULER), especially if you use OEM/Grid Control.

If you decide to create your own job scheduler (say, a PL/SQL job that runs every minute to find anything outstanding), you might add columns to the PROCESS_MASTER table. However, it would probably be a better solution if you create a new table to control the scheduling.

Process-Specific Tables

Some automated tasks might need extra information, such as your own stats-gathering job, where you gather specific statistics on particular tables, indexes, or extended columns statistics. We suggest that this extra task-specific information be implemented with a table dedicated to that information—and, of course, your application code will use that table and its data. You can use the four tables described earlier to hold the control information and logging/errors. You saw this in the section on automating the creation of new partitions, where we had a table named PARTITION_CONTROL to hold that information.

There is no need for any connection between these process-specific tables and the process-control tables, but you may want to add a column to PROCESS_MASTER to hold the name of the task-specific table, if only to help people track down where further information is held.

PL/SQL Packages for Aiding Database Developers and Administration

This book is about using SQL and PL/SQL, so we are not going to review all the built-in PL/SQL packages that come with Oracle. However, Oracle provides a lot of functionality via the built-in packages that can aid both the developer and administrator. For example, many tasks that are considered "DBA tools" provided via OEM are actually implemented via PL/SQL packages and can be used directly. We will look at one example of this, DBMS_WORKLOAD_REPOSITORY, which is used to produce AWR performance reports.

Other packages can provide information (often as SQL statements!) that is useful to developers and administrators, such as DBMS_METADATA (which is more capable than many realize) and the new Oracle 12c DBMS_UTILITY.EXPAND_SQL_TEXT.

Finally, there are packages that aid in both error handling and debugging by showing you where in your code stack errors occurred, as well as where you are. We will look at both DBMS_ UTILITY and the new UTL_CALL_STACK, which cover these requirements.

Built-in PL/SQL Packages Covered Elsewhere in This Book

Some built-in packages are covered extensively elsewhere in this book. For example, DBMS_ OUTPUT and DBMS_APPLICATION_INFO (for instrumenting PL/SQL) and the three packages for profiling PL/SQL (DBMS_TRACE, DBMS_PROFILER, and DBMS_HPROF) are covered in Chapter 7. DBMS_WARNING (to control PL/SQL compilation warnings) is also covered there (DBMS_RANDOM is partially discussed in that chapter, too). DBMS_SQL (used for dynamic SQL generation and execution) is covered in Chapter 8.

The packages used for limiting access to data (called Virtual Private Database, Row Level Security, or Fine Grained Access Control), DBMS_RLS and DBMS_SESSION.SET_CONTEXT, are covered in Chapter 16, which covers virtual private database and application contexts. DBMS_ ASSERT is covered in Chapter 15.

DBMS_WORKLOAD_REPOSITORY

DBMS_WORKLOAD_REPOSITORY contains procedures and functions for managing the Automatic Workload Repository (AWR) snapshots, running the reports you may have seen in OEM/Grid Control, and for creating baselines and coloring SQL (marking it so that information about it is always gathered).

This package is a prime example of how new functionality is often implemented in later versions of Oracle via PL/SQL packages. Many people think many of these DBA-type tools and the reports used in the OEM/Grid Control are part of OEM, but they can be used directly from SQL*Plus or any GUI SQL or PL/SQL development tool. Other examples are DBMS_ADDM for running the Automatic Database Diagnostic Monitor, DBMS_SQLTUNE for SQL Tuning Advisor, and DBMS_SPM for SQL plan management.

OEM is a great tool for managing AWR and running reports; however, you might not use or have access to OEM. Also, OEM is good for interactive use but you might want to run reports and such automatically. Pretty much everything you can do with AWR via OEM you can do via the PL/SQL packages.

Before we go any further, let's see what our AWR snapshot settings are and how to alter them. This is important because AWR reports compare information between snapshots. There is no function or procedure provided to show the current settings; instead, you look at the table DBA_HIST_WR_INTERVAL. However, you alter the settings with the procedure **dbms_workload_ repository.modify_snapshot_settings**.

```
select * from dba_hist_wr_control

      DBID SNAP_INTERVAL        RETENTION           TOPNSQL       CON_ID
```

```
---------- -------------------- -------------------- ---------- ----------
3937097240 +00000 01:00:00.0     +00008 00:00:00.0   DEFAULT            0

begin
  dbms_workload_repository.modify_snapshot_settings(retention =>42*24*60,interval  =>15);
end;
      DBID SNAP_INTERVAL        RETENTION            TOPNSQL    CON_ID
---------- -------------------- -------------------- ---------- ----------
3937097240 +00000 00:15:00.0     +00042 00:00:00.0   DEFAULT            0
```

NOTE
By default, AWR is running and takes snapshots every hour. However, you need the relevant license (Oracle diagnostics pack) to use the information, and Oracle audits if you look at the data. Also, if you have pluggable databases, the AWR settings have to be set in the root container, not at the pluggable database level. AWR runs at the instance level.

The defaults are hourly snapshots, retained for 8 days, with the top DEFAULT SQL statements being reported in any given section (which is 20). We changed the values to ones we typically use on production systems—a retention period of 42 days so we can compare month-on-month data and have a few days to do so, and a snapshot interval of 15 minutes. We changed the snapshot interval because the report is an average across the snapshot period, and an hour is typically too long to be able to attribute activity to a specific period of slow performance.

To see the snapshots that exist, we again look at the underlying tables, DBA_HIST_SNAPSHOTS plus DBA_HIST_DATABASE_INSTANCE, for some extra information:

```
--chk_snaps
select to_char(dhs.startup_time,' DD MON HH24:MI:SS')    inst_startup
      ,dhdi.instance_name inst_name ,dhdi.db_name       db_name
      ,dhs.dbid          dbid       ,dhs.snap_id        snap_id
      ,to_char(dhs.end_interval_time,'DD MON HH24:MI')   snap_time
      ,substr(to_char(dhs.flush_elapsed),7,13)           flush_elapsed
from dba_hist_snapshot dhs
    ,dba_hist_database_instance dhdi
where dhdi.dbid          = dhs.dbid
and   dhdi.instance_number = dhs.instance_number
and   dhdi.startup_time    = dhs.startup_time
and dhs.end_interval_time > systimestamp-nvl(&daysback,5)
order by snap_id desc

@chk_snaps
Enter value for daysback: 1
INST_STARTUP     INST_NAME    DB_NAME        DBID SNAP_ID SNAP_TIME    FLUSH_ELAPSED
---------------- ------------ -------- ---------- ------- ------------ -------------
 15 FEB 15:48:30 ora122       ORA122   3937097240    2477 29 FEB 14:00 00:00:00.1
                                                     2476 29 FEB 13:45 00:00:00.1
                                                     2475 29 FEB 13:30 00:00:00.4
                                                     2474 29 FEB 13:15 00:00:00.4
```

```
2473 29 FEB 12:55  00:00:00.2
2472 29 FEB 12:00  00:00:00.7
```

...

Having checked/altered our snapshot setting and seen how to find our snapshots, we can run some AWR reports. These reports pull out the top *n* SQL statements (top for physical reads, CPU, buffer gets, and a couple of others) and metrics for the period covered by the range of snapshots you state. If you ask for a large range (for example, a day), you are going to have a very broad and unfocused view of the activity of your database. This will allow you to see the outright most demanding SQL and the workload of your system, but it will likely be of limited use in solving performance issues. To do that, you need to identify the period of the performance issue and run reports for snapshots covering *only* that period. For example, if we had been informed of performance issues from 13:20 to 13:50 "today," we would run a report for snapshots 2474 to 2477 (that is, 13:15 to 14:00). If the performance problems spanned many hours, we would generate reports for each hour or part hour over the period so we could see the top SQL for each period.

In its simplest form, to run an AWR report you would use one of the functions that pass back a table type, which you convert into lines with the TABLE command, spooling the output to a file. You can run two versions, AWR_REPORT_TEXT and AWR_REPORT_HTML, which obviously produce a text and HTML report, respectively. Let's try the text version. You have to pass in the DBID, starting and ending SNAPSHOT_ID, and the INST_ID (1 for a non-RAC DB).

```
-- if using sql*plus, make your linesize and the specification for our column
-- wide enough for the report
Set lines 81 pages 0
Col output form a80
select output from table(dbms_workload_repository.awr_report_text
  (l_dbid =>3937097240
  ,l_bid  =>2464  ,l_eid  =>2468
  ,l_inst_num =>1   ))


WORKLOAD REPOSITORY report for
DB Name        DB Id        Instance      Inst Num Startup Time     Release      RAC
------------ ----------- ------------ -------- --------------- ----------- ---
ORA122       3937097240 ora122               1 15-Feb-16 15:48 12.1.0.2.0  NO


Host Name         Platform                            CPUs Cores Sockets Memory(GB)
---------------- ------------------------------ ---- ----- ------- ----------
MSI-MDW-LAPTOP   Microsoft Windows x86 64-bit        8     4       1      15.92


                Snap Id      Snap Time        Sessions Curs/Sess  CDB
             --------- ------------------- -------- --------- -----
Begin Snap:      2464 28-Feb-16 19:00:49       54      1.8 YES
  End Snap:      2468 28-Feb-16 23:00:19       58      1.7 YES
  Elapsed:            239.49 (mins)
  DB Time:              3.79 (mins)


Load Profile                    Per Second   Per Transaction Per Exec  Per Call
~~~~~~~~~~~~~~~~~               --------------- --------------- --------- ---------
            DB Time(s):              0.0             0.2      0.00      0.01
```

```
         DB CPU(s):               0.0            0.1       0.00      0.01
Background CPU(s):                0.0            0.0       0.00      0.00
 Redo size (bytes):           7,054.5       84,476.1
Logical read (blocks):          681.5        8,161.2
     Block changes:              44.6          533.6
```

. . .

The report will take a few seconds to run, depending on your settings. The report run duration does not depend on the width of the range because it compares the start and end snapshots, not the ones in between.

You can run the HTML version in a similar way, but the output for the file is wider, even though when viewed in a browser the layout is a similar width to the text version of the report. In SQL*Plus you need to set your line size and column size to 1500 (the size of VARCHAR2 the table function returns). You can run the report for a different snapshot range when you know you have some database activity:

```
--awr_html1
set lines 1500 pages 0
col output form a1500
set term off
spool awr_html.html
select output from table(dbms_workload_repository.awr_report_html
  (l_dbid =>3937097240
  ,l_bid  =>2462    ,l_eid   =>2463
  ,l_inst_num =>1  ))
/
spool off
set term on
```

You spool out to a file with an .html extension so that your browser recognizes it. Figure 9-1 shows the output for this example.

WORKLOAD REPOSITORY report for

DB Name	DB Id	Instance	Inst num	Startup Time	Release	RAC
ORA122	3937097240	ora122	1	15-Feb-16 15:02	12.1.0.2.0	NO

Host Name	Platform	CPUs	Cores	Sockets	Memory (GB)
MSI-MDW-LAPTOP	Microsoft Windows x86 64-bit	8	4	1	15.92

	Snap Id	Snap Time	Sessions	Cursors/Session	CDB
Begin Snap:	2454	27-Feb-16 23:00:55	53	1.7	YES
End Snap:	2469	29-Feb-16 00:00:23	58	1.7	YES
Elapsed:		1,499.48 (mins)			
DB Time:		15.05 (mins)			

Report Summary

Figure 9-1. *AWR HTML report*

Generating AWR reports "by hand" is fine, but really you want to automate them. Perhaps the best way is to create a directory and have reports run every hour or day, as you see fit. As mentioned before, daily reports lack the detail to properly investigate issues, but they provide a good way of looking for changing overall workload patterns and system-wide shifts in activity. Hourly reports are better for investigating issues and, of course, if you have the snapshots still you can create new reports manually as you see fit. You can make these reports available to people who do not have access to the production system.

First, create an OS directory for the reports and then an Oracle DIRECTORY object:

```
create or replace directory AWR_reports as 'D:\sqlwork\AWR_reports';
```

Here is code to run a daily AWR report for yesterday. The code gets the instance DBID and number, identifies the latest snapshot in the day before yesterday and the first snapshot today (you may need to consider what to do if no snapshot yet exists for today). The code uses UTL_FILE to open a file in the AWR_Reports DIR and return a file handle into **v_file_handle**. The AWR_REPORT_HTML is run and the output put into the file, which is then closed. Whenever you open files with UTL_FILE, it is good practice to close them again if any exceptions are raised.

```
declare
v_dir    varchar2(20)  :='AWR_REPORTS';
v_file   varchar2(30);
v_dbid   number;        v_inst   number;
v_snap_s pls_integer;    v_snap_e pls_integer;
v_file_handle utl_file.file_type;
begin
  select dbid              into v_dbid from v$database;
  select instance_number into v_inst from v$instance;
  select max(snap_id)     into v_snap_s
  from dba_hist_snapshot
  where dbid=v_dbid      and    instance_number = v_inst
  and end_interval_time between (trunc(systimestamp-2))
                       and      (trunc(systimestamp-1));
  select min(snap_id) into v_snap_e
  from dba_hist_snapshot
  where dbid=v_dbid      and    instance_number = v_inst
  and end_interval_time between (trunc(systimestamp))   and      (systimestamp);
  v_file :='AWR_'||to_char(sysdate-1,'YYMMDD')||'_'||to_char(v_snap_s)
          ||'-'||to_char(v_snap_e)||'.html';
  dbms_output.put_Line ('would run report for '||to_char(v_dbid)||' '
                       ||to_char(v_inst)||' for '||to_char(v_snap_s)||' to '
                       || to_char(v_snap_e));
  dbms_output.put_Line ('file '||v_file);
  v_file_handle :=utl_file.fopen(v_dir,v_file,'w',1500);
  for awr_lines in
    (select output from table(dbms_workload_repository.awr_report_html
                      (l_dbid =>v_dbid
                      ,l_bid  =>v_snap_s    ,l_eid  =>v_snap_e
                      ,l_inst_num => v_inst)  ) )                loop
    utl_file.put_line(v_file_handle,awr_lines.output);
  end loop;
  utl_file.fclose(v_file_handle);
```

```
exception
  when others then
    if utl_file.is_open(v_file_handle) then
      utl_file.fclose(v_file_handle);
    end if;
    raise;
end;

-- output
would run report for 3937097240 1 for 2454 to 2469
file AWR_160228_2454-2469.html
```

We then find the file created (**v_file := 'AWR_' || to_char(sysdate-1,'YYMMDD')…**) in our output directory and click on it, which should open it up in your web browser. By naming the AWR file by date and snap_id range, we can run other reports in this directory without overwriting any existing reports due to the naming convention (for example, we could also run hourly or 3-hourly reports into this directory). If this was a RAC database we would include the instance ID in the filename.

It would be a simple task for you to convert this code into a stored procedure or package and enhance it to run hourly reports as well. Of course, you could then automate it using the control and logging tables covered earlier in this chapter.

Just like with the text reports, there are global versions of these reports as well, to cover multiple instances of a RAC cluster, called, for example, AWR_GLOBAL_REPORT_HTML.

You can also run difference reports between snapshot periods, which is very useful for comparing, for example, your daily or hourly reports between normal running and when you had an issue. You can then see what metrics are changing, if there is a large discrepancy, or whether the top SQL statements have changed substantially (which is something we look for in particular). Figure 9-2 is an example of the HTML diff report. Just as with the standard reports, there are also GLOBAL and TEXT versions. As you can see in the following example, you simply provide two sets of snapshot information. One minor annoyance is that the AWR_REPORT_HTML has parameters with an "l_" prefix. The diff report has parameters without the prefix.

```
select output from table(dbms_workload_repository.awr_diff_report_html
  (dbid1 =>3937097240 ,bid1  =>2505 ,eid1  =>2506 ,inst_num1 =>1
  ,dbid2 =>3937097240 ,bid2  =>2506 ,eid2  =>2507 ,inst_num2 =>1 ))
```

We ran the report for two snaps next to each other (2505–2506 and 2506–2507) as we ran different workloads in each 15-minute period. The start of the report is shown in Figure 9-2.

If you encounter a performance issue and you want to take snapshots during the issue, or ideally before and after replicating the issue (so you can run AWR reports against snapshots that are focused on covering the time of the issue), you can do so easily, as the following example shows:

```
exec dbms_workload_repository.create_snapshot

-- We check the recent snapshots and see one not at the usual 15 min intervals
@chk_snaps
INST_STARTUP       INST_NAME      DB_NAME         DBID SNAP_ID SNAP_TIME    FLUSH_ELAPSED
----------------   ------------   --------   ---------- ------- ------------ -------------
 15 FEB 15:48:30 ora122         ORA122     3937097240    2501 29 FEB 19:50  00:00:00.7
                                                         2500 29 FEB 19:45  00:00:00.7
                                                         2499 29 FEB 19:30  00:00:00.1
```

WORKLOAD REPOSITORY COMPARE PERIOD REPORT

Report Summary

Snapshot Set	DB Name	DB Id	Instance	Inst num	Release	Cluster	Host	Std Block Size
First (1st)	ORA122	3937097240	ora122	1	12.1.0.2.0	NO	MSI-MDW-LAPTOP	
Second (2nd)	ORA122	3937097240	ora122	1	12.1.0.2.0	NO	MSI-MDW-LAPTOP	

Snapshot Set	Begin Snap Id	Begin Snap Time	End Snap Id	End Snap Time	Avg Active Users	Elapsed Time (min)	DB time (min)
1st	2505	29-Feb-16 20:45:09 (Mon)	2506	29-Feb-16 21:00:11 (Mon)	0.1	15.0	0.9
2nd	2506	29-Feb-16 21:00:11 (Mon)	2507	29-Feb-16 21:15:12 (Mon)	0.1	15.0	1.5
%Diff					66.7	0.0	67.3

Host Configuration Comparison

	1st	2nd	Diff	%Diff
Number of CPUs:	8	8	0	0.0
Number of CPU Cores:	4	4	0	0.0
Number of CPU Sockets:	1	1	0	0.0
Physical Memory:	16303.7M	16303.7M	0M	0.0
Load at Start Snapshot:				
%User Time:	4.84	5.35	.51	10.5
%System Time:	1.4	1.27	-.13	-9.3
%Idle Time:	93.77	93.4	-.38	-0.4

Load Profile

	1st per sec	2nd per sec	%Diff	1st per txn	2nd per txn	%Diff
DB time:	0.1	0.1	66.7	1.1	1.4	18.3
CPU time:	0.1	0.1	66.7	1.1	1.3	22.2
Background CPU time:	0.0	0.0	100.0	0.1	0.1	0.0
Redo size (bytes):	636,872.9	775,638.8	21.8	12,480,811.5	10,753,348.6	-13.8

Figure 9-2. *An HTML AWR diff report*

Next, we will show you how to get targeted information about a specific SQL statement and cover the concept of coloring a SQL statement.

You can run a text or HTML AWR report for a specific SQL statement. We will demonstrate this by looking for a specific statement run with part of the **pna_maint.pop_pers** procedure: SQL_ID "0agr573bs40nb" for a statement inserting records into PERSON (the SQL_ID was obtained from our AWR difference report but can be obtained in many ways). The SQL*Plus spooling and such is the same as in the other examples, so for brevity we will show just the raw statement. Figure 9-3 shows the start of the HTML report.

```
select output from table(dbms_workload_repository.awr_report_html
    (l_dbid =>3937097240 ,l_bid  =>2462  ,l_eid  =>2463  ,l_inst_num =>1  ))
```

WORKLOAD REPOSITORY SQL Report

Snapshot Period Summary

DB Name	DB Id	Instance	Inst num	Startup Time	Release	RAC
ORA122	3937097240	ora122	1	15-Feb-16 15:02	12.1.0.2.0	NO

	Snap Id	Snap Time	Sessions	Cursors/Session
Begin Snap:	2506	29-Feb-16 21:00:11	59	2.1
End Snap:	2507	29-Feb-16 21:15:12	56	2.2
Elapsed:		15.02 (mins)		
DB Time:		1.47 (mins)		

SQL Summary

SQL Id	Elapsed Time (ms)	Module	Action	SQL Text
0agr573bs40nb	2,268	Module: POP_PERS	CREATING FAMILIES	INSERT INTO PERSON (PERS_ID , SURNAME , FIRST_FORENAME , SECOND_FORENA...

Back to Top

SQL ID: 0agr573bs40nb

- 1st Capture and Last Capture Snap IDs refer to Snapshot IDs witin the snapshot range
- INSERT INTO PERSON (PERS_ID ,SURNAME ,FIRST_FORENAME ,SECOND_FORENAME ...

#	Plan Hash Value	Total Elapsed Time(ms)	Executions	1st Capture Snap ID	Last Capture Snap ID
1	824332917	2,268	59.933	2507	2507

Figure 9-3. *SQL ID specific AWR report*

Normally Oracle will include the top *n* SQL statements in a report for various factors (CPU, buffer gets, physical gets, and so on), but when a statement is swapping between several plans or alters its performance due to different values for bind variables, it will appear in some reports and not in others, depending on whether it happens to be in the top *n* during that snapshot. You may well want to always see this statement, and DBMS_WORKLOAD_REPOSITORY has the ability to "color" a statement so that it is always in the report (if the statement runs in that period). You need the SQL_ID of the statement, and you color it like so:

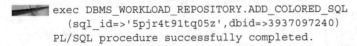

```
exec DBMS_WORKLOAD_REPOSITORY.ADD_COLORED_SQL
    (sql_id=>'5pjr4t91tq05z',dbid=>3937097240)
PL/SQL procedure successfully completed.
```

Now, whenever this statement runs in a period covered by a snapshot, information about it will be collected. You remove the coloring of a statement with the almost identical:

```
exec DBMS_WORKLOAD_REPOSITORY.REMOVE_COLORED_SQL
    (sql_id=>'5pjr4t91tq05z',dbid=>3937097240)
PL/SQL procedure successfully completed.
```

There are other aspects of DBMS_WORKLOAD_REPOSITORY, such as creating and using baselines and running ASH reports (which are very similar to AWR reports but use the more detailed Active Session History data held mostly in memory for the last hour or so). However, we just wanted to show you that by calling the provided PL/SQL package directly using SQL and PL/SQL, you can generate all the same reports you can via the OEM/Grid Control and you can also automate running these reports.

DBMS_METADATA

If you want to look up some aspect of your database objects, you can use the various dictionary views (DBA_, ALL_, USER_TABLE/INDEX/SEQUENCE, and so on) that hold everything about the objects you have access to. However, finding where the exact piece of information you want is held can take a bit of rooting out or joining across those dictionary views. Sometimes you need to duplicate parts of an Oracle Database structure or copy it with some minor changes. You could perform an object-only export and import, copy tables, and rebuild indexes, but this can be a lot of fiddly work, and you may well end up going back to the dictionary views and writing queries to generate creation scripts. But formatting the output of the queries on such views into executable scripts is not straightforward, and the time required to write the queries can be considerable.

These situations are where DBMS_METADATA comes in. This is a package Oracle introduced in version 9*i* that still seems to be overlooked at times or else only used in its most rudimentary way. It creates the DDL for *any object* in the database, including all the options. As new options and objects are introduced to Oracle, DBMS_METADATA is updated to include them.

Let's start with a simple example. We will retrieve the DDL to create the standard Oracle demonstration table HR.EMPLOYEES (you need access to the table to do this):

```
set pagesize 0
set lines 100
set long 20000
select dbms_metadata.get_ddl('TABLE','EMPLOYEES','HR') from dual;

CREATE TABLE "HR"."EMPLOYEES"
   (    "EMPLOYEE_ID" NUMBER(6,0),
        "FIRST_NAME" VARCHAR2(20),
        "LAST_NAME" VARCHAR2(25) CONSTRAINT "EMP_LAST_NAME_NN" NOT NULL ENABLE,
        "EMAIL" VARCHAR2(25) CONSTRAINT "EMP_EMAIL_NN" NOT NULL ENABLE,
        "PHONE_NUMBER" VARCHAR2(20),
        "HIRE_DATE" DATE CONSTRAINT "EMP_HIRE_DATE_NN" NOT NULL ENABLE,
        "JOB_ID" VARCHAR2(10) CONSTRAINT "EMP_JOB_NN" NOT NULL ENABLE,
        "SALARY" NUMBER(8,2),
        "COMMISSION_PCT" NUMBER(2,2),
        "MANAGER_ID" NUMBER(6,0),
        "DEPARTMENT_ID" NUMBER(4,0),
         CONSTRAINT "EMP_SALARY_MIN" CHECK (salary > 0) ENABLE,
         CONSTRAINT "EMP_EMAIL_UK" UNIQUE ("EMAIL")
USING INDEX PCTFREE 10 INITRANS 2 MAXTRANS 255 COMPUTE STATISTICS NOLOGGING
STORAGE(INITIAL 65536 NEXT 1048576 MINEXTENTS 1 MAXEXTENTS 2147483645
PCTINCREASE 0 FREELISTS 1 FREELIST GROUPS 1
BUFFER_POOL DEFAULT FLASH_CACHE DEFAULT CELL_FLASH_CACHE DEFAULT)
TABLESPACE "EXAMPLE"  ENABLE,
         CONSTRAINT "EMP_EMP_ID_PK" PRIMARY KEY ("EMPLOYEE_ID")
USING INDEX PCTFREE 10 INITRANS 2 MAXTRANS 255 COMPUTE STATISTICS NOLOGGING
STORAGE(INITIAL 65536 NEXT 1048576 MINEXTENTS 1 MAXEXTENTS 2147483645
PCTINCREASE 0 FREELISTS 1 FREELIST GROUPS 1
BUFFER_POOL DEFAULT FLASH_CACHE DEFAULT CELL_FLASH_CACHE DEFAULT)
TABLESPACE "EXAMPLE"  ENABLE,
         CONSTRAINT "EMP_DEPT_FK" FOREIGN KEY ("DEPARTMENT_ID")
          REFERENCES "HR"."DEPARTMENTS" ("DEPARTMENT_ID") ENABLE,
```

```
    CONSTRAINT "EMP_JOB_FK" FOREIGN KEY ("JOB_ID")
     REFERENCES "HR"."JOBS" ("JOB_ID") ENABLE,
    CONSTRAINT "EMP_MANAGER_FK" FOREIGN KEY ("MANAGER_ID")
     REFERENCES "HR"."EMPLOYEES" ("EMPLOYEE_ID") ENABLE )
SEGMENT CREATION IMMEDIATE
PCTFREE 10 PCTUSED 40 INITRANS 1 MAXTRANS 255
NOCOMPRESS NOLOGGING
STORAGE(INITIAL 65536 NEXT 1048576 MINEXTENTS 1 MAXEXTENTS 2147483645
PCTINCREASE 0 FREELISTS 1 FREELIST GROUPS 1
BUFFER_POOL DEFAULT FLASH_CACHE DEFAULT CELL_FLASH_CACHE DEFAULT)
TABLESPACE "EXAMPLE"  BUFFER_POOL DEFAULT FLASH_CACHE DEFAULT
CELL_FLASH_CACHE DEFAULT)
  TABLESPACE "USERS"
```

That gives us the full creation script. Perhaps the output contains too much detail about the EMPLOYEES table, but you will learn how to reduce the amount of details in the following steps.

We have set **pagesize** to 0 in SQL*Plus to suppress formatting information such as page breaks. The reason for setting **long** to 20000 is that the GET_DDL function returns a CLOB, and SQL*Plus only displays 80 bytes of a CLOB by default. We have increased it to 20000 bytes so that we can see the complete returned value of the CLOB.

By reading the command we ran, you might have already guessed the parameters required to call the GET_DDL function. Here is the specification for the procedure:

```
DBMS_METADATA.GET_DDL (
object_type      IN VARCHAR2,
name             IN VARCHAR2,
schema           IN VARCHAR2 DEFAULT NULL,
version          IN VARCHAR2 DEFAULT 'COMPATIBLE',
model            IN VARCHAR2 DEFAULT 'ORACLE',
transform        IN VARCHAR2 DEFAULT 'DDL')
RETURN CLOB;
```

As you can see, we have called the procedure with 'TABLE' as the **object_type**, 'EMPLOYEES' as the **name**, and 'HR' as the **schema** (the same as OWNER, as stated in many other data dictionary views), and we have relied on the default values for the rest of the parameters. If we had been logged on as HR we would not have needed to state the schema.

You need to consider an important point when calling GET_DDL, and in fact any procedure or function in DBMS_METADATA: unlike in many other packages where Oracle will handle the case of object names, the input parameters are case-sensitive; therefore, if 'employees' is supplied as the name parameter instead of 'EMPLOYEES', the following exception is thrown:

```
ORA-31603: object "employees" of type TABLE not found in schema "HR"
```

This is because you can force Oracle to create tables with lowercase or mixed-case names by putting the name in quotes. Many other databases allow such table names, so Oracle does too, if you really want to do it. Personally, we think it is a bad idea to do this because it makes referencing the specific table more problematic in other ways.

Note that you can state the VERSION and also the MODEL for GET_DDL. You can state any Oracle version from 9.2 onward to get the DDL for that version. You might expect MODEL to allow you to state other database languages, such as MySQL or SQL Server—but it only allows 'ORACLE'.

Controlling Output

Our DDL includes all aspects of the table—it has to because we could have altered any of those aspects, such as storage, compression, or segment information. Even if they are the defaults, some of those defaults might be overridden in the database or schema where we run this code. Rather than make things even more complex by trying to work out which defaults might be ignored, Oracle just gives us the full syntax of the DDL. But we might not want it all. Thankfully, to save us a lot of editing work, Oracle provides the **dbms_metadata.set_transform_param** procedure to enforce "transformations" on the output of the **get_ddl** function. In this case, we can disable reporting the STORAGE clause in the output of the function.

```
exec dbms_metadata.set_transform_param(dbms_metadata.session_transform
,'STORAGE',false)
```

Then we run the initial query again:

```
select dbms_metadata.get_ddl('TABLE','EMPLOYEES','HR') from dual;

CREATE TABLE "HR"."EMPLOYEES"
  (    "EMPLOYEE_ID" NUMBER(6,0),
...
        CONSTRAINT "EMP_EMAIL_UK" UNIQUE ("EMAIL")
USING INDEX PCTFREE 10 INITRANS 2 MAXTRANS 255 COMPUTE STATISTICS NOLOGGING
TABLESPACE "EXAMPLE"  ENABLE,
        CONSTRAINT "EMP_EMP_ID_PK" PRIMARY KEY ("EMPLOYEE_ID")
USING INDEX PCTFREE 10 INITRANS 2 MAXTRANS 255 COMPUTE STATISTICS NOLOGGING
TABLESPACE "EXAMPLE"  ENABLE,
...
  ) SEGMENT CREATION IMMEDIATE
PCTFREE 10 PCTUSED 40 INITRANS 1 MAXTRANS 255
NOCOMPRESS NOLOGGING
TABLESPACE "EXAMPLE"
```

As you can see, all STORAGE clauses are gone, including for the indexes created as part of constraint declarations.

Before we move on to describing how to control the display of other bits of the output, let's discuss a point about the **dbms_metadata.set_transform_param** procedure. This procedure has multiple interfaces. We used the following interface to call it:

```
DBMS_METADATA.SET_TRANSFORM_PARAM (
    transform_handle    IN NUMBER,
    name                IN VARCHAR2,
    value               IN BOOLEAN DEFAULT TRUE,
    object_type         IN VARCHAR2 DEFAULT NULL);
```

The **transform_handle** is a concept that facilitates two different use cases for functions such as DBMS_METADATA.GET_DDL:

- You might want to perform one unit definition retrieval using DBMS_METADATA at a time.
- You might want to handle multiple definition retrieval tasks one after the other in the same session.

You may have noticed we used **dbms_metadata.session_transform** as the value for the handle when we called the **set_transform_param** procedure. It means the transformation that we have chosen to apply will be applied to all GET_DDL and similar commands in the session from this point until we change the state of that transformation.

We will talk about the second use case (handling multiple definition retrieval tasks at the same time) when we cover examples of using DBMS_METADATA in PL/SQL.

If the table is created using the default segment attributes, reporting segment attributes might also not be necessary. As you can see the HR.EMPLOYEES table and the primary key and unique constraint indexes are created using the default segment attributes:

```
SEGMENT CREATION IMMEDIATE
  PCTFREE 10 PCTUSED 40 INITRANS 1 MAXTRANS 255
NOCOMPRESS LOGGING
  TABLESPACE "USERS"
```

We can disable the display of segment attributes with the following transform:

```
exec dbms_metadata.set_transform_param(dbms_metadata.session_transform
  ,'SEGMENT_ATTRIBUTES',false)

select dbms_metadata.get_ddl ('TABLE','EMPLOYEES','HR') from dual;

CREATE TABLE "HR"."EMPLOYEES"
  (    "EMPLOYEE_ID" NUMBER(6,0),
       "FIRST_NAME" VARCHAR2(20),
...
       CONSTRAINT "EMP_EMAIL_UK" UNIQUE ("EMAIL")
USING INDEX  ENABLE,
       CONSTRAINT "EMP_EMP_ID_PK" PRIMARY KEY ("EMPLOYEE_ID")
USING INDEX  ENABLE,
       CONSTRAINT "EMP_DEPT_FK" FOREIGN KEY ("DEPARTMENT_ID")
        REFERENCES "HR"."DEPARTMENTS" ("DEPARTMENT_ID") ENABLE,
       CONSTRAINT "EMP_JOB_FK" FOREIGN KEY ("JOB_ID")
        REFERENCES "HR"."JOBS" ("JOB_ID") ENABLE,
       CONSTRAINT "EMP_MANAGER_FK" FOREIGN KEY ("MANAGER_ID")
        REFERENCES "HR"."EMPLOYEES" ("EMPLOYEE_ID") ENABLE
  )
```

That is probably closer to the actual DDL we wanted originally.

The relationship between SEGMENT_ATTRIBUTES, STORAGE, and TABLESPACE transformation is an important one to remember. There is a hierarchy here: TABLESPACE transformation is a subset of STORAGE transformation, and STORAGE transformation is a subset of SEGMENT_ATTRIBUTES itself.

Therefore, if you disable the display of SEGMENT_ATTRIBUTES by enforcing the associated transformation, the state of STORAGE (and consequently TABLESPACE) transformations will be ignored and they will not be displayed.

The segment attributes encompass compression and logging as well, but the DBMS_METADATA does not provide any specific transformation to control the display of those attributes, and they both are controlled by the SEGMENT_ATTRIBUTES transformation.

It is possible to choose to not display constraints and referential constraints:

```
exec dbms_metadata.set_transform_param(dbms_metadata.session_transform
,'REF_CONSTRAINTS',false);
exec dbms_metadata.set_transform_param(dbms_metadata.session_transform
,'CONSTRAINTS',false);
```

You can also get DBMS_METADATA to put a SQL*Plus SQL terminator at the end of the script (but be warned, sometimes the output from GET_DDL won't run as it breaks over lines, depending on your column and line size settings):

```
exec dbms_metadata.set_transform_param(dbms_metadata.session_transform
,'SQLTERMINATOR', true)
```

Partitioned Tables

We will look at partitioned tables using the SH.SALES table. (Note that we still have SEGMENT_ATTRIBUTES, CONSTRAINTS, and REF_CONSTRAINTS disabled for the sake of space and clarity.)

```
Col output form a140
Set lines 140
SELECT DBMS_METADATA.GET_DDL ('TABLE','SALES','SH')  output FROM DUAL;

  CREATE TABLE "SH"."SALES"
   (    "PROD_ID" NUMBER,
        "CUST_ID" NUMBER,
        "TIME_ID" DATE,
        "CHANNEL_ID" NUMBER,
        "PROMO_ID" NUMBER,
        "QUANTITY_SOLD" NUMBER(10,2),
        "AMOUNT_SOLD" NUMBER(10,2)
   )
  PARTITION BY RANGE ("TIME_ID")
 (PARTITION "SALES_1995"  VALUES LESS THAN (TO_DATE(' 1996-01-01 00:00:00',
'SYYYY-MM-DD HH24:MI:SS', 'NLS_CALENDAR=GREGORIAN')) ,
 PARTITION "SALES_1996"  VALUES LESS THAN (TO_DATE(' 1997-01-01 00:00:00',
'SYYYY-MM-DD HH24:MI:SS', 'NLS_CALENDAR=GREGORIAN')) ,
 PARTITION "SALES_H1_1997"  VALUES LESS THAN (TO_DATE(' 1997-07-01 00:00:00',
'SYYYY-MM-DD HH24:MI:SS', 'NLS_CALENDAR=GREGORIAN')) ,
 PARTITION "SALES_H2_1997"  VALUES LESS THAN (TO_DATE(' 1998-01-01 00:00:00',
'SYYYY-MM-DD HH24:MI:SS', 'NLS_CALENDAR=GREGORIAN')) ,
 PARTITION "SALES_Q1_1998"  VALUES LESS THAN (TO_DATE(' 1998-04-01 00:00:00',
'SYYYY-MM-DD HH24:MI:SS', 'NLS_CALENDAR=GREGORIAN')) ,
 PARTITION "SALES_Q2_1998"  VALUES LESS THAN (TO_DATE(' 1998-07-01 00:00:00',
'SYYYY-MM-DD HH24:MI:SS', 'NLS_CALENDAR=GREGORIAN')) ,
 ...
 PARTITION "SALES_Q4_2003"  VALUES LESS THAN (TO_DATE(' 2004-01-01 00:00:00',
'SYYYY-MM-DD HH24:MI:SS', 'NLS_CALENDAR=GREGORIAN')) )
```

You may notice we used the SQL*Plus commands **set lines 140** and **col output form a140** and gave the column we are selecting (using the function GET_DDL) the column alias "output."

With much of the output of GET_DDL, the DDL statement is nicely formatted within 80 characters, but with partitions, it often exceeds this and splits wherever the (default) column size or line size falls, and you have to edit the script. We actually still had to edit the layout to fit within the page size of this book (but that is our problem, not yours).

You can suppress the partitioning information like so:

```
exec dbms_metadata.set_transform_param(dbms_metadata.session_transform
  ,'PARTITIONING', false);
PL/SQL procedure successfully completed.

select dbms_metadata.get_ddl ('TABLE','SALES') FROM DUAL;

CREATE TABLE "SH"."SALES"
  ( "PROD_ID" NUMBER,
    "CUST_ID" NUMBER,
    "TIME_ID" DATE,
    "CHANNEL_ID" NUMBER,
    "PROMO_ID" NUMBER,
    "QUANTITY_SOLD" NUMBER(10,2),
    "AMOUNT_SOLD" NUMBER(10,2)
  )
```

Why would you want a nonpartitioned version of a partitioned table? One reason is for partition exchange. You can load data for a new partition into this table and then perform a partition exchange. However, it needs to have exactly the same structure except for the partitioning, so you would need the constraint and index definition information as well.

You have no control over which PARTITION clauses you get or over the subpartitioning. It is either all partitions and subpartitions or no PARTITION clauses. If you are altering the PARTITION clauses in a fixed way, though, you could always write some PL/SQL to pull the information into an array and then edit it.

Separate Constraint Statements

In the examples so far all constraints have been declared within the table definition. We might want them stated outside the table definition so that we can create the table, load data, and then add the constraints (because having constraints/indexes in place can slow down DML on a table more than not having them in place and then adding them once all the data is in place).

```
exec dbms_metadata.set_transform_param(dbms_metadata.session_transform
  ,'CONSTRAINTS',true);
exec dbms_metadata.set_transform_param(dbms_metadata.session_transform
  ,'CONSTRAINTS_AS_ALTER', true);
exec dbms_metadata.set_transform_param(dbms_metadata.session_transform
  ,'SQLTERMINATOR', true)

select dbms_metadata.get_ddl ('TABLE','EMPLOYEES','HR') output from dual;

CREATE TABLE "HR"."EMPLOYEES"
  ( "EMPLOYEE_ID" NUMBER(6,0),
...
    "DEPARTMENT_ID" NUMBER(4,0)
  ) ;
```

```
ALTER TABLE "HR"."EMPLOYEES" ADD CONSTRAINT "EMP_SALARY_MIN"
CHECK (salary > 0) ENABLE;
ALTER TABLE "HR"."EMPLOYEES" ADD CONSTRAINT "EMP_EMAIL_UK"
UNIQUE ("EMAIL") USING INDEX  ENABLE;
ALTER TABLE "HR"."EMPLOYEES" ADD CONSTRAINT "EMP_EMP_ID_PK" PRIMARY KEY
("EMPLOYEE_ID") USING INDEX  ENABLE;
```

Note that we had to turn back on displaying constraints as well as the SQL terminator, so we have the semicolon (;) at the end of each statement, ready to be executed in SQL*Plus. We can now spool that output to a file, split it, and handle the tables and constraints independently.

DBMS_METADATA within PL/SQL

You may want to call DBMS_METADATA from PL/SQL for several reasons. You might want to automatically alter the metadata produced, you may want to schedule generating DDL via DBMS_SCHEDULER, and there are some capabilities of DBMS_METADATA that you cannot really take advantage of just via SQL.

Using DBMS_METADATA in a PL/SQL block is not like we did it in SQL using GET_DDL; it involves a process. The steps of this process are as follows:

1. Acquire an object type handler for your desired object type.

2. The handler facilitates your access to all objects of the desired type, in all schemas that are accessible from the schema that is running the PL/SQL block (remember, ROLES are ignored if the PL/SQL is not created with invoker rights).

3. You might want to remap the object names, schema, data file, or tablespace.

4. You might want to add transformations (for example, on SEGMENT_ATTRIBUTES).

5. Generate the metadata.

6. Close the object handler acquired in the first step.

This process requires other considerations as well. The best way to explain it is with an example rather than a load of package descriptions. Let's examine the following PL/SQL block, which we will run as the HR schema:

```
declare
   l_object_type_handler NUMBER;
   l_table_definition    CLOB;
begin
--1
   l_object_type_handler := dbms_metadata.open('TABLE');
--2
   dbms_metadata.set_filter(l_object_type_handler, 'SCHEMA', 'HR');
   dbms_metadata.set_filter(l_object_type_handler, 'NAME','EMPLOYEES');
--5
   l_table_definition := Dbms_metadata.fetch_clob(l_object_type_handler);
--6
   dbms_metadata.close(l_object_type_handler);
-- use the metadata
   dbms_output.put_line(l_table_definition);
END;
```

As you can see we have (the number of the steps correlates with the list of steps previously given):

1. Acquired an object type handler using the DBMS_METADATA.OPEN function, specifying that we would like to retrieve the metadata for a TABLE object.

2. Filtered the possible output to the ones in HR schema and object name EMPLOYEES using DBMS_METADATA.SET_FILTER.

5. Retrieved the definition using DBMS_METADATA.FETCH_CLOB into a CLOB variable.

6. Closed the object type handler. Finally we have echoed the output using DBMS_OUTPUT.PUT_LINE.

However, note that the output (which is reformatted and is heavily trimmed) isn't what we might have expected:

```
<?xml version="1.0" encoding="UTF-8"?>
<ROWSET>
    <ROW>
        <TABLE_T>
            <VERS_MAJOR>2</VERS_MAJOR>
            <VERS_MINOR>5</VERS_MINOR>
--
--trimmed
--
            </CON2_LIST>
            <REFPAR_LEVEL>0</REFPAR_LEVEL>
        </TABLE_T>
    </ROW>
</ROWSET>
```

This isn't a DDL statement! What went wrong? The answer is, nothing. If you remember our previous examples, we have only been using DBMS_METADATA.GET_DDL to retrieve object metadata. This returns plain-text SQL. However, not only it is possible to retrieve the metadata in XML format using DBMS_METADATA.GET_XML, but (as this example has demonstrated) XML is the default format for retrieving the metadata using DBMS_METADATA. Most of the procedures and functions return XML. However, we often want to get it in the normal textual format again. Can we do that? The answer is yes.

An overlooked "step" in the process of using DBMS_METADATA within PL/SQL that we defined earlier is that you need to decide about the output format. It is possible to use a transformation (step 4) to change the output format to generate a DDL statement rather than XML, but that decision has repercussions.

The transformation is applied using the object type handler and DBMS_METADATA.ADD_TRANSFORM. The following PL/SQL block generates a textual DDL statement, similar to the first example of using DBMS_METADATA.GET_DDL:

```
Set serveroutput on
Declare
  l_object_type_handler number;
  l_tranform_handler     number;
  l_table_definition     clob;
Begin
```

```
    l_object_type_handler := dbms_metadata.open('TABLE');
    dbms_metadata.set_filter(l_object_type_handler, 'SCHEMA',user);
    dbms_metadata.set_filter(l_object_type_handler, 'NAME','EMPLOYEES');
--1
    l_tranform_handler :=dbms_metadata.add_transform(l_object_type_
handler,'DDL');
    l_table_definition := dbms_metadata.fetch_clob(l_object_type_handler);
    dbms_metadata.close(l_object_type_handler);
    dbms_output.put_line(l_table_definition);
end;
/

    CREATE TABLE "HR"."EMPLOYEES"
    (    "EMPLOYEE_ID" NUMBER(6,0),
         "FIRST_NAME" VARCHAR2(20),
--
-- Trimmed
--
    ) SEGMENT CREATION IMMEDIATE
    PCTFREE 10 PCTUSED 40 INITRANS 1 MAXTRANS 255 NOCOMPRESS NOLOGGING
    STORAGE(INITIAL 65536 NEXT 1048576 MINEXTENTS 1 MAXEXTENTS 2147483645
    PCTINCREASE 0 FREELISTS 1 FREELIST GROUPS 1
    BUFFER_POOL DEFAULT FLASH_CACHE DEFAULT CELL_FLASH_CACHE DEFAULT)
    TABLESPACE "EXAMPLE"
```

Note that we had to create a variable, L_TRANFORM_HANDLER-type number, and then fetch a transform handler into it when we applied the transform (**--1**).

One of the major considerations in using XML or textual DDL relates to the use of transformations (for example, the suppression of sections such as the segment information we saw before). Such transformations can only be applied to the textual DDL output format, so if the transformation is required, our PL/SQL code would become this:

```
declare
    l_object_type_handler number;
    l_tranform_handler     number;
    l_table_definition     clob;
begin
    l_object_type_handler := dbms_metadata.open('TABLE');
    dbms_metadata.set_filter(l_object_type_handler, 'SCHEMA',user);
    dbms_metadata.set_filter(l_object_type_handler, 'NAME','EMPLOYEES');
    l_tranform_handler :=dbms_metadata.add_transform(l_object_type_handler,'DDL');
--1
dbms_metadata.set_transform_param(l_tranform_handler,'SEGMENT_
ATTRIBUTES',false);
    l_table_definition := DBMS_METADATA.FETCH_CLOB(l_object_type_handler);
    dbms_metadata.close(l_object_type_handler);
    dbms_output.put_line(l_table_definition);
end;
```

Note that to apply this transform to ignore segment attributes, we used the transform handler returned when we swapped to DDL.

REMAP to Alter the DDL

Using the XML version, we can use DBMS_METADATA.SET_REMAP_PARAM to map object/ schema/data file/tablespace names to new names. Again, to do this we need to acquire a transform handler, even though XML is the default output format, and then perform the transformation.

The following example demonstrates how to change references to 'HR' in the generated metadata to 'SH' and then transform it to DDL:

```
declare
  l_object_type_handler number;
  l_tranform_handler     number;
  l_table_definition     clob;
begin
  l_object_type_handler := dbms_metadata.open('TABLE');
  dbms_metadata.set_filter(l_object_type_handler, 'SCHEMA','HR');
  dbms_metadata.set_filter(l_object_type_handler, 'NAME','EMPLOYEES');
--1
  l_tranform_handler :=
      dbms_metadata.add_transform(l_object_type_handler, 'MODIFY');
  dbms_metadata.set_remap_param(l_tranform_handler,'REMAP_SCHEMA','HR','SH');
--2
  l_tranform_handler :=
      DBMS_METADATA.ADD_TRANSFORM(l_object_type_handler, 'DDL');
  dbms_metadata.set_transform_param(l_tranform_handler,'SEGMENT_
ATTRIBUTES',false);
  l_table_definition := dbms_metadata.fetch_clob(l_object_type_handler);
  dbms_metadata.close(l_object_type_handler);
  dbms_output.put_line(l_table_definition);
end;
/


-- output
CREATE TABLE "SH"."EMPLOYEES"
(    "EMPLOYEE_ID" NUMBER(6,0),
     "FIRST_NAME" VARCHAR2(20),
...
        CONSTRAINT "EMP_JOB_FK" FOREIGN KEY ("JOB_ID")
         REFERENCES "SH"."JOBS" ("JOB_ID") ENABLE,
        CONSTRAINT "EMP_MANAGER_FK" FOREIGN KEY ("MANAGER_ID")
         REFERENCES "SH"."EMPLOYEES" ("EMPLOYEE_ID") ENABLE
    )
```

You can see that HR became SH wherever the schema appears. We could have transformed it to null, in which case no schema owner is stated in the output and the object would be created as owned by whoever ran it. We had to get a transform handler (--1) to modify the XML—but we were then able to use the same variable when we acquired a transform handler to modify the XML to textual DDL and use *that* handle to transform the DDL to remove the segment details.

Note that this is the other version of the SET_TRANSFORM_PARAM—it is not being applied to our session but used against a single piece of DDL via L_TRANSFORM_HANDLER.

Such remap transformations can be applied to other aspects of the DDL: data file, object name, schema, and tablespace. For example, the following line will remap EMPLOYEES to EMPLOYEES_COPY:

```
DBMS_METADATA.SET_REMAP_PARAM(l_tranform_handler,'REMAP_NAME'
                             ,'EMPLOYEES','EMPLOYEES_COPY');
```

There is not enough space here to cover all the options, and to do so would simply be regurgitating the manual. All possible remappings and transformations can be found in the Oracle Database PL/SQL Packages and Types reference in the section on DBMS_METADATA.

UTL_FILE

In the previous section on DBMS_WORKLOAD_REPOSITORY, we used UTL_FILE to write daily AWR reports to a directory. That example is good enough to get going with UTL_FILE, but we thought we should add some further notes about it.

UTL_FILE is used to write and read files from the operating system. It was introduced with Oracle 8*i* and initially could only access directories specified in the initialization parameter UTL_FILE_DIR—which often got set to *, meaning all directories Oracle could access! This was done because altering this initialization parameter to add any locations was disruptive because you had to stop and start the instance for it to take effect. Of course, allowing access to all the directories the Oracle OS user could see was something of a security weakness!

In version 9*i*, Oracle introduced the concept of DIRECTORY objects, which could be defined to control where you read and write files from. Access to DIRECTORY objects by users can be controlled by grants, just as can access to most database objects. Unlike most database objects, DIRECTORIES are not owned by who created them. Despite DBA_DIRECTORIES containing the column OWNER, all directories are owned by SYS. Here is the directory we created in the DBMS_WORKLOAD_REPOSITORY section, and it was created via a schema called MDW2:

```
select * from dba_directories where directory_name like 'AWR%';
OWNER       DIRECTORY_NAME           DIRECTORY_PATH                   ORIGIN_CON_ID
----------  -----------------------  -------------------------------  -------------
SYS         AWR_REPORTS              D:\sqlwork\AWR_reports                       3
```

Obviously an Operating System directory has to exist for the Oracle DIRECTORY object to reference and the Oracle OS user must have access rights on the directory. If you use RAC, the file system the directory is on needs to be shared for all nodes to see it.

You can see another example of creating and using a directory object in Chapter 7 in the DBMS_HPROF section.

When you want to access a file, you must open it with the function **utl_file.fopen**, specifying the name of the directory, the filename, the method by which it will be accessed, and the maximum line size. The function returns a file handle, which we use in other functions and procedures to reference the file.

```
v_file_handle :=utl_file.fopen(v_dir,v_file,'w',1500);

utl_file.put_line(v_file_handle,'whatever text you want');
```

Just like DBMS_OUTPUT (covered extensively in Chapter 7) you use PUT, NEWLINE, and (most commonly) PUT_LINE commands to write to a file and GET and **get_line** procedures to get data from the file. There are NCHAR and RAW versions of PUT and GET commands for handling Unicode and raw data.

When you open a file you do so in one of three methods:

- **R** To read only from the file.
- **W** To read and write to the file, and the open command removes any existing contents of the file.
- **A** To read and write in append mode (that is, the existing data in the file is left intact).

Later versions of UTL_FILE introduced the ability to copy, remove, and rename files with the **fcopy**, **fremove**, and **frename** procedures. **fgetattr** gets the attributes of the file, and **fgetpos** and **fseek** allow you to find the current location in a file and move to a new location.

When you have finished with a file you should close it with the **fclose** procedure, as you saw in the DBMS_WORKLOAD_REPOSITORY AWR example. And, as also shown in that example, you should ensure you close your file(s) using **fclose** in any exception handlers. **fclose_all** will close all files you have open.

That should give you a feel for what you can do with UTL_FILE. In our experience, most people tend to simply **fopen** the file, PUT_LINE to it, and finally **fclose** it. Occasionally, people read from the files as well, but few people seem to be aware of the full capabilities of the package. See the Database PL/SQL Packages and Types reference for more details.

DBMS_UTILITY

DBMS_UTILITY is, as the name suggests, a package with some useful little tools in it that Oracle did not feel fit into other packages. Although the package has several useful items, we will highlight two of particular interest—EXPAND_SQL_TEXT, which is new to 12c, and the procedures for tracing back errors and your current position in your PL/SQL code stack (FORMAT_ERROR_STACK, FORMAT_ERROR_BACKTRACE, and FORMAT_CALL_STACK).

EXPAND_SQL_TEXT

The procedure **dbms_utility.expand_sql_text** is new in Oracle 12c and is used to show you what a SQL statement is expanded to before it is parsed. The most obvious of these is where a view is used in the query or an asterisk (*) is used in the select list. We will create a view and then perform a quick select operation on it:

```
create or replace view pers_sum
as select pers.surname
      ,pers.first_forename
      ,pers.dob
      ,pena.surname       prior_surname
      ,pena.first_forename prior_first_fn
      ,addr.post_code
from person      pers
   ,person_name pena
   ,address      addr
where pers.addr_id = addr.addr_id
and pers.pers_id   = pena.pers_id

select/* mdw_du2 */ * from pers_sum
```

```
where surname = 'WIDLAKE'
and dob between sysdate -(365*30)
        and      sysdate -(365*29)
SURNAME         FIRST_FORENAME  DOB           PRIOR_SURNAME   PRIOR_FIRST_FN
OST_COD
--------------- --------------- ------------  --------------- --------------- --------
WIDLAKE         ANNA            25-DEC-1986   WIDLAKE         ANNA            RG2 5WT
WIDLAKE         CHENG           07-JAN-1987   WIDLAKE         CHENG           BS18 2AW
WIDLAKE         DAVE            18-JUN-1986   WIDLAKE         DAVE            YO41 2WK
...
```

Here, DBMS_UTILITY.EXPAND_SQL_TEXT takes in a CLOB, the original text, and passes out a CLOB, the expanded text. You can just pass in the SQL as text, and it is implicitly converted to a CLOB. This is fine for a small SQL statement, but if you can find the SQL in V$SQLAREA, where it is held in a CLOB, you can pass that into the procedure, as we show here:

```
-- we need a clob holding the text of the SQL, so let's find it in V$SQLAREA
select sql_id,substr(sql_text,1,50)
from v$sqlarea
where sql_text like '%mdw_du2%'
and sql_text not like '%sql_text%'

SQL_ID          SUBSTR(SQL_TEXT,1,50)
-------------   --------------------------------------------------
4fx3zzc5m606b select/* mdw_du2 */ * from pers_sum_vw where surna

-- now let us get the full expanded text of it
declare
v_clobin    clob;
v_clobout   clob;
begin
  select sql_fulltext into v_clobin
  from v$sqlarea
  where sql_text like '%mdw_du2%'
  and sql_text not like '%sql_text%';
  dbms_utility.expand_sql_text(v_clobin,v_clobout);
  dbms_output.put_line(v_clobout);
end;

SELECT "A1"."SURNAME" "SURNAME","A1"."FIRST_FORENAME"
"FIRST_FORENAME","A1"."DOB" "DOB","A1"."PRIOR_SURNAME"
"PRIOR_SURNAME","A1"."PRIOR_FIRST_FN" "PRIOR_FIRST_FN","A1"."POST_CODE"
"POST_CODE" FROM  (SELECT "A4"."SURNAME" "SURNAME","A4"."FIRST_FORENAME"
"FIRST_FORENAME","A4"."DOB" "DOB","A3"."SURNAME"
"PRIOR_SURNAME","A3"."FIRST_FORENAME" "PRIOR_FIRST_FN","A2"."POST_CODE"
"POST_CODE" FROM MDWCH6."PERSON" "A4",MDWCH6."PERSON_NAME" "A3",MDWCH6."ADDRESS"
"A2" WHERE "A4"."ADDR_ID"="A2"."ADDR_ID" AND "A4"."PERS_ID"="A3"."PERS_ID") "A1"
WHERE "A1"."SURNAME"='WIDLAKE' AND "A1"."DOB">=SYSDATE-365*30 AND
"A1"."DOB"<=SYSDATE-365*29
```

By tidying up the text a bit, we can see that the simple four-line query was expanded to this:

```
SELECT "A1"."SURNAME"              "SURNAME"
      ,"A1"."FIRST_FORENAME"       "FIRST_FORENAME"
      ,"A1"."DOB"                  "DOB"
      ,"A1"."PRIOR_SURNAME"        "PRIOR_SURNAME"
      ,"A1"."PRIOR_FIRST_FN"       "PRIOR_FIRST_FN"
      ,"A1"."POST_CODE"            "POST_CODE"
FROM   (SELECT "A4"."SURNAME"  "SURNAME"
              ,"A4"."FIRST_FORENAME" "FIRST_FORENAME"
              ,"A4"."DOB"                 "DOB"
              ,"A3"."SURNAME"            "PRIOR_SURNAME"
              ,"A3"."FIRST_FORENAME" "PRIOR_FIRST_FN"
              ,"A2"."POST_CODE"         "POST_CODE"
        FROM MDWCH6."PERSON"        "A4"
            ,MDWCH6."PERSON_NAME" "A3"
            ,MDWCH6."ADDRESS"       "A2"
        WHERE "A4"."ADDR_ID"="A2"."ADDR_ID"
        AND    "A4"."PERS_ID"="A3"."PERS_ID") "A1"
WHERE "A1"."SURNAME"='WIDLAKE'
AND    "A1"."DOB"    >=SYSDATE-365*30
AND    "A1"."DOB"    <=SYSDATE-365*29
```

You can see that the **select *** is replaced with a full column select list and that the view is expanded out to the full text. Obviously in this case, we could have easily constructed what Oracle is doing, but as a DBA (or developer) you may not be aware of all the views, views-of-views, and so on, used in the application. Expanding the text shows you exactly what is being run. This can result in the "explain plan" output making a lot more sense, too. When a fairly simple SQL statement on two "tables" expands into a two-page explain plan, you should strongly suspect that views (and views on views) are involved. This DBMS_UTILITY feature shows you the exact details.

Why All the Quotation Marks (and Details)?

In our example of DBMS_UTILITY.EXPAND_SQL_TEXT, you may be wondering why all the quotation marks are there. This is because any central Oracle tool has to allow for anything that Oracle allows. You can force Oracle to allow lowercase or mixed-case object names using quotation marks, so any Oracle tool has to allow for this as well. Therefore, you see a lot of quotation marks appear in the output of the central tools.

We usually remove the quotation marks with a **replace** function, like so:

```
replace(v_clobout,'"','')
```

However, one day we will have a lowercase or mixed-case object name and something will break. If Oracle did the same, they would get a bug by an angry user raised against them.

If you have the privileges, you can run this against the dictionary views. We show an example here, including removing those quotation marks. We just pass in the SQL as text and let the procedure implicitly convert it to a CLOB:

```
declare
v_clob1  clob;
begin
  dbms_utility.expand_sql_text('select * from all_sequences',v_clob1);
  dbms_output.put_line('Original SQL is: select * from all_sequences');
  dbms_output.put_line('Expanded SQL is:');
  dbms_output.put_line(replace(v_clob1,'"',''));
end;


Original SQL is: select * from all_sequences
Expanded SQL is:

SELECT A1.SEQUENCE_OWNER SEQUENCE_OWNER,A1.SEQUENCE_NAME
SEQUENCE_NAME,A1.MIN_VALUE MIN_VALUE,A1.MAX_VALUE MAX_VALUE,A1.INCREMENT_BY
INCREMENT_BY,A1.CYCLE_FLAG CYCLE_FLAG,A1.ORDER_FLAG ORDER_FLAG,A1.CACHE_SIZE
CACHE_SIZE,A1.LAST_NUMBER LAST_NUMBER,A1.PARTITION_COUNT
PARTITION_COUNT,A1.SESSION_FLAG SESSION_FLAG,A1.KEEP_VALUE KEEP_VALUE FROM
(SELECT A2.NAME SEQUENCE_OWNER,A3.NAME SEQUENCE_NAME,A4.MINVALUE
MIN_VALUE,A4.MAXVALUE MAX_VALUE,A4.INCREMENT$
INCREMENT_BY,DECODE(A4.CYCLE#,0,'N',1,'Y')
CYCLE_FLAG,DECODE(A4.ORDER$,0,'N',1,'Y') ORDER_FLAG,A4.CACHE
CACHE_SIZE,A4.HIGHWATER
LAST_NUMBER,DECODE(A4.PARTCOUNT,0,TO_NUMBER(NULL),A4.PARTCOUNT)
PARTITION_COUNT,DECODE(BITAND(A4.FLAGS,64),64,'Y','N')
SESSION_FLAG,DECODE(BITAND(A4.FLAGS,512),512,'Y','N') KEEP_VALUE FROM SYS.SEQ$
A4,SYS.OBJ$ A3,SYS.USER$ A2 WHERE A2.USER#=A3.OWNER# AND A3.OBJ#=A4.OBJ# AND
(A3.OWNER#=USERENV('SCHEMAID') OR  EXISTS (SELECT 0 FROM SYS.OBJAUTH$ A6 WHERE
A3.OBJ#=A6.OBJ# AND  EXISTS (SELECT 0 FROM  (SELECT A8.ADDR ADDR,A8.INDX
INDX,A8.INST_ID INST_ID,A8.CON_ID CON_ID,A8.KZSROROL KZSROROL FROM SYS.X$KZSRO
A8 WHERE A8.CON_ID=0 OR A8.CON_ID=3) A7 WHERE A6.GRANTEE#=A7.KZSROROL)) OR
EXISTS (SELECT 0 FROM  (SELECT A9.PRIV_NUMBER PRIV_NUMBER,A9.CON_ID CON_ID FROM
(SELECT A10.PRIV_NUMBER PRIV_NUMBER,A10.CON_ID CON_ID FROM  (SELECT A11.INST_ID
INST_ID,(-A11.KZSPRPRV) PRIV_NUMBER,A11.CON_ID CON_ID FROM SYS.X$KZSPR A11) A10
WHERE A10.INST_ID=USERENV('INSTANCE')) A9 WHERE A9.CON_ID=0 OR A9.CON_ID=3) A5
WHERE A5.PRIV_NUMBER=(-109)))) A1
```

You might get errors like the following if you try to expand a database view where you lack privileges to see things:

```
ORA-24256: EXPAND_SQL_TEXT failed with ORA-28113: policy predicate has error
ORA-06512: at "SYS.DBMS_UTILITY", line 1525
ORA-06512: at line 25
```

This tool also shows your SQL after other changes have been applied—for example, VPD policies have been applied (that is, the extra WHERE clause of column filtering that occurs). You might want to be mindful of that if you use VPD and you want to protect the policies from prying eyes! It will also show you the SQL after the new 12c temporal clauses are applied to it.

All in all, the tool seems to show you what is actually passed to the optimizer but before any query transformations occur.

FORMAT_ERROR_STACK, _ERROR_BACKTRACK, and _CALL_STACK

Two functions in DBMS_UTILITY show information about errors in the PL/SQL you use in your exception handler. You saw examples of this back in the section about automating tasks:

■ Function **format_error_stack** returns the full error message(s) for the current error. Unlike the older SQLERRM function, which is limited to 512 bytes, this will show the error message to 2000 bytes. However, whereas you can pass an error code into SQLERRM and get the text for it, **format error_stack** takes no parameters.

■ Function **format_error_backtrace** returns a formatted string that describes the error stack at the point the last error occurred. One of its weaknesses is that when you use exception sections in your code to handle errors and then either re-raise them or raise a new error, *the backtrack is only to that latest RAISE*. Also, it shows only the line numbers within the code unit and not the unit names within a package. You can use the line numbers to look up the lines of the code in DBA_SOURCE, though occasionally things can confuse the numbers reported back in backtrace. (Using a PLSQL_OPTIMIZER_LEVEL greater than 0 such that Oracle may rewrite some of your PL/SQL on compilation time is one source; conditional compilation is another—and, sometimes, it just seems to go a bit odd).

A third function, called **dbms_utility.format_call_stack**, shows your call stack at the point you call it. This is actually of more use in debugging your code.

We will now demonstrate these functions. We create two new stored procedures, **test_depth1** and **test_depth2**, just to give us a couple levels of call. We also alter our TEST1 code in PNA_MAINT to call a function, **pna_maint.gen_err**, that purposefully errors, but does so after we have called **format_call_stack** and shown the output. We do not capture any exceptions except at the top level, **test_depth1**, because doing so unwinds the error backtrace to that point as just mentioned.

```
-- new procedure in PNA_MAINT
procedure gen_err_1 is
v_n1  number;     v_n2  number;
begin
  pv_call_stack := dbms_utility.format_call_stack;
  dbms_output.put_line('where are we in our code stack?');
  dbms_output.put_line(pv_call_stack);
  dbms_output.put_line (' should error now!');
  v_n1:=0;
  v_n2:=100/v_n1;
end gen_err_1;

--test1 code in PNA_MAINT
procedure test1 is
v_vc1 varchar2(100);
begin
  --
  -- removed code for this listing
  gen_err;
end test1;

create or replace procedure test_depth2 as
```

```
begin
  pna_maint.test1;
end test_depth2;

create or replace procedure test_depth1 as
pv_err_msg varchar2(2000);
pv_err_stack varchar2(2000);
pv_call_stack  varchar2(2000);
begin
  test_depth2;
exception
  when others then
    pv_err_msg:=dbms_utility.format_error_stack;
    pv_err_stack := dbms_utility.format_error_backtrace;
    pv_call_stack :=dbms_utility.format_call_stack;
    dbms_output.put_line (pv_err_msg);
    dbms_output.put_line('****************************************************');
    dbms_output.put_line (pv_err_stack);
    dbms_output.put_line('----------------------------------------------------');
    dbms_output.put_line (pv_call_stack);
end test_depth1;

-- run the code
exec test_depth1

where are we in our code stack?
----- PL/SQL Call Stack -----
  object        line  object
  handle      number  name
00007FFD64D23F98      357  package body MDWCH9.PNA_MAINT
00007FFD64D23F98      398  package body MDWCH9.PNA_MAINT
00007FFD5BE48FF8        3  procedure MDWCH9.TEST_DEPTH2
00007FFCE539D4A8        6  procedure MDWCH9.TEST_DEPTH1
00007FFD6CE8C578        1  anonymous block

should error now!
ORA-01476: divisor is equal to zero

****************************************************
ORA-06512: at "MDWCH9.PNA_MAINT", line 384
ORA-06512: at "MDWCH9.PNA_MAINT", line 398
ORA-06512: at "MDWCH9.TEST_DEPTH2", line 3
ORA-06512: at "MDWCH9.TEST_DEPTH1", line 6

----------------------------------------------------
----- PL/SQL Call Stack -----
  object        line  object
  handle      number  name
00007FFCE539D4A8       11  procedure MDWCH9.TEST_DEPTH1
00007FFD6CE8C578        1  anonymous block
```

So you can see that **format_call_stack** before the error ("where are we now") shows us the "path" to where we are when it is called, but it lacks information about units within packages. (The column headings not lining up with the output is not a layout mistake in this book; this is how it comes out). We then hit our error ("should error now").

Because our "ORA-01476: divisor is equal to zero" error is the only one raised, it is the only one returned by **format_error_stack** and **format_error_backtrack** shows us the "path" to where the last error occurred, which starts at **test_depth1**, goes to **test_depth2**, and then to **pna_maint**. We cannot see what unit(s) we are in within PNA_MAINT, only the lines.

Finally we show the **format_call_stack** information here in the error handler just to demonstrate that, being in **test_depth1**, the only stack information is that we called **test_depth1** from an anonymous block (in SQL*Plus).

We will now alter **test_depth2** to capture any error (WHEN OTHERS) and raise a NO_DATA_FOUND error:

```
create or replace procedure test_depth2 as
begin
  pna_maint.test1;
exception
  when others then raise no_data_found;
end test_depth2;
/

Exec test_depth1
-- NOTE: information from the DBMS_UTILITY.FORNMAT_CALL_STACK removed

 should error now!
ORA-01403: no data found
ORA-06512: at "MDW2.TEST_DEPTH2", line 5
ORA-01476: divisor is equal to zero

********************************************************
ORA-06512: at "MDW2.TEST_DEPTH2", line 5
ORA-06512: at "MDW2.TEST_DEPTH1", line 7
```

We now see three errors from the **format_error_stack**: our original 01476 error, a 06512 error (which is just a backtrack message), and our new 01403 No Data Found error. But now our FORMAT_ERROR_BACKTRACK data only takes us back to the "raise no data found" error in **test_depth2** and not the original error in PNA_MAINT. The assumption is that if we have an exception handler, we will handle all the processing of the error and its backtrack at that point before then raising the same error or a new error. But most commonly the exception at that point does not handle the backtrack information (which is not ideal but is very, very common). In practice, what you often end up doing in this situation is commenting out that simple, intermediate exception handler and letting the full error and backtrack come back to your more capable exception handler, where you can now get at the information about the source error. It is all a bit clunky, and removing that intermediate handler may not be possible if you cannot alter the production code.

Oracle 12c offers a new utility called UTL_CALL_STACK that you can use to get call stack information, which we cover next.

UTL_CALL_STACK

UTL_CALL_STACK allows you to examine the call stack in more detail and gives you control (and responsibility for!) the layout of the information. It also, at last, gives you information about the units within a package. It is a little harder to use than the DBMS_UTILITY functions we just covered, but if you want more detail in anything in the IT world, the price is usually handling more complexity. There are three stacks: the call stack, the error stack, and the error backtrace stack. You process the information for all three in a similar (but not identical) way. We will now repeat the tests we did for the DBMS_UTILITY exception handling and stack viewing.

You have to make multiple calls to the package to get the bits of each stack. Then, if you want the information nicely laid out, you need to format the information and allow for null values from some of the UTL_CALL_STACK functions.

We will replace the **dbms_utility.format_call_stack** in our original example with code using UTL_CALL_STACK. First, use the function DYNAMIC_DEPTH to get the number of levels of the call stack. For each one, you make calls to the functions UNIT_LINE, OWNER, and CONCATENATE_SUBPROGRAM (into which you pass the result of the function SUBPROGRAM) to get the information, which you then have to lay out. See the following code:

```
procedure gen_err is
v_n1  pls_integer;
v_n2  pls_integer;
v_stack_d pls_integer;
begin
  dbms_output.put_line(' lv    Line         Owner unit_name');
  dbms_output.put_line('--- ----- ------------ ------------------------------------');
  v_stack_d := utl_call_stack.dynamic_depth;
  for i in reverse 1..v_stack_d loop
   dbms_output.put_line(to_char(i,'99')||' '
      ||to_char(utl_call_stack.unit_line(i),'99999')||' '
      ||lpad(nvl(utl_call_stack.owner(i),' '),12)||' '
      ||utl_call_stack.concatenate_subprogram(utl_call_stack.subprogram(i)));
  end loop;
  ...

-- And our output looks like:

lv   Line        Owner unit_name
--- ----- ------------ -------------------------------
  5     1              __anonymous_block
  4     7        MDW2 TEST_DEPTH1
  3     5        MDW2 TEST_DEPTH2
  2   178        MDW2 PNA_MAINT.TEST1
  1   159        MDW2 PNA_MAINT.GEN_ERR
```

As you can see, we now get the procedure names for the stack entries for PNA_MAINT. However, there is little extra information beyond that, and it is a lot more effort to collect and handle the data than just using **dbms_utility.format_call_stack**. We can (and do) change the order of the output, though.

For handling the error stack, we replace the exception using **dbms_utility.format_error_stack** in TEST_DEPTH1 with code similar to that for processing the call stack, as shown next. We run the test twice: once with just the error generated in GEN_ERR and then with our intermediate error capturing in TEST_DEPTH2:

```
exception
  when others then
--    pv_err_stack := dbms_utility.format_error_backtrace;
--    dbms_output.put_line (pv_err_stack);
    pv_err_depth := utl_call_stack.error_depth;
    dbms_output.put_line ('error depth is '||to_char(pv_err_depth));
    for i in 1..pv_err_depth loop
      pv_err_msg :=utl_call_stack.error_msg(i);
      dbms_output.put_line(to_char(i,'99')||'  ORA-'
            ||to_char(utl_call_stack.error_number(i),'099999')
            ||' '||rtrim(pv_err_msg,chr(10))); -- removes a carriage return
    end loop;
end test_depth1;

--for our original test just generating ORA-001476 we now get
error depth is 1
  1  ORA- 001476 divisor is equal to zero

-- and for our second example where we catch WHEN OTHERS in TEST_DEPTH2
-- and raised NO_DATA_FOUND we get
error depth is 3
  1  ORA- 001403 no data found
  2  ORA- 006512 at "MDW2.TEST_DEPTH2", line 5
  3  ORA- 001476 divisor is equal to zero
```

As you can see, apart from the count of errors and the ability (or extra requirement, depending on how you see it) to lay out the data yourself, there is no extra information. You will also note that we had to handle the removal of a carriage return character at the end of the UTL_CALL_STACK .ERROR_MSG text.

Finally, you can get the error backtrace with similar calls, getting the depth of the backtrace and information for each level:

```
--    pv_err_stack := dbms_utility.format_error_backtrace;
--    dbms_output.put_line (pv_err_stack);
    pv_bt_depth :=utl_call_stack.backtrace_depth;
    dbms_output.put_line ('backtrace depth is '||to_char(pv_bt_depth));
    for i in 1..pv_bt_depth loop
      dbms_output.put_line(to_char(i,'99')||' Line'
      ||to_char(utl_call_stack.backtrace_line(i),'09999')
      ||' '||utl_call_stack.backtrace_unit(i) );
    end loop;

--for our original test just generating ORA-001476 we now get
backtrace depth is 4
  1 Line 00008 MDW2.TEST_DEPTH1
  2 Line 00003 MDW2.TEST_DEPTH2
  3 Line 00180 MDW2.PNA_MAINT
  4 Line 00166 MDW2.PNA_MAINT
```

```
-- and for our second example where we raised NO_DATA_FOUND in an intermediary
-- exception handler we get
backtrace depth is 2
  1 Line 00008 MDW2.TEST_DEPTH1
  2 Line 00005 MDW2.TEST_DEPTH2
```

It is rather disappointing that UTL_CALL_STACK error backtrace does not include the package unit information of the call stack, and just like **dbms_utility.format_error_backtrace** it only sees back to the last raise and not the original error.

All in all, UTL_CALL_STACK is more complex to use than the DBMS_UTILITY equivalents, with little extra to offer. So why have we covered it? Well, it does add the ability to see the depth of the stack or backtrace, and with the call stack functionality you can also see the package unit information. The DBMS_UTILITY functions are not deprecated, but they might be in the future, so we thought we would cover the new Oracle 12c take on examining your PL/SQL call stacks.

At present, we find UTL_CALL_STACK useful for reporting back our call stack due to it including the package unit information plus some other nice features, but the error message and error backtrack functionality does not add enough for us to replace DBMS_UTILITY.FORMAT_ERROR_STACK and FORMAT_ERROR_BACKTRACE in existing code. The ability to lay out the information as you see fit could be advantageous.

We will finish with two other bits of information available with UTL_CALL_STACK. The first is LEXICAL_DEPTH. This is simply the subnesting depth in the current program unit. The other is the current edition of the code, for use with edition based redefinition (see Chapter 5 for details of EBR).

We will add a new procedure just to add some subnesting to our call stack, TEST_DEPTH_NESTED:

```
create or replace procedure test_depth_nested as
procedure p1 is
  procedure p2 is
    procedure p3 is
    begin
      pna_maint.test1;
    end p3;
  begin
    p3;
  end p2;
begin
  p2;
end p1;
begin
  p1;
end test_depth_nested;
```

We will call this instead of TEST_DEPTH2. We will also add the two new pieces of information to our code in PNA_MAINT.GEN_ERR to show the call stack:

```
  dbms_output.put_line('    loc');
  dbms_output.put_line
    (' lv lev  Line         Owner unit_name                         Edition');
  dbms_output.put_line
    ('--- --- ----- ------------ -------------------------------- ---------');
```

```
v_stack_d := utl_call_stack.dynamic_depth;
for i in 1..v_stack_d loop
  dbms_output.put_line(to_char(i,'99')||' '||to_char(utl_call_stack.lexical_depth(i),'99')
    ||to_char(utl_call_stack.unit_line(i),'99999')||' '
    ||lpad(nvl(utl_call_stack.owner(i),' '),12)||' '
    ||rpad(utl_call_stack.concatenate_subprogram(utl_call_stack.subprogram(i)),32)
    ||nvl(utl_call_stack.current_edition(i),' cur'));
end loop;

--Output
```

| | loc | | | | |
lv	lev	Line	Owner	unit_name	Edition
1	1	399	MDWCH9	PNA_MAINT.GEN_ERR	cur
2	1	421	MDWCH9	PNA_MAINT.TEST1	cur
3	3	6	MDWCH9	TEST_DEPTH_NESTED.P1.P2.P3	cur
4	2	9	MDWCH9	TEST_DEPTH_NESTED.P1.P2	cur
5	1	12	MDWCH9	TEST_DEPTH_NESTED.P1	cur
6	0	16	MDWCH9	TEST_DEPTH_NESTED	cur
7	0	8	MDWCH9	TEST_DEPTH1	cur
8	0	1		__anonymous_block	cur

You can see how the LEXICAL_DEPTH works. If the code unit is a stored procedure (or function) with no nested code, the lexical depth is 0. When you are within a procedure or function in a package, the lexical depth is 1. With TEST_DEPTH_NESTED, we can see the level increasing with each nesting of the procedures. Personally, I think of it as the local level!

We don't have any EBR in our example, and we default "null" for CURRENT_EDITION to "cur," but you can see how it would work.

Summary

As you saw through this chapter, PL/SQL skills are invaluable for anyone administering Oracle Databases or automating tasks within Oracle.

Basic PL/SQL skills allow you to write simple scripts to handle LONG data types, process data that might otherwise need complex SQL (such as analytical functions), and gather data to help with issue analysis.

A plethora of PL/SQL built-in packages can help the DBA, some of which are covered in other chapters. Here, we looked at DBMS_WORKLOAD_REPOSITORY as an example of directly running performance reports normally associated with the OEM/Grid Control and how you could automate that task. Other PL/SQL built-ins allow you to access the DDL for any objects in the database and see how Oracle transforms your SQL before it is parsed.

This chapter also introduced a set of tables and code that can be used to control, manage, and log a range of background PL/SQL tasks—whether they are simple administrative tasks, that only need to be kicked off, or data processing tasks where the range of data being processed needs to be recorded and conserved. This control mechanism can be kept simple or expanded to allow for pausing and automatic restart functionality.

PART
IV

Advanced Analytics

CHAPTER
10

In-Database Data Mining
Using Oracle Data Mining

U nderstanding their data and gaining an insight into the behavior of their data (and hence their customers) is something that companies have been chasing for some time now. A myriad of technology solutions are available to help us achieve this understanding and insight, but just as we achieve this, some new challenge emerges to force us into looking at possible alternatives. One of the technologies that can help us achieve this deep insight into our data is the use of some of the advanced machine learning algorithms. These are commonly referred to as *data mining algorithms.*

Data mining algorithms can be considered a process of searching our data to discover patterns and trends that may have some competitive element to them. One of the most commonly used definitions of data mining is as follows:

> *Data mining is the non-trivial extraction of previously unknown and potentially useful information from data.*[1]

With in-database data mining, the data mining algorithms are built into the database. We no longer have another application and another server to run the data mining application. This is what Oracle has done with Oracle Data Mining. They have taken a suite of data mining algorithms and have built them into the kernel of the Oracle Database. A common phrase associated with this is "move the algorithms to the data, not the data to the algorithms."

In this chapter we show you the main components of Oracle Data Mining. This is an extra paid-for option that is available as part of the Enterprise Edition of the Oracle Database. We give examples of how you can use the main elements of Oracle Data Mining, and we step through the process of preparing your data for input to data mining, creating a classification data mining model using Oracle Data Mining, evaluating the model, and finally applying the Oracle Data Mining model to new data. All this is done using SQL and PL/SQL.

Overview of Oracle Advanced Analytics Option

The Oracle Advanced Analytics option comprises Oracle Data Mining and Oracle R Enterprise. The Oracle Advanced Analytics option is available as an extra license cost option with the Oracle Enterprise Edition of the Oracle Database. By combining the in-database advanced data mining algorithms with the power and flexibility of R, Oracle has provided a set of tools that allows everyone from data scientists to Oracle developers and DBAs to perform advanced analytics on their data, gaining a deeper insight into their data as well as giving them a competitive advantage over their competitors.

Oracle Data Mining contains a suite of advanced data mining algorithms that are embedded in the Oracle Database and allow you to perform advanced analytics on your data. The data mining algorithms are integrated into the Oracle Database kernel and operate natively on data stored in tables in the database. This removes the need for extraction or the transfer of data into stand-alone data mining/analytic servers, as is typical with most data mining applications. This can significantly reduce the timeframe of data mining projects by having near zero data movement.

In addition to the suite of data mining algorithms, which are listed in Table 10-1, Oracle has a variety of interfaces to allow you to use these algorithms. These interfaces include PL/SQL packages that allow you to build and apply models to new data, a variety of SQL functions for real-time scoring of data, and the Oracle Data Miner tool, which provides a graphical workflow

---

[1] W. Frawley, G. Piatetsky-Shapiro, and C. Matheus, "Knowledge Discovery in Databases: An Overview," *AI Magazine* (1992), 213–228.

Data Mining Technique	Data Mining Algorithms
Anomaly Detection	One-Class Support Vector Machine
Association Rule Analysis	Apriori
Attribute Importance	Minimum Description Length
Classification	Decision Tree Generalized Linear Model Naive Bayes Support Vector Machine
Clustering	Expectation Maximization k-Means Orthogonal Partitioning Clustering
Feature Extraction	Non-Negative Matrix Factorization Singular Value Decomposition Principal Component Analysis
Regression	Generalized Linear Model Support Vector Machine

TABLE 10-1. *Data Mining Algorithms Available in Oracle Data Mining*

interface for creating your data mining projects. Table 10-1 lists the various data mining algorithms available in the Oracle Database as part of the Oracle Advanced Analytics option.

Oracle R Enterprise (ORE) was introduced in 2011 and enables the open-source R statistical programming language and environment to be run on the database server and within the database. Oracle R Enterprise integrates R with the Oracle Database. When Oracle R Enterprise was released, it was combined with Oracle Data Mining to form the Oracle Advanced Analytics option.

While analysts interactively analyze data and develop R scripts, the data will be extracted from the Oracle Database so they can perform their analytics. With ORE, data scientists can still write their R scripts and analyze the data, but now the data can remain within the Oracle Database. No data has to be downloaded to the data scientist's computer, thus saving a significant amount of time and allowing the data scientist to concentrate on solving the business problem at hand. Having the R scripts run in the database allows for these scripts to utilize the ability of the database to manage the processing of many millions of records in an efficient manner, and they can utilize other database performance options, including the Parallel option. This overcomes many of the limitations of running R on the data scientist's computer.

Oracle Data Miner GUI Tool

The Oracle Data Miner (ODM) tool is a component of SQL Developer. The Oracle Data Miner tool is a GUI workflow-based tool that allows data scientists, data analysts, developers, and DBAs to quickly and simply build data mining workflows for their data and data mining business problem. The Oracle Data Miner workflow tool was first introduced in SQL Developer 3 and is available in all subsequent releases; more functionality has been added.

The Oracle Data Miner tool, shown in Figure 10-1, allows you to build workflows by defining nodes that allow you to do the following:

- Explore your data using statistics and various graphical methods.

- Build various data transformations that include sampling, build various data reduction techniques, create new features, apply complex filtering techniques, and create custom transformations on your data.

- Build data mining models using a variety of in-database data mining algorithms.

- Apply your data mining models to new data to produce a scored data set that can be acted upon by your business users.

- Create and use transient data mining models using predictive queries.

- Create and apply complex text analytics models on your semi-structured and unstructured data.

When the time comes to productionize your workflows, full support is provided by the generation of all the required SQL scripts needed to run the workflow. These can be easily scheduled in the Oracle Database to run on a regular basis.

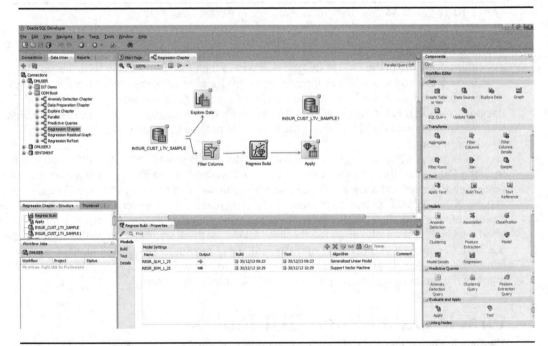

FIGURE 10-1.   *The Oracle Data Miner tool in SQL Developer*

Setting Up Oracle Data Miner and the Demo Data Sets

Before you can start using the Oracle Data Miner tool or using the in-database features, you need to ensure a few prerequisites are completed:

- You have installed Oracle 12c Enterprise Edition or Oracle 11 R2 Enterprise Edition.
- You have installed the sample schemas in the database.
- You have downloaded and installed the latest version of SQL Developer (version 4 or later is recommended).
- You have the SYS password or you have your DBA available for the steps that require this.
- You have created a schema that you want to use for your Oracle Data Mining work. You can create a new schema (for example, DMUSER) or use an existing schema.

The first step you need to take is to create a connection for your new DMUSER schema in SQL Developer. Select the green plus symbol in the Connections tab on the left side of SQL Developer. This opens the Create New Connection window. In this window you can enter the DMUSER connection details. Table 10-2 provides the details necessary to create the DMUSER schema.

When you have entered the connection details, click the Test button to check that the connection can be established. Any errors will be displayed. If all the details are correct, you will see a message on the left side of this screen stating "Status: Success." When you have a successful connection, you can click the Connect button to open the connection. The new connection will be added/saved to your list in the Connections tab and a SQL worksheet will open for your DMUSER schema.

Before you can start using Oracle Data Mining, you need to create an Oracle Data Mining repository in the Oracle Database. The simplest way to do this is to use the built-in functionality in SQL Developer. The alternative method is to use the scripts that come with SQL Developer to create the repository. You will need to have the SYS password to use either of these methods, or you can get your DBA to perform these steps for you.

Setting	Description
Connection Name	This is a label, and you can enter something meaningful here.
Username	Enter **DMUSER**, the name of your ODM schema.
Password	Enter **DMUSER**, the password for your ODM schema.
Hostname	The name of the server on which the database is located. If it is your local machine, you can enter **localhost**.
Port	Enter **1521**.
Service Name	You should select Service Name or SID for your Oracle Database. Enter the service name for your pluggable database (for example, pdb12c).

TABLE 10-2. *Creating the DMUSER Connection in SQL Developer*

SQL Developer maintains a separate listing of what schemas you use for Oracle Data Miner. To attach your DMUSER schema to this list, click the View menu, select the Data Miner option from the drop-down menu, and finally click Data Miner Connections. A new tab will open beside or under your existing Connection tab. You can reposition this tab to your preferred location. This new Data Miner tab will list any connections you have associated with Oracle Data Miner. To add your DMUSER schema to this list, click the green plus symbol to create a new connection. A window will open listing all the connections you have already created under the SQL Developer Connections list. Select the DMUSER schema from the drop-down list.

The DMUSER schema will now be added to your Oracle Data Miner Connections list. When you double-click the DMUSER schema, SQL Developer will check the database to see if the Oracle Data Miner Repository exists in the database. If the Repository does not exist, a message will be displayed asking if you would like to install the repository. Click the Yes button to proceed with the install. Next, you will be prompted with a Connection window that asks you to enter the password for SYS. If you have this password you can enter it, or you can get your DBA to enter it for you. After entering the password, click the OK button. In the new window you will be asked for the default and temporary tablespace names for the repository account/schema, ODMRSYS. The next window will chart the progress of creating the repository. Make sure that the Install Demo Data option is checked. You can then click the Start button to begin the install. SQL Developer then proceeds to create the repository in your Oracle Database, and the progress bar will be updated as the repository is created.

The repository install can take anywhere from approximately one minute for a local database to up to ten minutes for a remote database. When the repository install is complete, you will see a window stating "Task Completed Successfully." You can close this window and start using ODM.

As part of the repository install, the DMUSER will be granted all the Oracle system privileges necessary to create and use Oracle Data Mining objects. Additionally, the DMUSER schema will be granted access to the sample schemas. All the necessary views are created on the sample schemas, and a table containing some demo data will be created in the DMUSER schema. This table containing the demo data is called INSUR_CUST_LTV_SAMPLE. Some of this demo data will be used in this and the following two chapters of the book.

Creating an Oracle Data Miner Workflow

The Oracle Data Miner tool that comes as part of SQL Developer allows you to build your data mining models using a workflow-based approach. With Oracle Data Miner you get to create a series of nodes that are linked to form a workflow of steps. Oracle Data Miner comes with a number of nodes that define the most common steps in processing your data and creating your data mining models. Each node allows you to customize the default settings, including how to handle and process the data, what data should be included or excluded, what conditions need to be applied, adding specific SQL or R code to a step in the workflow, configuring the data mining algorithms, and using the data mining models to score your new data. Figure 10-2 shows a typical view of Oracle Data Miner with a workflow that creates a classification data mining model and then scores the new data.

When you create a workflow in the Oracle Data Miner tool, as shown in Figure 10-2, behind the scenes the tool is really running a series of SQL and PL/SQL scripts. The rest of this chapter shows you how you can create a similar workflow with SQL and PL/SQL.

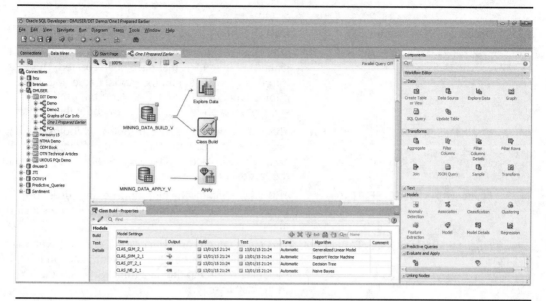

FIGURE 10-2. *Example of a workflow in Oracle Data Miner*

NOTE
If you would like to explore the full capabilities of the Oracle Data Miner tool and the SQL and PL/SQL functionality for performing data mining in Oracle, check out the Oracle Press book Predictive Analytics Using Oracle Data Miner *(2014).*

Oracle Data Mining Using SQL and PL/SQL

Oracle Data Mining comes with a number of Data Dictionary views, SQL functions, and PL/SQL packages to allow you to prepare data for data mining, build a data mining model, modify and tune the setting of the data mining algorithms, analyze and evaluate the model, and then apply the model to your new data. Because Oracle Data Miner is an in-database data mining tool, all objects and models created will be stored in the Oracle Database. This allows you to use SQL as the main interface for performing your data mining tasks. In this chapter, examples will be given on how you can use some of the ODM data dictionary views, the various SQL scoring functions, and the main PL/SQL packages.

The Oracle Data Mining models and other objects reside in the schema where they were created. They can be shared, queried, and used by any schema in the database that has been given access to them. A number of Oracle data dictionary views exist that allow you to query the Oracle Data Mining models and their various properties. Table 10-3 lists the data dictionary views specific to Oracle Data Mining. There are three versions of these (except for DBA_MINING_MODEL_SETTINGS), and they allow you to see what Oracle Data Mining objects you have access to in your local schema (using USER_), what ODM objects you have access to within the database (using ALL_), and what ODM objects are available to DBA users (using DBA_).

Dictionary View Name	Description
*_MINING_MODELS	This view contains the details of each of the Oracle Data Mining models that have been created. This information will contain the model name, the data mining type (or function), the algorithm used, and some other high-level information about the models.
*_MINING_MODEL_ATTRIBUTES	This view contains the details of the attributes that have been used to create the Oracle Data Mining model. If an attribute is used as a target, this will be indicated in the Target column.
*_MINING_MODEL_SETTINGS	This view contains the algorithm settings used to generate the Oracle Data Mining model for a specific algorithm.
DBA_MINING_MODEL_TABLES	This view, which is only accessible by users with the DBA privileges, lists all the tables that contain the metadata related to the data mining models that exist in the database.

TABLE 10-3. *Oracle Data Mining Data Dictionary Views*

In this table, * can be replaced by the following:

- **ALL_** Contains the Oracle Data Mining information that is accessible to the user
- **DBA_** Contains the Oracle Data Mining information that is accessible to DBA users
- **USER_** Contains the Oracle Data Mining information that is accessible to the current user

In the following example, the query can be used to retrieve all the classification data mining models you have in your schema and the data mining models for which you have been granted privileges. If you have not created any Oracle Data Mining models, no results will be returned.

```
SELECT model_name,
       algorithm,
       build_duration,
       model_size
FROM  ALL_MINING_MODELS
WHERE mining_function = 'CLASSIFICATION';

MODEL_NAME        ALGORITHM                        BUILD_DURATION MODEL_SIZE
----------------- -------------------------------- -------------- ----------
CLAS_GLM_1_13     GENERALIZED_LINEAR_MODEL                     13      .1611
CLAS_NB_1_13      NAIVE_BAYES                                  13       .061
CLAS_DT_1_13      DECISION_TREE                                13      .0886
CLAS_SVM_1_13     SUPPORT_VECTOR_MACHINES                      13      .0946
```

Oracle Data Mining PL/SQL API

Oracle Data Miner comes with some in-database PL/SQL packages. These packages allow you to perform all your data mining tasks. Three PL/SQL packages are associated with Oracle Data Miner:

- DBMS_DATA_MINING
- DBMS_DATA_MINING_TRANSFORM
- DBMS_PREDICTIVE_ANALYTICS

The DBMS_DATA_MINING PL/SQL package is the main package you will use to perform your data mining tasks. This includes creating new models, evaluating and testing the models, and then applying the models to new data. An overview of this package is given in the following sections, and examples of how to use the various procedures in this package to create a data mining model are given in the rest of this chapter.

The DBMS_DATA_MINING_TRANSFORM PL/SQL package allows you to define various data transformations that can be applied to your data sets to prepare them for input into the data mining algorithms.

The DBMS_PREDICTIVE_ANALYTICS PL/SQL package contains a number of procedures that allow you to perform an automated form of data mining. When you use this PL/SQL package, you are going to allow the Oracle Data Miner engine to determine what algorithm and settings to use. The output from the procedures will be the results, and any model produced will not exist after the procedures have completed. This PL/SQL package differs significantly from the DBMS_DATA_MINING package, as that package allows you to determine the algorithm, define the setting, investigate the model performance results, and so on.

The main package for Oracle Data Mining is the DBMS_DATA_MINING package. It is this package that is used by the Oracle Data Miner GUI tool, and the remainder of this chapter will illustrate how you can use the various components of this package.

The DBMS_DATA_MINING PL/SQL package contains the main procedures that allow you to create your data mining models, define all the necessary algorithm settings, investigate the results to determine the efficiency of the models, and apply the data mining models to your data. The Oracle Data Miner GUI tool that is part of SQL Developer is built upon this package and the procedures it contains.

Table 10-4 lists all the procedures you will find in the DBMS_DATA_MINING PL/SQL package.

Oracle Data Mining SQL Functions

One of the most powerful features of Oracle Data Mining is the ability to use SQL functions to run and score your data using the data mining models. The functions, listed in Table 10-5, can apply a mining model to your data, or they can dynamically mine the data by executing an analytic clause. SQL functions are available for all the data mining algorithms that support the scoring operation. By using these SQL functions, you can easily embed data mining functionality into all parts of your Oracle environment—be it your batch processing tasks, your reporting tools, your analytical dashboards, or your front-end applications.

Functions and Procedures	Description
add_cost_matrix	Adds a cost matrix to a classification model
alter_reverse_expression	Changes the reverse transformation expression to an expression that you specify
apply	Applies a model to a data set (scores the data)
compute_confusion_matrix	Computes the confusion matrix for a classification model
compute_lift	Computes the Lift for a classification model
compute_roc	Computes the Receiver Operating Characteristic (ROC) for a classification model
create_model	Creates a model
drop_model	Drops a model
export_model	Exports a model to a dump file
get_association_rules	Returns the rules from an association model
get_frequent_itemsets	Returns the frequent item sets for an association model
get_model_cost_matrix	Returns the cost matrix for a model
get_model_details_ai	Returns details about an Attribute Importance model
get_model_details_em	Returns details about an Expectation Maximization model
get_model_details_em_comp	Returns details about the parameters of an Expectation Maximization model
get_model_details_em_proj	Returns details about the projects of an Expectation Maximization model
get_model_details_glm	Returns details about a Generalized Linear Model
get_model_details_global	Returns high-level statistics about a model
get_model_details_km	Returns details about a k-Means model
get_model_details_nb	Returns details about a Naive Bayes model
get_model_details_nmf	Returns details about a Non-Negative Matrix Factorization model
get_model_details_oc	Returns details about an O-Cluster model
get_model_details_svd	Returns details about a Singular Value Decomposition model
get_model_details_svm	Returns details about a Support Vector Machine model with a linear kernel
get_model_details_xml	Returns details about a Decision Tree model
get_model_transformations	Returns the transformations embedded in a model
get_transform_list	Converts between two different transformation specification formats
import_model	Imports a model into a user schema
rank_apply	Ranks the predictions from the APPLY results for a classification model
remove_cost_matrix	Removes a cost matrix from a model
rename_model	Renames a model

TABLE 10-4. *Procedures and Functions in the DBMS_DATA_MINING PL/SQL Package*

Function Name	Description
prediction	Returns the best prediction for the target.
prediction_probability	Returns the probability of the prediction.
prediction_bounds	Returns the upper and lower bounds of the interval wherein the predicted values (linear regression) or probabilities (logistic regression) lie. This function only applies for GLM models.
prediction_cost	Returns a measure of the cost of incorrect predictions.
prediction_details	Returns detailed information about the prediction.
prediction_set	Returns the results of a classification model, including the predictions and associated probabilities for each case.
cluster_id	Returns the ID of the predicted cluster.
cluster_details	Returns detailed information about the predicted cluster.
cluster_distance	Returns the distance from the centroid of the predicted cluster.
cluster_probability	Returns the probability of a case belonging to a given cluster.
cluster_set	Returns a list of all possible clusters to which a given case belongs along with the associated probability of inclusion.
feature_id	Returns the ID of the feature with the highest coefficient value.
feature_details	Returns detailed information about the predicted feature.
feature_set	Returns a list of objects containing all possible features along with the associated coefficients.
feature_value	Returns the value of the predicted feature.

TABLE 10-5.   *Oracle Data Mining SQL Functions*

Classification Using Oracle Data Mining

One of the most commonly used data mining techniques is *classification*. With this data mining technique, you use a data set of previous known cases. You will use this data set as input to the data mining algorithms, which in turn generates a classification model. This model will be a representation of what attributes, the combination of those attributes, and their values contributed to a particular target value. A target value is an indicator represented by an attribute on the data set that distinguishes one set of cases from another. A typical application for classification is customer churn prediction. In this case, you would have a target attribute that contains a flag that indicates if a customer has churned or not churned. The data set you would use as input to the data mining algorithm is known as the *build data set*. This contains your historical data, and you can learn from the customer's past behavior. When you have a good data mining model that seems to give you good results, you can apply this model to new data. If we were to continue with this customer churn scenario, you would take the new customer data and apply the data mining model to it to see if these customers are likely to leave. Sometimes this is called *scoring the data*.

A common saying associated with this type of data mining is, "We learn from the past to predict the future." We will use the build data set to learn from the past.

Preparing Your Data

Data mining algorithms typically require your data to be prepared in a manner where there is one record for each case you want to feed as input to the data mining algorithms. Each of these case records will typically have a unique identifier that is called the CASE_ID. This case identifier can be based on one of the attributes that form the case record or can be generated automatically in some way by yourself or by a developer.

Typically when you are constructing the case records, you will want to perform a number of data preparation steps to get the data into the format you require and create the target attribute.

The following sections outline some of the typical tasks in data preparation and give some examples of how you can perform these tasks using the various functions available in SQL and PL/SQL.

Sampling and Creating Data Subsets

When our data sets are of a relatively small size, consisting of a hundred thousand records or fewer, we can explore the data in a relatively short period of time and build our data mining models using the entire data set. But if our data sets are larger than that, particularly as the size of the company increases, and we take into account all the data that might be available when we include the various Big Data data sources, we now have a new difficulty—it can now take a considerable amount of time to analyze the data and to build our data mining models. Sampling is a technique we can use that allows us to work with a subset of the data while maintaining the same characteristics of the entire data set. Sampling takes a "random" selection of records from our data set, up to the new number of records we have specified in the sample. For some of the data mining techniques, sampling can be used to divide our data set into two separate data sets that can be used for building our models and then for testing the effectiveness of those models.

In Oracle, the **sample** function takes a percentage figure. This is the percentage of the entire data set we want to have in the sampled result.

```
SELECT count(*)
FROM   mining_data_build_v
SAMPLE (20);

  COUNT(*)
----------
       319
```

CAUTION
*The **sample** function returns an estimate of the records for the sample size. Each time you run this query, you get a slightly different number of records being returned because Oracle completes an estimate based on the sample size and based on the default seed value used for the function.*

There is a variant of the **sample** function called **sample block**. In this case, you can still define a percentage value, but Oracle will take a random sample that closely relates to the percentage value from each block for the table.

```
SELECT count(*)
FROM   mining_data_build_v
SAMPLE BLOCK (20);

  COUNT(*)
----------
       150
```

CAUTION
*Just like the **sample** function, every time you run the **sample block** command you might get a different number of records being returned.*

Each time you use the **sample** function, Oracle will generate a random seed number that it uses as a seed for the **sample** function. If you omit a seed number (like in the previous examples), you get a different result set in each case, and the result set will have a slightly different number of records. If you run the sample code shown previously over and over again, you will see that the number of records returned varies by a small amount.

If you would like to have the same sample data set returned each time, you need to specify a seed value. The seed must be an integer between 0 and 4294967295.

```
SELECT count(*)
FROM   mining_data_build_v
SAMPLE (20) SEED (124);

  COUNT(*)
----------
       350
```

Again, if you run this query multiple times, you will still get some slightly different numbers being returned, but they are not as varied as the results when the seed is not used.

An alternative to using the **sample** function is to use the **ora_hash** function. The **ora_hash** function generates a hash value for a given expression, and it can be very useful when you want to generate a random sample based on a particular attribute. The following example illustrates how you can generate a subset of your data set consisting of 60 percent of the data that can be used for building your data mining model. The **ora_hash** value has three parameters. The first is the **case_id** for the data set/table. The second is the number of hash buckets that can be created. The numbering for the buckets starts at zero, so having a value of 99 for the **ora_hash** function creates 100 buckets. The third parameter is the seed value. In the following example, this is zero:

```
create view BUILD_DATA_SET_V
as
SELECT *
FROM   mining_data_build_v
WHERE ORA_HASH(CUST_ID, 99, 0) <= 60;
```

This example creates a view that contains 60 percent of the records from the data set. You can use this portion of the data as the build data set and input this into the data mining algorithms.

The rest of the original data set (40 percent) can then be used for your testing data set, as illustrated in this example, where a different range of the **ora_hash** values is used:

```
create view TEST_DATA_SET_V
as
SELECT *
FROM   mining_data_build_v
WHERE ORA_HASH(CUST_ID, 99, 0) > 60;
```

Data Transformations

The DBMS_DATA_MINING_TRANSFORM PL/SQL package provides a number of procedures and functions that allow you to perform certain types of data transformations on your data set. This PL/SQL package can be used in conjunction with the other types of transformations you will need to perform on your data.

There are two different ways of using the DBMS_DATA_MINING_TRANSFORM package. The first way is to use the package to define a list of transformations. These transformations form a list of what needs to be performed on the data. The output from this list of transformations will be a database view. This database view can then be used as the data source for your data mining algorithm. Every time you want to use the data mining model to score new data, you need to apply the list of transformations to the data before applying the model to the transformed data.

The second way to use this package is to define the list of transformations and then to pass this list of transformations as a parameter to the **create_model** procedure, which is used to create the data mining model. When you use this approach, the list of transformations is embedded into the data mining model. So when you want to apply the model to new data, you do not have to run the list of transformations as a separate step. Instead, the model will take the embedded transformations and apply these to the data before applying the model.

CAUTION
*When you embed the transformations in the data mining model,
you may still need to run some data transformations on the data set.
This is because the DBMS_DATA_MINING_TRANSFORM PL/SQL
package can handle a certain set of transformations. Using this PL/SQL
package can form one part of your data transformations.*

When you want to transform the data to replace the missing data with a mean or mode value, you need to follow a three-stage process. The first stage is to create a table that contains the updated transformed data. The second stage is to run the procedure that calculates the replacement value and then create the necessary records in the table created in the first stage. These two stages need to be followed for both numerical and categorical attributes. For stage three, you need to create a new view that contains the data from the original table and has the missing data rules generated in the second stage applied to it. The following example

illustrates these two stages for numerical and categorical attributes in the MINING_DATA_
BUILD_V data set:

```
-- Transform missing data for numeric attributes
BEGIN
    --
    -- Clean-up : Drop the previously created tables
    --
    BEGIN
       execute immediate 'drop table TRANSFORM_MISSING_NUMERIC';
    EXCEPTION
       WHEN others THEN
          null;
    END;
    BEGIN
       execute immediate 'drop table TRANSFORM_MISSING_CATEGORICAL';
    EXCEPTION
       WHEN others THEN
          null;
    END;

    --
    -- Transform the numeric attributes
    --
    dbms_data_mining_transform.CREATE_MISS_NUM (
       miss_table_name => 'TRANSFORM_MISSING_NUMERIC');

    dbms_data_mining_transform.INSERT_MISS_NUM_MEAN (
       miss_table_name => 'TRANSFORM_MISSING_NUMERIC',
       data_table_name => 'MINING_DATA_BUILD_V',
       exclude_list    => DBMS_DATA_MINING_TRANSFORM.COLUMN_LIST (
                          'affinity_card',
                          'cust_id'));

    --
    -- Transform the categorical attributes
    --
    dbms_data_mining_transform.CREATE_MISS_CAT (
       miss_table_name => 'TRANSFORM_MISSING_CATEGORICAL');

    dbms_data_mining_transform.INSERT_MISS_CAT_MODE (
       miss_table_name => 'TRANSFORM_MISSING_CATEGORICAL',
       data_table_name => 'MINING_DATA_BUILD_V',
       exclude_list    => DBMS_DATA_MINING_TRANSFORM.COLUMN_LIST (
                          'affinity_card',
                          'cust_id'));
END;
/
```

When this code completes, the two transformation tables will be in your schema. When you
query these two tables, you will find the attributes (numeric or categorical) listed along with the

value to be used to replace the missing values. For example, the following illustrates the missing data transformations for the categorical data:

```
column col format a25
column val format a25
SELECT col, val
FROM   transform_missing_categorical;

COL                         VAL
------------------------    ------------------------
CUST_GENDER                 M
CUST_MARITAL_STATUS         Married
COUNTRY_NAME                United States of America
CUST_INCOME_LEVEL           J: 190,000 - 249,999
EDUCATION                   HS-grad
OCCUPATION                  Exec.
HOUSEHOLD_SIZE              3
```

For stage three, you need to create a new view (MINING_DATA_V) that contains the data from the original table and has the missing data rules generated in the second stage applied to it. This is built in stages with an initial created view (MINING_DATA_MISS_V) that merges the data source and the transformations for the missing numeric attributes. This view (MINING_DATA_MISS_V) will then have the transformations for the missing categorical attributes applied to create a new view called MINING_DATA_V that contains all the missing data transformations.

```
BEGIN
    -- xform input data to replace missing values
    -- The data source is MINING_DATA_BUILD_V
    -- The output is MINING_DATA_MISS_V
    DBMS_DATA_MINING_TRANSFORM.XFORM_MISS_NUM(
        miss_table_name => 'TRANSFORM_MISSING_NUMERIC',
        data_table_name => 'MINING_DATA_BUILD_V',
        xform_view_name => 'MINING_DATA_MISS_V');

    -- xform input data to replace missing values
    -- The data source is MINING_DATA_MISS_V
    -- The output is MINING_DATA_V
    DBMS_DATA_MINING_TRANSFORM.XFORM_MISS_CAT(
        miss_table_name => 'TRANSFORM_MISSING_CATEGORICAL',
        data_table_name => 'MINING_DATA_MISS_V',
        xform_view_name => 'MINING_DATA_V');
END;
/
```

You can now query the MINING_DATA_V view and see that the data displayed does not contain any NULL values for any of the attributes.

The following example shows you how to transform the data to identify outliers and then how to transform them. In the example, a Winsorizing transformation is performed, where the outlier values are replaced by the nearest value that is not an outlier. The transformation process takes place in three stages. For the first stage, a table is created that contains the outlier transformation data. The second stage calculates the outlier transformation data and stores it in the table created in stage one. One of the parameters to the outlier procedure requires you to list the attributes you do not want the transformation procedure applied to (this is instead of listing the attributes you *do* want it applied to). The third stage creates a view (MINING_DATA_V_2) that contains the data set with the outlier transformation rules applied. The input data set to this stage can be the output from a previous transformation process (for example, DATA_MINING_V).

```
BEGIN
    -- Clean-up : Drop the previously created tables
    BEGIN
        execute immediate 'drop table TRANSFORM_OUTLIER';
    EXCEPTION
        WHEN others THEN
            null;
    END;

    -- Stage 1 : Create the table for the transformations
    -- Perform outlier treatment for: AGE and YRS_RESIDENCE
    --
    DBMS_DATA_MINING_TRANSFORM.CREATE_CLIP (
        clip_table_name => 'TRANSFORM_OUTLIER');

    -- Stage 2 : Transform the categorical attributes
    -- Exclude the number attributes you do not want transformed
    DBMS_DATA_MINING_TRANSFORM.INSERT_CLIP_WINSOR_TAIL (
        clip_table_name => 'TRANSFORM_OUTLIER',
        data_table_name => 'MINING_DATA_V',
        tail_frac       => 0.025,
        exclude_list    => DBMS_DATA_MINING_TRANSFORM.COLUMN_LIST (
                            'affinity_card',
                            'bookkeeping_application',
                            'bulk_pack_diskettes',
                            'cust_id',
                            'flat_panel_monitor',
                            'home_theater_package',
                            'os_doc_set_kanji',
                            'printer_supplies',
                            'y_box_games'));

    -- Stage 3 : Create the view with the transformed data
    DBMS_DATA_MINING_TRANSFORM.XFORM_CLIP(
        clip_table_name => 'TRANSFORM_OUTLIER',
        data_table_name => 'MINING_DATA_V',
        xform_view_name => 'MINING_DATA_V_2');
END;
/
```

The view MINING_DATA_V_2 will now contain the data from MINING_DATA_BUILD_V that has been transformed to process missing numeric and categorical data, and also has an outlier treatment for the AGE attribute.

The normalize procedures and the process of performing this transformation on your data follows a similar process to the previous transformations. Again, there is a three-stage process. The first stage involves the creation of a table that contains the normalization transformation data. The second stage applies the normalization procedures to your data source, defines the normalization required, and inserts the required transformation data into the table created during the first stage. The third stage involves defining a view that applies the normalization transformations to your data source and displaying the output via a database view. The following example illustrates how you can normalize the AGE and YRS_RESIDENCE attributes. The input data source is the view created as the output of the previous transformation (MINING_DATA_V_2). This is passed on to the original MINING_DATA_BUILD_V data set. The final output from this transformation step and all the other data transformation steps is MINING_DATA_READY_V.

```
BEGIN
    -- Clean-up : Drop the previously created tables
    BEGIN
        execute immediate 'drop table TRANSFORM_NORMALIZE';
    EXCEPTION
        WHEN others THEN
            null;
    END;

    -- Stage 1 : Create the table for the transformations
    -- Perform normalization for: AGE and YRS_RESIDENCE
    dbms_data_mining_transform.CREATE_NORM_LIN (
        norm_table_name => 'MINING_DATA_NORMALIZE');

    -- Step 2 : Insert the normalization data into the table
    dbms_data_mining_transform.INSERT_NORM_LIN_MINMAX (
        norm_table_name => 'MINING_DATA_NORMALIZE',
        data_table_name => 'MINING_DATA_V_2',
        exclude_list     => DBMS_DATA_MINING_TRANSFORM.COLUMN_LIST (
                            'affinity_card',
                            'bookkeeping_application',
                            'bulk_pack_diskettes',
                            'cust_id',
                            'flat_panel_monitor',
                            'home_theater_package',
                            'os_doc_set_kanji',
                            'printer_supplies',
                            'y_box_games'));
    -- Stage 3 : Create the view with the transformed data
    DBMS_DATA_MINING_TRANSFORM.XFORM_NORM_LIN (
        norm_table_name => 'MINING_DATA_NORMALIZE',
        data_table_name => 'MINING_DATA_V_2',
        xform_view_name => 'MINING_DATA_READY_V');

END;
/
```

You can now use the MINING_DATA_READY_V view as the data source for the Oracle Data Mining algorithms.

When you have prepared your data, performing all the necessary transformation on it, you are now ready to use the data as input to the data mining algorithms.

As an alternative to the previous approach, the following example illustrates how the transformed data created in the previous sections can be added as a data source to the data mining algorithms. Before you can create a data mining model, you need to create a settings table that contains all the algorithm settings necessary for the model. The following example illustrates a settings table where we want to create a Decision Tree classification model:

```
-- create the settings table for a Decision Tree model
CREATE TABLE demo_class_dt_settings
( setting_name  VARCHAR2(30),
  setting_value VARCHAR2(4000));

-- insert the settings records for a Decision Tree
-- Decision Tree algorithm. By Default Naive Bayes is used for classification
-- ADP is turned on. By default ADP is turned off.
BEGIN
  INSERT INTO demo_class_dt_settings (setting_name, setting_value)
  values (dbms_data_mining.algo_name, dbms_data_mining.algo_decision_tree);

  INSERT INTO demo_class_dt_settings (setting_name, setting_value)
  VALUES (dbms_data_mining.prep_auto,dbms_data_mining.prep_auto_on);
END;
/
```

When you have defined the settings, you can use the **create_model** procedure that is part of the DBMS_DATA_MINING PL/SQL package to create your data mining model. The following example shows how the **create_model** procedure uses the settings table from the previous example and uses MINING_DATA_READY_V as the data source to build the model:

```
BEGIN
    DBMS_DATA_MINING.CREATE_MODEL(
        model_name              => 'DEMO_CLASS_DT_MODEL',
        mining_function         => dbms_data_mining.classification,
        data_table_name         => 'MINING_DATA_READY_V',
        case_id_column_name     => 'cust_id',
        target_column_name      => 'affinity_card',
        settings_table_name     => 'demo_class_dt_settings');
END;
/
```

This example illustrates how you can create the data transformations, apply them to the data set, and then through a number of steps apply them to end up with a database view that can be used as the input data set for the **create_model** procedure. This transformed data set will have the various transformations included in it. These would be in addition to the more structural transformations you might need to write using PL/SQL (or some other programming language).

If you have a well-defined list of transformations, you might consider embedding them into your data mining model. To do this, you can pass a parameter that contains the list of transformations to the **create_model** procedure. This parameter takes the form

```
xform_list              IN TRANSFORM_LIST DEFAULT NULL
```

where **transform_list** has the following structure:

```
TRANFORM_REC      IS RECORD (
     attribute_name        VARCHAR2(4000),
     attribute_subname     VARCHAR2(4000),
     expression            EXPRESSION_REC,
     reverse_expression    EXPRESSION_REC,
     attribute_spec        VARCHAR2(4000));
```

You can use the **set_transform** procedure (in DBMS_DATA_MINING_TRANSFORM) to defined the transformations required. The following example illustrates the transformation of converting the BOOKKEEPING_APPLICATION attribute from a number data type to a character data type:

```
DECLARE
     transform_stack    dbms_data_mining_transform.TRANSFORM_LIST;
BEGIN
     dbms_data_mining_transform.SET_TRANSFORM(
               transform_stack,
               'BOOKKEEPING_APPLICATION',
               NULL,
               'to_char(BOOKKEEPING_APPLICATION)',
               'to_number(BOOKKEEPING_APPLICATION)',
               NULL);
END;
/
```

Alternatively, you can use the **set_expression** procedure and then create the transformation using it.

You can also stack the transforms together. Using the previous example, you could express a number of transformations and have these stored in the **transform_stack** variable. You can then pass this variable into your **create_model** procedure and have these transformations embedded in your data mining model (DEMO_TRANSFORM_MODEL). This is illustrated in the following example:

```
DECLARE
     transform_stack    dbms_data_mining_transform.TRANSFORM_LIST;
BEGIN
     -- Define the transformation list
     dbms_data_mining_transform.SET_TRANSFORM(
               transform_stack,
               'BOOKKEEPING_APPLICATION',
               NULL,
               'to_char(BOOKKEEPING_APPLICATION)',
               'to_number(BOOKKEEPING_APPLICATION)',
               NULL);
     -- Create the data mining model
     DBMS_DATA_MINING.CREATE_MODEL(
          model_name            => 'DEMO_TRANSFORM_MODEL',
          mining_function       => dbms_data_mining.classification,
          data_table_name       => 'MINING_DATA_BUILD_V',
          case_id_column_name   => 'cust_id',
          target_column_name    => 'affinity_card',
          settings_table_name   => 'demo_class_dt_settings',
          xform_list            => transform_stack);
END;
/
```

In the previous section, we gave examples of how you can create various transforms on your data set. These transformations were then used to create a view of the data set that included these transformations. If you would like to embed these transforms in your data mining model, instead of having to create the various views, you can use the **stack** procedures in the DBMS_DATA_MINING_ TRANSFORM package. The following examples illustrate the stacking of the transformations created in the previous section. These transformations are added (or stacked) to a transformation list. Then this transformation list is used in the **create_model** procedure call to embed the transformations in the model (MINING_STACKED_MODEL).

```
DECLARE
    transform_stack    dbms_data_mining_transform.TRANSFORM_LIST;
BEGIN
    -- Stack the missing numeric transformations
    dbms_data_mining_transform.STACK_MISS_NUM (
        miss_table_name    => 'TRANSFORM_MISSING_NUMERIC',
        xform_list         => transform_stack);

    -- Stack the missing categorical transformations
    dbms_data_mining_transform.STACK_MISS_CAT (
        miss_table_name    => 'TRANSFORM_MISSING_CATEGORICAL',
        xform_list         => transform_stack);

    -- Stack the outlier treatment for AGE
    dbms_data_mining_transform.STACK_CLIP (
        clip_table_name    => 'TRANSFORM_OUTLIER',
        xform_list         => transform_stack);

    -- Stack the normalization transformation
    dbms_data_mining_transform.STACK_NORM_LIN (
        norm_table_name    => 'MINING_DATA_NORMALIZE',
        xform_list         => transform_stack);

    -- Create the data mining model
    DBMS_DATA_MINING.CREATE_MODEL(
        model_name              => 'DEMO_STACKED_MODEL',
        mining_function         => dbms_data_mining.classification,
        data_table_name         => 'MINING_DATA_BUILD_V',
        case_id_column_name     => 'cust_id',
        target_column_name      => 'affinity_card',
        settings_table_name     => 'demo_class_dt_settings',
        xform_list              => transform_stack);
END;
/
```

To view the embedded transformations in your data mining model, you can use the **get_ model_transformations** procedure that is part of the DBMS_DATA_MINING PL/SQL package. The following example illustrates the embedded transformations that were added to the data mining model DEMO_STACKED_MODEL:

```
SELECT TO_CHAR(expression)
FROM TABLE
(dbms_data_mining.GET_MODEL_TRANSFORMATIONS('DEMO_STACKED_MODEL'));
```

```
TO_CHAR(EXPRESSION)
---------------------------------------------------------------------------
(CASE  WHEN (NVL("AGE",38.892)<18) THEN 18 WHEN (NVL("AGE",38.892)>70) THEN 70
ELSE NVL("AGE",38.892) END -18)/52

NVL("BOOKKEEPING_APPLICATION",.880667)
NVL("BULK_PACK_DISKETTES",.628)
NVL("FLAT_PANEL_MONITOR",.582)
NVL("HOME_THEATER_PACKAGE",.575333)
NVL("OS_DOC_SET_KANJI",.002)
NVL("PRINTER_SUPPLIES",1)
(CASE  WHEN (NVL("YRS_RESIDENCE",4.08867)<1) THEN 1 WHEN (NVL("YRS_RESIDENCE",4.
08867)>8) THEN 8 ELSE NVL("YRS_RESIDENCE",4.08867) END -1)/7

NVL("Y_BOX_GAMES",.286667)
NVL("COUNTRY_NAME",'United States of America')
NVL("CUST_GENDER",'M')
NVL("CUST_INCOME_LEVEL",'J: 190,000 - 249,999')
NVL("CUST_MARITAL_STATUS",'Married')
NVL("EDUCATION",'HS-grad')
NVL("HOUSEHOLD_SIZE",'3')
NVL("OCCUPATION",'Exec.')
```

Automatic Data Transformations in ODM

In Oracle, most of the data mining algorithms require some form of data transformation to be performed before the model is built. Oracle has built a lot of the necessary processing into the database, and the required data transformations are automatically performed on the data. This reduces the amount of time you have to spend on preparing the data for data mining and frees up this time for you to concentrate on your data mining project and its goals. Oracle Data Miner calls this Automatic Data Preparation (ADP).

During the building of a model, Oracle takes the specific data transformations that each algorithm requires and applies these to the input data. What's more, you can supplement these embedded data transformations with additional transformations of your own, or you can choose to manage all the transformations yourself.

ADP looks at the requirements of each algorithm and the input data set and applies the necessary data transformations, which may include binning, normalization, and outlier treatment.

Table 10-6 summarizes the Automatic Data Preparation that is performed for each algorithm.

When you are using the Oracle Data Miner tool, the Automatic Data Preparation feature is automatically turned on in each of the model build nodes. When you are using the Oracle Data Miner PL/SQL package DBMS_DATA_MINING to create your model, the default setting for Automatic Data Preparation is off (**prep_auto_off**). You can turn ADP on (**prep_auto_on**) by including a record in a settings table. An example of this is shown in the following code:

```
-- create the settings table for a Decision Tree model
DROP TABLE demo_class_dt_settings;
CREATE TABLE demo_class_dt_settings
( setting_name  VARCHAR2(30),
  setting_value VARCHAR2(4000));
```

```
-- insert the settings records for a Decision Tree
-- Decision Tree algorithm. By Default Naive Bayes is used for classification
-- ADP is turned on. By default ADP is turned off.
BEGIN
  INSERT INTO demo_class_dt_settings (setting_name, setting_value)
  values (dbms_data_mining.algo_name, dbms_data_mining.algo_decision_tree);

  INSERT INTO demo_class_dt_settings (setting_name, setting_value)
  VALUES (dbms_data_mining.prep_auto,dbms_data_mining.prep_auto_on);
END;
/
```

Building the Classification Model

The next stage in the process, after creating your data sets and applying all the necessary data transformations, is to create the data mining models. In this section we show you how to prepare for and create a classification model. With Oracle Data Mining, you have four data mining algorithms to choose from: Decisions Tree, Naive Bayes, GLM, and Support Vector Machine.

In this section we show you how to create a Decision Tree model. In most projects you will need to repeat the steps outlined in this discussion to create additional data mining models using the other Oracle Data Mining algorithms.

Algorithm	What Automatic Data Preparation Is Performed
Apriori	ADP has no effect on association rules.
Decision Tree	ADP has no effect on Decision Tree. Data preparation is handled by the algorithm.
Expectation Maximization	Single-column (non-nested) numerical columns that are modeled with Gaussian distributions are normalized with outlier-sensitive normalization. ADP has no effect on the other types of columns.
GLM	Numerical attributes are normalized with outlier-sensitive normalization.
k-Means	Numerical attributes are normalized with outlier-sensitive normalization.
MDL	All attributes are binned with supervised binning.
Naive Bayes	All attributes are binned with supervised binning.
NMF	Numerical attributes are normalized with outlier-sensitive normalization.
O-Cluster	Numerical attributes are binned with a specialized form of equi-width binning, which computes the number of bins per attribute automatically. Numerical columns with all NULLs or a single value are removed.
SVD	Numerical attributes are normalized with outlier-sensitive normalization.
Support Vector Machines	Numerical attributes are normalized with outlier-sensitive normalization.

TABLE 10-6. *Automatic Data Transformations Using Oracle Data Mining*

The Settings Table

To use a data mining algorithm to build a model, you need to list what settings you want to use for the algorithm. To specify the settings, you need to create a table that contains one record for each setting. The settings table will have two attributes:

- **setting_name** This contains the name of the setting parameter.
- **setting_value** This contains the value of the setting parameter.

You can define the name for the settings table, as illustrated in the previous example in "Data Transformation." Because you may have a number of these tables in your schema, you need to ensure that they have unique names and that each name is meaningful.

Typically the settings table will have two records in it. One of these records specifies the algorithm you want to use when building the model, and the second record specifies if you want to use the Automatic Data Processing (ADP) feature. ADP is turned on automatically when you are using the Oracle Data Miner tool, but when you are using the **create_model** PL/SQL function, ADP is turned off by default.

The following example provides the code to create a settings table and inserts two settings records. These records specify that the Decision Tree algorithm and ADP be used. This code can be run using a SQL worksheet in SQL Developer or using SQL*Plus or SQLcl. The schema that you use should be set up with the necessary permissions to use Oracle Data Miner (for example, you could use the DMUSER schema).

```
-- create the settings table for a Decision Tree model
DROP TABLE demo_class_dt_settings;
CREATE TABLE demo_class_dt_settings
( setting_name  VARCHAR2(30),
  setting_value VARCHAR2(4000));

-- insert the settings records for a Decision Tree
-- Decision Tree algorithm. By Default Naive Bayes is used for classification
-- ADP is turned on. By default ADP is turned off.
BEGIN
  INSERT INTO demo_class_dt_settings (setting_name, setting_value)
  values (dbms_data_mining.algo_name, dbms_data_mining.algo_decision_tree);

  INSERT INTO demo_class_dt_settings (setting_name, setting_value)
  VALUES (dbms_data_mining.prep_auto,dbms_data_mining.prep_auto_on);
END;
/

SELECT *
FROM   demo_class_dt_settings;

SETTING_NAME                    SETTING_VALUE
------------------------------  -----------------------------
ALGO_NAME                       ALGO_DECISION_TREE
PREP_AUTO                       ON
```

If you want to perform your own data preparation, you don't need to include the second INSERT statement, or you can change the setting value to **prep_auto_off**.

Algorithm Name	Description
ALGO_DECISION_TREE	Decision Tree
ALGO_GENERALIZED_LINEAR_MODEL	Generalized Linear Model
ALGO_NAIVE_BAYES	Naive Bayes
ALGO_SUPPORT_VECTOR_MACHINES	Support Vector Machine

TABLE 10-7. *Algorithm Names for Oracle Data Mining Algorithms*

You will need to create a separate settings table for each algorithm you want to use. In our example, we are only specifying the settings for creating a Decision Tree model. If you want to create additional classification models at the same time, you need to create a separate settings table for each of the other algorithms.

Table 10-7 lists the data mining algorithms available in Oracle.

Each algorithm has its own settings, and Table 10-8 shows the settings for each classification algorithm and the default values.

Algorithm	Setting	Values and Default Value
Naive Bayes	NABS_PAIRWISE_THRESHOLD	The value of the pairwise threshold for the algorithm. Values >= 0 and <= 1 0.001 (default)
	NABS_SINGLETON_THRESHOLD	The value of the singleton threshold for the algorithm. Values >= 0 and <= 1 0.001 (default)
Generalized Linear Model	GLMS_CONF_LEVEL	The confidence level for the intervals. Values > 0 and < 1 0.95 (default)
	GLMS_DIAGNOSTICS_TABLE_NAME	The name of the table that contains row-level diagnostic information, which is created during the model build. The default is determined by the algorithm.
	GLMS_REFERENCE_CLASS_NAME	The target value to be used as the reference value in a logistic regression model. The default is determined by the algorithm.
	GLMS_RIDGE_REGRESSION	Indicates whether ridge regression be enabled: GLMS_RIDGE_REG_ENABLE GLMS_RIDGE_REG_DISABLE The default is determined by the algorithm.
	GLMS_RIDGE_VALUE	The value of the ridge parameter used by the algorithm. Should only be set when ridge regression is enabled. Values > 0 The default is determined by the algorithm if set automatically; otherwise, a value must be provided.
	GLMS_VIF_FOR_RIDGE	Indicates whether Variance Inflation Factor statistics be created when ridge is used: GLMS_VIF_RIDGE_ENABLE GLMS_VIF_EIDGE_DISABLE (default)

TABLE 10-8. *Settings Available for Each Oracle Data Mining Algorithm* (Continues)

Algorithm	Setting	Values and Default Value
Support Vector Machine	SVMS_ACTIVE_LEARNING	Indicates whether active learning is enabled or disabled: SVMS_AL_DISABLE SVMS_AL_ENABLE (default)
	SVMS_COMPLEXITY_FACTOR	The value of the complexity factor. Values > 0 The default value is estimated by the algorithm.
	SVMS_CONV_TOLERANCE	The convergence tolerance for the algorithm. Values > 0 0.001 (default)
	SVMS_EPSILON	The value of the epsilon factor. Values > 0 The default value is estimated by the algorithm.
	SVMS_KERNEL_CACHE_SIZE	The value of the kernel cache size. For Gaussian kernels only. Values > 0 50MB (default)
	SVMS_KERNEL_FUNCTION	The kernel used by the algorithm: svm_gaussian svm_linear The default is determined by the algorithm.
	SVMS_OUTLINER_RATE	The rate of outlines in the training data for one-class models. Values > 0 and < 1 1 (default)
	SVMS_STD_DEV	The value of standard deviation for the algorithm using the Gaussian kernel. Values > 0 The default is estimated by the algorithm.
Decision Tree	TREE_IMPURITY_METRIC	The algorithm used to determine the best way to split the data for each node: TREE_IMPURITY_GINI (default) TREE_IMPURITY_ENTROPY
	TREE_TERM_MAX_DEPTH	Maximum depth of the tree (that is, the number of nodes between the root and the leaf nodes). Values >= 2 and <= 20 7 (default)
	TREE_TERM_MINPCT_NODE	Child nodes will not have a percentage record count below this value. Values >= 0 and <= 10 0.5 (default)
	TREE_TERM_MINREC_SPLIT	Minimum number of records in a parent node before a split will be considered. Values >= 0 and <= 20 20 (default)
	TREE_TERM_MINREC_NODE	Child nodes will not have a record count below this value. Values >= 0 10 (default)
	TREE_TERM_MINPCT_SPLIT	Minimum percentage of records needed to split a node. Values >= 0 .1 (default)

TABLE 10-8. *Settings Available for Each Oracle Data Mining Algorithm*

Creating the Classification Model

To create a new Oracle Data Mining model, you use the **create_model** procedure that is part of the DBMS_DATA_MINING package. The **create_model** procedure accepts the parameters listed in Table 10-9.

In the following examples, we will be creating a Decision Tree model based on the sample data set created early in the chapter. This sample data set contains the MINING_DATA_BUILD_V view. The **create_model** procedure will take all the cases in MINING_DATA_BUILD_V as inputs to create our model (in this example, a Decision Tree).

```
BEGIN
    DBMS_DATA_MINING.CREATE_MODEL(
         model_name             => 'DEMO_CLASS_DT_MODEL',
         mining_function        => dbms_data_mining.classification,
         data_table_name        => 'mining_data_build_v',
         case_id_column_name    => 'cust_id',
         target_column_name     => 'affinity_card',
         settings_table_name    => 'demo_class_dt_settings');
END;
/
```

Parameter	Description
model_name	This is the name of the model you are creating. This is a meaningful name you want to give to the model.
mining_function	The data mining function you want to use. The possible values are **association**, **attribute_importance**, **classification**, **clustering**, **feature_extraction**, and **regression**.
data_table_name	This is the name of the table or view that contains the build data set.
case_id_column_name	The CASE ID (PK) for the build data set.
target_column_name	The name of the target attribute in the build data set.
settings_table_name	The name of the settings table.
data_schema_name	The schema where the build data set is located. This can be left NULL if the build data set is in the current schema.
settings_schema_name	The schema where the settings table is located. This can be left NULL if the settings table is in the current schema.
xform_list	If you have a set of transformations you want to be embedded into the model, you can specify it here. These transformations can be instead of or in conjunction with the transformations performed by the ADP.

TABLE 10-9. *Parameters for the CREATE_MODEL Procedure*

NOTE
*If you want to drop a model, you can use the **drop_model** function.*
Here's an example:

```
BEGIN
    DBMS_DATA_MINING.DROP_MODE('DEMO_CLASS_DT_MODEL');
END;
/
```

If you want to create a number of classification models using the other classification algorithms, you will need to have a separate settings table for each of these. You then have to execute the CREATE_MODEL command for each model. The command is the same as the previous Decision Tree example, except you would have a different settings table and a different model name. The following example illustrates the settings table and the CREATE_MODEL command to generate a Support Vector Machine model for the same build data set:

```
-- create the settings table for a Support Vector Machine model
CREATE TABLE demo_class_svm_settings
( setting_name   VARCHAR2(30),
  setting_value VARCHAR2(4000));

-- insert the settings records for a Support Vector Machine
-- Support Vector Machine algorithm. By Default Naive Bayes is used for classification
-- ADP is turned on. By default ADP is turned off.
BEGIN
  INSERT INTO demo_class_svm_settings (setting_name, setting_value)
  values (dbms_data_mining.algo_name,
dbms_data_mining.algo_support_vector_machines);

  INSERT INTO demo_class_svm_settings (setting_name, setting_value)
  VALUES (dbms_data_mining.prep_auto,dbms_data_mining.prep_auto_on);
END;
/


BEGIN
    DBMS_DATA_MINING.CREATE_MODEL(
        model_name            => 'DEMO_CLASS_SVM_MODEL',
        mining_function       => dbms_data_mining.classification,
        data_table_name       => 'mining_data_build_v',
        case_id_column_name   => 'cust_id',
        target_column_name    => 'affinity_card',
        settings_table_name   => 'demo_class_svm_settings');
END;
/
```

The following code illustrates how to check that the classification model and the Support Vector Machine model have been built and what other classification models exist in your schema. We see our new Decision Tree model called DEMO_CLASS_DT_MODEL and our new Support Vector Machine called DEMO_CLASS_SVM_MODEL.

```
SELECT model_name,
       algorithm,
       build_duration,
       model_size
FROM ALL_MINING_MODELS
WHERE mining_function = 'CLASSIFICATION';
```

MODEL_NAME	ALGORITHM	BUILD_DURATION	MODEL_SIZE
CLAS_GLM_1_13	GENERALIZED_LINEAR_MODEL	13	.1611
CLAS_NB_1_13	NAIVE_BAYES	13	.061
CLAS_DT_1_13	DECISION_TREE	13	.0886
CLAS_SVM_1_13	SUPPORT_VECTOR_MACHINES	13	.0946
DEMO_CLASS_DT_MODEL	**DECISION_TREE**	**27**	**.0661**
DEMO_CLASS_SVM_MODEL	**SUPPORT_VECTOR_MACHINES**	**7**	**.1639**

To see what settings were used to build the models, you need to query the ALL_DATA_MINING_SETTINGS view, which shows you what settings were specified in the settings table and the other default settings for each algorithm.

```
SELECT setting_name,
       setting_value,
       setting_type
FROM  all_mining_model_settings
WHERE model_name = 'DEMO_CLASS_DT_MODEL';
```

SETTING_NAME	SETTING_VALUE	SETTING
TREE_TERM_MINREC_NODE	10	DEFAULT
TREE_TERM_MAX_DEPTH	7	DEFAULT
TREE_TERM_MINPCT_SPLIT	.1	DEFAULT
TREE_IMPURITY_METRIC	TREE_IMPURITY_GINI	DEFAULT
TREE_TERM_MINREC_SPLIT	20	DEFAULT
TREE_TERM_MINPCT_NODE	.05	DEFAULT
PREP_AUTO	ON	INPUT
ALGO_NAME	ALGO_DECISION_TREE	INPUT

Next, you can have a look at what attributes were used to build the Decision Tree model. A data mining algorithm might not use all the attributes available in the data source table or view to build its model. The algorithm will work out what attributes and their values contribute to the values in the target attribute. To see what attributes were used in the model, we can query the ALL_MINING_MODEL_ATTRIBUTES view:

```
SELECT attribute_name,
       attribute_type,
       usage_type,
       target
FROM  all_mining_model_attributes
WHERE model_name = 'DEMO_CLASS_DT_MODEL';
```

```
ATTRIBUTE_NAME                      ATTRIBUTE_T USAGE_TY TAR
------------------------------      ----------- -------- ---
AFFINITY_CARD                       CATEGORICAL ACTIVE   YES
YRS_RESIDENCE                       NUMERICAL   ACTIVE   NO
OCCUPATION                          CATEGORICAL ACTIVE   NO
HOUSEHOLD_SIZE                      CATEGORICAL ACTIVE   NO
EDUCATION                           CATEGORICAL ACTIVE   NO
CUST_MARITAL_STATUS                 CATEGORICAL ACTIVE   NO
AGE                                 NUMERICAL   ACTIVE   NO
```

Evaluating the Classification Model

When you create a new model using the **create_model** procedure, it uses all the records from the data source to build the model. When you are using the PL/SQL package DBMS_DATA_MINING, the testing and evaluation are separate steps that you need to complete. When using the DBMS_DATA_MINING package to create your models, you have to use a separate data source for testing your data. This separate data source can be a table or a view.

When the testing data set is ready, you can apply the model to it. You have two ways of doing this. The first is to use the APPLY procedure that is part of the DBMS_DATA_MINING package, or you can use the SQL functions **prediction** and **prediction_probability**. These are explained in more detail in following sections of this chapter. When you use the **apply** procedure, a new table is created to store the results. If you do not want your schema to get filled up with these tables, the alternative approach is to create a view using the SQL functions. This latter approach is illustrated in the upcoming examples. In the following scenario, a view is created that contains the primary key of the table that contains the data, the predicted target value, and the prediction probability. The CASE ID is needed so that we can link back to the testing data set, to compare the actual target values with the predicted values. The sample data has a view defined called MINING_DATA_TEST_V that we will be using for testing our Decision Tree model.

```
CREATE OR REPLACE VIEW demo_class_dt_test_result
AS
SELECT cust_id,
       prediction(DEMO_CLASS_DT_MODEL USING *)  predicted_value,
       prediction_probability(DEMO_CLASS_DT_MODEL USING *) probability
FROM   mining_data_test_v;

SELECT *
FROM demo_class_dt_test_result
FETCH first 8 rows only;

   CUST_ID PREDICTED_VALUE PROBABILITY
---------- --------------- -----------
    103001               0 .952191235
    103002               0 .952191235
    103003               0 .859259259
    103004               0 .600609756
    103005               1 .736625514
    103006               0 .952191235
    103007               1 .736625514
    103008               0 .600609756
```

The following sections use the views DEMO_CLASS_DT_TEST_RESULT and MINING_DATA_BUILD_V to build the confusion matrix as well as calculate the lift and the ROC (Receiver Operating Characteristic). All the results from these calculations will be numbers, and we will not have the Oracle Data Miner tool graphs to help us understand the results.

To calculate the confusion matrix for the model, use the **compute_confusion_matrix** procedure, which is part of the PL/SQL package DBMS_DATA_MINING. The confusion matrix can be used to test the classification models by comparing the predicted target values, generated by the model, with the actual target values in the testing data set. The procedure requires two sets of inputs that consist of the predictions (Case Id, Prediction, and Probabilities) and the actual target values from the testing data set (Case Id and Target attribute). Here is the syntax of the procedure:

```
DBMS_DATA_MINING.COMPUTE_CONFUSION_MATRIX (
    accuracy                       OUT NUMBER,
    apply_result_table_name        IN VARCHAR2,
    target_table_name              IN VARCHAR2,
    case_id_column_name            IN VARCHAR2,
    target_column_name             IN VARCHAR2,
    confusion_matrix_table_name    IN VARCHAR2,
    score_column_name              IN VARCHAR2 DEFAULT 'PREDICTION',
    score_criterion_column_name    IN VARCHAR2 DEFAULT 'PROBABILITY',
    cost_matrix_table_name         IN VARCHAR2 DEFAULT NULL,
    apply_result_schema_name       IN VARCHAR2 DEFAULT NULL,
    target_schema_name             IN VARCHAR2 DEFAULT NULL,
    cost_matrix_schema_name        IN VARCHAR2 DEFAULT NULL,
    score_criterion_type           IN VARCHAR2 DEFAULT 'PROBABILITY');
```

The following example shows how to create the confusion matrix for the Decision Tree model created earlier in the chapter using the testing data set and the view we created previously. The confusion matrix results will be stored in a new table called DEMO_CLASS_DT_CONFUSION_MATRIX.

```
set serveroutput on

DECLARE
    v_accuracy NUMBER;
BEGIN
    DBMS_DATA_MINING.COMPUTE_CONFUSION_MATRIX (
        accuracy                    => v_accuracy,
        apply_result_table_name     => 'demo_class_dt_test_result',
        target_table_name           => 'mining_data_test_v',
        case_id_column_name         => 'cust_id',
        target_column_name          => 'affinity_card',
        confusion_matrix_table_name => 'demo_class_dt_confusion_matrix',
        score_column_name           => 'PREDICTED_VALUE',
        score_criterion_column_name => 'PROBABILITY',
        cost_matrix_table_name      => null,
        apply_result_schema_name    => null,
        target_schema_name          => null,
        cost_matrix_schema_name     => null,
        score_criterion_type        => 'PROBABILITY');
```

```
    DBMS_OUTPUT.PUT_LINE('**** MODEL ACCURACY ****: ' || ROUND(v_accuracy,4));
END;
/
```

```
**** MODEL ACCURACY ****: .8187
```

Here's how to view the confusion matrix:

```
SELECT *
FROM    demo_class_dt_confusion_matrix;
```

ACTUAL_TARGET_VALUE	PREDICTED_TARGET_VALUE	VALUE
1	0	192
0	0	1074
1	1	154
0	1	80

To calculate the Lift for the model, use the **compute_lift** procedure that is part of the PL/SQL package DBMS_DATA_MINING. The *Lift* is a measurement of the degree to which the predictions of the positive class, by the model, are an improvement over random chance. The Lift is calculated based on the results from applying the model to the testing data set. These results are ranked by the probability and divided into quantiles. Each quantile has the score for the same number of cases.

The procedure requires two sets of inputs that consist of the predictions (Case Id, Prediction, and Probabilities) and the actual target values from the testing data set (Case Id and Target attribute). Here is the syntax for the procedure:

```
DBMS_DATA_MINING.COMPUTE_LIFT (
      apply_result_table_name      IN VARCHAR2,
      target_table_name            IN VARCHAR2,
      case_id_column_name          IN VARCHAR2,
      target_column_name           IN VARCHAR2,
      lift_table_name            .  IN VARCHAR2,
      positive_target_value        IN VARCHAR2,
      score_column_name            IN VARCHAR2 DEFAULT 'PREDICTION',
      score_criterion_column_name  IN VARCHAR2 DEFAULT 'PROBABILITY',
      num_quantiles                IN NUMBER DEFAULT 10,
      cost_matrix_table_name       IN VARCHAR2 DEFAULT NULL,
      apply_result_schema_name     IN VARCHAR2 DEFAULT NULL,
      target_schema_name           IN VARCHAR2 DEFAULT NULL,
      cost_matrix_schema_name      IN VARCHAR2 DEFAULT NULL
      score_criterion_type         IN VARCHAR2 DEFAULT 'PROBABILITY');
```

The following example shows how to create the Lift for the Decision Tree model from earlier in the chapter using the testing data set and the DEMO_CLASS_DT_TEST_RESULT view (created previously), which contains the results from applying the model. The Lift results will be stored in a new table called DEMO_CLASS_DT_LIFT.

```
BEGIN
    DBMS_DATA_MINING.COMPUTE_LIFT (
       apply_result_table_name      => 'demo_class_dt_test_result',
```

```
            target_table_name              => 'mining_data_test_v',
            case_id_column_name            => 'cust_id',
            target_column_name             => 'affinity_card',
            lift_table_name                => 'DEMO_CLASS_DT_LIFT',
            positive_target_value          => '1',
            score_column_name              => 'PREDICTED_VALUE',
            score_criterion_column_name => 'PROBABILITY',
            num_quantiles                  => 10,
            cost_matrix_table_name         => null,
            apply_result_schema_name       => null,
            target_schema_name             => null,
            cost_matrix_schema_name        => null,
            score_criterion_type           => 'PROBABILITY');
END;
/
```

After this code has been run, the quantile lift results are stored in the DEMO_CLASS_DT_LIFT table. This table has a number of attributes, and the core set of these (illustrated in the following SQL) shows the main Lift results:

```
SELECT quantile_number,
       probability_threshold,
       gain_cumulative,
       quantile_total_count
FROM   demo_class_dt_lift;
```

QUANTILE_NUMBER	PROBABILITY_THRESHOLD	GAIN_CUMULATIVE	QUANTILE_TOTAL_COUNT
1	.736625514	.1025641	24
2	.736625514	.205128199	24
3	.736625514	.307692317	24
4	.736625514	.410256398	24
5	.736625514	.508547003	23
6	.736625514	.606837582	23
7	.736625514	.705128211	23
8	.736625514	.803418791	23
9	.736625514	.90170942	23
10	.736625514	1	23

To calculate the ROC for the model, use the **compute_roc** procedure that is part of the PL/SQL package DBMS_DATA_MINING. The ROC is a measurement of the false-positive rate against the true positive rate. It can be used to assess the impact of changes to the probability threshold for a model. The probability threshold is the decision point used by the model for predictions. The ROC can be used to determine an appropriate probability threshold. This can be achieved by examining the true positive fraction and the false-positive fraction. The *true positive fraction* is the percentage of all positive cases in the test data set that were correctly predicted as positive. The *false-positive fraction* is the percentage of negative cases in the test data set that were incorrectly predicted as positive.

The procedure requires two sets of inputs that consist of the predictions (Case Id, Prediction, and Probabilities) and the actual target values from the testing data set (Case Id and Target attribute). Here is the syntax of the procedure:

```
DBMS_DATA_MINING.COMPUTE_ROC (
    roc_area_under_curve              OUT NUMBER,
    apply_result_table_name           IN VARCHAR2,
    target_table_name                 IN VARCHAR2,
    case_id_column_name               IN VARCHAR2,
    target_column_name                IN VARCHAR2,
    roc_table_name                    IN VARCHAR2,
    positive_target_value             IN VARCHAR2,
    score_column_name                 IN VARCHAR2 DEFAULT 'PREDICTION',
    score_criterion_column_name       IN VARCHAR2 DEFAULT 'PROBABILITY',
    apply_result_schema_name          IN VARCHAR2 DEFAULT NULL,
    target_schema_name                IN VARCHAR2 DEFAULT NULL);
```

The following example shows how to create the ROC statistics for the Decision Tree model created earlier in the chapter using the testing data set and the view DEMO_CLASS_DT_TEST_RESULT (created previously) that contains the results from applying the model. The ROC results will be stored in a new table called DEMO_CLASS_DT_ROC.

```
set serveroutput on
DECLARE
    v_area_under_curve NUMBER;
BEGIN
    DBMS_DATA_MINING.COMPUTE_ROC (
        roc_area_under_curve              => v_area_under_curve,
        apply_result_table_name           => 'demo_class_dt_test_results',
        target_table_name                 => 'mining_data_test_v',
        case_id_column_name               => 'cust_id',
        target_column_name                => 'affinity_card',
        roc_table_name                    => 'DEMO_CLASS_DT_ROC',
        positive_target_value             => '1',
        score_column_name                 => 'PREDICTED_VALUE',
        score_criterion_column_name       => 'PROBABILITY');

    DBMS_OUTPUT.PUT_LINE('**** AREA UNDER ROC CURVE ****: ' ||
        ROUND(v_area_under_curve,4));
END;
/

**** AREA UNDER ROC CURVE ****: .5
```

After this code has been run, the ROC results are stored in the DEMO_CLASS_DT_ROC table. This table has a number of attributes, and the core set of these, illustrated in the following SQL, shows the main ROC results:

```
SELECT probability,
       true_positive_fraction,
       false_positive_fraction
FROM   demo_class_dt_roc;
```

Applying the Classification Model to New Data

In this section we show you how to use the classification models produced in this chapter. You can embed the calling and scoring of new data in your applications as you are gathering the data or processing a record.

In the Oracle Database, you have two main ways of doing this. The first is using the SQL functions **prediction** and **prediction_probability** to score data as you are gathering it in your applications. The second way is to process a number of records in batch mode. This may be a part of an end-of-day process when you want to score your data and then perform another operation based on the outputs of this process. To do this, you use the **apply** procedure that is part of the DBMS_DATA_MINING package. The outputs of using this procedure are persisted as a table in the database.

Applying the Model Using Batch Mode

Applying an ODM model in batch mode involves using the **apply** procedure in the PL/SQL package DBMS_DATA_MINING. The main difference with using this package and procedure is that the outputs are stored in a new table in your schema. This method is best suited to scenarios where you want to process a number of records in a batch or for offline work. The syntax of the **apply** procedure is as follows:

```
DBMS_DATA_MINING.APPLY (
    model_name              IN VARCHAR2,
    data_table_name         IN VARCHAR2,
    case_id_column_name     IN VARCHAR2,
    result_table_name       IN VARCHAR2,
    data_schema_name        IN VARCHAR2 DEFAULT NULL);
```

Table 10-10 describes the parameters for the DBMS_DATA_MINING.APPLY procedure.

The table or view that contains the data to be scored (DATA_TABLE_NAME) needs to be in the same format and have the same column names as the original data source used to create the ODM model. Any data processing performed separately from the data processing performed by the model also needs to be performed before you run the **apply** procedure.

Parameter	Description
model_name	This is the name of the Oracle Data Mining model you want to use to score the data.
data_table_name	The name of the table or view that contains the data to be scored.
case_id_column_name	The Case Id attribute name.
result_table_name	The name of the table that will be created to store the results.
data_schema_name	The name of the schema that contains the data to be scored. If the table or view is in your schema, you can leave this parameter out or set it to NULL.

TABLE 10-10. *Parameters for the APPLY Procedure*

Columns	Description
CASE_ID	This is the Case Id attribute name from the data set to be scored.
PREDICTION	This will contain the predicted target attribute value.
PROBABILITY	This will contain the prediction probability for the Prediction.

TABLE 10-11. *Results Table Structure After Using the APPLY Procedure for Binary Classification*

The results from the **apply** procedure are stored in a new table (RESULT_TABLE_NAME). The **apply** procedure will create this new table and determine what attributes it will contain. Table 10-11 describes what attributes the results table will contain for the classification model.

The results table (RESULT_TABLE_NAME) will contain a record for each of the possible target variable values. In the case, where we have two target variable values (0 or 1), we will get two records in the results table for each record in the apply data set (DATA_TABLE_NAME). For each of these records, the prediction probability of each prediction will be given. You can then use this information to decide how you want to process the data.

Using our previously built Decision Tree model, the following example illustrates using the **apply** procedure to score the data in MINING_DATA_APPLY_V. The results table (DEMO_DT_DATA_SCORED) will contain the outputs from the **apply** procedure.

```
BEGIN
    dbms_data_mining.APPLY(model_name           => 'DEMO_CLASS_DT_MODEL',
                           data_table_name      => 'MINING_DATA_APPLY_V',
                           case_id_column_name  => 'CUST_ID',
                           result_table_name    => 'DEMO_DT_DATA_SCORED');
END;
/


SELECT *
FROM   demo_dt_data_scored
FETCH first 10 rows only;

   CUST_ID PREDICTION PROBABILITY
---------- ---------- -----------
    100001          0  .952191235
    100001          1  .047808765
    100002          0  .952191235
    100002          1  .047808765
    100003          0  .952191235
    100003          1  .047808765
    100004          0  .952191235
    100004          1  .047808765
    100005          1  .736625514
    100005          0  .263374486
```

There are two possible target values in our DEMO_CLASS_DT_MODEL data mining model. MINING_DATA_APPLY_V has 1500 records. The results table, DEMO_DT_DATA_SCORED, has

3000 records. A record is created for each of the target values and has the associated prediction probability for each possible target value.

Applying the Model in Real Time

With real-time data scoring, you can score the data as you are capturing it. This is particularly useful for applications where you need to score or label the data as it is being entered into an application. An example of this would be when you are entering the details of a new customer. As you are entering the values in each field in the application, Oracle Data Mining can be used to say if this customer will be a high-value customer or a low-value customer, or if you can make certain offers. Oracle has built this kind of functionality into their Fusion Applications.

The two functions you can use for this are **prediction** and **prediction_probability**. The **prediction** function returns the predicted value based on the input data and the Oracle Data Mining model. The **prediction_probability** function will return a value, in the range of 0 to 1, that indicates how strong of a prediction Oracle thinks it has made.

The **prediction** function returns the best prediction for the given model and the data inputted. The syntax of the function is as follows:

```
PREDICTION (model_name, USING attribute_list);
```

The attribute list can consist of attributes from a table. The ODM model will then process the values in these attributes to make the prediction. This function processes one record at a time to make the prediction, and the number of records to process is determined by your query. The following example illustrates how the **prediction** function can be used to score data that already exists in a table:

```
SELECT cust_id, PREDICTION(DEMO_CLASS_DT_MODEL USING *)
FROM    mining_data_apply_v
FETCH first 8 rows only;


    CUST_ID PREDICTION(DEMO_CLASS_DT_MODELUSING*)
---------- ------------------------------------
    100001                                     0
    100002                                     0
    100003                                     0
    100004                                     0
    100005                                     1
    100006                                     0
    100007                                     0
    100008                                     0
```

This example uses the Decision Tree model we created in the previous section (DEMO_CLASS_DT_MODEL). Note that USING * takes all the attributes and feeds their values into the Decision Tree model to make the prediction.

We can also use the **prediction** function in the WHERE clause to restrict what records are returned from a query, as shown here:

```
SELECT cust_id
FROM    mining_data_apply_v
WHERE   PREDICTION(DEMO_CLASS_DT_MODEL USING *) = 1
FETCH first 8 rows only;
```

```
   CUST_ID
----------
    100005
    100009
    100012
    100026
    100029
    100034
    100035
    100036
```

The second function that we can use is the **prediction_probability** function. It has the same syntax as the **prediction** function:

```
PREDICTION_PROBABILITY (model_name, USING attribute_list);
```

The **prediction_probabilty** function returns a value between 0 and 1 and is a measure of how strong a prediction ODM thinks it has made. You can use this function in the SELECT and WHERE parts of a query, just like the **prediction** function. Here's an example:

```
SELECT cust_id,
       PREDICTION(DEMO_CLASS_DT_MODEL USING *) Predicted_Value,
       PREDICTION_PROBABILITY(DEMO_CLASS_DT_MODEL USING *) Prob
FROM   mining_data_apply_v
FETCH first 8 rows only;
```

```
   CUST_ID PREDICTED_VALUE         PROB
---------- --------------- ----------
    100001               0 .952191235
    100002               0 .952191235
    100003               0 .952191235
    100004               0 .952191235
    100005               1 .736625514
    100006               0 .952191235
    100007               0 .952191235
    100008               0 .952191235
```

What-If Analysis Using Oracle Data Mining

These SQL functions can also be used on data as it is being captured and to apply the in-database data mining model to this data. We can easily integrate this functionality into our application, which allows us to perform real-time what-if analysis. In this kind of scenario we do not have the data in a table. Instead, we can feed the actual values being captured into the **prediction** and **prediction_probability** functions, as shown here:

```
SELECT prediction(DEMO_CLASS_DT_MODEL
       USING 'F' AS cust_gender,
             62 AS age,
          'Widowed' AS cust_marital_status,
             'Exec.' as occupation,
             2 as household_size,
```

```
              3 as yrs_residence)  Predicted_Value,
        prediction_probability(DEMO_CLASS_DT_MODEL, 0
      USING 'F' AS cust_gender,
              62 AS age,
        'Widowed' AS cust_marital_status,
            'Exec.' as occupation,
              2 as household_size,
              3 as yrs_residence) Predicted_Prob
FROM dual;



PREDICTED_VALUE PREDICTED_PROB
--------------- --------------
              0   .935768262
```

As you capture more data or change some of the values, the functions will return an updated value from the data mining model. The following example illustrates how the predicted value and the probability change as we capture more and more data:

```
SELECT PREDICTION(DEMO_CLASS_DT_MODEL using AGE) Pred_Value2,
     prediction_probability (DEMO_CLASS_DT_MODEL using AGE) Pred_Prob2,
     PREDICTION(DEMO_CLASS_DT_MODEL using AGE, HOUSEHOLD_SIZE) Pred_Value3,
     prediction_probability (DEMO_CLASS_DT_MODEL using AGE, HOUSEHOLD_SIZE) Pred_Prob3,
     PREDICTION(DEMO_CLASS_DT_MODEL using AGE, HOUSEHOLD_SIZE, EDUCATION) Pred_Value4,
     prediction_probability (DEMO_CLASS_DT_MODEL using AGE, HOUSEHOLD_SIZE, EDUCATION) Pred_Prob4,
     PREDICTION(DEMO_CLASS_DT_MODEL using *) Pred_Value,
     prediction_probability (DEMO_CLASS_DT_MODEL using *) Pred_Prob
FROM  MINING_DATA_BUILD_V WHERE cust_id = 101504;

PRED_VALUE2 PRED_PROB2 PRED_VALUE3 PRED_PROB3 PRED_VALUE4 PRED_PROB4 PRED_VALUE PRED_PROB
----------- ---------- ----------- ---------- ----------- ---------- ---------- ----------
          0 .746666667           0 .533994334           1 .736625514          1 .736625514
```

For example, a kind of what-if analysis can be built into your call center applications to give a real-time predicted outcome as each customer attribute is being entered. Another example would be with analyzing potential staff churn. As a manager, you can use an application built with Oracle Data Mining to see what impact a particular pay raise (or not) will have on the staff members and their potential risk of leaving or staying.

Oracle Data Mining: Other Techniques

In this chapter we illustrated how you can go about preparing data for data mining and how to build a classification data mining model using the SQL and PL/SQL features of Oracle Data Mining. When you are exploring your data and trying to work out what is the best data mining algorithm to use, you will probably build and test data mining models based on all the classification algorithms. Table 10-1 listed the various in-database Oracle Data Mining algorithms currently available to use.

As your data science projects evolve, you may end up using a combination of these algorithms to give you optional predictive solutions as well as combining them with some of the other techniques, like clustering. For example, you could use clustering to segment your data into related groups of customers and then build a classification model for each of these groups.

Being able to use SQL and PL/SQL allows you to easily embed the scoring of data into your everyday applications. It doesn't really matter what language your applications are built with; as long as you are using SQL to process data in your Oracle Database, you can perform predictive analytics using SQL without the need for any additional architectural changes. Table 10-5 listed the various SQL functions available to you to get the maximum out of using Oracle Data Mining within your applications.

Summary

Classification is a very powerful, and a very common, data mining technique and has many possible application areas. As your skills with data mining develop, you can use the many functions and procedures that are available in the database. Using these in-database functions and procedures, you can build data mining models and use a variety of methods to evaluate the models. Integrating the use of the data mining models into your organization's applications is a relatively simple task. Your Oracle developers can write some simple SQL code to use the data mining models in your database.

CHAPTER
11

Oracle R Enterprise

Oracle R Enterprise is one of the components of the Oracle Advanced Analytics (OAA) option, which is available as part of the Enterprise Edition of the Oracle Database. Chapter 10 provided an overview of how to use Oracle Data Mining and how you can build data mining models using the in-database data mining algorithms.

Oracle R Enterprise (ORE) enables the open-source R statistical programming language and environment to be run on the database server and within the database. Oracle R Enterprise integrates the R programming language with the Oracle Database and is installed in the Oracle Home directories on the Oracle Database server.

Oracle R Enterprise allows for the seamless translation of R code into Oracle SQL, where possible, and this allows the R programmer to utilize the performance and scalability features of the Oracle Database. They are no longer constrained by the computing power of the client machine. Oracle R Enterprise also has the ability to run R code that is embedded in SQL code. The data remains in the Oracle Database, and all operations that are defined in the R code are translated and performed on the data in the Oracle Database. This core ability of Oracle R Enterprise allows data analysts to work with larger data sets than they would typically be able to do. Using embedded R execution, you can store and run R scripts in the database through either the R programming environment or using SQL, or both. You can use the results generated by the R code in any SQL-enabled tool. The embedded R execution also allows you to utilize the vast graphical capabilities available in R within your tools, including Oracle Business Intelligence Enterprise Edition (OBIEE), Oracle BI Publisher, APEX, and others.

In this chapter we explore how you can get up and running with Oracle R Enterprise. We look at the installation process where you install Oracle R Enterprise as part of the Oracle Database on the server, how to install Oracle R Enterprise on the client machine, how to create a connection to the Oracle Database using ORE, how to explore data in your Oracle schema, how to build a data mining model, how to use the embedded R execution in SQL, and how you can include analytics and graphs generated by your R code in tools such as OBIEE, Oracle Publisher, APEX, and others.

The ORE Transparency Layer

One of the key features of Oracle R Enterprise is that it supports in-database analytics of your data. It achieves this by implementing a transparency layer. The transparency layer allows for some of your R code to be translated and run on your data in the Oracle Database. R programmers do not need to learn any new languages and, with minimal changes, can have their R code using the performance and scalability features of the Oracle Database. It also allows data analysts to work with all the available data instead of having to work with smaller samples of that data that can fit on their client machines.

The transparency layer looks to translate R functions into the equivalent SQL functions. These SQL functions are then run on the data, producing results. These results are then sent back to the R client and translated into R-formatted results. When a set of R functions is being run on a data set in the Oracle Database, these R functions are not immediately executed. Instead, they are accumulated, and it is only when the results are required for some computation or for viewing by the user that the actual functions will be executed. Additionally, the Oracle Database and the transparency layer will look to optimize these functions to ensure they are executed in an efficient manner.

In the following example, we have a view defined in our schema. In this particular example, the view is on the CUSTOMERS table in the SH schema. The view is assigned to a local R variable (**full_dataset**) via the transparency layer as an ORE data frame. This means that the data resides in the Oracle Database, and we have a pointer to it in our local R session. Any R functions we apply to this ORE data frame will be translated into the equivalent SQL function in the Oracle Database, if one exists. The R aggregate function will then perform an aggregation on the data, counting the number of people of each gender. The results are then displayed.

```
> full_dataset <- CUSTOMER_V
> AggData <- aggregate(full_dataset$CUST_ID,
        by = list(CUST_GENDER = full_dataset$CUST_GENDER),
        FUN = length)
> AggData

  CUST_GENDER      x
F            F 18325
M            M 37175
```

All of the preceding code was translated into an equivalent SQL function via the transparency layer. This query was run on the view in the schema, and the results were returned to us and displayed in our R session.

We can use the transparency layer to inspect what SQL was actually used. We can use the information produced by the transparency layer to inspect what SQL was actually generated and executed on the data in the schema. You can use the **str** R function to get all the details of what is produced by the transparency layer. It produces a lot of information, and we'll leave that for you to try out. The following example shows you how to extract the SQL query that was run in the Oracle Database by the transparency layer.

```
> AggData@dataQry

66_45
"( select \"CUST_GENDER\" NAME001, \"CUST_GENDER\" VAL001,count(*) VAL002 from
\"ORE_USER\".\"CUSTOMER_V\" where (\"CUST_GENDER\" is not null) group by
\"CUST_GENDER\" )"
```

Installing Oracle R Enterprise

Oracle R Enterprise is a component of the Oracle Advanced Analytics option of the Oracle Database Enterprise Edition. Before you can use Oracle R Enterprise, you need to complete a number of installation steps. The installation can be divided into two main parts. The first of these is the installation on the Oracle Database server. The second part is the installation on the client machines that will be used by the data analysts and data scientists. Additionally, this chapter looks at the various installation prerequisites that need to be completed before the installation can commence.

Installation Prerequisites

The following prerequisites are required before the installation of Oracle R Enterprise:

- You have installed the Enterprise Edition of Oracle Database 12c or 11gR2.
- You know the SID or the service name of the Oracle Database or Pluggable Database.
- You have the SYS password or you have your DBA available for the steps that require it.
- You have downloaded the Oracle R Enterprise Server and supporting packages installation files for your server operating system.
- You have installed the Oracle Client software on your client machine.
- You have downloaded the Oracle R Enterprise Client and supporting packages' installation files for your client operating system.

Another useful step is to install the Oracle sample schemas. Although these are not necessary for installing and using Oracle R Enterprise, what they do give you is an excellent group of prepared data sets that you can use to work with and learn how Oracle R Enterprise works.

Server Installation

Installing Oracle R Enterprise involves two major phases. The first of these phases involves installing R and Oracle R Enterprise on the database server. The second phase involves installing R and Oracle R Enterprise on the client machine.

It is important that you ensure that the same version of the Oracle R Enterprise packages are installed on the database server and on the client machine. You will also need to ensure that the database server and client ORE packages are upgraded at the same time. If these are different, you will get some error messages and your ORE code will not run or will run incorrectly.

Oracle R Enterprise is only supported on the Oracle 11.2g Database and the Oracle 12c Database. The requirements for installing Oracle R Enterprise on the Oracle Database server are as follows:

- Verify that your Oracle Database server platform is supported by Oracle R Enterprise.
- Enable Oracle Advanced Analytics.
- Obtain the SYS password and the name of the SID or service name of the Oracle Database.
- Obtain the tablespace name where the ORE metadata and system objects can be stored. This will typically be the SYSAUX tablespace.
- Check that there is sufficient space in this tablespace. If not, ask the DBA to allocate some more.
- Know the name of the temporary tablespace. This will typically be the TEMP tablespace.
- Know the default tablespace for the ORE user schema (for example, the USERS tablespace).
- Decide on the password for the ORE system account RQSYS (for example, RQSYS). This schema is created and only used during the ORE installation process. Once the installation is complete, the RQSYS schema will be locked with an expired password. The RQSYS schema does not have the **create session** privilege.

- Decide the name of your first ORE user schema and password. This will be created during the ORE installation (for example, **ore_user/ore_user**).
- Check that the ORACLE_HOME and SID environment variables are set.

Figure 11-1 outlines the steps involved in the installation of Oracle R Enterprise on your Oracle Database server. The following sections detail what is required for each of these steps.

Install R on the Server

To use Oracle R Enterprise on your Oracle Database server, you will need an installation of the R software. Two options are open to you for installing R. The first is to install the version of R that is provided by Oracle. This is called Oracle R Distribution. The second option is to install the required version of R that is needed for the version of Oracle R Enterprise you are installing. If you choose this second option, it is vital that you install the correct version of R; otherwise, Oracle R Enterprise may not work for you.

Oracle recommends that you use Oracle R Distribution. Oracle R Distribution is a separately maintained and supported version of R provided by Oracle. Additionally, Oracle has worked to integrate with certain libraries such as the Intel Math Kernel Library (MKL) and the Sun Performance Library. These libraries improve the performance of certain mathematical functions, including BLAS and LAPACK, to ensure that they utilize the underlying hardware preference.

To install Oracle R Distribution, you will need to download the software from the Oracle Open Source Download page. This is located at

https://oss.oracle.com/ORD

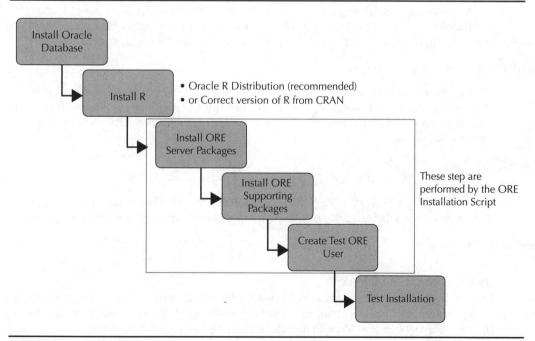

FIGURE 11-1. *Oracle R Enterprise installation steps on the Oracle Database server*

On this website, select the version of Oracle R Distribution you would like to download. When the download has completed, you can uncompress the file and then run the executable file to perform the installation. You are not required to enter any details during the installation process, and when this is complete you will have R (the Oracle R Distribution version) installed on your server.

On Linux you can use YUM to automatically download and install Oracle R Distribution. To enable YUM to perform this download and install Oracle R Distribution, you need to make the following edits to the YUM repository file located in /etc/yum.repos.d. The following example illustrates what steps you need to take and the changes you need to perform as the root user:

```
cd /etc/yum.repos.d
vi yum.repos.d
```

For Oracle Linux 5 or Oracle Linux 6, locate the following sections and make the changes highlighted in bold (note that olX is either ol5 or ol6 and depends on the version of Oracle Linux you are using):

```
[olX_latest]
enabled=1
[olX_addons]
enabled=1
```

If you are using Oracle Linux 7, you need to make an additional change to the YUM repository file:

```
[ol7_optional_latest]
enabled=1
```

After making these changes, you are now ready to run the yum.repos.d script to download and install Oracle R Enterprise. It will also download and run any other operating system updates available. To run the download and install it, you can run the following command:

```
yum install R.x86_64
```

This command installs the latest version of Oracle R Distribution. If you need to install a slightly older version of Oracle R Distribution, you can specify the version number. For example, for Oracle R Enterprise version 1.5, you will need to install Oracle R Distribution 3.2.0. An example of this is shown next:

```
yum install R.XXX
     Where XXX is the specific version number e.g. 3.2.0, 3.0.1, 3.1.1, etc
```

When the update is complete, Oracle R Distribution is installed. You can now run the R software and use the vast array of statistical functions by running the R command, like so:

```
$ R
```

Install ORE on the Server

The first step is to download and uncompress the Oracle R Enterprise server and supporting packages from the Oracle R Enterprise download webpage. Make sure you download the version of these files that corresponds with the operating system of your database server.

A user-created installation directory (for example, ORE_Server_Install) should be created, and both of these downloaded files should be uncompressed into this installation directory. After you do this, your installation directory should look like the following directory listing:

```
/ORE_Server_Install
      ore-server-linux-x86-64-1.5.zip
      ore-supporting-linux-x86-64-1.5.zip
      server.sh
      /server
      /supporting
```

NOTE
It is important to have the server and the supporting packages uncompressed into the same directory, as shown here, as this will simplify the installation of Oracle R Enterprise. Otherwise, you will have to install the supporting R packages as a separate step after completing the installation of the server packages.

The server.sh (or server.bat on a Windows server) file is the batch file you can run to install the Oracle R Enterprise server and supporting packages. You have two options for running this file. The first is in batch mode, where you can specify all the arguments on the command line. To see all the available parameters you can run

```
./server.sh –help
```

An alternative way to run this script is in inactive mode:

```
./server.sh
```

Before running this server installation script, you should have set up the ORACLE_HOME and ORACLE_SID environment variables.

If you are running Oracle 12c Database, you can set the ORACLE_SID to your pluggable database (PDB) name. When you are prompted for the SYS password during the installation, you will need to add the PDB name after the password. If you are using an Oracle 11gR2 Database, you do not need to add anything after entering the SYS password.

```
[oracle@localhost ORE_install]$ ./server.sh –i
```

Additionally, you will be prompted to enter the names of the permanent (SYSAUX) and temporary (TEMP) tablespaces, a password for the ORE owner schema called RQSYS, the name and password of your first ORE-enabled schema (ORE_USER), and the permanent (USERS) and temporary (TEMP) tablespaces for this user.

Client Installation
Any data analysts who will be using Oracle R Enterprise will need to have the R software installed on their machines as well as the necessary Oracle R Enterprise and supporting Oracle R Enterprise packages installed on their client machines. Figure 11-2 illustrates the client installation process.

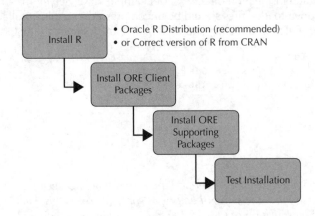

FIGURE 11-2. *Client installation of Oracle R Enterprise*

It is important that the version of R that is installed on the client machine matches the version of R or Oracle R Distribution installed on the Oracle Database server. If a different version of R is used, then when you try to establish an ORE connection to the database, you will get an error.

Install R on the Client

This step is exactly the same as what was done to install R on your Oracle Database server, but this time you are installing R on your client machine. You can download and install the correct version of R for your Oracle R installation from the R CRAN site, or you can go to the following Oracle website to download the version of the Oracle R Distribution you require:

https://oss.oracle.com/ORD

The only post-installation step you will need to perform is to add the full path to the Oracle R Distribution bin directory (or your R bin directory) to the PATH environment variable.

You can now perform a quick check that Oracle R Distribution or R has been installed. Open a command window and enter the following command:

```
> R
```

Install ORE Client and Supporting Packages

To install Oracle R Enterprise on your client machine, you need to download and unzip the Oracle R Enterprise client and Oracle R Enterprise supporting packages from the Oracle R Enterprise website. Care should be taken to download the correct version of these packages and that the version matches the one that was installed on the Oracle Database server.

After downloading the compressed files, you can uncompress these into the same directory (for example, ORE_Client_Install). After you uncompress these files, your directory should contain the following (for ORE 1.5):

```
...\ORE_Client_Install
            \client
                    \ORE_1.5.zip
                    \OREbase_1.5.zip
                    \OREcommon_1.5.zip
                    \OREdm_1.5.zip
                    \OREeda_1.5.zip
                    \OREembed_1.5.zip
                    \OREgraphics_1.5.zip
                    \OREmodels_1.5.zip
                    \OREpredict_1.5.zip
                    \OREstats_1.5.zip
                    \ORExml_1.5.zip
            \supporting
                    \arules_1.1-9.zip
                    \Cairo_1.5-8.zip
                    \DBI_0.3.1.zip
                    \png_0.1-7.zip
                    \randomForest_4.6-10
                    \Roracle_1.2-1.zip
                    \statmod_1.4.21.zip
```

To install these packages, you have two options available. The first of these is to use the **install.packages** function in R. To use this function, you need to start R and then run the commands shown next to install the core Oracle R Enterprise packages and the supporting packages:

```
> ## Install the Oracle R Enterprise Client Packages
> ##
> ## Need to ensure your Client has the correct version of R or Oracle R
> ## Distribution
> ##
> install.packages("C:/app/ORE_Client_Install/client/ORE_1.5.zip")
> install.packages("C:/app/ORE_Client_Install/client/OREbase_1.5.zip")
> install.packages("C:/app/ORE_Client_Install/client/OREcommon_1.5.zip")
> install.packages("C:/app/ORE_Client_Install/client/OREdm_1.5.zip")
> install.packages("C:/app/ORE_Client_Install/client/OREeda_1.5.zip")
> install.packages("C:/app/ORE_Client_Install/client/OREembed_1.5.zip")
> install.packages("C:/app/ORE_Client_Install/client/OREgraphics_1.5.zip")
> install.packages("C:/app/ORE_Client_Install/client/OREmodels_1.5.zip")
> install.packages("C:/app/ORE_Client_Install/client/OREpredict_1.5.zip")
> install.packages("C:/app/ORE_Client_Install/client/OREstats_1.5.zip")
> install.packages("C:/app/ORE_Clien_Install/client/ORExml_1.5.zip")

> ## Install the ORE Supporting packages
> install.packages("C:/app/ORE_Client_Install/supporting/arules_1.1-9.zip")
> install.packages("C:/app/ORE_Client_Install/supporting/Cairo_1.5-8.zip")
> install.packages("C:/app/ORE_Client_Install/supporting/DBI_0.3.1.zip")
> install.packages("C:/app/ORE_Client_Install/supporting/png_0.1-7.zip")
> install.packages("C:/app/ORE_Client_Install/supporting/randomForest_4.6-10.zip")
> install.packages("C:/app/ORE_Client_Install/supporting/ROracle_1.2-1.zip")
> install.packages("C:/app/ORE_Client_Install/supporting/statmod_1.4.21.zip")
```

RStudio
The R language comes with a command-line interface and with a very simple GUI interface. A very popular alternative tool, used by many data analysts and data scientists, is RStudio (www.rstudio.com). RStudio is available in open-source and commercial editions. RStudio provides an integrated development environment (IDE) that allows you to work with all components of your R projects in one integrated tool.

Using Oracle Pre-Built Appliances

To use Oracle R Enterprise, you will need access to an Oracle Database (version 11gR2 or 12c). If you don't have ready access to a suitable Oracle Database environment or you are not allowed to install Oracle R Enterprise on your Oracle Database server, then you are a bit stuck. One option open to you is to build a virtual machine on your client machine. This will involve the installation of the operating system, installing the Oracle Database, and setting up schemas and data sets. However, you may not be comfortable with this option.

As an alternative, you could use one of the Oracle pre-built appliances that come preconfigured with loads of Oracle software installed, configured, and with some sample data sets. These pre-built appliances are a great way to try the software before you have to install in your development environments. You can import these appliances into Oracle VirtualBox to have your own personal Oracle virtual machine.

If you want to try out Oracle R Enterprise, you can use one of these pre-built appliances as a learning environment and try out the various features of Oracle R Enterprise. Oracle provides a number of pre-built appliances that are suitable for you to use with Oracle R Enterprise, with the Oracle OBIEE Sample App and the Oracle Big Data Lite appliances having Oracle R Enterprise already installed and configured for you.

Alternatively, you can use the Oracle Database Developer pre-built appliance. Unfortunately, it doesn't have Oracle R Enterprise installed on it, but you can easily install Oracle R Enterprise using the instructions given in the section on Oracle Database server installation.

Getting Started and Connecting to the Oracle Database

After completing the server and client installation of Oracle R Enterprise, you are now ready to perform an initial test to make sure the installation has been completed correctly. The following code example illustrates the creation of a database connection using the **ore.connect** command. This example connects to the ORE_USER schema created during the Oracle R Enterprise Server installation. This example also connects to an Oracle 12c Database using SERVICE_NAME. If you're using Oracle Database 11gR, you can use SID instead of SERVICE_NAME.

```
> # First you need to load the ORE library
> library(ORE)

> # Create an ORE connection to your Oracle Schema
> ore.connect(user="ore_user", password="ore_user", host="localhost",
            service_name="PDB12C", port=1521, all=TRUE)
```

This example uses "localhost" for the server name. Alternatively, you can use the name of the Oracle Database server or the IP address of the Oracle Database server.

We can now perform some simple checks. The first is to check that we are connected to the database. The response to this is TRUE to indicate that we have an open connection to the database; otherwise, we would get FALSE.

```
> # Test that we are connected
> ore.is.connected()
 [1] TRUE
```

Next, we can list all the objects that exist in the Oracle schema (ORE_USER). These objects include all tables and views. The ORE_USER schema was created during the Oracle R Enterprise Server installation. At this point, we have no objects in this schema, and this is indicated with the **character(0)** response:

```
> # List the objects that are in the Oracle Schema
> ore.ls()
 character(0)
```

An additional test to verify the embedded R execution is to run the following **ore.doEval** function. To run this function, the ORE_USER will need to have the **rqadmin** database privilege granted to it:

```
> ore.doEval(function() .libPaths() )
```

This **ore.doEval** function lists the R library paths on your Oracle Database server. It is in these directories that the Oracle Database will look for the necessary R packages and code to run.

The **ore.exec** function allows you to execute SQL statements in your schema. These statements will typically be DDL and DML statements that do not return a value or result, unless there is an error. You can also use this command to set any optimizer or session-level settings, use the In-Memory option, and so on.

The following example illustrates using **ore.exec** to drop some views, create some views, create a table, and put the table into memory. This example assumes you have been granted SELECT privilege on the tables in the SH schema and have the Oracle In-Memory option configured. If you do not have the Oracle In-Memory option, you can ignore the last ORE.EXEC statement.

```
> ore.exec("DROP VIEW customers_v")
> ore.exec("DROP VIEW products_v")
> ore.exec("DROP VIEW countries_v")
> ore.exec("DROP VIEW sales_v")
> # You will need select privileges on the tables in the SH schema
> ore.exec("CREATE VIEW customers_v AS SELECT * FROM sh.customers")
> ore.exec("CREATE VIEW products_v AS SELECT * FROM sh.products")
> ore.exec("CREATE VIEW countries_v AS SELECT * FROM sh.countries")
> ore.exec("CREATE VIEW sales_v AS SELECT * FROM sh.sales")
> # create a view for Customers who live in USA
> ore.exec("CREATE TABLE customers_usa
            AS SELECT * FROM customers_v WHERE COUNTRY_ID = 52790")
> # put the new Customers table in memory
> ore.exec("ALTER TABLE customers_usa inmemory")
```

Note that ORE.EXEC should only be used on SQL statements when there is no return value.

The views and table created in this example are not included in the R environment because no ORE proxy objects have been created for them; plus, they have not been added to the R search space. You can see this if you use the **ore.ls()** function. These objects do not exist. You will need to run the **ore.sync** function to make these objects accessible to your R environment.

```
> ore.sync()
> ore.ls()
[1] "COUNTRIES_V"   "CUSTOMERS_USA" "CUSTOMERS_V"   "PRODUCTS_V"    "SALES_V"
```

When working with data in an Oracle table or view, you can use the ORE proxy object to perform your analysis and such, or you might prefer to use a local R variable to refer to the object in the database. The following example illustrates this kind of assignment and the display of some basic information and statistics about the data:

```
> # create a local variable ds that points to SALES_V in the database
> ds <- ore.get("SALES_V")
> # list the attributes of the SALES_V. This is the same as using DESC in SQL
> names(ds)
[1] "PROD_ID"        "CUST_ID"       "TIME_ID"       "CHANNEL_ID"    "PROMO_ID"
[6] "QUANTITY_SOLD"  "AMOUNT_SOLD"
> # We can verify we are pointing at the object in the database
> class(ds)
[1] "ore.frame" attr(,"package")
[1] "OREbase"
> # How many rows and columns are in the table
> dim(ds)
[1] 918843        7
> # Display the first 6 records from the table
> head(ds)
    PROD_ID CUST_ID    TIME_ID CHANNEL_ID PROMO_ID QUANTITY_SOLD AMOUNT_SOLD
1        13     987 1998-01-10          3      999             1     1232.16
2        13    1660 1998-01-10          3      999             1     1232.16
3        13    1762 1998-01-10          3      999             1     1232.16
4        13    1843 1998-01-10          3      999             1     1232.16
5        13    1948 1998-01-10          3      999             1     1232.16
6        13    2273 1998-01-10          3      999             1     1232.16
Warning messages:
1: ORE object has no unique key - using random order
2: ORE object has no unique key - using random order
> # Get the Summary statistics for each attribute in SALES_V
> summary(ds)
    PROD_ID           CUST_ID          TIME_ID            CHANNEL_ID       PROMO_ID
Min.   : 13.00   Min.   :      2   Min.   :1998-01-01   Min.   :2.000   Min.   : 33.0
1st Qu.: 31.00   1st Qu.:   2383   1st Qu.:1999-03-13   1st Qu.:2.000   1st Qu.:999.0
Median : 48.00   Median :   4927   Median :2000-02-17   Median :3.000   Median :999.0
Mean   : 78.18   Mean   :   7290   3rd Qu.:2001-02-15   Mean   :2.862   Mean   :976.4
3rd Qu.:127.00   3rd Qu.:   9163   Max.   :2001-12-31   3rd Qu.:3.000   3rd Qu.:999.0
Max.   :148.00   Max.   : 101000                        Max.   :9.000   Max.   :999.0
QUANTITY_SOLD   AMOUNT_SOLD
Min.   :1   Min.   :   6.40
1st Qu.:1   1st Qu.:  17.38
Median :1   Median :  34.24
Mean   :1   Mean   : 106.88
3rd Qu.:1   3rd Qu.:  53.89
Max.   :1   Max.   :1782.72
```

If you would prefer to work with the data on your local machine (PC or laptop), you can use the **ore.pull** function to create a local copy of the data. You need to be careful when using this function because, depending on the volume of data, this may take a lot of time. Plus, you will not be using any of the performance features available by default in the database. This function should only be used on rare occasions.

```
> # Create a local copy of the SALES_V data
> sales_ds <- ore.pull(SALES_V)
 Warning message:
 ORE object has no unique key - using random order
> # Check to see that this is a local data frame and not an ORE object
> class(sales_ds)
 [1] "data.frame"
> # Get details of the local data
> dim(sales_ds)
 [1] 918843      7
```

You can use the **ore.push** function to take a local data frame and move it to your schema in the database. A temporary table will be created in your schema with a name beginning with ORE$. This will be followed by some set of numbers. The following example takes the MTCARS data set that comes with R and pushes the data set to a temporary table in the database:

```
> cars_ore_ds<-ore.push(mtcars)
```

The **cars_ore_ds** variable will now be an ORE object pointing to a table in the database. You can see this table if you log into your schema in the database.

You can perform many of your typical data manipulation and analytics operations on this data, and all of these operations will be performed in the database.

In a previous example we showed how you can take a local R data frame and push this to the database as a temporary table. In the following example, this same data frame will instead be created as a table in the schema.

```
> ore.create(mtcars, "CARS_DATA")
```

The **ore.create** function accepts two parameters. The first is the name for the data frame you want to persist in the schema. The second parameter is the name of the table in the database schema.

When you run the **ore.ls** function, you will now see that the new table is listed. The **ore.create** function also performs an **ore.sync** and **ore.attach** for this new object. This makes it available for use without you needing to run any additional functions.

We have the **ore.drop** function to drop and remove an object from the database. In this case, we can drop a database table or a database view from our schema using the **ore.drop** function.

The following example illustrates the dropping of the CARS_DATA table that we created using the **ore.create** function in the previous example:

```
> ore.drop("CARS_DATA")
```

When you are finished working with your ORE connection, you will need to issue the **ore.disconnect** command to cleanly exit your ORE connection and disconnect from the Oracle Database. Any temporary objects created in your schema and not explicitly saved will be removed before your connection to the database is closed. All temporary ORE objects will have a name beginning with ORE$.

```
> ore.disconnect()
```

ORE will issue an implicit **ore.disconnect** command when you quit your R session or issue a new ORE connection using **ore.connect**.

However, if the session is abnormally disconnected (for example, the session dies, you kill it, your machine hibernates, and so on), then any temporary objects that were created during your ORE session will remain as objects in the database. When a normal disconnect happens, ORE will clean up and remove any temporary objects from your schema.

Exploring Your Data Using ORE

The R language has a vast array of functions you can use when exploring your data. There are lots of books and websites available to you to learn about them. Instead of exploring all of the various explorative data analysis (EDA) functions here, we will look at some of the ORE-specific functions, as listed in Table 11-1.

In addition to the functions listed in Table 11-1, Oracle R Enterprise has, via the transparency layer, mapped most of the typical statistical functions found in the R base package and the R stat package to their equivalent in SQL.

The R language has a vast array of statistical functions, and there is a multitude of resources available to help you learn the R language and utilize these statistical functions. It would be impossible to cover everything here in this chapter; instead, the following examples illustrate how you can use some of the highly tuned ORE functions listed in Table 11-1.

ORE Function	Description
ore.corr	Used to perform correlation analysis across numeric columns.
ore.crosstab	Used to build cross-tabulations and supports multiple columns. Also allows optional aggregations, weighting, and ordering options.
ore.esm	Builds an exponential smoothing model on data that is in an ordered **ore.vector** function.
ore.freq	Using the output of the **ore.crosstab** function, **ore.freq** determines if two-way cross-tabulation or N-way cross-tabulation tables should be used for the results.
ore.rank	Allows you to investigate the distribution of values along numeric columns.
ore.sort	Allows you to sort the data in a variety of ways.
ore.summary	Provides a series of descriptive analytics based on the data in an ORE data frame.
ore.univariate	Provides distribution analysis of numeric columns in an ORE data frame. Gives all the statistics from an **ore.summary** function, plus signed rank test and extreme values.

TABLE 11-1. *Oracle R Enterprise Exploratory Data Analysis Functions*

The **ore.summary** function calculates descriptive statistics using a large number of statistical functions based on numerical attributes. By default, the statistical functions used include frequency or count of nonmissing values, mean, minimum value, and maximum value.

The following example illustrates how you can use the **ore.summary** function at a basic level for one numeric attribute. If you want to include additional numeric attributes, you can include them in the **var** list.

```
> # EDA - Examples
> #
> # Use the CUSTOMERS_V data. It is in our schema in the Database
> full_dataset <- V
> # list the attributes of the CUSTOMERS_USA table in the database.
> names(full_dataset)
> # Generate the summary statistics
> ore.summary(full_dataset, var="CUST_YEAR_OF_BIRTH")

    FREQ     N    MEAN MIN  MAX
1 55500 55500 1957.404 1913 1990
```

This example illustrates how **ore.summary** uses the default list of statistical functions. If you want to use some of the other functions available with **ore.summary**, you will need to list out all the statistical functions as shown in the following example:

```
> ore.summary(full_dataset, var="CUST_YEAR_OF_BIRTH",
            stats=c("n", "nmiss", "min", "max", "var", "range") )

    FREQ     N NMISS  MIN  MAX     VAR RANGE
1 55500 55500     0 1913 1990 225.388    77
```

The **ore.summary** function also allows us to add a grouping to the calculations. Adding a grouping produces statistics for the numeric attribute based on all the values in the grouping attribute. The following example illustrates the calculation of the statistics for each of the values we have in the CUST_GENDER attribute. The third row of the results gives us the overall statistics for the CUST_YEAR_OF_BIRTH attribute. This is the same as what we had in our previous example. Then, for the first and second rows we get the statistics for the values M and F in the CUST_GENDER attribute.

```
> ore.summary(full_dataset, class="CUST_GENDER", var="CUST_YEAR_OF_BIRTH")

  CUST_GENDER  FREQ TYPE     N     MEAN MIN  MAX
1           F 18325    0 18325 1957.577 1913 1990
2           M 37175    0 37175 1957.318 1913 1990
3        <NA> 55500    1 55500 1957.404 1913 1990
```

You can add more levels to the grouping set of attributes listed for **class**. For each attribute listed, you will get different grouping levels. For example, if we add CUST_CITY to the class list, we get the statistics for the males and females for each city in the data set. This is illustrated in the following example, which shows a partial set of the output:

```
> ore.summary(full_dataset, class=c("CUST_CITY", "CUST_GENDER"),
            var="CUST_YEAR_OF_BIRTH", ways=2)
```

	CUST_CITY	CUST_GENDER	FREQ	TYPE	N	MEAN	MIN	MAX
1	Ede	F	54	0	54	1955.704	1922	1985
2	Ede	M	100	0	100	1958.420	1917	1986
3	Opp	F	10	0	10	1963.800	1944	1983
4	Opp	M	14	0	14	1952.357	1942	1972
5	Ulm	F	15	0	15	1968.733	1939	1989
6	Ulm	M	30	0	30	1961.367	1923	1984
7	Alma	F	37	0	37	1958.000	1922	1986
8	Alma	M	74	0	74	1957.257	1926	1986

...

The **ore.corr** function allows you to perform a correlation analysis on your data. The correlation analysis can include the Pearson, Spearman, and Kendall correlations on your numeric attributes. By default, the **ore.corr** function will create a Pearson correlation analysis. The following example illustrates the correlation analysis of CUST_POSTAL_CODE and CUST_CITY. In the table in the Oracle Database, these attributes are defined with a character data type. However, these are really number values, and we can remap them to numeric.

```
> # Use the CUSTOMERS_V data. It is in our schema in the Database
> full_dataset <- CUSTOMERS_V
> # add an index to the data frame
> row.names(full_dataset) <- full_dataset$CUST_ID
> # Remap the following to numeric data type
> full_dataset$CUST_POSTAL_CODE <- as.numeric(full_dataset$CUST_POSTAL_CODE)
> full_dataset$CUST_CITY_ID <- as.numeric(full_dataset$CUST_CITY_ID)
```

We can then perform the correlation analysis using the following:

```
> # Correlation analysis using Pearson
> ore.corr(full_dataset, var="CUST_POSTAL_CODE, CUST_CITY_ID")
```

	ROW	COL	PEARSON_T	PEARSON_P	PEARSON_DF
1	CUST_POSTAL_CODE	CUST_CITY_ID	0.05713612	1.6e-14	55498

As you would expect, this is highly correlated, which is indicated in the value under the PEARSON_P column. We can add other attributes to the **var** list, and the correlation analysis of each pair of attributes will be calculated.

If you would like to perform a Spearman or Kendall correlation analysis, you can do so by changing the default value for the **stats** setting, as shown here:

```
> # Correlation analysis using Spearman
> ore.corr(full_dataset, var="CUST_POSTAL_CODE, CUST_CITY_ID",
stats="spearman")
```

	ROW	COL	SPEARMAN_T	SPEARMAN_P	SPEARMAN_DF
1	CUST_POSTAL_CODE	CUST_CITY_ID	0.06935903	3.737711e-60	55498

The **ore.crosstab** function allows you to create some cross-tabulations analyses based on the attributes in your data set. The cross-tabulations will create a frequency count table based on the attributes you specify.

The following example shows how you can use **ore.crosstab** to create a simple frequency count of the males and females in your data set:

```
> # Use the CUSTOMERS_V data. It is in our schema in the Database
> full_dataset <- CUSTOMERS_V
> # add an index to the data frame
> row.names(full_dataset) <- full_dataset$CUST_ID
> # Crosstab example
> ore.crosstab(~CUST_GENDER, data=full_dataset)

   CUST_GENDER ORE$FREQ ORE$STRATA ORE$GROUP
 F           F   18325          1         1
 M           M   37175          1         1
```

You can add any number of attributes to be included in the crosstab calculations, and you can also add different groups for the calculations. For example, suppose you want to get the calculations of the number of males and females for each age range. This is illustrated in the following example, along with a sample of the output:

```
> full_dataset$AGE <- as.numeric(format(Sys.time(), "%Y")) -
                       full_dataset$CUST_YEAR_OF_BIRTH
> # Analyze Age by Customer Gender
> ore.crosstab(AGE~CUST_GENDER, data=full_dataset)

        AGE CUST_GENDER ORE$FREQ ORE$STRATA ORE$GROUP
 26|F   26            F       10          1         1
 26|M   26            M       21          1         1
 27|F   27            F       28          1         1
 27|M   27            M       29          1         1
 28|F   28            F       30          1         1
 28|M   28            M       52          1         1
 29|F   29            F       54          1         1
 29|M   29            M       97          1         1
 30|F   30            F      102          1         1
 30|M   30            M      179          1         1
 ...
```

When processing the data set, you many want to sort it so that the records are ordered based on the ranks that have been calculated. The following example illustrates how you can create a data set that contains the original data plus the new attribute that contains the rank values. You can then use the **ore.sort** function to create an ordered data set based on the values in the RANK attribute.

```
> # Create a Sorted dataset of the Ranked Data
> ranked_data <- ore.rank(full_dataset, var="CUST_CREDIT_LIMIT=Rank_CL",
                          group.by="CUST_CITY", percent=TRUE, ties="dense")
> sorted_ranked_data <- ore.sort(ranked_data, by=c("CUST_CITY", "Rank_CL"))
> head(sorted_ranked_data,30)
```

When you start working with your data sets, you can easily use R to extract the data from the database and to process this data locally on your laptop or PC. However, as you venture into the Big Data world, the size of the data sets, including the number of records and the number of attributes or features, can increase dramatically. In these situations, the data sets become too large to work with on our local machines. Traditionally using R you would extract the data to your local machine and then create different subsets of the data locally. When working with Big Data, we need an alternative approach. With Oracle R Enterprise, we can use a variety of data sampling techniques that are executed in the Oracle Database. This is achieved by the transparency layer of Oracle R Enterprise. The typical data sampling techniques available to you in Oracle R Enterprise are outlined in Table 11-2.

When you use the data sampling techniques outlined in Table 11-2, the data sampling and corresponding process will occur on the Oracle Database. The resulting sampled data set will then exist in the Oracle Database, and you can access this via an ORE proxy object. You can then choose to leave this object and data in the database or to pull the data set to your local machine.

With stratified sampling, you are looking to produce a sample data set that is based on the values from one or more particular attributes. This is a very common sampling technique that is used with building classification data mining models. With stratified sampling, you want the sampled data set to have the same proportions as the original data set.

The following example illustrates how to create a stratified sample set based on the proportion of values for the CUST_GENDER attribute. This example uses the same data set of CUSTOMER_V, and it will create a sample data set of 1000 records. The **do.call** constructs and executes a function. The data set is split into subgroups according to the value of the split attributes (CUST_GENDER)

Sampling Technique	Description
Random	This method takes a random sample from the input data set and creates a subset that contains a specified number of records. This method takes as input the number of records to be in the sample data set.
Stratified	This method looks to create a randomized selection of data that is based on a particular attribute. For example, if the attribute contains the value 0 and 1, the sampled data set will have records selected in proportion to the number of records for 0 and 1 in the original data set. This is a very common technique for building data sets used for building and testing classification data mining models.
Split	You use the split sampling technique to divide your data set into a number of smaller data sets. For example, you can use this method to create a training and test data set. This approach is different from the stratified sampling technique in that there is no attribute used to proportion the partitioning of the data.
Cluster	Cluster sampling allows you to base the sample of data on randomly selected groups based on the values in a certain attribute.
Systematic	Systematic sampling selects rows from the data set at regular intervals. You can also give a starting position for the first record to be selected.

TABLE 11-2. *Data Sampling Techniques*

and selects a random sample from this subgroup based in proportion to the number of records for that group. The output from each of these sampled subgroups is then merged using **rbind** to form an **ore.frame** object.

```
> # Stratified Sampling example
> #
> full_dataset <- CUSTOMERS_V
> # add an index to the data frame
> row.names(full_dataset) <- full_dataset$CUST_ID
> # Check the class of the object. It should be an ore.frame pointing
> #   to the object in the Database
> class(full_dataset)
 [1] "ore.frame"
 attr(,"package")
 [1] "OREbase"
> # Set the sample size
> SampleSize <- 1000
> # Calculate the total number of records in the full data set
> NRows_Dataset = nrow(full_dataset)
> # Create the Stratified data set based on using the CUST_GENDER attribute
> stratified_sample <- do.call(rbind,
            lapply(split(full_dataset, full_dataset$CUST_GENDER),
            function(y) {
                NumRows <- nrow(y)
                y[sample(NumRows, SampleSize*NumRows/NRows_Dataset), , drop=FALSE]
            }))
> class(stratified_sample)
 [1] "ore.frame"
 attr(,"package")
 [1] "OREbase"
> nrow(stratified_sample)
 [1] 999
```

In this particular example, the sampled data set only contains 999 records, although we asked for 1000 records. When stratified sampling is performed, the data set is divided and proportioned based on the values of the attribute being used. This can result in the sampled data set having a slightly smaller number than what was asked for. If you change the attribute (for example, to COUNTRY_ID), you will get a sample data set with a slightly different number of records.

ORE has many other data sampling techniques, as listed in Table 11-2. You can follow a similar approach to what has been illustrated here when sampling your data using these techniques.

One of the final steps you may perform on your data is to organize it so that the records are listed in a particular order. This may involve ordering by one particular attribute (for example, when sorting data for time series analysis). When sorting data you can use any combination of attributes from the data set, and you can specify whether they should be sorted in ascending or descending order.

The following code example illustrates some of the various ways you can sort your data:

```
> # Sorting Data
> # Sort the data set by COUNTRY_REGION (in ascending order by default)
> ore.sort(data = customers, by = "COUNTRY_REGION")
```

```
> # Sort the data by COUNTRY_REGION in descending order
> ore.sort(data = customers, by = "COUNTRY_REGION", reverse=TRUE)

> # Sort the data set by COUNTRY_REGION and AGE_BIN
> ore.sort(data = customers, by = c("COUNTRY_REGION","AGE_BIN"))

> # Sort the data by COUNTRY_REGION ascending and by CUST_YEAR_OF_BIRTH in
> # descending order
> #   You will notices a different way for indicating Descending order. This
> #   is to be used when sorting your data using a combination of 2 or more
> #   attributes.
> cust_sorted <- ore.sort(data = customers, by = c("COUNTRY_REGION",
                          "-CUST_YEAR_OF_BIRTH"))

> # Sorted data is stored in an ORE data frame called 'cust_sorted'
> #   This allows you to perform additional data manipulations on the data set
> #   The following displays 3 of the attributes from the sorted data set
> head(cust_sorted[,c("AGE_BIN","COUNTRY_REGION","CUST_YEAR_OF_BIRTH")], 20)
```

Exploring your data to gain additional insights is a very important part of any data science project. Additionally, you'll need to modify and process your data in a variety of ways. In this section we looked at some of the typical Oracle R Enterprise methods for exploring your data. This list is by no means exhaustive, and we encourage you to spend some time researching and trying out the other capabilities of the R language and Oracle R Enterprise.

Building Data Mining Models Using ORE

Oracle R Enterprise comes with a number of data mining algorithms. These algorithms have been designed to use the full functionality, scalability, and performance features of the Oracle Databases. These Oracle R Enterprise algorithms run on the data inside the Oracle Database. The Oracle R Enterprise data mining algorithms are grouped into two types. First, there are the data mining algorithms that already exist in the Oracle Database and can be accessed using SQL. These data mining algorithms are part of the Oracle Data Mining product and can be accessed using the OREdm package that comes as part of Oracle R Enterprise. The second set of data mining algorithms is part of the OREmodels package. This is an additional set of data mining algorithms that have been highly tuned to work with and use the Oracle Database. All of these algorithms are listed in Table 11-3.

Unfortunately we do not have the space to show you how to use all of these examples; instead we will show you how to use the **ore.odmAssocRules** and **ore.odmDT** algorithms from the OREdm package, and **ore.neural** from the OREmodels package.

Association Rule Analysis

Association rule analysis is an unsupervised data mining technique that looks for frequent item sets in your data. This data mining technique is often used in the retail sector to discover what products are frequently purchased together. A common example used to illustrate association rule analysis is that bread and milk are two products commonly purchased together in a grocery store.

ORE Algorithm	ORE Package	Description
ore.odmAI	OREdm	Uses the Minimum Description Length algorithm to generate attribute importance.
ore.odmAssocRules	OREdm	Uses the Apriori algorithm to perform association rule analysis.
ore.odmDT	OREdm	Uses the Decision Tree algorithm to create a classification model.
ore.odmGLM	OREdm	Uses the Generalized Linear Model algorithm to create either a classification or regression model.
ore.odmKMeans	OREdm	Uses the k-Means algorithm to create a clustering model.
ore.odmNB	OREdm	Uses the Naive Bayes algorithm to create a classification model.
ore.odmNMF	OREdm	Uses the Non-Negative Matrix Factorization algorithm for feature extraction.
ore.odmOC	OREdm	Uses the Orthogonal Partitioning Cluster algorithm to create a clustering model.
ore.odmSVM	OREdm	Uses the Support Vector Machine algorithm to create a classification or regression model.
ore.glm	OREmodels	Creates a generalized linear model on the data in your ORE data frame.
ore.lm	OREmodels	Creates a linear regression model on the data in your ORE data frame.
ore.neural	OREmodels	Creates a neural network model on the data in your ORE data frame.
ore.stepwise	OREmodels	Creates a stepwise linear regression model on the data in your ORE data frame.
Ore.RandomForest	OREmodels	Creates a random forest model on the data in your ORE data frame.

TABLE 11-3.   *Data Mining Algorithms Available in Oracle R Enterprise*

This type of data mining is very common in the retail sector and is sometimes referred to as *market basket analysis*. By analyzing what products previous customers have bought, you can then prompt a new customer with products they might be interested in. Every time you look at a product (for example, a data mining book) on Amazon.com, you are presented with a list of other products that previous customers bought, in addition to the product you are looking at. By using association rule analysis, you can start to answer questions about your data and the patterns that may exist in the data.

For association rules analysis, you can use the **ore.odmAssocRules** function. This function uses the Apriori algorithm that is embedded in the Oracle Database. The **ore.odmAssocRules** function has the following syntax and default values:

```
> ore.odmAssocRules(formula,
          data,
          case.id.column,
          item.id.column = NULL,
          item.value.column = NULL,
          min.support = 0.1,
          min.confidence = 0.1,
          max.rule.length = 4,
          na.action = na.pass)
```

The data set you need to use for association rule analysis must consist of transactional records, and the algorithm will look at the co-occurrence of items (in the following example, Products). First, you need to construct the input data set. This is done by creating a view over the transactional data and creating a single attribute as the identifier of each record and product name. This information is then passed into the **ore.odmAssocRules** algorithm, along with the values for the support and confidence measures. You may need to spend some time adjusting these measures. If you set them too high, no association rules will be produced, whereas if you set them too low, you will end up with too many rules being produced. The following code example illustrates the generation of an association rule model for our transactional data:

```
> # Build an Association Rules model using ore.odmAssocRules
> ore.exec("CREATE OR REPLACE VIEW AR_TRANSACTIONS
  AS
  SELECT s.cust_id || s.time_id  case_id,
         p.prod_name
  FROM   sh.sales s,
         sh.products p
  WHERE s.prod_id = p.prod_id")
> # You need to sync the meta data for the newly created view to be visible in
> #  your ORE session
> ore.sync()
> ore.ls()
> # List the attributes of the AR_TRANSACTION view
> names(AR_TRANSACTIONS)
> # Generate the Association Rules model
> ARmodel <- ore.odmAssocRules(~., AR_TRANSACTIONS, case.id.column = "CASE_ID",
        item.id.column = "PROD_NAME", min.support = 0.06, min.confidence = 0.1)
> # List the various pieces of information that is part of the model
> names(ARmodel)
> # List all the information about the model
> summary(ARmodel)

Call:   ore.odmAssocRules(formula = ~., data = AR_TRANSACTIONS, case.id.column =
"CASE_ID",
        item.id.column = "PROD_NAME", min.support = 0.06, min.confidence = 0.1)

Settings:                           value
asso.min.confidence        0.1
asso.min.support           0.06
```

```
odms.item.id.column.name prod.name
prep.auto                        off
```

```
Rules:     RULE_ID NUMBER_OF_ITEMS                                  LHS
1              38               2           CD-RW, High Speed Pack of 5
2              38               2 CD-R, Professional Grade, Pack of 10
3              37               2     CD-R with Jewel Cases, pACK OF 12
4              37               2 CD-R, Professional Grade, Pack of 10
5              39               2           CD-RW, High Speed Pack of 5
...
                                   RHS     SUPPORT CONFIDENCE      LIFT
1    CD-R with Jewel Cases, pACK OF 12 0.06122021  0.9064860  8.772463
2    CD-R with Jewel Cases, pACK OF 12 0.06122021  0.9064860  8.772463
3          CD-RW, High Speed Pack of 5 0.06122021  0.8566820  9.733656
4          CD-RW, High Speed Pack of 5 0.06122021  0.8566820  9.733656
5 CD-R, Professional Grade, Pack of 10 0.06122021  0.8412211  9.746766
...
```

This is only a partial listing of the output and the association rules. If you would like to explore these association rules and associated item sets, you can pull them from the Oracle Database to a local data frame and then use the ARULES package that is available in the R language to explore them in more detail. The following code example illustrates how you can perform this additional analysis, but the output is not shown due to space restrictions:

```
> # Bring the Association Rules to the client & use the 'arules' package
> #  to see more details of the association rules
> #install.packages("arules")
> library(arules)
> ARrules <- rules(ARmodel)
> local_ARrules <- ore.pull(ARrules)
> inspect(local_ARrules)
> ARitemsets <- itemsets(ARmodel)
> local_ARitemsets <- ore.pull(ARitemsets)
> inspect(local_ARitemsets)
```

Building a Decision Tree Model and Scoring New Data

A Decision Tree is a very popular technique for building a model for classification types of problems. Classification is a supervised data mining method that takes a data set of prelabeled data and builds a classification model, using one or more algorithms. The prelabeled data set is called the *training data set,* which consists of the data for which we already know the outcome. For example, if we want to run a customer churn analysis, we would take all our customers who registered up to a certain date. We can write some code that can easily determine which of these customers have remained as customers (that is, they are still active) and those who are no longer active customers (that is, they have left). We will create a new attribute for each customer. This attribute is typically called the *target variable,* and it is this target variable that contains the label (0 or 1) that will be used by the classification algorithms to build the models. We can then use one of these models to score a new group of customers and determine which ones are likely to stay and those who will leave (churn).

We learn from the past to predict the future.

There are a number of algorithms available in Oracle R Enterprise that can be used for classification problems. The examples shown in this section illustrate how you can build a Decision Tree data mining model using the **ore.odmDT** algorithm. This points to the in-database Decision Tree algorithm that can be accessed using SQL and PL/SQL.

NOTE
In Chapter 10, we showed you how to create an Oracle Data Mining Decision Tree model using SQL. In the following example, we are creating a similar Oracle Data Mining Decision Tree model using Oracle R Enterprise.

The first step in building a classification data mining model is to prepare the data input to the data mining algorithm. This may require you to integrate data from various sources, perform a variety of data transformations on the data, decide how to handle missing data, generate additional attributes, and so on. When you have your data ready, you can then input it to the data mining algorithm. The following code example illustrates the creation of a view in the Oracle database that contains the data we will input to the data mining algorithm. It then uses the **ore.odmDT** function to create the data mining model.

```
> ore.exec(" CREATE OR REPLACE VIEW ANALYTIC_RECORD
  AS
  SELECT a.CUST_ID,
  a.CUST_GENDER,
  2003-a.CUST_YEAR_OF_BIRTH AGE,
  a.CUST_MARITAL_STATUS,
  c.COUNTRY_NAME,
  a.CUST_INCOME_LEVEL,
  b.EDUCATION,
  b.OCCUPATION,
  b.HOUSEHOLD_SIZE,
  b.YRS_RESIDENCE,
  b.AFFINITY_CARD,
  b.BULK_PACK_DISKETTES,
  b.FLAT_PANEL_MONITOR,
  b.HOME_THEATER_PACKAGE,
  b.BOOKKEEPING_APPLICATION,
  b.PRINTER_SUPPLIES,
  b.Y_BOX_GAMES,
  b.OS_DOC_SET_KANJI
  FROM sh.customers a,
       sh.supplementary_demographics b,
       sh.countries c
  WHERE a.CUST_ID = b.CUST_ID
  AND a.country_id  = c.country_id
  AND a.cust_id between 101501 and 103000")
> # You need to run the ore.sync function to bring the meta data of this
> #   view into your session
> ore.sync()
```

```
> ore.ls()
> # Build a Decision Tree model using ore.odmDT
> DTmodel <- ore.odmDT(AFFINITY_CARD ~., ANALYTIC_RECORD)
> class(DTmodel)
> names(DTmodel)
> summary(DTmodel)
```

The lengthy output from **summary(DTmodel)** is not shown here (it would take up about two pages in this book). When you run the previous code and examine the output generated by **summary(DTmodel),** you will be able to see some of the Decision Tree properties, including the various nodes that form the Decision Tree.

The second step is to evaluate the model produced. To do this, you need to use a separate data set from what was used to build the data mining model. This data set should also contain the known target value. In our example, the target value is in the AFFINITY_CARD variable.

To create the training data set, we create another view on the SH schema. This view will have the exact same structure as the one used to create the ANALYTICS_RECORD view, except that the last line is replaced with the following:

```
AND a.cust_id between 103001 and 104500
```

You can call this view TEST_DATA. Make sure to run the **ore.sync()** function after creating the view to make its metadata available in your R session. The following code example illustrates how you can apply the Decision Tree model to this new data and then present the results using a confusion matrix format, which is similar to type I and type II errors in statistics:

```
> # Test the Decision Tree model
> DTtest <- predict(DTmodel, TEST_DATA, "AFFINITY_CARD")
> # Generate the confusion Matrix
> with(DTtest, table(AFFINITY_CARD, PREDICTION))
               PREDICTION
  AFFINITY_CARD    0     1
             0  1074    80
             1   192   154
```

The confusion matrix allows us to measure the accuracy of the data mining model and from that, access its usefulness for our situation. For example, this confusion matrix is very accurate at predicting when the AFFINITY_CARD value is 0, but it is not as accurate as predicting when the value is 1.

If you decide to use this data mining model on new data, you can use the **predict** function to apply the model to the new data and to score the data; for example, if we had a new data set called NEW_DATA that was in the exact same format and had the exact same steps performed to prepare it, as was done to prepare the data we used for building the data mining model. The following code example illustrates how you score this new data:

```
> # Add an index to the data set. This is needed when using the cbing
> DTnew <- predict(DTmodel, NEW_DATA, "AFFINITY_CARD")
> # Combine the New Data Set with the scored values
> DTresults <- cbind(TEST_DATA, DTnew)
> head(DTresults, 5)
```

Building a Neural Network Model and Scoring New Data

A neural network is another popular data mining technique used for classifying numeric or binary target variables. Neural networks can be used to capture complex nonlinear relationships between the inputs and the output and hence find the patterns in the data. The next code example follows the same process used for the Decision Tree model in the previous section. The same data set is used to build the data mining model. We can examine some of the properties of the data mining model using the **summary** function, and then use the model to score or label new data.

```
> # Build a Neural Network using ore.neural
> Nmodel <- ore.neural(AFFINITY_CARD ~., data = ANALYTIC_RECORD)
> summary(Nmodel)

> Ntest <- predict(Nmodel, TEST_DATA, supplemental.cols=c("CUST_ID"))
> row.names(Ntest) <- Ntest$CUST_ID
> Nresult <- cbind(TEST_DATA, Ntest )
> head(Nresult, 5)
```

We encourage you to explore the capabilities of all the other Oracle R Enterprise data mining algorithms that are listed in Table 11-3.

Embedded R Execution

Embedded R execution is a major feature of Oracle R Enterprise that provides the ability to store and run R scripts inside the Oracle Database. When these scripts are run, via SQL or PL/SQL, the Oracle Database will execute one or more R engines that run on the database server. These R engines are completely managed by the Oracle Database. Using the embedded R execution allows us to not only run the ORE features in the Oracle Database but also use and run the open-source CRAN packages. Oracle provides two main interfaces for running embedded R execution: an R interface and a SQL interface.

In this section of the book we only show you some of the features of the embedded R execution using the SQL interfaces. Table 11-4 lists the SQL interfaces for performing embedded R execution.

Before you can use the embedded R execution feature, your Oracle schema will need an additional database privilege. You can ask your Oracle DBA to grant the RQADMIN privilege to your schema.

SQL Interface	Description
rqEval()	Invokes a stand-alone R script
rqTableEval()	Invokes an R script for inputting all the data from a table
rqRowEval()	Invokes an R script on one row at a time, or on groups of rows at a time
rqGroupEval()	Invokes an R script on data that is partitioned based on a grouping column

TABLE 11-4. *Embedded R Execution Interfaces in SQL*

Using rqEval to Call Functions and Return a Data Set

One of the key aspects of using the SQL interfaces and for using the embedded R execution features is that you need to write all the R code you want executed on your data in a script. This script can then be stored in the Oracle Database and is available for others to use with their analytics and in their applications. The following example illustrates a simple script that outputs a typical "Hello World." The first step is to create a script called HelloWorld. This creates a data frame that contains the string 'Hello World'. An additional formatting step is needed to convert the attribute in the data set from a factor to a string. In the last step, **res** returns the 'Hello World' string.

```
BEGIN
--    sys.rqScriptDrop('HelloWorld');
    sys.rqScriptCreate('HelloWorld',
        'function() {
            res <- data.frame(Ans="Hello World", stringsAsFactors=FALSE)
            res} ');
END;
/
```

The first line in this example is commented out. This line issues a DROP SCRIPT command. You will need to include this line of code if you run or re-create this function subsequent times.

This script will be stored in an ORE data store in the Oracle Database, and you will be the owner of that script. The next step is to call this ORE script using a SELECT statement and to display the results. In this particular scenario, we are just calling a function that performs a predefined set of steps. In scenarios like this we can use the **rqEval** interface to call the ORE script. This **rqEval** interface takes four parameters. The first is the parameter values needed by the function. In our case, the function does not take any parameters, and we can set this value as NULL. The second parameter details how the results are to be formatted and displayed. The third parameter is the name of the ORE script. When we run this query, we get the result from the HelloWorld script being displayed:

```
SELECT *
FROM    table ( rqEval( NULL,
                'select cast(''a'' as varchar2(14)) "Ans" from dual',
                'HelloWorld'));


ANS
--------------
Hello World
```

The next example illustrates creating a script that selects some random numbers from a range of values. Performing something like this can be useful in various scenarios.

```
BEGIN
--    sys.rqScriptDrop('Example1');
    sys.rqScriptCreate('Example1',
        'function() {
            ID <- sample(seq(100), 11)
            res <- data.frame(ID = ID)
            res } ');
```

```
END;
/

SELECT *
FROM   table( rqEval(NULL,
                     'select 1 id from dual',
                     'Example1'));

        ID
----------
        54
        23
        40
        44
        33
        84
        58
        66
        38
        57
        86
```

We can add greater flexibility to this function by parameterizing the function in our ORE script. For example, we could add two parameters to our Example1 script. We could add a parameter for the number of data points to consider and then a second parameter for the sample size. This is a simple example of parameterizing a function, but hopefully you can see that by doing so you are making your functions more dynamic and usable in many different situations. A new version of the ORE script called Example2 is created that contains these new parameters for the function. This is shown in the following code:

```
BEGIN
--       sys.rqScriptDrop('Example2');
       sys.rqScriptCreate('Example2',
          'function(NumPoints, SampleSize) {
              ID <- sample(seq(NumPoints), SampleSize)
              res <- data.frame(ID = ID)
              res } ');
END;
/
```

Again the **drop script** function has been commented out. If you need to rerun this code, you will need to include this function.

In Example1 we showed you how to call the ORE script and to run the function within it. Example1 did not require any parameters to be passed into the call and hence why we had a NULL as the first parameter to the **rqEval** interface. For Example2, we now have parameters and we need to include these in the call to **rqEval**. The following query illustrates how parameters can be passed to this function. In the call to Example2, we want to pass in a value of 50 for the number of data points (**NumPoints**) and a value of 6 for the random sample size (**SampleSize**).

There is a bit of formatting to the passing of these parameters. This consists of a **SELECT from DUAL** and then wrapping that in a **cursor** function.

```
SELECT *
FROM
    table( rqEval(cursor(select 50 "NumPoints", 6 "SampleSize" from dual),
                  'select 1 id from dual',
                  'Example2'));
```

When we run this query, we get a randomized set of six numbers appearing every time. Every time you run this query you will get a different random set of values:

```
       ID
----------
       50
       28
       39
       23
        8
       22
```

As you have seen from using these SQL interfaces to the embedded R execution feature of Oracle R Enterprise, you can perform a wide variety of analytics incorporating R code within your Oracle Database. In the next section, we explore some of the other capabilities and how these can be used.

Using rqTableEval to Apply a Data Mining Model to Your Data

The **rqTableEval** function allows us to pass in a data set to a function and for this data set to be processed and a result to be returned and displayed by the SELECT statement. We have many options available to us to aggregate data. By far the easiest way to do this is with a SELECT statement with a GROUP BY. As an alternative, there is a very commonly used R package called PLYR that allows us to process data sets and perform a variety of statistical analysis actions on the data.

In the following example, a data set is passed into the function and the PLYR R package will be used to perform an aggregation based on one of the attributes. This is an example of how you can use one of the many thousands of packages available for the R language. You can install these R packages into your Oracle R Enterprise environment that is part of your Oracle Home on your database server. Once they are installed, you can then use these R packages via the embedded R execution feature of Oracle R Enterprise. Check out the Oracle R Enterprise documentation for more details on how to install additional R packages into your Oracle R Enterprise environment.

The first step is to create an R script that will be stored in the Oracle Database. This script will contain all the R code you want to perform. This script accepts one input—the data set that will be used and processed within the script. The second step is to load the R library/package that contains the function(s) you want to use. The third step is to read the data and then perform the aggregation of the data using the **plyr** function. The final step, as with all your in-database R scripts, is to return the results of the function.

```
BEGIN
--    sys.rqScriptDrop('plyrExample');
    sys.rqScriptCreate('plyrExample',
        'function(dat) {
```

```
                   library(plyr)
                   df3 <- dat
                   res <- ddply(df3, .(CUST_GENDER), summarize, freq=length(CUST_ID))
                   res } ');
END;
```

The first line in this PL/SQL code is commented out. If you have to rerun this script, you will need to include this first command to delete the existing script.

Next, you need to perform a call to this R script using SQL. In this scenario, we'll use the **rqTableEval** function because we want to pass in the contents of a table. You can pass in all the contents of a table, or you can write a query that selects all the required data for input to the function.

```
SELECT *
FROM   table( rqTableEval( cursor(select * from customers_v),
           NULL,
           'select cast(''a'' as varchar2(14)) "Cust_Gender", 1 as freq from dual',
           'plyrExample'));


Cust_Gender          FREQ
-------------- ----------
F                   18325
M                   37175
```

In the previous section of this chapter, we showed you how to create and use a Decision Tree data mining model using the in-database data mining Decision Tree algorithm. What would be useful is if you could package this data mining code and its capabilities into an in-database R script. This script can then be used within all your applications that can use SQL. We are not going to use the exact same scenario we used in the previous section; instead, we are going to show you how you can use one of the generally available data mining algorithms that come with the standard install of R. By showing you this, we are showing you some of the flexibility and additional capabilities of Oracle R Enterprise. In the following example, we create a data mining model using the **glm** algorithm that comes standard with the R language.

The first step with all data mining projects is to create the data mining model using a training data set. The data sets we use in these examples are available in the DMUSER schema created in Chapter 10. If you are going to use the DMUSER schema, you will need to grant that schema the additional privilege of **rqadmin**. This will give the DMUSER schema the privilege to run the embedded R execution feature of Oracle R Enterprise.

The first thing we need to do is to create an in-database R script that will create the data mining and then save this model to the database. The following code shows this:

```
-- Build & save the R script, called Demo_GLM in the DB
--   This builds a GLM  DM model in the DB
--
BEGIN
--    sys.rqScriptDrop('Demo_GLM');
      sys.rqScriptCreate('Demo_GLM',
         'function(dat,datastore_name) {
             mod <- glm(AFFINITY_CARD ~ CUST_GENDER + AGE + CUST_MARITAL_STATUS +
                     COUNTRY_NAME + CUST_INCOME_LEVEL + EDUCATION + HOUSEHOLD_SIZE
                     + YRS_RESIDENCE, dat, family = binomial())
          ore.save(mod, name=datastore_name, overwrite=TRUE)    }');
END;
```

The second thing we need to do is to call or run this script in the Oracle Database. By running this script, we create the **glm** data mining model and store this R-generated data mining model in an Oracle R Enterprise data store called **datastore_name**. The following SELECT statement is used to run the Demo_GLM script and uses the **rqTableEval** function to define what data is used as input to this script:

```
--
-- After creating the script you need to run it to create the GLM model
--
SELECT *
FROM table(rqTableEval(
    cursor(select CUST_GENDER,
                  AGE,
                  CUST_MARITAL_STATUS,
                  COUNTRY_NAME,
                  CUST_INCOME_LEVEL,
                  EDUCATION,
                  HOUSEHOLD_SIZE,
                  YRS_RESIDENCE,
                  AFFINITY_CARD
           from mining_data_build_v),
    cursor(select 1 as "ore.connect", 'myDatastore' as "datastore_name" from dual)
               'XML', 'Demo_GLM' ));
```

When this is complete, we get one record being returned that contains some XML with no values within it. At this point, we know that the **glm** data mining model has been created and stored within the Oracle Database.

The next step is to apply the data mining model, built using the preceding code, to new data. Again, we need to write an R script to be stored in the Oracle Database that defines all the R code that needs to run. The following example illustrates such a script. It uses the **glm** data mining model built previously and returns the scored or labeled data.

```
-- Script to apply the GLM data mining model to your new data
BEGIN
--    sys.rqScriptDrop('Demo_GLM_Batch');
    sys.rqScriptCreate('Demo_GLM_Batch',
        'function(dat, datastore_name) {
        ore.load(datastore_name)
        prd <- predict(mod, newdata=dat)
        prd[as.integer(rownames(prd))] <- prd
        res <- cbind(dat, PRED = prd)
        res}');
END;
/
```

Just like before, we can use the **rqTableEval** function to call this script and feed in a data set that contains the data we want to score or label with the predicted values.

```
SELECT *
FROM table(rqTableEval(
        cursor(select CUST_GENDER, AGE, CUST_MARITAL_STATUS, COUNTRY_NAME,
                      CUST_INCOME_LEVEL, EDUCATION, HOUSEHOLD_SIZE, YRS_RESIDENCE
```

```
                    from    MINING_DATA_APPLY_V
                    where rownum <= 10),
        cursor(select 1 as "ore.connect", 'myDatastore' as "datastore_name"
                from dual),
        'select CUST_GENDER, AGE, CUST_MARITAL_STATUS, COUNTRY_NAME,
                CUST_INCOME_LEVEL, EDUCATION, HOUSEHOLD_SIZE, YRS_RESIDENCE,
                1 PRED from MINING_DATA_APPLY_V','Demo_GLM_Batch'))
ORDER BY 1, 2, 3;
```

The previous query selects ten rows from the MINING_DATA_APPLY_V view and feeds them into the function. This data will form the data set that is processed by the stored R script. The function scores the data with the predicted value and then returns a data set that contains the original data set that was input into the R script, along with an attribute that contains the predicted value.

In this section, we have looked at how you can use the **rqTableEval** function to pass a data set into R scripts stored in your Oracle Database. These data sets are based on a query of your data and can contain all the data from a table, a subset of the records, or they can combine data from many tables. We also illustrated a couple of different ways to use these stored R scripts and how you can utilize the various functions and packages available with the R language to expand your analytic capabilities within the SQL language.

Creating and Using ORE Graphics in Your Dashboards

The R language comes with a wide range of libraries for creating graphics. Perhaps this is one of the R language's strongest features. Most of the typical reporting tools come with a limited set of graphics you can create. These would seem a tiny portion of what is available when compared to what is available in the R language.

With the embedded R execution feature of Oracle R Enterprise, you can now use the graphing capabilities of the R language within the Oracle Database. We showed you in the previous section how you can make use of newly installed R packages on the Oracle Database server. Now you can install the various R graphing packages and use these to produce various graphs of your data.

However, the problem we have when using the embedded R execution feature of Oracle R Enterprise is that SQL is not a language that allows us to display these graphs. With Oracle R Enterprise, you can define the format of the output. For graphics, you have the option of creating them using XML or PNG. Oracle R Enterprise comes with the PNG package as part of the install. With this feature, you can now integrate your R graphics into your Oracle Business Intelligence Enterprise Edition (OBIEE) dashboards, Oracle BI Publisher, APEX, and so on. For OBIEE, you can stream the PNG graphic into a BLOB column and, from there, display it on your OBIEE dashboard. For Oracle BI Publisher, you can use the XML format.

The following example illustrates an R script that aggregates data from our ANALYTIC_RECORD table, counting the number of records for each unique value of the AGE attribute. The final command uses the standard **plot** function in R to produce a line plot of the aggregated data.

```
BEGIN
--    sys.rqScriptDrop('AgeProfile');
    sys.rqScriptCreate('AgeProfile',
        'function(dat) {
            mdbv <- dat
            aggdata <- aggregate(mdbv$AFFINITY_CARD,
                            by = list(Age = mdbv$AGE),
```

```
                            FUN = length)
            res <- plot(aggdata$Age, aggdata$x, type = "l") } ');
END;
/
```

After creating this script in your schema, you can then use the following code to call this script and produce the chart. You can take the following query and embed it into the different layers of the RPD of OBIEE and then make it available on your OBIEE dashboards. For instance, the previous example would create the chart shown in Figure 11-3. You can also view this chart using SQL Developer.

```
SELECT *
FROM table(rqTableEval(
        cursor(select * from ANALYTIC_RECORD),
                cursor(select 1 "ore.connect" from dual),
                'PNG', 'AgeProfile'));
```

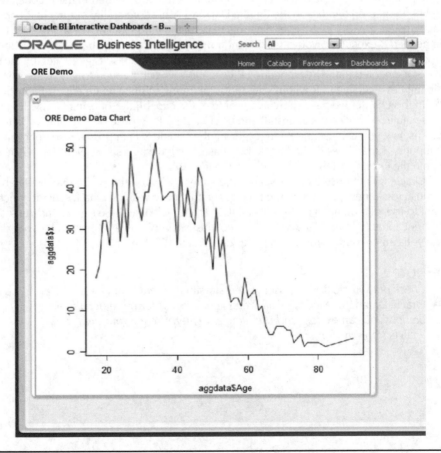

FIGURE 11-3.   *Oracle R Enterprise graphic in an OBIEE dashboard*

Summary

Oracle R Enterprise, part of the Oracle Advanced Analytics option, allows you to expand your analytic capabilities while using the Oracle Database. With Oracle R Enterprise, you can now overcome many of the limitations of using R and use the performance and scalability features of the Oracle Database. This allows you to greatly expand the volume of data you can include in your analytics, perform your analytics significantly quicker, and use the parallel features of the Oracle Database to run your advanced analytics on various portions of your data set, all at the same time.

With the integration with the Oracle Database, you can use the SQL and PL/SQL languages to run R code on the Oracle Database server. By using the SQL and PL/SQL languages, you can incorporate the R language analytical capabilities within your traditional applications, your analytic dashboards, and reporting.

Oracle R Enterprise allows for the seamless translation of R code into Oracle SQL where possible, and this allows R programmers to utilize the performance and scalability features of the Oracle Database. They are no longer constrained by the computing power of the client machine. Oracle R Enterprise also has the ability to run R code that is embedded in SQL code. The data remains in the Oracle Database, and all operations that are defined in the R code are translated and performed on the data in the Oracle Database. This core ability of Oracle R Enterprise allows data analysts to work with larger data sets than they would typically be able to do. Using embedded R execution, you can store and run R scripts in the database through either the R programming environment or SQL, or both. You can use the results generated by the R code in any SQL-enabled tool. The embedded R execution also allows you to utilize the vast graphical capabilities available in R within your tools, including OBIEE and Oracle BI Publisher.

In this chapter we have shown you some of the capabilities of using Oracle R Enterprise. These included how you can install and use Oracle R Enterprise on the Oracle Database server, as well as how you can use the R language, via the Oracle R Enterprise transparency layer, to use the computing capabilities of the Oracle Database. We have also shown you how to create R scripts within the Oracle Database and call them using SQL.

Oracle R Enterprise greatly expands the analytic capabilities of the Oracle Database. If you come across a new package in the R language that provides you with a specific function that you want to use, all you need to do is install it on the Oracle Database server, and you can then call this functionality from SQL. As you can see, this is a very powerful feature for your data analysts, and you can encourage more of them to use Oracle R Enterprise.

NOTE
Check out Oracle R Enterprise: Harnessing the Power of R in the Oracle Database *(McGraw-Hill Professional, 2016) for more details on how you can explore and use Oracle R Enterprise for your data analytics and in your applications.*

CHAPTER
12

Predictive Queries
in Oracle 12c

In the previous two chapters, we looked at how you can use the Oracle Data Mining features and greatly expand the analytic capabilities of your database by running R code within SQL. To fully utilize these features, you need to have a good understanding of them as well as how and where they should be implemented and used.

But what if you didn't want to go into all that complexity? What if you wanted to use these advanced machine learning algorithms without having to know or understand what they do and how they do it? What if you knew what kind of business problems they could be applied to, and all you wanted was an answer. Additionally, what if you're not too concerned about how accurate they are? Instead, you're just interested in something that gives an indication, an approximate result, and some details about the attributes that lead to the prediction? What if you want these predictions to be scalable without having to write any additional code?

If the answers to some of these questions are "yes," then perhaps Predictive Queries are what you're looking for. The new Predictive Queries feature introduced in the Oracle Database 12c allows you to create and apply data mining models to your data without any of the additional coding shown in the previous two chapters. All the work and processing are performed in the background, the data is scored, and when all the work is completed, the models are removed and the results are displayed.

In this chapter, we show you how to use Predictive Queries to perform classification, regression, anomaly detection, and clustering using the new powerful features available in some of the analytic functions found in the Oracle Database.

What Are Predictive Queries and Why Do You Need Them?

One of the new SQL features introduced into the Oracle Database 12c is the ability to create on-the-fly predictive models for your data. All you need to do is write a SQL query that builds a predictive model and then apply this model to your data. This is all done in one step and does not require knowledge of its inner workings. The predictive models that are built during the execution of the Predictive Query only exist while the query is being run. When the query is finished, all the models and associated settings are deleted. These are called *transient models*.

NOTE
When looking for details of Predictive Queries in the Oracle documentation, you need to be careful because it seems to go by many names. In the documentation it can be found under On-the-Fly Models, and sometimes it is called Dynamic Queries. This feature is also part of the Oracle Data Miner tool that is part of SQL Developer, where it goes by the name Predictive Queries. In other words, On-the-Fly Models = Dynamic Queries = Predictive Queries. Yes, that is a bit confusing!

Predictive Queries enable you to build and score data quickly using the in-database data mining algorithms, without the complexity of needing to understand the required settings and fine-tuning of the models. All models created during the execution of the Predictive Query will not exist once the Predictive Query is finished executing. You cannot inspect or tune the algorithms being used or the models that are generated. Therefore, you have to trust what Oracle is doing behind the scenes. If you are a data scientist type of person, you will typically want to tune the models, so this approach might not be for you. However, if you want to build models very quickly and score your data without wanting to know what is involved in doing this, then Predictive Queries are something you should consider.

A major advantage of using Predictive Queries is that you can partition the data so that predictive models can be built specific to each partition. This is achieved by using the Partitioning clause. This will divide your data into the relevant partitions and then create a predictive model specific to a partition and then score the data in that partition. Typically for most data mining tools, you will have to specifically define the creation of the data subset for the partition, define how to build the model, and then run the model to score the data. All of these steps have to be manually defined. By defining a partition in the Predictive Query, all of this work will be done automatically for you. There are two major advantages to this. The first is that as new data partitions (that is, a new value exists for the partition attribute) are created, the Predictive Query will automatically pick this up and do all the work for you. The second is that Predictive Queries allow you to use the Parallel Query option to speed up the process of scoring the data. This is particularly useful when you are working with Big Data.

There are two ways you can go about creating your Predictive Queries. The first option is to write a SQL statement to prompt the database to use the in-database data mining algorithms. The second option is to use the Predictive Queries nodes in the Oracle Data Miner tool. This chapter concentrates on showing you how to use Predictive Queries using SQL. A section later in this chapter shows you how to build a Predictive Query using the Oracle Data Mining tool that is part of SQL Developer.

NOTE
The sample data set used in this chapter to illustrate Predictive Queries is the same data set that was used in Chapter 10 when we looked at using Oracle Data Mining. This sample data set mainly consists of some views on the tables in the sample schemas provided by Oracle. These views and tables are created automatically when you create the Oracle Data Miner Repository using SQL Developer. Alternatively, you can run the instDemoData.sql script that comes with SQL Developer and is located in the following directory under the main SQL Developer directory: ...\sqldeveloper\dataminer\scripts.

Oracle Analytic Functions

Analytic functions first appeared in the Oracle Database starting back in Oracle 8*i* Database (or even earlier). With each release of the database, we have more functions being added. We now have over 46 functions in the Oracle Database 12*c*. Table 12-1 lists the analytic functions, with the Predictive Query–related functions highlighted with an asterisk.

As shown in Table 12-1, there are ten predictive analytic functions. The first set of these functions begins with **cluster** and can be used to perform cluster analysis and to see the details of each cluster.

avg	max
cluster_details*	min
cluster_distance*	nth_value
cluster_id*	ntile
cluster_probability*	percent_rank
cluster_set*	percentile_cont
corr	percentile_disc
count	prediction*
covar_pop	prediction_cost*
covar_samp	prediction_details*
cume_dist	prediction_probability*
dense_rank	prediction_set*
feature_details	rank
feature_id	ratio_to_report
feature_set	regr_ (Linear Regression)
feature_value	row_number
first	stddev
first_value	stddev_pop
lag	stddev_samp
last	sum
last_value	var_pop
lead	var_samp
listagg	variance

TABLE 12-1. *Analytic Functions in Oracle Database 12c*

The second set of these functions (in the right column of Table 12-1), beginning with **prediction**, can be used for classification, regression, anomaly detection, and feature sets. These sets of functions are powerful, so you need to be careful of how you write the Predictive Query because you may end up getting a type of prediction you didn't expect.

An analytic function has three main parts to the syntax. First there is the definition of the function. Within this syntax, we have the other two parts: the Partition and Window clauses, as illustrated in Figure 12-1.

The Magic of the Partitioning Clause

When we use Predictive Queries, we are asking Oracle to build and apply predictive models on our data. These predictions can then be used to gain additional insight on our data and to make decisions.

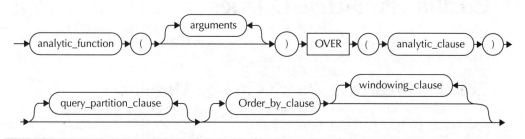

FIGURE 12-1.   *Analytic functions syntax*

When we use the Partitioning clause, we are telling the Oracle Database to treat the data for each partition of the data differently. That means for Predictive Queries, the Oracle Database will build and apply a separate data mining model for each set of values that the Partition clause defines.

For example, in Figure 12-2, we can see that approximately 90 percent of the data comes from one country. In this kind of scenario, it does not make sense to use the same data mining model for all countries. What we should do is create a separate model for each country.

When we use the Partitioning clause, we can specify how we want the Predictive Queries to create these separate data mining models. Using the data illustrated in Figure 12-2, we can add COUNTRY_NAME to the Partition clause. By doing this, Oracle Database groups the data into separate partitions for each of the values for COUNTRY_CODE. Data mining models will be created in the database for each partition, and then the data is scored. The data mining models do not exist after they have been used to score the data.

Similarly, if we wanted to refine our data mining to a more granular level, we could add more attributes to the Partition clause. This is illustrated in the various examples given throughout this chapter.

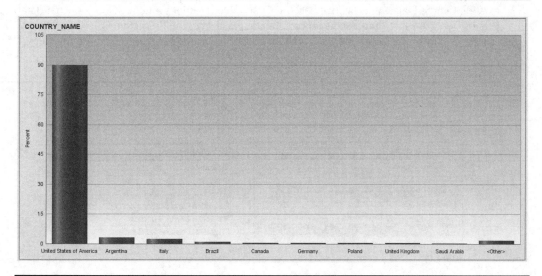

FIGURE 12-2.   *Distribution of transactional records by country*

Creating Predictive Queries

When starting out with Predictive Queries, it can be a little bit difficult to get the syntax of your queries correct. To help you overcome this and get up to speed quickly with Predictive Queries, Oracle has provided two simple ways to get going.

Creating Predictive Queries in SQL Developer

The first of these is to use the Snippets section of SQL Developer, as shown in Figure 12-3. Snippets are code fragments that give you an example of a prebuilt query that uses a particular function. For Predictive Queries, the snippets give us sample code for using the various types of Predictive Queries, as well as using the **dbms_predictive_analytics** functions. You can open the snippets in SQL Developer by selecting View from the main menu and then selecting Snippets. This opens the Snippets window. In this window, select Predictive Analytics from the drop-down lists, as shown in Figure 12-3. When Predictive Analytics is selected, the window will display the snippets we are looking for.

To get the snippet details to display, you need to click one of the listed functions and drag it to your SQL Developer worksheet. For example, if you select Prediction Classification Function from the Snippet list, you get a sample Predictive Query that is based on the sample data set for Oracle Data Mining. A SQL Developer worksheet with the snippet code for a Classification Predictive Query is shown in Figure 12-4. This snippet code also illustrates how to use the **prediction**, **prediction_details**, **prediction_probability**, and **prediction_set** functions.

Creating Predictive Queries in Oracle Data Miner

The second way to try out Predictive Queries is to use the Oracle Data Miner tool that comes as part of Oracle SQL Developer. First, you need to open Oracle Data Miner. The Predictive Queries section of the Components window only becomes visible when you are connected to an Oracle Database 12c, as shown in Figure 12-5.

To create Predictive Queries in the Oracle Data Miner tool, you need to create or open an existing Oracle Data Miner worksheet. The Oracle Data Miner tool checks to see what database version you are using. If it detects an Oracle Database 12c, the Predictive Queries section will appear as part of the Components Workflow Editor, as shown in Figure 12-5. The four template

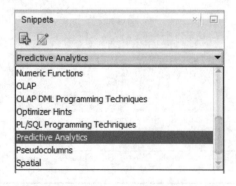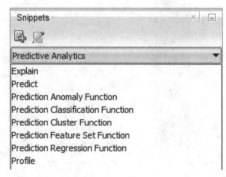

FIGURE 12-3. *Snippets in Oracle SQL Developer*

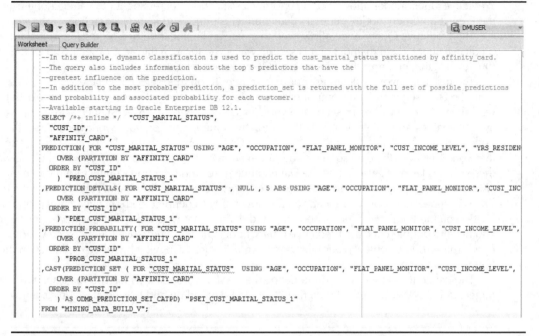

FIGURE 12-4. *Sample Predictive Query from the SQL Developer Snippets section*

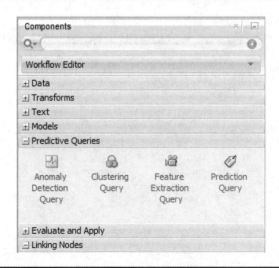

FIGURE 12-5. *Predictive Queries in Oracle Data Miner*

Predictive Query nodes allow you to perform classification, regression (both can be done using the Prediction Query node), anomaly detection, clustering, and feature extraction.

The Predictive Query node allows you to create a classification or a regression model for your predictive query. The remainder of this section walks you through the steps of setting up a Predictive Query node that performs the same as the SQL code version given later in this chapter.

The first step involves defining your data source. To do this, select the Data Source node from the Data section of the Components Workflow Editor. Then click on your new or existing worksheet. A node will be created, and you can select MINING_DATA_BUILD_V from the list of available tables and views. To create the Predictive Query node on your worksheet, select this node from the Predictive Queries section of the Components Workflow Editor and click again on the worksheet near the data source node. You now need to define the connection or link between these two nodes by right-clicking the Data Source node and selecting Connect from the menu. Then move your mouse over to the Predictive Query node and click again. An arrow connection line will appear on your worksheet. You are now ready to define the Predictive Query properties.

To edit the Predictive Query properties and define what type of predictive query to perform, you need to double-click the Predictive Query node. The Edit Predictive Query Node window will open. This window contains four tabs, as shown in Figure 12-6, which will be explained in the following paragraphs.

The Predictions tab allows you to define the CASE ID if one exists for your data set and the target attributes you want the Predictive Query to be based on and to predict. In our example, you

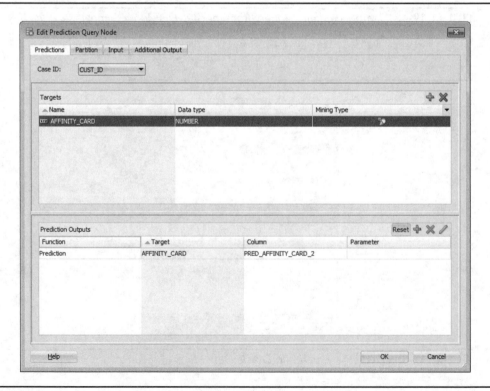

FIGURE 12-6. *The Predictions tab for the Predictive Query node*

will want to set the CASE_ID to CUST_ID. To define the attribute(s) you want to predict, you need to click the green plus icon above the Targets section of the window. A window opens that lists the attributes for the data source. Select the attribute(s) you want to predict. In our example, you can select the AFFINITY_CARD attribute and then click the OK button to close. The AFFINITY_ CARD attribute will now appear in the Targets section of the window. To tell Oracle what type of data mining to perform, you may need to change the mining type for the TARGET attribute. In our example, we want a classification to be performed. To ensure this happens, change the Mining Type setting to Categorical (and click OK for the warning message). If the mining type was left as numerical, a regression model would be created. The next step you need to perform is to define what predictions you want created for this target attribute. By default, the Prediction, Prediction Details, and Prediction Probability attributes will be created. Select Prediction Details and Prediction Probabilities (in the Prediction Outputs section of the window) and then click the red X icon to remove them. Figure 12-6 shows the setting of the Predictions tab.

The Partition tab allows you to define what partitions you want applied to the model build and scoring processes. If a partition is applied, the Oracle Database will create a separate model for each value of the partition attribute(s). These separate models will then be applied to the data set to score it based on the values of the partition. To create the partition, click the green plus icon on the Partitions tab. Select the CUST_GENDER attribute from the list and then click the OK button to finish. The Partitions tab will be updated to contain this attribute, as illustrated in Figure 12-7.

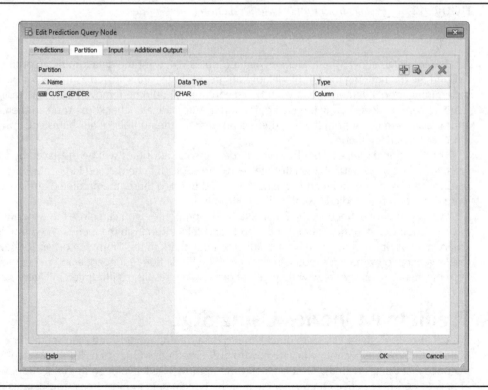

FIGURE 12-7.   *The Partition tab for the Predictive Query node*

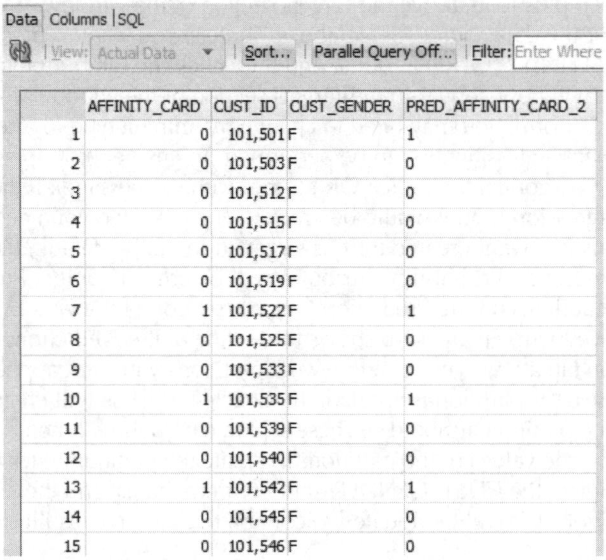

	AFFINITY_CARD	CUST_ID	CUST_GENDER	PRED_AFFINITY_CARD_2
1	0	101,501	F	1
2	0	101,503	F	0
3	0	101,512	F	0
4	0	101,515	F	0
5	0	101,517	F	0
6	0	101,519	F	0
7	1	101,522	F	1
8	0	101,525	F	0
9	0	101,533	F	0
10	1	101,535	F	1
11	0	101,539	F	0
12	0	101,540	F	0
13	1	101,542	F	1
14	0	101,545	F	0
15	0	101,546	F	0

FIGURE 12-8. *Results from running the Prediction Query node*

The Input tab allows you to define what attributes you want the data mining algorithm to use to build the data mining model. By default, all the attributes are selected as inputs for building the data mining model. If there are any attributes you think should be removed as inputs, you can remove them by de-selecting the Determine Input Automatically checkbox. You can then click an attribute and remove it from the list. There is no limit on the number of attributes you can use as input to Predictive Queries.

The Additional Output tab allows you to define what attributes will be displayed by the Predictive Query. By default, the attribute set as the CASE_ID, the defined target attribute, and any partition attributes are included in the output. In addition to these, the predicted attributes that were defined in the Predictions tab will be outputted.

When you have defined all the Predictive Query properties, you can close the window. To run the Prediction Query node, right-click the node and select Run from the menu. When the Prediction Query node is finished, it will have a small green tick mark in the top-right corner. To view the results generated by the node, you can right-click the Prediction Query node and select View Data from the menu. A new window will open that displays the results, as illustrated in Figure 12-8.

Predictive Queries Using SQL

We can use Predictive Queries to quickly build data mining models and then score our data using SQL. In the previous section, you saw how to build Predictive Queries using the wizard-type interface that comes with the Oracle Data Miner tool in SQL Developer. In this section, we look at how to build Predictive Queries for each of the typical data mining areas. These areas include classification, regression, anomaly detection, and data clustering.

Classification Using Predictive Queries

In this first example, we are going to look at how to perform a simple classification Predictive Query in SQL. If you have already built an Oracle Data Mining classification model, as shown in Chapter 10, you are able to use the **prediction** and **prediction_probability** functions to apply that model to your data. You can also use these functions for Predictive Queries, but they need some additional specification to enable the Predictive Queries to work.

The following example shows a Predictive Query that uses the data in the MINING_DATA_ BUILD_V view to build one data mining model, and it uses this model to score our data. In this particular example, we can compare what customers actually took out an affinity card versus what customers were predicted to take out an affinity card:

```
SELECT cust_id, affinity_card,
       PREDICTION( FOR to_char(affinity_card) USING *) OVER ()
                                      pred_affinity_card
FROM mining_data_build_v;
```

In this query, we are asking Oracle to take all the data in the MINING_DATA_BUILD view (**USING *** in the query) and work out what data mining algorithm to use, what setting to use, and to optimize itself using this data. Only one data mining model will be created in this case because we have not specified any attributes in the Partition clause. This query produces the following output (note that only a subset of the results is shown):

```
   CUST_ID AFFINITY_CARD PRED_AFFINITY_CARD
---------- ------------- -------------------
...
    101523             0 0
    101524             0 1
    101525             0 0
    101526             1 1
    101527             0 0
    101528             0 0
    101529             0 0
    101530             1 1
    101531             0 0
    101532             0 0
    101533             0 0
    101534             0 0
    101535             1 0
    101536             1 1
    101537             0 1
    101538             1 1
    101539             0 0
    101540             0 0
    101541             1 1
    101542             1 0
    101543             1 0
    101544             0 0
...
```

In these results, we get to see and compare the actual value with the predicted value. You may notice that it got some of the predictions incorrect. This is typical in data mining. It will not get everything 100 percent correct, but that is okay. Part of the reason for this is that the data mining algorithm is trying to figure out what works best for all the data across all the records. One way to improve the accuracy is to look at building data mining models based on different groupings of the data. In this case, we use the Partition clause to divide the data into the groups.

Using the PARTITION Clause

When you want a separate data mining model created for separate groups on the data, you can use the PARTITION BY clause to achieve this. For example, we have a COUNTRY_NAME attribute, but maybe it would be better to build separate data mining models for each country. This way, the data mining algorithm can build models that better reflect the behavior of the data in each grouping. This should then lead to us getting better accuracy with the predicted values for each group.

In our example, we can add COUNTRY_NAME to the PARTITION BY clause. When the query is run, a separate data mining model will be created for each country (Partition). These models will then be used to score or label the data with the predicted value. The following query extends our previous example by using the PARTITION BY clause:

```
SELECT cust_id, affinity_card,
       PREDICTION( FOR to_char(affinity_card) USING *) OVER
                  (PARTITION BY "COUNTRY_NAME") pred_affinity_card
FROM mining_data_build_v;
```

When we examine the results from running this query, we find that we now have a very high degree of accuracy in the predictions. This is what we would expect because we now have a highly tuned data model.

If we wanted to add more refinement to the data mining models, we could add some more attributes to the views. For example, we could add CUST_GENDER. In this case, we would get two data mining models being produced for each of the countries. Thus, we would have 38 mining models (19 countries × 2 genders). We can also calculate how strong of a prediction has been made. We do this by calling the **prediction_probability** function. The closer the probability value is to 1, the stronger the prediction.

```
SELECT cust_id, affinity_card,
       PREDICTION( FOR to_char(affinity_card) USING *) OVER
            (PARTITION BY "COUNTRY_NAME", "CUST_GENDER") pred_affinity_card,
       PREDICTION_PROBABILITY( FOR to_char(affinity_card) USING *) OVER
            (PARTITION BY "COUNTRY_NAME", "CUST_GENDER") prod_affinity_card
FROM mining_data_build_v;
```

One of the problems with Predictive Queries is that these very efficient data mining models no longer exist in the database. They only exist for the duration of the query execution, and only as part of the execution of the analytic function. No Oracle data mining models are persisted, even for a short time period, in the database.

TIP

*For your typical classification type of problem, your target attribute will need to be a character data type. If it isn't, you will need to convert it. For example, if it is defined as a number, you will need to apply the **to_char** function to the target attribute to convert it into a categorical value. If you don't apply the **to_char** function to the number attribute, the Predictive Queries will treat the data as a regression data mining problem.*

Regression Using Predictive Queries

With regression-type problems and applications, we are looking to predict some continuous-value variable. Typically applications involve predicting monetary spending, lifetime value, value of claim, and so on. To illustrate the use of regression with Predictive Queries, we are going to use another of the sample data sets that comes with the installation of the Oracle Data Miner repository. One of these tables is called INSUR_CUST_LTV_SAMPLE. What we want to do with this data is to predict what the potential life-time value (LTV) is for each customer. We can then compare the predicted value with the calculated value and then determine if there are any customers who are generating significantly more or less revenue when compared with all the other customers.

The following example shows a Predictive Query that calculates a predicted LTV and displays this with the current values. For records where you don't have the LTV value, the predicted value will give you an idea of what the LTV would be.

```
SELECT customer_id,
       ltv,
       PREDICTION( FOR ltv USING *) OVER ( ) pred_ltv
FROM   insur_cust_ltv_sample
ORDER BY customer_id;


CUSTOMER_ID                 LTV    PRED_LTV
-------------------- ---------- ----------
CU100                  24891.25 24635.6722
CU10006                 23638.5 23550.5382
CU10011                 35600.5  35384.337
CU10012                   26070 26317.024
CU10020                25092.75 24870.8761
CU10025                   27149 26898.858
CU10041                 27342.5 27177.981
CU10044                   23786 24003.0287
CU1005                 25530.25 25782.2133
CU10110                 20978.5 20766.2043
CU10119                    9603 9333.17705
CU10148                18586.75 18763.5533
CU1015                    20439 20376.9408
CU10154                19845.75 19756.1573
CU10161                 20400.5 20475.0282
CU10168                18977.75 19183.9125
```

Using the PARTITION Clause

Just like we did for the previous example of using Predictive Queries, we can ask the database to create multiple data mining models that are based on the values of an attribute or a set of attributes. In the following example, our LTV Predictive Query is expanded so that it will create separate data mining models for each combination of STATE and SEX. In this case, it will be creating 44 different data mining models because we have 22 distinct states in the data set and two distinct values for SEX.

```
select customer_id,
       ltv,
       PREDICTION( FOR ltv USING *)
                  OVER ( PARTITION BY STATE, SEX ) pred_ltv
from   insur_cust_ltv_sample;


CUSTOMER_ID                LTV    PRED_LTV
-------------------- ---------- ----------
CU100                 24891.25 24585.7955
CU10006                23638.5 22684.1578
CU10011                35600.5 35327.8755
CU10012                  26070 23770.4415
CU10020               25092.75 24877.3583
CU10025                  27149 26946.9569
CU10041                27342.5 27123.4588
CU10044                  23786 24667.3585
CU1005                25530.25 24676.8757
CU10110                20978.5 20567.8927
CU10119                   9603 9627.61307
CU10148               18586.75 19284.6848
CU1015                   20439  19502.895
CU10154               19845.75 19942.1711
CU10161                20400.5 19999.6592
CU10168               18977.75 19189.9201
```

The results generated by this query are closer to the actual value than what were generated by the previous query. We can expand this query to include percentage differences and other statistics to gain a clear picture of the differences. For example, if you look at Customer CU10012, you will notice that their calculated LTV value is significantly different from all the other customers' results being displayed. You can use this additional information as a way of being able to focus in on the customers who need closer attention.

TIP
For each new state added to the data set, no additional coding or alternations are needed to the preceding code. The dynamic nature of Predictive Queries will automatically pick up the new values, and they will be processed. This is a major advantage of using Predictive Queries because they can be easily built into your reports and dashboards.

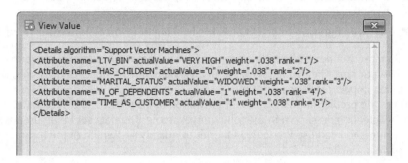

FIGURE 12-9.   *Viewing the PREDICTION_DETAILS results*

The **prediction_details** function can be used with classification, regression, and anomaly detection Predictive Queries to see details of the decisions made by the data mining algorithms. This kind of information is particularly useful as the decisions, the attributes used to make the decisions, and their values can be different for each of the records. For example, if we are using the LTV example, we can use the information given by **prediction_details** to decide how we might interact with the customer. The following code example extends our previous example to include the **prediction_details** function:

```
SELECT customer_id,
       ltv,
       PREDICTION( FOR ltv USING *)
                    OVER ( PARTITION BY STATE, SEX ) pred_ltv,
       PREDICTION_DETAILS( FOR ltv USING *)
                    OVER ( PARTITION BY STATE, SEX ) details_ltv
FROM   insur_cust_ltv_sample;
```

The **prediction_details** function returns the results in XML format. The easiest way to view the formatted output of this function is to use SQL Developer. For each record in the results, double-click the field under **prediction_details** and you will get a window like the one shown in Figure 12-9 that displays the formatted XML.

Anomaly Detection Using Predictive Queries

When you are analyzing data, there are times when you will want to identify what data items or records are different from the other data items or records. Anomaly detection is the searching for and identification of case records that do not conform to the typical pattern of case records. These nonconforming cases are often referred to as *anomalies* or *outliers*.

Anomaly detection can be applied to many problem domains, including the following:

■ Financial transaction monitoring by clearinghouses to identify transactions that require further investigation for potentially fraudulent or money-laundering transactions

■ Detecting fraudulent credit card transactions

■ Insurance claims analysis to identify possible claims that are not in keeping with the typical claims

■ Network intrusion to detect possible hacking or atypical behavior by employees

With these examples, the type of transactions we are interested in discovering will be uncommon or rare. They will only occur in a very small percentage of the cases, but they may have a high impact for their scenario.

To use the **prediction** function to identify anomalous records, we need to tell it to perform anomaly detection, as shown in the following example. The data set being used is from insurance policy claims. You can use Predictive Queries to quickly see which of the insurance claims records are anomalous.

```
SELECT policynumber,
       PREDICTION( OF ANOMALY USING *) OVER ()  ANOMALY_PRED
FROM   claims;

POLICYNUMBER ANOMALY_PRED
------------ ------------
           1            0
          29            1
          53            0
          54            1
          80            1
          95            1
          97            1
         101            1
         114            0
         118            1
         119            1
         120            0
```

For anomaly detection, the **prediction** function will give a value of zero or one as the result. When a zero is given, this indicates that the Predictive Query has identified this record as an anomalous record. These are the records you will want to pay attention to and will require additional investigation.

In addition to the **prediction** function, you can use the **prediction_probability** and **prediction_details** functions to gain a deeper insight into the anomalous records. For example, you could use the **prediction_probability** function to rank the predictions in order of probability that the records are anomalous. Then the investigating analyst can use the information and insight given by the **prediction_details** function to see what particular attributes and their values have been identified as causing the anomaly.

The following example illustrates the use of these functions on the insurance claims data set:

```
SELECT policynumber,
       PREDICTION( OF ANOMALY USING *) OVER ()  ANOMALY_PRED,
       PREDICTION_PROBABILITY( OF ANOMALY USING *) OVER ()  ANOMALY_PROB,
       PREDICTION_DETAILS( OF ANOMALY USING *) OVER ()  ANOMALY_DETAILS
FROM   claims
ORDER BY policynumber;
```

```
POLICYNUMBER ANOMALY_PRED ANOMALY_PROB ANOMALY_DETAILS
------------ ------------ ------------ ------------------------------
           1            0      0.60092 <Details algorithm="Support Ve
                                        ctor Machines" class="0">
                                        <Attribute name="ADDRESS
          29            1      0.51399 <Details algorithm="Support Ve
                                        ctor Machines" class="1">
                                        <Attribute name="WEEKOFM
          53            0      0.51583 <Details algorithm="Support Ve
                                        ctor Machines" class="0">
                                        <Attribute name="ACCIDEN
          54            1      0.55443 <Details algorithm="Support Ve
                                        ctor Machines" class="1">
                                        <Attribute name="WEEKOFM
          80            1      0.50958 <Details algorithm="Support Ve
                                        ctor Machines" class="1">
                                        <Attribute name="FRAUDFO
```

If you examine the ANOMALY_DETAILS results for the two anomalous records in the previous listing, where ANOMALY_PRED is zero, you will see that the attributes and their values are very different. The ANOMALY_PRED for these two records is shown in Figure 12-10.

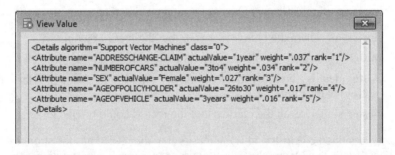

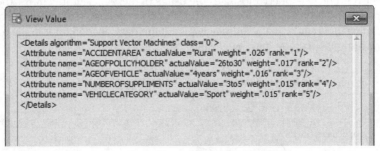

FIGURE 12-10. *Differences in anomaly detection attributes*

Just like with our previous examples for classification and regression, we can expand the number of anomaly detection models by adding attributes to the PARTITION clause:

```
SELECT policynumber,
       PREDICTION( OF ANOMALY USING *)
               OVER ( PARTITION BY VEHICLECATEGORY )   ANOMALY_PRED,
       PREDICTION_PROBABILITY( OF ANOMALY USING *)
               OVER ( PARTITION BY VEHICLECATEGORY )   ANOMALY_PROB,
       PREDICTION_DETAILS( OF ANOMALY USING *)
               OVER ( PARTITION BY VEHICLECATEGORY )   ANOMALY_DETAILS
FROM   claims
ORDER BY policynumber;
```

Clustering Using Predictive Queries

Clustering is an unsupervised data mining technique. You can use the clustering algorithms to find groupings of data that are more related to each other (a cluster) and less related to other groupings (other clusters). Examples of when the clustering data mining technique is used include customer segmentation, marketing, insurance claims analysis, outlier detection, image pattern recognition, biology, and security.

Clustering is the process of dividing the data into smaller related subsets. Each of these subsets is called a *cluster*. For each cluster, the data in it is similar, and also dissimilar to the data in the other clusters.

For clustering using Predictive Queries, we have a different set of functions available to us:

- **cluster_id**   Gives the cluster identifier that the record belongs to
- **cluster_probability**   Indicates how strong a link the record has with the cluster
- **cluster_details**   Provides the details of the attributes and their values that form the centroid of the cluster
- **cluster_set**   Lists all the clusters that the record could be part of

The cluster identified by **cluster_id** is the cluster that the record has the strongest bond with.

The next Predictive Query illustrates the usage of these cluster functions. The main difference between the cluster Predictive Query functions and the previous functions is that we have to tell the Predictive Query how many clusters we want the data divided into. In the following example, we are dividing the data set into ten clusters:

```
SELECT cust_id,
       CLUSTER_ID( INTO 10 USING *) OVER ()   CLUS_ID,
       CLUSTER_PROBABILITY( INTO 10 USING *) OVER ()   CLUS_PROB,
       CLUSTER_DETAILS( INTO 10 USING *) OVER ()      CLUS_DETAILS,
       cast(CLUSTER_SET( INTO 10 USING *) OVER () AS ODMR_CLUSTER_SET_NUMPD) CLUS_SET
FROM   mining_data_build_v

   CUST_ID    CLUS_ID  CLUS_PROB CLUS_DETAILS
---------- ---------- ---------- -------------------------------------------
CLUS_SET(CLUSTER_ID, PROBABILITY)
-------------------------------------------
    101501         7    0.77232 <Details algorithm="K-Means Clustering" cl
                                 uster="7">
                                 </Details>
```

```
ODMR_CLUSTER_SET_NUMPD(ODMR_CLUSTER_NUMPD(
7, 0.77232), ODMR_CLUSTER_NUMPD(4, 0), OD
MR_CLUSTER_NUMPD(6, 0), ODMR_CLUSTER_NUMPD
(8, 0), ODMR_CLUSTER_NUMPD(9, 0))
    101502        9    0.84828 <Details algorithm="K-Means Clustering" cl
                                uster="9">
                                </Details>
ODMR_CLUSTER_SET_NUMPD(ODMR_CLUSTER_NUMPD(
9, 0.84828), ODMR_CLUSTER_NUMPD(4, 0), OD
MR_CLUSTER_NUMPD(6, 0), ODMR_CLUSTER_NUMPD
(7, 0), ODMR_CLUSTER_NUMPD(8, 0))
    101503        6    0.98450 <Details algorithm="K-Means Clustering" cl
                                uster="6">
                                </Details>
ODMR_CLUSTER_SET_NUMPD(ODMR_CLUSTER_NUMPD(
6, 0.98450), ODMR_CLUSTER_NUMPD(4, 0), OD
MR_CLUSTER_NUMPD(7, 0), ODMR_CLUSTER_NUMPD
(8, 0), ODMR_CLUSTER_NUMPD(9, 0))
```

The easiest way to view the results generated by the **cluster_details** and **cluster_set** functions is to use SQL Developer. Figure 12-11 illustrates the **cluster_details** outputs, and Figure 12-12 illustrates the **cluster_sets** outputs.

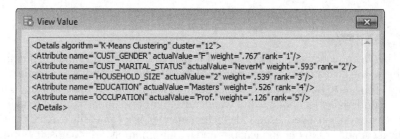

FIGURE 12-11.   *Output generated by cluster_details*

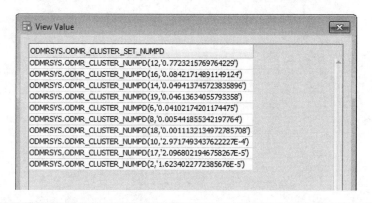

FIGURE 12-12.   *Output generated by cluster_sets*

Similar to the previous examples of using Predictive Queries, these cluster functions can be extended to include attributes in the Partition clause.

Working with Predictive Queries

You have seen in this chapter that Predictive Queries are a powerful feature within the Oracle Database 12c. It allows us to focus on the use of in-database advanced machine learning algorithms that come as part of the Oracle Advanced Analytics option. Their simplicity allows all developers to use them in building their custom applications and their back-end processing, as part of workflow management, and in their business intelligence (BI) and analytics environments.

The use of Predictive Queries does have some limitations. When you run a Predictive Query, Oracle creates a transient or temporary data mining model. This model is only available during the execution of the query. The model produced by the Predictive Query does not exist afterward and is not available for inspection or tuning. If you need to inspect the model to correlate scoring results, specify special algorithm settings, or execute multiple scoring queries that use the same model, you must create a predefined model using the Oracle Data Miner model nodes in the Oracle Data Miner tool that is part of SQL Developer. Alternatively, you can use the Oracle Data Mining PL/SQL package called DBMS_DATA_MINING. You are most likely to use the Oracle Data Mining PL/SQL package to build custom data mining models and integrate this functionality in a dynamic manner with your front-end and back-end applications. Examples of building such models was given in Chapter 10.

Summary

Oracle has been working on making the advanced analytics features that exist in the database more available to the data analyst. With Predictive Queries, we have another example of this. Predictive Queries allow us to build advanced analytics into our queries without having to understand or know the underlying technology. But we can use our basic understanding to gain additional insight on our data in a very easy and efficient manner. We can easily expand the statistical and analytical capabilities in our applications and in our reporting dashboards. If we want to build more complex solutions, we need to use the Oracle Data Miner tool or use the underlying Oracle Data Mining SQL and PL/SQL functionality that was demonstrated in Chapter 10.

PART
V

Database Security

CHAPTER
13

Redaction and Masking

D
ata security has always been at the center of attention, thanks not only to mandates by many regulations such as SOX and HIPAA, but to the security consciousness of company management not wanting to be embarrassed—or, worse, a target of a lawsuit in the case of data theft. Data security has received a more-than-usual share of attention following several recent events of data breach. Information security departments all over the world are working overtime to mitigate the threats coming from different sources. However, data security is not the responsibility of the Information Security department alone; it starts with the foundation—code development. And, yes, that includes PL/SQL coding. Security is akin to a chain, and everyone knows that a chain is only as strong as the weakest link. A highly protected database is severely exposed when accessed by a compromised application vulnerable to SQL injection attacks. To offer true security, the code must be built from the ground up with security in mind.

In this chapter you learn several tips and techniques for developing code, not just for functionality and efficiency, but also for security and reliability. We have divided the security topics into four different parts. Chapter 13 describes data redaction and data masking; Chapter 14 describes the techniques of data encryption at rest and data hashing using PL/SQL; Chapter 15 covers coding to avoid common vulnerabilities such as SQL injection attacks and to develop security around the code itself, such as wrapping and preventing unauthorized calls. Finally, Chapter 16 covers using Virtual Private Database (VPD), also known as Row Level Security, to implement a restricted view of the data using PL/SQL. After reading these chapters, you will be able to sharpen your skills for developing secure code and, consequently, secure systems. Let's get on with this chapter on redaction and masking. These are related but different, as you will learn in the next few sections.

Why Redaction?

Suppose you regularly move data from the production database to the nonproduction ones, such as staging, QA, development, and so on. Typically these nonproduction databases are less protected compared to the production one. For starters, they have more users. The development database, of course, has developers who would not normally have access to production. These users need to have access to the database with a lot less restriction in order to write code. These databases may also have lax firewall protection—at least compared to the production servers— and perhaps are accessed by third-party contractors developing code. Therefore, it may be important, or even required by some regulation or policy, that some of the sensitive data be altered rather than being in the original value. Take, for instance, the SALARY column in the EMP table. When you move the production database table to the nonproduction database, you may have to alter the value of the columns to hide the original value. In the simplest case, you may have to set the column value to NULL for all the rows in nonproduction. That is known as *redaction,* which is hiding data. However, that may not be good for all cases. If the developers want the value to test some matching conditions, NULL values will always yield one result, thus making the tests inconclusive. If the DBAs are doing performance testing for indexes, the presence of NULL values will always cause indexes to be skipped, making these tests inconclusive as well. Therefore, instead of making the column completely NULL, you may have to just alter it to another random value. Or you may need to make all the values a specific number, such as 0000, which could be XXXX for character-based columns. This process is known as *masking.*

Sometimes you may need to *partially*—not entirely—hide the value. Consider the case of the Social Security Number (SSN) in the United States. It's a nine-digit number, but because it might start with 0 (which can't be dropped), it's usually stored as a character string. It may be important to show only a part of that number for verification purposes (for example, the last four digits). Hiding the first five digits makes the overall SSN impossible to identify, but making the last four digits visible enables a rudimentary validation of the customer. This is called *partial masking.*

The need for redaction and masking does not apply to nonproduction systems alone. Consider the SALARY column discussed earlier. While it makes sense for those applications and users who deal with salary to see the column value, it doesn't makes sense for other users. However, you can't just update the column values to mask them because the genuine applications still need to use them. This brings up the second type of redaction—keeping the actual value intact but showing a redacted value to a user who is not authorized otherwise. This is called *in-place redaction.*

Although the objectives may differ, the overall solutions for both problems are the same. For in-place redaction, we need to present the data differently depending on who is asking for it. For permanent redaction, we will simply need an additional step to update the values using the same approach used for in-place redaction. For the purpose of simplicity, this book will cover the techniques for in-place redaction only.

To demonstrate the concept, we will use the EMP table in the SCOTT schema available as an example in the Oracle Database. Let's grant the HR user SELECT privilege on this table, as shown here:

```
SQL> conn scott/tiger
Connected.
SQL> grant select on emp to hr;
Grant succeeded.
```

Now connect as HR and issue this statement:

```
SQL> conn hr/hr
SQL> select deptno, empno, ename, hiredate, sal
  2  from scott.emp;
```

Here is the result:

DEPTNO	EMPNO	ENAME	HIREDATE	SAL
20	7369	SMITH	17-DEC-80	800
30	7499	ALLEN	20-FEB-81	1600
30	7521	WARD	22-FEB-81	1250
20	7566	JONES	02-APR-81	2975
30	7654	MARTIN	28-SEP-81	1250
30	7698	BLAKE	01-MAY-81	2850
10	7782	CLARK	09-JUN-81	2450
20	7788	SCOTT	19-APR-87	3000
10	7839	KING	17-NOV-81	5000
30	7844	TURNER	08-SEP-81	1500
20	7876	ADAMS	23-MAY-87	1100
30	7900	JAMES	03-DEC-81	950
20	7902	FORD	03-DEC-81	3000
10	7934	MILLER	23-JAN-82	1300

Column Name	How to Mask the Values	Example Output
ENAME	Random characters with no numeric value. Random length.	**KXPWD**
HIREDATE	The date and month of hiring should be visible, but the year should be updated to 1900.	**17-DEC-1980** should become **17-DEC-1900**
SAL	Any random number between 0 and 1000.	**500**

TABLE 13-1. *Requirements for Redaction in the EMP Table*

The result shows all the values clearly, and you do not want that. You want the data to be scrambled, as shown in Table 13-1.

Remember, you can't just update the columns because this is a production database. If you need to update the data, we show you a way later in this chapter. Obviously the schema owner—SCOTT—should see the actual values, but not the user HR or any other user authorized to access the table.

All these objectives are possible to accomplish through PL/SQL relatively easily. Oracle provides an add-on to the database called the Data Masking and Subsetting Pack, which is an extra-cost option. However, you can do much of the same using plain PL/SQL without incurring the extra expense. Let's explore both solutions.

PL/SQL-Only Solution for Redaction

This solution uses plain PL/SQL without the need for any special packs or options. It also works in any version of the Oracle database.

Here is the general sequence of tasks:

1. Create functions or procedures to produce randomized data outputs.

2. Create views on the actual tables to produce randomized outputs.

3. Create synonyms to point to the views, not the tables.

4. Revoke all privileges from the original tables and grant all necessary privileges to the views.

5. If data changes are also expected, create INSTEAD OF triggers on the view to affect the data changes on the tables after the changes on the views.

Let's explore these tasks in detail.

Randomization

First, we need to develop some code to generate random values to fit our specific needs. Fortunately, Oracle supplies a package called DBMS_RANDOM to generate random values, but it's too generic for our needs. We can use this package to develop some pointed, specific routines.

Random Numbers

Let's create some user-friendly functions to get specific random numbers. Here is one to create random numbers between two specified numbers and with a pre-specified length after the decimal point:

```
create or replace function get_num (
    p_highval    number,
    p_lowval     number := 0,
    p_scale      pls_integer := 0
)
    return number
is
    l_ret    number;
begin
    l_ret := round (dbms_random.value (p_lowval, p_highval), p_scale);
    return l_ret;
end;
```

This function returns a random number between two numbers passed as a parameter. It also allows us to specify the precision (that is, the number of digits after the decimal point). The default precision is 0, which means the generated number will be a whole one, not a fraction. Here is how you use the function to get a random number with two decimal points between 100 and 200:

```
SQL> select get_num(100,200,2)
  2  from dual;

GET_NUM(100,200,2)
------------------
          104.46
```

Of course, your output may differ; this is a *random* number. Although this function is great for generating random numbers that are positive (account numbers, serial numbers, salaries, and so on), in some cases you may need to generate negative numbers. Consider bank account balances, which may realistically be negative when the accounts are overdrawn. But not all the account balances will be negative. The negative balance should also be randomly occurring. This is easy to accomplish with a slight modification of the previous function:

```
create or replace function get_num (
    p_highval                number,
    p_lowval                 number := 0,
    p_negatives_allowed      boolean := false,
    p_scale                  pls_integer := 0
)
    return number
is
    l_ret    number;
    l_sign   number := 1;
begin
    if (p_negatives_allowed)
    then
```

```
      l_sign := sign (dbms_random.random);
   end if;
   l_ret := l_sign * round (dbms_random.value (p_lowval, p_highval), p_scale);
   return l_ret;
end;
```

What Is Seeding?

What makes random numbers truly random? To visualize the mechanism, here is an exercise: quickly think of a number, any number. What number came to mind? That number is very likely significant to you in some way: your age, a part of your telephone number, your street address number—something that you are either familiar with or just happened to see at that time. That number, in other words, was not randomly selected and is, therefore, likely to be repeated or predicted.

Fine, you might say. You want a random number? I will close my eyes and punch at keys randomly on my calculator. Surely that will result in a random number.

Probably not. If you examine the number closely, you will notice that some digits are repeated next to each other. That is natural: if you hit a key (say, 9), it's likely that you will hit 9 again next because your finger was hovering in the general vicinity of that key.

As you can see after these simple thought exercises, it is quite difficult for a human being to come up with a truly random number. Similarly, a machine can't just pull a number from thin air. There are several methods to achieve true randomness based on complex mathematical formulas that are beyond the scope of this book. The most common component of any random number generator is some randomizer found elsewhere, such as system time, which is guaranteed to be different between two points in time. This randomizer component, which is conceptually similar to the general area where your finger was hovering over the calculator keypad to produce a random number, is called a *seed*. If the seed chosen is sufficiently random, the generated number will be truly random. If the seed is constant, the random number generated may not be truly random. The pattern might be repeated and might be easy to guess. Therefore, a seed is very important in random number generation.

The DBMS_RANDOM package contains an **initialize** procedure that provides an initial seed that will then be used by its randomizer function. Here is an example of a call to this program:

```
begin
   dbms_random.initialize (239076190);
end;
```

This procedure accepts a BINARY_INTEGER argument and sets that value as the seed. The larger the number of digits in this seed, the higher the degree of randomness for the generated number. You would generally want to use a number greater than five digits to achieve an acceptable degree of randomness.

Explicitly calling the **initialize** procedure is purely optional and is not required when you are using the DBMS_RANDOM package. By default, Oracle will automatically initialize with the date, user ID, and process ID if no explicit initialization is performed.

For true randomness, though, the number should not be a constant. A good variable for this seed is the system time, which is guaranteed to be different every time it is used within a 24-hour period. Here's an example:

```
begin
    dbms_random.initialize (
        to_number (to_char (sysdate, 'mmddhhmiss')));
end;
```

Here we have fed the month, day, hour, minute, and second as the seed. This seed is used initially; however, if the same seed is used throughout the session, the randomness might be compromised. Hence, you will need to supply a new seed at regular intervals. This can be accomplished via the **seed** procedure, which, like **initialize**, accepts a **binary_integer** as a parameter:

```
begin
    dbms_random.seed (to_char (sysdate, 'mmddhhmiss'));
end;
```

When the session does not need any further generation of new seeds, you can issue the **terminate** procedure as follows to stop generating new random numbers (and stop wasting CPU cycles):

```
begin
    dbms_random.terminate;
end;
```

Random Strings

Next, we need to generate random characters for scrambling the employee names. The package DBMS_RANDOM provides a function for that as well. It's named **string()**. Like its sister function **value()**, it's a bit generic for our taste, so let's build our own function, shown next. We will pass the length of the string we want to generate and the type of the string (all lowercase, all uppercase, all mixed, and so on).

```
create or replace function get_random_string (
    p_len     in    number,
    p_type    in    varchar2 := 'a'
)
    return varchar2
as
    l_retval    varchar2 (200);
begin
    l_retval := dbms_random.string (p_type, p_len);
    return l_retval;
end;
```

p_type	Type of String Generated	Example
u	Uppercase alphabets only	**WFKHSL**
l	Lowercase alphabets only	**wfkhsl**
a	Mixed-case alphabets	**WfKhsL**
x	A mixture of uppercase alphabets and numbers	**A1GH45KL**
p	Any printable characters	**@FH*k9L**

TABLE 13-2.   *Parameter Values for Producing Random Strings*

The parameter **p_type** specifies what type of character value needs to be generated. Table 13-2 shows the possible values passed to the parameter and the results they produce.

To be truly random, the employee names should not be of the same size. The length of each randomized name should not only be different from the original length, the length itself should be randomized as well. Therefore, we need a modified function that can accept the upper and lower bounds of the lengths and produce a random string of a random length between these. Here is the code for that function:

```
create or replace function get_random_string (
    p_minlen    in    number,
    p_maxlen    in    number,
    p_type      in    varchar2 := 'a'
)
    return varchar2
as
    l_retval    varchar2 (200);
begin
    l_retval :=
        dbms_random.string (p_type
                        , dbms_random.value (p_minlen, p_maxlen));
    return l_retval;
end;
```

Here is how we use this function to generate a random string of a random value between 3 and 13 characters:

```
SQL> select get_random_string(3,13,'a') from dual;
GET_RANDOM_STRING(3,13,'A')
---------------------------------------------------
LszXXmgGGJK
```

Calling it once more:

```
SQL> select get_random_string(3,13,'a') from dual;
GET_RANDOM_STRING(3,13,'A')
---------------------------------------------------
rTZVn
```

As you can see, not only is the string random, its length is random as well. Now we have all the tools in place to redact the data.

The View for Redaction

Now we can build the redaction solution using the view. Remember, this solution will work with any version of Oracle and without the need for any expensive option or pack.

1. As the user SCOTT, revoke access to the table from HR:

```
SQL> conn scott/tiger
Connected.
SQL> revoke select on emp from hr;
Revoke succeeded.
```

2. Create a view called, say, VW_EMP_REDACTED, to show the data as redacted:

```
create or replace view vw_emp_redacted
as
  select empno,
    cast(get_random_string(3,10,'a') as varchar2(10)) as ename,
    job,
    mgr,
    to_date(to_char(hiredate,'dd-mon')
    ||'-1900','dd-mon-yyyy') as hiredate,
    get_num(3000,1000)        as sal,
    comm,
    deptno
  from emp;
```

3. Grant SELECT on this view to HR user:

```
Grant select, update, insert, delete on vw_emp_redacted to hr;
```

NOTE
It is very important to revoke the privilege from the main table and grant it on the view. The redaction occurs in the view, and the only way to make sure the user experiences it is by selecting from the view, not from the table accidentally.

4. For the HR user, create a synonym to point to the view:

```
SQL> conn hr/hr
Connected.
SQL> create synonym emp for scott.vw_emp_redacted;
Synonym created.
```

5. If the HR user does not do anything other than SELECT from the view, there is nothing else to do. Connecting as the HR user, execute a SELECT:

```
SQL> select * from emp;
     EMPNO ENAME         JOB         MGR HIREDATE      SAL       COMM     DEPTNO
---------- ---------- ---------- ----- --------- ------- ---------- ----------
      7369 wgquNdu       CLERK      7902 17-DEC-00    2132                    20
      7499 ZZxFP         SALESMAN   7698 20-FEB-00    2770        300         30
      7521 nanfB         SALESMAN   7698 22-FEB-00    1789        500         30
```

```
      7566 yAVIH         MANAGER      7839 02-APR-00    2606                        20
      7654 oFPXYQQWk     SALESMAN     7698 28-SEP-00    1804          1400          30
      7698 CMD           MANAGER      7839 01-MAY-00    1253                        30
      7782 KwfpE         MANAGER      7839 09-JUN-00    2100                        10
      7788 FewCzBDWj     ANALYST      7566 19-APR-00    2336                        20
      7839 xxOVleg       PRESIDENT         17-NOV-00    2656                        10
      7844 AiHkauf       SALESMAN     7698 08-SEP-00    1452             0          30
      7876 khyTB         CLERK        7788 23-MAY-00    1682                        20
      7900 ZUmFTB        CLERK        7698 03-DEC-00    1023                        30
      7902 aYr           ANALYST      7566 03-DEC-00    2789                        20
      7934 nJqnkcgZb     CLERK        7782 23-JAN-00    1536                        10
14 rows selected.
```

6. You may want to compare that against the actual table. Connecting as the SCOTT user, execute the same SELECT statement:

```
SQL> select * from emp;
    EMPNO ENAME        JOB          MGR HIREDATE      SAL       COMM     DEPTNO
---------- ---------- --------- ----- --------- ------- ---------- ----------
      7369 SMITH        CLERK        7902 17-DEC-80     800                     20
      7499 ALLEN        SALESMAN     7698 20-FEB-81    1600         300         30
      7521 WARD         SALESMAN     7698 22-FEB-81    1250         500         30
      7566 JONES        MANAGER      7839 02-APR-81    2975                     20
      7654 MARTIN       SALESMAN     7698 28-SEP-81    1250        1400         30
      7698 BLAKE        MANAGER      7839 01-MAY-81    2850                     30
      7782 CLARK        MANAGER      7839 09-JUN-81    2450                     10
      7788 SCOTT        ANALYST      7566 19-APR-87    3000                     20
      7839 KING         PRESIDENT         17-NOV-81    5000                     10
      7844 TURNER       SALESMAN     7698 08-SEP-81    1500           0         30
      7876 ADAMS        CLERK        7788 23-MAY-87    1100                     20
      7900 JAMES        CLERK        7698 03-DEC-81     950                     30
      7902 FORD         ANALYST      7566 03-DEC-81    3000                     20
      7934 MILLER       CLERK        7782 23-JAN-82    1300                     10
14 rows selected.
```

7. If you want the user to update, delete, or insert on this view, you need to create an INSTEAD OF trigger on this view, which will perform the appropriate actions on the actual table. Here is the trigger code:

```
create or replace trigger tr_io_vw_emp_red instead of
  insert or
  update or
  delete on vw_emp_redacted
begin
if (inserting) then
  insert
  into emp values
    (
      :new.empno,
      :new.ename,
      :new.job,
      :new.mgr,
      :new.hiredate,
      :new.sal,
      :new.comm,
```

```
      :new.deptno
    );
elsif (deleting) then
  delete emp where empno = :old.empno;
elsif (updating) then
  update emp
  set ename   = :new.ename,
    job       = :new.job,
    mgr       = :new.mgr,
    hiredate  = :new.hiredate,
    sal       = :new.sal,
    comm      = :new.comm,
    deptno    = :new.deptno
  where empno = :new.empno;
else
  null;
end if;
end;
```

8. With this in place, let's test an update. First, as SCOTT, let's see the actual value:

```
SQL> select sal, comm from emp where empno = 7902;
     SAL       COMM
---------- ----------
     3000
```

9. Then, as HR user, let's update it:

```
SQL> conn hr/hr
SQL> update emp set sal = 2250 where empno = 7902;
1 row updated.
SQL> commit;
Commit complete.
```

10. Check from SCOTT (so that it's not redacted):

```
SQL> conn scott/tiger
SQL> select sal, comm from emp where empno = 7902;
     SAL       COMM
---------- ----------
     2250
```

11. Check again from HR:

```
SQL> conn hr/hr
SQL> select sal, comm from emp where empno = 7902;
     SAL       COMM
---------- ----------
     1298
```

The value is 1298, which is a completely random value because the HR user is not supposed to see the actual value. Earlier we checked via SCOTT whether the actual value in the table is 2250, as updated by HR. Therefore, although HR is allowed to update the table, HR is not supposed to see the actual value. We just made sure that is indeed the case.

12. Similarly, you can test the DELETE and INSERT statements as well. That's it! You are done.

This exercise shows you a way to provide a complete redaction and masking solution using only PL/SQL. We have shown only a simple rudimentary masking of data. You can make the masking solution as complex as you want so it is as close to your specific requirements as possible.

NOTE
If you want to show some sensitive columns merely as NULL and not altered in any other way, there is a much easier way to do that using Virtual Private Database, which you will learn about in Chapter 15.

Cleanup

Before ending the section, let's drop all the new objects created and clean up anything we introduced earlier:

```
drop function get_num
/
drop function get_random_string
/
drop view vw_emp_redacted
/
```

The INSTEAD OF triggers will be automatically dropped when the view is dropped.

Redaction and Masking Pack

The PL/SQL-based solution is effective for many purposes, but it requires you to create the view and revoke the privileges on the original table. This may not be acceptable to many organizations. Oracle Database 12c introduced a new Redaction and Masking Pack as an extra-cost option that performs the redaction and masking at the SQL layer. This makes the SQL layer execute the masking automatically on the SQL statements against the table without the need to create a view. All you have to do is define a "masking policy" on the table. In that policy you specify the columns, the type of masking, and so on. Let's see how that works using an example—on the same EMP table with the same requirements as shown earlier. Table 13-3 details the requirements once again.

Column Name	How to Mask the Values	Example Output
ENAME	Random characters with no numeric value. Random length.	**KXPWD**
HIREDATE	The date and month of hiring should be visible, but the year should be updated to 1900.	**17-DEC-1980** should become **17-DEC-1900**
SAL	Any random number between 0 and 1000.	**500**

TABLE 13-3. *Requirements for Masking the EMP Table*

Let's create a policy on the table on the first column to be masked—ENAME. You can define the policy on one column at a time. Here is the code to do that:

```
begin
    dbms_redact.add_policy (
            object_schema      => 'SCOTT',
            object_name        => 'EMP',
            policy_name        => 'Employee Mask',
            expression         => 'SYS_CONTEXT(''USERENV'',''CURRENT_
USER'')!=''SCOTT''',
            column_name        => 'ENAME',
            function_type      => dbms_redact.random,
            policy_description    => 'Emp Masking Policy',
            column_description    => 'Employee Name. Full Random'
    );
end;
```

Table 13-4 explains the parameters. Once the policy is created, we will add the other two columns using the **alter_policy** procedure available in the same package:

```
begin
    dbms_redact.alter_policy (
            object_schema        => 'SCOTT',
            object_name          => 'EMP',
            policy_name          => 'Employee Mask',
            action               => dbms_redact.add_column,
            column_name          => 'HIREDATE',
            function_type        => dbms_redact.partial,
            function_parameters  => 'MDy1900'
    );
end;
```

Most of the parameters for this procedure have already been described. Table 13-5 explains the others.

Finally, we will add the third column—SAL—to the policy as follows:

```
begin
    dbms_redact.alter_policy (
            object_schema    => 'SCOTT',
            object_name      => 'EMP',
            policy_name      => 'Employee Mask',
            action           => dbms_redact.add_column,
            column_name      => 'SAL',
            function_type    => dbms_redact.random
    );
end;
```

Parameter Name	Description
object_schema	Schema where the table is located.
object_name	The table name.
policy_name	Name of the policy. Choose a name that represents the policy correctly.
expression	When the data is to be redacted. This is a logical expression that should evaluate to TRUE or FALSE at run time. In this case, we want redaction to be applied only when other users select the data. When the owner—SCOTT—selects, we do not want the redaction to apply. Hence, we have put in an expression that returns FALSE when SCOTT logs in and TRUE for the rest of the cases. Therefore, the data will not be redacted when SCOTT manipulates the data.
column_name	The column that needs to be masked.
function_type	The type of masking to be applied. In this case, we have mentioned that it should be a random value; that is, the ENAME column should show some random strings not dependent on the original values.
policy_description	Choose a description to document the purpose of the policy.
column_description	The description of the redaction applied on the column. Remember, the policy is for the entire table, which may have more than one column.

TABLE 13-4. *Parameters of ADD_POLICY()*

Parameter Name	Description
action	This designates the action to be performed. For instance, in this case, it shows **add_column**; that is, the objective of this execution is to add a column to the policy named ENAME Mask.
function_type	This was explained earlier. However, unlike in the earlier invocation, this **function_type** shows partial redaction, that is, masking only part of the value, not the entire value. The exact pattern to apply to the original value is governed by the next parameter.
function_parameters	This parameter governs how the pattern has to be applied. In this case, it is **MDy1900**, which means keep the month (M) and day (D) as they were but change the year (y) to 1900. We will explore more options for this parameter later in this section.

TABLE 13-5. *Additional Parameters of ALTER_POLICY()*

After the policy is placed on the table, when a user selects from it, he will get the masked values:

```
SQL> conn hr/hr
SQL> select * from scott.emp;
```

```
    EMPNO ENAME       JOB          MGR HIREDATE      SAL       COMM     DEPTNO
---------- ---------- --------- ----- --------- ------- ---------- ----------
     7369 @}Nxd       CLERK       7902 17-DEC-00      51                    20
     7499 mC4xy       SALESMAN    7698 20-FEB-00     932        300         30
     7521 xRL]        SALESMAN    7698 22-FEB-00     962        500         30
     7566 S |:U       MANAGER     7839 02-APR-00    2261                    20
     7654 U!bid_      SALESMAN    7698 28-SEP-00     707       1400         30
     7698 1du/O       MANAGER     7839 01-MAY-00    2123                    30
     7782 Ig$$s       MANAGER     7839 09-JUN-00    1028                    10
     7788 [$`1/       ANALYST     7566 19-APR-00    1723                    20
     7839 )QLk        PRESIDENT        17-NOV-00     791                    10
     7844 r%o){       SALESMAN    7698 08-SEP-00       5          0         30
     7876 yk 4z       CLERK       7788 23-MAY-00     697                    20
     7900 Prc9S       CLERK       7698 03-DEC-00     142                    30
     7902 y%KY(       ANALYST     7566 03-DEC-00     420                    20
     7934 bNGaAk      CLERK       7782 23-JAN-00     875                    10
14 rows selected.
```

But when SCOTT selects from it, he will get the real values. This should be sufficient for many cases.

Fixed Values

You just saw a tiny glimpse of the power of the redaction package. Before examining the remaining features, let's cover another important variation. In the previous example, the values are randomized; that is, every time you select the SAL column for a specific employee, you will get a different, random value. What if that is not something you want? Perhaps all you want is to mask the value (that is, replace with some number that does not represent the actual salary of the employee). It's possible to get a fixed value from the package instead of an always-randomized value. The trick is to set a different value for a parameter while calling the package. Here is how we called it earlier:

```
function_type    => dbms_redact.random
```

Instead, we will need to call the following:

```
function_type    => dbms_redact.full
```

To set this new value, we need to first drop the policy before re-creating it. Or, we could just modify the policy to set the **function_type** parameter to the new value, as shown here:

```
begin
    dbms_redact.alter_policy (
            object_schema    => 'SCOTT',
            object_name      => 'EMP',
```

```
            policy_name      => 'Employee Mask',
            action           => dbms_redact.modify_column,
            column_name      => 'SAL',
            function_type    => dbms_redact.full
    );
end;
```

After this change, when the HR user selects the SAL column, the SAL column comes back as 0 instead of a random number, as shown here:

```
SQL> conn hr/hr
SQL> select sal from scott.emp;

       SAL
----------
         0
         0
… output truncated …
14 rows selected.
```

This may make sense for some types of applications where you need to set a fixed value for masking. The columns with the NUMBER data type show up as 0; the VARCHAR2 columns will show up as NULL.

Other Types of Redaction

Earlier in the chapter you witnessed only a few of the entire gamut of capabilities of the redaction package. We've only scratched the surface. Let's explore other features. To fully demonstrate the features, we will create a table to hold bank account information in the SCOTT schema:

```
create table accounts
   (
    accno         number,
    accname       varchar2(30) not null primary key,
    ssn           varchar2(9),
    phone         varchar2(12),
    email         varchar2(30),
    last_trans_dt date
   );
```

Before proceeding, it would be prudent to explain what these columns are. ACCNO and ACCNAME are pretty self-explanatory; they represent the number and name of the account holder, respectively. The SSN column represents the Social Security Number in the United States, which is a nine-digit number that may begin with a zero. This is a unique identifier for citizens and legal residents of the United States. Other countries have similar identifiers. We will explore them later in the chapter. The column PHONE represents the telephone number of the account holder, which is in the U.S. format of 999-999-9999. Other countries may have different formats, and we will explore them later. The column EMAIL is pretty standard. It has two parts joined by the "@" character. The column LAST_TRANS_DT shows the date and time of the last transaction made by the account holder.

Let's insert some rows into this table:

```
insert into accounts values (
   123456,
   'Arup Nanda',
   '123456789',
   '203-555-1212',
   'arup@proligence.com',
   to_date('10-JUL-2015 15:12:33','dd-MON-YYYY hh24:MI:SS')
)
/
insert into accounts values (
   234567,
   'Heli Helskyaho',
   '234567890',
   '516-555-1212',
   'heli.helskyaho@miracleoy.fi',
   to_date('11-JUL-2015 12:11:23','dd-MON-YYYY hh24:MI:SS')
)
/
insert into accounts values (
   345678,
   'Martin Widlake',
   '345678901',
   '201-555-1213',
   'mwidlake@btinternet.com',
   to_date('12-JUL-2015 11:21:35','dd-MON-YYYY hh24:MI:SS')
)
/
insert into accounts values (
   456789,
   'Alex Nuijten',
   '456789012',
   '212-555-2134',
   'alexnuijten@gmail.com',
   to_date('13-JUL-2015 21:15:21','dd-MON-YYYY hh24:MI:SS')
)
/
insert into accounts values (
   567890,
   'Brendan Tierney',
   '567890123',
   '860-555-3138',
   'brendan.tierney@oralytics.com',
   to_date('14-JUL-2015 18:34:32','dd-MON-YYYY hh24:MI:SS')
)
/
commit
/
```

Let's select to make sure we got all the values right:

```
SQL> select * from accounts;

  ACCNO ACCNAME           SSN       PHONE        EMAIL                       LAST_TRAN
-------- ----------------  --------- ------------ --------------------------- ----------
  123456 Arup Nanda        123456789 203-555-1212 arup@proligence.com         10-JUL-15
  234567 Heli Helskyaho    234567890 516-555-1212 heli.helskyaho@miracleoy.fi 11-JUL-15
  345678 Martin Widlake    345678901 201-555-1213 mwidlake@btinternet.com     12-JUL-15
  456789 Alex Nuijten      456789012 212-555-2134 alexnuijten@gmail.com       13-JUL-15
  567890 Brendan Tierney   567890123 860-555-3138 brendan.tierney@oralytics.com 14-JUL-15
```

Since we will need to test with a different user—not the owner SCOTT—accessing the table, let's grant the privileges on the table to the user HR:

```
grant select, insert, update, delete on accounts to hr;
```

With this in place, let's put in some complex rules for redactions. Table 13-6 shows how we want redaction for the columns of this new table, ACCOUNTS.

The package DBMS_REDACT makes it simple and easy to bring these requirements into reality. The **function_type** parameter in the **add_policy** procedure we used earlier can be used to create all types of interesting and complex masks to hide the original. Take, for instance, the requirement to mask the SSN column. It has nine numbers. Our objective is to hide the first five numbers (that is, from position 1 through position 5) and replace them with *. The **function_parameters** parameter

Column	Redaction Method	Example After Redaction
ACCNO	No redaction.	
ACCNAME	Full redaction with random characters.	**Q@FRCV^&**
SSN	Only last four digits are to be displayed; all others should be replaced by *.	**123456789** is displayed as *******6789**
PHONE	Only the first three numbers (usually an area code in the U.S.) should be displayed. The rest should be replaced by X, and the overall length should be retained.	**203-555-1234** may be displayed as **203-XXX-XXXX**
EMAIL	The first part of the e-mail (that is, before the @ sign) should be redacted, and the domain name (that is, the part after the @ sign) should be left intact.	**arup@proligence.com** should be displayed as **XXXX@proligence.com**
LAST_TRANS_DT	The year should be masked to 1900. The month and date should remain as is.	**12-JAN-2015** should be **12-JAN-1900**

TABLE 13-6.   *Redaction Requirements for ACCOUNTS Table*

accepts a string that tells the redaction function how to do it. This string has five parts, separated by commas:

- The type of characters in the original value. In this case, the original value is composed of nine numbers. Therefore, this part is written as nine V's (that is, VVVVVVVVV).

- What positions to consider for display. In this case, we want to display all nine numbers (although some will be masked). Therefore, we employ the same value we used earlier (that is, VVVVVVVVV).

- The character to be used for masking (in this case, *).

- The first position where the masking begins. In this case, we want to start masking at the first character, so this value is 1.

- The last position the masking should continue to. In this case, it should be the fifth position, so this value needs to be 5.

This is how the final value of the **function_parameters** parameter looks like:

```
function_parameters => 'VVVVVVVVV,VVVVVVVVV,*,1,5'
```

With this in place, we can create the policy. This should be performed by a privileged user, not the owner of the table that needs to be redacted. For simplicity, we will use the SYS schema:

```
begin
    dbms_redact.add_policy (
        object_schema       => 'SCOTT',
        object_name         => 'ACCOUNTS',
        policy_name         => 'ACCOUNTS_Redaction',
        expression   => 'SYS_CONTEXT(''USERENV'',''CURRENT_USER'') != ''SCOTT''',
        column_name         => 'SSN',
        function_type       => dbms_redact.partial,
        function_parameters => 'VVVVVVVVV,VVVVVVVVV,*,1,5'
    );
END;
```

Now we will add the other columns to this policy. The next column to add is the LAST_TRANS_DT column. Because this is a DATE data type, the **function_parameters** value has to be in that context. The value takes M, Y, and D for month, year, and date, without any changes. If you need to change any one, you should use **m**, **y**, and **d** instead and put the new value right alongside. For instance, in this case we have to preserve the month and day, but the year should be masked to 1900. Here is how it would look:

```
function_parameters => 'MDy1900'
```

We use this format to add the column to the policy:

```
begin
    dbms_redact.alter_policy (
        object_schema       => 'SCOTT',
        object_name         => 'ACCOUNTS',
        policy_name         => 'ACCOUNTS_Redaction',
```

```
        action              => dbms_redact.add_column,
        column_name         => 'LAST_TRANS_DT',
        function_type       => dbms_redact.partial,
        function_parameters => 'MDy1900'
    );
end;
```

Next, let's take the phone number. It's similar to the SSN column for masking, but with a slight twist. Unlike the SSN column, this phone number column has hyphens between the different parts of the number. We have to make sure we don't count them as characters to be redacted. To make sure the redaction procedure understands the difference between a value and filler such as hyphens or spaces, we need to use the special character F. Because it's a set of 10 numbers with three hyphens, we will make the first value VVVFVVVFVVVV. Note how fillers are placed at the appropriate positions. It does not matter what the filler character is. In this case it happens to be a hyphen (-), but it could be anything: a period (.), a space ( ), a forward slash (/), or any other character.

For the second value, we need to reproduce all the characters, even though some will be masked. We will also use the hyphen (-) as the delimiter. Therefore, the second part should be VVV-VVV-VVVV. The masking character, from the requirements, is *X*, so we will use that character as the third value.

We need to mask all characters except the first three (that is, positions 4 through 10). Therefore, for the fourth and fifth values, we will use 4 and 10, respectively. Here is what the final **function_parameters** value looks like:

```
function_parameters => 'VVVFVVVFVVVV,VVV-VVV-VVVV,X,4,10'
```

And here is the complete code block to add this column to the policy:

```
begin
    dbms_redact.alter_policy (
        object_schema       => 'SCOTT',
        object_name         => 'ACCOUNTS',
        policy_name         => 'ACCOUNTS_Redaction',
        action              => dbms_redact.add_column,
        column_name         => 'PHONE',
        function_type       => dbms_redact.partial,
        function_parameters => 'VVVFVVVFVVVV,VVV-VVV-VVVV,X,4,10'
    );
end;
```

Next, let's take a more complex requirement—masking the EMAIL column. We need to make sure we identify the two different parts of the e-mail address on either side of the @ character. The filler we used earlier will not work in this case because the filler is a character, as are all the other characters of the value. Fortunately, the package provides a special value for the **function_type** to analyze regular expressions in the values. We need to set the value of **function_type** to **dbms_redact.regexp**, as shown here:

```
function_type => dbms_redact.regexp
```

Because e-mail addresses are often masked, the package provides built-in mechanisms to use regular expressions for masking them. We can let the package know that by setting the following value:

```
regexp_pattern => dbms_redact.re_pattern_email_address
```

Our objective is to redact the first part of the e-mail address. Here are the parameters you need to set for the policy procedure:

```
regexp_replace_string => dbms_redact.re_redact_email_name,
regexp_position       => dbms_redact.re_beginning,
regexp_occurrence     => dbms_redact.re_all
```

Here is how the complete **alter_policy()** procedure looks now:

```
begin
    dbms_redact.alter_policy (
        object_schema         => 'SCOTT',
        object_name           => 'ACCOUNTS',
        policy_name           => 'ACCOUNTS_Redaction',
        action                => dbms_redact.add_column,
        column_name           => 'EMAIL',
        function_type         => dbms_redact.regexp,
        regexp_pattern        => dbms_redact.re_pattern_email_address,
        regexp_replace_string => dbms_redact.re_redact_email_name,
        regexp_position       => dbms_redact.re_beginning,
        regexp_occurrence     => dbms_redact.re_all
    );
end;
```

Finally, we will add the complete random redaction for the ACCNAME column:

```
begin
     dbms_redact.alter_policy (
         object_schema => 'SCOTT',
         object_name   => 'ACCOUNTS',
         policy_name   => 'ACCOUNTS_Redaction',
         action        => dbms_redact.add_column,
         column_name   => 'ACCNAME',
         function_type => dbms_redact.random
     );
  end;
```

After you execute the procedures, log in as the HR user and select from this table. Here is what you will see:

```
SQL> conn hr/hr
SQL> select * from scott.accounts;
```

ACCNO	ACCNAME	SSN	PHONE	EMAIL	LAST_TRAN
123456	x6xKvA|\!>	*****6789	203-XXX-XXXX	xxxx@proligence.com	10-JUL-00

```
234567  EHC-/s%0MPK57{    *****7890 516-XXX-XXXX xxxx@miracleoy.fi   11-JUL-00
345678  76?O7+-[?>GW?3    *****8901 201-XXX-XXXX xxxx@btinternet.com 12-JUL-00
456789  'L\90%[[/TdA      *****9012 212-XXX-XXXX xxxx@gmail.com      13-JUL-00
567890  7<])b@2Z?De1jH:   *****0123 860-XXX-XXXX xxxx@oralytics.com  14-JUL-00
```

We did it! We created the masking solution on this table as per the requirements.

The regular expression syntax is pretty powerful because it's flexible. Anything that can be used to match a regular expression syntax in Oracle can be used. You should follow this set of rules in that case:

1. Set **function_type** to **dbms_redact.regexp**.

2. Omit specifying anything for **function_parameters**.

3. Set the regex-specific parameters: **regexp_pattern**, **regexp_replace_string**, **regexp_position**, **regexp_occurrence**, and **regexp_match_parameter**.

Table 13-7 shows the settings for the regex-specific parameters.

Parameter	Description
regexp_position	The position where the pattern matching should start in the input value. Remember, the first position is counted as 1.
regexp_occurrence	How many occurrences of the pattern to be searched for. For instance, if we want to replace @ by at in the input value, should we do that for all instances of @ or just the first one? If set to 1, it will replace only the first occurrence. Setting it to 2 will replace the second occurrence only, leaving the first one. If you need to replace all occurrences, set this to 0.
regexp_pattern	The pattern to be searched, in regular expression format. Should be a maximum of 512 bytes.
regexp_replace_string	The replacement pattern in regular expression format, up to a maximum length of 4000 characters.
regexp_match_parameter	This parameter specifies how to match the pattern. Here are the possible values and their behavior: **i** Pattern matching is case insensitive. **c** Pattern matching is case sensitive. **n** The period character (.) is a wildcard character in regular expressions. It matches any character but not the newline. If you set this value to **n**, the newline character is also matched by ".". **m** If your input has multiple lines, then Oracle treats the entire input as a single line unless the regex-specific characters ^ and $ are used for the beginning and the end of lines, respectively. Specifying this parameter as **m** treats each line as a separate line. **x** Ignores the whitespace as characters to match. You can specify multiple values in the parameter. Here's an example to specify both case-insensitive matching and the period character to match any character, including newlines: `regexp_match_parameter => 'ni'`

TABLE 13-7. *Specific Parameters for Regular Expression-Based Redactions*

If you are daunted by the complex rules of the regular expression syntax to define the redaction policies, don't worry. Oracle has provided a lot of built-in formats for common use cases to redact familiar types of data. The current example shows one such type of built-in pattern matching. Here is how we defined the policy for the EMAIL column:

```
function_type          => dbms_redact.regexp,
regexp_pattern         => dbms_redact.re_pattern_email_address,
regexp_replace_string  => dbms_redact.re_redact_email_name,
regexp_position        => dbms_redact.re_beginning,
regexp_occurrence      => dbms_redact.re_all
```

The EMAIL column is masked by a built-in:

```
regexp_pattern         => dbms_redact.re_pattern_email_address,
regexp_replace_string  => dbms_redact.re_redact_email_name,
```

In reality, here are the actual parameters used in the **add_policy** procedure:

```
regex_pattern          => '([A-Za-z0-9._%+-]+)@([A-Za-z0-9.-]+\.[A-Za-z]{2,4})'
regex_replace_string   => ' xxxx@\2'
```

If you examine these carefully, you will be able to notice the regular expression syntax to identify various parts of the e-mail address. But rather than you writing this complex syntax, you simply used the user-friendly constant **re_pattern_email_address** provided in the DBMS_REDACT package.

Table 13-8 shows the built-ins you can use for the value of the **function_parameters** parameter.

Built-in	Description	Example
redact_us_ssn_f5	Masks the first five numbers of the U.S. Social Security Number.	**123-45-6789 becomes XXX-XX-6789**
redact_us_ssn_l4	Masks the last four numbers of the U.S. SSN.	**123-45-6789 becomes 123-45-XXXX**
redact_us_ssn_entire	Masks all the numbers of the U.S. SSN.	**123-45-6789 becomes XXX-XX-XXXX**
redact_num_us_ssn_f5	Masks the first five numbers of the U.S. SSN when the input is a number. Output is still VARCHAR2.	**123456789 becomes XXXXX6789**
redact_num_us_ssn_l4	Masks the last four numbers of the U.S. SSN when the input is a number. Output is still VARCHAR2.	**123456789 becomes 12345XXXX**

TABLE 13-8. *Built-ins for Function Types* (Continues)

Built-in	Description	Example
redact_num_us_ssn_ entire	Masks the entire U.S. SSN.	**123456789** becomes **XXXXXXXXX**
redact_zip_code	Masks the five-digit U.S. ZIP code when the input is a VARCHAR2.	**12345** becomes **XXXXX**
redact_num_zip_code	Masks the five-digit U.S. ZIP code when the input is a NUMBER.	**12345** becomes **XXXXX**
redact_ccn16_f12	Masks the first 12 digits of a 16-digit credit card number.	**1234 5678 9012 3456** becomes ******_****_****_ 3456**
redact_date_ millennium	Masks the input date value with a constant— the beginning of the millennium.	All dates become **01-JAN-2000**
redact_date_epoch	Masks all dates with 01-JAN-70.	

TABLE 13-8. *Built-ins for Function Types*

As you can see, you don't have to reinvent the wheel for many of the common types of data in need of redaction. The package already provides for them using the built-ins. For instance, in our previous example we used the following for masking the SSN:

```
function_parameters => 'VVVVVVVVV,VVVVVVVVV,X,1,5'
```

We could have used this instead:

```
function_parameters => dbms_redact.redact_us_ssn_f5
```

Credit card numbers are a good example. If we used

```
function_parameters  => dbms_redact.redact_ccn16_f12
```

to mask credit cards, the following would have been used internally:

```
function_parameters  => 'VVVVFVVVVFVVVVFVVVV,VVVV-VVVV-VVVV-VVVV,*,1,12',
```

These built-ins are beneficial when you use the most common types of data to be redacted. However, they don't cover all the different types of data that may need to be redacted. E-mail is such a type. Or, they may not display the way you want them to. For instance, instead of masking the first 12 numbers of a credit card, you may want to show the first six digits (which generally specify the issuing bank) and the last four digits while masking the rest of the data. You can write regex-style redaction parameters. Fortunately, Oracle provides more built-ins for the regular expression parameters. When the **function_type** parameter is set to DBMS_REDACT.regexp, you can use the following combinations for the parameters **regexp_pattern** and **regexp_replace_string**:

1. To replace any digit with 1, set the following:

    ```
    regexp_pattern          => dbms_redact.re_pattern_any_digit
    regexp_replace_string => dbms_redact.re_redact_with_single_1
    ```

2. To replace any digit with X, set the following:

    ```
    regexp_pattern          => dbms_redact.re_pattern_any_digit
    regexp_replace_string => dbms_redact.re_redact_with_single_x
    ```

3. Here is how to display the first six and last four digits of a 16-digit credit card number and to mask the rest with X:

    ```
    regexp_pattern          => dbms_redact.re_pattern_cc_16_t4
    regexp_replace_string => dbms_redact.re_redact_cc_middle_digits
    ```

4. Here is how to take any U.S. phone number and mask the last seven numbers:

    ```
    regexp_pattern          => dbms_redact.re_pattern_us_phone
    regexp_replace_string => dbms_redact.re_redact_us_phone_l7
    ```

5. We saw an example of the EMAIL redaction earlier, but there is more to it. This sets the input value as an e-mail address:

    ```
    regexp_pattern          => dbms_redact.re_pattern_cc_16_t4
    ```

    ■ To mask only the user name (the part before the @ sign in an e-mail address), set the following:

    ```
    regexp_replace_string => dbms_redact.re_redact_email_name
    ```

    ■ To mask the domain (the part after the @ sign), set the following:

    ```
    regexp_replace_string => dbms_redact.re_redact_email_domain
    ```

    ■ To mask everything in the e-mail address, set the following:

    ```
    regexp_replace_string => re_redact_email_entire
    ```

6. To mask the IP addresses, use the following:

    ```
    regexp_pattern          => dbms_redact.re_pattern_ip_address
    regexp_replace_string => dbms_redact. re_redact_ip_l3
    ```

    This replaces the last section of the IP address with 999.

You can apply these to any suitable type of data. For instance, there is a built-in for credit card numbers, but you can also use the following:

```
regexp_pattern          => dbms_redact.re_pattern_any_digit
regexp_replace_string => dbms_redact.re_redact_with_single_x
```

This will mask any 16-digit or 15-digit credit card. For instance, 1234 5678 9012 3456 will become XXXX XXXX XXXX XXXX. This is how you can mask other types of data for which no built-ins exist yet. For instance, the National Insurance Number is the identifier for healthcare consumers in the United Kingdom. It's a nine-character code usually written in two-character blocks at a time (for example, AB 12 34 56 C). Because it follows the same nine-digit U.S. SSN, you can use the built-in for SSN, or you can use a regular expression to mask parts of it.

SQL Developer Access

You can also create and manage redaction activities via SQL Developer, which may be an easier option for some, being a graphical user interface. In SQL Developer, navigate to the table name and right-click it to bring up the table-specific menu, as shown in Figure 13-1. Click Redaction and then Add/Alter Redaction Polices. This will bring up the redaction policies on the table already, as shown in Figure 13-2. Note that the SCOTT user should have the privilege to select from two views. If it doesn't, you will get an error. Execute the two statements shown next to grant the privileges.

```
grant select on sys.redaction_policies to scott;
grant select on sys.redaction_columns to scott;
```

These grants are needed only for the SQL Developer interface. In the SQL*Plus examples shown earlier, you had connected as the SYS user, which already has these privileges.

Notice the tab named SQL in Figure 13-2. If you click it, you will see the PL/SQL block to execute that action. This is helpful if you don't remember the syntax or are too lazy to type it. This is also useful for putting the PL/SQL code in a script to be deployed to a different database as a part of structured code deployment not possible through a GUI interface.

Looking at Figure 13-1, you'll notice the other things you can do with the Redaction menu—namely, you can enable or disable a policy as well as drop it.

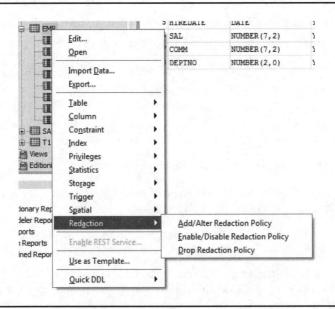

FIGURE 13-1. *Redaction menu in SQL Developer*

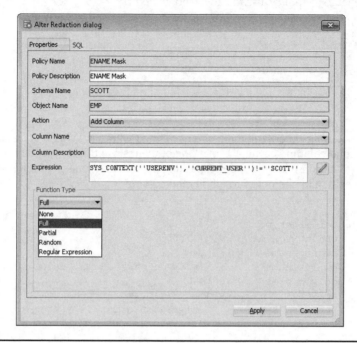

FIGURE 13-2. *Main panel of redaction*

Policy Administration

If you want to temporarily allow everyone to see the actual values and not mask anything, you can disable the policy. This does not drop the policy; it just disables its effect. When you want to start masking again, you can just enable it, like so:

```
begin
    dbms_redact.disable_policy (
            object_schema    => 'SCOTT',
            object_name      => 'EMP',
            policy_name      => 'Employee Mask'
    );
end;
```

After this, if you check the table as the HR user, you can see all the values came up as present:

```
SQL> select ename, hiredate, sal from scott.emp;
ENAME        HIREDATE        SAL
----------   ---------   ----------
SMITH        17-DEC-80       800
ALLEN        20-FEB-81      1600
WARD         22-FEB-81      1250
... output truncated ...
```

To re-enable the policy, use the code shown here:

```
begin
    dbms_redact.enable_policy (
            object_schema    => 'SCOTT',
            object_name      => 'EMP',
            policy_name      => 'Employee Mask'
    );
end;
```

Enabling a policy masks all the columns defined within it. What if you just want to suppress masking of one column, leaving the masking of the rest? In this case, disabling the policy is not going to work because it will suppress masking of all the columns and not just one. Therefore, you will need to alter the policy to modify the column:

```
begin
    dbms_redact.alter_policy (
            object_schema    => 'SCOTT',
            object_name      => 'EMP',
            policy_name      => 'Employee Mask',
            column_name      => 'SAL',
            action           => dbms_redact.modify_column,
            function_type    => dbms_redact.none
    );
end;
```

Setting the value of the **function_type** parameter to **dbms_redact.none** does the trick. With this in place, when the HR user selects from the table:

```
SQL> select ename, hiredate, sal from scott.emp;

ENAME       HIREDATE        SAL
----------  ---------   ----------
VP, !W      17-DEC-00        800
03Xy@       20-FEB-00       1600
Q=1R        22-FEB-00       1250
... output truncated ...
```

the ENAME and HIREDATE columns have been masked, but not the SAL column, which shows the actual value.

Note that you can perform these activities using SQL Developer as well.

Cleanup

Before ending the section, let's drop all the new objects created and clean up anything we introduced earlier:

```
drop table accounts
/
```

Summary

In many cases you may want to hide the actual data in the database from some users. When these "nonprivileged" users select the data, you want them to see a masked (or redacted) representation of the data such as X's instead of characters, or random values instead of actual values, or just blanks in some cases. The key to this requirement is that the data itself is not updated in the database. When the privileged users select the data, they should see the actual values. It differs from encryption (which you will learn about in Chapter 14), where the data is actually updated in the database itself.

In this chapter you learned how to develop such a mechanism using plain PL/SQL, which works in all versions of Oracle without any special options, and using the DBMS_REDACT package, which is available as an extra-cost option only in Oracle 12c. Using DBMS_REDACT allows you to create "policies" that specify the particulars of the redaction for the columns of the table. You can disable policies temporarily to allow clear data to be seen, or you can disable the redaction on specific columns. Clearly the redaction package gives you an advantage because it intercepts the SQL access directly. Your own solution with PL/SQL requires you to filter the access through a view, which may create its own complexities. In the end, you will need to balance the extra cost of the package with the added management overhead of your homegrown solution.

CHAPTER
14

Encryption and Hashing

What is the biggest threat to data security? It's often believed to be hackers who break into the database using various forms of authentication hacks or man-in-the-middle attacks, stealing data by the shovelfuls. While these threats do occur, it's not correct to say that this is the usual cause of database leaks. History has shown that the biggest threat to the database comes from insiders who have more privileges than they actually need to do their job, either because of lazy administrators or privilege escalations. You will learn how to reduce the possibility of privilege abuse in Chapter 15. The second-biggest threat comes from stolen backups. Consider this: a thief steals your backup tapes, mounts them on a server, and starts the recovery process. The thief does not need to know the password; being the "oracle" user in that server with the "dba" group gives the thief the ability to connect as SYS without a password using the very simple **sqlplus / as sysdba**. Once the database is restored, the thief gets access to all the data, including sensitive data such as credit card numbers, names, diseases, convictions, and so on. Here are the important points about this vulnerability:

- Even if you find out about the theft, you can do nothing about protecting the data. The thief can do everything on the remote server at his leisure. The data is lost—forever.

- Any kind of strong password and complex authentication mechanism wouldn't have helped. The thief would have gotten access to the SYS password, thus defeating everything else.

- Any carefully planned authorization models or minimum privilege sets would not have helped either because the thief has the SYSDBA role (that is, the ability to select, update, delete, and insert any table).

In other words, you just suffered an utter defeat. So, how can you protect yourself from such an incident?

This is where encryption comes in. If you alter the actual data stored on the disks, which can be deciphered only by those who have knowledge of the deciphering mechanism, the thief who stole the backup will be stopped. At that time, the "deciphering knowledge" is needed to see the actual data for any user, including the SYS user. Therefore, unless that knowledge is available to him, the thief is left with nothing but completely useless information. If you store that knowledge separate from the backup or the database itself, you will have accomplished your objective of protecting the data in case of theft. In this chapter, you learn how to build a system for encryption.

What Is Encryption?

In the simplest terms, *encryption* means disguising data, or altering the contents in such a way that only the creator of the original data knows the secret of how to put the data back together again. This is different from redaction, which you learned in Chapter 13. Redaction involves the masking of data, which can be applied to the data to alter it forever or applied during selection so that the data appears to be different, without the original data being altered. Encryption involves actually changing the data. But more than that, encryption allows the owner of the secret to find out what the original value was; no one can decipher the original from the redacted data. This chapter describes Oracle's support for encryption, focusing on the concepts and features of most use to PL/SQL developers.

There are two approaches to building an encryption solution: building your own in the PL/SQL language from scratch using Oracle's built-in package DBMS_CRYPTO, and using Oracle's

Transparent Data Encryption (TDE), which is an extra-cost option. We also focus on the protection of data on disk, as opposed to the protection of data being transmitted between the client and the database, or the protection of data during authentication, both of which require the use of Oracle's extra-cost Advanced Security Option (ASO). The only exception to the rule is the transmission of passwords, which are always encrypted, regardless of the use of ASO.

In this chapter you learn how to build a basic encryption system that will protect sensitive data from access by unauthorized users. You learn how to build a key management system that effectively protects your encryption keys while seamlessly providing the application users unrestrained access to the data. In addition, you learn about cryptographic hashing and the use of message authentication codes (MACs). We also describe Transparent Data Encryption (TDE)—at both the column level and tablespace level. TDE can be used to encrypt sensitive data in a way that allows you to comply with many regulations with the least amount of effort.

This book does not discuss algorithms and the art and science of computer encryption, a field that usually demands much more detailed coverage than this book attempts to accomplish. The objective of this book is to help you start using the built-in tools to create an encryption system—not to reinvent the wheel by writing algorithms.

Introduction to Encryption

It's very hard for me to remember a number such as my ATM card's PIN number, which, by the way, is 3451. If I write it down on a piece of paper, it doesn't really solve the problem because I need to carry the paper along with the ATM card. Therefore, I do the easiest thing—I write it down directly on the ATM card. One day, however, my wallet was stolen. The thief not only found the card but the PIN number as well and pulled all the money out of my account.

I learned my lesson. When I got my new card from the bank, I still wrote down the PIN on it, but not being a complete idiot this time, I didn't write that exact number. Instead, I made up a secret number that I always remember—for example, 6754. Using this number, I modified the PIN by adding the corresponding digits:

3 + 6 = 9
4 + 7 = 11
5 + 5 = 10
1 + 4 = 5

The resulting numbers are 9, 11, 10, and 5. Using my secret key 6754, I transformed the number 3451 into 9-11-10-5, and that's the number I wrote on the ATM card, not the actual PIN. To get the PIN, I just have to read that number and use my magic number 6754 to reverse the logic I applied earlier so I can use the number 3451 to unlock the key. The number 9-11-10-5 is for the whole world to see, but the thief still won't be able to use the card unless he also knows the key, 6754.

What did I just do? I *encrypted* the number, albeit in a very rudimentary manner. The number 6754 is the *key* to the encryption process. This type of encryption I've performed here is known as *symmetric* encryption because the same key is used to encrypt and decrypt. (In contrast, with asymmetric encryption, described later in this chapter, there are two distinct keys: a public key and a private key.) The logic I just described to encrypt the PIN is a very simplistic implementation of an encryption *algorithm*.

Block and Stream Ciphering

Encryption can be performed on a block of data at a time via a process known as *block ciphering*. This method is the most common and the easiest to implement. However, some systems may not have the luxury of getting data in uniform chunks—for example, encrypted content relayed through the public media or other outlets. In such cases, the content must be encrypted as and when it comes in. This is known as *stream ciphering*.

Encryption Components

Let's summarize what we have learned so far. An encryption system has three basic components:

- The algorithm
- The key
- The type of encryption (symmetric, in this case, because the same key is used both to encrypt and to decrypt)

Let's assume that a thief intent on stealing from my account is trying to use the ATM card PIN. What does he need in order to succeed? First, he has to know the algorithm; let's assume here that he knows it, perhaps because I boasted about my cleverness at a party, or he read this book, or this algorithm is public knowledge. Second, he needs to learn the key. That is something I can protect. Even if the thief knows about the algorithm, I can still hide the key and make the security effective. However, because there are only four digits in the key, it takes only up to 10 × 10 × 10 × 10, or 10,000, attempts by the thief to guess the key. And because each attempt has an equal probability of getting it right or wrong, in theory, the thief has a 1 in 5000 chance to guess the right key. It's theoretically possible to know the PIN. Suddenly, I don't feel so secure anymore.

How can I protect my PIN?

- I can hide the algorithm.
- I can make the key difficult to guess.
- Better yet, I can take both of these steps together.

The first option is impossible if I am using a publicly known algorithm. I could develop my own, but the time and effort may not be worth it. It might later be found out anyway, and changing an algorithm is a very difficult, nearly impossible task. That rules out the third option, too, leaving the second option as the only viable one.

The Effect of Key Length

An ATM card PIN is the digital equivalent of sensitive data. If a hacker wants to crack the encrypted key, 10,000 iterations to guess the code is trivial—he'll be able to crack it in under a second. What if I use an alphanumeric key instead of an all-numeric one? That gives 36 possible values for each character of the key, so the hacker will have to guess up to 36 × 36 × 36 × 36, or 1,679,616, combinations—more difficult than 10,000, but still not beyond the reach of even ancient smartphones. The key must be strengthened, or "hardened," by making it longer than four characters. Therefore, the secret to hardening the key is to increase the length of the key. The longer the key, the more difficult it is to crack the encryption. But longer keys also extend the elapsed time needed to do encryption and decryption because the CPU has to do more work. In designing an encryption infrastructure, you may need to make a compromise between key size and reduced security.

Symmetric vs. Asymmetric Encryption

In our earlier example, the same key is used to encrypt and decrypt. As mentioned, this type of encryption is known as *symmetric* encryption. There is an inherent problem with this type of encryption: because the same key is used to decrypt the data, the key must be made known to the recipient. Either the key, which is generally referred to as the *secret key,* has to be known by the recipient before he or she receives the encrypted data (that is, there needs to be a "knowledge-sharing agreement") or the key has to be sent as a part of the data transmission. For data at rest (on disk), the key will have to be stored as a part of the database in order for an application to decrypt it. There are obvious risks in this situation. A key that is being transmitted may be intercepted by a hacker, and a key that is stored in the database may be stolen.

To address this problem, another type of encryption is often used, one in which the key used to encrypt is different from the one used to decrypt. Because the keys differ, this is known as *asymmetric* encryption. Because two keys are generated—a public key and a private key—it is also known as public key encryption. The public key, which is required for the encryption, is made known to the sender and, in fact, can be freely shared. The other key, the private key, is used only to decrypt the data encrypted by the public key and must be kept secret.

Let's see how public key encryption might work in real life. As shown in Figure 14-1, Sam (on the left) is expecting a message from Rita (on the right). Here are the steps in the encryption process:

■ Sam generates two keys—a public key and a private key.

■ He sends the public key to Rita.

■ Rita has an original message in cleartext that she encrypts using the public key, and she sends the encrypted message to Sam.

■ Sam decrypts it using the private key he generated earlier.

Note carefully here that there is no exchange of decryption keys between the parties. The public key is sent to the sender in advance, but because that is not what is needed to decrypt the value, it does not pose a threat from a potential key theft.

However, you should be aware of the effect of spoofing in this process, which can render this process of data encryption insecure. Here is a scenario:

■ Sam generates a public and private key pair and hands the public key over to Rita.

■ A hacker is sniffing the communication line and obtains Sam's public key. Sometimes that's not even necessary since the public key may have been made available to the public anyway.

■ The hacker creates another public-private key pair with his software (using Sam's name so the public key looks like it was from him).

■ The hacker sends "his" new public key that he generated with his software, not the original one created by Sam. Rita does not know the difference; she thinks it is Sam's real public key.

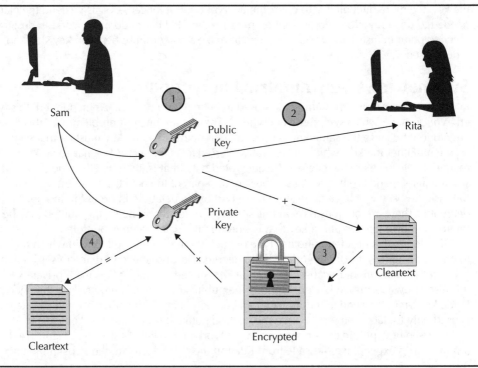

Figure 14-1. *Basic asymmetric encryption*

- Rita encrypts the message using this public key and sends the encrypted message to Sam.

- However, the hacker is still sniffing on the line and intercepts this message. Since he has the private key for the public key, he can decrypt the message. In an instant, the whole point of intended security advantage is lost.

- There is a slight problem, though. When Sam eventually gets the encrypted message and tries to decrypt it, he will be unsuccessful because the private key that needs to be used is not the correct one. He will get suspicious. To prevent this, the hacker will just have to re-encrypt the message using Sam's real public key and pass on the encrypted message to him. Sam is unlikely to know that something like this has happened.

Scary? Of course. So, what's the solution? The solution is to somehow verify the authenticity of the public key and ascertain its source as the correct sender. This can be done using a fingerprint match. The topic is beyond the scope of this book, but essentially when Rita encrypts with the public key, she checks the fingerprints of the key to make sure the key indeed belongs to Sam. This also highlights how the communication lines between the source and the destination must be highly secure.

The key used to encrypt is not the key used to decrypt, so how does the decryption process know the key used during the encryption process? Recall that both keys are generated at the same time by the receiver, which ensures that there is a mathematical relationship between them. One is simply the inverse of the other: whatever one does, the other simply undoes it. The decryption process can therefore decipher the value without knowing the encryption key.

Because public and private keys are mathematically related, it is theoretically possible to guess the private key from the public key, albeit a rather laborious process that requires factoring an extremely large number. Therefore, to reduce the risk of brute-force guessing, very high key lengths are used, typically 1024-bit keys, instead of the 56-, 64-, 128-, or 256-bit keys used in symmetric encryption. Although a 1024-bit key is typical, keys of shorter lengths are also used.

Oracle provides asymmetric encryption at two points:

- During transmission of data between the client and the database
- During authentication of users

Because asymmetric encryption systems use different keys to encrypt and decrypt, the source and destination need not know the key that will be used to decrypt. In contrast, symmetric encryption systems do use the same key, so safeguarding the keys when using such systems is very important.

Encryption Algorithms

There are many widely used and commercially available encryption algorithms, but we'll focus here on the symmetric key algorithms supported by Oracle for use in PL/SQL applications. All three of the following algorithms are supported by both of Oracle's built-in encryption packages: DBMS_CRYPTO:

- **Digital Encryption Standard (DES)**   Historically, DES has been the predominant standard used for encryption. It was developed more than 30 years ago for the National Bureau of Standards (which later became the National Institute of Standards and Technology, or NIST), and subsequently DES became a standard of the American National Standards Institute (ANSI). There is a great deal to say about DES and its history, but our purpose here is not to describe the algorithm but simply to summarize its adaptation and use inside the Oracle database. This algorithm requires a 64-bit key, but discards 8 of them, using only 56 bits. A hacker would have to use up to 72,057,594,037,927,936 combinations to guess the key.

  DES was an adequate algorithm for quite a while, but the decades-old algorithm shows signs of age. Today's powerful computers might find it easy to crack open even the large number of combinations needed to expose the key.

- **Triple DES (DES3)**   NBS/NIST went on to solicit development of another scheme based on the original DES that encrypts data twice or thrice, depending on the mode used. A hacker trying to guess a key would have to face 2112 then 2168 combinations in two-pass and three-pass encryption routines, respectively. DES3 uses a 128-bit or 192-bit key, depending on whether it is using a two-pass or three-pass scheme.

  Triple DES is now also showing signs of age and, like DES, has become susceptible to determined attacks.

- **Advanced Encryption Standard (AES)**   In November 2001, the Federal Information Processing Standards Publication (FIPS) 197 announced the approval of a new standard, the Advanced Encryption Standard, which became effective in May 2002. The full text of the standard can be obtained from NIST at http://csrc.nist.gov/CryptoToolkit/aes/round2/r2report.pdf.

Later in this chapter we'll show how you can use these algorithms by specifying options or selecting constants in Oracle's built-in packages.

Padding and Chaining

When a piece of data is encrypted, it is not encrypted as a whole by the algorithm. It's usually broken into chunks of 8 bytes each, and then each chunk is operated on independently. Of course, the length of the data may not be an exact multiple of eight; in such a case, the algorithm adds some characters to the last chunk to make it exactly 8 bytes long. This process is known as *padding*. This padding also has to be done right so a hacker won't be able to figure out what was padded and then guess the key from there. To securely pad the values, you can use a pre-developed padding method, available in Oracle, known as *Public Key Cryptography System #5* (PKCS#5). There are several other padding options that allow for padding with zeros and for no padding at all. Later in this chapter we'll show how you can use padding by specifying options or selecting constants in Oracle's built-in packages.

When data is divided into chunks, there needs to be a way to reconnect the adjacent chunks, a process known as *chaining*. The overall security of an encryption system also depends on how chunks are connected and encrypted—independently or in conjunction with the adjacent chunks. Oracle supports the following chaining methods:

- **CBC** Cipher Block Chaining, the most common chaining method
- **ECB** Electronic Code Book
- **CFB** Cipher Feedback
- **OFB** Output Feedback

Later in this chapter we'll show how you can use these methods by specifying options or selecting constants in Oracle's built-in packages.

The Crypto Package

Now that we've introduced the most basic building blocks of encryption, it's time to see encryption in action in the Oracle database using PL/SQL. The built-in package DBMS_CRYPTO allows us to build this pretty quickly.

Recall that to encrypt something, you need four components in addition to the input value itself:

- The encryption key
- The encryption algorithm
- The padding method
- The chaining method

Let's explore each of these activities.

Generating Keys

It should be apparent from our discussion so far that the weakest link in the encryption chain is the encryption key. To successfully decrypt the encrypted data, the key is literally that—the *key*. To protect the encryption, you must make that key extremely difficult to guess. There are two important points to remember about using a proper encryption key:

- The longer the key is, the more difficult it is to guess. To have an acceptable level of encryption, you should use a key as large as it can be; but keep in mind that the longer the key, the more CPU cycles it takes to encrypt and decrypt.

- In addition to being long, the key should be one that does not follow a pattern or format prone to guessing. The value 1234567890123456 is a bad choice as a key because the sequence of numbers appears in a predictable order. This is not acceptable. A value of a2H8s7X40Ys8346yp2 is better (though still too short).

As you learned in Chapter 13, you can use the **string()** function available in the DBMS_RANDOM package to generate any random string to serve as the key. However, it may not be random enough to be considered *cryptographically* secure. Fortunately, the package has a function called **randombytes** that produces cryptographically secure keys. This function takes the number of bytes you want the length to be and returns a value in the RAW data type.

Also in Chapter 13 you learned the value of a "seed" in generating random values. This seed determines the randomness of the value generated. The **randombytes()** function in DBMS_CRYPTO gets the seed from the parameter **sqlnet.crypto_seed** inside the file SQLNET.ORA in $ORACLE_HOME/network/admin directory. This parameter must have a valid value of any combination of characters between 10 and 70 bytes long. Here is an example setting of the parameter:

```
SQLNET.CRYPTO_SEED =
weipcfwe0cu0we98c0wedcpoweqdufd2d2df2dk2d2d23fv43098fpiwef02uc2ecw1x982jd23d908d
```

Let's create a function called **get_key** that returns a key of a specified length. All you need is execute privilege on the DBMS_CRYPTO package owned by SYS.

```
create or replace function get_key
(
   p_length in pls_integer
)
   return raw
is
   l_ret   raw (4000);
begin
   l_ret := dbms_crypto.randombytes (p_length);
   return l_ret;
end;
```

NOTE
The package DBMS_CRYPTO may not have been granted to public by default or there may not be a public synonym for it. If you want all developers to be able to use DBMS_CRYPTO, make sure you have a public synonym and proper grants in place. You can execute these two statements as SYS to accomplish this:

```
grant execute on dbms_crypto to public;
create public synonym dbms_crypto for sys.dbms_crypto;
```

If the public synonym already exists, that statement will fail; but that is no cause for concern because it will not cause any problems in your database.

The **randombytes** function is a very simple one, and you may decide that you do not need a wrapper function to simplify it further. However, you may still want to wrap the function inside **get_key** for the following reasons:

- If your existing code contains a **get_key** function because you used it earlier, you would have to create a function to ensure backward compatibility anyway.
- It takes fewer characters to type **get_key**, which can enhance code readability.
- Uniformity usually helps in developing quality code, so creating a wrapper function may be beneficial for that reason alone.

In addition to generating keys via the **randombytes** function, DBMS_CRYPTO can be used to produce numbers and binary integers. The **randominteger** function generates a binary integer key, as shown in this code segment:

```
l_ret := dbms_crypto.randominteger;
```

The **randomnumber** function generates a key of the integer data type with a length of 128 bits, as follows:

```
l_ret := dbms_crypto.randomnumber;
```

You may be wondering why we need an integer and a binary integer when the encryption relies on the RAW data type only. These are not really important, strictly speaking, for encryption, but they may be useful in generating pseudo-random numbers for other processing. Hence, they are mentioned here.

The encrypt Function
After the key is generated, we have to encrypt the data. Another function in the DBMS_CRYPTO package, named **encrypt**, does the job. This function is overloaded—that is, it provides both function and procedure variants. The function variant accepts only a RAW data type as an input value, whereas the procedure variant accepts only CLOB and BLOB as input values. Before

exploring the cause of these variants, let's look at the simplest case of encryption of an input value of the RAW data type using the **encrypt** function. Here is the declaration of the function:

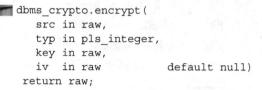

```
dbms_crypto.encrypt(
    src in raw,
    typ in pls_integer,
    key in raw,
    iv  in raw          default null)
  return raw;
```

You should already be familiar with two of these parameters:

- **src**   The input value to be encrypted
- **key**   The encryption key

The parameter **typ**, however, is new and requires a more detailed explanation. This parameter allows you to specify the type of encryption algorithm, padding, and chaining. It accepts an integer as an input. Passing appropriate integers to the function sets the desired type of encryption algorithm, padding, and chaining. Let's see how.

DBMS_CRYPTO provides several constants to specify the algorithm. Table 14-1 shows the algorithms available in the encryption process and their corresponding constants. You specify the desired constant in the form *PackageName.ConstantName*. To select DES, for example, you would use the constant DBMS_CRYPTO.ENCRYPT_DES. Similarly, you choose the desired chaining method by selecting the appropriate constant shown in Table 14-2. It's also specified in the same *PackageName.ConstantName* form (for example, DBMS_CRYPTO.CHAIN_OFB). Finally, you choose the desired padding method by selecting the appropriate constant from Table 14-3 in the same format (for example, DBMS_CRYPTO.PAD_PKCS5).

Constant	Description	Effective Key Length
ENCRYPT_DES	Digital Encryption Standard (DES)	56
ENCRYPT_3DES_2KEY	Modified Triple Digital Encryption Standard (3DES); operates on a block three times with two keys	112
ENCRYPT_3DES	Triple Digital Encryption Standard (3DES); operates on a block three times	156
ENCRYPT_AES128	Advanced Encryption Standard	128
ENCRYPT_AES192	Advanced Encryption Standard	192
ENCRYPT_AES256	Advanced Encryption Standard	256
ENCRYPT_RC4	Streaming cipher (the only one)	

Table 14-1.   *Types of Encryption in DBMS_CRYPTO*

Constant	Description
CHAIN_CBC	Cipher Block Chaining format
CHAIN_ECB	Electronic Code Book format
CHAIN_CFB	Cipher Feedback format
CHAIN_OFB	Output Feedback format

Table 14-2. *Chaining Methods in DBMS_CRYPTO*

Constant	Description
PAD_PKCS5	Padding with Public Key Cryptography System #5.
PAD_ZERO	Padding with zeros.
PAD_NONE	No padding is done; the data must be an exact multiple of the block size to be encrypted (a multiple of eight).

Table 14-3. *Types of Padding in DBMS_CRYPTO*

Now let's see how to put these various options together. Suppose that you want to select these options during encryption:

- **Padding method**   Pad with zeros (PAD_ZERO)
- **Encryption algorithm**   128-bit Key Advanced Encryption Standard (ENCRYPT_AES128)
- **Chaining method**   Block chaining via Cipher Feedback (CHAIN_CFB)

You can set the **typ** parameter as follows to express this combination of different settings—a rather lengthy string of values:

```
typ => dbms_crypto.pad_zero + dbms_crypto.encrypt_aes128 + dbms_crypto.chain_cfb
```

Using the same principle, you can specify any combination of options to the **encrypt** function. Here is a typical complete call to the function:

```
declare
    l_enc    raw(2000);
    l_in     raw(2000);
    l_key    raw(2000);
begin
    l_enc :=
        dbms_crypto.encrypt (
            src      => l_in,
            key      => l_key,
            typ      =>    dbms_crypto.pad_zero
                        + dbms_crypto.encrypt_aes128
                        + dbms_crypto.chain_cfb
        );
end;
```

Constant	Encryption	Padding	Block Chaining
DES_CBC_PKCS5	ENCRYPT_DES	PAD_PKCS5	CHAIN_CBC
DES3_CBC_PKCS5	ENCRYPT_3DES	PAD_PKCS5	CHAIN_CBC

Table 14-4. *DBMS_CRYPTO Constants with Predefined Sets for the typ Parameter*

To make things more convenient, the package provides two constants with a predefined combination of values for these three parameters. Table 14-4 shows these constants and the set of encryption, padding, and chaining options they represent.

Assuming that we still want to specify the DES algorithm, PKCS#5 padding, and CBC block chaining, we would use the combination constant as follows:

```
declare
    l_enc    raw(2000);
    l_in     raw(2000);
    l_key    raw(2000);
begin
    l_enc :=
        dbms_crypto.encrypt (
            src      => l_in,
            key      => l_key,
            typ      => dbms_crypto.des_cbc_pkcs5
        );
end;
```

With this, we can now develop a function that accepts an input value and key of the RAW data type and returns the encrypted value (also in RAW), as follows. Note that we decided to change the padding to PKCS#5 for this example because it is the most commonly used.

```
create or replace function get_enc_val (
    p_in_val    in    raw,
    p_key       in    raw,
    p_iv        in    raw := null
)
    return raw
is
    l_enc_val    raw (4000);
begin
    l_enc_val :=
        dbms_crypto.encrypt (
            src      => p_in_val,
            key      => p_key,
            iv       => p_iv,
            typ      =>   dbms_crypto.encrypt_aes128
                       + dbms_crypto.chain_cbc
                       + dbms_crypto.pad_pkcs5
        );
    return l_enc_val;
end;
```

Handling and Converting RAW Data

This function accepts the input values in RAW and assumes we want to use the 128-bit AES encryption algorithm, PKCS#5 padding, and Cipher Block Chaining. In real-world applications, these assumptions may be too constraining. For instance, the input values are usually in VARCHAR2 or some numeric data type, not RAW. Let's make the function more generic by letting it accept VARCHAR2 instead of RAW. Because the **encrypt** function requires RAW input, we will have to convert our original input to RAW. We can do that via the package UTL_I18N. Here is a code fragment to show how we change a VARCHAR2 input (l_in_varchar2) to RAW:

```
l_in_raw := utl_i18n.string_to_raw (l_in_varchar2, 'AL32UTF8');
```

The UTL_I18N package is provided as part of Oracle's Globalization Support and is used to perform globalization (or *internationalization,* which is often shortened to "I18N"; the name is made up of the starting letter *i,* the ending letter *n,* and the 18 letters in between).

Also, the **encrypt** function returns a RAW data type, which may not be convenient to store in the database or easy to manipulate. We can convert the value from RAW to a hexadecimal number as follows:

```
l_enc_val := rawtohex(l_enc_val);
```

Or we can convert to a VARCHAR2 data type by using another function:

```
l_enc_val := utl_i18n.raw_to_char (l_enc_val, 'AL32UTF8');
```

It's always best not to convert RAW to anything, if possible. See the sidebar "When You Should Use RAW Encryption."

Flexible Encryption Algorithm

Even though AES algorithms are more secure and efficient, you may have to use something else, such as DES. For additional security, you might want to use 3DES (but be aware that it is slower than DES). In many cases you may need to choose different algorithms to satisfy different conditions, while the other two modifiers—padding and chaining—will remain the same. Unfortunately, the **encrypt** function does not allow us to define the type of encryption algorithm directly; it must be passed as a parameter along with other modifiers (e.g., padding and chaining). We can accomplish this ourselves, however, by introducing a new parameter (**p_algorithm**) in our user-defined generic encryption package, which can be used to specify the algorithm. That parameter will accept only the following values, indicating the types of algorithms supported by DBMS_CRYPTO:

- DES
- 3DES_2KEY
- 3DES
- AES128
- AES192
- AES256
- RC4

The passed value is then appended to the term "ENCRYPT_" and passed to the **encrypt** function. The following code fragment does just that:

```
l_enc_algo :=
    case lower(p_algorithm)
        when 'des'
            then dbms_crypto.encrypt_des
        when '3des_2key'
            then dbms_crypto.encrypt_3des_2key
        when '3des'
            then dbms_crypto.encrypt_3des
        when 'aes128'
            then dbms_crypto.encrypt_aes128
        when 'aes192'
            then dbms_crypto.encrypt_aes192
        when 'aes256'
            then dbms_crypto.encrypt_aes256
        when 'rc4'
            then dbms_crypto.encrypt_rc4
    end;
```

Putting everything together, the **get_enc_val** function now looks like this:

```
create or replace function get_enc_val (
    p_in_val       in    varchar2,
    p_key          in    varchar2,
    p_algorithm    in    varchar2 := 'aes128',
    p_iv           in    varchar2 := null
)
    return varchar2
is
    l_enc_val      raw (4000);
    l_enc_algo     pls_integer;
    l_in           raw (4000);
    l_key          raw (4000);
    l_ret          varchar2 (4000);
begin
    l_enc_algo :=
        case lower(p_algorithm)
            when 'des'
                then dbms_crypto.encrypt_des
            when '3des_2key'
                then dbms_crypto.encrypt_3des_2key
            when '3des'
                then dbms_crypto.encrypt_3des
            when 'aes128'
                then dbms_crypto.encrypt_aes128
            when 'aes192'
                then dbms_crypto.encrypt_aes192
            when 'aes256'
                then dbms_crypto.encrypt_aes256
```

```
            when 'rc4'
                then dbms_crypto.encrypt_rc4
        end;
    l_in := utl_i18n.string_to_raw (p_in_val, 'al32utf8');
    l_key := utl_i18n.string_to_raw (p_key, 'al32utf8');
    l_enc_val :=
        dbms_crypto.encrypt (src       => l_in,
                             key       => l_key,
                             typ       =>  l_enc_algo
                                    + dbms_crypto.chain_cbc
                                    + dbms_crypto.pad_pkcs5
                            );
    l_ret := rawtohex (l_enc_val);
    return l_ret;
end;
```

After this function is created, let's test it:

```
SQL> select get_enc_val ('Test','1234567890123456')
  2> from dual;
GET_ENC_VAL('TEST','1234567890123456')
--------------------------------------
2137F30B29BE026DFE7D61A194BC34DD
```

That's it; we have just built a generic encryption function that can optionally take the encryption algorithm. It assumes PKCS#5 padding and ECB chaining, which are common practices. If these encryption characteristics meet your requirements, this program could become your wrapper function to perform everyday encryption.

Decrypting Data

On the other side of the coin is the decryption process, which decodes the encrypted string using the same key used originally for encryption. Let's write a new function for decryption, called **get_dec_val**, using the DBMS_CRYPTO package as follows:

```
create or replace function get_dec_val (
    p_in_val       in    varchar2,
    p_key          in    varchar2,
    p_algorithm    in    varchar2 := 'aes128'
)
    return varchar2
is
    l_dec_val      raw (4000);
    l_enc_algo     pls_integer;
    l_in           raw (4000);
    l_key          raw (4000);
    l_ret          varchar2 (4000);
begin
    l_enc_algo :=
        case lower(p_algorithm)
            when 'des'
                then dbms_crypto.encrypt_des
```

```
        when '3des_2key'
            then dbms_crypto.encrypt_3des_2key
        when '3des'
            then dbms_crypto.encrypt_3des
        when 'aes128'
            then dbms_crypto.encrypt_aes128
        when 'aes192'
            then dbms_crypto.encrypt_aes192
        when 'aes256'
            then dbms_crypto.encrypt_aes256
        when 'rc4'
            then dbms_crypto.encrypt_rc4
        end;
    l_in := hextoraw(p_in_val);
    l_key := utl_i18n.string_to_raw (p_key, 'al32utf8');
    l_dec_val :=
        dbms_crypto.decrypt (src       => l_in,
                             key       => l_key,
                             typ       =>   l_enc_algo
                                          + dbms_crypto.chain_cbc
                                          + dbms_crypto.pad_pkcs5
                            );
    l_ret := utl_i18n.raw_to_char (l_dec_val, 'al32utf8');
    return l_ret;
end;
```

Let's test this function. To decrypt the value we encrypted earlier, we can use:

```
SQL> select get_dec_val ('2137F30B29BE026DFE7D61A194BC34DD',
'1234567890123456')
  2> from DUAL;
GET_DEC_VAL('2137F30B29BE026DFE7D61A194BC34DD','1234567890123456')
------------------------------------------------------------------------
Test
```

There it is; we just got back our original value. Note how we have used the same key we used to encrypt earlier. When you are decrypting an encrypted value, you must use exactly the same key, algorithm, padding method, and chaining method used during encryption. This is the essence of symmetric encryption.

You might consider using **get_dec_val** as your generic program to decrypt encrypted values. For simplicity, ease of management, and security, you might want to place this set of encryption and decryption functions inside a package of your own construction.

Before closing the section, let's consider a very important concept. In the previous two examples we have used the input and output values as VARCHAR2. Recall, however, that the encryption and decryption are done inside the database as RAW, so we converted the data and key from RAW to VARCHAR2 and then back to RAW again. Although it simplifies the presentation, it may not be acceptable in some cases. See the sidebar "When Should You Use RAW-Only Encryption?" later in the chapter.

Initialization Vector or Salt

If you use the same key to encrypt several values, there may be a pattern visible in the encrypted values that could help hackers guess the input data. To prevent this, you can add a non-data-related random value to the actual data. For example, if your actual data is 12345678, you could affix a random value (say, 6675) before it to make it 667512345678, which can then be encrypted. The header information then contains some value related to 6675, not the actual data. Therefore, the hackers will not be able to determine a pattern, or if they do, that pattern will be bogus. When decrypting, you need to make sure to remove these random characters.

The random characters affixed to the real data are known as an *initialization vector* (IV) or a *salt*. In the **encrypt** function of the Crypto package, an optional parameter (**iv**) allows you to specify this value. Let's modify our encryption function to accept this parameter:

```
create or replace function get_enc_val (
    p_in_val      in    varchar2,
    p_key         in    varchar2,
    p_iv          in    varchar2 := null,
    p_algorithm   in    varchar2 := 'aes128'
)
    return varchar2
is
    l_enc_val     raw (4000);
    l_enc_algo    pls_integer;
    l_in          raw (4000);
    l_key         raw (4000);
    l_iv          raw (4000);
    l_ret         varchar2 (4000);
begin
    l_enc_algo :=
        case lower(p_algorithm)
            when 'des'
                then dbms_crypto.encrypt_des
            when '3des_2key'
                then dbms_crypto.encrypt_3des_2key
            when '3des'
                then dbms_crypto.encrypt_3des
            when 'aes128'
                then dbms_crypto.encrypt_aes128
            when 'aes192'
                then dbms_crypto.encrypt_aes192
            when 'aes256'
                then dbms_crypto.encrypt_aes256
            when 'rc4'
                then dbms_crypto.encrypt_rc4
        end;
    l_in := utl_i18n.string_to_raw (p_in_val, 'al32utf8');
    l_key := utl_i18n.string_to_raw (p_key, 'al32utf8');
    l_iv := utl_i18n.string_to_raw (p_iv, 'al32utf8');
    l_enc_val :=
```

```
        dbms_crypto.encrypt (
            src       => l_in,
            key       => l_key,
            iv        => l_iv,
            typ       =>    l_enc_algo
                            + dbms_crypto.chain_cbc
                            + dbms_crypto.pad_pkcs5
            );
    l_ret := rawtohex (l_enc_val);
    return l_ret;
end;
```

If you use the IV during encryption, you have to use the same IV while decrypting. Here is our decryption function to accept the IV or salt as a parameter:

```
create or replace function get_dec_val (
    p_in_val       in    varchar2,
    p_key          in    varchar2,
    p_iv           in    varchar2 := null,
    p_algorithm    in    varchar2 := 'aes128'
)
    return varchar2
is
    l_dec_val      raw (4000);
    l_enc_algo     pls_integer;
    l_in           raw (4000);
    l_key          raw (4000);
    l_iv           raw (4000);
    l_ret          varchar2 (4000);
begin
    l_enc_algo :=
        case lower(p_algorithm)
            when 'des'
                then dbms_crypto.encrypt_des
            when '3des_2key'
                then dbms_crypto.encrypt_3des_2key
            when '3des'
                then dbms_crypto.encrypt_3des
            when 'aes128'
                then dbms_crypto.encrypt_aes128
            when 'aes192'
                then dbms_crypto.encrypt_aes192
            when 'aes256'
                then dbms_crypto.encrypt_aes256
            when 'rc4'
                then dbms_crypto.encrypt_rc4
        end;
    l_in := hextoraw(p_in_val);
    l_key := utl_i18n.string_to_raw (p_key, 'al32utf8');
    l_iv := utl_i18n.string_to_raw (p_iv, 'al32utf8');
```

```
   l_dec_val :=
      dbms_crypto.decrypt (
         src      => l_in,
         key      => l_key,
         iv       => l_iv,
         typ      =>   l_enc_algo
                     + dbms_crypto.chain_cbc
                     + dbms_crypto.pad_pkcs5
      );
   l_ret := utl_i18n.raw_to_char (l_dec_val, 'al32utf8');
   return l_ret;
end;
```

In a way, the IV acts as a key or a part of the key, but it can't be relied on as a key as such. Why? Consider the following code, where we first encrypt a value using a key and an IV value of "Salt":

```
SQL> select get_enc_val ('Test','1234567890123456','Salt')
  2  from dual;
GET_ENC_VAL('TEST','1234567890123456','SALT')
--------------------------------------------------------------------------
704D23228C0D7688CC9E2E76A6B46191
```

Then we decrypt the value using the same key but a slightly different IV ("Sale" instead of "Salt"):

```
SQL> select get_dec_val ('124314C068287BCC2740517E8E48C97A', '1234567890123456','Sale')
  2  from dual;
GET_DEC_VAL('124314C068287BCC2740517E8E48C97A','1234567890123456','SALE')
--------------------------------------------------------------------------
Clep??"!xt Data
```

The IV parameter is Salt during encryption but Sale during decryption; only the fourth character has changed. That's because the decrypted value is not exactly the same as the input value; the middle characters are some nonprintable ones. Although the returned data is not exactly the same, it might be easier to guess by supplying random values for the initialization vector, a procedure known as a *brute-force attack*. Because IVs are typically shorter than keys, that guess may take less time, so you should not rely on the IV as a key.

The initialization vector simply modifies the input cleartext value to prevent repetition; it is not a substitute for the encryption key.

TIP
Many regulations and mandates require that you use a salt or initialization vector during encryption, so it makes sense to always use it.

Key Management

You've learned the basics of how to use encryption and decryption, as well as how to generate keys. But that's the easy part; for the most part, we've simply used Oracle's supplied programs and built wrappers around them to get the job done. Now comes the most challenging part of the encryption infrastructure—managing the key. Our applications will need to have access to the key to decrypt the encrypted values, and this access mechanism should be as simple as possible. On the other hand, the key should not be so simple as to be accessible to hackers. A proper key management system balances the simplicity of key access against prevention of unauthorized access to the keys.

There are essentially three different types of key management:

- A single key for the entire database
- A different key for each row of tables with encrypted data
- A combination approach

The following sections describe these different approaches to key management. The discussions in this chapter use features available in all versions of the Oracle Database.

Using a Single Key

With this approach, a single key is used to access any data in the database. The encryption routine reads only one key from the key location and encrypts all the data that needs to be protected. This key could be stored in a variety of locations:

- **In the database**   This is the simplest strategy of all. The key is stored in a relational table, perhaps in a schema created specifically for this purpose. Because the key is inside the database, it is automatically backed up as a part of the database; older values can be obtained by flashback queries or the database, and the key is not vulnerable to theft from the operating system. The simplicity of this approach is also its weakness: because the key is just data in a table, anyone with the authority to modify that table (such as any DBA or a hacker, who could assume SYSDBA privileges after stealing your backup) could alter the key and compromise the security.

- **In the file system**   The key is stored in a file, which may then be read by the encryption procedure using the UTL_FILE built-in package. By setting the appropriate privileges on that file, you can ensure that it cannot be changed from within the database. This is probably better because the file is outside of the database; therefore, the database backup will not have the file. This way, a thief stealing your backup tapes will not be able to decrypt.

- **On some removable media controlled by the end user**   This approach is the safest one; no one except the end user can decrypt the values or alter the key, not even the DBA or system administrator—and definitely not the hacker. Examples of removable media include a USB stick, a DVD, and a removable hard drive. A major disadvantage of removable media is the possibility of key loss or key theft. The responsibility for keeping the key safe lies with the end user. If the key is ever lost, the encrypted data is also lost— *permanently.*

The biggest advantage of using a single key is that the encryption/decryption routines will not need to select keys from tables or store them every time a record is manipulated in the base table. The result is that performance is generally better because of reduced CPU cycles and I/O operations. The biggest disadvantage of this approach is its dependence on a single point of failure. If a hacker breaks into the database and determines the key, the entire database becomes immediately vulnerable. In addition, if you want to change the key, you will need to change all the rows in all the tables, which may be quite an extensive task in a large database.

Because of these disadvantages, particularly the consequences of key theft, this approach isn't frequently used. However, there are a few cases where it may be useful. One example is a data publication system where a key is generally used only once during the transmission of data. After the transmission, the key is destroyed and a new key is used for the next transmission. Such a system might be used by financial data publication houses sending analytical data to customers or in a situation where one division of a company is sending confidential corporate data to the other divisions or to company headquarters. The key and the encrypted data travel separately to reduce the possibility of compromise.

Using a Key for Each Row

With the second approach, a different key is used for each row of a table. This approach is far more secure than the one discussed in the previous section. Even if a thief succeeds in stealing a key, only one row will be compromised, not the entire table or the database. There are some disadvantages to this approach. For one, the proliferation of keys makes it extremely difficult to manage them. Also, because encryption and decryption operations need to generate or retrieve a different key for each row, performance will suffer. Nevertheless, the added security provided by this approach makes it preferable in most encryption systems.

Using a Combined Approach

In some cases, neither of the approaches we've described so far is suitable. Let's examine the pros and cons of the two options.

- **With the one-key approach:**

    - The key management is extremely simple. There is only one key to manage—create, access, and back up.

    - The key can be located in many places convenient for the applications to access.

    - On the other hand, if the key is ever stolen, the entire database becomes vulnerable.

- **With the one-key-per-row approach:**

    - The number of keys equates to the number of rows, thus increasing the complexity of key management—more data to back up, more storage, and so on.

    - On the other hand, if a single key is stolen, only that corresponding row is compromised, not the entire database. This adds to the overall security of the system.

Clearly, neither approach is perfect, and you will have to find a middle ground—that is, choose an approach somewhere between the two approaches we've discussed. Perhaps you will use a single key per column, where the same key applies to all the rows; or a key per table regardless of the number of columns; or a key per schema, and so on. The number of keys to be managed would decrease dramatically with any of these approaches, but of course the vulnerability of the data would increase.

Let's take a look at a third approach—we will adopt a *combination* of keys:

- One key for each row, plus
- A key modifier for the entire database

This is not the same as encrypting the encrypted value (in fact, that isn't even possible). Although we have defined one key per row, the actual key used during encryption is not the key stored for the row; it is, instead, the bitwise exclusive OR (XOR) of two values—the stored key and a key modifier. The key modifier can be stored in a location different from the location of the other keys. A hacker must find both keys if he or she is to successfully decrypt an encrypted value.

The built-in UTL_RAW package provides the **bit_xor** function, which we can use to perform a bitwise XOR operation. Here, we'll perform a bitwise XOR for the values 12345678 and 87654321:

```
declare
    l_bitxor_val    raw (2000);
    l_val_1         varchar2 (2000) := '12345678';
    l_val_2         varchar2 (2000) := '87654321';
begin
    l_bitxor_val :=
        utl_raw.bit_xor (
            utl_i18n.string_to_raw (l_val_1, 'al32utf8'),
            utl_i18n.string_to_raw (l_val_2, 'al32utf8')
        );
    dbms_output.put_line (
        'raw val_1:      ' ||
        rawtohex (utl_i18n.string_to_raw (l_val_1,'al32utf8'))
    );
    dbms_output.put_line (
        'raw val_2:      ' ||
        rawtohex (utl_i18n.string_to_raw (l_val_2,'al32utf8'))
    );
    dbms_output.put_line ('after bit xor: ' || rawtohex (l_bitxor_val));
end;
```

To perform a bitwise operation, we first need to convert the values to the RAW data type, as shown on line 8, where the call to the **utl_i18n.string_to_raw** function converts the value to RAW. On line 7, we call the bitwise XOR function, and at the end we display the two input values converted to RAW, along with the XOR'ed value.

After executing the preceding block, we get this output:

```
raw val_1:      3132333435363738
raw val_2:      3837363534333231
after bit xor: 0905050101050509
```

Note how the bitwise XOR'ed value is quite different from both of the input values. Using this technique, if we pull one value as the stored key for the row and the other as a key modifier, we can generate a different key that will be used in the actual encryption. We need both of the values, not just one, to arrive at the XOR'ed value. Therefore, even someone who knows one of the values will not be able to decipher the XOR'ed value and thus get the actual encryption value.

This approach is not the same as re-encrypting the encrypted value with a different key. The DBMS_CRYPTO package does not allow you to re-encrypt an encrypted value. If you attempt to do so, you will encounter the "ORA-28233 source data was previously encrypted" error.

We can change our original encryption/decryption program to use this key modifier, as shown next. We add a new variable called **l_key_modifier** on line 6, which accepts a value from the user (the substitution variable **&key_modifier**). In lines 15 through 17, we have XOR'ed the key and the key modifier, which was used instead of the **l_key** variable as the encryption key on line 22.

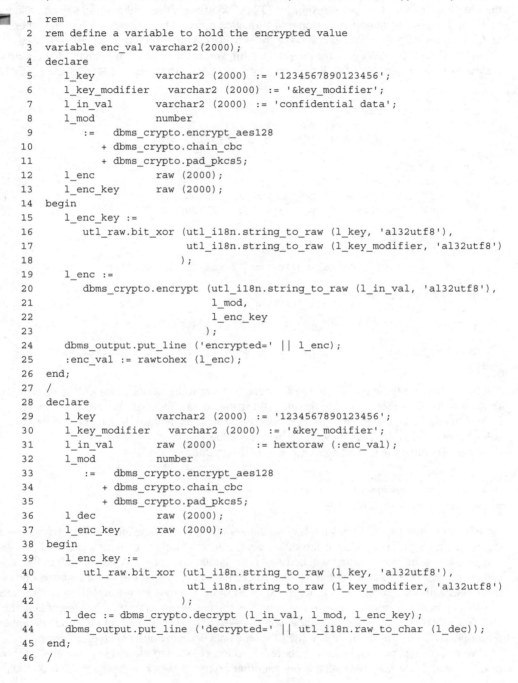

```
 1   rem
 2   rem define a variable to hold the encrypted value
 3   variable enc_val varchar2(2000);
 4   declare
 5      l_key            varchar2 (2000) := '1234567890123456';
 6      l_key_modifier   varchar2 (2000) := '&key_modifier';
 7      l_in_val         varchar2 (2000) := 'confidential data';
 8      l_mod            number
 9         :=   dbms_crypto.encrypt_aes128
10            + dbms_crypto.chain_cbc
11            + dbms_crypto.pad_pkcs5;
12      l_enc            raw (2000);
13      l_enc_key        raw (2000);
14   begin
15      l_enc_key :=
16         utl_raw.bit_xor (utl_i18n.string_to_raw (l_key, 'al32utf8'),
17                          utl_i18n.string_to_raw (l_key_modifier, 'al32utf8')
18                         );
19      l_enc :=
20         dbms_crypto.encrypt (utl_i18n.string_to_raw (l_in_val, 'al32utf8'),
21                              l_mod,
22                              l_enc_key
23                             );
24      dbms_output.put_line ('encrypted=' || l_enc);
25      :enc_val := rawtohex (l_enc);
26   end;
27   /
28   declare
29      l_key            varchar2 (2000) := '1234567890123456';
30      l_key_modifier   varchar2 (2000) := '&key_modifier';
31      l_in_val         raw (2000)        := hextoraw (:enc_val);
32      l_mod            number
33         :=   dbms_crypto.encrypt_aes128
34            + dbms_crypto.chain_cbc
35            + dbms_crypto.pad_pkcs5;
36      l_dec            raw (2000);
37      l_enc_key        raw (2000);
38   begin
39      l_enc_key :=
40         utl_raw.bit_xor (utl_i18n.string_to_raw (l_key, 'al32utf8'),
41                          utl_i18n.string_to_raw (l_key_modifier, 'al32utf8')
42                         );
43      l_dec := dbms_crypto.decrypt (l_in_val, l_mod, l_enc_key);
44      dbms_output.put_line ('decrypted=' || utl_i18n.raw_to_char (l_dec));
45   end;
46   /
```

When we execute these two blocks of code, this is what the output looks like. Note that first we supply the key modifier to encrypt the value and then we provide the same key modifier while decrypting.

```
Enter value for key_modifier: Keymodifier01234
old   3:      l_key_modifier varchar2(2000) := '&key_modifier';
new   3:      l_key_modifier varchar2(2000) := 'Keymodifier01234';
Encrypted=C2CABD4FD4952BC3ABB23BD50849D0C937D3EE6659D58A32AC69EFFD4E83F79D

PL/SQL procedure successfully completed.

Enter value for key_modifier: Keymodifier01234
old   3:      l_key_modifier varchar2(2000) := '&key_modifier';
new   3:      l_key_modifier varchar2(2000) := 'Keymodifier01234';
Decrypted=ConfidentialData

PL/SQL procedure successfully completed.
```

Our program asked for the key modifier, which we supplied correctly, and the correct value came up. But what if we supply a wrong key modifier?

```
Enter value for key_modifier: Keymodifier01234
old   3:      l_key_modifier varchar2(2000) := '&key_modifier';
new   3:      l_key_modifier varchar2(2000) := 'Keymodifier01234';
Encrypted=C2CABD4FD4952BC3ABB23BD50849D0C937D3EE6659D58A32AC69EFFD4E83F79D

PL/SQL procedure successfully completed.

Enter value for key_modifier: WrongKeymodifier
old   3:      l_key_modifier varchar2(2000) := '&key_modifier';
new   3:      l_key_modifier varchar2(2000) := 'WrongKeymodifier';
declare
*
ERROR at line 1:
ORA-28817: PL/SQL function returned an error.
ORA-06512: at "SYS.DBMS_CRYPTO_FFI", line 67
ORA-06512: at "SYS.DBMS_CRYPTO", line 41
ORA-06512: at line 15
```

Note the error here: the use of a wrong key modifier did not expose the encrypted data. This enhanced security mechanism relies on two different keys, and both keys must be present to successfully decrypt it. If you hide the key modifier, it will be enough to prevent unauthorized decryption.

Because the key modifier is stored with the client, and it is sent over the network, a potential hacker could use a tool to "sniff" the value as it passes by. To prevent this from occurring, you can use a variety of approaches:

- You could create a virtual LAN (VLAN) between the application server and the database server that protects the network traffic between them to a great extent.

- You could modify the key modifier in some predetermined way, such as by reversing the characters so that a hacker could potentially get the key modifier that passed over the network but not the key modifier actually used.

- Finally, for a really secure solution, you could use Oracle Advanced Security to secure the network traffic between the client and the server.

There is no "perfect" key management solution. The approach you choose will be determined by the nature of your application and your best attempts to balance security against ease of access. The three approaches described in the previous sections represent three major types of key management techniques and are intended to give you a jump start on figuring out your own key management approach. You might very well come up with a better idea that could be more appropriate to your specific situation. For example, you might consider a hybrid approach, such as using different keys for critical tables.

There are some out-of-the-database solutions that offer slightly better protection for the storage of the key modifier. Here are some of those options:

- **Oracle Wallet**   This is a wallet manager to store, among other things, passwords, keys, and so on. In a Microsoft Windows environment, you can even put the Oracle Wallet inside a Microsoft Wallet.

- **Hardware security modules (HSMs)**   These are hardware appliances designed to store items such as keys or key modifiers securely.

- **Third-party key vaults**   These are the software equivalent of the HSM, designed to run on a server (which could be the database server itself, or a different one for more security) to store keys or modifiers securely.

A complete discussion of these topics is beyond the scope of this book.

Protecting the Data from the DBA

Do you need to protect the encrypted data from the DBA? It's a question that is bound to come up while designing the system, so you will have to address it in one way or another.

A key is stored either in the database or file system. If the key store is the database, then because the DBA is authorized to select from any table, including the table where the keys are stored, he can thus decrypt any encrypted data. If the key store is the file system, it has to be available to the Oracle software owner to be read using UTL_FILE, which the DBA may have access to. So either way, protecting encrypted data from the DBA is probably a fruitless exercise. Is that an acceptable risk in your organization? The answer depends on your organization's security policies and guidelines. In many cases the risk is managed by placing trust in the DBA, so this may be a moot point. But in some cases the encrypted data must be protected even from the DBA.

The most definitive solution is to define multiple realms in Oracle Database Vault, which is an extra-cost option. Realms can provide the separation you need for protection from the DBA. Database vaults are beyond the scope of this book. A PL/SQL-only solution is to store the keys at a location the DBA will not be able to access—such as on the application server. But that makes key management difficult. You have to ensure the keys are backed up and protected from theft.

You can employ a more complex system for key management using the key modifier approach described earlier. The key modifier is placed in a digital wallet, and the application server requests the key every time it needs to encrypt and decrypt the data. Although it makes the key inaccessible to the DBA, it makes the system complex and adds increasing processing times.

If the objective is only to prevent the DBA from altering the key but still be able to see it, you can use the same key modifier approach. The key modifier can be placed in a file system that is read-only but accessible to the Oracle software owner to read it. This enables the database (and the DBA) to use it in encryption, but the DBA will not be able to alter it.

However, to keep the system manageable, especially if you want to make sure the applications are minimally affected, then you have to make the keys available to the Oracle software owner, either in a file system or inside the database in a table. In that case, it will be impossible to hide the keys from a DBA.

Encrypting RAW Data

In the examples so far, the parameters passed were of data type VARCHAR2, but we had to convert them to RAW because that's the data type for the functions of the Crypto package. The encrypted value is also in RAW, but we may decide to convert it to VARCHAR2 for easy display. The UTL_I18N package and the **rawtohex()** function make it easy to convert between RAW and VARCHAR2.

However, the additional processing required for conversion between the RAW and VARCHAR2 data types might actually hurt performance rather than help it. In my tests, this version for the VARCHAR2 and NUMBER data types underperformed the plain string version by about 50 percent. Because encryption is a CPU-intensive process, this measurement may vary widely based on the host system. However, the general rule of thumb is to avoid this raw manipulation if possible if your data is primarily character based and you use only one type of character set.

When Should You Use RAW-Only Encryption?

One situation in which you should use RAW encryption is when are you are using the BLOB data type, as explained earlier.

Another situation is when non-English characters are used in the database. If you are using Oracle Globalization Support (also known as National Language Support, or NLS), RAW encryption and decryption can handle such characters very well without necessitating any additional manipulations, especially while exporting and importing data. The encrypted data can be moved across databases without fear of corruption.

A Complete Encryption Solution

Let's put all that you've learned in this chapter so far to build a complete encryption solution. Suppose we have a table named ACCOUNTS that looks like this:

```
SQL> desc accounts
 Name                                      Null?    Type
 ----------------------------------------- -------- -------------
 ACCOUNT_NO                                NOT NULL NUMBER
 BALANCE                                            NUMBER
 ACCOUNT_NAME                                       VARCHAR2(200)
```

We want to protect the data by encrypting the columns BALANCE and ACCOUNT_NAME. As stated many times, the most important element is the key, and it must be an appropriate one. We can generate a key, use it to encrypt the column value, and then store the key and the encrypted value somewhere to be retrieved later. How exactly can we do this? We have a few options.

Option 1: Alter the Table

Here are the general steps:

1. Add the columns ENC_BALANCE and ENC_ACCOUNT_NAME to the table to store the encrypted values of the corresponding columns. Because the encrypted values are in RAW, these columns should be RAW as well.

2. Add another column named ENC_KEY to store the key used for encryption. It should also be in RAW.

3. Create a view called VW_ACCOUNTS, defined as follows:

```
create or replace view vw_accounts
as
select account_no,
       enc_balance as balance,
       enc_account_name as account_name
from accounts;
```

4. Create INSTEAD OF triggers to handle updates and inserts to the view, if needed.

5. Create a public synonym ACCOUNTS for the view VW_ACCOUNTS.

6. Grant all privileges on VW_ACCOUNTS and revoke all privileges on ACCOUNTS.

This arrangement ensures that the schema owner, as well as any users who have been given direct privileges on the ACCOUNTS table and can access the table with the *schema.tablename* convention, will see the cleartext values. All others will see only the encrypted values.

Option 2: Encrypt the Columns Themselves, and Use the View to Show the Decrypted Data

Here are the general steps:

1. Add a column called ENC_KEY to store the key for that row. It should be the RAW data type.

2. Store the encrypted values of BALANCE and ACCOUNT_NAME in those columns.

3. Create a view named VW_ACCOUNTS, as follows:

```
create or replace view vw_accounts
as
select account_no,
       get_dec_val (balance, enc_key) as balance,
       get_dec_val (enc_account_name, enc_key) as account_name
from accounts;
```

4. Now, the table will show the encrypted value, but the view will show the cleartext values; privileges on those values can be granted to users.

5. Create triggers on the table to convert the values to encrypted values before inserting or updating the columns.

The advantage of this approach is that the table itself need not be changed.

Store the Keys Separate from the Table

Both of the approaches just described have a serious flaw—the key is stored in the table. If someone has the access required to select from the table, he or she will be able to see the key and decrypt the values. A better approach is to store the keys separately from the source table. Follow these steps:

1. Create a table called ACCOUNT_KEYS with only two columns:

    ■ **ACCOUNT_NO**   Corresponds to the ACCOUNT_NO of the record in the ACCOUNTS table

    ■ **ENC_KEY**   The key used to encrypt the value

2. Make the original table ACCOUNTS contain the *encrypted* values, not the cleartext values.

3. Create triggers on the ACCOUNTS table. The AFTER INSERT trigger generates a key, uses it to encrypt the actual value given by the user, changes the value to the encrypted value before storing, and, finally, stores the key in the ACCOUNT_KEYS table.

4. Create a view to display decrypted data by joining both of the tables.

Storing the Keys

Storing the keys is the most crucial part of the encryption exercise. If you don't do this properly, the whole point of safeguarding data by encrypting it becomes moot. You have a variety of storage options:

■ **In database tables**   This approach, illustrated in the preceding example, is the most convenient way to handle keys. It suffers from a serious drawback, however: it offers no protection from the DBA, who is able to access all tables.

■ **In an operating system file**   The file can be created at run time by the client process via either the built-in package UTL_FILE or external tables, and it can then be used for decryption. After the read, the file can be destroyed. This approach offers protection from all other users, including the DBA.

■ **Issued by the user**   At run time, the user can provide the key to the function for decryption. This is the most secure (as well as the most impractical) approach of the three. The disadvantage is that the user may forget the key, which means that it will be impossible to ever decrypt the encrypted data.

At the end of this chapter you will see a more robust encryption solution.

Transparent Data Encryption

When you store the encryption key and the encrypted data both in the database, another potential security hole opens up—if the disks containing the entire database are stolen, the data becomes immediately vulnerable. One way around this problem is to encrypt all the data elements and store the keys separately in a different location away from the disk drives where the data resides.

   If your database is completely isolated, you may not feel that you need to encrypt its data. However, you may still want to protect the data in case of disk theft. One solution would be to create a view to show the decrypted value. In this case, if the key is stored elsewhere, physical disk theft will not make the data vulnerable. This approach works, but it requires an extensive and elaborate setup.

To address these types of situations, Oracle has introduced a feature in 10.2 known as Transparent Data Encryption (TDE). TDE uses a combination of two keys—one *master key* stored outside the database in a wallet and one key for each table. The same key is used for all rows in a table, and a unique key is generated for each table. The keys used to encrypt the data values are stored in a table called ENC$ and are themselves encrypted by the master key.

There are two different types of TDE—column level and tablespace level. With column-level TDE, you may define only some columns of the table as encrypted. For example, if a table has four columns, and columns 2 and 3 are encrypted, Oracle will generate a key and use it to encrypt those columns. On the disk, columns 1 and 4 will be stored as cleartext, and the other two as encrypted text. In case of tablespace-level TDE, Oracle encrypts all the columns of the table.

When a user selects encrypted columns, Oracle transparently retrieves the key from the wallet, decrypts the columns, and shows them to the user. If the data on the disk is stolen, it cannot be retrieved without the keys, which reside in the wallet encrypted by the master key, which is not stored as cleartext itself. The result is that the thief can't decrypt the data, even he steals the disks or copies the files.

The goal of TDE is to satisfy the need to protect data stored on media such as disks and tapes, a requirement for compliance with many national and international regulatory frameworks and rules such as Sarbanes-Oxley, HIPAA, Payment Card Industry, and so on. It is a quick fix for companies with regulations and mandates to meet; however, it may not be a solution in all cases. Note, for example, that it automatically decrypts all the encrypted columns regardless of who actually selects them—a scenario that may not satisfy your security needs. For more comprehensive solutions, you need to build your own tool using the techniques described in this chapter.

To take advantage of TDE, add an ENCRYPT clause (available in Oracle Database 10g Release 2 only) to your table-creation statement for each column to be encrypted. We can simply define a table to be under TDE as follows:

```
create table accounts
  (
    acc_no        number not null,
    first_name    varchar2(30) not null,
    last_name     varchar2(30) not null,
    ssn           varchar2(9) encrypt using 'aes128',
    acc_type      varchar2(1) not null,
    folio_id      number encrypt using 'aes128',
    sub_acc_type  varchar2(30),
    acc_open_dt   date not null,
    acc_mod_dt    date,
    acc_mgr_id    number
  )
```

Here we have decided to encrypt the columns SSN and FOLIO_ID using AES 128-bit encryption. Using the ENCRYPT USING clause in the column definition instructs Oracle to intercept the cleartext values, encrypt them, and then store the encrypted format. When a user selects from the table, the column value is transparently decrypted. Note that you cannot enable Transparent Data Encryption on tables owned by SYS.

Setting Up TDE

Before you start using TDE, you have to set up the wallet where the master key is stored and secure it. Here is a step-by-step approach to wallet management:

1. Set the wallet location.

   When you enable TDE for the first time, you need to create the wallet where the master key is stored. By default, the wallet is created in the directory $ORACLE_BASE/admin/$ORACLE_SID/wallet. You can also choose a different directory by specifying it in the file SQLNET.ORA. For instance, if you want the wallet to be in the /oracle_wallet directory, place the lines in the SQLNET.ORA file as shown here (in this example we assume that the nondefault location is chosen):

   ```
   ENCRYPTION_WALLET_LOCATION =
     (SOURCE=
         (METHOD=file)
         (METHOD_DATA=
             (DIRECTORY=/oracle_wallet)))
   ```

   Make sure to include the wallet as a part of your regular backup process.

2. Set the wallet password.

   Now you have to create the wallet and set the password to access it. This is done in one step by issuing the following command:

   ```
   alter system set encryption key identified by "abcd1234";
   ```

   This command does three things:

   - It creates the wallet in the location specified in Step 1.

   - It sets the password of the wallet as "abcd1234".

   - It opens the wallet for TDE to store and retrieve keys.

   The password is case-sensitive, and you must enclose it in double quotes.

3. Open the wallet.

   The previous step opens the wallet for operation. However, after the wallet is created once, you do not need to re-create it. After the database comes up, you just have to open it using the same password via the following command:

   ```
   alter system set encryption wallet open authenticated identified by
   "abcd1234";
   ```

   This step is needed after the database comes up. You can close the wallet by issuing this command:

   ```
   alter system set encryption wallet close;
   ```

   The wallet needs to be open for TDE to work. If the wallet is not open, all nonencrypted columns are accessible, but the encrypted columns are not.

Adding TDE to Existing Tables

In the example in the previous section you saw how to use TDE while creating a brand-new table. You can encrypt a column of an existing table as well. To encrypt the column SSN of the table ACCOUNTS, specify the following:

```
alter table accounts modify (ssn encrypt);
```

This operation does two things:

- It creates a key for the column SSN.
- It converts all values in the column to encrypted format.

It does not do anything else, such as change the data type or size of the column or create a trigger or view. The encryption is then performed inside the database. By default, it uses AES with a 192-bit key algorithm for the encryption. You can choose a different algorithm by specifying it in the command. For instance, to choose 128-bit AES encryption, you would specify this:

```
alter table accounts modify (ssn encrypt using 'AES128');
```

You can choose AES128, AES256, or 3DES168 (168-bit Triple DES algorithm) as parameters. After encrypting a column, let's look at the table:

```
SQL> desc accounts
 Name          Null? Type
 ---------     ----- ------------
 ACC_NO              NUMBER
 ACC_NAME            VARCHAR2(30)
 SSN                 VARCHAR2(9) ENCRYPT
```

Note the clause ENCRYPT after the data type. To find out the encrypted columns in the database, you can search the new data dictionary view DBA_ENCRYPTED_COLUMNS.

What about the performance impact on TDE? There is no overhead when you select the nonencrypted columns; it's no different from regular Oracle table processing. When encrypted columns are accessed, there is a small performance overhead while the columns are decrypted. You may want to encrypt columns selectively. If encryption is no longer required, you can turn it off for a column by specifying the following:

```
alter table account modify (ssn decrypt);
```

Tablespace TDE

The problems with TDE, and to a lesser extent user-written encryption in general, in the application performance area can be summed up in two key points:

- TDE negates the use of indexes for queries with a range scan. The encrypted data gets little to no help from indexes for queries in a range scan because there is no pattern correlation of the table data to the index entry. User-written encryption offers only limited opportunities to use indexes.

- Querying the encrypted data means decryption of that data, which means significant additional CPU consumption.

To address these drawbacks, Oracle Database 11*g* Release 1 added a new feature to TDE—at the tablespace level—that allows a user to define an entire tablespace, not a few columns of a table, as encrypted. Here is an example of creating an encrypted tablespace:

```
create tablespace securets1
    datafile '+dg1/securets1_01.dbf'
    size 10m
    encryption using 'aes128'
    default storage (encrypt);
```

Whenever you create an object in this tablespace, it will be converted to an encrypted format via an AES algorithm using a 128-bit key. Of course, you would have set up the wallet and opened it as described in the "Setting Up TDE" section. The encryption key is stored in the ENC$ table in an encrypted manner, and the key to that encryption is stored in the wallet, as it is in TDE.

You may be wondering how an encrypted tablespace can avoid the problems of table-based encryption. The key difference is that the data in the tablespace is encrypted only on disk—not in memory. When the data is pulled into the SGA, or more specifically to the database buffer cache, the encrypted data is decrypted and placed in the buffer cache as cleartext. The index scans use the data buffers, not those on the disk; therefore, the issue of not matching encrypted data does not arise. Similarly, because the data is decrypted and placed in the buffer cache only once (at least until it is aged out), the decryption occurs just once—not every time that data is accessed. As a consequence, as long as the data remains in the buffers, the performance is not affected by encryption. It's the best of both worlds—security by encryption and minimized performance impact.

Because the issues seem to be resolved, does TDE spell the doom for the user-written encryption procedures shown in this chapter? Not at all!

When you encrypt a tablespace, all the objects—indexes and tables—inside it are encrypted, regardless of whether you need them to be encrypted or not. That's fine when you need to encrypt all or most of the data in the tablespace. What if, on the other hand, you only need encryption for a fraction of the total data volume? In the example shown earlier, only the column SSN of the table ACCOUNTS has been encrypted. But in this case, if the table ACCOUNTS is in the tablespace USERS, all the columns will be encrypted—name, address, and all that. So when you query the nonsensitive columns, unless the data is already in the SGA, it will have to be decrypted and there will be a performance hit. Sooner or later the block will have to be aged out of the buffer cache and the decryption will need to occur. You can't prevent it because you can't control the selective encryption or decryption of columns.

Finally, encrypted tablespaces can only be created; you can't convert an existing tablespace from cleartext to encrypted (nor can you change an encrypted tablespace to cleartext). Instead, you must create a tablespace as encrypted and then move your objects into it. When you decide to introduce encryption to an existing database, that approach may not be feasible, given the enormous volumes of many production databases. User-written encryption gives you tight control and will come in handy in such cases where you can control how much of the data will be encrypted—and then decrypted. By the way, you also can't alter an encrypted tablespace back to cleartext.

Clearly, user-written PL/SQL-based encryption still has its charm and its place in real-world applications. You can implement TDE much more quickly and easily, but you will need to validate that the "brute-force" approach of total encryption works for your application.

The biggest appeal of the TDE feature is that you can use it to quickly encrypt the existing database without spending a lot of time coding. If you can afford to live with the limitations, it's worth it. But if you can't, you still have selective encryption using PL/SQL.

Performing TDE Key and Password Management

What if someone somehow discovers the TDE keys? You can simply re-create the encrypted values by issuing a simple command. While you are at it, you may also want to choose a different encryption algorithm such as AES256. You can do both by issuing the following command:

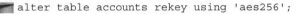

```
alter table accounts rekey using 'aes256';
```

What if someone discovers the wallet password? Can you can change it? The password can be changed using a graphical tool called *Oracle Wallet Manager*. From the command line, type **owm**, which brings up the tool shown in Figure 14-2. From the top menu, select Wallet | Open and choose the wallet location you have specified. You will have to supply the password of the wallet. After that, choose Wallet | Change Password to change the password. Note that changing the password does not change the keys.

Adding Salt

Encryption is all about hiding data, and sometimes encrypted data is easier to guess if there is repetition in the cleartext. For example, a table that contains salary information is quite likely to contain repeated values, and in that case, the encrypted values will also be the same. Even if a hacker can't decrypt the actual values, he will be able to tell which entries have the same salary, and this information may be valuable. To prevent such a thing from happening, "salt" is added to the data, which makes the encrypted value different even if the input data is the same. TDE, by default, applies a salt.

In some cases, patterns of data may improve your database performance, and adding salt may degrade it. With certain indexes, for example, a pattern may establish a b-tree structure and make it faster to search LIKE predicates, as in the following query:

```
select … from accounts where ssn like '123%';
```

In this case, b-tree indexes will have to travel along only one branch to get the data because all account numbers start with the digits 123. If a salt is added, the actual values will be stored all over the b-tree structure, making index scans more expensive, so the Optimizer will most likely choose a full table scan. In such cases, you may want to remove the salt from the indexed columns. You can do so by specifying the following:

```
alter table accounts modify (ssn encrypt no salt);
```

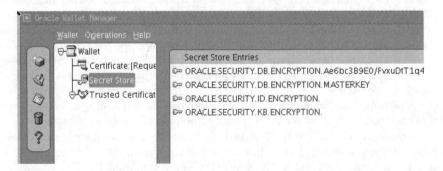

Figure 14-2. *Oracle Wallet Manager*

You can't use TDE on columns that have any of the following characteristics:

- Contain the data types BLOB or CLOB
- Are used in indexes other than regular b-tree indexes, such as bitmap indexes, function-based indexes, and so on
- Are used as a partitioning key

The lack of support for TDE in these cases is another reason why TDE is not a candidate for all types of encryption.

Cryptographic Hashing

Encryption provides a way to ensure that only authorized people can see your data. It does so by disguising sensitive data. In some cases, however, you may not be interested in disguising data, but simply in protecting it from manipulation. Suppose that you have stored payment information for vendors. That data by itself may not be sensitive enough to require encryption, but you may want a way to ensure that someone does not alter the numbers to increase a payment amount. How can you do that? The answer lies in a process known as cryptographic hashing. Let's start by looking at a nontechnical example.

The Case of the Suspicious Sandwich

Let's suppose you leave your sandwich open on your desk when you go over to the fax machine to pick up an important fax. When you come back, you feel somehow that the sandwich has shifted a little to the left. Has someone tampered with your sandwich, perhaps placing a barbiturate in it to knock you out so he can steal your cool new Apple watch? Or perhaps he's after the PL/SQL book hidden in your drawer? Maybe it's not drugs, but sand, in your sandwich? The possibilities spin madly through your mind and you lose your appetite.

To calm your fears, you decide to check the integrity of the sandwich. Being the careful fellow you are, you had previously weighed the sandwich before leaving the room and recorded its weight. After encountering the possibility of an altered sandwich, you weigh the sandwich again and compare the results. They are exactly the same. A sigh of relief signifies that all is well. If someone had actually changed the sandwich in any way (for example, by adding barbiturates or sand), the weights would have been different, thus revealing the adulteration.

Pay close attention to the concepts presented here. You did not "hide" the sandwich (that is, encrypt it); you simply created your own method of calculating a value that represents the sandwich. You could then compare the before and after values and know that something changed if the values differ. The value you arrive at could be based on any algorithm—in this case, it was the weight of the sandwich.

If you were examining data rather than sliced bread and meat, a pretty sophisticated algorithm could be used to generate the value. This process is known as *hashing*. It's different from encryption in that it is one-way only—you can decrypt encrypted data, but you can't de-hash hashed values. Hashing the same piece of data produces the same value regardless of when or how often it is done. If data has been modified in any way (that is, tampered with), the generated hash value will not be the same, thus revealing the contamination.

There is always a theoretical risk that two different pieces of data will hash to the same value, but this probability can be minimized to almost nothing using a sufficiently sophisticated hashing algorithm. One such algorithm is known as a Message Digest (MD). One MD variant known as MD5 was once a standard, but it did not prove secure enough to maintain its standardization; a newer standard called Secure Hash Algorithm Version 1 (SHA-1) is more often used today. SHA-2, an even more advanced version, is available with Oracle Database 12c.

Hashing with PL/SQL

Let's see how we can use hashing in real-life database administration. When a sensitive piece of information is sent to a different location, you might calculate the hash value beforehand and send it in another shipment or transmission. The recipient can then calculate the hash value of the received data and compare it against the hash value you sent out.

As mentioned, the MD5 protocol is not considered sufficiently secure for modern data protection, and the Secure Hash Algorithm (SHA-1) is often used instead. In Oracle Database 12c, you have yet another choice: SHA-2. Here is the declaration of the function:

```
dbms_crypto.hash (
    src in raw,
    typ in pls_integer)
 return raw;
```

Because HASH accepts only the RAW data type as input, we have to convert the input character string to RAW using the technique described earlier for encryption:

```
l_in := utl_i18n.string_to_raw (p_in_val, 'AL32UTF8');
```

This converted string can now be passed to the hash function.

In the **typ** parameter (which must be declared in the PLS_INTEGER data type), you specify the algorithm to use for hashing. You can select any of the algorithms in Table 14-5.

For example, to get the SHA-1 hash value for a RAW data type variable, you might write a function as follows:

```
create or replace function get_sha1_hash_val (p_in raw)
    return raw
is
    l_hash    raw (4000);
begin
    l_hash := dbms_crypto.hash (src => p_in, typ => dbms_crypto.hash_sh1);
    return l_hash;
end;
```

Constant	Description	Size in Bits
DBMS_CRYPTO.HASH_MD5	Message Digest 5	128
DBMS_CRYPTO.HASH_MD4	Message Digest 4	128
DBMS_CRYPTO.HASH_SH1	Secure Hashing Algorithm 1	160
DBMS_CRYPTO.HASH_SH256	Secure Hashing Algorithm 2	256
DBMS_CRYPTO.HASH_SH384	Secure Hashing Algorithm 2	384
DBMS_CRYPTO.HASH_SH512	Secure Hashing Algorithm 2	512

Table 14-5. *Hashing Algorithms in DBMS_CRYPTO*

For 384-bit SHA-2 hashing, you would change the value of the parameter **typ** from **dbms_crypto .hash_sh1** to **dbms_crypto.hash_sh384**. In our function, to get the hash value, we can make it generic enough to accept any algorithm.

Finally, because the return value is in RAW, we need to convert it to VARCHAR2 as follows:

```
l_enc_val := rawtohex (l_enc_val, 'AL32UTF8');
```

Putting everything together, this is what the function looks like:

```
create or replace function get_hash_val (
    p_in_val     in    varchar2,
    p_algorithm  in    varchar2 := 'sh1'
)
    return varchar2
is
    l_hash_val    raw (4000);
    l_hash_algo   pls_integer;
    l_in          raw (4000);
    l_ret         varchar2 (4000);
begin
    l_hash_algo :=
      case lower(p_algorithm)
          when 'sh1'
              then dbms_crypto.hash_sh1
          when 'md4'
              then dbms_crypto.hash_md4
          when 'md5'
              then dbms_crypto.hash_md5
          when 'sh256'
              then dbms_crypto.hash_sh256
          when 'sh384'
              then dbms_crypto.hash_sh384
          when 'sh512'
              then dbms_crypto.hash_sh512
        end;
    l_in := utl_i18n.string_to_raw (p_in_val, 'al32utf8');
    l_hash_val := dbms_crypto.hash (src => l_in, typ => l_hash_algo);
    l_ret := rawtohex(l_hash_val);
    return l_ret;
end;
```

Let's see how we can use it in an example by calling this function with different parameters for different algorithms:

```
begin
    dbms_output.put_line('MD5  ='||get_hash_val ('Test Data','MD5'));
    dbms_output.put_line('SH1  ='||get_hash_val ('Test Data','SH1'));
    dbms_output.put_line('SH256='||get_hash_val ('Test Data','SH256'));
    dbms_output.put_line('SH384='||get_hash_val ('Test Data','SH384'));
    dbms_output.put_line('SH512='||get_hash_val ('Test Data','SH512'));
end;
```

Here is the output:

```
MD5 =F315202B28422ED5C2AF4F843B8C2764
SH1 =CAE99C6102AA3596FF9B86C73881154E340C2EA8
SH256=BCFE67172A6F4079D69FE2F27A9960F9D62EDAE2FCD4BB5A606C2EBB74B3BA65
SH384=18500E642FAA93323D8B94E288AB0FBE835A403F0DDF2EA0AF0453786D3F2616237D85D7
4214EB207CAD29A70BD9D4EB
SH512=439E4CEED9312FEF2E554042C3D27D6AC31DA9CF72BA866BA9B0E00328D06280797482BF
2CD007E0808296DB0B987B73FE1F953E97E25883263B9783513C2949
```

Note how the hash values are different based on the key length and hashing algorithms used.

NOTE
*There are two important differences between hashing and encryption.
First, in hashing, there is no key. Because no key is involved, there is
no need to store or supply the key at any point of the send-receive
process, which makes a hashing system extremely simple. Second, you
can't get the original value from the hashed value.*

The function returns an identical value each time for the same input string, a fact that can be used in validating the integrity of that particular piece of data. Note that here we are referring to the integrity of the data, not the database; the latter is ensured by the Oracle database in enforcing constraints and in transactions. When a legitimate user updates a value that does not violate defined constraints, the data (but not the database) becomes corrupt. For example, if someone updates an account balance via ad hoc SQL from $12,345.67 to $21,345.67, that fact may not be detected at all unless the organization provides tracking capabilities.

Some organizations do have extensive tracking systems that aim to reduce such occurrences. In a banking system that one of us helped build, the account balances are updated through transactions; in this system, a mere update of the balance without the corresponding addition, deletion, and update of transaction records will clearly expose such malicious activity. But even in this system, certain other types of data, such as Social Security Numbers, names, product codes, and so on, can be easily updated without violating the accounting rule. This is where hashing is effective. If the hash value for a column such as Social Security Number was calculated beforehand and stored somewhere, and then after retrieval the recalculated hash value is compared against the stored one, it signals a possibly malicious data manipulation because the hash values will not be the same. Let's see how this works:

```
declare
    l_data    varchar2 (200);
begin
    l_data := 'social security number = 123-45-6789';
    dbms_output.put_line ('hashed = ' || get_hash_val (l_data));
    --
    -- someone manipulated the data and changed it
    --
    l_data := 'social security number = 023-45-6789';
    dbms_output.put_line ('hashed = ' || get_hash_val (l_data));
end;
```

Here is the output:

```
Hashed = 098D833A81B279E54992BFB1ECA6E428
Hashed = 6682A974924B5611FA9D809357ADE508
```

Note how the hash values differ. The resulting hash value will be different if the data was modified in any way, even if the value itself is unchanged. If a space, punctuation, or anything else is modified, the hash value will not be the same.

It is theoretically possible that two different input values will produce the same hash value. However, by relying on widely used algorithms such as MD5 and SHA-1, you are assured that the probability of a hash conflict is a statistically remote 1 in 10 to the 38th power (depending on the algorithm chosen). If you cannot afford to even take that chance, you will need to write conflict-resolution logic around your use of the hash function.

Other Uses of Hashing

Hashing has many uses beyond cryptography—for example, in web programming and virus detection.

Web applications are stateless: they do not keep the connection open to the database server for the duration of the transaction. In other words, there is no concept of a "session," and therefore there is no locking of the type Oracle users rely on. This means that there is no easy way to find out whether data on a web page has changed. But if a hash value is stored along with the data, a new hash value can be recalculated and compared with the stored value. If the two values do not agree, the data has changed.

Hashing is also helpful in determining whether data can be trusted. Consider the case of a virus that updates critical documents stored inside the database. This is not something that can be easily caught by a trigger. However, if the document contains a hash value, then by comparing a computed hash value with the stored value, you can determine whether the document has been tampered with, and you will know whether you can trust that document.

Message Authentication Code

The type of hashing we have discussed so far in this section is a very helpful technique, but it has certain limitations:

- Anyone can verify the authenticity of transmitted data by using the hash function. In certain types of ultra-secure systems, where only a particular recipient is expected to verify the authenticity of the message or data, this may not be appropriate.

- Anyone can calculate the same hash value if the algorithm is known and can then update the values in the checksum columns, hiding the compromise in the data.

- For the reason stated in the previous problem, the hash value cannot be stored along with the data in a reliable manner. Anyone with update privileges on the table can update the hash value as well. Similarly, someone can generate the hash value and update the data in transit. For this reason, the hash value cannot accompany the data. It has to travel separately, which adds to the complexity of the system.

These limitations can be overcome by a modified implementation of hashing, one in which the exclusivity of the hashing mechanism at the receiver's end can be ascertained by a password or key. This special type of hash value is known as a *message authentication code* (MAC). The sender calculates the MAC value of the data using a predetermined key that is also known to the receiver but not sent with the data. The sender then sends the MAC to the receiver along with the data, not separate from it. After receiving the data, the receiver also calculates the MAC value using the same key and matches it with the MAC value sent with the data.

Like hashing, MAC also follows the standard algorithms (MD, SHA-1, and SHA-2). As with the HASH function, the parameter **typ** is used to specify the algorithm to be used. Select one of the following: **dbms_crypto.hmac_md5**, **dbms_crypto.hmac_sh1**, **dbms_crypto.hmac_sh256**, **dbms_crypto.hmac_sh384**, or **dbms_crypto.hmac_sh512**. Here is how we calculate the MAC value of an input string using the SHA-1 algorithm:

```
create or replace function get_sha1_mac_val (
    p_in raw,
    p_key raw
)
    return raw
is
    l_mac   raw (4000);
begin
    l_mac :=
        dbms_crypto.mac (
            src => p_in,
            typ => dbms_crypto.hmac_sh1,
            key => p_key);
    return l_mac;
end;
```

Using our hashing function as a model, we can also create our own generic MAC calculations:

```
create or replace function get_mac_val (
    p_in_val      in    varchar2,
    p_key         in    varchar2,
    p_algorithm   in    varchar2 := 'sh1'
)
    return varchar2
is
    l_mac_val     raw (4000);
    l_key         raw (4000);
    l_mac_algo    pls_integer;
    l_in          raw (4000);
    l_ret         varchar2 (4000);
begin
    l_mac_algo :=
        case p_algorithm
            when 'sh1'
                then dbms_crypto.hmac_sh1
            when 'md5'
                then dbms_crypto.hmac_md5
            when 'sh256'
                then dbms_crypto.hmac_sh256
            when 'sh384'
```

```
         then dbms_crypto.hmac_sh384
      when 'sh512'
         then dbms_crypto.hmac_sh512
   end;
   l_in := utl_i18n.string_to_raw (p_in_val, 'al32utf8');
   l_key := utl_i18n.string_to_raw (p_key, 'al32utf8');
   l_mac_val := dbms_crypto.mac (src => l_in, typ => l_mac_algo, key=>l_key);
   l_ret := rawtohex (l_mac_val);
   return l_ret;
end;
```

Let's test this function to get the MAC value of a data "Test Data" and the key "Key" using various parameters:

```
begin
    dbms_output.put_line('MD5   ='||get_mac_val ('Test Data','Key','MD5'));
    dbms_output.put_line('SH1   ='||get_mac_val ('Test Data','Key','SH1'));
    dbms_output.put_line('SH256='||get_mac_val ('Test Data','Key','SH256'));
    dbms_output.put_line('SH384='||get_mac_val ('Test Data','Key','SH384'));
    dbms_output.put_line('SH512='||get_mac_val ('Test Data','Key','SH512'));
end;
```

Here is the output:

```
MD5   =DD6414C75D97B4AA2A02ED26A452F70C
SH1   =8C36C24C767E305CD95415C852E9692F53927761
SH256=94309013EB37E7F013F6FFD0B65E3C178D2F3D0567B06D5E180F20286F8CC88F
SH384=C78D10E66230578ADD8A995D3607A53C5519C2F9FC450BF26AE58D0BB0F2DA0387678168
B4C96866CEEC786E3649E9D0
SH512=C233A2148A682267791E2A8BB7F835856DE9A77210CB0346C9DD31AE2689A1D338BEB21D
7369D7F3FA91243C3A9C1463EF6B2E5E239E4237DD47116351E1C28B
```

Because a key is required to generate the checksum value, the MAC method provides more security than the hashing method. For example, in a banking application, the integrity of character data, such as a Social Security Number (SSN), in a bank account is important. Assume that the ACCOUNTS table looks like this:

```
ACCOUNT_NO      NUMBER(10)
SSN             CHAR(9)
SSN_MAC         VARCHAR2(200)
```

When an account is created, the MAC value is calculated on the SSN field using a predetermined key, such as "Humpty Dumpty Fell Off the Wall". The column SSN_MAC is updated by the following statement:

```
update accounts
    set ssn_mac = get_mac_val (ssn, 'Humpty Dumpty Fell Off the Wall')
 where account_no = <AccountNo>;
```

Now assume that sometime afterward, a hacker updates the SSN field. If the SSN_MAC field contains the hash value of the column SSN, the hacker can calculate the hash value himself and update the column with the new value as well. Later, when the hash value is calculated on the SSN column and compared to the stored SSN_MAC value, they would match, thus hiding the fact that the data was compromised! However, if the column contains the MAC value of the column, rather than the hash value, the calculation of the new value would require the key (Humpty Dumpty Fell Off the Wall). Because the hacker does not know that, the updated value will not generate the same MAC value, thus revealing that the data was compromised.

Putting It All Together: A Project

In this section, we wrap up the chapter by describing a practical, real-world system that illustrates the encryption and hashing concepts we've been discussing throughout this chapter. And we will do this without needing to change the existing application running against the table.

Sometimes your encrypted data will need to be matched with incoming data. For instance, many Customer Relationship Management (CRM) applications use different attributes of customers, such as credit card numbers, passport numbers, and so on, to identify unique customers. Medical applications may need to go through the patients' diagnosis history to project a pattern and suggest treatment options. Insurance applications may need to search patient diagnoses to assess the validity of the claims, and so on. Because these data items are stored in an encrypted manner, the matching applications cannot simply match against the stored data.

There are two options for handling such situations, as described next.

Option 1

You encrypt the data to be matched and match it against the stored encrypted values. This option is possible only if the encryption key is known. If your approach is to have one key per database (or table or schema), then you know the exact key that must have been used to encrypt the values. On the other hand, if your approach is to use one key per row, you will have an idea of what key must have been used to encrypt the value in that particular row. Hence, you can't use this approach.

The other issue with using this option is indexing. If you have an index on this encrypted column, the index will be useful when an equality predicate is specified. Here's an example:

```
"ssn = encrypt ('123-45-6789')"
```

The query will locate on the index the encrypted value of the string **'123-45-6789'** and then get the other values of the row. Because this is an equality predicate, an exact value on the index is searched and located. However, if you specified a likeness predicate (for example, **"ssn like '123-%'"**), the index will be useless. Because the b-tree structure of the index stores the data starting with a specific value close together, this like operation would have been helped by the index had it been in cleartext. For instance, index entries for **'123-45-6789'** and **'123-67-8945'** would have been close together in an index. But when they are encrypted, the actual values could be something like this:

```
076A5703A745D03934B56F7500C1DCB4
178F45A983D5D03934B56F7500C1DCB4
```

Because the first characters are very different, they will be on different parts of the index. Using an index match first to determine the location in the table will be slower than doing a full table scan.

Option 2

Decrypt the encrypted data in each row and match it against the cleartext value to be matched. If you use one single key per row, this is your only option. But each decryption consumes several precious CPU cycles, which may adversely affect performance.

So, how can you design a system that matches against encrypted columns faster? The trick is to match against a hash value, not the encrypted value. Creating a hash value is significantly faster than encryption, and it consumes fewer CPU cycles. Because the hashing of an input value will always produce the same value, we could store the hash value of the sensitive data, create a hash value of the data to be compared, and match it against the stored hash value.

Here is a proposed system design. Assume that you have a table named CUSTOMERS where the credit card numbers are stored. This is how the table looks today:

```
SQL> desc customers
 Name                                      Null?    Type
 ----------------------------------------- -------- -------------
 CUST_ID                                   NOT NULL NUMBER
 CC                                        NOT NULL VARCHAR2(128)
```

Applications are already written against it, and you don't want to change them. You want to encrypt the credit card numbers in the CUSTOMERS table with no impact to the applications. How can you accomplish this?

Instead of storing the credit card number in the CUSTOMERS table, you would create two additional tables, like so:

CUSTOMERS table:

- CUST_ID (primary key)
- CC (the hash value of the credit card, not the actual credit card number itself)

CC_MASTER table:

- CC_HASH (primary key)
- ENC_CC# (the encrypted value of the credit card number)

CC_KEYS table:

- CC_HASH (primary key)
- ENC_KEY (the encryption key used to encrypt the credit card number)

The cleartext entry of the credit card is not stored anywhere. You could write a before-row INSERT or UPDATE trigger on the table that follows the pseudo-code shown here:

```
1    Calculate the hash value
2    Set the value of the column CC to the hash value calculated earlier
3    Search for this hash value in CC_MASTER table
4    IF found THEN
5        Do nothing
6    ELSE
```

```
7        Generate a key
8        Use this key to generate the encrypted value of the clear text credit card number
9        Insert a record into the CC_KEYS table for this hash value and the key
10        Insert a record in the CC_MASTER table with the encrypted value and the key.
11    END IF
```

This logic ensures that the cleartext credit card is not stored in the database. Applications will continue to insert the cleartext value, but the trigger will change it to a hash value.

Create the tables for the project:

```
create table customers
(
    cust_id          number not null primary key,
    cc               varchar2(128) not null
);
create table cc_master
(
    cc_hash          raw(32) not null primary key,
    enc_cc           varchar2(128) not null
);
create table cc_keys
(
    cc_hash          raw(32) not null primary key,
    enc_key          varchar2(128) not null
);
```

Because we will be matching on the CC column a lot, you should create an index on it:

```
create index in_cust_cc on customers (cc);
```

You need to have already created the functions **get_enc_val()**, **get_dec_val()**, and **get_key()** described earlier in the chapter.

Here is the actual code for the trigger:

```
create or replace trigger tr_aiu_customers
    before insert or update
    on customers
    for each row
declare
    l_hash    varchar2 (64);
    l_enc     raw (2000);
    l_key     raw (2000);
begin
    l_hash := get_hash_val (:new.cc);
    begin
        select enc_cc
          into l_enc
          from cc_master
         where cc_hash = l_hash;
    exception
        when no_data_found
        then
```

```
        begin
           l_key := get_key (8);
           l_enc := get_enc_val (:new.cc, l_key);
            insert into cc_master
                        (cc_hash, enc_cc)
                values (l_hash, l_enc);
            insert into cc_keys
                        (cc_hash, enc_key)
                values (l_hash, l_key);
        end;
      when others then
         raise;
   end;
   :new.cc := l_hash;
end;
```

Now, let's test this trigger by inserting a row:

```
SQL> insert into customers values (1,'1234567890123456');
1 row created.
```

This insert should have triggered insertion into the other tables. Let's check them to confirm:

```
SQL> select * from cc_master;
CC_HASH
----------------------------------------------------------------
ENC_CC
----------------------------------------------------------------
DEED2A88E73DCCAA30A9E6E296F62BE238BE4ADE
1E06059F7D97197DB8B3C47815AC1C2241E32625199FD4499F89A69A1D28AA85
SQL> select * from cc_keys;
CC_HASH
----------------------------------------
ENC_KEY
----------------------------------------
DEED2A88E73DCCAA30A9E6E296F62BE238BE4ADE
F16B2C803F937565
```

As you can see, the actual credit card number (1234567890123456) doesn't appear anywhere. But by joining the encrypted values with the keys table on the CC_HASH column, you will be able to decrypt the card, as shown here:

```
select cust_id,
       get_dec_val
       (m.enc_cc,k.ENC_KEY) as cc
from customers c, cc_master m, cc_keys k
where c.cc = m.cc_hash
and k.cc_hash = m.cc_hash;

   CUST_ID CC
---------- ------------------------------------------------
         1 1234567890123456
```

We can see the actual credit card number now. We can use this query to define a view, as shown here:

```
create or replace view vw_customers
as
select cust_id,
   cast (
     get_dec_val
     (m.enc_cc,k.ENC_KEY)
   as varchar2(16)) as cc
from customers c, cc_master m, cc_keys k
where c.cc = m.cc_hash
and k.cc_hash = m.cc_hash;
```

Let's check from the view to confirm:

```
SQL> select * from vw_customers;
   CUST_ID CC
---------- ----------------
         1 1234567890123456
```

Grant access to this view to those who are expected to see the credit card (privileged users). Suppose one of those privileged users is HR. Here is how you grant privileges:

```
SQL> conn scott/tiger
SQL> grant select, insert, delete, update on vw_customers to hr;
Grant succeeded.
```

Everyone else should have the privileges on the table only. Thus, the privileged users will be able to see the cleartext credit card while others will see the hash value, which they can use to match the card but never actually decipher the real card number.

Because users will execute DML against this view, we need to create an INSTEAD OF trigger on it so that the table will be updated when DML is issued against the view:

```
create or replace trigger tr_io_iud_vw_cust
   instead of
   insert or
   update or
   delete on vw_customers
begin
  if (inserting) then
    insert
    into customers values
    (
      :new.cust_id,
      :new.cc
    );
  elsif (deleting) then
    delete customers where cust_id = :old.cust_id;
  elsif (updating) then
    update customers
```

```
      set cc = :new.cc
      where cust_id = :new.cust_id;
   else
      null;
   end if;
end;
```

The HR user, which usually operates on the CUSTOMERS table, can no longer do so because it has to see the cleartext; therefore, it has to operate on VW_CUSTOMERS. However, recall that we don't want to change any applications. Therefore, changing the applications to point to VW_ CUSTOMERS from CUSTOMERS is not acceptable. We can solve this simply by creating a synonym:

```
SQL> conn hr/hr
SQL> create synonym customers for scott.vw_customers;
Synonym created.
```

With these in place, let's see the application when connected as the HR user. Remember, the application connected as the HR user selects the CC column from the CUSTOMERS table and is used to get the cleartext value. What will be the case now? Let's see:

```
select * from customers;
   CUST_ID CC
---------- ----------------
         1 1234567890123456
```

Perfect! It got the *cleartext* value—not the encrypted value that is actually stored in the CUSTOMERS table—because the object CUSTOMERS actually points to the VW_CUSTOMERS view, which does the decryption and shows the cleartext value automatically.

What about DML statements issued by the application? Let's see:

```
SQL> insert into customers values (2,'2345678901234567');
1 row created.
SQL> update customers set cc = '3456789012345678' where cust_id = 2;
1 row updated.
SQL> delete customers where cust_id = 2;
1 row deleted.
```

In all these cases, the INSTEAD OF trigger kicked in and executed the INSERT, UPDATE, and DELETE statements against the original table.

What happens when another user (say, SH) who is non-privileged (that is, one who should *not* see the cleartext value) wants to see the credit card number? In that case, you would not have created the synonym to point to the view. Instead, the synonym would have pointed to the table, so the CUSTOMERS object would point to the table CUSTOMERS. Suppose SH selects the following:

```
select * from scott.customers;
   CUST_ID CC
---------- -----------------------------------------
         1 DEED2A88E73DCCAA30A9E6E296F62BE238BE4ADE
```

In this case, the user sees the hash value, not the cleartext. This is what you wanted.

For matching card numbers, instead of decrypting the values, all the users have to do is create the hash value and match it with the stored data. For instance, suppose you just want to find out the customer with the credit card number 1234567890123456. Instead of decrypting the table via the view, all you need to do is filter the CC column with the hash value. Let's look at the results with autotrace enabled so that we can see the execution path and the statistics.

```
SQL> conn hr/hr
SQL> set autot on explain stat
SQL> select cust_id from customers where cc = get_hash_val ('1234567890123456');


   CUST_ID
----------
         1
Execution Plan
----------------------------------------------------------
Plan hash value: 1492748282

-------------------------------------------------------------------------------------
| Id  | Operation                            | Name        | Rows  | Bytes | Cost (%CPU)| Time     |
-------------------------------------------------------------------------------------
|   0 | SELECT STATEMENT                     |             |     1 |    79 |     2   (0)| 00:00:01 |
|   1 |  TABLE ACCESS BY INDEX ROWID BATCHED | CUSTOMERS   |     1 |    79 |     2   (0)| 00:00:01 |
|*  2 |   INDEX RANGE SCAN                   | IN_CUST_CC  |     1 |       |     1   (0)| 00:00:01 |
-------------------------------------------------------------------------------------

Predicate Information (identified by operation id):
---------------------------------------------------

   2 - access("CC"="GET_HASH_VAL"('1234567890123456'))

Note
-----
   - dynamic statistics used: dynamic sampling (level=2)


Statistics
----------------------------------------------------------
         24  recursive calls
          0  db block gets
         18  consistent gets
          0  physical reads
          0  redo size
        586  bytes sent via SQL*Net to client
        551  bytes received via SQL*Net from client
          2  SQL*Net roundtrips to/from client
          0  sorts (memory)
          0  sorts (disk)
          1  rows processed
```

Now let's see the effect when the user searches for a specific credit card number (for example, 1234567890123456), not searching for the hash value:

```
select cust_id from vw_customers where cc = '1234567890123456';

   CUST_ID
----------
         1


Execution Plan
----------------------------------------------------------
Plan hash value: 3308188567

---------------------------------------------------------------------------------------------------
| Id | Operation                               | Name        | Rows | Bytes | Cost (%CPU)| Time     |
---------------------------------------------------------------------------------------------------
|  0 | SELECT STATEMENT                        |             |    1 |   247 |     5   (0)| 00:00:01 |
|  1 |  NESTED LOOPS                           |             |    1 |   247 |     5   (0)| 00:00:01 |
|  2 |   NESTED LOOPS                          |             |    1 |   247 |     5   (0)| 00:00:01 |
|  3 |    NESTED LOOPS                         |             |    1 |   163 |     4   (0)| 00:00:01 |
|  4 |     TABLE ACCESS FULL                   | CC_MASTER   |    1 |    84 |     3   (0)| 00:00:01 |
|  5 |     TABLE ACCESS BY INDEX ROWID BATCHED | CUSTOMERS   |    1 |    79 |     1   (0)| 00:00:01 |
|* 6 |      INDEX RANGE SCAN                   | IN_CUST_CC  |    1 |       |     0   (0)| 00:00:01 |
|* 7 |    INDEX UNIQUE SCAN                    | SYS_C0010519|    1 |       |     0   (0)| 00:00:01 |
|* 8 |   TABLE ACCESS BY INDEX ROWID           | CC_KEYS     |    1 |    84 |     1   (0)| 00:00:01 |
---------------------------------------------------------------------------------------------------

Predicate Information (identified by operation id):
---------------------------------------------------

   6 - access("C"."CC"=RAWTOHEX("M"."CC_HASH"))
   7 - access("K"."CC_HASH"="M"."CC_HASH")
   8 - filter(CAST("GET_DEC_VAL"("M"."ENC_CC","K"."ENC_KEY") AS
             varchar2(16))='1234567890123456')

Note
-----
   - dynamic statistics used: dynamic sampling (level=2)
   - this is an adaptive plan


Statistics
----------------------------------------------------------
         38  recursive calls
          0  db block gets
         47  consistent gets
          0  physical reads
          0  redo size
```

```
541  bytes sent via SQL*Net to client
551  bytes received via SQL*Net from client
  2  SQL*Net roundtrips to/from client
  0  sorts (memory)
  0  sorts (disk)
  1  rows processed
```

Because there is an index on the CC column, it was used as an index range scan instead of a full table scan. Contrast this with the case when you selected the cleartext credit card number from the view created earlier. In this case, 47 consistent get operations were performed, compared to 18 earlier—not to mention the fact that some cycles were spent in the decryption process as well.

This is merely a demonstration to show how you can leverage various concepts explained in this chapter to build a PL/SQL-based encryption solution. You can take off from here and enhance it any way you want. For instance, in this case, we stored the keys in a table. To add further security, you can use the key modifier concept described earlier in the chapter to store a key modifier in the file system and use it to modify the actual key using bitwise XOR. The important thing is that you can create all this without the need to change the application.

Quick Reference

This section contains specifications for all the procedures and functions provided in the built-in package DBMS_CRYPTO.

GETRANDOMBYTES

Generates a cryptographically secure key for encryption. This function accepts one input parameter and returns the key as a RAW data type.

Parameter	Data Type	Description
number_bytes	BINARY_INTEGER	Length of the random value to be generated

ENCRYPT

Produces encrypted values from input values. This program is overloaded as a function and two procedures, and is further overloaded for different data types.

Function Version   Accepts four input parameters and returns the encrypted value as a RAW data type.

Parameter	Data Type	Description
src	RAW	Value to be encrypted. This value may be of any length.
typ	BINARY_INTEGER	Combines the encryption algorithm, padding method, and chaining method.
key	RAW	Encryption key.

Parameter	Data Type	Description
iv	RAW	Initialization vector. This value is added to the input value to reduce the repetition of encrypted values. This parameter must be specified if it was used during encryption, and it must be the same as the value used for encryption.

Procedure: Version 1   Encrypts LOBs. To encrypt non-LOB values, use the function version of **encrypt**. This version accepts four input parameters and returns the encrypted value as a RAW data type.

Parameter	Data Type	Description
dst	BLOB	**out** parameter; the encrypted value is passed back to the user in this parameter.
src	BLOB	BLOB value or resource locator to be encrypted.
typ	BINARY_INTEGER	Combines the encryption algorithm, padding method, and chaining method.
key	RAW	Encryption key.
iv	RAW	Initialization vector. This value is added to the input value to reduce the repetition of encrypted values. It is optional.

Procedure: Version 2   Identical to the first procedure version, except that it is used to encrypt CLOB data.

Parameter	Data Type	Description
dst	BLOB	**out** parameter; the encrypted value passed back to the user in this parameter.
src	CLOB	CLOB value or resource locators to be encrypted.
typ	BINARY_INTEGER	Combines the encryption algorithm, padding method, and chaining method.
key	RAW	Encryption key.
iv	RAW	Initialization vector. This value is added to the input value to reduce the repetition of encrypted values. It is optional.

DECRYPT

This program decrypts encrypted values. Like **encrypt**, this program is overloaded as a function and two procedures, and is further overloaded for different data types.

Function Version   Accepts four input parameters and returns the decrypted value as a RAW data type.

Parameter	Data Type	Description
src	RAW	Encrypted value to be decrypted.
typ	BINARY_INTEGER	Combines the encryption algorithm, the padding method, and the chaining method. It must be the same as that used during the encryption process.
key	RAW	Encryption key. It must be the same one used during encryption.
iv	RAW	Initialization vector. This value is added to the input value to reduce the repetition of encrypted values. This parameter must be specified if it was used during encryption, and it must be the same as the value used for encryption.

Procedure: Version 1   Decrypts encrypted LOBs. To decrypt encrypted non-LOB values, use the function variant of **decrypt** instead. This version accepts four input parameters and returns the decrypted value in the BLOB data type.

Parameter	Data Type	Description
dst	BLOB	Decrypted value is placed here.
src	BLOB	Encrypted BLOB value or resource locator to be decrypted.
typ	BINARY_INTEGER	Combines the encryption algorithm, the padding method, and the chaining method. It must be the same one used during encryption.
key	RAW	Encryption key. It must be the same one used during encryption.
iv	RAW	Initialization vector. This value is added to the input value to reduce the repetition of encrypted values. This parameter must be specified if it was used during encryption, and it must be the same as the value used for encryption.

Procedure: Version 2   Identical to the first procedure version, except that it is used to decrypt encrypted CLOB data.

Parameter	Data Type	Description
dst	CLOB	Decrypted value is placed here.
src	BLOB	Encrypted BLOB value or resource locator to be decrypted.
typ	BINARY_INTEGER	Combines the encryption algorithm, padding method, and chaining method. This value must be the same as the one used for encryption.
key	RAW	Encryption key. It must be the same as the one used during encryption.
iv	RAW	Initialization vector. This value is added to the input value to reduce the repetition of encrypted values. This parameter must be specified if it was used during encryption, and it must be the same as the value used for encryption.

HASH

This program generates cryptographic hash values from the input values. You can generate either Message Digest 5 (MD5) or Secure Hash Algorithm 1 or 2 (SHA-1/SHA-2) hash values by specifying the appropriate **typ** parameter. This program is overloaded with three functions.

Function: Version 1   Generates hash values of non-LOB data types. This version accepts two parameters and returns the hash value as a RAW data type.

Parameter	Data Type	Description
src	RAW	The input value whose hash value is to be generated
typ	BINARY_INTEGER	The hash algorithm to be used, as per the table shown next

The hash algorithm is specified by setting one of the following constants defined in DBMS_CRYPTO as the value of the **typ** parameter.

Use This Value for typ Parameter	Description	Size in Bits
dbms_crypto.hash_md5	Message Digest 5	128
dbms_crypto.hash_md4	Message Digest 4	128
dbms_crypto.hash_sh1	Secure Hashing Algorithm 1	160
dbms_crypto.hash_sh256	Secure Hashing Algorithm 2	256
dbms_crypto.hash_sh384	Secure Hashing Algorithm 2	384
dbms_crypto.hash_sh512	Secure Hashing Algorithm 2	512

Function: Version 2   Generates hash values of BLOB data types. This version accepts two parameters and returns the hash value as a RAW data type.

Parameter	Data Type	Description
src	BLOB	Input BLOB value or resource locator whose hash value is to be generated
typ	BINARY_INTEGER	The hash algorithm to be used

Function: Version 3   Generates hash values of CLOB data types. This version accepts two parameters and returns the hash value as a RAW data type.

Parameter	Data Type	Description
src	CLOB	Input CLOB value or resource locator whose hash value is to be generated
typ	BINARY_INTEGER	Hash algorithm to be used

MAC

This program generates message authentication code (MAC) values from the input values. MAC values are similar to hash values but they have an added key. You can generate either Message Digest 5 (MD5) or Secure Hash Algorithm 1 or 2 (SHA-1 or SHA-2) MAC values by specifying the appropriate **typ** parameter. Like HASH, this program is overloaded with three functions.

Function: Version 1   Generates MAC values of non-LOB data types. This version accepts three parameters and returns the MAC value as a RAW data type.

Parameter	Data Type	Description
src	RAW	Input value whose MAC value is to be generated
typ	BINARY_INTEGER	MAC algorithm to be used as per the table shown next
key	RAW	Key used to build the MAC value

The MAC algorithm is specified by setting one of the following constants defined in DBMS_CRYPTO as the value of **typ** parameter.

Use This Value for typ Parameter	Description	Size in Bits
dbms_crypto.hmac_md5	Message Digest 5	128
dbms_crypto.hmac_sh1	Secure Hashing Algorithm 1	160
dbms_crypto.hmac_sh256	Secure Hashing Algorithm 2	256
dbms_crypto.hmac_sh384	Secure Hashing Algorithm 2	384
dbms_crypto.hmac_sh512	Secure Hashing Algorithm 2	512

Function: Version 2   Generates hash values of BLOB data types. This version accepts two parameters and returns the hash value as a RAW data type.

Parameter	Data Type	Description
src	BLOB	Input value whose MAC value is to be generated
typ	BINARY_INTEGER	MAC algorithm to be used
key	RAW	Key used to build the MAC value

Function: Version 3   Generates hash values of CLOB data types. This version accepts two parameters and returns the hash value as a RAW data type.

Parameter	Data Type	Description
src	CLOB	Input value whose MAC value is to be generated
typ	BINARY_INTEGER	MAC algorithm to be used
key	RAW	Key used to build the MAC value

Summary

In this chapter we looked at encryption, key management, hashing, and related concepts. Encryption of data is the disguising of the data so its true meaning is not visible. It requires three basic ingredients—the input data, an encryption key, and an encryption algorithm. There are two fundamental methods of encryption: key encryption, where the keys used to encrypt and decrypt are different, and symmetric key encryption, where the keys are the same. The former is typically used in data transmission and requires elaborate setup, whereas the latter is relatively simple to implement.

The most important and challenging aspect of building an encryption infrastructure is not using the APIs themselves, but building a reliable and secure key management system. There are a variety of different ways to do that: you can use the database, the file system, or both as a key store. You can use a single key for the entire database, one key per row of the table, or something in between. You can use two different keys: one regular key stored somewhere and a key modifier stored at a different location. The key that is used to encrypt data is not the one stored, but is a bitwise XOR operation of the modifier and stored keys. If either one is compromised, the encrypted data cannot be decrypted.

Sometimes, it is not necessary to hide data, but we nevertheless have to ensure that it has not changed. This is done via cryptographic hashing. A hash function will always return the same value for a given input value. Therefore, if we determine that a calculated hash value differs from the value originally calculated, we know that the source data has changed. A variation of hashing called Message Authentication Code (MAC) involves hashing with a key.

Oracle 10*g* Release 2 introduced a feature called Transparent Database Encryption (TDE) that transparently encrypts and decrypts data before storing it in data files. With TDE, sensitive columns in data files, archived log files, and database backups are stored encrypted, so a theft of the files will not reveal the sensitive data. Oracle 11*g* Release 1 introduced a variant of TDE known as tablespace TDE that encrypts all the data in a tablespace on the disk but decrypts it in the buffer cache. This makes joins and index range scans very easy. TDE is a quick way to encrypt the data for immediate compliance, but because it performs the encryption and decryption transparently without discrimination, it might not address all scenarios. You still need to build your own infrastructure if you want to control who will see the decrypted values and who will not.

Finally, you learned how to put all these ideas together to build a project to encrypt an existing table without disturbing the application running against it.

CHAPTER
15

SQL Injection and Code Security

O nce again, let's ponder the question posed at the beginning of Chapter 14. What is the biggest threat to data security?

Security in databases used to be a DBA-only activity. Back in those days, the databases used to be islands processing batch applications. With the advent of online processing, and the ever-increasing importance of interactive data, ease of access takes the center stage in most system development. Unfortunately, that's where the clash with the concepts of security occurs. Some see the need to make data easily accessible and coding even easier—especially with the now-popular agile programming methodology—to be more important than the need to make it secure. And that's where the walls of security fall apart. For instance, you may have granted privilege to the EMPLOYEE table to the application user alone assuming that no one else can access it. What if the application allows the query to be transformed in such a way that it includes *another* query selecting from the SALARY table as well? Sure, the database allows this because it is supposed to, but, of course, that is not what you intended.

As you learned in the previous chapters, making the database secure is only half the battle. The other half is making the manipulation of data secure, which starts and ends with application development. We covered some aspects of application security such as data redaction, encryption, and hashing in the previous chapters. In the next chapter, you will learn how to make data selectively visible using Virtual Private Database. In this chapter, we explain the techniques of coding that incorporate elements of security from inception to deployment, thus eliminating or at least reducing the vulnerabilities. We call it secure or defensive coding. We will discuss how to safeguard our code against unintended execution, close vulnerabilities, and avoid SQL injection attacks.

Execution Models

Stored PL/SQL code such as procedures and functions can reference underlying objects in the code. For instance, assume there is a table known as T1 in the SCOTT schema created by the following SQL:

```
-- as SCOTT
create table t1 (col1 number);
-- SCOTT inserts a row into the table and commits it:
insert into t1 values (1);
commit;
```

Here is a procedure owned by the user SCOTT:

```
create or replace procedure myproc
as
    l_col1   number;
begin
    select col1
    into l_col1
    from t1
    where rownum <2;
    dbms_output.put_line('col1='||l_col1);
end;
```

Assume, another user (in this case, SH) also has a table called T1 and a row with the value 10:

```
-- As user SH
create table t1 (col1 number);
insert into t1 values (10);
commit;
```

SCOTT grants the execute privilege on the newly created procedure to SH:

```
grant execute on myproc to sh;
```

After this, SH can execute the procedure. When he does, the procedure selects from a table named T1. Both SH and SCOTT own a table with that name, and both have a column called COL1. Which table will be selected? Let's see with an actual execution. First, SCOTT executes the procedure:

```
SQL> conn scott/tiger
Connected.
SQL> set serveroutput on
SQL> exec myproc
col1=1
PL/SQL procedure successfully completed.
```

In this case, the output is 1, which is the value in the COL1 in T1 owned by SCOTT. That's no surprise. Now, SH executes the procedure:

```
SQL> conn sh/sh
Connected.
SQL> set serveroutput on
SQL> exec scott.myproc
col1=1
PL/SQL procedure successfully completed.
```

It also outputs 1, which is from the table owned by SCOTT. This is also not a surprise. SH executed the procedure owned by SCOTT; therefore, any objects inside that procedure will be deemed to be owned by SCOTT. Of course, if any such object is qualified by a schema name (for example, SYS.DBA_USERS), then that object will be assumed to be owned as specified. If a table is not qualified, the schema is deemed to be the owner of the procedure. Hence, the table T1 of the SCOTT schema was selected. This is the default behavior.

What if SH wants to select from its own table T1 instead of that of SCOTT? Well, conventional wisdom says that in that case, SH should create its own version of the procedure **myproc**. This procedure, because it's owned by SH, will automatically point to its own table T1. That's probably fine, but in reality it may be undesirable. You may want to create a code that can be easily used by everyone without duplicating the effort. If everyone created their own procedures, the code would be different and inconsistent. You could mandate that everyone copy the code from a common source, but that's also impractical. What if someone doesn't copy? You may have wrong code, and it will be difficult to track what precisely is the discrepancy in the case of issues. Therefore, you want to have just a single procedure, but the procedure should be smart enough to look into the objects owned by the user *executing* them, not those of who *created* them. It's possible to create a procedure that way using a special directive—**authid current_user**. Here is the same procedure, created by SCOTT, but using the special directive:

```
-- As user SH
create or replace procedure myproc
authid current_user
as
    l_col1 number;
begin
    select col1
    into l_col1
    from t1
    where rownum <2;
    dbms_output.put_line('col1='||l_col1);
end;
```

Note the second line where the **authid current_user** is defined. After the procedure is defined this way, when the user SH executes it, the procedure gets the data from the T1 table owned by SH, not that of SCOTT:

```
SQL> conn sh/sh
Connected.
SQL> set serveroutput on
SQL> exec scott.myproc
col1=10
```

Because it accesses the objects owned by the invoker (or executor) of the program, this method of creating the procedure is known as the *invoker rights model*. The other method, where the authority of the creator (or definer) of the program is used, is known as the *definer rights model*, which is the default behavior. You can also optionally set the **authid** by this line in the code for procedure creation:

```
authid definer
```

It's very important to understand the implications of these two methods of procedure creation. The code could be identical, but the logic may be completely different, and if you don't pay attention, you will not only have buggy code, but will open vulnerabilities for malicious users to exploit it. For example, suppose SCOTT develops a small procedure that counts the number of tables in the schema:

```
create or replace procedure count_tables
as
    l_cnt   number;
begin
    select count(*)
    into l_cnt
    from user_tables;
    dbms_output.put_line('Total Number of tables in my schema='||l_cnt);
end;
```

When SCOTT runs this procedure, the expected result is returned:

```
SQL> exec count_tables
Total Number of tables in my schema=2
```

Assume that everyone wants to use this new "utility" by SCOTT. Being pretty generous by nature, SCOTT grants execute privileges to PUBLIC:

```
grant execute on scott.count_tables to public;
```

Now, suppose user SH executes it:

```
SQL> exec scott.count_tables
Total Number of tables in my schema=2
```

The output shows only two tables, which is a wrong result. SH has more than two tables. Why did the procedure show the wrong results? It's because the procedure does not have an **authid** clause, which causes it to default to the definer rights model, which assumes the objects inside the procedure are owned by the owner of the procedure—SCOTT. Hence, it displayed the number of tables owned by SCOTT, not SH.

To make the procedure truly generic, SCOTT has to re-create it with the invoker rights model (that is, using **authid current_user**), as shown here:

```
-- As SCOTT
create or replace procedure count_tables
authid current_user
as
    l_cnt   number;
begin
    select count(*)
    into l_cnt
    from user_tables;
    dbms_output.put_line('Total Number of tables in my schema='||l_cnt);
end;
```

After that, when SH executes the procedure, the correct results are returned:

```
-- as SH
SQL> exec scott.count_tables
Total Number of tables in my schema=18
```

In fact, any other user can execute the procedure to get the results within the scope of their own authority and not that of the creator of the program. Here is user HR executing it:

```
SQL> conn hr/hr
Connected.
SQL> set serveroutput on
SQL> exec scott.count_tables
Total Number of tables in my schema=7
```

So, when do you choose one model over the other? There seems to be an urban myth floating around that the invoker rights model is more secure than the definer rights model. That is simply not true. The degree of security depends on understanding what is possible but not intended and then mitigating those risks. Let's examine that with an example. Assume there is a user named SCHEMAUSER who owns all the tables, procedures, and so on, and the applications connect as the user EXECUSER. Let's create the two users and grant the appropriate privileges:

```
-- as SYS
create user schemauser identified by schemauser;
grant create session, create table, create procedure,
unlimited tablespace to schemauser;
create user execuser identified by execuser;
grant create session to execuser;
```

We deliberately granted as few privileges as possible to demonstrate the effects of various settings. It's a good practice anyway to grant as few privileges as needed. Now, we will create a table to hold the account information in the SCHEMAUSER schema:

```
-- As SCHEMAUSER
create table accounts
(
    accno               number,
    accname             varchar2(30),
    ssn                 varchar2(9),
    birthday            date,
    principal           number,
    interest            number,
    created_dt          date
);
```

We also need to insert some data into this table. The following code inserts 100 records with some test data:

```
-- As SCHEMAUSER
begin
  for i in 1..100 loop
    insert into accounts values (
      i,
      dbms_random.string('u',30),
      ltrim (to_char(dbms_random.value
        (100000000, 999999999), '999999999')),
      sysdate - 30*365 - dbms_random.value(1,60*365),
      dbms_random.value(1,100000),
      dbms_random.value(1,10000),
      sysdate - dbms_random.value(1,365*5)
    );
  end loop;
end;
/
commit
/
```

You probably have many applications, but not all of them need access to all the columns of the table. For instance, many applications are interested in the total number of accounts in the table, but not all should be authorized to see sensitive columns such as SSN. To get the count of all records in the table, the users need SELECT access on the table, but we don't want to give them that. Instead, we create a simple function that counts and returns the number of records of a specific table:

```
create or replace function get_accounts_count
return number
as
    l_cnt    number;
begin
    select count(*)
    into l_cnt
    from schemauser.accounts;
    return l_cnt;
end;
```

We then grant the execute privileges on this function to public:

```
grant execute on get_accounts_count to public;
```

Now, when EXECUSER wants to know the total number of records, it can execute the function:

```
SQL> conn execuser/execuser
SQL> select schemauser.get_accounts_count from dual;

GET_ACCOUNTS_COUNT
------------------
               100
```

This works as expected. Now consider what would happen if we had created the function with invoker rights. Let's re-create the function:

```
-- as SCHEMAUSER
create or replace function get_accounts_count
return number
authid current_user
as
    l_cnt    number;
begin
    select count(*)
    into l_cnt
    from schemauser.accounts;
    return l_cnt;
end;
```

Now when EXECUSER executes the procedure, the following error is returned because the procedure references the SCHEMAUSER.ACCOUNTS table inside it:

```
SQL> select schemauser.get_accounts_count from dual;
select schemauser.get_accounts_count from dual
       *
ERROR at line 1:
ORA-00942: table or view does not exist
ORA-06512: at "SCHEMAUSER.GET_ACCOUNTS_COUNT", line 7
```

Because this is under the invoker rights model, the authority of the invoker (EXECUSER), not the creator (SCHEMAUSER), applies. The user EXECUSER doesn't have any privileges on the table, so the execution fails.

To make it work, we have to grant EXECUSER the select privileges on the table:

```
SQL> connect schemauser/schemauser
SQL> grant select on accounts to execuser;
Grant succeeded.
SQL> conn execuser/execuser
Connected.
SQL> set serveroutput on
SQL> select schemauser.get_accounts_count from dual;
GET_ACCOUNTS_COUNT
------------------
               100
```

This works now, but is it desirable? Maybe not. Because EXECUSER has the privileges on the table now, it can select anything else from the table, including sensitive columns such as SSN, PRINCIPAL, and so on. It's definitely not desirable. The Invoker Rights model does not work in this case. This is a great use case for the definer rights model.

So, what are the use cases of the invoker rights model? You've already seen one example of a "utility" program—one where the logic is same for all users but the objects referenced in them are owned by the calling user. However, because this program uses the caller's authority, not the definer's, you must be aware of some interesting ramifications. Consider the earlier example where we created a function to return the number of rows in the USER_TABLES view. Now we want to make it generic enough so that it can count the number of records in any table or view accessible by the calling user, with the name of the table or view passed to it as a parameter. This sounds simple enough. All we have to do is call something like the following pseudo-code:

1. Get the name of the table passed as a parameter.

2. Select **count(*)** from the table.

3. Store the count in some variable.

4. Return the value in the variable.

Will this work? No. Because we won't know the name of the table during the creation of the procedure, which is needed for the compilation, this function won't compile. Therefore, we have to resort to dynamic SQL, not static. We need to create a statement at run time and execute it. Here is how the program looks:

```
-- As SCHEMAUSER
create or replace function get_table_rec_count
(
    p_table_name in varchar2
)
return number
authid current_user
as
    l_cnt    number;
    l_stmt   varchar2(32767);
```

```
begin
   l_stmt := 'select count(*) from '||p_table_name;
   execute immediate l_stmt into l_cnt;
   return l_cnt;
end;
```

Now we grant the execute privileges to all users so that they can execute it:

```
grant execute on get_table_rec_count to public;
```

After this, if EXECUSER needs to know the count of records in a table or view to which it has access (for example, ACCOUNTS by SCHEMAUSER), it can call the function:

```
SQL> select schemauser.get_table_rec_count('SCHEMAUSER.ACCOUNTS') from dual;

SCHEMAUSER.GET_TABLE_REC_COUNT('SCHEMAUSER.ACCOUNTS')
-----------------------------------------------------
                                                  100
```

So far, so good. The usage of this "utility" continues to spread. Now, a user named ARUP has a very powerful privilege—SELECT ANY DICTIONARY—that allows him to select from any of the data dictionary tables that are generally off limits to regular users. The user SYS grants the following to ARUP:

```
grant create session, select any dictionary,
select any table to arup identified by arup;
```

Unfortunately, the user ARUP is bit naïve and doesn't fully understand the ramifications of executing everything. During a debugging exercise, some developer wants to find out the counts from various tables in multiple schemas. Instead of writing the SQL and sending it to various groups to execute and get the results back, the developer approaches ARUP with the script and asks him to run it. Because ARUP has the privilege to select from any table (and he is a nice guy), he runs it and gets the results quickly. The script looks like this:

```
select schemauser.get_table_rec_count('SCHEMA1.TABLE1') from dual;
select schemauser.get_table_rec_count('SCHEMA2.TABLE2') from dual;
select schemauser.get_table_rec_count('SCHEMA3.TABLE3') from dual;
... and so on ...
```

Sounds innocuous. However, unbeknownst to ARUP, the developer slips this SELECT statement into the script:

```
select schemauser.get_table_rec_count('SYS.DBA_USERS') from dual;
```

Because the function runs with the privilege of the user ARUP, and ARUP can select from this view (DBA_USERS), the statement will work. Ideally data dictionary views are not supposed to be exposed to any regular user, but this works because the regular user asks the program to be run as a privileged user. This example merely illustrates a point. The count from the DBA_USERS view may not be that dangerous, but the concept definitely is. What if the malicious developer had chosen to select something more sensitive, such as how many accounts are in the table (which is a trade secret of the company)? Or, what if the function had selected some specific column instead of just a count, and the developer had passed those column names as a parameter? It would have exposed underlying data that is not supposed to be exposed. Later in the chapter you will learn about a grave danger to PL/SQL code where an attacker can alter the exact code executed at run time—a concept called SQL injection.

In summary, the definer and invoker rights models, by themselves, do not offer any more (or less) security. Security is as strong as your understanding of the implications of various actions and the steps you take to mitigate the risks. In this chapter, you will learn about various risks and how to reduce the possibilities of an attack.

Program Security

Going back to the previous example, recall that the applications connect as user EXECUSER. As a routine activity, this user needs to update the table ACCOUNTS owned by SCHEMAUSER. Because EXECUSER doesn't own the table, this user can't just update it; instead, update privileges are needed. However, allowing users to update the table directly may not be desirable. Many applications could have the code written in different ways. Ideally, you want the business logic to be in a single place. Allowing applications to write the update code makes the logic inconsistent and potentially erroneous. To avoid this issue, you should put the logic in a stored procedure (or function, as appropriate) and allow the users to simply call this stored code. If the logic of a business function ever changes, along with the changes in the business, you just need to update the code in one place.

Let's assume one such business function is updating interest on the balances of accounts. You create a stored procedure—called upd_int_amt—to perform this interest calculation and perform the update. This procedure is owned by SCHEMAUSER, which owns the table as well. To avoid the possibility of SQL injection (described later), you would want to make this procedure's security model the *invoker rights model*—that is, the actions inside the procedure are executed only to the extent of the authority of the user executing them, not the owner of the procedure. Conceptually, this is shown in Figure 15-1.

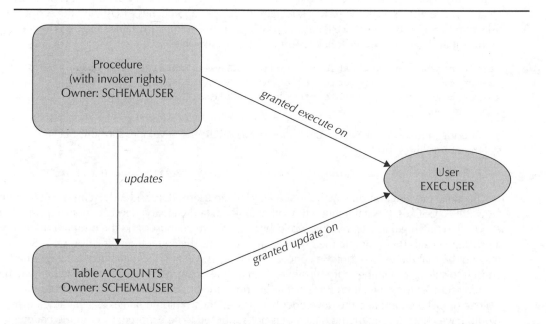

FIGURE 15-1. *Traditional approach to procedure security*

The Traditional Approach

Traditionally how you would have created the procedure is shown next. Because it's supposed to be under invoker rights security, you had to put in the **authid current_user** explicitly during the creation of the procedure.

```
-- As user SCHEMAUSER
create or replace procedure upd_int_amt
(
    p_accno in schemauser.accounts.accno%type
)
authid current_user
is
begin
    update schemauser.accounts
    set interest = principal * 0.01
    where accno = p_accno;
end;
```

Because EXECUSER is going to execute the procedure, you will need to grant the execute privileges on this procedure to that user:

```
grant execute on schemauser.upd_int_amt to execuser;
```

And because the procedure is created under the invoker rights model, the user EXECUSER needs the update privilege on the table explicitly as well to execute it:

```
grant update on schemauser.accounts to execuser;
```

Now EXECUSER can execute this procedure to update the accounts. For instance, as user EXECUSER, you can execute the following to update the interest amount of account number 100:

```
execute schemauser.upd_int_amt (100)
```

It works; the interest amount for account number 100 is computed and updated. So, what's wrong with it? The big problem here is the ability of the user EXECUSER. You created the procedure to update the accounts instead of letting the users update the table directly because the code to update the table for the interest application would remain consistent regardless of who performs the update. However, the user EXECUSER does have the privileges to update the table directly, so what prevents the user from making the update directly? Unfortunately, nothing. The user can easily make an update to the table instead of calling the procedure, thus violating your one-code arrangement.

How can you prevent the user from making a direct update on the table? Revoking the grant will not work because the procedure needs the privileges of the executor at run time. Will a role be helpful (that is, you create a role and assign the privileges to the role instead of the user and then grant that role to EXECUSER instead of giving direct access to the table)? Let's examine it. First, revoke the privilege granted earlier to EXECUSER (as user SYS):

```
revoke update on accounts from execuser;
```

Now, create the appropriate roles and grant the necessary privileges:

```
-- As a DBA user
create role upd_int_role;
grant update on schemauser.accounts to upd_int_role;
grant upd_int_role to execuser;
```

Conceptually, this is shown in Figure 15-2. To test whether this new setup works, let's reconnect as EXECUSER and make sure the role (UPD_INT_ROLE) is enabled in the session:

```
SQL> conn execuser/execuser
SQL> select * from session_roles;
ROLE
----------------------------------
RESOURCE
SELECT_CATALOG_ROLE
HS_ADMIN_SELECT_ROLE
UPD_INT_ROLE
```

The role UPD_INT_ROLE is enabled, as you can see from the output. Now when EXECUSER wants to update the interest by calling the procedure, it will succeed:

```
SQL> execute schemauser.upd_int_amt(1)
PL/SQL procedure successfully completed.
```

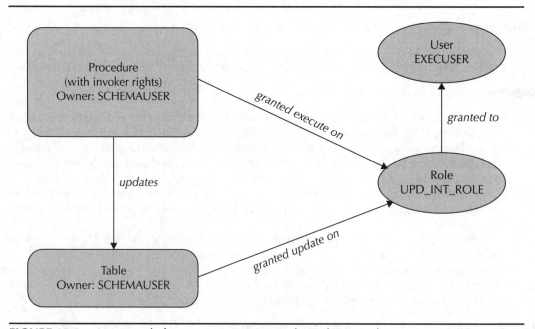

FIGURE 15-2. *Using a role for program security (traditional approach)*

Success? Not at all. Since it has the privilege, the user EXECUSER can also bypass the procedure and update the table directly, which is the very possibility you wanted to avoid:

```
SQL> update schemauser.accounts
  2   set interest = 1
  3   where accno = 100;
1 row updated.
```

Clearly, we have failed. We have to be able to put the update code in the stored procedure and provide the ability to update the ACCOUNTS table only via the procedure and remove any ability to update the table directly while under the invoker rights model. However, the invoker rights model requires the privileges to be granted to the executor (EXECUSER). These are mutually contradictory requirements. So what's the solution?

Role-Based Program Security

This is where a feature introduced in Oracle 12*c* Release 1 comes to the rescue. Instead of granting the role to a user, you can assign it to a procedure. Yes, that's correct: assign the *role* to the procedure. If you are wondering how that is possible, you are not alone. Prior to Oracle 12*c,* roles could only be granted to users or other roles, not to other objects such as procedures. But that changes with Oracle 12*c.* Granting a role to a procedure makes the arrangement you want possible. Conceptually, this is shown in Figure 15-3.

Let's look at how it works. First, revoke the privileges granted earlier:

```
-- As a DBA user
revoke execute on schemauser.upd_int_amt from execuser;
revoke update on schemauser.upd_int_amt from execuser;
revoke upd_int_role from execuser;
```

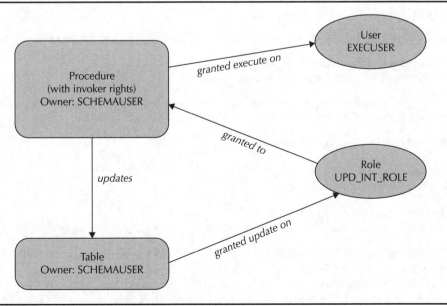

FIGURE 15-3. *Role-based program security*

Some of these may throw an error because the privilege may have been revoked already. Next, grant the execute privilege on the procedure to the user who will be calling it (that is, EXECUSER), as we did in the earlier case:

```
grant execute on schemauser.upd_int_amt to execuser;
```

Grant the update privilege to the role as well:

```
grant update on schemauser.accounts to upd_int_role;
```

Now perform two steps you didn't have to do earlier. First, grant the role to the user SCHEMAUSER:

```
grant upd_int_role to schemauser;
```

This may seem redundant because the user SCHEMAUSER owns the tables and hence does not need any role-based privilege to update it. However, this step is needed here. The second step uses the new syntax introduced in Oracle Database 12c. You grant the role to the procedure:

```
grant upd_int_role to procedure schemauser.upd_int_amt;
```

If you get the message

```
ORA-01924: role 'UPD_INT_ROLE' not granted or does not exist
```

that means you forgot to grant the role to the user SCHEMAUSER.

With this in place, connect as EXECUSER and check the roles enabled in the session:

```
SQL> conn execuser/execuser
SQL> select * from session_roles;
no rows selected
```

This confirms that the user does not have any roles enabled. Execute the procedure now:

```
SQL> execute schemauser.upd_int_amt(1)
PL/SQL procedure successfully completed.
```

It works; the procedure has updated the interest as expected. However, what happens if the user attempts to update the table directly?

```
SQL> update schemauser.accounts
  2   set interest = 1
  3   where accno = 100;
update schemauser.accounts
               *
ERROR at line 1:
ORA-00942: table or view does not exist
```

The user's action fails simply because it does not have any privileges on the table. The only way for this user to execute the interest calculation and update is to execute the procedure; it can't update the table directly. This is precisely what we wanted. You can apply this new role-based security to programs to enforce singular and consistent code logic while keeping the security model as invoker rights to reduce the possibility of SQL injection. In summary, here is what you need to do to enforce role-based program security:

1. Create a stored procedure (or function) for the business logic.
2. Create a role specifically for this purpose.
3. Grant this role to the schema owner only—no other user.
4. Grant privileges on the table to that role.
5. Grant execute privilege on the procedure to the application user. Do not grant anything on the table to this user.
6. Grant this role to the procedure. So, this role is granted only to the procedure and schema owner, not to any application users executing the procedure.

Here is a comparison of the steps between the traditional approach and the new approach to program security.

Traditional Approach	New Approach
Grant execute on procedure to SCOTT	Grant execute on procedure to SCOTT
Grant update on table to SCOTT	*Not needed*
Not needed	Grant update on table to role
Not possible	Grant role to procedure

Code Whitelisting

Modularization is an excellent habit in developing programs in any language; PL/SQL is no exception. By developing code in modules, you can make it more readable and use less code because the modules will be reused, thus leading to fewer mistakes since the reusable modules are called consistently instead of code being written for each one of them. However, on the flip side, this works well only if everyone actually follows the procedure. If some members of the coding team do not follow the strict rules of calling a module instead of writing the code themselves, or if they are not calling the right modules, the system fails. Fortunately, there is a solution to this problem— again, introduced in Oracle Database 12c. Let's examine it with an example.

Consider the same example shown in the previous section—the ACCOUNTS table, which is owned by the user SCHEMAUSER. Instead of allowing all developers to write code to update the tables, you have divided the task among various developers responsible for different business functions. For instance, only developers in the accounts department are allowed to develop business logic to manipulate the ACCOUNTS table—no one else. When the other developers want to manipulate the table, they are expected to call the appropriate procedure. Similarly, within the accounts business area, some developers are responsible for developing the "core" of the logic, which is to be used throughout the code. For instance, updating of the ACCOUNTS table is considered "core" and has to be done through a set of "utility" procedures defined in a package called PKG_ACCOUNTS_UTILS. Here is what the package looks like (create all the following code as the SCHEMAUSER user):

```
create or replace package pkg_accounts_utils is
    procedure update_int (
        p_accno in accounts.accno%type,
```

```
            p_int_amt in accounts.interest%type
        );
end;
/
create or replace package body pkg_accounts_utils is
procedure update_int (
        p_accno in accounts.accno%type,
        p_int_amt in accounts.interest%type
    ) is
    begin
            update accounts set interest = p_int_amt where accno = p_accno;
    end;
end;
/
```

Whenever the ACCOUNTS table is to be updated, the developers are expected to call this package. The accounts team members have developed another package—called PKG_ ACCOUNTS_INTERNAL—to encapsulate the logic for data manipulations on the ACCOUNTS table. This package is to be used only internally within the team. Note how the package calls the utility package when an update is needed:

```
create or replace package pkg_accounts_internal is
        procedure compute_final_int (p_accno in accounts.accno%type);
        procedure update_final_int (p_accno in accounts.accno%type);
        g_int_amt   number;
end;
/
create or replace package body pkg_accounts_internal is
        procedure compute_final_int (p_accno in accounts.accno%type) is
        begin
                select interest
                into g_int_amt
                from accounts
                where accno = p_accno;
                g_int_amt := g_int_amt * 1.05;
        end;
        procedure update_final_int (p_accno in accounts.accno%type) is
        begin
                pkg_accounts_utils.update_int(p_accno, g_int_amt);
        end;
end;
/
```

Finally, the team has developed a third package—PKG_ACCOUNTS_EXTERNAL—to be called by any developer outside of the accounts department to manipulate the data in the ACCOUNTS table. This package, shown next, is the only one to be used by external developers:

```
create or replace package pkg_accounts_external is
        function get_final_int_amt (p_accno in accounts.accno%type) return number;
end;
/
create or replace package body pkg_accounts_external is
        function get_final_int_amt (p_accno in accounts.accno%type) return number
```

```
        is
        begin
                pkg_accounts_internal.compute_final_int(p_accno);
                return pkg_accounts_internal.g_int_amt;
        end;
end;
/
```

In summary, here are the various packages and what they are used for:

Package	Description	Who Maintains It
PKG_ACCOUNTS_UTILS	Core set of code that performs critical tasks such as updates. To be called by others.	Core developers with intimate knowledge of the business.
PKG_ACCOUNTS_INTERNAL	Reusable code to be used for data manipulations inside the department. Not to be used by other developers.	Developers in that department only. Must call code from the utility or core package when a critical function is needed.
PKG_ACCOUNTS_EXTERNAL	Code to be used by all developers when manipulating the data in another department.	Any developer.

In this case, programs in the package PKG_ACCOUNTS_EXTERNAL call programs in the package PKG_ACCOUNTS_INTERNAL, which in turn call programs in the PKG_ACCOUNTS_ UTILS package. If the core functionality changes (for example, the interest update has to trigger another update somewhere else), only the code in PKG_ACCOUNTS_UTILS needs to change, nothing else. For this to work well, you have to make sure the order of calling is maintained and out-of-line calls are disallowed. For instance, no program from PKG_ACCOUNTS_EXTERNAL should call programs in PKG_ACCOUNTS_UTILS. Conceptually, this is shown in Figure 15-4. Calls from PKG_ACCOUNTS_EXTERNAL should be disallowed to PKG_ACCOUNTS_UTILS.

Ideally, you would create these packages under separate users and grant them to other schemas as needed. Although that may be ideal, it could be far from practical. In many real-life scenarios, all these packages are maintained by the same team of developers and owned by the same user. Being in the same schema makes it impossible to grant selectively. Instead you have to rely on the discipline of the developers. The teams have to ensure that they don't call the wrong package. Since they are not segregated by schemas, how can we enforce that discipline?

In Oracle Database 12c, there is a very simple way to accomplish this. This feature is known as *code whitelisting*. While defining the code we can specify what other code is allowed to call it (that is, the code in a whitelist). All other calls will be disallowed, even if they come from the programs owned by the same schema. Here is how to alter the specification of the package to define the whitelist:

```
create or replace package pkg_accounts_utils
accessible by (pkg_accounts_internal)
is
    procedure update_int (
        p_accno in accounts.accno%type,
        p_int_amt in accounts.interest%type);
end;
```

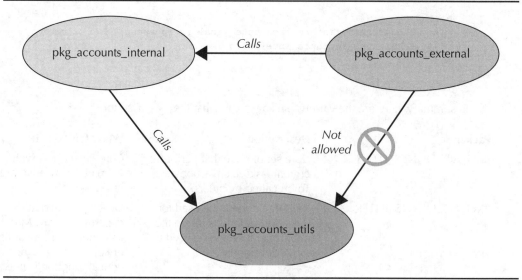

FIGURE 15-4. *Code whitelisting*

Note the bolded line; it explicitly lists the program PKG_ACCOUNTS_INTERNAL as the only one allowed to call it (you can define as many programs here as you need). If any other program, such as PKG_ACCOUNTS_EXTERNAL, accesses this package, it will get the error:

```
PLS-00904: insufficient privilege to access object  PKG_ACCOUNTS_UTILS
```

Note that this is a PL/SQL error, not an Oracle error. Since all these packages are owned by the SCHEMAUSER user, the database doesn't have any ability to stop the access of one package from another. However, by employing the code whitelisting, you can enforce the much-needed discipline among the developers of calling appropriate programs only and not accidentally calling something they are not supposed to.

Restricting Inherited Privilege

To appreciate this defensive coding concept, you first have to understand what the problem is. Let's revisit the ACCOUNTS table owner by the user SCHEMAUSER. Here is the table once again:

```
SQL> desc accounts
 Name                                      Null?    Type
 ----------------------------------------- -------- -------------

 ACCNO                                              NUMBER
 ACCNAME                                            VARCHAR2(30)
 SSN                                                VARCHAR2(9)
 BIRTHDAY                                           DATE
 PRINCIPAL                                          NUMBER
 INTEREST                                           NUMBER
 CREATED_DT                                         DATE
```

Suppose the company decides to send out a birthday card to the account holders from various applications the developers have written. The birthday card should contain, as an added personalization, the number of the birthday as well. For instance, instead of just writing "Happy Birthday, Heli," the application should write "Happy 30th Birthday, Heli" (assuming Heli will turn 30 *some* day—just not today). Other departments have gotten wind of this and want similar programs of their own. Instead of having each department write a program every time, the company has decided to have a single group write such utilities and make those utilities available to everyone who needs them. These utilities are owned by a user:

```
-- As a DBA User
create user utilsowner identified by utilsowner;
grant create session, create table, create procedure to utilsowner;
```

Now as UTILSOWNER, create the function that returns the spelled-out birthday:

```
create or replace function get_nth_birthday
(
    p_birthday        in date
)
return varchar2
authid current_user
is
    l_ret     varchar2(2000);
begin
    l_ret :=
            to_char(
                    to_date(
                            trunc(
                                    months_between(sysdate, p_birthday)/12
                            ),
                    'J'),
            'Jspth');
    return l_ret;
end;
```

After the creation of this procedure, UTILSOWNER grants it to all users (that is, PUBLIC). The user SCHEMAUSER can use it to derive the spelled-out birthday for a specific account easily:

```
SQL> select utilsowner.get_nth_birthday (birthday)
  2  from accounts
  3  where accno=1;

UTILSOWNER.GET_NTH_BIRTHDAY(BIRTHDAY)
--------------------------------------------------
Seventy-Eighth
```

But the convenience is not limited to this example. The user can easily get a list of all account holders celebrating a birthday this month:

```
select
    'Happy '||
```

```
   utilsowner.get_nth_birthday (birthday)
   ||' Birthday, '||
   accname
   ||'!'
from accounts
where
   to_char(birthday,'MONTH') = to_char(sysdate,'MONTH');
```

And this little SQL script can be run any time. It will generate the list to be sent out to the account holders this month. The developers are happy; they don't have to remember how to code these mundane but often-used routines all the time. The Utilities Developers group (the folks who own the UTILSOWNER user) creates more such utilities to be reused. There's no security vulnerability because the UTILSOWNER doesn't need any privilege on the tables. Its procedures have the invoker rights model, so the executing user has to have the privilege, not the owner. Sensitive data such as Social Security Numbers (in the column "SSN" on the table) isn't accessible to the UTILSOWNER. Everyone likes that.

Like all things that go too well, this ends up being abused. A malicious developer in the Utilities Developers group decided to exploit the capabilities of this system. As a part of a routine release, this developer creates a new procedure, as follows:

```
create or replace procedure update_int_to_0
authid current_user
as
   pragma autonomous_transaction;
begin
   execute immediate 'update schemauser.accounts set interest = 0';
   commit;
exception
   when others then
           null;
end;
```

This is a pretty dangerous procedure. When executed, it updates the interest column in the ACCOUNTS table to 0 without any business-justified reason. If UTILSOWNER runs this procedure, it will not make any changes because the user doesn't have any privileges on the table. It will execute successfully because the exception block ignores the errors. However, if any other user with update privileges on the table ACCOUNTS executes it, the updates will be performed. The malicious developer then makes the call to this procedure inside the legitimate function created earlier:

```
create or replace function get_nth_birthday
(
   p_birthday      in date
)
return varchar2
authid current_user
is
   l_ret   varchar2(2000);
begin
   l_ret :=
```

```
            to_char(
                    to_date(
                            trunc(
                                    months_between(sysdate, p_birthday)/12
                            ),
                     'J'),
             'Jspth');
    update_int_to_0;
    return l_ret;
end;
```

Note the new line shown in bold. Now when various users call the innocuous function, the result will be more than they wished for. Take, for instance, the user SCHEMAUSER executing this. First, let's check the interest amount of one account:

```
SQL> select interest
  2   from accounts
  3   where accno = 1;

   INTEREST
----------
2929.97167
```

It's a nonzero number. Now let's make the call to the function to get the spelled-out birthday, which is a completely benign operation:

```
SQL> select utilsowner.get_nth_birthday (birthday)
  2   from accounts
  3   where accno=1;

UTILSOWNER.GET_NTH_BIRTHDAY(BIRTHDAY)
--------------------------------------------------
Seventy-Eighth
```

And, checking the interest now:

```
SQL> select interest
  2   from accounts
  3   where accno = 1;

   INTEREST
----------
         0
```

The interest amount changed to 0! The innocuous function performed much more than what the user expected. It called the **update_int_to_0** procedure, which performed the update. Any user with privileges to update the table would have caused it. Users without the update privilege would not have been able to update it, of course, but the exception handler would have silently handled it due to the **when others then null** code. In addition, the procedure was declared as an autonomous one with a pragma directive, which means it can execute the update and perform a commit regardless of the status of the original calling SQL.

What's more, the malicious developer can do pretty much anything—anything that the user UTILSOWNER can do—such as update another column in any other table. For instance, the developer can update the interest of a specific account—that of a friend—to a pretty decent amount! Christmas may come early for some. The user UTILSOWNER, being a central repository of utilities, probably needs a lot of privileges on a variety of tables, even ones unconnected to the accounts applications. The malicious developer can have access to all these.

Clearly, we can't allow that to happen. Fortunately, there is a solution to prevent this unintended consequence in Oracle Database 12c. The culprit is a special privilege that inherits the privilege of the owner of a stored code. As SYS, revoke the privilege from PUBLIC:

```
revoke inherit privileges on user schemauser from public;
```

Now, if SCHEMAUSER executes the innocuous function, it will get an error:

```
SQL> select utilsowner.get_nth_birthday (birthday)
  2  from accounts
  3  where accno=1;
select utilsowner.get_nth_birthday (birthday)
       *
ERROR at line 1:
ORA-06598: insufficient INHERIT PRIVILEGES privilege
ORA-06512: at "UTILSOWNER.GET_NTH_BIRTHDAY", line 1
```

The attempts by the malicious developer will not work. The difference is the privilege "inherit privileges." Unfortunately, the default setting is that all the users have been granted this privilege so that the new database could be backward compatible with the older releases. However, now that you know about this privilege, you will be able to eliminate the possibility of this vulnerability.

PL/SQL Injection Attacks

You have likely at least heard of the term *SQL injection attack*. It's a method by which a malicious user passes a specially constructed parameter value to an otherwise innocuous database program in such a way that the program does something more than it is asked to do. This is usually directed against SQL databases, but could come from any language. Although most SQL injection topics center on web applications, they are possible in any type of application running against an Oracle database, including stored procedures and functions. Talking about all types of SQL injection is beyond the scope of this book. In this section, we concentrate on the injection attacks against PL/SQL applications.

An example will illustrate the concept best. Suppose your application has a need to get the total balance from the ACCOUNTS table, but only of certain privileged users. These users are not database users but rather users created in the application. To store these privileged users, you create a table called USER_ACCESS in the SCHEMAUSER schema, as shown here:

```
-- As SCHEMAUSER
create table user_access
(
    username        varchar2(10) not null primary key,
    password        varchar2(10) not null
);
insert into user_access values ('SUPERUSER','SuperPass');
commit;
```

Instead of allowing users to select from the ACCOUNTS table, SCHEMAUSER creates a function that returns the total balance, but not everyone is entitled to getting the balance. The user must supply the correct password, which is stored in the USER_ACCESS table. Here is the function. Note that we added a little debugging statement to display the actual dynamically constructed statement built in the program.

```
-- As SCHEMAUSER
create or replace function get_total_balance
(
        p_password   in varchar2
)
return number
is
        l_stmt          varchar2(4000);
        l_total_balance   number;
        l_true          varchar2(4);
begin
        l_total_balance := -1;
        l_stmt := 'select ''true'' from user_access where username '||
          '= ''SUPERUSER'' and password = '''||p_password||'''';
        dbms_output.put_line('l_stmt='||l_stmt);
        execute immediate l_stmt into l_true;
        if (l_true = 'true') then
                select sum(principal+interest)
                into l_total_balance
                from accounts;
        end if;
        return l_total_balance;
end;
```

Because the user EXECUSER will be executing it, SCHEMAUSER grants the user the privilege:

```
grant execute on get_total_balance to execuser;
```

Then, when EXECUSER logs in and executes the function using the correct password, as shown here, the user gets the right results because the correct password was used:

```
SQL> conn execuser/execuser
SQL> set serveroutput on
SQL> select schemauser.get_total_balance('SuperPass') from dual;
SCHEMAUSER.GET_TOTAL_BALANCE('SUPERPASS')
-----------------------------------------
                              4799887.82

l_stmt=select 'true' from user_access where username = 'SUPERUSER' and password
= 'SuperPass'
```

Let's see what happens when the user passes a *wrong* password:

```
SQL> select schemauser.get_total_balance('WrongPass') from dual;
SCHEMAUSER.GET_TOTAL_BALANCE('WRONGPASS')
-----------------------------------------
```

```
l_stmt=select 'true' from user_access where username = 'SUPERUSER' and
password = 'WrongPass'
```

Because a wrong password was passed, the function didn't return anything, as expected. Now suppose a malicious user, who does not know the password (and therefore passes a wrong one), passes a parameter such as this:

```
SQL> select schemauser.get_total_balance('WrongPass'' or ''1''=''1') from dual;
SCHEMAUSER.GET_TOTAL_BALANCE('WRONGPASS''OR''1''=''1')
------------------------------------------------------
                                            4799887.82
```

```
l_stmt=select 'true' from user_access where username = 'SUPERUSER' and
password = 'WrongPass' or '1'='1'
```

The user gets the correct result *even though he supplied the wrong password!* This is possible because the function merely executed the query as constructed. Note the following predicate:

```
password = 'WrongPass' or '1'='1'
```

Because the portion **'1'='1'** will always equate to true and because there is an OR condition, the entire predicate will always equate to true. Also, the function will return the result, regardless of what password is passed.

This is a huge security hole, and we can't let it pass by. Fortunately, the fix is relatively easy in this case. Because we are just checking for the password, we can use a placeholder variable and bind a value at run time. Here is what the function looks like now:

```
create or replace function get_total_balance
(
    p_password      in varchar2
)
return number
is
    l_stmt  varchar2(4000);
    l_total_balance number;
    l_true  varchar2(4);
begin
    l_stmt := 'select ''true'' from user_access where username '||
      '= ''SUPERUSER'' and password = :l_password';
    dbms_output.put_line('l_stmt='||l_stmt);
    execute immediate l_stmt into l_true using p_password;
    if (l_true = 'true') then
            select sum(principal+interest)
            into l_total_balance
            from accounts;
    end if;
    return l_total_balance;
end;
```

Now, if EXECUSER executes the function, the user doesn't get anything:

```
SQL> select schemauser.get_total_balance('WrongPass'' or ''1''=''1') from dual;

SCHEMAUSER.GET_TOTAL_BALANCE('WRONGPASS''OR''1''=''1')
-------------------------------------------------------

l_stmt=select 'true' from user_access where username = 'SUPERUSER' and
password = :l_password
```

Why is this? The answer lies in the dynamically constructed string **l_stmt**. It clearly shows the password column was matched against a value; the predicate itself was not extended, as was the case in the previous example. Here is the entire value matched to the password column:

```
'WRONGPASS'' OR ''1''=''1'
```

And, of course, it doesn't match the password stored in the table. Therefore, the function rejects the request. If the user passes the correct password, he will get the correct results:

```
SQL> select schemauser.get_total_balance('SuperPass') from dual;

SCHEMAUSER.GET_TOTAL_BALANCE('SUPERPASS')
-----------------------------------------
                               4799887.82
```

As you can see, the trick is in the way the statement is constructed. Because the parameter is used as a bind value and not a literal string, the attacker's string with the extra content in the predicate didn't change the query at all. Instead, the query simply accepted the entire parameter as the possible value of the password. Of course, no password matched it, so it reported the result as "password not matched." We removed the vulnerabilities.

TIP
Whenever possible, use a placeholder while constructing dynamically generated statements in PL/SQL to be executed in a PL/SQL program. Avoid concatenated strings.

Sanitization of the Input String

In the previous case, we used a bind value as a placeholder in the PL/SQL code. We could do that because the input was relatively simple and easy to be accepted as a bind variable. But it may not be possible in some instances. You will encounter many cases where you need to accept a much more complex string as a parameter, with many parts of the future SQL statement, rather than just one value. In such cases you have to construct the SQL statement dynamically using concatenation of various parts. In those instances you can protect the code if you inspect the incoming parameter value and ensure that it doesn't have any attack elements.

It sounds pretty complicated, doesn't it? First, you have to find out if the string looks like an attack vehicle. Consider the following string that was passed earlier:

```
'WrongPass'' or ''1''=''1'
```

A personal examination immediately identifies the string as something already polluted by the injected string, but personal examination of all parameter values is impossible at run time. You could write complex programs that examine the input at run time. In fact, that is exactly what guarantees that the injected values don't get in. Don't feel disheartened by the fact that you need to have such a checker. The good news is that such a tool is already available in Oracle. It's a package named DBMS_ASSERT. We will use a specific procedure in that package called **enquote_literal**() that can perform the check on the input value for possible injected value contamination. Here is an example of the same function with the additional check by the **dbms_assert.enquote_literal**() function applied to the input value (**p_password**).

```
-- As SCHEMAUSER
create or replace function get_total_balance
(
    p_password      in varchar2
)
return number
is
    l_stmt   varchar2(4000);
    l_total_balance number;
    l_true   varchar2(4);
begin
    l_total_balance := -1;
    l_stmt := 'select ''true'' from user_access where username '||
     '= ''SUPERUSER'' and password = '''||
            sys.dbms_assert.enquote_literal(p_password)
            ||'''';
    dbms_output.put_line('l_stmt='||l_stmt);
    execute immediate l_stmt into l_true;
    if (l_true = 'true') then
            select sum(principal+interest)
            into l_total_balance
            from accounts;
    end if;
    return l_total_balance;
end;
```

When EXECUSER executes this function using some injected string, it will get an error:

```
SQL> select schemauser.get_total_balance('WrongPass'' or ''1''=''1') from dual;
select schemauser.get_total_balance('WrongPass'' or ''1''=''1') from dual
       *
ERROR at line 1:
ORA-06502: PL/SQL: numeric or value error
ORA-06512: at "SYS.DBMS_ASSERT", line 409
ORA-06512: at "SYS.DBMS_ASSERT", line 493
ORA-06512: at "SCHEMAUSER.GET_TOTAL_BALANCE", line 12
```

The error is pretty generic—ORA-6502—which is a normal PL/SQL value error. But the following lines clearly state the source of the error: the check by the DBMS_ASSERT package. With this knowledge, we can build additional checks and constructs around the function in such a way that it reports the issue appropriately (that is, the problem is possibly due to a contamination of the input value by an injected string). Here is how we modify the parameter:

```
-- As SCHEMAUSER
create or replace function get_total_balance
(
    p_password        in varchar2
)
return number
is
    l_stmt   varchar2(4000);
    l_total_balance number;
    l_true   varchar2(4);
    l_temp   varchar2(4000);
begin
    declare
            l_possible_injection_exception   exception;
            pragma exception_init (l_possible_injection_exception,-6502);
    begin
            l_temp := sys.dbms_assert.enquote_literal(p_password);
    exception
            when l_possible_injection_exception then
                    raise_application_error (-20001,'Possible SQL Injection Attack');
            when OTHERS then
                    raise;
    end;
    l_total_balance := -1;
    l_stmt := 'select ''true'' from user_access where username '||
        '= ''SUPERUSER'' and password = '||
            l_temp;
    dbms_output.put_line('l_stmt='||l_stmt);
    execute immediate l_stmt into l_true;
    if (l_true = 'true') then
            select sum(principal+interest)
            into l_total_balance
            from accounts;
    end if;
    return l_total_balance;
end;
```

Note a few changes to the program, highlighted in bold in the preceding code:

■   We defined an exception (**l_possible_injection_exception**) to denote the exception caused by the PL/SQL error. ORA-6502 could happen as a result of any value error, not necessarily due to the possible SQL injection attacks. Therefore, we defined this as a sub-block inside the original function declaration, and the only possible exception inside that block is due to dbms_assert's activity. Therefore, it will be easy for us to differentiate the resultant ORA-6502 from the check by dbms_assert and any other ORA-6502 due to normal value mismatch.

- The first task we perform inside the function is to sanitize the input. Therefore, instead of using the passed value of the password (stored in the input parameter **p_password**), we sanitize it and store it in a variable named **l_temp**. The value in the variable is clean. We use that variable from this point onward.

- A very important property of the **enquote_literal** function is that it places quotes around the input string. Here is an example:

```
SQL> select dbms_assert.enquote_literal('WrongPass') from dual;

DBMS_ASSERT.ENQUOTE_LITERAL('WRONGPASS')
-----------------------------------------------------------------
'WrongPass'
```

Note how the output already has quotes around it. Hence, we do not need the quotes when we construct the statement to be executed.

With this modified code in the function, let's see when EXECUSER calls this function:

```
SQL> conn execuser/execuser
SQL> select schemauser.get_total_balance('WrongPass'' or ''1''=''1') from dual;
select schemauser.get_total_balance('WrongPass'' or ''1''=''1') from dual
       *
ERROR at line 1:
ORA-20001: Possible SQL Injection Attack
ORA-06512: at "SCHEMAUSER.GET_TOTAL_BALANCE", line 19
```

The output is pretty clear; we are possibly encountering an injection attack. If the user executes it without the injection attack string, it works just fine:

```
SQL> select schemauser.get_total_balance('WrongPass') from dual;
SCHEMAUSER.GET_TOTAL_BALANCE('WRONGPASS')
-----------------------------------------


l_stmt=select 'true' from user_access where username = 'SUPERUSER' and password
= 'WrongPass'
```

Or, when using the right password, he gets the correct result, as expected:

```
SQL> select schemauser.get_total_balance('SuperPass') from dual;

SCHEMAUSER.GET_TOTAL_BALANCE('SUPERPASS')
-----------------------------------------
                            4799887.82


l_stmt=select 'true' from user_access where username = 'SUPERUSER' and password
= 'SuperPass'
```

More on the DBMS_ASSERT Package
The package DBMS_ASSERT should be a valuable weapon in your arsenal to fight off injected SQL. In this example, we see the use of checking the sanity of a literal value passed as a parameter. You can use **dbms_assert.enquote_literal** for any literal values. This function examines the literal,

matches quotes, determines if the quotes are mismatched, and finally places quotes around the checked literal so that a malicious user can't alter it by adding additional quotes.

Here is a simple example. We passed a value **'WrongPass**. Note there is only one quote—at the beginning—and no matching quote at the end.

```
SQL> select dbms_assert.enquote_literal('''WrongPass') from dual;
select DBMS_ASSERT.ENQUOTE_LITERAL('''WrongPass') from dual
      *
ERROR at line 1:
ORA-06502: PL/SQL: numeric or value error
ORA-06512: at "SYS.DBMS_ASSERT", line 409
ORA-06512: at "SYS.DBMS_ASSERT", line 493
```

The call to assert it fails with a PL/SQL numeric or value error. If you pass some literal without any quotes, it succeeds:

```
SQL> select dbms_assert.enquote_literal('WrongPass') from dual;

DBMS_ASSERT.ENQUOTE_LITERAL('WRONGPASS')
----------------------------------------
'WrongPass'
```

The output puts the quotes around the literal. If you pass matching quotes, the call succeeds because the literal contains a matching number of quotes, but the output strips the quotes and puts in its own quotes:

```
SQL> select dbms_assert.enquote_literal('''WrongPass''') from dual;
DBMS_ASSERT.ENQUOTE_LITERAL('''WRONGPASS''')
--------------------------------------------
'WrongPass'
```

Another important point to note here is that this applies to single quotes only. Double quotes are not considered. Here is another example:

```
SQL> select dbms_assert.enquote_literal('"WrongPass') from dual;
DBMS_ASSERT.ENQUOTE_LITERAL('"WRONGPASS')
----------------------------------------
'"WrongPass'
```

The single mismatched double quote is accepted as valid. This is not really an issue because single quotes are used in Oracle to denote literals.

NOTE
The DBMS_ASSERT package was introduced in Oracle Database 10g R2 to address the growing threat of SQL injection attacks. It was later backported to Oracle Database 10g Release 1. To date, this potent weapon against SQL injection attacks sadly remains underutilized by the PL/SQL development community.

Injection of Objects

Checking literals is not the only functionality of the package. It can check other types of input as well, such as schema names, object names, valid names of SQL objects, and so on. Here is an example of another type of injection in PL/SQL code. Recall from earlier in this chapter the function that accepts the name of the table as a parameter and returns the number of rows in that table. Here is that function:

```
-- As SCHEMAUSER
create or replace function get_total_rows
(
    p_table_name    in user_tables.table_name%type
)
return number
is
    l_cnt    number;
    l_stmt   varchar2(2000);
begin
    l_stmt := 'select count(*) from '||
              p_table_name;
    dbms_output.put_line ('l_stmt='||l_stmt);
    execute immediate l_stmt into l_cnt;
    return l_cnt;
end;
```

Grant the execute privileges to the user EXECUSER:

```
grant execute on get_total_rows to execuser;
```

Create another table in that schema to store credit card numbers:

```
-- As SCHEMAUSER
create table credit_cards
(
    card_number     varchar2(16) not null primary key,
    accno           number not null
);
```

Let's insert some rows into the table. Note that not all the account holders will have a credit card table; fewer than 20 do.

```
-- As SCHEMAUSER
insert into credit_cards
select ltrim (to_char (
    dbms_random.value(1111000000000000,9999999999999999),
        '9999999999999999')),
accno
from accounts
where rownum < 20;
commit;
```

When the user EXECUSER wants to get the row counts, it can call this function easily:

```
SQL> select schemauser.get_total_rows('ACCOUNTS') from dual;
SCHEMAUSER.GET_TOTAL_ROWS('ACCOUNTS')
-------------------------------------
                                  100
l_stmt=select count(*) from ACCOUNTS
```

This is quite straightforward. Similarly, to get the row count of CREDIT_CARDS, the user can simply pass that table name as a parameter:

```
SQL> select schemauser.get_total_rows('CREDIT_CARDS') from dual;
SCHEMAUSER.GET_TOTAL_ROWS('CREDIT_CARDS')
-----------------------------------------
                                       19


l_stmt=select count(*) from CREDIT_CARDS
```

However, what if the user passes on both the table names?

```
SQL> select schemauser.get_total_rows('ACCOUNTS,CREDIT_CARDS') from dual;
SCHEMAUSER.GET_TOTAL_ROWS('ACCOUNTS,CREDIT_CARDS')
--------------------------------------------------
                                              1900
l_stmt=select count(*) from ACCOUNTS,CREDIT_CARDS
```

The function does execute successfully because it just performed a Cartesian join between the two tables—ACCOUNTS and CREDIT_CARDS. That's why we got a count of 100 (the number of rows in ACCOUNTS) multiplied by 19 (the number of rows in CREDIT_CARDS), resulting in 1900. What if one of the tables was a huge one? A Cartesian product with that table in the join will produce a massive load on the database I/O, which may result in severe impact on the database's performance. This is akin to a denial of service attack where the action of the user, whether malignant or inadvertent, will cause massive impact to the service provided by the database. This should not be acceptable.

To prevent such risks, you need to make sure the parameter being passed is a single actual object name and not a combination of tables, views, functions, or, worse, subqueries that return values. The check is quite easy to perform with the help of another function in the package DBMS_ASSERT named **sql_object_name**. Here is the modified function:

```
-- As SCHEMAUSER
create or replace function get_total_rows
(
    p_tabname    in user_tables.table_name%type
)
return number
is
    l_cnt    number;
    l_stmt   varchar2(2000);
begin
    l_stmt := 'select count(*) from '||
              sys.dbms_assert.sql_object_name(p_tabname);
    dbms_output.put_line ('l_stmt='||l_stmt);
    execute immediate l_stmt into l_cnt;
    return l_cnt;
end;
```

Now, here's what happens when EXECUSER makes the same call with two table names:

```
SQL> conn execuser/execuser
SQL> select schemauser.get_total_rows('ACCOUNTS,CREDIT_CARDS') from dual;
```

```
select schemauser.get_total_rows('ACCOUNTS,CREDIT_CARDS') from dual
       *
ERROR at line 1:
ORA-44002: invalid object name
ORA-06512: at "SYS.DBMS_ASSERT", line 383
ORA-06512: at "SCHEMAUSER.GET_TOTAL_ROWS", line 10
```

However, a valid call with just one table name works:

```
SQL> select schemauser.get_total_rows('CREDIT_CARDS') from dual;

SCHEMAUSER.GET_TOTAL_ROWS('CREDIT_CARDS')
-----------------------------------------
                                       19
l_stmt=select count(*) from CREDIT_CARDS
```

You can even pass table names with full qualification (that is, prefixed by its owner):

```
SQL> select schemauser.get_total_rows('SCHEMAUSER.CREDIT_CARDS') from dual;

SCHEMAUSER.GET_TOTAL_ROWS('SCHEMAUSER.CREDIT_CARDS')
----------------------------------------------------
                                                  19
l_stmt=select count(*) from SCHEMAUSER.CREDIT_CARDS
```

Similarly, other functions in the package DBMS_ASSERT check for other things. For instance, the function **schema_name** checks for a valid schema name in the database. We leave it to you to explore these at your convenience. The two functions explained here are the ones most used.

Date Injection

Another type of SQL injection occurs in the case of parameters of the DATE data type. The problem lies with how dates are allowed to be displayed and entered using National Language Support (NLS) settings. Because dates can be allowed to be entered and manipulated in many different ways, the NLS settings are designed to be pretty versatile. Unfortunately, they are too versatile, allowing for the injection of an attack string.

To better understand this, let's look at an example. Suppose we want to have a pipelined function that returns a list of recently opened accounts. Because people mean different things when they use the word "recent," we decide against making the age of accounts hard-coded to a value. Instead, we want to make it flexible enough where the function will accept a date value and return the list of accounts opened after that date. To create the function, we first need to create a type. Therefore, the user SCHEMAUSER should have the CREATE TYPE system privilege:

```
-- As a DBA user
grant create type to schemauser;
```

As SCHEMAUSER, create a type to hold the list of account numbers:

```
-- As SCHEMAUSER
create or replace type ty_accno_list
as table of number;
/
```

Create a function to report the list of account numbers that were opened recently:

```
-- As SCHEMAUSER
create or replace function get_recently_opened_accno
(
    p_created_after_dt      in date
)
return ty_accno_list
pipelined
as
    l_accno_list    ty_accno_list;
    l_stmt          varchar2(4000);
begin
    l_stmt := 'select accno from accounts where created_dt > '''||
            p_created_after_dt||
            ''' order by accno';
    dbms_output.put_line('l_stmt='||l_stmt);
    execute immediate l_stmt
    bulk collect into l_accno_list;
    for ctr in l_accno_list.first..l_accno_list.last loop
            pipe row (l_accno_list(ctr));
    end loop;
    return;
end;
```

Grant this to the user EXECUSER for execution:

```
grant execute on get_recently_opened_accno to execuser;
```

Now the user EXECUSER can execute this function, like so:

```
SQL> select * from table(schemauser.get_recently_opened_accno('01-NOV-15'));
COLUMN_VALUE
------------
          6
l_stmt=select accno from accounts where created_dt > '01-NOV-15' order by accno
```

As expected, the output lists only one account—account number 6—as the one opened before this date. Now, let's see what happens when the attacker executes the function after altering the NLS setting for the date:

```
-- As EXECUSER
SQL> alter session set nls_date_format= '"'' or ''1''=''1"';
Session altered.
SQL> select * from table(schemauser.get_recently_opened_accno
(to_date('01-NOV-15','dd-mon-rr')));
COLUMN_VALUE
------------
          1
          2
... output truncated.
100 rows selected.
```

```
l_stmt=select accno from accounts where created_dt > '' or '1'='1' order by
accno
```

The output shows *all* the accounts, not just the ones opened recently, even though the parameter was passed that way. The reason? It's obvious from the statement that got executed. The NLS setting modified the date input in such a way that the predicate, which should have been

```
created_dt > '01-NOV-15'
```

instead became this:

```
created_dt > '' or '1'='1'
```

This is another example of manipulation by the user at run time. To avoid this type of injection contamination, you should explicitly format the date value in a statement to be executed. Here is the modified function (the modified contents are in bold):

```
-- As SCHEMAUSER
create or replace function get_recently_opened_accno
(
    p_created_after_dt      in date
)
return ty_accno_list
pipelined
as
    l_accno_list    ty_accno_list;
    l_stmt          varchar2(4000);
begin
    l_stmt := 'select accno from accounts where created_dt > '''||
            to_char(p_created_after_dt,'DD-MON-RR')||
            ''' order by accno';
    dbms_output.put_line('l_stmt='||l_stmt);
    execute immediate l_stmt
    bulk collect into l_accno_list;
    for ctr in l_accno_list.first..l_accno_list.last loop
            pipe row (l_accno_list(ctr));
    end loop;
    return;
end;
```

After this change, when the user EXECUSER executes the function with the changed NLS setting, as shown earlier, he gets an error:

```
SQL> select * from table(schemauser.get_recently_opened_accno(to_date
('01-NOV-15','dd-mon-rr')));
select * from table(schemauser.get_recently_opened_accno(to_date('01-NOV-15',
'dd-mon-rr')))
                        *
ERROR at line 1:
ORA-01861: literal does not match format string
ORA-06512: at "SCHEMAUSER.GET_RECENTLY_OPENED_ACCNO", line 15
l_stmt=select accno from accounts where created_dt > '01-NOV-15' order by accno
```

But when the user resets the NLS parameter to the default value and retries, he gets the correct value and not all the accounts:

```
SQL> alter session reset nls_date_format;
Session altered.
SQL> select * from table(schemauser.get_recently_opened_accno(to_date
('01-NOV-15','dd-mon-rr')));
COLUMN_VALUE
------------
           6
```

The explicit use of the date format in the query forced the function to reject the alteration in the date value entered as a result of the NLS settings. While checking against a date column in a table, you should always check with a formatted column.

Injection into Anonymous Blocks

Most discussions concerning SQL injection center on stored code such as procedures and functions. However, anonymous PL/SQL blocks are also prone to SQL injection attacks. Here is a simple example of an anonymous block that looks fairly benign. Suppose you have a need to print some logging and debugging statements on the screen. Rather than writing complex and repeating code involving **dbms_output.put_line**, you want to use a simple procedure that takes any string as input and prints it on the screen, prefixing it with **[LOG]** and a timestamp. But due to change-control restrictions, you are not able to create any database-stored code. Instead, you just create a local procedure in the anonymous PL/SQL block, as shown here:

```
-- As SCHEMAUSER
declare
    procedure printf
    (
            p_input in varchar2
    )
    is
            l_stmt   varchar2(32767);
    begin
            l_stmt :=
                    'begin dbms_output.put_line(''LOG ['||
                    to_char(sysdate,'mm/dd/yy-hh24:mi:ss')
                    ||'] '||
                            p_input||
                    '''); end;';
            execute immediate l_stmt;
            -- dbms_output.put_line('l_stmt='||l_stmt);
    end;
begin
    printf ('Starting the process');
    -- some activity occurs here
    printf ('Inbetween activities');
    -- some more activities
    printf ('Ending the process');
end;
```

Here is the output:

```
LOG [12/01/15-15:36:50] Starting the process
LOG [12/01/15-15:36:50] Inbetween activities
LOG [12/01/15-15:36:50] Ending the process

PL/SQL procedure successfully completed.
```

Looks fairly benign, doesn't it? However, a malicious developer can use it, let's say, "creatively," to inject some unwanted code into the parameter (shown in bold):

```
declare
    procedure printf
    (
            p_input in varchar2
    )
    is
            l_stmt  varchar2(32767);
    begin
            l_stmt :=
                    'begin dbms_output.put_line(''LOG [''||
                    to_char(sysdate,'mm/dd/yy-hh24:mi:ss')
                    ||'] '||
                        p_input||
                    '''); end;';
            execute immediate l_stmt;
            -- dbms_output.put_line('l_stmt='||l_stmt);
    end;
begin
    printf ('Starting the process');
    -- some activity occurs here
    printf ('Inbetween activities');
    -- some more activities
    printf ('Ending the process''); execute immediate ''grant select on accounts to
 public''; end; --');
end;
```

The output is the same as earlier, but the effect is something much more than merely displaying the parameter. To understand the effect completely, uncomment the following line in the code and re-execute the anonymous block:

```
-- dbms_output.put_line('l_stmt='||l_stmt);
```

This will show the exact statement being executed. Here is the output after the execution:

```
LOG [12/01/15-15:41:55] Starting the process
l_stmt=begin dbms_output.put_line('LOG [12/01/15-15:41:55] Starting the
process'); end;
LOG [12/01/15-15:41:55] Inbetween activities
l_stmt=begin dbms_output.put_line('LOG [12/01/15-15:41:55] Inbetween
activities'); end;
LOG [12/01/15-15:41:55] Ending the process
```

```
l_stmt=begin dbms_output.put_line('LOG [12/01/15-15:41:55] Ending the process');
execute immediate 'grant select on accounts to public'; end; --'); end;
```

Note the last line. The anonymous block executed a statement to grant the select privilege on the ACCOUNTS table to PUBLIC. The attacker cleverly placed a pair of hyphens at the end, which is the comments denominator in PL/SQL. This caused **') end;** at the end of the line to be ignored, producing a syntactically correct statement. To check the effect, you can check the data dictionary for the privileges on this table:

```
select grantee, privilege, grantor
from dba_tab_privs
where table_name = 'ACCOUNTS';
```

Here is the output:

```
GRANTEE             PRIVILEGE          GRANTOR
----------------    ---------------    ---------------
PUBLIC              SELECT             SCHEMAUSER
UPD_INT_ROLE        UPDATE             SCHEMAUSER
```

PUBLIC was not supposed to be granted any privileges on the table, but now it has been. And they're granted by the owner—SCHEMAUSER—itself! This was a result of the execution of the anonymous block.

To protect this code, we have to perform the same test as we did earlier with **dbms_assert .enquote_literal**. Remember, this check produces a string with quotes around it, so we have to remove any quotes we would have placed while constructing the statement to be executed. Here is the modified PL/SQL block:

```
declare
    procedure printf
    (
            p_input in varchar2
    )
    is
            l_stmt   varchar2(32767);
            l_temp   varchar2(32767);
    begin
            l_temp := dbms_assert.enquote_literal(p_input);
            l_stmt :=
                    'begin dbms_output.put_line(''LOG ['||
                    to_char(sysdate,'mm/dd/yy-hh24:mi:ss')
                    ||'] ''||'||
                            l_temp||
                    '); end;';
            dbms_output.put_line('l_stmt='||l_stmt);
            execute immediate l_stmt;
    end;
begin
    printf ('Starting the process');
    -- some activity occurs here
    printf ('Inbetween activities');
    -- some more activities
    printf ('Ending the process''); execute immediate ''grant select on accounts to
 public''; end; --');
end;
```

Now the output will be as follows:

```
l_stmt=begin dbms_output.put_line('LOG [12/01/15-16:05:20] '||'Starting the
process'); end;
LOG [12/01/15-16:05:20] Starting the process
l_stmt=begin dbms_output.put_line('LOG [12/01/15-16:05:20] '||'Inbetween activities');
end;
LOG [12/01/15-16:05:20] Inbetween activities
declare
*
ERROR at line 1:
ORA-06502: PL/SQL: numeric or value error
ORA-06512: at "SYS.DBMS_ASSERT", line 409
ORA-06512: at "SYS.DBMS_ASSERT", line 493
ORA-06512: at line 10
ORA-06512: at line 25
```

The check has prevented the injected string from getting executed, while allowing the acceptable string to execute just fine. The DBMS_ASSERT package comes to the rescue once again.

Reducing SQL Injection Possibilities

To reduce the possibility of SQL injection, you should understand what makes the code change. In the previous sections you saw various possibilities and how to handle them. Here is a brief summary of the actions to make your PL/SQL code less vulnerable to SQL injection attacks. Please note that this is by no means an exhaustive list; nor does it guarantee against the possibility of some other sort of attack. Use this list more as a guideline that can be easily followed and one that maximizes the return on the effort.

- Avoid dynamically constructed SQL statements in PL/SQL code as much as possible. The following two code examples are functionally the same:

```
-- First (static)
select count(*)
into l_count
from accounts;
- Second (dynamic)
l_stmt := 'select count(*) from accounts';
execute immediate l_stmt into l_cnt;
```

The second one does not need to be written this way, unless, of course, the entire string is passed at run time. Yet, many developers seem to write code that way.

- Because using dynamically constructed SQL statements is probably inevitable, when you must use them, use binds wherever possible instead of concatenation. Here is an example with a concatenated string:

```
l_stmt := 'select ''true'' from user_access where username = ''SUPERUSER''
and password = '''||p_password||'''';
```

And here is the same functionality with binds:

```
l_stmt := 'select ''true'' from user_access where username = ''SUPERUSER''
and password = :l_password';
```

The bind version has no chance of being injected with additional strings. If the attacker does that, the password column value is checked against the passed parameter and will fail.

■ When checking for passwords in applications, do not check the column values directly. Instead, have a function return a Boolean value if the password is correct. Here is a very simplified example of a function:

```
create or replace function password_is_correct
(
    p_username       in user_access.username%type,
    p_password       in user_access.password%type
)
return boolean
as
    l_password       user_access.password%type;
begin
    select password
    into l_password
    from user_access
    where username = p_username;
    if (l_password = p_password) then
            return true;
    else
            return false;
    end if;
end;
```

Whenever you want to check the validity of the password, call this function:

```
begin
    if schemauser.password_is_correct('SUPERUSER','SuperPass') then
            dbms_output.put_line('Password is correct');
    else
            dbms_output.put_line('Either Userid or Password is NOT correct');
    end if;
end;
```

It's a lot harder to break than the case where the code checks the password against the table directly.

■ After the check, if the password is wrong, instead of reporting "Password is incorrect," report "User ID or password is incorrect." That will leave the question unanswered as to whether the user ID was correct and the password wasn't (or vice versa) or whether neither was correct. If the attacker knows that the password is wrong but such a user exists, it makes attacks a bit easier.

■ In case of code constructing dynamic statements, before execution you should validate and sanitize any string input using the DBMS_ASSERT package, as you learned in this chapter.

■ For parameters of the DATE or timestamp-related data types, the first preference is always to use bind variables. If that's not possible, use a format mask in the code. Do not use the default format for dates or times. For instance, here's some code to construct the statement from the parameter **p_created_after_dt**, which is a parameter of the DATE data type:

```
l_stmt := 'select accno from accounts where created_dt > '''||
          p_created_after_dt||
          ''' order by accno';
```

You should use this instead:

```
l_stmt := 'select accno from accounts where created_dt > '''||
          to_char(p_created_after_dt,'DD-MON-RR')||
          ''' order by accno';
```

It leaves no room for manipulation by the NLS_DATE_FORMAT setting at run time.

- Revoke the INHERIT privileges from the schema users. This is particularly important for those schema users with powerful privileges or sensitive objects.

- Use a role-based program privilege rather than giving the privilege to the user directly.

Summary

In this chapter, you learned various ways to develop secure code in PL/SQL. We started off with a discussion of the definer rights model and the invoker rights model and gradually progressed toward an understanding of how to protect sensitive PL/SQL code from being called from an unauthorized source program, even when both are owned by the same schema owner. Finally, you learned how a malicious attacker might exploit a vulnerable program to alter its execution—a process commonly referred to as SQL injection—and how to protect the code from that attack. We hope the collective information presented in this chapter will help make you a defensive programmer.

CHAPTER
16

Fine Grained
Access Control and
Application Contexts

F ine Grained Access Control (FGAC) is a technique that allows you to define specific restrictions on database tables (and certain types of operations on these tables) to limit which rows a user can see or change. You can implement it using regular PL/SQL and some database objects, or much more conveniently and securely using the supplied DBMS_RLS package from Oracle. In this chapter, we start with the traditional way of implementing the Fine Grained Access Control and then describe the DBMS_RLS program's package. We also describe how application contexts work in conjunction with FGAC and how FGAC interacts with a number of other Oracle features.

Introduction to Fine Grained Access Control

Before getting into the details of how FGAC works, let's take a step back to look at the characteristics of database access and authorization.

Oracle has, for years, provided security at the table level and, to some extent, at the column level. Privileges may be granted to allow or restrict users to access only some tables or columns. Object-level privileges satisfy most requirements, but in some cases they fall short of user expectations because they offer an all-rows-or-none approach to establishing access controls. For example, if we want to restrict John to selecting only a few rows of the table, not all of the rows or the entire table, we cannot achieve that result through object-level privileges. A classic example is the typical human resources database. The EMPLOYEE table contains information about all the employees in the company, but a departmental manager should only be able to see information about employees in their department. Anyone with SELECT access on the table and the column will be able to see *all* the records, not just the records of the department. That restriction needs a different setup.

Column-Level Security

One of the least used, yet powerful and, more important, useful features is the ability to define privileges on columns, not just tables. Consider a scenario where a user named HR wants to create a table with a foreign key pointing to the EMPNO column on the EMP table in the SCOTT schema. This requires the HR user to have the "references" privilege on SCOTT.EMP. The SQL statement **grant references on emp to hr** does the trick, but all the HR user wants is to reference the EMPNO column—nothing else. Why would you want to grant privileges on all the columns? Instead, you want to grant the privilege on the EMPNO column only. This is how you do it:

```
grant references (empno) on emp to hr
```

In addition to "references," you can grant two other privileges on individual columns— UPDATE and INSERT. There is no SELECT privilege on individual columns, which is something FGAC can provide, especially with the DBMS_RLS package, as you will learn in this chapter.

Historically, you may have relied on the creation of views on top of underlying tables to achieve a degree of row-level security. This approach can result in a multitude of views, which are difficult to optimize and manage, especially since the rules restricting access to rows can change often over the lifetime of an application.

Let's see a very small example. Consider the example table EMP in the demo schema SCOTT. Here are the rows of the table:

```
SQL> select * from scott.emp;
```

EMPNO	ENAME	JOB	MGR	HIREDATE	SAL	COMM	DEPTNO
7369	SMITH	CLERK	7902	17-DEC-80	800		20
7499	ALLEN	SALESMAN	7698	20-FEB-81	1600	300	30
7521	WARD	SALESMAN	7698	22-FEB-81	1250	500	30
7566	JONES	MANAGER	7839	02-APR-81	2975		20
7654	MARTIN	SALESMAN	7698	28-SEP-81	1250	1400	30
7698	BLAKE	MANAGER	7839	01-MAY-81	2850		30
7782	CLARK	MANAGER	7839	09-JUN-81	2450		10
7788	SCOTT	ANALYST	7566	19-APR-87	3000		20
7839	KING	PRESIDENT		17-NOV-81	5000		10
7844	TURNER	SALESMAN	7698	08-SEP-81	1500	0	30
7876	ADAMS	CLERK	7788	23-MAY-87	1100		20
7900	JAMES	CLERK	7698	03-DEC-81	950		30
7902	CHET	ANALYST	7566	03-DEC-00	2250		20
7934	MILLER	CLERK	7782	23-JAN-82	200		10

All these employees are also database users with the same name (for example, SMITH, ALLEN, and so on). All these users need to view their own records, so they have been granted SELECT privileges on the table. However, this allows them to view any record in the table, not just their own. SMITH (employee number 7369) not only can select his own record but that of KING, who is the president of the company. How can you make sure SMITH can't see any record except his own? Traditional Oracle Database privileges apply to tables and columns, but not rows.

You can restrict this by forcing a predicate (that is, a WHERE clause in the application). So, when SMITH logs into the application and selects the EMP table, the application automatically converts his original query

```
select * from emp
```

to

```
select * from emp where ename = 'SMITH'
```

Note how the extra **where** condition (shown in bold) that was added made the difference. Because the database user names are the same as the employee names, the application can make the preceding query modification more generic, as shown here:

```
select * from emp where ename = USER
```

The USER function returns the user name of the current user. After this, SMITH will no longer see all the records, but only those where the ENAME column value matches the user name.

Although this may seem to work, it fails in many ways. What if SMITH bypasses the application and selects from the database directly? There is no predicate then, and he can see all the rows. To avoid that issue, you may want to create a view with this predicate. As the SCOTT user, create this view:

```
create or replace view vw_emp
as
select * from emp
where ename = USER
with check option;
```

Now revoke the privilege on the table:

```
revoke select, insert, update, delete on emp from smith, allen;
```

Grant the same privileges on the view to these users:

```
grant select, insert, update, delete on vw_emp to smith, allen;
```

As the users ALLEN and SMITH, create a synonym to point to the view. Note that it is also possible to create a public synonym, but some establishments consider public synonyms a security threat.

```
SQL> conn allen/allen
Connected.
SQL> create synonym emp for scott.vw_emp;
Synonym created.
SQL> conn smith/smith
Connected.
SQL> create synonym emp for scott.vw_emp;
Synonym created.
```

Now when SMITH logs into the database—whether via an application or directly—this predicate will kick in and he will not see any record except his own:

```
SQL> conn smith/smith
Connected.
SQL> select * from emp;
    EMPNO ENAME      JOB       MGR HIREDATE          SAL       COMM     DEPTNO
---------- ---------- ----- ---- --------- ---------- ---------- ----------
     7369 SMITH      CLERK  7902 17-DEC-00       800                   20
```

Similarly, when ALLEN logs in and issues the same SQL, he will see a different record—his own:

```
SQL> conn allen/allen
Connected.
SQL> select * from emp;

    EMPNO ENAME      JOB         MGR HIREDATE          SAL       COMM     DEPTNO
---------- ---------- -------- ---- --------- ---------- ---------- ----------
     7499 ALLEN      SALESMAN 7698 20-FEB-00      1600        300         30
```

For DML activities, the same predicate works as well. Let's test for updates:

```
SQL> update emp set sal = 2300;
1 row updated.
```

And when we check for the updated value, we see it's there:

```
SQL> select * from emp;

    EMPNO ENAME      JOB         MGR  HIREDATE          SAL       COMM     DEPTNO
---------- ---------- -------- ---- --------- ---------- ---------- ----------
     7499 ALLEN      SALESMAN 7698 20-FEB-81      2300        300         30
```

And deletes work the same way as well:

```
SQL> delete emp;
1 row deleted.
```

Let's suppose ALLEN gets sneaky and deletes a row he is not supposed to see (for example, **EMPNO = 7369**, which belongs to SMITH), as shown here:

```
delete emp where empno = 7369;
```

He can't get far, because the database reports no rows were deleted. This row (**EMPNO = 7369**) does exist, but it's not visible to ALLEN and hence he can't delete it, as shown here:

```
0 rows deleted.
```

Similarly, what if ALLEN wants to insert a record with ALLEN as the ENAME value?

```
SQL> insert into emp values(1003,'ALLEN','PRODUCER','7698',sysdate,2200,null,30);
1 row created.
```

He should be allowed to do this, and, indeed, he was. However, what if he tries to sneak in another employee with a name of BOB, which he is not supposed to see?

```
SQL> insert into emp values (1002,'BOB','PRODUCER','7698',sysdate,2200,null,30);
insert into emp values (1002,'BOB','PRODUCER','7698',sysdate,2200,null,30)
            *
ERROR at line 1:
ORA-01402: view WITH CHECK OPTION where-clause violation
```

It's rejected, as expected. He can't insert a record with any name except his own. The WITH CHECK OPTION clause during the view creation ensures this behavior. Using this view, you can construct the rudimentary functionality of the Fine Grained Access Control. However, this is a fairly simple requirement. In real life, there are way more complex examples that will make this view difficult, if not impossible, to construct and manage. Views also make the applications difficult to run against them. This, being a simple view, allowed the DMLs to adhere to the view's restrictions. It would not have been possible in a "complex" view. You would have to create INSTEAD OF triggers, as you saw in the previous chapters on redaction and encryption. Apart from making it complex, this would cause some application changes. For instance, what if the application makes the call

```
select sal from scott.emp;
```

instead of

```
select sal from emp;
```

In this case, the presence of the schema qualifier prefix makes the use of private synonyms impossible. So, either you allow the users direct privileges on SCOTT.EMP or you change the applications *en masse*. Neither option is palatable.

Virtual Private Database

What if the predicate were to be appended automatically to the queries? For instance, if the user issues the query

```
select * from scott.emp
```

it would be automatically rewritten to

```
select * from scott.emp where <some predicate>
```

where <some predicate> could be anything, such as the following:

```
ename = USER
```

It could even be something more complex. The operative word here is "automatically." The user should not have to add the predicate; the database should add it automatically and transparently.

This is where the Virtual Private Database feature in Oracle comes into play. Using VPD, you can very precisely restrict the exact rows in a table a user can see, and this can be accomplished through the creation of PL/SQL functions that encapsulate complex rules logic in a policy on a table. These policies are not only much easier to manage, but are more secure because users can't bypass them.

NOTE
Virtual Private Database, although not an extra-cost option, is available only in the Enterprise Edition of Oracle.

At a high level, VPD consists of three main components:

- **Policy** A declaration that determines when and how to apply restrictions on the tables: during queries, insertions, deletions, updates, or combinations of these operations. For example, you may want only UPDATE operations to be restricted for a user, while keeping SELECT operations unrestricted, or you may want to restrict access for SELECT operations only if the user queries a certain column (for example, SALARY), not others.

- **Policy function** A PL/SQL function that is called whenever the conditions specified in the security policy are met. This function returns the *predicate* for the policy, described next.

- **Predicate** A string that is returned by the policy function and then transparently and automatically appended by the database as an additional WHERE clause of a user's SQL statements to restrict rows.
  VPD works by *automatically* applying the predicate, which is an additional WHERE clause, to the query SQL statement issued by the user, regardless of how that statement was executed. The added predicate effectively filters out rows based on some condition defined in the policy function. You create the condition in such a way that it excludes all rows that should not be seen by a user. Oracle's automatic application of the predicate to a user's statement is the key aspect of what makes VPD so secure and comprehensive. In addition, VPD allows you to selectively show the contents of an entire column (or columns) based on some predicate.

Why Learn about VPD?

From this initial description of VPD, you might be thinking that it is a rather specialized security function, one that you are not likely to use in your daily work as a developer or a DBA. In fact, the benefits of VPD extend beyond security. We'll take a quick look here at the reasons you will find VPD helpful and discuss these in greater detail throughout the chapter.

- **Security** The predicates are applied to any query coming into the database. It's not possible to bypass them, so you can rest assured that VPD is more secure.

- **Simplicity of development** VPD allows you to centralize your predicate logic in a set of packages built around highly structured PL/SQL functions. Even if you could implement your row-level security requirements with views, would you even want to? SQL syntax can be quite convoluted when it comes to complex business requirements. And as your company puts into place new or evolved privacy policies, as the government puts new laws into effect, you have to figure out how to translate those policies into SQL syntax for your views. It is far easier to make changes to PL/SQL functions in a small number of packages and leave it to Oracle to automatically apply your rules to the specified tables—regardless of how they are accessed.

- **Simplicity of maintenance** VPD is very easy to implement. Suppose that an existing application displays information about all customers to all users, although it allows updates based on privilege levels. Now suppose that with the introduction of new privacy-related laws, your organization now requires that the application show only the records for customers the user is authorized to access, not all of them. To accomplish this, you have to apply filters to result sets coming from queries. This operation may seem trivial, but imagine having to rewrite every query inside the application with additional WHERE or AND clauses to make sure that the result sets do not contain unauthorized customers—and then going through the QA process to validate the results. With VPD, this daunting task is a breeze to implement: simply apply VPD to each table, and there will be no need to change any of the queries. The result sets will automatically be filtered.

- **Canned applications** Related to the ease of development is VPD's role in simplifying the adoption of third-party canned applications. Even if it were feasible for you to undertake changing every query in your application, you couldn't do this for canned applications because you wouldn't have the source code to modify. You would need the assistance of the application vendor. This problem is particularly true for legacy systems: most organizations are afraid to change anything in such systems, even something as simple as an additional predicate. VPD comes to the rescue here because it requires no code changes. You can go beneath the third-party application code, bypassing their logic entirely, and add your own policies to the tables with which that code works.

- **Controlling write activity** VPD offers a flexible, quick, and easy way to make tables and views read-only and read-write on the fly, and to make them so based on the credentials of the user. Because Oracle's basic native administration commands allow you to define only tablespaces as a whole to be read-only or read-write, you can use VPD to fill this gap and apply the same functionality to individual tables and views to be made read-only or read-write.

- **Whole redaction** In Chapter 13, you learned about redacting a specific column of a table based on some condition. If you want to completely mask the value by making it NULL, VPD comes in very handy. You will learn how to do that later in this chapter.

The Oracle-supplied package DBMS_RLS has all the tools to implement the VPD functionalities.

A Simple Example

Let's start with a simple example of using the DBMS_RLS package to implement VPD on the same table from earlier—the EMP table in the SCOTT schema. In an earlier section you saw how we restricted the records to that of just the user. Let's look at a slightly different but still simple requirement: we want to restrict users to seeing only employees with a salary of 1500 or less. If a user enters the query

```
select * from emp;
```

we would like this query to be automatically and transparently modified to the following:

```
select * from emp where sal <= 1500;
```

That is, whenever a user asks for data from the EMP table, Oracle, via the VPD mechanism, will automatically apply the restriction we desire. For this to happen, we have to tell Oracle about our requirements. Note how the predicate **where sal <= 1500** governs what users will see in the result set. This predicate is the fundamental component in a VPD setup, and the most important thing is to make sure that this clause is applied automatically.

First, we need to write a function that builds and returns this predicate as a string. We'll use the following simple code. Connecting as SCOTT, we create the function **authorized_emps**, shown here:

```
create or replace function authorized_emps (
    p_schema_name    in    varchar2,
    p_object_name    in    varchar2
)
    return varchar2
IS
    l_return_val    varchar2 (2000);
BEGIN
    l_return_val := 'SAL <= 1500';
    return l_return_val;
END;
```

Notice that the two arguments—the schema name and the object name—are not used inside the function. They are still required by the VPD architecture. Every predicate function, in other words, must pass those two arguments; this topic is explained in more detail later in the chapter.

When the function is executed, it will return the required predicate string **SAL <= 1500**. Let's just confirm that by using the following code segment:

```
declare
    l_return_string    varchar2 (2000);
begin
    l_return_string := authorized_emps ('X', 'X');
    dbms_output.put_line ('Return String = ' || l_return_string);
end;
```

The output is

```
Return String = SAL <= 1500
```

The function will always return the same value regardless of the value of the parameters passed, so why pass the parameters? You'll learn the answer a bit later in this chapter.

Now that we have a function that returns the required predicate, we can take next step: set up the predicate string to be applied for VPD enforcement. A VPD policy defines when and how the predicate will be applied to SQL statements. To define the row-level security for the table EMP, connect as SYS or some other DBA account and execute this:

```
begin
    dbms_rls.add_policy (
        object_schema          => 'SCOTT',
        object_name            => 'EMP',
        policy_name            => 'EMP_POLICY',
        function_schema        => 'SCOTT',
        policy_function        => 'AUTHORIZED_EMPS',
        statement_types        => 'INSERT, UPDATE, DELETE, SELECT'
    );
END;
```

Let's look more carefully at what is going on here: we are adding a policy named EMP_POLICY on the table EMP owned by the schema SCOTT. The policy will apply the filter coming out of the function **authorized_emps** owned by schema SCOTT whenever any user performs an INSERT, UPDATE, DELETE, or SELECT operation.

After the policy is in place, we can immediately test it with a query against the EMP table by the user ALLEN. First, we may need to grant the privileges on the table to ALLEN:

```
grant select, insert, update, delete on scott.emp to allen;
```

Now, let's connect as ALLEN and select from the table directly:

```
SQL> conn allen/allen
SQL> select * from scott.emp;
    EMPNO ENAME      JOB        MGR  HIREDATE         SAL       COMM     DEPTNO
---------- ---------- --------- ---- --------- ---------- ---------- ----------
     7369 SMITH      CLERK      7902 17-DEC-80        800                    20
     7521 WARD       SALESMAN   7698 22-FEB-81       1250        500         30
     7654 MARTIN     SALESMAN   7698 28-SEP-81       1250       1400         30
     7844 TURNER     SALESMAN   7698 08-SEP-81       1500          0         30
     7876 ADAMS      CLERK      7788 23-MAY-87       1100                    20
     7900 JAMES      CLERK      7698 03-DEC-81        950                    30
     7934 MILLER     CLERK      7782 23-JAN-82        200                    10
7 rows selected.
```

Note how only 7 rows are selected, not all 14 of them. If you look closely, you'll notice that all the rows selected have a SAL value less than or equal to 1500, which was enforced by the predicate function. So the user's original query

```
select * from scott.emp;
```

was transformed automatically by the RDBMS (even though the user did not specify the predicate) to this:

```
select * from scott.emp
where SAL <= 1500;
```

Similarly, if users try to delete from or update all the rows in the table, as shown next, only those rows made visible by the RLS policy will be removed:

```
SQL> delete scott.emp;
7 rows deleted.
```

Only 7 rows are deleted, not all 14. Along the same lines, here's what happens when the user updates the COMM column in the table:

```
SQL> update scott.emp set comm = 100;
7 rows updated.
```

And because Oracle applies this filtering at the SQL execution level, users are not aware of the filtering—and that is another valuable feature of VPD from the standpoint of security.

CAUTION: Do Not Grant Execute to Public

Policies are not database schema objects: in other words, no user owns them. Any user with the EXECUTE privilege on the DBMS_RLS package can create a policy. Consequently, any user with that same EXECUTE privilege can also drop any policy. Therefore, it's important that you grant the execute privilege on DBMS_RLS very carefully. If someone has granted the EXECUTE privilege on the package to PUBLIC, revoke it immediately.

You can write policy functions as complex as you want to meet virtually any application requirements. Each function must, however, conform to these rules:

- It must be a stand-alone or packaged function, never a procedure.
- It must return a VARCHAR2 value, which will be applied as the predicate.
- It must have exactly two input parameters in the following order:
    - The schema that owns the table on which the policy has been defined.
    - The object name (table or view) to which the policy is being applied.

To see the policies defined on a table, you can check the data dictionary view DBA_POLICIES, which shows the name of the policy, the object on which it is defined (and its owner), the policy function name (and its owner), and much more. Here is a sample output:

```
select policy_name, pf_owner, function, sel, ins,
       upd, del, idx, chk_option
from dba_policies
where object_owner = 'SCOTT'
and object_name = 'EMP';
```

```
POLICY_NAME       PF_OWNER          FUNCTION          SEL INS UPD DEL IDX CHK
---------------   ---------------   ---------------   --- --- --- --- --- ---
EMP_DEPT_POLICY SCOTT               AUTHORIZED_EMPS YES YES YES YES NO  YES
```

The columns SEL, INS, DEL, UPD, and IDX denote whether the policy is active for selects, inserts, deletes, updates, and indexes, respectively. The columns PF_OWNER and FUNCTION denote the policy function's owner and the name.

If you want to drop an existing VPD policy, you can do so using the DROP_POLICY program in the DBMS_RLS package. Later in this chapter, you will see examples of using this program.

VPD Policies in a Nutshell

- A policy is a set of instructions used to place a table under row-level security. It is not a schema object, and no user owns it.
- Oracle uses the policy to determine when and how to apply a predicate to all the queries against the table.
- The predicate is created by and returned from the policy function, which is written by you—the user.

Intermediate VPD

Now that you have seen an example of VPD fundamentals and know the basics of how VPD works, let's look at some examples that take advantage of different aspects of VPD functionality.

Performing an Update Check

Let's consider a slight twist on our earlier example. Instead of updating the COMM column, the user now updates the SAL column. Because SAL is the column used in the predicate, it will be interesting to see the result. The following is done by either ALLEN or SMITH:

```
SQL> update scott.emp set sal = 1200;
7 rows updated.
SQL> update scott.emp set sal = 1100;
7 rows updated.
```

Only seven rows are updated, as expected. Now, let's change the updated amount. After all, everyone deserves a better salary.

```
SQL> update scott.emp set sal = 1600;
7 rows updated.
SQL> update hr.emp set sal = 1100;
0 rows updated.
```

Let's roll the changes back:

```
SQL> rollback
```

Note the last update. How come no rows were updated?

The answer lies in the first update. The first operation updated the SAL column to 1600, which causes all the visible rows of the table to not be satisfied by the filtering predicate **SAL <= 1500**. Thus, after the first update, all the rows become invisible to the user.

This is a potentially confusing situation: the user can execute a SQL statement against rows that changes the visibility of those rows. During application development, this seemingly instability of data may create bugs or at least introduce some degree of unpredictability that makes debugging a challenge. To counter this behavior, we can take advantage of another ADD_POLICY parameter called **update_check**. Let's take a look at the impact of setting this parameter to TRUE when we create a policy on the table. First, drop the policy:

```
begin
    dbms_rls.drop_policy (
        object_schema        => 'SCOTT',
        object_name          => 'EMP',
        policy_name          => 'EMP_POLICY'
    );
end;
```

Add the policy back to the table with the added parameter:

```
begin
    dbms_rls.add_policy (
        object_schema        => 'SCOTT',
        object_name          => 'EMP',
        policy_name          => 'EMP_POLICY',
        function_schema      => 'SCOTT',
        policy_function      => 'AUTHORIZED_EMPS',
        statement_types      => 'INSERT, UPDATE, DELETE, SELECT',
        update_check         => TRUE
    );
end;
```

After this policy is placed on the table, if a user attempts to perform the same update, he gets an error:

```
SQL> update scott.emp set sal = 1600;
update scott.emp set sal = 1600
                *
ERROR at line 1:
ORA-28115: policy with check option violation
```

The ORA-28115 error is raised because the policy now prevents any updates to the columns in a row that will cause a change in the visibility of that row with the specified predicate. Users can still make changes to other columns that do not affect the visibility of the rows.

TIP
*I recommend that you set the **update_check** parameter to TRUE every time you declare a policy to prevent unpredictable and probably undesirable behavior in the application later on.*

Static vs. Dynamic Policies

In our example, the policy function always returns a static value, which doesn't change even if the circumstances under which it is called changes. This is called a *static* policy. VPD need not execute the function every time a query is issued against the table. The value can be determined only once, cached, and then reused from the cache as many times as needed. This will improve the performance significantly. To make a policy behave that way, we have to explicitly define it as a static policy by setting the value of the parameter **static_policy** to TRUE, as shown here:

```
begin
    dbms_rls.drop_policy (
        object_schema        => 'SCOTT',
        object_name          => 'EMP',
        policy_name          => 'EMP_POLICY'
    );
end;
/
begin
    dbms_rls.add_policy (
        object_schema     => 'SCOTT',
        object_name       => 'EMP',
        policy_name       => 'EMP_POLICY',
        function_schema   => 'SCOTT',
        policy_function   => 'AUTHORIZED_EMPS',
        statement_types   => 'INSERT, UPDATE, DELETE, SELECT',
        update_check      => TRUE,
        static_policy     => TRUE
    );
end;
/
```

As of Oracle 12.1.0.2, the default value of the **static_policy** parameter is FALSE, which makes the policy dynamic rather than static and causes the policy function to be re-executed for each operation on the table.

There are many situations in which a static predicate policy is what is really needed, even when that doesn't appear to be the case. Consider a merchandise warehouse that is servicing several customers. Here, a predicate might be used to limit the entries to only the relevant records for a customer. For example, the table BUILDINGS may contain a column named CUSTOMER_ID. The predicate **CUSTOMER_ID = customer_id** must be appended to the queries, where customer_id is based on the user who is logged in. When a user logs in, his or her customer ID can be retrieved via a LOGON trigger, and the RLS policy can use that ID to evaluate which rows should be displayed. During a session, the value of this predicate does not change, so it makes sense to set **static_policy** to TRUE in such a situation.

Problems with Static Policies

Static policies can enhance performance, but they can also introduce bugs in applications because the predicate remains constant. If the predicate derives from or depends on a changing value, such as time, IP address, or client identifier, you will need to define a dynamic policy rather than a static one. Here is an example that shows why.

Let's look again at our original policy function, but now assume that the predicate depends on a changing value, such as the value of seconds in the current system timestamp. This may not be a very likely real-life example, but it is close enough to explain the concept. Let's create a table as the user SCOTT:

```
create table func_execs
(
    val number
);
```

Insert just a single row into the table:

```
insert into func_execs values (1);
commit;
```

Now let's make some modifications to the **authorized_emps** function we created earlier:

```
create or replace function authorized_emps (
    p_schema_name    in    varchar2,
    p_object_name    in    varchar2
)
    return varchar2
is
    l_return_val    varchar2 (2000);
    pragma autonomous_transaction;
begin
    l_return_val := 'sal <= ' ||
        to_number (to_char (sysdate, 'ss')) * 100;
    update func_execs
        set val = val + 1;
    commit;
    return l_return_val;
end;
```

In this example, the function takes the seconds part of the current time, multiplies it by 100, and returns a predicate that shows the value of the column SAL less than or equal to this number. Because the seconds part will change with time, consecutive executions of this function will yield different results. In addition, every time the function is invoked, the VAL column in the table FUNC_EXECS is updated by 1. This update occurs via an autonomous transaction, so it does not depend on the outcome of the query. Note that this autonomous transaction is merely for our instrumentation purpose; it is neither required nor relevant for the VPD implementation.

The table EMP should already have a VPD policy on it from the previous examples. If it's not there already, re-create it (and, optionally, drop it in case it's there already with some other attributes). While re-creating the policy, make sure that the parameter **static_policy** is FALSE (which is the default).

```
begin
    dbms_rls.drop_policy (
        object_schema        => 'SCOTT',
        object_name          => 'EMP',
        policy_name          => 'EMP_POLICY'
    );
end;
```

Now add the policy back to the table with the added parameter:

```
begin
    dbms_rls.add_policy (
        object_schema          => 'SCOTT',
        object_name            => 'EMP',
        policy_name            => 'EMP_POLICY',
        function_schema        => 'SCOTT',
        policy_function        => 'AUTHORIZED_EMPS',
        statement_types        => 'INSERT, UPDATE, DELETE, SELECT',
        update_check           => TRUE,
        static_policy          => FALSE
    );
end;
```

It's time to test the policy. The user ALLEN tries to find out the number of employees in the table:

```
SQL> select count(*) from scott.emp;
  COUNT(*)
----------
         0
```

Because the table is under VPD security, the policy function is invoked to provide the predicate string to be applied to the query. It depends on the seconds part of the current timestamp, so it is some value between 0 and 60. In this particular case, the value was such that none of the records matched the predicate, and hence no rows were satisfied.

Because the policy function updates the column VAL in the table FUNC_EXECS, we can check to see how many times the function was called. As the user SCOTT, check the value of VAL in the table FUNC_EXECS:

```
select * from func_execs;
       VAL
----------
         3
```

Because the policy function was called twice—once during the parse phase and once during the execution—the value was incremented by 2 from 1. ALLEN can issue the query again to know the number of employees:

```
select count(*) FROM scott.emp
  COUNT(*)
----------
        10
```

This time the policy function returned the predicate, which was satisfied by 10 records in the table. Again, let's check the value of VAL in the table FUNC_EXECS:

```
select * from func_execs;
       VAL
----------
         5
```

The value is incremented by 2, from 3—proof that the policy function was executed multiple times. You can repeat the exercise as many times as you wish to verify that the policy function is executed each time the operation occurs on the table.

Now, declare the policy as static and repeat the test. Because there is no VPD operation or API to alter a policy, you will need to drop the policy and then re-create it. Interestingly, there is an **alter_policy** procedure, but it does something entirely different, as you will see later.

```
begin
    dbms_rls.drop_policy (
        object_schema          => 'SCOTT',
        object_name            => 'EMP',
        policy_name            => 'EMP_POLICY'
    );
end;
```

Add the policy back to the table with the added parameter:

```
begin
    dbms_rls.add_policy (
        object_schema          => 'SCOTT',
        object_name            => 'EMP',
        policy_name            => 'EMP_POLICY',
        function_schema        => 'SCOTT',
        policy_function        => 'AUTHORIZED_EMPS',
        statement_types        => 'INSERT, UPDATE, DELETE, SELECT',
        update_check           => TRUE,
        static_policy          => TRUE
    );
end;
```

As the SCOTT user, reset the VAL column in the table FUNC_EXECS to 1:

```
SQL> conn scot/tiger
SQL> update func_execs set val = 1;
SQL> commit;
```

As user ALLEN, select the number of rows from the table:

```
SQL> conn allen/allen
SQL> select count(*) from scott.emp;
  COUNT(*)
----------
        8
```

As user SCOTT, check the value of the column VAL in FUNC_EXECS:

```
SQL> conn scott/tiger
SQL> select * from func_execs;
       VAL
----------
        2
```

The value was incremented by one, because the policy function was executed only once, not twice as it was before. Repeat the selection from the table EMP several times as user ALLEN:

```
SQL> conn allen/allen
SQL> select count(*) from scott.emp;
  COUNT(*)
----------
         8
SQL> select count(*) from scott.emp;
  COUNT(*)
----------
         8
SQL> select count(*) from scott.emp;
  COUNT(*)
----------
         8
SQL> select count(*) FROM scott.emp;
  COUNT(*)
----------
         8
```

In all cases, the same number is returned, unlike the previous case where a different number was returned. Why? It's because the policy function was executed only once and the predicate that was used by the policy was cached. Because the policy function was never executed after the first execution, the predicate did not change. To confirm that, select from the table FUNC_EXECS as user SCOTT:

```
select * from func_execs;
       VAL
----------
         2
```

The value is still 2; it has not been incremented at all since the first time it was called. This output confirms that the policy function was not called during subsequent SELECT operations on the table EMP.

By declaring a policy as static, you have effectively instructed the policy function to execute only once, and the policy to reuse the predicate originally created, even though the predicate might have changed in the course of time. This behavior might produce unexpected results in your application, so you should use static policies with great caution. The only time you're likely to want to use static policies is when the function positively results in a definitive predicate regardless of any of the variables, except those set at session startup and never changed—for example, the user name.

Preventing Static Policy Bugs

Here you see the potential issues surrounding the use of static policies. On one hand, static policies are great for performance because they execute a function once and cache the result. But that is also the problem because the function is not re-executed and hence the predicate remains the same where it is not supposed to. How can you prevent writing a static policy function that may inadvertently not be static?

Simple. Apart from plain diligence, Oracle helps you by preventing your function from using a pragma declaration to suppress any database operations. Instead of using a stand-alone function for the policy function, you can use a packaged function. Here is the package specification to be created in the SCOTT schema:

```
create or replace package vpd_pkg
as
    function authorized_emps (
        p_schema_name    in    varchar2,
        p_object_name    in    varchar2
    )
        return varchar2;

    pragma restrict_references (authorized_emps, WNDS, RNDS, WNPS, RNPS);
end;
```

Note how we have defined a pragma to bring this function to these purity levels:

- **WNDS**   Write No Database State
- **RNDS**   Read No Database State
- **WNPS**   Write No Package State
- **RNPS**   Read No Package State

Next, we create the package body where we put the logic into the function **authorized_emps**. Recall that this function selects the current timestamp in its code.

```
create or replace package body vpd_pkg
as
    function authorized_emps (
        p_schema_name    in    varchar2,
        p_object_name    in    varchar2
    )
        return varchar2
    is
        l_return_val    varchar2 (2000);
    begin
        l_return_val :=
            'sal <= ' || to_number (to_char (sysdate, 'ss')) * 100;
        return l_return_val;
    end;
end;
```

The package creation fails with the following message:

```
Warning: Package Body created with compilation errors.

Errors for PACKAGE BODY RLS_PKG:

LINE/COL ERROR
-------- ----------------------------------------------------------------
2/4      PLS-00452: Subprogram 'AUTHORIZED_EMPS' violates its associated
         pragma
```

This is good. Oracle has performed this check for us. Declaring a pragma protects us from falling into potentially erroneous situations. When you are creating a static policy, make sure that the predicate returned by the policy function will never have a different value within the session.

TIP
Even if you think a function will always return a static value, use a pragma to enforce that, even if you rely on the code. This will prevent potential bugs in the future.

Defining a Dynamic Policy

In the previous sections, we talked about a policy that returns a predicate string that is always constant—for example, **SAL <= 1500**. In real life, such a scenario is not very common, except in some specialized applications such as goods warehouses. In most cases, you will need to build a filter based on the user issuing the query. For instance, the HR application may require that users see only their own records, not all records in a table. This is a dynamic requirement, because it needs to be evaluated for each employee who logs in. The policy function can be rewritten as follows:

```
create or replace function authorized_emps (
    p_schema_name   in   varchar2,
    p_object_name   in   varchar2
)
    return varchar2
is
    l_return_val   varchar2 (2000);
begin
    l_return_val := 'ename = user';
    return l_return_val;
end;
```

In line 9, the predicate will compare the ENAME column with the USER—that is, the name of the current logged-in user. If ALLEN logs in and selects from the table, he sees only one row—his own:

```
SQL> select * from scott.emp;
```

EMPNO	ENAME	JOB	MGR	HIREDATE	SAL	COMM	DEPTNO
7499	ALLEN	SALESMAN	7698	20-FEB-81	1600	300	30

Now let's expand this model to let ALLEN see more records—not just his own, but his entire department's records. The policy function now becomes the following:

```
create or replace function authorized_emps (
    p_schema_name   in   varchar2,
    p_object_name   in   varchar2
)
    return varchar2
is
    l_deptno        number;
```

```
      l_return_val    varchar2 (2000);
begin
   select deptno
     into l_deptno
     from emp
    where ename = user;

   l_return_val := 'deptno = ' || l_deptno;
   return l_return_val;
end;
```

But there is a small problem. In the previous code, the function selects from the table EMP. However, the table is protected by the VPD policy whose policy function is owned by the user SCOTT. When the function executes under the privileges of the user SCOTT, it will find only one row, because there is just one employee with the name SCOTT—making the predicate an incorrect one. To prevent this from happening, we have two options:

- Grant a special privilege to the user SCOTT so that VPD policies do not apply to it.
- Inside the policy function, indicate whether the calling user is the schema owner; if so, ignore the check.

If you use the first approach, you will not need to change the policy function. As a DBA user, you must grant the special privilege to HR as follows:

```
grant exempt access policy to scott;
```

This removes from the application any VPD policies from the user SCOTT. Because no policy, regardless of which table it is defined on, will be applied, you should use this approach with great caution. In fact, considering the breach it places in the security model, we do not recommend this approach for regular schema owners.

The second approach is to have a special schema named, say, VPDOWNER, which creates all the VPD policies and owns all the policy functions. Only this user, and no others, is granted the EXEMPT ACCESS POLICY system privilege.

Using the second approach, the policy function has to include the logic to bypass the filter for the schema owner, as shown next. First, we will create a special user named VPDOWNER to create the policies and functions. As SYS or another DBA user, execute the following SQL statements:

```
create user vpdowner identified by vpdowner;
grant exempt access policy, create session, create procedure to vpdowner;
grant execute on dbms_rls to vpdowner;
```

We also need to grant select privileges on the EMP table to this user:

```
grant select on scott.emp to vpdowner;
```

With these grants in place, create the following function as the VPDOWNER user. Note that this should be created as VPDOWNER, not the owner of the table (that is, SCOTT).

```
create or replace function authorized_emps (
   p_schema_name    in    varchar2,
   p_object_name    in    varchar2
```

```
)
   return varchar2
is
   l_deptno          number;
   l_return_val      varchar2 (2000);
begin
   if (p_schema_name = user)
   then
      l_return_val := null;
   else
      select deptno
        into l_deptno
        from scott.emp
       where ename = user;
      l_return_val := 'deptno = ' || l_deptno;
   end if;
   return l_return_val;
end;
```

This version of the function is very similar to the previous ones; the new lines are shown in bold. Here, we are checking to see if the calling user is the owner of the table; if so, we return NULL. A NULL value in the predicate returned by the function is equivalent to no policy at all— that is, no rows are filtered.

Drop any existing policies on the table and re-create them using the newly created function:

```
begin
   dbms_rls.drop_policy (
      object_schema          => 'SCOTT',
      object_name            => 'EMP',
      policy_name            => 'EMP_POLICY'
   );
end;
/
begin
   dbms_rls.add_policy (
      object_schema          => 'SCOTT',
      object_name            => 'EMP',
      policy_name            => 'EMP_POLICY',
      function_schema        => 'VPDOWNER',
      policy_function        => 'AUTHORIZED_EMPS',
      statement_types        => 'INSERT, UPDATE, DELETE, SELECT',
      update_check           => TRUE,
      static_policy          => FALSE
   );
end;
/
```

Note the line in bold where we have used the new function owned by VPDOWNER.

Now, when ALLEN executes the same query as before, all of the returned rows are from his department (30):

```
SQL> conn allen/allen
SQL> select * from scott.emp;
 EMPNO ENAME      JOB         MGR HIREDATE    SAL   COMM DEPTNO
 ------ ---------- ---------- ------ --------- ------ ------ ------
  7499 ALLEN      SALESMAN    7698 20-FEB-81 1,600   300     30
  7521 WARD       SALESMAN    7698 22-FEB-81 1,250   500     30
  7654 MARTIN     SALESMAN    7698 28-SEP-81 1,250 1,400     30
  7698 BLAKE      MANAGER     7839 01-MAY-81 2,850           30
  7844 TURNER     SALESMAN    7698 08-SEP-81 1,500     0     30
  7900 JAMES      CLERK       7698 03-DEC-81   950           30
6 rows selected.
```

As you can see, the policy function is crucial in building the VPD policy. The policy will be able to place filters on the rows with whatever predicate value the function can spin out, as long as it is syntactically correct. You can create quite elaborate and sophisticated predicates using policy functions.

Following the same approach, you can have the VPD filters applied to any table in the database. For instance, you could have a policy on the table DEPT, as shown here:

```
begin
    dbms_rls.add_policy (
        object_schema        => 'SCOTT',
        object_name          => 'DEPT',
        policy_name          => 'DEPT_POLICY',
        function_schema      => 'VPDOWNER',
        policy_function      => 'AUTHORIZED_EMPS',
        statement_types      => 'SELECT, INSERT, UPDATE, DELETE',
        update_check         => TRUE,
        static_policy        => FALSE
    );
end;
```

Here, the same function—**authorized_emps**—is used as the policy function. Because the function returns the predicate **DEPTNO = deptno**, it can easily be used in the table DEPT as well as any other table containing a DEPTNO column. We can confirm it is working by connecting as ALLEN and selecting from the DEPT table. First, you need to grant select privilege to ALLEN:

```
SQL> conn scott/tiger
SQL> grant select on dept to allen;
SQL> conn allen/allen
SQL> select * from scott.dept;
    DEPTNO DNAME          LOC
---------- -------------- -------------
        30 SALES          CHICAGO
```

Note how only one row (DEPTNO = 30, which is the department number of ALLEN) was returned, thanks to the policy function, or more specifically, the predicate returned by the policy function.

A table that does not have a DEPTNO column probably has another column through which it has a foreign key relationship with the EMP table. For instance, the table BONUS has a column called ENAME through which it is tied to the EMP table. Therefore, we could rewrite our policy function as follows (owned by VPDOWNER schema):

```
create or replace function allowed_enames (
    p_schema_name   in    varchar2,
    p_object_name   in    varchar2
)
    return varchar2
is
    l_deptno        number;
    l_return_val    varchar2 (2000);
    l_str           varchar2 (2000);
begin
    if (p_schema_name = user)
    then
        l_return_val := null;
    else
        select deptno
          into l_deptno
          from scott.emp
         where ename = user;
        l_str := '(';
        for emprec in (select ename
                         from scott.emp
                        where deptno = l_deptno)
        loop
            l_str := l_str || '''' || emprec.ename || ''',';
        end loop;
        l_str := rtrim (l_str, ',');
        l_str := l_str || ')';
        l_return_val := 'ename in ' || l_str;
    end if;
    return l_return_val;
end;
```

Before going further, you may want to confirm that this does return what you expect it to. Since this is owned by VPDOWNER, grant execute privilege on it to ALLEN and let ALLEN execute it. It's important to know that this is just for the purpose of confirmation. You should revoke the privilege immediately afterward.

```
SQL> conn vpdowner/vpdowner
SQL> grant execute on allowed_enames to allen;
SQL> conn allen/allen
SQL> select vpdowner.allowed_enames ('SCOTT','BONUS') from dual;

VPDOWNER.ALLOWED_ENAMES('SCOTT','BONUS')
-----------------------------------------------------------------
ENAME IN ('BOB','ALLEN','WARD','MARTIN','BLAKE','TURNER','JAMES')
```

This confirms it; we get the predicate string as we expect. It's a list of all employees in the department where ALLEN—the current user—works. Now, revoke the privilege:

```
SQL> conn vpdowner/vpdowner
SQL> revoke execute on allowed_enames from allen;
```

If you define a policy on the BONUS table with the following policy function, this places the VPD policy on the BONUS table as well:

```
begin
    dbms_rls.add_policy (
        object_schema          => 'SCOTT',
        object_name            => 'BONUS',
        policy_name            => 'BONUS_POLICY',
        function_schema        => 'VPDOWNER',
        policy_function        => 'ALLOWED_ENAMES',
        statement_types        => 'SELECT, INSERT, UPDATE, DELETE',
        update_check           => TRUE
    );
end;
```

The BONUS table in Oracle's sample schema is empty. Let's put some records there:

```
SQL> conn scott/tiger
SQL> insert into bonus select ename, job, sal, comm from emp;
15 rows created.
SQL> commit;
Commit complete.
SQL> grant select on scott.bonus to allen;
```

Now, as ALLEN, select from this table:

```
SQL> conn allen/allen
SQL> select * from scott.bonus;
ENAME        JOB              SAL        COMM
---------- --------- ---------- ----------
BOB          PRODUCER         2200
ALLEN        SALESMAN         1600         300
WARD         SALESMAN         1250         500
MARTIN       SALESMAN         1250        1400
BLAKE        MANAGER          2850
TURNER       SALESMAN         1500           0
JAMES        CLERK             950
7 rows selected.
```

ALLEN got only 7 rows instead of the 15 that are actually in the table.

In this manner, you can define VPD polices on all related tables in the database driven from one table. Because the facility we've described in this section essentially provides a private view of the tables in the database based on the user or another parameter (such as time of the day or IP address), it is known as Virtual Private Database (VPD).

Improving Performance

Let's assume that our requirements have changed again (that's not surprising in a typical organization, is it?), and now you have to set up the policy in such a way that all employees and departments will be visible to a user who is a manager; otherwise, only the employees of only the user's department are visible. To accommodate this requirement, your policy function might look like this:

```
create or replace function authorized_emps (
    p_schema_name    in    varchar2,
    p_object_name    in    varchar2
)
    return varchar2
is
    l_deptno        number;
    l_return_val    varchar2 (2000);
    l_mgr           boolean;
    l_empno         number;
    l_dummy         char (1);
begin
    if (p_schema_name = user)
    then
        l_return_val := null;
    else
        select deptno, empno
        into l_deptno, l_empno
        from scott.emp
        where ename = user;

        begin
            select '1'
              into l_dummy
              from scott.emp
             where mgr = l_empno and rownum < 2;

            l_mgr := true;
        exception
            when no_data_found
            then
                l_mgr := false;
            when others
            then
                raise;
        end;

        if (l_mgr)
        then
            l_return_val := null;
        else
            l_return_val := 'deptno = ' || l_deptno;
        end if;
    end if;

    return l_return_val;
end;
```

Look at the complexity in selecting the data. This complexity will surely add to our response time (and, of course, in your real-world applications, the logic will be considerably more complex). Can we simplify the code and improve performance?

We certainly can. Look at the first requirement—checking to see if the employee is a manager. In the preceding code we checked the EMP table for that information, but the fact that an employee is a manager does not change very often. Similarly, a manager's manager might change, but the status of the employee as a manager remains the same. So, the title of a manager is actually more like an attribute of the employee when he logs in, not something that changes during a session. Therefore, if we can somehow, during the login process, pass to the database the fact that the user is a manager, that check will not be needed later in the policy function.

How do we pass a value of this kind? Global variables come to mind. We could assign the value **'Y'** or **'N'** to designate the manager status and then create a package to hold the variable:

```
create or replace package mgr_check
is
    is_mgr    char (1);
end;
```

The policy function looks like this:

```
create or replace function authorized_emps (
    p_schema_name    in    varchar2,
    p_object_name    in    varchar2
)
    return varchar2
is
    l_deptno        number;
    l_return_val    varchar2 (2000);
begin
    if (p_schema_name = user)
    then
        l_return_val := null;
    else
        select distinct deptno
                    into l_deptno
                    from scott.emp
                   where ename = user;

        if (mgr_check.is_mgr = 'y')
        then
            l_return_val := null;
        else
            l_return_val := 'deptno = ' || l_deptno;
        end if;
    end if;

    return l_return_val;
end;
```

Notice how much less code is now required to check for manager status. It merely checks the status from a global packaged variable. This variable has to be set during the login process and therefore is a perfect job for an AFTER LOGON database trigger:

```
create or replace trigger tr_set_mgr
    after logon on database
declare
    l_empno    number;
    l_dummy    char (1);
begin
    select distinct empno
                into l_empno
                from scott.emp
               where ename = user;
    select '1'
      into l_dummy
      from scott.emp
     where mgr = l_empno and rownum < 2;
    vpdowner.mgr_check.is_mgr := 'y';
exception
    when no_data_found
    then
        vpdowner.mgr_check.is_mgr := 'n';
    when others
    then
        raise;
end;
```

The trigger sets the value of the packaged variable to designate the manager status of the employee, which is then picked up by the policy function. Let's do a quick test. Connecting as KING (who is a manager) and ALLEN (who is not), we can see that the setup works. We assume that KING has select privilege on the table.

```
SQL> conn allen/allen
SQL> select count(1) from scott.emp;
  COUNT(1)
----------
         7
SQL> conn king/king
SQL> select count(1) from scott.emp;
  COUNT(1)
----------
        15
```

ALLEN's query retrieves fewer employees, as expected, whereas KING's query retrieves all rows.

You can often use this packaged variable approach to improve performance. In the first example, where the check for manager status was done inside the policy function, the query took 102 centiseconds. Using the global variable approach, it took only 53 centiseconds, which represents a significant improvement.

Controlling the Type of Table Access

VPD has many uses beyond security and the simplification of application development models. It is also very helpful if you need to switch a table between read-only and read-write status, as determined by a variety of circumstances. Prior to Oracle 11g, you had to make an entire tablespace read-only or read-write, but not the individual tables inside it. Even if you could live with this approach, a tablespace could not be made read-only if the database had any active transactions. Since it may be impossible to find a period of time during which there are no transactions in a database, especially in an OLTP database, a tablespace may never actually be able to be made read-only. In Oracle 11g and beyond, we have the ALTER TABLE READ ONLY command to make a tablespace read-only, but it's a DDL command and needs a TM lock, which means the table mustn't be accessed. The VPD approach is the only option in that case.

Now, to be honest, VPD does not actually make a table read-only; it simply emulates that behavior with a way to get the same effect by disallowing attempts to change the contents of the table. The simplest way to do this is to apply a predicate to any UPDATE, DELETE, and INSERT statements. If the predicate evaluates to FALSE (for example, "1=2"), the DML statement will not match any row. This will appear like the table is read-only.

Here is an example. If you want a quick way to make the EMP table read-only with this most basic of predicate functions, you can create a very simple policy function that returns that predicate as follows, in the VPDOWNER schema:

```
create or replace function make_read_only (
    p_schema_name   in    varchar2,
    p_object_name   in    varchar2
)
    return varchar2
is
    l_deptno        number;
    l_return_val    varchar2 (2000);
begin
    -- only the owner of the table can change
    -- the data in the table.
    if (p_schema_name = user)
    then
        l_return_val := null;
    else
        l_return_val := '1=2';
    end if;
    return l_return_val;
end;
```

Using this policy function, we can create a VPD policy on the table EMP for the DML statements that change data: INSERT, UPDATE, and DELETE.

First, drop the existing policy, if any:

```
begin
    dbms_rls.drop_policy (
        object_schema => 'SCOTT',
        object_name   => 'EMP',
        policy_name   => 'EMP_POLICY'
    );
end;
```

Add the policy with this function:

```
begin
    dbms_rls.add_policy (
        object_schema      => 'SCOTT',
        object_name        => 'EMP',
        policy_name        => 'EMP_READONLY_POLICY',
        function_schema    => 'VPDOWNER',
        policy_function    => 'MAKE_READ_ONLY',
        statement_types    => 'INSERT, UPDATE, DELETE',
        update_check       => TRUE
    );
end;
```

Note that the **statement_types** parameter does not include the SELECT statement because that statement will be freely allowed. The function we wrote earlier is designated as the policy function.

When ALLEN issues the following statements, he sees what is expected:

```
SQL> conn allen/allen
SQL> delete scott.emp;
0 rows deleted.
```

But notice what happens when he selects from the table:

```
SQL> select count(*) from scott.emp;
  COUNT(*)
----------
        14
```

He can select all 14 rows, but cannot delete, update, or insert anything in the table, making the table effectively read-only. When the time comes to make the table read-write again, we can simply disable the policy:

```
begin
    dbms_rls.enable_policy (
        object_schema => 'SCOTT',
        object_name   => 'EMP',
        policy_name   => 'EMP_READONLY_POLICY',
        enable        => FALSE
    );
end;
```

Now ALLEN and other users can successfully complete DML operations on the table. Later on, if we need to make the table read-only again, we can execute the previous code segment again with a slight difference:

```
enable              => TRUE
```

This enables the policy and applies the predicate **WHERE 1=2** to every DML statement, thus preventing changes to the table. Note that you can have more than one policy on the table. The presence of this "read-only" policy does not replace the policies currently existing on the table, so the current row-level access control requirements in place remain intact.

The table is never actually set to read-only; the policy just makes sure that no rows are affected when the user issues DML statements against the table. Because no error is returned and the policy simply ignores any DML statements, you need to be careful to examine all of the application code that uses this functionality. You may inadvertently mistake the no-error condition as a successful DML operation.

But the power of this feature doesn't stop here. More than making tables read-only/read-write on demand, this restriction can be created dynamically and applied automatically based on any user-defined conditions you wish. For instance, we could write a policy function that takes the time of the day and makes the table read-only between 5:00 P.M. and 9:00 A.M. for all users, except for the batch job user, BATCHUSER. We can write the policy function as shown here:

```
create or replace function make_read_only (
    p_schema_name    in    varchar2,
    p_object_name    in    varchar2
)
    return varchar2
is
    l_hr            pls_integer;
    l_return_val    varchar2 (2000);
begin
    if (p_schema_name = user)
    then
        l_return_val := null;
    else
        l_hr := to_number (to_char (sysdate, 'hh24'));
        if (user = 'BATCHUSER')
        -- you can list all users here that should be
        -- read only during the daytime.
        then
            if (l_hr between 9 and 17)
            then
                -- make the table read only
                l_return_val := '1=2';
            else
                l_return_val := null;
            end if;
        else
            -- users which need to be read only during after-hours
            if (l_hr >= 17 and l_hr <= 9)
            then
                -- make the table read only
                l_return_val := '1=2';
            else
                l_return_val := null;
            end if;
        end if;
    end if;
    return l_return_val;
end;
```

Based on the timestamp, you can let the table be controlled granularly on multiple fronts. The example we've shown here can be extended to cover other attributes as well (for example,

IP address, authentication type, client information, terminal, OS user, and many others). All you have to do is get the appropriate variable from the system context (SYS_CONTEXT; this feature is explored later in the chapter) of the session and check it. For example, assume that you have a requirement that the user KING (the president of the company) is allowed to see every record only if he does both of the following:

- Connects from his laptop KINGLAP with a fixed IP address (192.168.1.1) and from the Windows NT domain ACMEBANK
- Connects to Windows as user KING

The policy function would now look like this:

```
create or replace function emp_policy (
    p_schema_name    in    varchar2,
    p_object_name    in    varchar2
)
    return varchar2
is
    l_deptno          number;
    l_return_val      varchar2 (2000);
begin
  if (p_schema_name = user)
  then
      l_return_val := null;
  elsif (user = 'KING')
  then
      if (
              -- check client machine name
              sys_context ('userenv', 'host') = 'ACMEBANK\KINGLAP'
          and
              -- check os username
              sys_context ('userenv', 'os_user') = 'KING'
          and
              -- check ip address
              sys_context ('userenv', 'ip_address') = '192.168.1.1'
          )
      then
          -- all checks satisfied for king; allow unrestricted access.
          l_return_val := null;
      else
          -- return the usual predicate
          l_return_val := 'sal <= 1500';
      end if;
  else   -- all other users
      l_return_val := 'sal <= 1500';
  end if;

  return l_return_val;
end;
```

Here we are using the built-in function SYS_CONTEXT to return the context attributes. We'll discuss system contexts later in the "Application Contexts" section; all you need to understand now is that the function call returns the name of the client terminal from which the user is connected. The other lines using the function call also return the appropriate values.

You can use SYS_CONTEXT to get a variety of information about the user connection. By using this information, you can easily customize your policy function to build a filter to cater to your specific needs. For a complete list of attributes available via SYS_CONTEXT, refer to the SQL Reference Manual in the Oracle documentation.

Column-Sensitive VPD

Let's revisit the example of the HR application used in earlier sections. We designed the policy with the requirement that no user except KING should have permission to see all records. Any other user can see only data about the employees in his or her department. But there may be cases in which that policy is too restrictive. Suppose that we want to protect the data so people can't snoop around for salary information. Consider the following two queries:

```
select empno, sal from emp;
select empno from emp;
```

The first query shows salary information for employees, the very information you want to protect. In this case, you want to show only the employees in the user's own department. But the second query shows only the employee numbers. Should you filter that as well so that it shows only the numbers for the employees in the user's own department?

The answer might vary depending on the security policy in force within your organization. There may be a good reason to let the second query show all employees, regardless of the department to which they belong. In such a case, will VPD be effective?

Fortunately, yes. The parameter **sec_relevant_cols** in the **add_policy**() procedure makes it easy. In the preceding scenario, you want the filter to be applied only when the SAL or COMM column is selected, not any other columns. You can write the policy as follows. Note the new parameter shown in bold:

```
begin
    -- drop the policy first, if exists.
    dbms_rls.drop_policy (
        object_schema      => 'SCOTT',
        object_name        => 'EMP',
        policy_name        => 'EMP_POLICY'
    );
end;
/
begin   --
    -- add the policy
    dbms_rls.add_policy (
        object_schema           => 'SCOTT',
        object_name             => 'EMP',
        policy_name             => 'EMP_POLICY',
        function_schema         => 'VPDOWNER',
        policy_function         => 'AUTHORIZED_EMPS',
        statement_types         => 'INSERT, UPDATE, DELETE, SELECT',
```

```
        update_check           => TRUE,
        sec_relevant_cols      => 'SAL, COMM'
    );
end;
/
```

After this policy is put in place, ALLEN's queries perform differently:

```
SQL> -- "harmless" query, only EMPNO is selected
SQL> select empno from scott.emp;
… rows come here …
14 rows selected.
SQL> -- sensitive query:, SAL is selected
SQL> select empno, sal from scott.emp;
… rows come here …
6 rows selected.
```

Note that when the column SAL is selected, the VPD policy kicks in, preventing the display of all rows; it filters out the rows where DEPTNO is something other than 30—that is, the DEPTNO of the user (ALLEN) executing the query.

Column sensitivity does not apply just to being in the SELECT list, but applies whenever the column is referenced, either directly or *indirectly*. Consider the following query:

```
SQL> select deptno, count (*) from scott.emp where sal > 0 group by deptno;
    DEPTNO    COUNT(*)
---------- ----------
        30          6
```

Here, the SAL column has been referenced in the WHERE clause, so the VPD policy applies, causing only the records from department 30 to be displayed.

Consider another example, in which we try to display the value of SAL:

```
SQL> select * from scott.emp where deptno = 10;
no rows selected
```

Here, the column SAL has not been referenced explicitly, but it is *implicitly* referenced by the **SELECT *** clause, so the VPD policy filters all but the rows from department 30. Because the query called for department 10, no rows were returned.

Let's examine a slightly different situation now. In the previous case, we did protect the SAL column values from being displayed for those rows for which the user is not authorized. However, in the process we suppressed the display of the entire row, not just the column. Suppose the new requirements call for masking only the column, not the entire row, and for displaying all other nonsensitive columns. Can this be done?

It's easy with another ADD_POLICY parameter called **sec_relevant_cols_opt**. All you have to do is re-create the policy with the parameter set to the constant DBMS_RLS.ALL_ROWS, as follows:

```
begin
    dbms_rls.drop_policy (
        object_schema     => 'SCOTT',
        object_name       => 'EMP',
        policy_name       => 'EMP_POLICY'
```

```
     );
     dbms_rls.add_policy (
        object_schema          => 'SCOTT',
        object_name            => 'EMP',
        policy_name            => 'EMP_POLICY',
        function_schema        => 'VPDOWNER',
        policy_function        => 'AUTHORIZED_EMPS',
        statement_types        => 'SELECT',
        update_check           => TRUE,
        sec_relevant_cols      => 'SAL, COMM',
        sec_relevant_cols_opt  => DBMS_RLS.all_rows
     );
end;
```

If ALLEN issues the same type of query now, the results will be different (in the following output, we request that a "?" be shown for NULL values):

```
SQL> -- Show a "?" for the NULL values in the output.
SQL> set null ?
SQL> select * from scott.emp order by deptno;
EMPNO ENAME      JOB        MGR HIREDATE     SAL   COMM DEPTNO
------ ---------- --------- ------ --------- ------ ------ ------
 7782 CLARK      MANAGER    7839 09-JUN-81 ?      ?         10
 7839 KING       PRESIDENT ?    17-NOV-81 ?      ?         10
 7934 MILLER     CLERK      7782 23-JAN-82 ?      ?         10
 7369 SMITH      CLERK      7902 17-DEC-80 ?      ?         20
 7876 ADAMS      CLERK      7788 12-JAN-83 ?      ?         20
 7902 FORD       ANALYST    7566 03-DEC-81 ?      ?         20
 7788 SCOTT      ANALYST    7566 09-DEC-82 ?      ?         20
 7566 JONES      MANAGER    7839 02-APR-81 ?      ?         20
 7499 ALLEN      SALESMAN   7698 20-FEB-81 1,600    300     30
 7698 BLAKE      MANAGER    7839 01-MAY-81 2,850 ?         30
 7654 MARTIN     SALESMAN   7698 28-SEP-81 1,250  1,400     30
 7900 JAMES      CLERK      7698 03-DEC-81   950 ?         30
 7844 TURNER     SALESMAN   7698 08-SEP-81 1,500      0     30
 7521 WARD       SALESMAN   7698 22-FEB-81 1,250    500     30

14 rows selected.
```

Notice how all 14 rows are shown, along with all the columns, but the values for SAL and COMM are NULL for the rows that the user is not supposed to see—that is, the employees of departments other than 30. It was possible to do without the use of views. Another method was shown in Chapter 13 on redaction, but it needs an extra-cost option, whereas this approach does not need it.

Although it may sound attractive, we must warn you to use this feature with extreme caution because it may produce unexpected results. Consider the following query issued by user ALLEN:

```
SQL> select count(1), avg(sal) from scott.emp;
COUNT(SAL)   AVG(SAL)
---------- ----------
        14 1566.66667
```

The result shows 14 employees, and the average salary is 1566, but that salary is actually the average of only the 6 employees ALLEN is authorized to see, *not all 14 employees*. This may create some confusion as to which values are correct.

When the schema owner, SCOTT, issues the same query, we see a different result:

```
SQL> CONN scott/tiger
SQL> SELECT COUNT(1), AVG(sal) FROM scott.emp;
COUNT(SAL)   AVG(SAL)
---------- ----------
        14 2073.21429
```

Because results vary by the user issuing the query, you need to be very careful to interpret the results accordingly; otherwise, this feature may introduce difficult-to-trace bugs into your application.

Other Classes of Dynamism

We've already discussed static vs. dynamic policies, but there is more than just one type of "dynamism."

First, let's review the difference between static and dynamic policies. With a dynamic policy type, the policy function is executed to create a predicate string every time the policy places filters on access to the table. Although using a dynamic policy guarantees a fresh predicate every time it is called, the additional overhead resulting from multiple executions of the policy function can be quite substantial. In most real-life cases, the policy function does not need to be re-executed because the predicate will never change inside a session, as shown earlier in the discussion of static policies.

The best approach, from a performance point of view, would be to design the policy function in such a way that if some specific value changes, the policy function will be re-executed. Oracle Database does offers such a feature: if the application context on which the program depends is changed, the policy can force re-execution of the function; otherwise, the function will not be run again. You'll see how this works in the following sections.

The trick is to use the **policy_type** parameter. Recall that the **static_policy** parameter in the ADD_POLICY procedure can be set to either TRUE (indicating a static policy) or FALSE (indicating a dynamic policy). If this parameter is TRUE, then the value of **policy_type** is set to DBMS_RLS .STATIC. If **static_policy** is FALSE, then **policy_type** is set to DBMS_RLS.DYNAMIC. The default for **static_policy** is TRUE, but the **policy_type** can take other values, as shown in the following list:

- DBMS_RLS.DYNAMIC for completely dynamic policies
- DBMS_RLS.CONTEXT_SENSITIVE for context-sensitive policies
- DBMS_RLS.SHARED_CONTEXT_SENSITIVE for shared context-sensitive policies
- DBMS_RLS.STATIC for completely static policies
- DBMS_RLS.SHARED_STATIC for "shared" static policies.

If you state a **policy_type** in your ADD_POLICY statement, the value is used and overrides the setting for **static_policy**. Let's explore the valid values of **policy_type** in depth.

Shared Static Policy

The shared static policy type is similar to the static type, except that the same policy function is used in policies on multiple objects. In a previous example you saw how the function **authorized_emps** was used as the policy function in the policies on both the DEPT and the EMP tables. Similarly, you can have the same policy defined on both tables, not merely the same function. This is known as a shared policy. If it can also be considered static, then the policy is known as a shared static policy and the **policy_type** parameter is set to the constant DBMS_RLS.SHARED_STATIC. Using this policy type, here is how we can create the same policy on our two tables:

```
-- drop policies if they exist already
begin
    dbms_rls.drop_policy (
        object_schema      => 'SCOTT',
        object_name        => 'DEPT',
        policy_name        => 'EMP_DEPT_POLICY'
    );
    dbms_rls.drop_policy (
        object_schema      => 'SCOTT',
        object_name        => 'EMP',
        policy_name        => 'EMP_DEPT_POLICY'
    );
end;
/
begin
    dbms_rls.add_policy (
        object_schema      => 'SCOTT',
        object_name        => 'DEPT',
        policy_name        => 'EMP_DEPT_POLICY',
        function_schema    => 'VPDOWNER',
        policy_function    => 'AUTHORIZED_EMPS',
        statement_types    => 'SELECT, INSERT, UPDATE, DELETE',
        update_check       => TRUE,
        policy_type        => DBMS_RLS.shared_static
    );

    dbms_rls.add_policy (
        object_schema      => 'SCOTT',
        object_name        => 'EMP',
        policy_name        => 'EMP_DEPT_POLICY',
        function_schema    => 'VPDOWNER',
        policy_function    => 'AUTHORIZED_EMPS',
        statement_types    => 'SELECT, INSERT, UPDATE, DELETE',
        update_check       => TRUE,
        policy_type        => DBMS_RLS.shared_static
    );
end;
```

By declaring a single policy on both tables, we are effectively instructing the database to cache the outcome of the policy function once and then use it multiple times.

Context-Sensitive Policy

As you saw earlier, static policies, although quite efficient, can be dangerous because they do not re-execute the function every time. Therefore, they may produce unexpected and unwanted results. Hence, Oracle provides another type of policy—the context-sensitive policy—that re-executes the policy function only when the application context changes in the session. (See the "Application Contexts" section later in this chapter.) Here is a parameter definition in a block of code that defines such a policy:

```
policy_type => dbms_rls.context_sensitive
```

When you use a context-sensitive policy type (DBMS_RLS.CONTEXT_SENSITIVE), performance can increase dramatically. The following block of code shows the time differences in the query issued by ALLEN. To measure the time, we will use the built-in time function, DBMS_UTILITY.GET_TIME, to help us calculate elapsed time down to the hundredth of a second.

```
declare
    l_start    pls_integer;
    l_count    pls_integer;
begin
    l_start := dbms_utility.get_time;

    select count (*)
      into l_count
      from scott.emp;

    dbms_output.put_line (
        'elapsed time = '
        || to_char (dbms_utility.get_time - l_start)
        );
end;
```

We then apply each of the types of policies shown in the following table and run the block of code. As you can see from this table, the purely static policy results in the fastest time (just a single execution of the policy function), but the context-sensitive policy was very close:

```
select dbms_utility.get_time cstime from dual;
select count (*) from scott.emp;
select dbms_utility.get_time - &timevar from dual;
```

The difference in the output of the function call between the beginning and the end is the time elapsed in centiseconds (hundredths of seconds). When the previous query is run under different conditions, we get different response times. As shown in the table, the times are significantly faster than the 100 percent dynamic version.

Policy Type	Response Time (cs)
Dynamic	133
Context Sensitive	84
Static	37

Shared Context-Sensitive Policy

Shared context-sensitive policies are similar to context-sensitive policies, except that the same policy is used for multiple objects, as you saw with shared static policies.

NOTE
How do you decide which types of policy to use? We recommend that you do the following: Initially use the default type (dynamic). Then, once the upgrade is complete, try to re-create the policy as context-sensitive and test the results thoroughly, with all possible scenarios to eliminate any potential caching issues. Finally, for those policies that can be made static, convert them to static and test thoroughly.

VPD and Performance

We can't complete a treatise on VPD without warning you about the potential performance issues. Since VPD policies apply the predicate automatically, every query will contain the predicate (or the WHERE condition). This adds yet another line to the execution steps and affects performance. Therefore, the presence of indexes on the columns mentioned in the automatic predicate affects the performance, often negatively. When tables under VPD are joined with others, the predicate also gets in the join, which may change the behavior. Therefore, you must carefully analyze the impact of this non-user-supplied predicate on the query performance and take adequate steps to avoid a performance problem later.

Troubleshooting

VPD is a somewhat complex feature that interacts with a variety of elements in the Oracle architecture. You may encounter errors, either as a result of problems in your design or through misuse by users. Fortunately, for most errors, RLS produces a detailed trace file in the trace directory, which, in Oracle 10g and below, is the directory specified by the database initialization parameter USER_DUMP_DEST and, in Oracle 11g and above, the Automatic Diagnostic Repository. This section describes how you can trace VPD operations and resolve common error conditions.

ORA-28110: Policy Function or Package Has Error

The most common error you will likely encounter and the easiest to deal with is "ORA-28110: policy function or package has error." The culprit here is a policy function with one or more compilation errors. Fixing your compilation errors and recompiling the function (or the package containing the function) solves the problem.

ORA-28112: Failed to Execute Policy Function

You may also encounter run-time errors, such as an unhandled exception, a data type mismatch, or a situation in which the fetched data is much larger than the variable fetched into. In these cases,

Oracle raises the "ORA-28112: failed to execute policy function" error and produces a trace file. You can examine that file to find out the nature of the error. Here is an excerpt from a trace file:

```
------------------------------------------------------------
Policy function execution error:
Logon user      : ALLEN
Table/View      : SCOTT.EMP
Policy name     : EMP_DEPT_POLICY
Policy function: VPDOWNER.AUTHORIZED_EMPS
ORA-01422: exact fetch returns more than requested number of rows
ORA-06512: at "VPDOWNER.AUTHORIZED_EMPS", line 14
ORA-06512: at line 1
```

The trace file shows that ALLEN was executing the query when this error occurred. Here the policy function simply fetched more than one row. Examining the policy function, you notice that the policy function has the following segment:

```
select deptno
into l_deptno
from scott.emp
where ename = user;
```

It seems there is more than one employee with the name ALLEN—hence, the number of rows fetched is more than one, thus causing this problem. The solution is to either handle the error via an exception or just use something else as a predicate to get the department number.

ORA-28113: Policy Predicate Has Error

This error occurs when the policy function does not construct the predicate clause correctly. Like the previous error, it produces a trace file. Here is an excerpt from the trace file:

```
Error information for ORA-28113:
Logon user      : ALLEN
Table/View      : SCOTT.EMP
Policy name     : EMP_DEPT_POLICY
Policy function: VPDOWNER.AUTHORIZED_EMPS
RLS predicate   :
DEPTNO = 10,
ORA-00907: missing right parenthesis
```

It shows that the predicate returned by the policy function is

```
DEPTNO = 10,
```

This string is syntactically incorrect inside a SQL query, so the policy application failed, and so did ALLEN's query. This can be fixed by correcting the policy function logic to return a valid value string as the predicate.

Direct-Path Operations

If you are using direct-path operations—for example, SQL*Loader Direct Path Load, Direct Path Inserts using the APPEND hint (**INSERT /*+ APPEND */ INTO** ...), and Direct Path Export—you may run into trouble when using VPD. Because these operations bypass the SQL layer, the VPD policy on these tables is not invoked, and hence the security is bypassed. How do we get around this problem?

In the case of exports, it's rather easy. Here is what happens when you export the table EMP, which is protected by one or more VPD policies, with the DIRECT=Y option:

```
About to export specified tables via Direct Path ...
EXP-00080: Data in table "EMP" is protected. Using conventional mode.
EXP-00079: Data in table "EMP" is protected. Conventional path may only be
 exporting partial table.
```

The export is successfully done, but as you can see, the output is a conventional path, not the direct path we wanted it to be. And in the process of performing the operation, the export still applied the VPD policies to the table—that is, the user can export only the rows he is authorized to see, not all of them.

Because exporting a table under VPD may still successfully complete, you might get a false impression that all rows have been exported. However, be aware that only the rows the user is allowed to see, not all rows of the table, are exported.

Now, when you try to do a direct-path load to the table under RLS, using SQL*Loader or Direct Path Insert, you get an error:

```
insert /*+ append */
into scott.emp
select *
from scott.emp;
```

Here is the output:

```
FROM scott.emp
        *
ERROR at line 4:
ORA-28113: policy predicate has error
```

The error is self-explanatory; you can fix this situation either by temporarily disabling the policy on the table EMP or by exporting through a user who has the EXEMPT ACCESS POLICY system privilege.

Checking the Query Rewrite

During debugging, it may be necessary to see the exact SQL statement rewritten by Oracle when an RLS policy is applied. In this way, you will leave nothing to chance or interpretation. You can see the rewritten statement either via a data dictionary view or by setting an event.

Data Dictionary View

The view V$VPD_POLICY shows all the query transformations made by the VPD policy:

```
select sql_text, predicate, policy, object_name
from v$sqlarea , v$vpd_policy
where hash_value = sql_hash
/
SQL_TEXT
------------------------------------------------------------------------
```

```
PREDICATE
-------------------------------------------------------------------------
POLICY                          OBJECT_NAME
-----------------------------   ----------------------------------
select count(*) from hr.emp     DEPTNO = 10
DEPTNO = 10
EMP_DEPT_POLICY                 EMP
```

The column SQL_TEXT shows the exact SQL statement issued by the user, while the column PREDICATE shows the predicate generated by the policy function and applied to the query. Using this view you can identify the statements issued by the users and the predicates applied to them.

Event-Based Tracing

The other option is to set an event in the session and examine the trace file. When ALLEN issues the query, he specifies an additional command to set the event before issuing the query:

```
alter session set events '10730 trace name context forever, level 12';
select count(*) from scott.emp;
```

After the query finishes, he sees a trace file generated. Here is what the trace file shows:

```
Logon user      : ALLEN
Table/View      : SCOTT.EMP
Policy name     : EMP_DEPT_POLICY
Policy function: VPDOWNER.AUTHORIZED_EMPS
RLS view :
SELECT   "EMPNO","ENAME","JOB","MGR","HIREDATE","SAL","COMM","DEPTNO" FROM
 "HR"."EMP"  "EMP" WHERE (DEPTNO = 10)
```

This clearly shows the statement as it was rewritten by the RLS policy.

Using either of these methods you will be able to see the exact way that the user queries are rewritten.

Interactions with Other Oracle Features

VPD, like any other powerful feature, presents its share of potential concerns, issues, and complexities. This section describes the interactions between VPD and several other Oracle features.

Referential Integrity Constraints

If a table has a referential integrity constraint pointing to a parent table that is under VPD, there could be a possible security concern in the way Oracle deals with the resulting errors. Let's see that in an example. Suppose that the EMP table is not under VPD, but the table DEPT has a VPD policy defined on it that lets the user see only his department number's row. In this case, an "all rows" query against DEPT reveals just a single row:

```
SQL> conn allen/allen
SQL> select * from scott.dept;
    DEPTNO DNAME          LOC
---------- -------------- -------------
        10 ACCOUNTING     NEW YORK
```

Table EMP has a referential integrity constraint on the column DEPTNO that references the DEPTNO column in table DEPT. Since the EMP table is not under any VPD policy, the user can freely select from it. A user can, therefore, be made aware that there is more than one department.

```
select distinct deptno from scott.emp;
    DEPTNO
----------
        10
        20
        30
```

The user can see only the details of department 10, the one to which he belongs, but with this query he knows that there are others too. As per the VPD policy on the DEPT table, he is not supposed to know how many other departments there are.

The problem doesn't stop right there. Let's see what happens when he tries to update the EMP table to set the department number to 50:

```
update scott.emp
set deptno = 50
where empno = 7369;
```

Here is the output:

```
update scott.emp
*
ERROR at line 1:
ORA-02291: integrity constraint (SCOTT.FK_EMP_DEPT) violated - parent key not
 found
```

The error indicates that the integrity constraint is violated; this makes sense because the DEPT table does not have a row with DEPTNO equal to 50. Oracle Database is doing its job, but now ALLEN knows more about the DEPT table than was intended by the security policy. By running such updates multiple times, he can find out whether or not a department number exists. Revealing such data, under some circumstances, could be as severe a security breach as showing the data that is in the table. It is something you should be aware of.

Replication

In multimaster replication, the receiver and propagator schemas have to be able to select data from tables in an unrestricted manner. Hence, you will need to either modify the policy function to return a NULL predicate for these users or grant the EXEMPT ACCESS POLICY system privilege to them.

Materialized Views

When defining materialized views, you should be careful to make sure that the owner of the materialized view has unrestricted access to the underlying tables. Otherwise, only the rows satisfied by the predicate will be returned to the query defining the materialized view, and that will be incorrect. As in the case of replication, you can either modify the policy function to return a NULL predicate or grant the EXEMPT ACCESS POLICY system privilege to the schemas.

Application Contexts

In the discussion of row-level security so far, we have assumed a critical fact—that the predicate (that is, the string denoting the WHERE condition that restricts the rows of the table) is constant or fixed at the time of login. But what if we have a new requirement: users can now see employee records based not on fixed department numbers but on a list of privileges maintained for that reason? A table named EMP_ACCESS maintains the information about which users can access which employee information. Let's create and populate the table. Connect as SYS and give the necessary privileges to the user VPDOWNER:

```
grant create table to vpdowner;
alter user vpdowner quota unlimited on users;
```

Connect as VPDOWNER and create the table:

```
create table emp_access (
    username          varchar2(30) not null,
    deptno            number not null
);
```

Now insert the rows:

```
insert into emp_access values ('ALLEN',10);
insert into emp_access values ('ALLEN',20);
insert into emp_access values ('KING',10);
insert into emp_access values ('KING',20);
insert into emp_access values ('KING',30);
insert into emp_access values ('KING',40);
```

Don't forget to commit the changes. Now, let's check the table:

```
SQL> desc emp_access
 Name                     Null?    Type
 ------------------ -------- ------------
 USERNAME                          VARCHAR2(30)
 DEPTNO                            NUMBER
```

And, here is the data in it:

```
USERNAME                             DEPTNO
------------------------------- ----------
ALLEN                                    10
ALLEN                                    20
KING                                     20
KING                                     10
KING                                     30
KING                                     40
```

We note that ALLEN can see departments 10 and 20, but KING can see 10, 20, 30, and 40. If an employee's name is not in this table, he cannot see any records. This new rule requires that we change the predicate as well as the policy function. The requirements also state that a user's privilege can be reassigned dynamically by updating the EMP_ACCESS table. The new privileges must take effect immediately; it's not an option to log off and then log in again. Hence, a LOGON trigger will not help in this case to set all the values needed for use in the policy function.

What's the solution? One possible option for meeting this requirement is to create a package with a variable to hold the predicate and let the user execute some PL/SQL code program to assign the value to the variable before selecting from the EMP table. The policy function can then pick up the value cached in the package. Is this an acceptable approach? Consider this situation carefully: if the user can assign a value to the package variable, what prevents him from assigning a very high security level to this value, such as that for KING? ALLEN could log in, set the variable to provide access to *all* departments, and then SELECT from the table to see all the records. There is no security in this case, and that is unacceptable.

The possibility that a user may change the value of the package variable dynamically requires us to rethink our strategy. We need a way to set a global variable by some secure mechanism so that unauthorized alteration will not be possible. Fortunately, Oracle provides this capability through *application contexts*. An application context is analogous to a global package variable; once set, it can be accessed throughout the session and can also be reset.

An application context is similar to a structure (struct) in the C language or a record in PL/SQL; it consists of a series of attributes, each of which is made up of a name-value pair. Unlike its counterparts in C and PL/SQL, however, the attributes are not named during the creation of the context; instead, they are named and assigned at run time. Application contexts, by default, reside in the Program Global Area (PGA), not the System Global Area (SGA). Therefore, they are not visible outside the session. You can also define *global* application contexts, which are visible to all sessions.

But more than just a variable, application context is a mechanism by which a value inside it can be set more securely than a package variable. You can change the value of an application context only by calling a specific named PL/SQL program, not by PL/SQL assignment, as is the case in a package variable. Let's explore this further with an example.

A Simple Example

Let's explore application contexts further with an example. We'll start by using the CREATE CONTEXT command to define a new context named DEPT_CTX. Any user with the CREATE ANY CONTEXT system privilege and execute privilege on the package DBMS_SESSION can create and set a context:

```
create context dept_ctx using set_dept_ctx;
```

Note the special clause **using set_dept_ctx**. This clause indicates that an attribute of the DEPT_CTX context can only be set and changed through a procedure named **set_dept_ctx**, and that *only* that procedure can set or change attributes of the context DEPT_CTX; this cannot be done any other way.

We have not yet specified any attributes of the context; we have simply defined the overall context (its name and the secure mechanism for changing it). Next let's create the procedure. Inside this procedure, we will assign values to the context attributes using the **set_context** function from the built-in package DBMS_SESSION, as shown in the following example:

```
create or replace procedure set_dept_ctx (
    p_attr in varchar2, p_val in varchar2)
is
begin
    dbms_session.set_context ('dept_ctx', p_attr, p_val);
end;
```

Now, to set the attribute named DEPTNO to a value of 10, you would issue

```
exec set_dept_ctx ('deptno','10')
```

To obtain the current value of an attribute, you call the **sys_context** function, which accepts two parameters—the context name and the attribute name. Here is a sample PL/SQL segment to demonstrate. Issue **set serveroutput on size 999999** before executing this code segment to enable the output display from **dbms_output** calls:

```
declare
    l_ret    varchar2 (20);
begin
    l_ret := sys_context ('dept_ctx', 'deptno');
    dbms_output.put_line ('value of deptno = ' || l_ret);
end;
```

Here is the output:

```
value of deptno = 10
```

You may have noticed that we used this **sys_context** function earlier in the chapter to obtain the IP address and terminal name of the client.

The Security in Application Contexts

Let's go back to the procedure design again; all that the procedure does is call **set_context** with appropriate parameters. Why do we need to use a procedure to do that? Can't we just call the built-in function directly? Let's see what happens if a user calls the same code segment to set the value of the attribute DEPTNO to 10:

```
SQL> begin
  2      dbms_session.set_context ('dept_ctx', 'deptno', 10);
  3  end;
  4  /
begin
*
ERROR at line 1:
ORA-01031: insufficient privileges
ORA-06512: at "SYS.DBMS_SESSION", line 82
ORA-06512: at line 2
```

Note the error, "ORA-01031: insufficient privileges." That's puzzling, because the user ALLEN does have the required Execute privilege on DBMS_SESSION (it would have been impossible to compile **set_dept_ctx** without that privilege). So that is clearly not the issue here. You can verify this by granting the execute privilege on this package again and re-executing the same code segment—you will still get the same error.

The reason is, the insufficient privilege refers not to the use of DBMS_SESSION, but to the attempt to set the context value *outside* of the **set_dept_ctx** procedure. Oracle only "trusts" the **set_dept_ctx** procedure to set the application context values for DEPT_CTX. Therefore, Oracle refers to the program referenced by the USING clause of CREATE CONTEXT as the *trusted* procedure.

The only schemas that can execute a trusted procedure are

■ The schema that owns the procedure

■ Any schema to which execute authority is granted on that trusted procedure

So if you are careful about how you grant that execute authority, you can tightly control who can set that context's values.

Contexts as Predicates in VPD

So far you have learned that a procedure must be used to set a context value, which is similar to a global package variable. You might be tempted to ask, where is that going to be useful? Doesn't it increase the complexity rather unnecessarily without achieving any definite purpose?

Not at all. Since the trusted procedure is the *only* way to set the value of a context attribute, the biggest advantage is that you can use it in maintaining execution control. Inside the trusted procedure, you can place all types of checks to ensure that the variable assignments are legitimate. Remember, the user must call the trusted procedure to set a value; he can't simply assign it. So there is no way to bypass the check for legitimacy of the call. You can even completely eliminate the passing of parameters and set the values from predetermined values without the any input (and therefore influence) from the user. Going back to our requirement for employee access, for instance, we know that we need to set the application context value to a string of department numbers, picked from the table EMP_ACCESS, not passed in by the user. Let's see how to meet this requirement.

We will use the application context in the policy function itself. First, we need to grant proper privileges to the VPDOWNER user. As SYS, issue

```
grant execute on dbms_session to vpdowner;
grant create any context to vpdowner;
```

As the VPDOWNER user, create the context:

```
create context dept_ctx using set_dept_ctx;
```

We will create the trusted function **set_dept_ctx** a bit later. Coming back to the VPD, we need to modify the policy function so that it returns the predicate reading from the application context instead of a string created inside the function:

```
create or replace function authorized_emps (
    p_schema_name   in   varchar2,
    p_object_name   in   varchar2
)
    return varchar2
is
    l_deptno        number;
    l_return_val    varchar2 (2000);
begin
    if (p_schema_name = user)
    then
        l_return_val := null;
    else
```

```
      if (sys_context ('dept_ctx', 'deptno_list')) is null
      then
        l_return_val := '1=2';
      else
        l_return_val := sys_context ('dept_ctx', 'deptno_list');
      end if;
   end if;
   return l_return_val;
 end;
```

Here the policy function expects the department numbers to be passed through the attribute DEPTNO_LIST of the context DEPT_CTX. To set this value, we need to write the trusted procedure of the context, as shown here:

```
create or replace procedure set_dept_ctx
is
    l_str    varchar2 (32767);
    l_ret    varchar2 (32767);
begin
    for deptrec in (select deptno
                        from emp_access
                        where username = user)
    loop
       l_str := l_str || deptrec.deptno || ',';
    end loop;

    if l_str is null
    then
       -- no access records found, no records
       -- should be displayed.
       l_ret := '1=2';
    else
       l_str := rtrim (l_str, ',');
       l_ret := 'deptno in (' || rtrim (l_str, ',') || ')';
       dbms_session.set_context ('dept_ctx', 'deptno_list', l_ret);
    end if;
end;
```

Again, as VPDOWNER, grant the execute privileges on this function to ALLEN:

```
grant execute on set_dept_ctx to allen;
```

If the VPD policy does not exist on the table, you should add it. Drop it if it already exists:

```
begin
    dbms_rls.drop_policy (
        object_schema        => 'SCOTT',
        object_name          => 'EMP',
        policy_name          => 'EMP_DEPT_POLICY'
    );
end;
/
```

```
begin
    dbms_rls.add_policy (
        object_schema          => 'SCOTT',
        object_name            => 'EMP',
        policy_name            => 'EMP_DEPT_POLICY',
        function_schema        => 'VPDOWNER',
        policy_function        => 'AUTHORIZED_EMPS',
        statement_types        => 'SELECT, INSERT, UPDATE, DELETE',
        update_check           => TRUE,
        policy_type            => DBMS_RLS.context_sensitive,
        namespace              => 'DEPT_CTX',
        attribute              => 'DEPTNO_LIST'
    );
end;
```

The final two parameters, shown in bold, do the trick. They tell the policy not to re-execute the policy function if the DEPTNO_LIST attribute of the DEPT_CTX context does not change. This is important. If the allowed department changes, the user must call the **set_dept_ctx** procedure to set the values. Only in that case could the predicate change. Otherwise, the predicate doesn't change and the policy function shouldn't be re-executed.

It's time to test the function. First, ALLEN logs in and counts the number of employees. Before he issues the query, he needs to set the context:

```
SQL> conn allen/allen
SQL> exec vpdowner.set_dept_ctx
```

Now, let's see what happens when ALLEN checks the value of the attribute:

```
SQL> select sys_context ('dept_ctx','deptno_list') from dual;
SYS_CONTEXT('DEPT_CTX','DEPTNO_LIST')
--------------------------------------
DEPTNO IN (20,10)
```

This is good. Now ALLEN selects from the table itself:

```
SQL> select distinct deptno from scott.emp;
    DEPTNO
----------
        10
        20
```

Here, ALLEN sees only the employees of departments 10 and 20, as per the EMP_ACCESS table.

Suppose ALLEN's access is now changed from 10 and 20 to only 30. All we have to do is to change the EMP_ACCESS table as the VPDOWNER user. Remember to commit the changes.

```
delete emp_access where username = 'ALLEN';
insert INTO emp_access values ('ALLEN',30);
```

Now when ALLEN issues the same query, he will see different results. First, he executes the stored procedure to set the context attribute:

```
exec vpdowner.set_dept_ctx
```

When he issues the same query he issued before, he sees only department 30, as expected:

```
select distinct deptno from hr.emp;
    DEPTNO
----------
        30
```

Note that ALLEN did not set which department he was allowed to see; he simply called the stored procedure **set_dept_ctx**, which set the context attributes *automatically*. Because ALLEN can't set the context attributes himself, this arrangement is inherently more secure than setting a global package variable, which can be set directly by him. Not only that, but the policy type being context sensitive also prevented unnecessary re-execution of the policy function—a huge performance boost.

What if ALLEN does not execute the procedure **set_dept_ctx** at all before issuing the SELECT query? In that case, the attribute DEPTNO_LIST of the application context DEPT_CTX will be set to NULL and hence the predicate from the policy function will return "1=2", which will suppress all department numbers. As a result, ALLEN will not be able to see any employee.

Analyze the previous situation carefully. All we have done so far is to create a policy predicate (in other words, a WHERE condition) to be applied to a user's query. We have decided to set the application context attribute first and have the policy function selected from the context attribute instead of selecting from the table EMP_ACCESS. We could have also made the policy function select directly from the table EMP_ACCESS and construct the predicate, which could have made the policy function very easy to write, and the user would not have to execute the policy function every time he logged on. Is there an added advantage in the policy function selecting from application contexts instead of tables directly?

The answer is yes. Here is some rough pseudo-code for the policy function to select from the table EMP_ACCESS to return the predicate string:

```
1    Get the username
2    Loop
3        Select department numbers from EMP_ACCESS table
4        which are accessible to the username
5        Compile a list of department numbers
6    End loop
7    Return the list as a predicate
```

On the other hand, the rough pseudo-code for the context route will move the previous logic to the **set_dept_ctx** procedure.

Note the differences in the two approaches in the **set_dept_ctx** procedure:

```
1    Get the userid
2    Loop
3        Select department numbers from EMP_ACCESS table
4        which are accessible to the username
5        Compile a list of department numbers
6    End loop
7    Set the attribute DEPTNO_LIST to the value as in the list above
Inside the policy function:
8    Look up the context attribute DEPTNO_LIST
9    Return that as a policy predicate
```

When a user logs in, his username does not change in a session. Therefore, he has to execute the **set_dept_ctx** function only once when the session starts to set the context attribute. If we had built our policy function to select from the context attribute, then for every query by the user, the policy function would merely access the context attribute. Since that's in memory, the access is fast and the policy function can return the predicates faster. If we used the policy function to select from the table instead, it would have taken longer because each query would cause a selection from the table. This is yet another reason policies with selection from context attributes increase the performance significantly.

Identifying Nondatabase Users

Application contexts are useful well beyond the situations we've described so far. A key use of application contexts is to distinguish between different users who cannot be identified through unique sessions. This is quite common in web applications that typically use a connection pool—a group of database connections using a single user named, for example, CONNPOOL. Web users connect to the application server, which in turn uses one of the connections from the pool to get to the database. This is shown in Figure 16-1.

Here, the users Martin and King are *not* database users, they are web users, and the database has no specific knowledge of them. The connection pool connects to the database using the user ID CONNPOOL, which is a *database* user. When Martin requests something from the database, the pool might decide to use the first connection to get it from the database. After the request is complete, the connection becomes idle. If at this point King requests something, the pool might decide to use the same connection. Hence, from the database perspective, a session (which is actually the connection from the pool) is from the user CONNPOOL. As a consequence, the examples shown earlier (where the USER function identifies the actual user connected) will not work to uniquely identify the user making the calls. The USER function will always return the value "CONNPOOL" because that is the database user known to the database.

This is where the application context comes into the picture. Assume that there is a context named WEB_CTX with the attribute name WEBUSER. This value is set to the name of the actual user (for example, MARTIN) by the connection pool when it gets the request from the client.

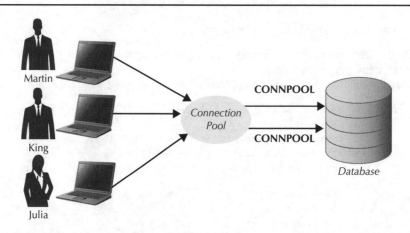

FIGURE 16-1. *Web users using a connection pool*

The VPD policy can be based on this value instead of on the database username. Let's see this in action. Suppose you have a sales application where several account managers access the clients' records. You need to build a VPD system that allows an account manager to see only his or her clients, not those of the other managers. The table has a column—ACC_MGR—that holds the user name of the account manager for that account. Therefore, the policy predicate should be

```
where acc_mgr = AccountManagerUserName
```

The AccountManagerUserName value should be the Windows user ID of the account manager—something the database does not know. This value needs to be passed by the connection pool to the database using contexts.

First, we will create the context:

```
create context web_ctx using set_web_ctx;
```

Then, our main procedure to set the context looks like this:

```
create or replace procedure set_web_ctx (
    p_webuser in varchar2
) is
begin
    dbms_session.set_context ('web_ctx', 'webuser', p_webuser);
end;
```

This procedure takes one parameter—the actual website user (p_webuser). This is exactly what will be used by the application to set the application context WEB_CTX. After the procedure is created, we will make sure it works. Let's assume website user MARTIN logs in. The application will make the following call:

```
exec set_web_ctx ('MARTIN')
```

If you want to make sure the context is properly set, use the following SQL:

```
SQL> exec dbms_output.put_line(sys_context('WEB_CTX','WEBUSER'))
MARTIN
```

Note that the context setting procedure shown here—**set_web_ctx**—is extremely simple and rudimentary. All it does is set a context attribute. In real life, you will probably need to place several lines of code to perform various checks to make sure the caller of the procedure is authorized and so on. One example may be a Windows-based application server, which pulls the user name from the client machine directly and passes it to the context using the preceding procedure.

Once the context is set, you can easily use it to build the policy function. Your policy function looks like the following. You should execute it as VPDOWNER.

```
create or replace function authorized_accounts (
    p_schema_name    in    varchar2,
    p_object_name    in    varchar2
)
    return varchar2
is
    l_deptno         number;
    l_return_val     varchar2 (2000);
```

```
begin
   if (p_schema_name = user)
   then
      l_return_val := null;
   else
      l_return_val :=
                   'acc_mgr = ''' || sys_context ('web_ctx', 'webuser')
                   || '''';
   end if;

   return l_return_val;
end;
```

This policy function returns the predicate **acc_mgr = 'the username'**, which is applied to the policy. The following code adds the VPD policy on the table:

```
begin
   dbms_rls.add_policy (
      object_schema          => 'SCOTT',
      object_name            => 'ACCOUNTS',
      policy_name            => 'ACCMAN_POLICY',
      function_schema        => 'VPDOWNER',
      policy_function        => 'AUTHORIZED_ACCOUNTS',
      statement_types        => 'SELECT, INSERT, UPDATE, DELETE',
      update_check           => TRUE,
      policy_type            => DBMS_RLS.context_sensitive,
      namespace              => 'WEB_CTX',
      attribute              => 'WEBUSER'
   );
end;
```

Since the web user name only changes once, when the user logs into the application, the WEBUSER attribute of WEB_CTX context will only change once. Therefore, this policy function should not be re-executed for every call on the ACCOUNTS table. Instead, it will be re-executed *only* when the web user name changes. This makes the policy faster.

Sometimes, the context value itself changes. For instance, consider a case where the context value is set by reading from a table. If you update the table, the context value changes and you would want that new value reflected. In this case, you would want to force the policy function to re-execute. To do this, use the following PL/SQL code segment:

```
begin
  dbms_rls.refresh_policy(
      object_schema          => 'SCOTT',
      object_name            => 'EMP',
      policy_name            => 'EMP_DEPT_POLICY'
  );
end;
```

As requirements change, you may want to add or remove an application context from a VPD policy. The procedure **alter_policy()** in the DBMS_RLS package is the mechanism to do so.

As a final step, you might be interested in checking the policies defined on the table, the columns, and so on. The data dictionary views for the policies are described later in the chapter in the section "Quick Reference."

Clean Up

To clean up the objects used in this chapter, use the following commands:

- As SCOTT:

  ```
  drop table accounts;
  ```
- As SYS:

  ```
  drop user vpdowner cascade;
  ```

This will remove all created policies on the EMP table.

Quick Reference

This section provides a quick reference for the DBMS_RLS package and the various data dictionary views used with RLS.

Package DBMS_RLS

The Oracle built-in package DBMS_RLS contains all of the programs used to implement row-level security.

ADD_POLICY   The **add_policy** procedure adds a VPD policy on a table.

Parameter	Description
object_schema	Owner of the table on which the RLS policy is placed. The default is the current user.
object_name	Name of the table on which the RLS policy is placed.
policy_name	Name of the RLS policy being created.
function_schema	Owner of the policy function. This function produces the predicate that is applied to the query to restrict rows. The default is the current user.
policy_function	Name of the policy function.
statement_types	Types of statements to which this policy is applied—SELECT, INSERT, UPDATE, and/or DELETE. The default is all.
update_check	Boolean—TRUE or FALSE. If set to TRUE, the policy makes sure that the user sees the rows even after the change. The default is FALSE.
enable	Boolean—TRUE or FALSE. Indicates whether the policy is enabled.
static_policy	Boolean, included if the policy is static.

Parameter	Description
policy_type	Dynamism of the policy; STATIC, SHARED_STATIC, CONTEXT_ SENSITIVE, SHARED_ CONTEXT_SENSITIVE or DYNAMIC. Prefix with DBMS_RLS, as in **policy_type=> dbms_rls.static**. The default is DYNAMIC.
long_predicate	If the length of the predicate returned by the policy function is more than 4000 bytes, you must set this parameter to TRUE; that allows the policy function to return predicates up to 32,000 bytes long. The default is FALSE.
sec_relevant_cols	Specifies the list of columns whose selection causes the RLS policy to be applied; otherwise, the RLS policy is not applied to the query.
sec_relevant_cols_opt	If there are specific columns whose selection triggers use the RLS policy, then there is a choice: when the user selects the sensitive columns, should the row be displayed with the values of the columns shown as NULL, or should the row not be displayed at all? Setting this parameter to ALL_ROWS chooses the former behavior. Prefix with DBMS_RLS, as in **sec_relevant_cols_opt => dbms_rls.all_ rows**. The default is NULL, which indicates that the rows containing these values should not be displayed.

DROP_POLICY   The **drop_policy** procedure drops an existing VPD policy on a table.

Parameter	Description
object_schema	Owner of the table on which the RLS policy is placed. The default is the current user.
object_name	Name of the table on which the RLS policy is placed.
policy_name	Name of the RLS policy to be dropped.

ENABLE_POLICY   The **enable_policy** procedure enables or disables an RLS policy on a table.

Parameter	Description
object_schema	Owner of the table on which the RLS policy is placed. The default is the current user.
object_name	Name of the table on which the RLS policy is placed.
policy_name	Name of the RLS policy to be enabled or disabled.
enable	Boolean. TRUE means enable this policy; FALSE means disable this policy.

REFRESH_POLICY   The **refresh_policy** procedure refreshes the predicate on an RLS policy. When a policy is defined as being anything other than DYNAMIC, the policy predicate may not execute. The predicate cached in memory will be used until the expiring condition specified for that predicate occurs. When you want to refresh the policy, simply call the **refresh_policy** procedure. It re-executes the policy function and refreshes the cached predicate.

Parameter	Description
object_schema	Owner of the table on which the RLS policy is placed. The default is the current user.
object_name	Name of the table on which the RLS policy is placed.
policy_name	Name of the RLS policy to be refreshed.

Data Dictionary Views

This section summarizes the data dictionary views and columns that are relevant to RLS.

DBA_POLICIES   This view shows all the RLS policies on the database, whether they are enabled or not.

Column Name	Description
OBJECT_OWNER	Owner of the table on which the policy is defined.
OBJECT_NAME	Name of the table on which the policy is defined.
POLICY_GROUP	If this is part of a group, this is the name of the policy group.
POLICY_NAME	Name of the policy.
PF_OWNER	Owner of the policy function that creates and returns the predicate.
PACKAGE	If the policy function is a packaged one, this is the name of the package.
FUNCTION	Name of the policy function.
SEL	Indicates that this is a policy for SELECT statements on this table.
INS	Indicates that this is a policy for INSERT statements on this table.
UPD	Indicates that this is a policy for UPDATE statements on this table.
DEL	Indicates that this is a policy for DELETE statements on this table.
IDX	Indicates that this is a policy for CREATE INDEX statements on this table.
CHK_OPTION	Indicates whether the update check option was enabled when the policy was created.
ENABLE	Indicates whether the policy is enabled.
STATIC_POLICY	Indicates whether this is a static policy.
POLICY_TYPE	Dynamism of the policy (for example, STATIC).
LONG_ PREDICATE	Indicates whether this policy function returns a predicate longer than 4000 bytes.
OBJECT_SCHEMA	Owner of the table on which the RLS policy is placed. The default is the current user.
OBJECT_NAME	Name of the table on which the RLS policy is placed.
POLICY_NAME	Name of the RLS policy being created.

Summary

Virtual Private Database is a very important tool for securing databases at the row level. Although VPD is very useful in security-conscious applications and databases, its utility extends beyond security. It can also be used to restrict access to certain rows of the table, eliminate the need to maintain applications for changing query conditions, and even selectively make a table effectively read-only. Using many combinations of variables inside the policy function, you can create a customized view of the data inside a table, and in this way both satisfy the needs of users and create more maintainable applications.

Index

Symbols

* (asterisk), 105
\ (backslash), 102
^ (caret), 105, 112
{ } (curly brackets), 100
% (percentage sign) wildcard, 96
| (pipe character), 101
'/'' (quotation marks), 608–609
; (semicolon), 200, 309
[ ] (square brackets). *See* bracket expressions
_ (underscore), 94

A

ACID-compliant databases, 203
add_policy procedure, 673–674
addresses, 348–352
Advanced Security Option (ASO), 527
AES (Advanced Encryption Standard), 531, 538
After Redaction dialog (SQL Developer), 521
algorithms. *See also* data mining algorithms
    DBMS_CRYPTO encryption, 535, 536, 538–540
    DBMS_CRYPTO hashing, 560–563
    encryption, 527, 528, 531–532
ALL_MINING_MODELS data dictionary view, 406
ALL_MINING_MODELS_ATTRIBUTES data dictionary view, 406, 427–428
ALL_MINING_MODELS_SETTINGS data dictionary view, 406
ALTER SESSION command, 153–154
American National Standards Institute (ANSI), 531
analytics. *See* Oracle Advanced Analytics
anomalies, 487–490
ANSI (American National Standards Institute), 531
application contexts for VPD
    about, 663–664
    example, 664–665
    identifying non-database users, 670–673
    security in, 665–666
    serving as predicates, 666–670
applications
    built-in instrumentation for, 223
    calling PL/SQL functions from SQL, 166
    executing procedures securely, 590–595

677

E

Join the Largest Tech Community in the World

 Download the latest software, tools, and developer templates

 Get exclusive access to hands-on trainings and workshops

 Grow your professional network through the Oracle ACE Program

 Publish your technical articles – and get paid to share your expertise

Join the Oracle Technology Network
Membership is free. Visit community.oracle.com

🐦 @OracleOTN   ⓕ facebook.com/OracleTechnologyNetwork

Climb the Career Ladder

Think about it—97 percent of the Fortune 500 companies run Oracle solutions. Why wouldn't you choose Oracle certification to secure your future? With certification through Oracle, your resume gets noticed, your chances of landing your dream job improve, you become more marketable, and you earn more money. It's simple. Oracle certification helps you get hired and get paid for your skills.

93%
Hiring managers who say IT certifications are beneficial and provide value to the company[1]

7%
Salary growth for Oracle Certified professionals[5]

70%
Believe that Oracle certification improved their earning power[2]

90%
Say that Oracle certification gives them credibility when looking for a new job[2]

68%
Think that certification has made them more in demand[3]

6x
Increased LinkedIn profile views for people with certifications, boosting their visibility and career opportunities[4]

Take the next step
http://education.oracle.com/certification/press

[1] "Value of IT Certifications," CompTIA, October 14, 2014, [2] Oracle Certification Survey, [3] "Certification: It's a Journey Not a Destination," Certification Magazine 2015 Salary Edition, [4] "The Future Value of Certifications: Insights from LinkedIn's Data Trove," ATP 2015 Innovations in Testing, [5] Certification Magazine 2015 Annual Salary Survey

Push a Button
Move Your Java Apps to the Oracle Cloud

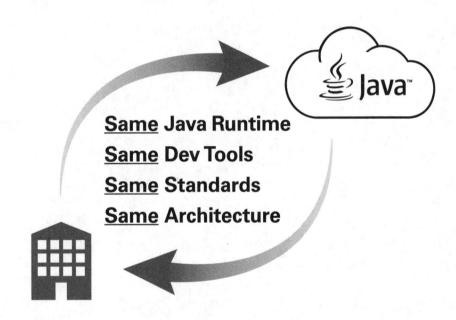

Same Java Runtime
Same Dev Tools
Same Standards
Same Architecture

... or Back to Your Data Center

Reach More than 640,000 Oracle Customers with Oracle Publishing Group

Connect with the Audience that Matters Most to Your Business

Oracle Magazine
The Largest IT Publication in the World
Circulation: 325,000
Audience: IT Managers, DBAs, Programmers, and Developers

Profit
Business Insight for Enterprise-Class Business Leaders to Help Them Build a Better Business Using Oracle Technology
Circulation: 90,000
Audience: Top Executives and Line of Business Managers

Java Magazine
The Essential Source on Java Technology, the Java Programming Language, and Java-Based Applications
Circulation: 225,00 and Growing Steady
Audience: Corporate and Independent Java Developers, Programmers, and Architects

For more information or to sign up for a FREE subscription: Scan the QR code to visit Oracle Publishing online.

Beta Test Oracle Software

Get a first look at our newest products—and help perfect them. You must meet the following criteria:

- ✓ **Licensed Oracle customer or Oracle PartnerNetwork member**

- ✓ **Oracle software expert**

- ✓ **Early adopter of Oracle products**

Please apply at: pdpm.oracle.com/BPO/userprofile